ACTS OF
REBELLION

◆◆◆◆◆◆◆◆◆◆◆◆◆◆◆◆◆◆◆◆◆◆

ALSO BY WARD CHURCHILL

Authored

Fantasies of the Master Race: Literature, Cinema, and the Colonization of American Indians
(1992, 1998)

Struggle for the Land: Native North American Resistance to Genocide, Ecocide, and Colonization
(1993, 1999)

Indians 'R' Us: Culture and Genocide in Native North America (1994, 2002)

Since Predator Came: Notes from the Struggle for American Indian Liberation (1995)

Que Sont les Indiens Devenue? Culture et génocide chez les Indiens d'Amerique du Nord (1996)

From a Native Son: Essays in Indigenism, 1985–1995 (1996)

Perversions of Justice: Indigenous Peoples and Angloamerican Law (2002)

Co-authored

Culture versus Economism: Essays on Marxism in the Multicultural Arena,
with Elisabeth R. Lloyd (1984)

*Agents of Repression: The FBI's Secret Wars Against the Black Panther Party and
the American Indian Movement*, with Jim Vander Wall (1988, 2002)

*The COINTELPRO Papers: Documents from the FBI's Secret Wars Against Dissent
in the United States*, with Jim Vander Wall (1990, 2002)

Pacifism as Pathology: Reflections on the Role of Armed Struggle in North America,
with Mike Ryan (1996)

Edited

Marxism and Native Americans (1983)

Critical Issues in Native North America, Volumes 1 and 2 (1989–1990)

*Die indigen Nationen Nordamerikas und die Marxistishe Tradition: Debatte über eine revolu-
tionäre Theorie der Kultur* (1993)

In My Own Voice: Explorations in the Sociopolitical Context of Art and Cinema,
by Leah Renae Kelly (2001)

Co-edited

Cages of Steel: The Politics of Imprisonment in the United States, with J.J. Vander Wall (1992)

*Islands in Captivity: The Record of the International Tribunal on the Rights of Indigenous Hawai-
ians, Volumes 1, 2, and 3*, with Sharon H. Venne (2002)

ACTS OF
REBELLION

◆◆◆◆◆◆◆◆◆◆◆◆◆◆◆◆◆◆◆

THE
WARD CHURCHILL
READER

WARD CHURCHILL

ROUTLEDGE
New York London

Published in 2003 by
Routledge
29 West 35th Street
New York, New York 10001
www.routledge-ny.com

Published in Great Britain by
Routledge
11 New Fetter Lane
London EC4P 4EE
www.routledge.com

Routledge is an imprint of the Taylor & Francis Group.

Printed in the United States of America on acid-free paper.

10   9   8   7   6   5   4   3   2   1

Library of Congress Cataloging-in-Publication Data

Churchill, Ward.
    Acts of rebellion : The Ward Churchill reader / Ward Churchill.
        p. cm.
    Includes bibliographical references and index.
    ISBN 0-415-93155-X (Hardcover : alk. paper) — ISBN 0-415-93156-8 (Paperback : alk.
        paper)
    1. Indians of North America—Government relations. 2. Indians of North America—
        Social conditions. 3. Indians of North America—Land tenure.
    I. Title.
    E93 .C58 2002
    973.0497—dc21   2002002693

in memory of Leah Renae Kelly (Kizhiibaabinesik)
February 19, 1970–June 1, 2000
lost love of my life

FOREWORD

I want my words to be as eloquent
As the sound of a rattle snake.

I want my actions to be as direct
As the strike of a rattle snake.

I want the results to be as conclusive
As the bite of a beautiful red and black coral snake.

—Jimmie Durham
Columbus Day

ACKNOWLEDGMENTS

MANY PEOPLE HAVE EXTENDED THEIR SUPPORT AND/OR CONTRIBUTED ADVICE and criticism as, over the years, I've written the essays included in this book. Among the more consistent have been Faith Attaguille, Aunt Bonnie, Bobby Castillo, Michelle Cheung, Vine Deloria, Jr., Dan Debo, Don Grinde, Moana Jackson, Elaine Katzenberger, Lilikala Kameʻeleihiwa, Steve Kelly, Barbara Mann, Barb and Harv Mathewes, Russ Means, Glenn Morris, Jim Page, Bob Robideau, Mike Ryan, George Tinker, Haunani-Kay Trask, Jim and Jenny Vander Wall, and Sharon Venne. I owe them each an eternal debt of gratitude for being there when and how it counted. Many thanks are also due Natsu Saito for having proofed every page and offered suggestions for improving most of them. As well, to my editors, Eric Nelson and Vik Mukhija at Routledge, for their good work and steady encouragement.

CONTENTS

PART IV. THE INDIGENIST ALTERNATIVE

ACTS OF REBELLION

Notes on the Interaction of History and Justice

✦✦✦✦✦✦✦✦✦✦✦✦✦

As ye sow, so shall ye reap.

—*Galatians*, 6:7

ON SEPTEMBER 11, 2001, A DATE NOW AND FOREVER EMBLAZONED IN THE shorthand of popular consciousness as a correlation to the emergency dialing sequence, "9-1-1," a quick but powerful series of assaults were carried out against the paramount symbols of U.S. global military/economic dominance, the Pentagon and the twin towers of New York's World Trade Center (WTC). About one-fifth of the former structure was left in ruins, the latter in a state of utter obliteration. Some 3,000 U.S. citizens were killed, along with 78 British nationals, come to do business in the WTC, and perhaps 300 other "aliens," the majority of them undocumented, assigned to scrub the floors and wash the windows of empire.[1]

In the immediate aftermath, while the identities of the attackers was still to some extent mysterious, a vast wail was emitted by the American body politic, asking in apparent bewilderment, "Who are they and why do they hate us?"[2] The answer came shortly, in the form of a videotaped and briefly televised statement by Usama bin Laden, expatriate Saudi head of al-Qaida, one of a plethora of terrorist organizations spawned by the CIA over the past half-century to carry out a broad range of "dirty" assignments for the United States (al-Qaida parted company with "The Company" during the 1990–91 U.S. war against Iraq).[3]

Bin Laden's message was quite clear:[4] The attacks were carried out in response to blatant and ongoing U.S. violations of the laws of war, together with almost every aspect of international public and humanitarian law. The matter, as he pointed out, is of no mere academic concern: over the past decade well upwards of a half-million Iraqi children and at least a million of their adult counterparts have died as the result of palpably criminal U.S. actions against their country.[5] United Nations officials have resigned in protest, denouncing what one of them, Assistant Secretary General Denis Halliday, was widely quoted in the press describing as America's "policy of deliberate genocide" against the people of Iraq.[6] The accuracy of Halliday's—and bin Laden's—assessment of the situation was, moreover, bluntly corroborated on NBC's *60 Minutes* by no less senior a U.S. spokesperson than U.N. Ambassador, and subsequent Secretary of State, Madeleine Albright.[7]

Reaction among average Americans to revelations of the horror perpetrated in their name has been to all intents and purposes nonexistent. Since it can hardly be argued that the public was "uninformed" about the genocide in Iraq, its lack of response can only be seen as devolving upon a condition of collective ignorance—that is, of having information but ignoring it because it is considered inconsequential[8]—as profound as it must be intolerable to those whose children lie murdered en masse. How, under these conditions, are the victims to claim the attention necessary to impress upon their tormentors the fact that they, too, count for something, that they are of consequence, that in effect they will no longer accept the lot of being slaughtered, conveniently out of sight and mind or with impunity?

It is all well and good to observe, as others have, that those who struck on 9-1-1 should instead have taken their case before "the World Court."[9] Genocide is, without doubt, the worst of all crimes against humanity. In this instance, it has been effectively admitted, and the plaintiffs would thus undoubtedly have received a favorable ruling. These truisms uttered, however, a serious question must be posed: To what effect might the victims have pursued such an option? The U.S., its lofty rhetoric to the contrary notwithstanding, self-evidently disdains the rule of law.[10] It long ago repudiated notions that the venerable International Court of Justice (ICJ) holds the least authority over it.[11] The same pertains, and more so, to the newly established International Criminal Court (ICC).[12] Plainly, the U.S. is a "rogue state" which,[13] like the Third Reich before it, imagines itself possessed of a "sovereign right" to operate in a manner unfettered by any but its own customs and conventions of comportment.[14]

The ICJ might nonetheless have entered a ruling. And then? The issue would immediately become one of enforcement.[15] The means decreed in this regard by the United Nations Charter and numerous other international instruments are mostly constrained to imposing economic and/or diplomatic sanctions upon offenders.[16] It is assumed that such embargoes, pressed with sufficient vigor by the world community, will compel targeted states to correct their behavior. No provision is made, however, for dealing with violators like the U.S., which exercises not only an undeniable global economic suzerainty, but formal veto power over U.N. sanctions.[17] Other countries are thereby left in the position of having to elect between attempting to militarily enforce international law against the "world's only remaining superpower" or acquiescing in its ever-expanding pattern of gross illegalities.

There is but one route out of this particular box. It traces the trajectory of an obligation inherent in the citizens of each country to do *whatever* is necessary to ensure that their government complies with the requirements of international law.[18] Enunciated as part of the postwar Nuremberg Doctrine with the Germans in mind, the principle applies no less to Americans.[19] Yet it is *precisely* this civic/human responsibility upon which Americans have defaulted so conspicuously in the aggregate of their willful ignorance concerning the ghastly toll exacted from Iraq.

The question reverts thus to whether, under the conditions at hand, there might have been some "more appropriate means" by which the victims of U.S. aggression might have conveyed the consequences of their agony. Posing it may best be left to the moral cretins who, having done so much to foment the situation in the first place, now revile and seek to exterminate the messengers, demanding "defense" against the truth of their statement.[20] For the rest of us, the method of communication employed was what it was, a mere pinprick when measured against the carnage America so routinely inflicts on others, more akin to a wake-up call than anything else.

In retrospect it will be seen that September 11, 2001, marked the point at which the U.S. was put on notice that business-as-usual would no longer prevail: if Americans wish ever again to be secure from the ravages of terrorism, their top priority must at long last become that of preventing their own government from instigating and participating in it;[21] if, in substance, they desire safety for their own children, they will first have to "stop killing other people's babies."[22] While there remain tremendous disparities in the scales of lethality involved, a nonetheless unmistakable symmetry is embodied in these grim equations. Some might even call it justice, and from justice there can be no ultimate escape.

ON THE MATTER OF SELF-CONCEPT

This said, it must be admitted that there remains a considerable potency to the fantasy of a forum not unlike the Nuremberg Trials in which America's international criminals would take their proper place in the defendants' dock. While the near-term prospect of any such scenario materializing is virtually nil—absent the unlikely emergence of an alliance among secondary powers both capable and willing to literally pound the U.S. into submission—reveries of malignant toads like Henry Kissinger, Madeleine Albright, and Jesse Helms squatting in the shadow of the gallows are simply too pleasant to be suppressed.[23] This gives rise to more serious contemplation of how such worthy objectives might actually be attained over the longer run. Fortunately, there are possibilities in this regard.

The trials precipitated by their total military defeat and occupation forced the Germans into an unprecedented form of self-reckoning. Compelled to face what Karl Jaspers termed the "Question of German Guilt" because of overwhelming courtroom evidence concerning their societal responsibility for the crimes of nazism, they were left no viable alternative but to search for a coherent explanation of their behavior.[24] Eventually, the process led them to collectively embrace an "internationalization of [their] 'national' history" as an antidote to the "collective, narcissistic self-exaltation" enshrined in previous narratives of German identity.[25] In this manner, the duality of triumphalism and denial forming the Germans' "mass psychology of fascism" was gradually transformed into its antithesis.[26]

By 1959, shortly after West Germany regained its autonomy, their psychointellectual denazification had evolved to such an extent that the Germans themselves could undertake the first of what by 1981 would total nearly 6,000 trials of nazi criminals in their country's domestic courts.[27] Concomitantly, although its record in this respect remains far from perfect, Germany has voluntarily paid—in fact, continues to pay—billions of dollars in compensation to those it victimized during World War II (or, in some cases, their descendants).[28] Imposition of the death penalty has all along been constitutionally prohibited, as has, until very recently, the deployment for any purpose whatever of German troops abroad.

One wonders whether the transformative process evident in postwar Germany might not yield similarly constructive results if undertaken through a reversed sequence in the contemporary United States. In theory, rather than international trials serving as the catalyst for a radical reinterpretation of national history, hence national character, a reconfigured history might serve to galvanize popular initiatives culminating in international trials (and/or domestic trials evoking international law).[29] A surmounting of America's well-nurtured public evasion of such "unpleasantness" is of course necessary, as it so obviously was in Germany, yet it seems possible that the means are already at hand. Taken together with a growing awareness that there are likely other, much heavier shoes ready to drop unless Americans show signs of getting their house in order—biochemical weapons? a nuclear device?—9-1-1 may well have injected the essential element of self-interested incentive to change.[30]

Thus must the country at last and in the fullest sense commence the task of coming face to face with the stark horrors of which its historical burden is comprised: not just what has been done to the Iraqis, but, as bin Laden himself pointed out, to the Palestinians as well.[31] And, to be sure, there are others: the millions of Timorese,[32] Guatemalans,[33] Indonesians[34] and comparable victims of America's client regimes since 1945;[35] the millions of Indochinese slaughtered by U.S. troops during the "Vietnam Era";[36] the untold numbers of Koreans massacred at places like No Gun Ri;[37] the million-odd Japanese civilians deliberately burned alive not just at Hiroshima and Nagasaki, but in the massive incendiary raids flown against Tokyo and other cities during World War II;[38] the hundreds of thousands of Filipinos butchered during the American conquest of their homeland at the dawn of the twentieth century.[39]

To this, still more must be added: the millions lost to the Middle Passage, shipped as livestock from Africa to fuel the rise of America's economy through their slavery;[40] the millions of their relatives worked to death as chattel labor, both before and *since* "Emancipation";[41] the thousands of blacks lynched during the Klan's century-long postreconstruction "festival of violence";[42] the Chinese who stood not "a Chinaman's chance" of surviving their indenture while building America's railroads and sinking its deep shaft mines;[43] the Mexican migrant laborers dead of pesticides in California fields;[44] the twelve-million-or-more Third World kids who perish each year of poverty-induced afflictions, their very subsistence siphoned into providing the cellphones and other paraphernalia now deemed all-important to the average American's "quality of life."[45]

These are but a few of the highlights—more accurately, the low points—of the history American triumphalism has sought not only to silence, but to transmute into the opposite of itself.[46] Recasting the country's narrative self-conception in a form wherein such matters assume their proper place as defining ingredients would go far towards dispelling the illusion that the words "innocent" and "American" are synonymous.[47] From there, it should be possible to break down the intricate codes of disunderstanding through which average Americans have come to see themselves, both individually and collectively, as being somehow entitled to possess, control, and/or consume that which belongs to others (including even their very lives, "where need be").[48] On this basis, it would at least be arguable that the U.S. polity had intellectually equipped itself to participate as responsible citizens within the world community it now purports to "lead."[49]

IN SEARCH OF A METHOD

The question arises of how best to approach the mass of information upon which any radical (re)interpretation of "The American Experiment" must proceed.[50] The sheer volume of what has been shunted aside in canonical recountings threatens to overpower the most intrepid of counternarratives, dissolving into a fine mist of contrarian detail. How then to give shape to the whole, ordering and arranging its contents in ways that explicate rather than equivocating or obscuring their implications, making the conclusions to be drawn not just obvious but unavoidable? How, in other words, to forge an historical understanding which in itself amounts to an open demand for the sorts of popular action precipitating constructive social change?[51]

There are several methodological contenders in this connection, beginning with Howard Zinn's commendable effort in *A People's History of the United States* to more or less straightforwardly rewrite Samuel Eliot Morison's *Oxford History of the American People* in reverse polarity, effigizing rather than celebrating the status quo.[52] Historical materialism,[53] functionalism,[54] structuralism,[55] hermeneutics,[56] and even some of the less tedious variants of postmodernism offer themselves as alternatives (usually as *the* alternative).[57] So, too, do subgenres of postcolonialism like subaltern studies.[58] Each of these "visions of history," at least in some of their aspects, are of utility to the development of a bona fide U.S. historical praxis.[59] At face value, however, none are able to avoid the fate of either descending into a state of hopeless atomization,[60] or, alternately, overreaching themselves to the point of producing one or another form of reductionist metahistorical construction.[61]

Perhaps the surest route to avoiding these mirrored pitfalls will be found in the Nietzschean method of "historical genealogy" evolved by Michel Foucault in works such as *The Archaeology of Knowledge*.[62] This is a highly politicized endeavor in which the analyst, responding to circumstances s/he finds objectionable in the present, traces its "lineage" back in time until a fundamental difference is discerned (this "historical discontinuity" is invariably marked by an "epistemological disjuncture"). Having thus situated the source of the problem in its emergence from a moment of historical transition, the analyst can proceed to retrace the unfolding of the specific history at issue forward in time, with an eye toward what would need to be "undone"—and how—if the future is to be rendered more palatable than the current state of affairs. In this, whatever set of circumstances prevailed prior to the discontinuity is mined for its potentially corrective features.[63]

> Instead of condemning the barbarism of pre-modern society, its inhumanity, injustice, and irrationality, Foucault presents the difference of the pre-modern system by demonstrating that, on its own terms, it makes sense and is coherent. The reason for doing so, let it be noted, is not to present a revised picture of the past, nostalgically to glorify [its] charms . . . but underline the transitory nature of the present system and therefore remove the pretense of legitimacy it holds by dint of a naïve, rationalist contrast with the past.[64]

Although firmly grounded in Nietzsche, Foucault's model also incorporates a "post-structuralist strategy of detotalization oriented to the particularity of the phenomena" studied, and "a structuralist strategy oriented to remove the analysis from the register of subjectivist humanism."[65] To this might be added occasional forays into a strategy of immanent critique in which the contemporary order is held strictly accountable to the standards and ideals it typically claims as being descriptive of its own composition and character.[66] Overall, the object is to reveal in all their squalor the pretensions of "modern" morés and institutions, "undermining the [illusion of] naturalness" in which they seek to cloak themselves, and to make explicit thereby both the necessity and tangible possibility of their being dismantled or transcended.[67]

This book follows Foucauldian procedure. In the U.S., irrespective of which among the earlier-sketched grotesqueries is emphasized—be it America's voracious greed and genocidal disregard for the wellbeing of others, the concomitants of militarism and virulent racism, or the weird psychic stew in which imperial/racial arrogance has been blended in equal part with the most sanctimonious professions of peaceful innocence—its lineage traces to precisely the same source: the invasion(s) of Native North America by Europeans during the sixteenth and seventeenth centuries.[68] Absent that profound and violently imposed rupture in historical continuity, nothing else that is objectionable in American history—slavery, for instance—or in contemporary American life—"globalization," to name a salient example—would have been materially possible (or, in the main, conceivable). The relationship between Euroamericans and American Indians is therefore the most fundamental of any on the continent. It is the bedrock upon which all else is built, the wellspring from whence all else flows.[69]

Hence, in tracing the course and temper of Indian-white relations, a considerable light is shed upon the relationship of the U.S. "mainstream" population and virtually every other people it has encountered over the past two and a quarter centuries, both "domestically" and abroad. It might indeed be argued that Euroamerica's attitude towards and treatment of the peoples indigenous to the "homeland" it has seized for itself has been in many respects definitive of those it has accorded all Others, including not least—and in some cases increasingly—certain sectors of its own nominal racial/ethnic constituency.[70] The postinvasion history of Native America thus provides the lens through which all of American history must be examined if it is to be in any sense genuinely understood. To put it more personally, it is essential, if one is to truly appreciate the implications of one's own place in American society, that one "read" them in terms of U.S./Indian relations.[71]

It follows that correction of the socioeconomic, political, and other repugnancies marking modern American life is, in the final analysis, entirely contingent upon rectification of nonindian America's abecedarian relationship to American Indians. Here, history provides the agenda concerning what must be done. So long as Native North America remains internally colonized, subject to racial codes, unindemnified for the genocide and massive expropriations we've suffered—and *continue* to suffer—genocide, colonialism, racism, and wholesale theft will remain the signal attributes of American mentality and behavior.[72] Insofar as this is so, the U.S. will undoubtedly continue to comport itself in the world as it has in the past. And this, in turn, will inevitably result in responses far more substantial than that made on 9-1-1.

ACTS OF REBELLION

Plainly, there are choices to be made. Arriving at the right choices, however, depends to a considerable extent upon being able to see things clearly. *Acts of Rebellion*, then, although it is a reader, and therefore by both intent and design far from comprehensive, is meant to facilitate the attainment of the insights requisite to deciding where one stands on many of the core issues confronting American Indians. Call it, if you will, an exercise in values clarification. In any event, I flatter myself to think that one cannot read it and, without entering into active falsehood, afterwards claim "not to know" what has been/is being done to Native North America. Knowledge, of course, associated as it is with power, demands action. To possess knowledge and ignore its demands is to nullify claims of innocence. Ignorance, in effect, equates to complicity, a variety of guilt.[73]

Since the book is a reader it seeks to accomplish a number of things. Not only does it cover a fairly broad range of discrete but related topics, for instance, but it does so by employing a variety of styles. The majority of the essays—"The Law Stood Squarely on Its Head," "The Nullification of Native America?" and "A Breach of Trust," for example—are "formal," at least in the sense that they were originally prepared for publication in academic journals and rely upon extensive annotation. Others, such as "False Promises" and "The New Face of Liberation," have been developed from the transcripts of lectures delivered at various universities. "Let's Spread the 'Fun' Around" was written as an op-ed piece,[74] while "Confronting Columbus Day" was originally prepared as a legal brief. One object of this "eclectic" arrangement is to demonstrate that in writing—which may in itself be viewed as a mode of activism[75]—it is unnecessary to pull one's punches, regardless of the venue in which one seeks to publish.

A word on annotation is in order. Mine is almost always extensive, sometimes notoriously so. There are reasons for this that go well beyond the "scholarly" imperative of demonstrating "command of the literature" bearing upon whatever topic I may be writing. Many of my notes amplify points raised in my texts, offering caveats or digressions that would, if incorporated into the body of the essay itself, disrupt its flow. The notes thus serve in a literal sense as a conscious and deliberate "subtext," and should be approached as such. Still, the citations appearing in my notes are quite extensive, and this is because I want no reader to have to simply "take my word for" anything I say. Anyone wishing to know more than I observe about anything I mention, or apprehend the concrete basis upon which I've said what I've said, is empowered by my citations to examine things for themselves—without necessarily having to do thirty years of intensive research in the process—and appreciate for themselves how I've "connected the dots."

Acts of Rebellion is divided into four sections. The first, which concerns the application of European/Euroamerican legality to North America's indigenous peoples, is designed to debunk the smug lie that the U.S. is or ever has been "a nation of laws, not men."[76] Particularly in "The Law Stood Squarely on Its Head," great care is taken to demonstrate exactly how both the Law of Nations and the constitutional requirements of U.S. domestic law itself have been cynically and consistently subverted by American jurists almost from the inception of the republic, always for purposes of political/military dominance and material gain. "The Law" has always been used as toilet paper by the status quo where American Indians are concerned, a circumstance to be heeded by anyone naïve enough to believe—or duplicitous enough to argue without really believing—that the problems we face can somehow be resolved through recourse to the sort of "due process" available to us in the courts of our colonizers. The lesson should be taken especially to heart by other "out groups" in American life, all of whom are subject to at least some of the illegitimate juridical principles articulated by the U.S. judiciary vis-à-vis the continent's native inhabitants.[77]

The second essay, "The Nullification of Native America?," explores a specific example of how legalistic rationalizations have lately been employed to subvert the most intimate aspect of native self-determination: the question of identity (in both individual and collective terms). The third and final essay of the first section, "Confronting Columbus Day," examines, again in a very specific way, the manner in which the tenets of U.S. jurisprudence and statutory legality conflict with the requirements of international law. The latter argument in particular, in that it was successfully employed by the defense in an actual criminal proceeding, can be mined for its utility to others in similar situations.

As should have become apparent in reading the first section, if it wasn't already, a purportedly strict adherence to legality has been absolutely central to the false image of itself America has persistently projected to the world. Hence, law serves as an ideal medium by which to perform immanent critique (analyzing, that is, the question of whether or to what extent the realities of American comportment differ from its enunciated self-description).[78] The reader will find it regularly deployed for this purpose not only in the opening section, but throughout the remainder of the book. This is especially true in the second section, wherein "The Earth Is Our Mother" investigates the historical process by which Native North Americans were/are dispossessed of some 98 percent of our property, "A Breach of Trust" examines America's internal colonial structure in the specific connection of uranium mining (thus confirming Sartre's equation of colonialism to genocide), and "Like Sand in the Wind" discusses the creation of an American Indian diaspora in North America.

The final essay in this sequence, "The Bloody Wake of Alcatraz," details the gruesome counterinsurgency campaign mounted by the Federal Bureau of Investigation and collaborating military and police agencies during the mid-1970s against the American Indian Movement on and around the Pine Ridge Reservation in South Dakota. Since many of the techniques employed by the FBI against AIM were patently illegal, even in terms of U.S. law, and because the entire operation was undertaken to prevent AIM from asserting rights held by native people under a host of treaties, covenants, and conventions, the gulf separating America's often flowery verbiage on "law enforcement" from the sordid realities of its practice in this regard have seldom revealed themselves in bolder relief. The distinctions will, however, be readily appreciated by similarly targeted dissident groups ranging from the United Negro Improvement Association to the Black Panther Party,[79] and should be studied closely by all who set upon the task of forging a positive future.

The third section is devoted to examining the instrumentalities of popular culture through which the settler society has sought to disguise the conditions it has imposed upon native people, vigorously denying the reality even (or especially) to itself, meanwhile degrading its indigenous victims in an ever more ubiquitous and refined fashion. The centerpiece of this ugly endeavor has been cinema—movies—as is discussed in "Fantasies of the Master Race." Film is by no means the sole offender, however, as is brought out in "Let's Spread the 'Fun' Around," which deals with the issue of sports team mascots, and "Indians 'R' Us," which takes up the matter of the "Men's Movement" and the question of "New Age" sensibilities more generally. The moral of the story, so to speak, is that words and images *do* hurt, as is witnessed by the fact that nazi propagandist Julius Streicher was tried at Nuremberg,[80] convicted of crimes against humanity, and executed for having engaged in derogations of Jews no worse than those to which American Indians are routinely subjected. That criminal activities of the sort engaged in by Streicher are protected under the rubric of U.S. domestic law is a circumstance imbued with negative implications for any group suffering the psychic ravages of Euroamerica's customary racist discourse.[81]

To conclude, three essays are offered which explore in various ways the kinds of action and alternatives pointed to in the preceding three sections. "False Promises" endeavors to explain in capsule form exactly how and why marxism is an unsatisfactory paradigm for the attainment of native rights. "The New Face of Liberation" explores the indigenist alternative from yet another angle, finding more common ground with anarchism than any other European praxis. The section's—and the book's—last essay, "I Am Indigenist," concerns itself with explaining what the consummation of the indigenist agenda in the U.S. portion of North America might look like, and why no other progressive program can succeed unless something of the sort actually occurs. A message on priorities is obviously embedded therein.

As I said, *Acts of Rebellion* is far from comprehensive. It should, nonetheless, provide sufficient stimulation to set at least some readers on what I see as the right track, empowering them to make contributions of their own. If so, it will have accomplished its purpose. No more can be asked by an author of any book than that it be put to such use.

PART I

IN MATTERS OF LAW

✦✦✦✦✦✦✦✦✦✦✦✦✦✦

Although the United States did not have to exercise great legal imagination in incorporating [indigenous nations] within its boundaries, it made a great effort to do so. From the recognition of the treaty system as the most appropriate method of legal dealings with [native peoples], to the early-nineteenth-century "Cherokee cases" that gave the legal system meaning, to the "plenary power" decisions that ended the century and the notion of tribal sovereignty, U.S. law helped structure not only U.S. Indian policy but also Indian-white relations . . . Law was used to perpetrate murder and land frauds of all sorts and the legal rights of American Indians were ignored by state and federal courts. The product of this great concern with the "legality" of nineteenth century federal Indian policy was genocide: more than 90 percent of all Indians died, and most native land was alienated, the balance occupied by Indians "owned" by the United States. Indian people were under the control of Indian agents, political hacks sent out from Washington to manage the lives of native people and backed by the army.

—Sydney L. Harring
Crow Dog's Case

"THE LAW STOOD SQUARELY ON ITS HEAD"
U.S. Doctrine, Indigenous Self-Determination, and the Question of World Order

◆ ◆ ◆ ◆ ◆ ◆ ◆ ◆ ◆ ◆ ◆ ◆ ◆

There's no precedent in law for the way American jurists, beginning with Chief Justice of the Supreme Court John Marshall, have elected to assert their country's "right" to own territories in which the peoples native to this continent had resided since time immemorial. Marshall himself quite simply invented the "legal principles" upon which he based his doctrine of settler dominion, in the process standing a large portion of existing international law squarely on its head, and his successors have continued to treat these distortions as gospel right up to the present moment.

—Glenn T. Morris, 1990

As anyone who has ever debated or negotiated with U.S. officials on matters concerning American Indian land rights can attest, the federal government's first position is invariably that its title to/authority over its territoriality was acquired incrementally, mostly through provisions of cession contained in some 400 treaties with Indians ratified by the Senate between 1778 and 1871.[1] When it is pointed out that the U.S. has violated the terms of every one of the treaties at issue, thus voiding whatever title might otherwise have accrued therefrom, there are usually a few moments of thundering silence.[2] The official position, publicly framed by perennial "federal Indian expert" Leonard Garment as recently as 1999, is then shifted onto different grounds: "If you don't accept the treaties as valid, we'll have to fall back on the Doctrine of Discovery and Rights of Conquest."[3] This rejoinder, to all appearances, is meant to be crushing, forestalling further discussion of a topic so obviously inconvenient to the status quo.

While the idea that the U.S. obtained title to its "domestic sphere" by discovery and conquest has come to hold immense currency among North America's settler population, one finds that the international legal doctrines from which such notions derive are all but unknown, even among those holding degrees in law, history, or political philosophy. The small cadre of arguable exceptions to the rule have for the most part not bothered to become acquainted with the relevant doctrines in their original or customary formulations, instead contenting themselves with reviewing the belated and often transparently self-serving "interpretations" produced by nineteenth-century American jurists, most notably those of John Marshall, third Chief Justice of the Supreme Court.[4] Overall, there seems not the least desire—or sense of obligation—to explore the matter further.

The situation is altogether curious, given Marshall's own bedrock enunciation of America's self-concept, the hallowed proposition that the U.S. should be viewed above all else as "a nation governed by laws, not men."[5] Knowledge of/compliance with the law is presupposed, of course, in any such construction of national image. This is especially true with respect to laws which, like those pertaining to discovery and conquest, form the core of America's oft and loudly proclaimed contention that its acquisition and consolidation of a transcontinental domain has all along been "right," "just," and therefore "legal."[6] Indeed, there can be no questions of law more basic than those of the integrity of the process by which the United States has asserted title to its landbase and thereby claims jurisdiction over it.

The present essay addresses these questions, examining U.S. performance and the juridical logic attending it through the lens of contemporaneous international legal custom and convention, and drawing conclusions accordingly. The final section explores the conceptual and material conditions requisite to a reconciliation of rhetoric and reality within the paradigm of explicitly American legal (mis)understandings. It should be noted, however, that insofar as so much of this devolves upon international law, and with the recent emergence of the U.S. as "the world's only remaining superpower,"[7] the implications are not so much national as global.

THE DOCTRINE OF DISCOVERY

Although there are precursors dating back a further 200 years, the concepts which were eventually systematized as discovery doctrine for the most part originated in a series of Bulls promulgated by Pope Innocent IV during the late thirteenth century to elucidate material relations between Christian crusaders and Islamic "infidels."[8] While the pontiff's primary objective was to establish a legal framework compelling "Soldiers of the Cross" to deliver the fruits of their pillage abroad to such beneficiaries as the Vatican and Church-sanctioned heads of Europe's incipient states, the Innocentian Bulls embodied the first formal acknowledgment in Western law that rights of property ownership were enjoyed by non-Christians as well as Christians. "In Justice," then, it followed that only those ordained to rule by a "Divine Right" conferred by the "One True God" were imbued with the prerogative to "rightly" dispossess lesser mortals of their lands and other worldly holdings.[9]

The law remained as it was until 1492, when the Columbian "discovery" of what proved to be an entire hemisphere, very much populated but of which most Europeans had been unaware, sparked a renewed focus upon questions of whether and to what extent Christian sovereigns might declare proprietary interest in the assets of

Others.[10] Actually, the first problem was whether the inhabitants of the "New World" were endowed with "souls," the criterion of humanity necessary for us to be accorded any legal standing at all. This issue led to the famous 1550 debate in Valladolid between Frey Bartolomé de las Casas and Juan Ginés de Sepúlveda, the outcome of which was papal recognition that American Indians were human beings and therefore entitled to exercise at least rudimentary rights.[11]

As a corollary to the Valladolid proceedings, Spanish legal theorists such as Franciscus de Vitoria and Juan Matías de Paz were busily revising and expanding upon Innocent's canonical foundation as a means of delineating the property rights vested in those "discovered" by Christian (i.e., European) powers as well as those presumably obtained in the process by their "discoverers."[12] In the first instance, Vitoria in particular posited the principle that sovereigns acquired outright title to lands discovered by their subjects only when the territory involved was found to be literally unoccupied (*terra nullius*).[13] Since almost none of the land European explorers ever came across genuinely met this description, the premise of *territorium res nullius*, as it was called, was essentially moot from the outset (albeit, as will become apparent, the English— and much more so their American offshoot—would later twist it to their own ends).

In places found to be inhabited, it was unequivocally acknowledged in law that native residents held inherent or "aboriginal" title to the land.[14] What the discoverer obtained was a monopolistic right vis-à-vis other powers to acquire the property from its native owners, in the event they could be persuaded through peaceful means to alienate it. On balance, the formulation seems to have been devised more than anything as an attempt to order the relations between the European states in such a way as to prevent them from shredding one another in a mad scramble to glean the lion's share of the wealth all of them expected to flow from the Americas.[15]

> Under the right of discovery, the first European nation to discover American [or other] lands previously unknown to Europe had what is similar to an exclusive European franchise to negotiate for Indian land within the discovered [area]. International law forbade European nations from interfering with the diplomatic affairs each carried on with the Indian nations within their respective "discovered" territories. The doctrine thus reduced friction and the possibility of warfare between the competing European nations.[16]

That this principle was well developed in international law and understood perfectly by America's "Founding Fathers" is confirmed in an observation by no less luminous a figure than Thomas Jefferson.

> We consider it as established by the usage of different nations into a kind of *Jus gentium* for America, that a white nation settling down and declaring such and such are their limits, makes an invasion of those limits by any other white nation an act of war, but gives no right of soil against the native possessors . . . That is to say, [we hold simply] the sole and exclusive right of purchasing land

from [indigenous peoples within our ostensible boundaries] whenever they should be willing to sell. . . .[17]

The requirement that the consent of indigenous peoples was needed to legitimate cessions of their land was what prompted European states to begin entering into treaties with "the natives" soon after the invasion of North America had commenced in earnest.[18] While thus comprising the fundamental "real estate documents" through which the disposition of land title on the continent must be assessed, treaties between European and indigenous nations also served to convey formal recognition by each party that the other was its equal in terms of legal stature ("sovereignty").[19] To quote Jefferson again, "the Indians [have] full, undivided and independent sovereignty as long as they choose to keep it, and . . . this might be forever."[20] Or, as U.S. Attorney General William Wirt would put it in 1828:

> [Be it] once conceded, that the Indians are independent to the purpose of treating, their independence is to that purpose as absolute as any other nation . . . Nor can it be conceded that their independence as a nation is a limited independence. Like all other nations, they have the absolute power of war and peace. Like any other nation, their territories are inviolable by any other sovereignty . . . They are entirely self-governed, self-directed. They treat, or refuse to treat, at their pleasure; and there is no human power that can rightly control their discretion in this respect.[21]

From early on, the English had sought to create a loophole by which to exempt themselves in certain instances from the necessity of securing land title by treaty, and to undermine the discovery rights of France, whose New World settlement patterns were vastly different from those of England.[22] Termed the "Norman Yoke," the theory was that an individual—or an entire people—could rightly claim only such property as they'd converted from wilderness to a state of domestication (i.e., turned into townsites, placed in cultivation, and so forth).[23] Without regard for indigenous methods of land use, it was declared that any area found to be in an "undeveloped" condition could be declared *terra nullius* by its discoverer and clear title thus claimed.[24] By extension, any discovering power such as France which failed to pursue development of the sort evident in the English colonial model forfeited its discovery rights accordingly.[25]

The Puritans of Plymouth Plantation and Massachusetts Bay Colony experimented with the idea during the early seventeenth century—arguing that while native property rights might well be vested in their towns and fields, the remainder of their territory, since it was uncultivated, should be considered unoccupied and thus unowned—but the precedent never evolved into a more generalized English practice.[26] Indeed, the Puritans themselves abandoned such presumption in 1629.[27]

Whatever theoretical disagreements existed concerning the nature of the respective ownership rights of Indians and Europeans to land in America, practical realities shaped legal relations between the Indians and colonists. The necessity of getting along with powerful Indian [peoples], who outnumbered the European settlers for several decades, dictated that as a matter of prudence, the settlers buy lands that the Indians were willing to sell, rather than displace them by other methods. The result was that the English and Dutch colonial governments obtained most of their lands by purchase. For all practical purposes, the Indians were treated as sovereigns possessing full ownership of [all] the lands of America.[28]

So true was this that by 1750 England had dispatched a de facto ambassador to conduct regularized diplomatic relations with the Haudenosaunee (Iroquois Six Nations Confederacy)[29] and, in 1763, in an effort to quell native unrest precipitated by his subjects' encroachments upon unceded lands, King George III issued a proclamation prohibiting English settlement west of the Allegheny Mountains.[30] This foreclosure of the speculative interests in "western lands" held by George Washington and other members of the settler élite—and the less grandiose aspirations to landed status of rank-and-file colonials—would prove a major cause of the American War of Independence.[31]

Although it is popularly believed in the U.S. that the 1783 Treaty of Paris through which England admitted defeat also conveyed title to all lands east of the Mississippi River to the victorious insurgents, the reality was rather different. England merely quitclaimed its interest in the territory at issue. All the newly established American republic thus acquired was title to such property as England actually owned—the area of the original thirteen colonies situated east of the 1763 demarcation line—plus an exclusive right to acquire such property as native owners might be convinced to cede by treaty as far westward as the Mississippi.[32] The same principle pertained to the subsequent "territorial acquisitions" from European or euroderivative countries—the 1803 Louisiana Purchase and the 1848 impoundment of the northern half of Mexico through the Treaty of Guadelupe Hidalgo, to cite two prominent examples—through which the present territoriality of the forty-eight contiguous states was eventually consolidated.[33]

As a concomitant to independence, moreover, the Continental Congress found itself presiding over a pariah state, defiance—much less forcible revocation—of Crown authority being among the worst offenses imaginable under European law. Unable to obtain recognition of its legitimacy in other quarters,[34] the federal government was compelled for nearly two decades to seek it through treaties of peace and friendship, with indigenous nations along its western frontier—all of them recognized as sovereigns in prior treaties with the very European powers then shunning the U.S.—meanwhile going to extravagant rhetorical lengths to demonstrate that, far from being an outlaw state, it was really the most legally oriented of all nations.[35]

The fledgling country could hardly peddle a strictly law-abiding image while openly trampling upon the rights of indigenous peoples. As a result, although George Washington had secretly and successfully recommended the opposite policy even before being sworn in as president,[36] one of the earliest acts of Congress was to pass the

Northwest Ordinance, in which it solemnly pledged that "the utmost good faith shall always be observed towards the Indians; their lands and property shall never be taken without their consent; and, in their property, rights, and liberty, they shall never be invaded or disturbed."[37] For the most part, then, it was not until the U.S. had firmed up its diplomatic ties with France, and the demographic/military balance in the west had begun to shift decisively in its favor,[38] that it started to make serious inroads on native lands.

THE MARSHALL OPINIONS

The preliminary legal pretext for U.S. expansionism, set forth by John Marshall in his 1810 *Fletcher v. Peck* opinion,[39] amounted to little more than a recitation of the Norman Yoke theory, quite popular at the time with Jefferson and other American leaders.[40] The proposition that significant portions of Indian Country amounted to *terra nullius*, and was thus open to assertion of U.S. title without native agreement, was, however, contradicted by the country's policy of securing by treaty at least an appearance of indigenous consent to the relinquishment of each parcel brought under federal jurisdiction.[41] The presumption of underlying native land title lodged in the Doctrine of Discovery thus remained the most vexing barrier to America's fulfillment of its territorial ambitions.

In the 1823 *Johnson v. McIntosh* case, Marshall therefore undertook a major (re)interpretation of the doctrine itself.[42] While demonstrating a thorough mastery of the law as it had been previously articulated, and an undeniable ability to draw all the appropriate conclusions therefrom, the Chief Justice nonetheless managed to invert it completely. Although he readily conceded that title to the territories they occupied was vested in indigenous peoples, Marshall denied that this afforded them supremacy within their respective domains. Rather, he argued, the self-assigned authority of discoverers to constrain alienation of discovered lands implied that prepotency inhered in the discovering power, not only with respect to other potential buyers but vis-à-vis the native owners themselves.[43]

Since the sovereignty of discoverers—or derivatives like the U.S.—could in this sense be said to overarch that of those discovered, Marshall held that discovery also conveyed to the discoverer an "absolute title" or "eminent domain" underlying the aboriginal title possessed by indigenous peoples. The native "right of possession" was thereby reduced at the stroke of a pen to something enjoyed at the "sufferance" of the discovering (superior) sovereign.[44]

> The principle was, that discovery gave title to the government by whose subjects, or by whose authority, it was made, against all other European governments whose title might be consummated by possession. The exclusion of all other Europeans necessarily gave to the nation making the discovery the sole right of acquiring the soil from the natives, and establishing settlements upon it . . . In the establishment of these relations, the rights of the original inhabi-

tants were, in no instance, entirely disregarded; but were, to a considerable extent, diminished . . . [T]heir rights to complete sovereignty, as independent nations, were necessarily diminished, and their power to dispose of the soil, at their own will, to whomever they pleased, was denied by the original fundamental principle, the discovery gave exclusive right to those who made it . . . [T]he Indian inhabitants are [thus] to be considered merely as occupants.[45]

"However extravagant [my logic] might appear," Marshall summed up, "if the principle has been asserted in the first instance, and afterwards, sustained; if a country has been acquired and held under it; if the property of the great mass of the community originates in it, it cannot be questioned."[46] In other words, violations of law themselves become law if committed by those wielding enough power to get away with them. For all the elegant sophistry embodied in its articulation, then, the *Johnson v. McIntosh* opinion reduces to the gutter cliché that "might makes right." In this manner, Marshall not only integrated "the legacy of 1,000 years of European racism and colonialism directed against nonwestern peoples" into the canon of American law, but did so with a virulence unrivaled even by European jurists upon whose precedents he professed to base his own.[47]

There were of course loose ends to be tied up, and these Marshall addressed through opinions rendered in the "Cherokee Cases," *Cherokee v. Georgia* (1831) and *Worcester v. Georgia* (1832).[48] In his *Cherokee* opinion, the Chief Justice undertook to resolve questions concerning the precise standing to be accorded indigenous peoples. Since the U.S. had entered into numerous treaties with them, it was bound by both customary international law and Article 1§ 10 of its own constitution to treat them as coequal sovereigns. Marshall's verbiage in *McIntosh* had plainly cast them in a very different light. Hence, in *Cherokee*, he conjured a whole new classification of politicolegal entity "marked by peculiar and cardinal distinctions which nowhere else exist."[49]

[I]t may well be doubted whether those tribes which reside within the acknowledged boundaries of the United States can, with strict accuracy, be denominated foreign nations. They may, more correctly, perhaps, be denominated *domestic dependent nations.* They occupy a territory to which we assert a title independent of their will . . . Their relation to the United States resembles that of a ward to his guardian [emphasis original].[50]

"The Indian territory is admitted to compose a part of the United States," he continued. "In all our maps, geographical treatises, histories, and laws, it is so considered . . . [T]hey are [therefore] considered to be within the jurisdictional limits of the United States [and] acknowledge themselves to be under the protection of the United States."[51] What Marshall had described was a status virtually identical to that of a protectorate, yet as he himself would observe in *Worcester* a year later, "the settled doctrine of the law of nations is that a weaker power does not surrender its independence—its right of self-government—by associating with a stronger, and taking its protection. A weak state, in order to provide for its safety, may place itself under the protection of one more powerful, without stripping itself of the right of government, and ceasing to be a state."[52] It follows that a protectorate would also retain its land rights, unimpaired by its relationship with a stronger country.[53]

At another level, the Chief Justice was describing a status similar to that of the states of the union (i.e., subordinate to federal authority, while retaining a residue of sovereign prerogative). Yet he, better than most, was aware that if this were so, the federal government would never have had a basis in either international or constitutional law to enter into treaties with indigenous peoples in the first place, a matter which would have invalidated any U.S. claim to land titles accruing therefrom. Small wonder, trapped as he was in the welter of his own contradictions, that Marshall eventually threw up his hands in frustration, unable or unwilling to further define Indians as either fish or fowl. In the end, he simply repeated his assertion that the U.S./Indian relationship was "unique . . . perhaps unlike [that of] any two peoples in existence."[54]

Small wonder, too, all things considered, that the Chief Justice's *Cherokee* opinion was joined by only one other member of the high court.[55] The majority took exception, Justices Henry Baldwin and William Johnson writing separate opinions,[56] and Smith Thompson, together with Joseph Story, entering a strongly worded dissent which laid bare the only reasonable conclusions to be drawn from the facts (both legal and historical).[57]

> It is [the Indians'] political condition which determines their *foreign* character, and in that sense must the term *foreign* be understood as used in the Constitution. It can have no relation to local, geographical, or territorial position. It cannot mean a country beyond the sea. Mexico or Canada is certainly to be considered a foreign country, in reference to the United States. It is the political relation in which one country stands to another, which constitutes it [as] foreign to the other [emphasis original].[58]

Nonetheless, Marshall's views prevailed, a circumstance allowing him to deploy his "domestic dependent nation" thesis against both the Cherokees *and* Georgia in *Worcester.*[59] First, he reserved on constitutional grounds relations with all "other nations" to the federal realm, thereby dispensing with Georgia's contention that it possessed a "state's right" to exercise jurisdiction over a portion of the Cherokee Nation falling within its boundaries.[60] Turning to the Cherokees, he reiterated his premise that they—and by implication all Indians within whatever borders the U.S. might eventually claim—occupied a nebulous quasisovereign status as "distinct, independent political communities" subject to federal authority.[61] In practical effect, Marshall cast indigenous nations as entities inherently imbued with a sufficient measure of sovereignty to alienate their territory by treaty when- and wherever the U.S. desired they do so, but never with enough to refuse.[62]

As legal scholars Vine Deloria, Jr., and David E. Wilkins have recently observed, the cumulative distortions of both established law and historical reality bound up in

Marshall's "Indian opinions" created a very steep and slippery slope, with no bottom anywhere in sight.

> [T]he original assumption [was] that the federal government is authorized and empowered to protect American Indians in enjoyment of their lands. Once it is implied that this power also involves the ability of the federal government by itself to force a purchase of the lands, there is no way the implied power can be limited. If the government can force the disposal of lands, why can it not determine how the lands are to be used? And if it can determine how the lands are to be used, why can it not tell Indians how to live? And if it can tell Indians how to live, why can it not tell them how to behave and what to believe?[63]

By the end of the nineteenth century, less than seventy years after *Cherokee* and *Worcester*, each of these things had happened. Within such territory as was by then reserved for indigenous use and occupancy the traditional mode of collective land tenure had been supplanted by federal imposition of a "more civilized" form of individual title expressly intended to compel agricultural land usage.[64] Native spiritual practices had been prohibited under penalty of law,[65] and entire generations of American Indian youngsters were being shipped off, often forcibly, to boarding schools where they were held for years on end, forbidden knowledge of their own languages and cultures while they were systematically indoctrinated with Christian beliefs and cultural values.[66] The overall policy of "assimilation," under which these measures were implemented, readily conforms to the contemporary legal definition of cultural genocide.[67]

Meanwhile, American Indians had been reduced to utter destitution, dispossessed of approximately 97.5 percent of our original landholdings,[68] our remaining assets held in a perpetual and self-assigned "trust" by federal authorities wielding what Marshall's heirs on the Supreme Court described as an extraconstitutional or "plenary"—that is, unlimited, absolute, and judicially unchallengeable—power over our affairs.[69] Suffice it here to observe that nothing in the Doctrine of Discovery empowered any country to impose itself on others in this way. On the contrary, the "juridical reasoning" evident in the Marshall opinions and their successors has much in common with, and in many respects prefigured, the now discredited body of law—repudiated first by an International Court of Arbitration opinion in the 1928 *Island of Palmas* case,[70] then more sweepingly in the 1945 United Nations Charter and the United Nations' 1960 Declaration on the Granting of Independence to Colonial Countries and People[71]—which purported to legitimate the imperialism manifested by Europe during the early twentieth century.[72]

RIGHTS OF CONQUEST

Although they are usually treated as an entirely separate consideration, conquest rights in the New World accrued under the law of nations as a subpart of discovery doctrine.

Under international law, discoverers could acquire land only through a voluntary alienation of title by native owners, with one exception—when they were compelled to wage a "Just War" against native people—by which those holding discovery rights might seize land and other property through military force.[73] The U.S. clearly acknowledged that this was so in the earlier-mentioned Northwest Ordinance, where it pledged that indigenous nations would "never be invaded or disturbed, unless in just and lawful wars authorized by Congress."[74]

The criteria for a Just War were defined quite narrowly in international law. As early as 1539, Vitoria and, to a lesser degree, Matías de Paz asserted that there were only three: the natives had either to have refused to admit Christian missionaries among them, to have arbitrarily refused to engage in commerce with the discovering power, or to have mounted some unprovoked physical assault against its representatives/subjects.[75] Absent at least one of these conditions, any war waged by a European state or its derivative would be "unjust"—the term was changed to "aggressive" during the twentieth century—and resulting claims to title unlawful.[76] One searches in vain for an example in American history where any of the criteria were realized.

A more pragmatic problem confronting those claiming that the U.S. holds conquest rights to native lands is that, while the federal government recognizes the existence of approximately 400 indigenous peoples within its borders, its own count of the number of "Indian Wars" it has fought "number [about] 40."[77] Plainly, the United States cannot exercise "conquest rights" over the more than 300 nations against which, by its own admission, it has never fought a war. Yet, as is readily evident in its 1955 *Tee-Hit-Ton* opinion, the Supreme Court, mere facts to the contrary notwithstanding, has anchored U.S. land title in a pretense that exactly the opposite is true.

> Every American schoolboy knows that the savage tribes of this continent were deprived of their ancestral ranges by force and that, even when the Indians ceded millions of acres by treaty in return for blankets, food and trinkets, it was not a sale but the conquerors' will that deprived them of their land.[78]

Particularly in his *McIntosh* opinion, but also in *Cherokee*, John Marshall sought to transcend this issue by treating discovery and conquest as if they were synonymous, a conflation evidencing even less legal merit than the flights of fancy discussed in the preceding section. In fact, the high court was ultimately forced to distinguish between the two, acknowledging that the "English possessions in America were not claimed by right of conquest, but by right of discovery," and, resultingly, that the "law which regulates, and ought to regulate in general, the relations between the conqueror and conquered, [is] incapable of application" by the U.S. to American Indians.[79]

A further complication is that as early as 1672 legal philosophers like Samuel Pufendorf had mounted a serious challenge to the idea that even such territory as was seized in the course of a Just War might be permanently retained.[80] Although Hugo Grotius, Emmerich de Vattel, William Edward Hall, John Westlake, and other such theorists continued to aver the validity of conquest rights through the end of the nineteenth century,[81] by the 1920s a view very similar to Pufendorf's had proven ascendant.

Oddly, given its stance concerning American Indians, as well as its then recent forcible acquisitions of overseas colonies like Hawai'i, Puerto Rico, and the Philippines,[82] the U.S. assumed a leading role in this respect. Although the Senate refused to allow the country to join, President Woodrow Wilson was instrumental in creating the League of Nations, an organization intended "to substitute diplomacy for war in the resolution of international disputes."[83] In some ways more important was its centrality in crafting the 1928 General Treaty on the Renunciation of War, also known as the "Kellogg-Briand Pact" or "Pact of Paris."[84]

> With the [treaty], almost all the powers of the world, including all the Great Powers, renounced the right to resort to war as an instrument of state policy. By Article 1, "[t]he High Contracting Parties solemnly declare, in the names of their respective peoples, that they condemn war for the solution of international controversies, and renounce it as an instrument of national policy in their relations with one another." By Article 2, the Parties "agree that the settlement or solution of all disputes or conflicts, of whatever nature or of whatever origin they may be, which may arise among them, shall never be sought except by pacific means."[85]

In 1932, Secretary of War Henry Stimson followed up by announcing that the U.S. would no longer recognize title to territory seized by armed force.[86] This "new dictum of international law,"[87] shortly to be referred to as the "Stimson Doctrine of Non-Recognition," was expressly designed to "effectively bar the legality hereafter of any title or right sought to be obtained by pressure or treaty violation, and [to] lead to the restoration to [vanquished nations] of rights and titles of which [they] have been unjustly deprived."[88] Within a year, the doctrine's blanket rejection of conquest rights had been more formally articulated in a League of Nations Resolution and legally codified in the Chaco Declaration, the Saaverda Lamas Pact, and the Montevideo Convention on the Rights and Duties of States.[89] In 1936, the Inter-American Conference on the Maintenance of Peace also declared a "proscription of territorial conquest and that, in consequence, no acquisition made through violence shall be recognized."[90] The principle was again proclaimed in the Declaration on the Non-Recognition of the Acquisition of Territory by Force advanced by the Eighth Pan-American Conference in 1938.

> As a fundamental of the Public Law of America . . . the occupation or acquisition of territory or any other modification of territorial or boundary arrangement obtained through conquest by force or non-pacifistic means shall not be valid or have legal effect . . . The pledge of non-recognition of situations arising from the foregoing conditions is an obligation which cannot be avoided either unilaterally or collectively.[91]

By the time the Supreme Court penned its bellicose opinion in *Tee-Hit-Ton*, the Stimson Doctrine had already served as a cornerstone in formulating the charges of planning and waging aggressive war pressed against the major nazi defendants at Nuremberg and the Japanese in Tokyo (tribunals instigated and organized mainly by the U.S.).[92] It had also served as a guiding principle in the (again, effectively U.S. instigated) establishment of both the Organization of American States and the United Nations, entities which by their very charters, like the ill-fated League of Nations before them, are devoted to the "the progressive codification of [international] law . . . for purposes of preventing war."[93] Correspondingly, Stimson's "new dictum" found its most refined and affirmative expression in the charters' provisos, reiterated almost as boilerplate in a host of subsequent U.N. resolutions, declarations, and conventions, concerning the "equal rights and self-determination of all peoples."[94]

Contradictory as the *Tee-Hit-Ton* court's blatant conquest rhetoric was to the lofty posturing of the U.S. in the international arena, it was even more so with respect to a related subterfuge unfolding on the home front. By 1945, the United States was urgently seeking a means of distinguishing its own record of territorial expansion from that of the nazis it was preparing to hang for having undertaken very much the same course of action.[95] The workhorse employed in this effort was the so-called Indian Claims Commission (ICC), established to make retroactive payment to indigenous peoples whose property had been "unlawfully taken" over the years.[96] The purpose of the commission was, as President Harry Truman explained upon signing the enabling legislation on August 14, 1946, to foster an impression that the U.S. had acquired *none* of its landbase by conquest.

> This bill makes perfectly clear what many men and women, here and abroad, have failed to recognize, that in our transactions with Indian tribes we have . . . set for ourselves the standard of fair and honorable dealings, pledging respect for all Indian property rights. Instead of confiscating Indian lands, we have purchased from the tribes that once owned this continent more than 90 percent of our public domain.[97]

The game was rigged from the outset, to be sure, since the ICC was not empowered to return land to native people even in cases where its review of the manner in which the U.S. had acquired it revealed the grossest sorts of illegality. The terms of compensatory awards, moreover, were restricted to payment of the estimated value of the land at the time it was taken—often a century or more before—without such considerations as interest accrual or appreciation in land values during the intervening period.[98] Still, despite its self-serving and mostly cosmetic nature, the very existence of the ICC demonstrated quite clearly that, in terms of legality, U.S. assertion of title to/jurisdiction over Indian Country can no more be viewed as based in "conquest rights" than in "rights of discovery." All U.S. pretensions to ownership of property in North America must therefore be seen as treaty-based.

THROUGH THE LENS OF THE LAW

When Congress established the ICC in 1946, it expected within five years to "resolve" all remaining land rights issues concerning American Indians.[99] The commission was to identify and catalogue the basis in treaties, agreements, and statutes by which the U.S. had assumed lawful ownership of every disputed land parcel within its purported domain, awarding "just compensation" in each case where the propriety of the transaction(s) documented might otherwise be deemed inadequate.[100] By 1951, however, the 200-odd claims originally anticipated had swelled to 852.[101] The lifespan of the ICC was extended for another five years, then another, a process which was repeated until the "third generation" of commissioners finally gave up in exhaustion.[102]

By the time the commission suspended operations on September 30, 1978, it had processed 547 of the 615 dockets into which the 852 claims had been consolidated, none in a manner satisfactory to the native claimants (nearly half were simply dismissed).[103] Title to virtually the entire state of California, for instance, was supposedly "quieted" in the "Pit River Land Claims Settlement" of the mid-1960s by an award amounting to 47 cents per acre, despite the fact that the treaties by which the territory had ostensibly been ceded to the U.S. had never been ratified by the Senate.[104]

Most important, in its final report the ICC acknowledged that after three decades of concerted effort, it had been unable to discern a legal basis for U.S. title to what the federal Public Lands Law Review Commission had already described as "one third of the nation's land."[105]

> The fact is that about half the area of the country was purchased by treaty or agreement at an average price of less than a dollar per acre; another third of a [billion] acres, mainly in the West, was confiscated without compensation; another two-thirds of a [billion] acres was claimed by the United States without pretense of [even] a unilateral action extinguishing native title.[106]

There can be no serious question of the right of indigenous nations to recover property to which their title remains unclouded, or that their right to recover lands seized without payment equals or exceeds that of the United States to preserve its "territorial integrity" by way of paltry and greatly belated compensatory awards.[107] Restitution rather than compensation is, after all, the guiding principle of the tort provisions embodied in international public law.[108] Nor is this the end of it. Within the area ostensibly acquired by the U.S. through treaties or agreements, many of the instruments of cession are known to have been fraudulent or coerced. These must be considered invalid under Articles 48–53 of the Vienna Convention on the Law of Treaties.[109]

A classic illustration of a fraud involves the 1861 Treaty of Fort Wise, in which not only did federal commissioners forge the signatures of selected native leaders—several of whom were not even present during the "negotiations"—but the Senate altered many of the treaty's terms and provisions *after* it was supposedly signed, then ratified the result without so much as informing the Indians of the changes. On this basis, the U.S. claimed to have obtained the "consent" of the Cheyennes and Arapahos to its acquisition of the eastern half of what is now the State of Colorado.[110] Comparable examples abound (e.g., the above-mentioned California treaties).

Examples of coercion are also legion, but none provides a better illustration than does the 1876–77 proceeding in which federal authorities suspended distribution of rations to the Lakotas, at the time directly subjugated by and therefore dependent upon the U.S. military for sustenance, and informed them that they'd not be fed again until their leaders had signed an agreement relinquishing title to the Black Hills region of present-day South Dakota.[111] Thus did the Congress contend that the 1851 and 1868 treaties of Fort Laramie, in each of which the Black Hills were recognized as an integral part of the Lakota homeland, had been "superseded" and U.S. ownership of the area secured.[112]

Without doubt, North America's indigenous nations are no less entitled to recover lands expropriated through such travesties than they are the territories already discussed. Although it is currently impossible to offer a precise estimate regarding the extent of the acreage involved—to do so would require a contextual review of each U.S./Indian treaty, and a parcel-by-parcel delineation of the title transfers accruing from invalid instruments—it is safe to suggest that adding it to the 35-odd percent of the continental U.S. which was never ceded would place something well over half the present gross "domestic" territoriality of the United States (see Map 4.1, p. 69).[113]

The U.S. of course holds the power to simply ignore the law in inconvenient contexts such as these. Doing so, however, will never serve in itself to legitimate its comportment. Instead, its continued possession of a vast expanse of illegally occupied territory[114]—an internal colonial empire, as it were[115]—can only destine it to remain what it was at its inception: an inherently criminal or "rogue" state.[116] It is through this lens that U.S. pronouncements and performance from Nuremberg to Vietnam must inevitably be evaluated.[117] So, too, President George Herbert Walker Bush's 1990 rhetoric concerning America's moral/legal obligation to kill more than a million Iraqis while militarily revoking their government's forcible annexation of neighboring Kuwait.[118]

On the face of it, the only reasonable conclusion to be drawn is that the unsavory stew of racial/cultural arrogance, duplicity, and abiding legal cynicism defining U.S. relations with indigenous nations from the outset has come long since to permeate America's relationship to most other countries. How else to understand Bush's 1991 declaration that the display of U.S. military might he'd ordered in Iraq was intended more than anything else to put the entire world on notice that, henceforth, "what *we* say, goes"?[119] In what other manner might we explain the fact that while Bush claimed the "New World Order" he was inaugurating would be marked by nothing so much as "the rule of law among nations," the United States was and remains unique in the consistency with which it has rejected both the authority of international courts and any body of law other than its own.[120]

For the past fifty years, federal policymakers have been increasingly adamant in their refusal of the proposition that the U.S. might be bound by customs or conventions conflicting with its sense of self-interest.[121] More recently, American delegates to the United Nations have taken to arguing that new codifications of international law must be written in strict conformity to their country's constitutional and even statutory requirements, and that, for interpretive purposes, the distortions of existing law advanced by American jurists such as John Marshall be considered preeminent.[122] In effect, the U.S. is seeking to cast an aura of legitimacy over its ongoing subjugation of American Indians by engineering a normalization of such relations in universal legal terms.

A salient example will be found in the ongoing U.S. rejection of language in the United Nations Draft Declaration on the Rights of Indigenous Peoples—and a similar declaration drafted by the OAS—reiterating that self-determination is guaranteed *all* peoples by the U.N. Charter.[123] Instead, American diplomats have been instructed to insist that indigenous peoples the world over must be accorded only a "right of *internal* self-determination" which is "not . . . synonymous with more general understandings of self-determination under international law" but which conforms perfectly with those set forth in the United States' own Indian Self-Determination and Educational Assistance Act of 1975.[124] Most specifically, as was stated in an official cable in January 2001, "the U.S. understanding of the term 'internal self-determination' indicates that it does not include a right of independence or permanent sovereignty over natural resources."[125]

The standard "explanation" offered by U.S. officials when queried about the legal basis for their government's position on native rights has been that "while the United States once recognized American Indian [peoples] as separate, distinct, and sovereign nations, it long since stopped doing so."[126] This, however, is the same, legally speaking, as saying nothing at all. According to no less an authority than Lassa Oppenheim, author of the magisterial *International Law*, voluntary relinquishment is the sole valid means by which any nation may be divested of its sovereignty.[127] Otherwise, "recognition, once given is irrevocable unless the recognized [nation] ceases to exist."[128] As always, the U.S. is simply making up its own rules as it goes along.

As should be obvious, the implications of such maneuvers are by no means confined to a foreclosure upon the rights of native peoples. The broader result of American "unilateralism" is that, just as it did with respect to North America's indigenous nations, the U.S. is now extrapolating its presumptive juridical primacy to global dimensions.[129] The initiative is especially dangerous, given that the place now held by the U.S. within the balance of world military power closely resembles the lopsided advantage it enjoyed against American Indians during the nineteenth century.[130] The upshot is that, should the present trend be allowed to continue, the United States will shortly have converted most of the planet into an equivalent of "Indian Country."[131] In fact, especially with regard to the so-called Third World, this has already to all practical intents and purposes come to pass.[132]

THE NATURE OF MODERN EMPIRE

"It's an old story, really," writes Phyllis Bennis, one of "a strategically unchallenged do-minion, at the apogee of its power and influence, rewriting the global rules for how to manage its empire. Two thousand years ago, Thucydides described how Mylos, the island the Greeks conquered to ensure stability for their Empire's golden age, was invaded and occupied according to laws wholly different from those governing demo-cratic (if slavery dependent) Athens. The Roman empire followed suit, creating one set of laws for Rome's own citizens, imposing another on its far-flung possessions. In the last couple of hundred years the sun-never-sets-on-us British empire did much the same thing. And then, at the end of the twentieth century, having achieved once unimaginable heights of military, economic, and political power, it was Washington's turn."[133]

> The American-style *fin de 20th siecle* law of empire took the form of the U.S. exempting itself from UN-brokered treaties and other agreements that it de-manded others accept. It was evident in Washington's rejection of the Interna-tional Criminal Court in 1998, its refusal to sign the 1997 Convention against anti-personnel land mines, its failures [to accept] the Convention on the Rights of the Child, the Law of the Sea, the Comprehensive Test Ban Treaty and more.[134]

Actually, the roots of the current U.S. posture run much deeper than Bennis sug-gests. As its record concerning the earlier-mentioned California Indian treaties readily demonstrates, the United States had by the mid-1850s already adopted a policy of se-lectively exempting itself from compliance with treaties to which it asserted others were nonetheless bound.[135] The Supreme Court's 1903 opinion in *"Lone Wolf" v. Hitchcock* effectively extended this procedure to encompass all treaties and agreements with indigenous nations.[136] From there, it became only a matter of time before the U.S. would begin to approach the remainder of its foreign relations in a comparable manner.[137] This parallels the attitude, first explicated with regard to Indians and now displayed quite prominently on the global stage, that America is endowed with a ple-nary authority to dictate the "permissible" forms of other countries' governmental and political processes, the modes of their economies, and so on.[138]

Legal scholar Felix S. Cohen once and accurately analogized American Indians as a "miner's canary" providing early warning of the fate in store for other sectors of the U.S. populace.[139] The principle can now be projected to worldwide proportions. Given the scale of indignity and sheer physical suffering the U.S. has inflicted—and continues to inflict—upon indigenous peoples trapped within its "domestic" domain,[140] it is self-evidently in the best interests of very nearly the entire human species to forcefully reject the structure of "unjust legality" by which the U.S. is attempting to rationalize its ambition to consolidate a position of planetary suzerainty.[141] The only reasonable question is how best to go about it.

Here, the choice is between combating the endless array of symptoms emanating from the problem or going after it at its source, eradicating it root and branch, once and for all. Again, the more reasonable alternative is self-revealing. Unerringly, then, the attention of those desiring to block America's increasingly global reach must be focused upon unpacking the accumulation of casuistic jurisprudence employed by the U.S. as a justification for its own geographical configuration.[142] Since, as has been established herein, there is no viable basis for the United States to assert territorial rights based on the concept of *terra nullius* or any other aspect of discovery doctrine, and even less on rights of conquest, it is left with a legally defensible claim to only those parcels of the continent where it obtained title through a valid treaty. As has also been shown herein, this adds up to something less than half its professed North American landbase. To its "overseas possessions" such as Guam, Puerto Rico, and Hawai'i, the U.S. holds no legal right at all.[143]

Viewed from any angle, the situation is obvious. Shorn of its illegally occupied territories, the U.S. would lack the critical mass and internal jurisdictional cohesion necessary to impose itself as it does at present. This is all the more true in that even the fragments of land still delineated as Indian reservations are known to contain up to two-thirds of the uranium, a quarter of the readily accessible low sulfur coal, a fifth of the oil and natural gas, and all of the zeolites available to feed America's domestic economy.[144] Withdrawal of these assets from federal control would fatally impair the ability of the U.S. to sustain anything resembling state-corporate business as usual. By every reasonable standard of measure, the decolonization of Native North America must thus be among the very highest priorities pursued by anyone, anywhere, who is seriously committed to achieving a positive transformation of the global status quo.[145]

A major barrier to international coalescence around this sort of "deconstructionist" agenda, among sworn enemies of the U.S. no less than its allies, has been the exclusively statist "world order"[146]—or "world system," as Immanuel Wallerstein terms it[147]—in which both sides are invested. Only *states* are eligible for membership in the United *Nations*, for instance, a conflation which once caused American Indian Movement leader Russell Means to quip that "the organization would more rightly have been called the United States, but the name was already taken."[148] Although it may be no surprise to find a veritable U.S. appendage like Canada citing John Marshall's *McIntosh* opinion as "the *locus classicus* of the principles governing aboriginal title" in the formulation of its own judicial doctrine,[149] it is quite another matter to find the then still decolonizing countries of Africa adopting the thinking embodied in *Cherokee* to ensure that the "national borders" demarcated by their European colonizers would be preserved in international law.[150]

This came about during United Nations debates concerning the 1960 Declaration of the Granting of Independence to Colonial Countries and Peoples. Belgium, in the process of relinquishing its grip on the Congo, advanced the thesis that if terms like decolonization and self-determination were to have meaning, the various "tribal" peoples whose homelands it had forcibly incorporated into its colony would each have to be accorded the right to resume independent existence. Otherwise, the Belgians argued, colonialism would simply be continued in another form, with the indigenous peoples involved arbitrarily subordinated to a centralized authority presiding over a territorial dominion created not by Africans but by Belgium itself.[151] To this, European-educated Congolese insurgents like Patrice Lumumba, backed by their colleagues in the newly-emergent Organization of African Unity (OAU), counterposed what is called the "Blue Water Principle," that is, the idea that to be considered a bona fide colony—and thus entitled to exercise the self-determining rights guaranteed by both the Declaration and the U.N. Charter—a country or people had to be separated from its colonizer by at least thirty miles of open ocean.[152]

Although the Blue Water Principle made no more sense during the early 1960s than it had when Justice Smith Thompson rebutted John Marshall's initial iteration of it in 1831, it was quickly embraced by U.N. member states and Third World revolutionary movements alike.[153] For the member states, whether capitalist (First World) or socialist (Second World), adoption of the principle served to consecrate the existing disposition of their "internal" territoriality, irrespective of how it may have been obtained. For the Third World's marxian revolutionaries, it offered the same prospect, albeit quite often with regard to positions of "postcolonial" state authority to which they were at the time still aspiring.[154] For either side to acknowledge that a "Fourth World" comprised of indigenous nations[155] might possess the least right to genuine self-determination would have been—and remains—to dissolve the privileged status of the state system to which both sides are not only conceptually wedded but owe their very existence.[156]

The stakes embodied in this denial are staggering. There are twenty different indigenous peoples along the peninsula British colonizers called Malaya (now Malaysia), 380 in "postcolonial" India, 670 in the former Dutch/Portuguese colony of Indonesia.[157] In South America, the numbers range from 35 in Ecuador to 210 in Brazil.[158] There are scores, including such large nationalities as the Yi, Manchus, and Miao, encapsulated within the Peoples Republic of China.[159] In Vietnam, two dozen-odd "montagnard tribes" of the Annamese Cordillera have been unwillingly subsumed under authority of what the Vietnamese constitution unilaterally proclaims "a multinational state."[160] The same situation prevails for the Hmongs of Laos.[161] Not only the Chechens of the south but at least three-dozen smaller northern peoples remain trapped within the Russian rump state resulting from the breakup of the Soviet Union.[162] In Iraq and Turkey, there are the Kurds;[163] in Libya and Morocco, the Bedouins of the desert regions.[164] Throughout subsaharan Africa, hundreds more, many of them partitioned by borders defended at gunpoint by statist régimes, share the circumstance of the rest.[165] Similar situations prevail in every quarter of the earth.[166]

Observed from this standpoint, it's easy enough to see why no state, regardless of how bitterly opposed it might otherwise be to the United States, has been—or could be—willing to attack the U.S. where it is most vulnerable. The vulnerability being decidedly mutual, any precedent thus established would directly contradict the attacking state's sense of self-preservation at the most fundamental level. Hence, the current process of militarily enforced politicoeconomic "globalization"[167]—world imperialism, by any other name[168]—must be viewed as a collaborative endeavor, involving even those states which stand to suffer most as a result (and which have therefore been most vociferously critical of it). It follows that genuine and effective opposition can only accrue from locations outside "official" venues, at the grassroots, among those who understand their interests as being antithetical not only to globalization, per se, but to the entire statist structure upon which it depends.[169]

RETURNING THE LAW TO ITS FEET

It's not that native peoples are especially accepting of their lot, as has been witnessed by such bloody upheavals as Katanga and Biafra since 1960.[170] In 1987, cultural anthropologist Bernard Nietschmann conducted a global survey in which he discovered that of 125 armed conflicts occurring at the time, fully 85 percent—amounting to a "third world war," in his view—were being fought between indigenous nations and states claiming an inherent right to dominate them.[171] Among the sharper clashes have been the ongoing guerrilla struggles waged by the Kurds, the Nagas of the India/Burma border region,[172] the southern Karins and northern Kachens of Burma (Myanmar),[173] the Tamils of Sri Lanka (formerly Ceylon),[174] the Pacific islanders of Belau, Fiji and elsewhere,[175] the so-called Moro peoples of the southern Philippines,[176] the Timorese and Papuans of Indonesia,[177] as well as the Miskito and other native peoples of Nicaragua's Atlantic coast.[178] To this list may now be added the series of revolts in Chechnya[179] and the recent Mayan insurgency in the Mexican province of Chiapas.[180]

The list extends as well to the venerable states of western Europe. In Spain, the Basques, and to a lesser degree the Catalans, have been waging a protracted armed struggle to free themselves from incorporation into a country of which they never consented to be a part.[181] In France, aside from the Basques around Navarre, there are the Celtic Bretons of the Channel coast.[182] The Irish are continuing their eight-century-long military campaign to reclaim the whole of their island,[183] while, on the "English Isle" itself, the Welsh, Scots, and Cornish—Celtic peoples all—have increasingly taken to asserting their rights to autonomy.[184] So, too, the Celtic Manxmen on the Isle of Man.[185] Far to the north, the Saamis ("Lapps") are also pursuing their right to determine for themselves the relationship of Saamiland (their traditional territory, usually referred to as "Lapland") vis-à-vis Norway, Sweden, Finland, and Russia.[186] In Greenland, the primarily Inuit population, having already achieved a "home rule" arrangement with their Danish colonizers, are pushing for full independence.[187] In Canada, there have been armed insurgencies by native peoples at Oka, Gustafsen Lake, and elsewhere, as well as the emergence of a tentatively autonomous Inuit territory called Nunavut.[188]

Those who see dismantlement of the present U.S. territorial/power configuration as the pivot point of constructive change are thus presented with the prospect of linking up with a vibrantly global Fourth World liberation movement, one which has never been quelled, and which cannot be satisfied until what Leopold Kohr once called the "breakdown of nations"—by which he actually meant the breakdown of *states*—has been everywhere accomplished.[189] Dire predictions concerning the horrors supposedly attending "the coming anarchy"[190] blink the fact that the hegemony of statism has generated an estimated fifty million corpses from wars alone over the past half-century.[191] Adding in those lost to the "underdevelopment" and "diseconomies of scale" inherent to the world system as it is now constituted would increase the body count at least twenty times over.[192] Also to be considered is the radical and rapidly accelerating truncation of fundamental rights and liberties undertaken by all states—the "freedom-loving" U.S. far more than most of those it condemns as "totalitarian"—in order to concretize and reinforce their imposition of centralized authority.[193] As well, the massive and unprecedented degree of cultural "leveling" entailed in the systematic and state-anchored transnational corporate drive to rationalize production and unify markets the world over.[194]

Rectifying John Marshall's seminal inversion of international legal principle—negating his negation, so to speak[195]—and thus "returning the law to its feet"[196] would serve to undermine one of the most potent components of the master narrative through which statism and its imperial collaterals have been presented as though they were natural, inevitable, and somehow beneficial to all concerned.[197] General exposure, in their own terms, of the falsity intrinsic to such "truths" stands to evoke a "legitimation crisis" of such proportions and intractability that the statist system could not sustain itself.[198] This "end of world order"[199]—or, more accurately, transformative reordering of international relations[200]—in favor of a devolution of state structures into something resembling the interactive clusters or federations of "mininationalisms"[201] which were the norm before the advent of European hegemony,[202] restoring human scale and bioregional sensibility to the affairs of peoples, can only be seen as a positive trajectory.[203]

Putting a name to it is a more difficult proposition, however. Insofar as its thrust centers in a wholesale (re)assertion of the rights of Fourth World peoples, such a path might correctly be depicted as an "indigenist alternative."[204] Still, given so sweeping a reconfiguration of humanity's relationship with itself and its habitat must encompass those who are of the Fourth World in neither identity nor present orientation, the old standby of "anarchism" might well prove a more apt descriptor.[205] Regardless of its labeling, the result will inevitably be far more just, and thus more liberatory, than that which it will replace.

2

THE NULLIFICATION OF NATIVE AMERICA?

An Analysis of the 1990 American Indian Arts and Crafts Act

♦♦♦♦♦♦♦♦♦♦♦♦♦♦

> An Indian is an Indian no matter what kind of Indian [s/he] is.
> —E. Alan Morinis, 1982

ON NOVEMBER 29, 1990, PUBLIC LAW 104-644, TITLED "AN ACT FOR THE Protection of American Indian Arts and Crafts Act" and best known as simply the "Arts and Crafts Act," was signed by U.S. President George Bush.[1] Through this measure, the federal government of the United States arrogated unto itself and its state-level subordinates the ultimate authority to determine who is/is not entitled to identify themselves as an American Indian "for purposes of selling arts and crafts," usurping and in fact criminalizing the self-determining prerogatives of indigenous peoples in the process. According to Sec. 104 § 1159 of the Act:

(a) It is unlawful to offer for sale or display any good, with or without a Government trademark, in a manner that falsely suggests it is Indian produced, an Indian product, or the product of a particular Indian or Indian tribe or Indian arts and crafts organization, resident within the United States.

(b) Whoever knowingly violates subsection (a) shall—

    (1) in the case of a first violation, if an individual, be fined not more than $250,000 or imprisoned not more than five years, or both, and if a person other than an individual, be fined not more than $1,000,000; and

    (2) in the case of subsequent violations, if an individual, be fined not more than $1,000,000 or imprisoned not more than fifteen years, or both, and, if a person other than an individual, be fined not more than $5,000,000.

(c) As used in this section—

    (1) the term "Indian" means any individual who is a member of an Indian tribe, or for purposes of this section is certified as an artisan by an Indian tribe;

    (2) the terms "Indian product" and "product of a particular tribe or Indian arts and crafts organization" has the meaning given in regulations which may be promulgated by the Secretary of the Interior;

(3) the term "Indian tribe" means—

    (A)any Indian tribe, band, nation, Alaska Native village, or other orga-
nized group or community which is recognized as eligible for the
special programs and services provided by the United States to Indians because of their status as Indians; or

    (B)any Indian group that has been formally recognized as an Indian
tribe by a State legislature or by a State commission of similar organization legislatively vested with State tribal recognition authority; and

    (4) the term "Indian arts and crafts organization" means any legally es-
tablished arts and crafts marketing organization composed of members of Indian tribes.

Plainly, while certain things are spelled out reasonably well in the legislative language—criminal penalties, for example, and a highly restrictive definition of what it
means to be "Indian" in the United States—the matter of what constitutes, or is
meant to constitute, "arts and crafts" is left not merely ambiguous but virtually unaddressed. This, in turn, has led a number of observers to question whether the intent of
the Act's sponsors, and thus of Congress itself, was to "cast the net" far more widely
than it appears on the surface.

Are arts and crafts to be construed in a more or less conventional sense—i.e.,
painting, drawing, printmaking, sculpture, ceramics, photography, beadwork and
jewelry, basketry, weaving, and the like—or should they be considered more broadly,
as including such things as dance, music, drama, cinema, poetry, and literature? If the
latter is to be considered an "artform," as it usually is, shouldn't the production of
nonfiction writing—history, for instance, or philosophy, or political theory—also be
included? After all, fiction, nonfiction, and even technical writing are all produced
through essentially the same "craft" process.

The dominoes keep right on falling. If it is so easily conceivable that scholarly,
journalistic, and scientific writing might be taken as falling within the Act's provisions, then how about the professional occupations associated with such publishing?
This might be taken as encompassing everyone from reporters to research technicians
and university professors. And, if the latter are at issue, then what about elementary
and secondary school teachers? Educational administrators? Public speakers and commentators of all sorts? Day care workers? School bus drivers and custodial staff?

The question of where all this stops, or even where it is supposed to stop, is far
from clear, a matter compounded by the fact that organizations devoted to enforcing
the Act's constraints upon definitions of native identity have recently emerged not
only in connection with what would normally be seen as "arts and crafts production,"
but filmmaking, acting, and university-level teaching as well.[2] Active discussions are
also occurring in preexisting organizations concerned with science and engineering,
journalism, and the like.[3] At least some of the Act's original supporters have openly
called for its expansion to explicitly encompass each of these areas and more.[4]

The slippery slope embodied in the 1990 Arts and Crafts Act is thus readily apparent. In the end, as critics point out, it requires no great flight of fancy to imagine a setting in which anyone desiring, for whatever reason, to identify themselves as an American Indian would be required to obtain what amounts to the express permission of the U.S. government or its delegates to do so. In the alternative, they would face criminal prosecution, hefty fines, and the possibility of imprisonment. That any such development would set in place the mechanism for nullifying one of the last vestiges of genuine self-determination among the indigenous nations of North America—that of deciding for ourselves the composition of our respective polities—is, or at least should be, self-evident.[5]

Proponents of the Act, on the other hand, variously pooh-pooh the idea that any such dire results might occur and argue, often vociferously, that it is in any event worth the risk. The reason for this, they claim, is that passage of the measure has in itself served to drive a number of "counterfeit" Indians out of the commercial venues in which native arts and crafts are sold, thereby opening up increased sales opportunities for "real" Indians. Expansion of the law into other areas of activity, advocates continue, along with rigorous enforcement, would stand to amplify and extend such beneficial effects across the board, alleviating the dire poverty they accurately describe as presently afflicting far too many native people.[6]

Perhaps predictably, the mutual exclusivity of the two positions has engendered a sharp polarization among Indians in the U.S. and, to a lesser extent, in Canada as well. Marked by squadrons of self-styled and -appointed "purity police" on the one side, and increasingly angry denunciations of such tactics on the other, the resulting turmoil has proven extraordinarily ugly and divisive.[7] Nor does it show signs of abating at any point in the foreseeable future.

The purpose of this essay is to attempt a clarification of the situation by lifting the veil of sheer contentiousness which has shrouded the 1990 Act from its inception, offering instead a more balanced assessment. The method selected is that of cost-benefit analysis: What have American Indians lost as a consequence of the law, and what have we gained? The intent of the endeavor is, as it should be, to provide a better and more comprehensive basis for reasonable people to go about making reasoned rather than emotional choices on whether and to what extent they should support either the current law or some evolutionary counterpart in the years ahead. Alternatives to it are suggested in the concluding section.

OPENING ROUNDS

Probably the first thing of consequence happening in the wake of the Act's passage was that the Cherokee Cultural Heritage Center outside Tahlequah, Oklahoma, was forced to close its doors. It seems that the facility's central exhibit, a large sculpture in wood depicting the Cherokees' "Trail of Tears," had been carved by the late Willard Stone, a man who'd never entered his name on the tribal rolls. Under the new law, this made Stone an "ethnic impostor"—and the Cherokee museum guilty of perpetrating "ethnic fraud" by displaying his work—despite the fact that he'd always been considered unquestionably Cherokee by Cherokees. Indeed, Stone was/is generally considered to have been the preeminent Cherokee wood carver of his era, a standing which led to his having been asked to render the Great Seal of the Cherokee Nation.[8]

Nor was Stone the only artist or craftsperson at issue in the museum's collection. Given the sustained history of resistance to enrollment manifested in some of the more traditional sectors of Cherokee society, it was soon discovered that literally scores of "offenders" were involved.[9] Although we Cherokees have long since devised our own methods of determining the validity of claims to Cherokee identity, the new law not only nullified but criminalized us. In order to reopen the museum—and, presumably, to continue using its own Great Seal—the Cherokee Nation of Oklahoma was compelled to implement a special procedure whereby Stone and many of his contemporaries could be posthumously certified or enrolled.[10]

The living were and remain another matter entirely. Often decrying the "insult" to their ancestors of imposing upon them after death something they'd rejected in life, a number of currently practicing Cherokee artists have refused to enroll even though they may be eligible to do so. Such people are hardly cultural/aesthetic also-rans. One of them, the accomplished painter Jeanne Walker Rorex, is Willard Stone's niece.[11] Another is Cherokee Master Artist Bert Seabourn.[12] Still another is Jimmie Durham, a man whose mixed-media and installation work is very prominent in the conceptual art scene, and whose postmodernist theoretical writings on "hybridity" have been internationally embraced as "exceedingly important."[13]

Durham's experience is in many ways indicative. Scheduled for a solo exhibition at the U.S. Bureau of Indian Affairs-sponsored Gallery of American Indian Contemporary Arts (AICA) in San Francisco at the time the Act was passed, he suddenly found himself canceled. Upon inquiry, he was informed that, while the gallery's all-native staff fully accepted his self-identification as a Wolf Clan Cherokee, and that they had "fought hard for the right to mount [his] show as planned," the BIA had confronted them with the stark alternatives of either calling it off or suffering an abrupt and complete withdrawal of the federal funds upon which the gallery's very existence depended.[14]

Although an ad hoc group of native community members quickly took up a collection, rented private loft space, printed a poster and carried through with Durham's exhibition on their own, both the official cancellation and the nakedly coercive means by which it had been achieved emboldened other elements to launch a concerted drive aimed at "purifying" such events throughout the Bay Area.[15] In short order, this self-proclaimed body of "identity police" had adopted a strategy of disrupting—often physically—all manner of native activities, refusing in each case to disengage until participants produced "satisfactory proof" that they met the "standard of Indianness" articulated in the Arts and Crafts Act.[16]

For the next three years, the list of such interventions lengthened and expanded to include, not just arts-related events, but numerous powwows and public lectures, the local Leonard Peltier Support Group, various church-supported shelters and community outreach centers, programming at Pacifica radio station KPFA and other local broadcast facilities, as well as the San Francisco School District's Title-V Indian Education Program and the Native American Studies Department at San Francisco State University.[17]

It was not until the spring of 1994 that the situation began to ease, and then only because the occupation and resulting suspension of services by a native AIDS clinic led to the death of one of the facility's clients.[18] Faced with the possibility of felony murder charges, and finding it impossible to explain how such results could in any way be construed as "beneficial" to the victim or his counterparts, the group quickly de-escalated the physical dimension of its effort in favor of a lower keyed and less risky, but in some ways more insidious, whispering campaign conducted via the Internet as well as such time-honored expedients as letters, phone calls, and word of mouth.

As one longtime resident of the San Francisco native community recently put it, "It got so bad out here for a while that nobody could do or say anything without somebody else popping up to claim they weren't an Indian. It's as if the people doing it—whoever they are, a lot of them like to operate anonymously—are of the opinion that if you've actually accomplished something, or if you actually have things to say that people might find worth hearing, then by that definition alone you must not be a 'real' Indian. And that, of course, raises the question of whether these so-called identity policers are themselves really Indians. I, for one, suspect that a lot of them aren't, but to say so is just to join the vicious circle we've gotten trapped in."[19]

"They've got us chasing our tails," another San Franciscan concludes. "It's humiliating. It's frustrating. We're Indians. We're supposed to know who we are, and to be proud of it. But the appearance is not only that we don't, but that we need the goddamned federal government to sort it out for us. The whole thing just makes us all look like a bunch of idiots. You can almost hear the White Man snickering at the spectacle we're presenting. Now I ask you, where's the pride in that?"[20]

ESCALATION

While eastern Oklahoma and San Francisco may represent particularly striking examples of the internecine squabbling unleashed by the Act, they are neither alone nor necessarily the worst. Santa Fe, New Mexico, for instance, was another flashpoint. There, a sort of roving patrol composed of members of a locally-based group touting itself as the "Native American Artists Association" (NAAA) went virtually from gallery to gallery, demanding to see "proof of identity" for each "allegedly Indian" artist or craftsperson exhibited therein.[21]

Among the NAAA's more noteworthy accomplishments was heading off a prospective show by Phoenix-area maskmaker El Zarco Guerrero, whom they accused of being "a Chicano, not an Indian." (Ironically, Guerrero was later revealed to be an enrolled Juaneño, although he flatly rejected the idea that he was obliged to produce paperwork to document the fact.[22]) A comparable "success" was registered when the group's head, David Bradley, managed to engineer the rejection of paintings by imprisoned American Indian Movement leader Leonard Peltier, an unenrolled Chippewa/Sioux, from a group exhibit at Santa Fe's Institute of American Indian Arts Museum.[23]

Soon, NAAA was seeking to extend its reach internationally. In 1992, for instance, members attempted to convince the curator of a landmark exhibition of First Nations art at the National Gallery of Canada to remove work by Jimmie Durham in favor of that produced by someone within their own ranks.[24] Although this and similar maneuvers have proven unsuccessful over the short run, it has become apparent that a longer-term strategy may be involved. At Alberta's University of Lethbridge, for example, Santa Fe expatriate Alfred Young Man uses his faculty position to indoctrinate students, native and non-native alike, with Arts and Crafts Act-style definitions of Indianness.[25]

Meanwhile, back in the United States, *Indian Country Today* (*ICT*; formerly *Lakota Times*), a widely circulated publication which strongly supported passage of the Act, inaugurated a series of "exposés" concerning the nonenrolled status of several well-published native authors, most prominently the award-winning Modoc writer, Michael Dorris.[26] This, in turn, generated a spate of similar "revelations" in such lesser publications as *News From Indian Country* and the now defunct *Smoke Signals* during 1994 and '95.[27] For his part, *ICT* publisher and nationally syndicated columnist Tim Giago helped things along by repackaging what was appearing in the native press for consumption by the readers of more mainstream papers.[28]

Those who resisted the onslaught were themselves targeted. My own case is in many ways illustrative. In 1991, I published a strong defense of Jimmie Durham which included sharp criticism both of the 1990 Act and of motives I saw as prompting identity policers to conduct themselves as they did.[29] As a consequence, although I am an enrolled Keetoowah Band Cherokee and served as codirector of the Colorado chapter of the American Indian Movement since 1980,[30] I was subjected to a concerted campaign to brand me an "impostor," both nationally and in my home town press.[31]

My publishers were contacted by "representatives of the Indian community" who threatened dire consequences unless my books were withdrawn and I was dropped from their rosters of authors.[32] Agencies handling my public appearances were approached in much the same fashion, while universities and other fora at which I was scheduled to speak were informed that disruptive protests would occur unless they canceled my talks.[33] I was included in *ICT*'s series on "pseudo-Indian writers," showcased in one of Giago's columns, and was for a time the focus of sustained "controversy" in *News From Indian Country*.[34] Needless to say, the Internet came alive with all manner of unsubstantiated assertions.[35]

In early 1993, a small group met secretly with administrators at the University of Colorado to demand that I be summarily fired from my faculty position on grounds of "ethnic fraud."[36] Failing this, they quickly submitted a list of allegations ranging from embezzlement to physical intimidation of students in hopes of forcing my dismissal.[37] Although I was eventually exonerated on all counts, Colorado law is such that this could occur only by way of an official inquiry. Meanwhile, the fact that a mandated investigation process had been convened was itself used by my accusers to cast an aura of validity over their charges.[38]

For me, things have not worked out badly at all. Somewhat ironically, the stench of McCarthyism surrounding the situation may have contributed to my receiving a major teaching award from my college during the year of the Great Investigation, and I've since been promoted to full professor. I've published eight new books since 1993, revised editions of two others, seen translation of still another, and have three more in press.[39] I also continue to receive more invitations to lecture publicly than I can possibly handle.[40]

An untenured junior faculty member would likely not have fared so well, however. Nor would a writer less established than I. Or a young painter, journalist, or filmmaker. Even a senior professor with solid publishing or gallery connections, but less seasoning in the incessant sectarian backbiting and duplicity of both institutional and radical politics, might well have found him- or herself in serious trouble. And, of course, an undetermined number have. More problematic yet is the fact that universities—and publishers, museums, and art galleries, for that matter—are hardly solicitous of the kinds of headaches mine experienced. Given the choice between bringing aboard an undistinguished Indian bearing proper proof of pedigree on the one hand, and a promising but uncertified scholar—or writer, sculptor, or painter—on the other, many may choose to do without native participation altogether.[41]

BENEFITS, REAL AND IMAGINARY

Advocates of the Arts and Crafts Act argue that the ill effects sketched above are more than offset by the benefits which have already accrued to Indians as a result of its passage. In this connection, they often point first to a 1985 Commerce Department report estimating that the importation of ersatz "Indian" crafts from Korea, Taiwan, and other foreign sources siphons off somewhere between ten and twenty percent of the annual $400–800 million "industry value" of such goods from the native craftspeople who should have received it.[42] Unquestionably, the potential revenue lost each year to people as endemically impoverished as American Indians is a problem of the first magnitude.

With that said, however, there is no indication that the Act has had the least favorable impact on the situation, or that it really lends itself to such a result. This is perhaps because, if the intent of policymakers had been to staunch the flow of Asian-produced items, or at least to prevent them from being foisted off by unscrupulous dealers as "Indian made," there was no particular reason to write new legislation pertaining to Indian arts and crafts, per se. Instead, weight might have been more fruitfully placed on beefing up the Tariff Act of 1930, which already required that all imported products be clearly labeled with their countries of origin.[43]

Such convenient rationalizations—or diversions—aside, the real thrust of the 1990 Act is, as it clearly states, to sharply restrict the range of persons allowed to identify themselves as being American Indians within the United States itself. As one

NAAA spokesperson framed the sentiments of its supporters in a letter submitted during the "fact finding" process leading up to the Act's passage:

> Too long have I observed and yes, voiced my outrage over the non-Indian who pushes and elbows the real Indian artist out of Indian art shows, galleries, museums and historical places. Many of these silver, forked-tongued non-Indians, and most of us know who they are, have risen to prominence through fraudulently representing themselves as Indian artists . . . These frauds have one object, and that is to make money.[44]

Indeed. Apart from the writer's uncomfortably whiny tone, suggesting as it does that "real" native artists are somehow inherently inferior to and therefore can't be expected to compete with nonindian "pretenders," there are other problems embedded in the missive. These begin with the question of exactly what economic stakes for Native America undergird such animus projection. The answer, as even the NAAA's most dogmatic adherents were ultimately forced to concede, is not much.[45] While nothing resembling a solid estimate exists—a situation which in itself seems an odd basis upon which to enact federal laws—the best guess advanced has been that it might add up to "several million dollars" per year.[46]

Then there is the matter of who, exactly, it is who's "risen to prominence" on the basis described by the NAAA. Parsing out people like Seabourn, Rorex, and Durham, the strongest example the organization could come up with of someone who is "absolutely not an Indian," but who demonstrably makes a living by claiming otherwise, was an obscure individual in Oklahoma who calls himself "John Redtail Freesoul," peddles "sacred pipes" and, more often, hawks "native ceremonies."[47] Others, like Paul Pletka, whose name came up, and who did in fact achieve a certain prominence during the 1970s while painting neosurrealist depictions of indigenous subject matter, have never actually identified themselves as being Indians.[48]

By the same token, a respectable number of indisputably Indian artists over the past generation have not only achieved prominence in their field, but have become rather wealthy in the bargain. These include the late T.C. Cannon, Fritz Scholder, R.C. Gorman, and the now-deceased Earl Biss, to name but an obvious handful.[49] Taken in combination with the examples offered by Pletka and others, this suggests that certain forms, styles, or manners of expression, and perhaps even content itself, are likely to sell if well-executed, *regardless* of the ethnicity claimed by the artist producing it.[50] It also presents the possibility that, as one rather successful—and enrolled— Oklahoma painter recently put it, "If these guys [NAAA members] would spend half as much time in the studio improving the quality of their art as they do running around worrying about other people's identity cards, they'd have a helluva lot less to complain about."[51]

The acrimony attending NAAA's denunciation of an artistic nobody like "Freesoul" suggests that many of those provoking the organization's ire are involved in arts and crafts production only peripherally, if at all. Instead, they belong to a growing legion of "plastic medicine men" and "New Age hucksters" whose increasingly lucrative trade consists of peddling bogus "Native American rituals" and/or pseudoreligious tracts designed to "share" ersatz renderings of beliefs and practices which indigenous societies all but invariably hold to be most sacred (and private). The problems here are manifest. First of all, there is nothing at all in the 1990 Act which prohibits these activities by nonindians impersonating Indians. Even if there were, or the Act were somehow expanded to encompass such things, the fact is that many of the worst offenders—the late "Sun Bear" (Vincent LaDuke), for example, "Eagle Man" (Ed McGaa) and numerous others—are themselves enrolled in federally recognized tribes (LaDuke as a White Earth Chippewa, McGaa as an Oglala Lakota).[52] Conversely, few if any of the nonindians involved—Lynn Andrews, Robert Bly, and Carlos Castaneda to name but three of the more prominent from a steadily lengthening list—have ever pretended that they themselves *are* Indians.[53]

At issue in this connection are matters mostly of attitude and content rather than identity.[54] It follows that the best antidote to the malady—and probably the *only* one available in a country like the United States, where even the most objectionable expressions of New Age sensibility are swathed in a blanket of First Amendment protections—will be found not in legislation but within the arena of public discourse (i.e., critical analysis, rebuttal, and ridicule). Ironically, some of those who have proven most committed and effective in this respect—I feel no hesitancy about including myself in any such list, along with people like Cherokee anthropologist Rayna Green—have been undermined by identity police attacks resulting from their opposition to the 1990 Act.[55] This situation has, in turn, been seized upon by New Age polemicists like Stephen Harrod Buhner as a means of bolstering their own positions.[56]

FURTHER CONTRADICTIONS

In 1992, conservative nonindian columnist James J. Kilpatrick, writing with reference to the situation of Jeanne Rorex, remarked that the Arts and Crafts Act appeared to have more to do with "restraint of trade" than it did with ensuring the legitimacy of arts and crafts.[57] In this, he was to some extent reflecting a view expressed two years earlier by Wilma Mankiller, who observed that many of the Act's most vociferous supporters seemed to be motivated more by the prospect of personal financial gain and/or resolving psychological insecurities concerning their own identities than by any discernible interest in reinforcing indigenous sovereignty.[58]

The example used by Chief Mankiller was that of a man who was "an artist himself, a 1/64th degree Cherokee who has been a member of the Cherokee Nation for only two years. Prior to that time, he entered several Indian art shows . . . Now, he is attempting to prevent others from doing the same."[59] Such a characterization would certainly appear to fit a number of key players, beginning with the Act's primary congressional sponsor, Colorado Representative (now Senator) Ben Campbell, who has been quoted as saying that only "a few so-called Cherokees who could not prove their ancestry have complained that it is unfair."[60]

Long before he was enrolled as a Northern Cheyenne in 1980, Campbell, working under the name "Ben Nighthorse," fashioned a highly lucrative career as an American Indian jeweler in the Southwest. By his own account, Campbell's "impersonation of an Indian" during the period in which he was neither enrolled nor otherwise certified resulted in his averaging $150,000 per year in profits. This translated into an opulent lifestyle graced by an upscale ranch near Durango, Colorado, a collection of thoroughbred horses and "expensive sports cars that he bought new every year."[61] Moreover, although he contends that a "real" Indian "should have no problem tracing his background" in compliance with the Act,[62] Campbell's own experience readily attests to the opposite. After expending what he himself has estimated as fourteen years and $40,000 in a quest to document his identity—sums of both time and money which are surely beyond the means of most people—he failed rather spectacularly to do so.[63]

This is doubly interesting in that, while rules governing Northern Cheyenne enrollment require documentation that applicants be at least one-half Cheyenne by "blood," Campbell has publicly conceded that he is unsure of his own "quantum" and "that therefore no specific percentage of Indian blood is claimed."[64] The situation is complicated even further by the fact that the one tenuous bit of evidence linking Campbell to *any* native ancestry suggests he is more likely of Jicarilla Apache, Ute, or Puebloan than Cheyenne descent.

In the winter of 1916, a boy calling himself Albert Baldez appeared at the Crow Agency, in Montana. When questioned by agency superintendent Even W. Estep, the boy said he "thought" he was part Jicarilla Apache. On this "very meager" basis, never verified, Estep enrolled the boy as a "half Apache" in the reservation boarding school. There, young Baldez remained only three months before running away to take up residence with the Black Horse family at nearby Northern Cheyenne. Then, on July 10, 1919, he enlisted in the army under the name Albert B. Campbell, turned "his back on his Indian ancestry," and eventually sired Ben Campbell. Based upon the name used by his father upon enlistment, Ben Campbell has adduced that little Albert Baldez was actually Alexander Valdez, son of a Mexican immigrant named Vanceslado Valdez and Fortunata Campbell, who lived in Tierra Amarilla, New Mexico, and Pagosa Junction, Colorado, near the Jicarilla Apache Reservation. While Fortunata may well have been a genizaro (mixed-blood), there is no evidence that she was actually of Jicarilla rather than Ute or Puebloan extraction. Indeed, her mother, Ramona Mestas, grew up in Taos and, while Mestas is certainly the name of a genizaro family—to which she may or not have belonged—it is associated with the Utes, not the Jicarillas. As to the supposed "Cheyenne connection," aside from young Baldez's two-year stint with the Black Horses—from which Ben Campbell's "Nighthorse" obviously derives—it is based upon the thoroughly speculative assumption that Ramona Mestas was actually a young Cheyenne woman whom the Cheyennes themselves record as having been killed during the 1864 Sand Creek Massacre. Although there is absolutely nothing to support his contention, Ben Campbell claims to have "just sort of accepted" the proposition that, instead, she survived, made her way to Taos, and was then adopted into one or another Mestas family. As the senator himself now declaims with staggering circularity of logic, "Indians have their own ways of putting things together." And *this* is the man who professes a belief that others' "unproven" assertions of native identity constitute "fraud"?[65]

One can, and probably should, feel considerable sympathy for the senator's plight. No more so, however, than for the "many others" in the same situation mentioned by Little Big Horn Community College President Janine Pease Windy Boy while remarking upon Campbell's example.[66] The fact is that these many others are not customarily privileged to resolve their difficulties by enrolling on the basis of such nebulous documentation as Campbell's. On the contrary, people with far better proof that "they are who they say they are" are routinely turned down by tribal enrollment committees.

This raises the question of why the Northern Cheyennes opted to treat Campbell in such preferential fashion. The answer, unfortunately, may be as simple as the fact that, as he himself has recounted, he has long been strategically lavish in his bestowal of gifts upon them, for example the creation of a "handsome ceremonial pipe . . . richly inlaid with stones and silver and decorated with beads and feathers" for the tribe as a whole, the crafting of a drum and minting of fifty commemorative medals for the politically important Crazy Dog Society, the fashioning of a beautifully inlaid buffalo skull for the reservation's Dull Knife Community College, the making of a unique gold and blue coral ring for a key elder, and so on.[67] An additional incentive may be discerned from the view expressed by Cheyenne elder Austin Two Moons that it might be useful for the Cheyennes to have "one of their own" in Washington, D.C., even if he weren't, strictly speaking, a Cheyenne.[68]

While naturalization of citizens is of course the right of any nation, indigenous no less than any other, the context at issue here obviously opens up the prospect of rich and powerful nonindians being officially enrolled as tribal members while powerless and impoverished Indians are regularly denied the recognition of their identity conveyed by such enrollment. By all appearances, then, an exception of the sort not readily available to more run-of-the-mill applicants was made when it came time to process the senator's paperwork.

Much the same reputedly pertains to the enrollment as a Southern Cheyenne of federal lobbyist Suzan Shown Harjo, elsewhere described as "one of the prime movers behind the Indian Arts and Crafts Act."[69] Although Harjo has publicly denied having been enrolled by the Southern Cheyennes long after she'd established herself as a professional "American Indian spokesperson," she also identifies herself as a Muscogee (Creek), a people with whom she is not enrolled at all.[70] While it may be true that there is nothing intrinsically wrong with the latter practice—Harjo is undeniably related to the Muscogees by marriage—hers is exactly the sort of "unauthorized self-identification" she has proven so vituperative in denouncing as ethnic fraud when employed with equal or greater validity by others.[71] Such problems attend the status of virtually every major figure among the identity police.[72]

Nor do supporters of the Act fare better when extending claims that they are somehow defending native aesthetic tradition from encroachment or corruption by "outsiders."[73] Ben Nighthorse, for one, has stated explicitly that he considers traditional styles to be "overworked and worn out," and that the whole point of his own jewelry designs—as well as those of the famed Charles Loloma, Preston Monongye, and others—has been to *depart* from traditional patterns by incorporating both new materials and influences as diverse as Tiffany, Cellini, Boucheron, and Fabergé.[74]

With respect to the "fine arts" approach to aesthetic expression embraced by virtually all members of the NAAA, as well as their counterparts in cinema and photography, there is quite literally no tradition either to defend or to depart from. As J.J. Brody framed the matter more than a quarter-century ago:

> Except for a few years at San Ildefonso Pueblo, Indian easel painting was always a nontribal art with only the most tenuous roots in any tribal art system. Produced for urban-industrial consumers . . . it was assumed to be tribal, but as it developed in nontribal, antitribal, or pan-Indian environments, its forms could never be anything but nontribal, antitribal or pan-Indian. If ever an art can be described as schizoid, it was Indian easel painting until it reached its most recent phase. In this phase, the problems cease to exist: It has no style, manner, tradition, nor anything else that identifies it as Indian; the artist simply happens to be Indian.[75]

This is not to say that specifically native values and perspectives cannot be brought to bear with good effect in such work (they can be and obviously have been by a broad range of artists), just that there is nothing inherently "Indian" in the media themselves. Further, for a displaced and thoroughly assimilated Chippewa like the NAAA's David Bradley—adopted by a white family at a very early age, never a functioning part of his own culture and unable as a result even to speak his language or practice his ceremonies—to advance *himself* as a sort of repository/protector of traditional values and perspectives is ludicrous to the point of insult. Fraud, be it said, comes in many forms.[76]

ON THE MATTER OF SOVEREIGNTY

Probably the strongest, or at least most appealing, argument put forth by proponents of the 1990 Act concerns the need to reinforce the sovereignty of indigenous nations. As Bradley articulated the idea, "We are sovereign nations, and we have the right to determine who is a member of our nation and who is a citizen of our nation . . . We need to protect [Indian art] not because of its economic impact, but for the preservation of the Indian people. You talk about culture. The majority of Native American

Indian artists are involved because of culture. As a sovereign nation [*sic*: there are *many* indigenous nations], we have a right to protect our rights."[77]

Speaking on behalf of the National Congress of American Indians, of which she was then executive director, Suzan Harjo seconded such sentiments in 1989, informing the House panel convened to hear concerns regarding the then-proposed legislation that "we see this as a sovereign issue" involving recognition of "the inherent sovereign right of the Indian nations to determine sovereignty."[78] And again, to quote a representative of the Eight Northern Pueblos Council during the same hearings:

> We feel strongly that tribes should determine who is Indian or who is recognized by the tribe. Statements were made about the Indianness of various individuals. I strongly feel and relate that to other racial and ethnic groups. I think there's a very strong distinction here. Tribes are recognized by the Federal Government as sovereign nations, and we're the only racial or ethnic group that's [so] recognized. So I don't think it's fair to compare one's ethnicity and one's racial background. And so we strongly feel that tribes should determine who is a member and who is not a member, whether they're recognized by the Government or not recognized by the Government.[79]

To put it most charitably, such statements, and the record is filled with many more, are simply incoherent. First of all, despite the radical rhetoric with which Harjo larded her presentation, decrying "the terms of colonialism" imposed upon native peoples in the U.S. (she mentions substitution of the word "member" for "citizen" in describing the status connoted by enrollment in a "federally-recognized tribe"), the reality is that the very term "tribe," which she and her colleagues bandy about so freely, is itself a colonialist imposition.[80] In addition, the paradigm of federal recognition/authority they sought to invoke via the Act constitutes the essential doctrinal apparatus rationalizing U.S. colonial dominion over Native North America.[81]

Second, contrary to assertions made by the Pueblo representative and many others, the United States did *not* enter into treaties with or otherwise recognize the sovereign standing of American Indian peoples as "racial or ethnic groups." By constitutional provision, the federal government has always been legally precluded from entering into treaty relations with *any* entity, including "tribes," aside from other *nations* (that is, entities which are politically rather than racially, ethnically, and/or culturally defined).[82] As recently as 1977, the U.S. Supreme Court has unequivocally reaffirmed this crucial distinction in *U.S. v. Antelope.*

> Federal regulation of tribes . . . is governance of once-sovereign *political* communities; it is *not* to be viewed as legislation of a "racial" group consisting of "Indians" (emphasis added).[83]

Third, and most important, proponents' wholesale "confusion of the political with the cultural (or ethnic) and both with the racial" in the formulation of federal identity criteria threatens to undermine what little residual sovereignty has been left to indigenous nations at the dawn of the twenty-first century, most especially with respect to our ability to determine the composition of our own citizenry.[84] This is because, at base, it is no more logically necessary for a person to be an "enrolled member of a federally-recognized tribe" to be ethnically Indian than it is for another person to be a citizen of a European country in order to be construed as "Euroamerican," or of Italy in order to be described, with greater ethnic precision, as an "Italo-American."[85]

Italian nationals are, of course, imbued with a spectrum of rights, privileges, entitlements, and responsibilities which are not automatically shared by their noncitizen ethnic Italian counterparts. Precisely the same principle of differentiation pertains with respect to enrolled and unenrolled American Indians. The two groups are politically distinct, or at least distinguishable, even though they in many ways hold a cultural/historical heritage in common.[86] And, whatever the differences in respective political standings, neither group is sociologically/anthropologically more valid than the other.[87]

A serious legal rub enters into the 1990 Act's substitution of nationality for ethnicity when it is taken in combination with its advocates' contention that the law is necessary to protect their version of native identity as an "intellectual property right" and/or "marketable commodity."[88] Since such rights are vested primarily in individuals rather than in governments, the conjuncture at issue makes it virtually inevitable that at least some indigenous governments "will end up being defendants in legal challenges by disgruntled nonmembers who are denied [enrollment or other] certification or who are certified but question the assumed authority of the tribe over them."[89]

> If Indian identity is property, in which one has intellectual property rights, then the question arises whether those individuals who have a legitimate claim to being Indian by some accepted standard, but who are not Indians under this statute, have been deprived of their property without due process of law.[90]

It might be argued, as it has been by Harjo and others, that due process guarantees accrue under the Fifth Amendment to the U.S. Constitution and thus have no bearing on the internal mechanisms by which tribal governments determine their enrollment procedures. The 1978 *Martinez* opinion is often cited as evidence in this regard. *Martinez*, however, concerned how such governments went about defining their own constituents, while the Arts and Crafts Act is expressly aimed at *non*members.[91] Moreover, in demanding promulgation of a federal statute on the matter of native identity, both tribal officials and "independents" like Harjo implicitly conceded federal jurisdiction over such questions (one can hardly demand federal intervention and claim "sovereign immunity" from it at the same time).

Litigation will therefore necessarily occur in federal courts, subject to inquiries as to whether the Act creates a legal classification based upon race. Since—leaving aside statements like that of the above-quoted Pueblo Council spokesperson—the requirement for enrollment in the vast majority of all federally recognized tribes at this point *begins* with some minimum "degree of Indian blood," there can be no serious doubt that it does.[92] From there, since all such classifications are inherently "suspect" under U.S. law, the question becomes whether, "subject to the most exacting scrutiny" required by the Fourteenth Amendment to its Constitution, the federal government can demonstrate to a juridical certainty that the "classification is necessary to a compelling interest," *not* of indigenous governments but of the United States itself.[93]

For native peoples, this is, completely and utterly, a "no win" situation. While "our side"—which in this instance can only be construed, with ultimate absurdity, as our federal colonizers—may prevail in a few or even many potential cases, the unfortunate truth is that "*any* law, statutory or not, has the potential to change the entire legal structure of its context . . . Law and social change is not a one-way street, but interactional."[94] In other words, it will likely require only a single loss in court for *all* racial constructions of Indian identity, including those pertaining to tribal enrollment, to be ruled impermissible.

At that point, federal intervention will be judicially mandated, not with respect to the self-identification of ethnic Indians, but with regard to how native governments themselves go about determining the qualifications for indigenous citizenship. The United States will then be back in the business of directly administering tribal rolls in exactly the same sense it was a century ago, during the era of allotment and the Dawes Commissions.[95] Assertions—or, more properly, reassertions—of native sovereignty will be set back a hundred years or nullified altogether. Worst of all, perhaps, it can be said with no small measure of accuracy that this time "we" asked for it.

THE MAGNITUDE OF ETHNICITY

It's not that there haven't been ample warnings. Beyond the statements of native leaders like Wilma Mankiller, unenrolled artists like Durham and Jeanne Rorex, and academic activists like myself, even a U.S. Senator, Jeff Bingaman of New Mexico, offered a thoroughly negative assessment in 1991 as to what implementation of the Act might mean. "It is simply not sufficient or logical," he argued, "to say that nonenrolled Indians can continue with their art, so long as they refrain from talking about it in connection with their heritage."[96]

> The act appears to create the odious spectacle of requiring American citizens to carry paperwork establishing their racial or ethnic purity before they can fully practice their chosen professions.[97]

Bingaman went on to predict that suits would arise on the basis of the First, Fifth, and Fourteenth Amendments, and that the courts would be "unlikely" to uphold the statute in the face of such challenges. The outcome, he suggested, might well be an infringement upon rather than a bolstering of the sovereignty presently enjoyed by native governments.[98]

Meanwhile, all efforts by ad hoc identity policers to finesse the situation by articulating some sort of definitional reconciliation between the parameters of ethnicity and the constraints of tribal enrollment have failed. Representative of the genre was the postulation offered by self-styled "Cherokee genealogist" David Cornsilk when he opined in 1991 that, to be considered Indian in even a generalized ethnic sense, one must be directly and demonstrably descended from persons who "stayed with the tribe, enrolled when required to, and otherwise lived an Indian life."[99]

Apart from the fact that in this rendering "living an Indian life" comes dangerously close to "doing what one is told to do, whenever one is told to do it," a concept which would undoubtedly prove startling to some of Native America's more significant historical figures, Cornsilk begs even the most obvious questions. As analyst Gail K. Sheffield has pointed out, the "American Indian experience . . . also includes people who, *because they were Indian,* were separated from the tribal context. In addition to those who chose to avoid government rolls [or resist forced removal], there were significant dislocations created by the federal government through policies that encouraged adoption of Indian children by whites and relocation of rural Indians to cities (emphasis original)."[100] What of them?

On these "equally authentic Indian experiences," Cornsilk and his colleagues remain alternately silent and contemptuously dismissive, postures which leave the "ethnics" little recourse but to take to the courts now that such arbitrary denials of their identity have become law.[101] The magnitude of the threat to indigenous sovereignty thus posed may in some ways be calibrated in direct proportion to the size of the ethnic Indian population comprising the pool of potential plaintiffs. Here, a 1991 statement by Jonathan Taylor, then-Principal Chief of the Eastern Band of Cherokee (North Carolina), is instructive:

> There are many people in this country—including an inordinate percentage of whom live in the Southeast—that have varying degrees of Indian blood in their veins . . . There are, without question, hundreds of thousands of people in the Southeast and in Oklahoma who have some degree of Cherokee ancestry and who are proud of that ancestry [but who are not enrolled members of any officially recognized body].[102]

Comparable observations might be made, of course, about a number of other federally- or state-recognized peoples besides the Cherokees.[103] Further, there are a number of nations such as the Klamaths whose federal recognition was terminated pursuant to House Resolution 108 during the 1950s, and who therefore—although they continue to be considered Indians for certain purposes pertaining to treaty rights—are no longer "Indians" within the meaning of the 1990 Act.[104] Finally, there are literally hundreds of groups, sometimes whole peoples, whose existence has, for whatever reason, never been formally acknowledged by either a state or the federal government. The Abenakis of the Maine/Vermont area are a prime example of the latter.[105]

Exactly how many people fall into the overall category of unenrolled ethnic Indians is open to discussion and has been subject to broad interpretation. Of the

1,878,285 persons initially identified as American Indians in the 1990 U.S. census, only 746,175 were actually enrolled.[106] While this data suggests that the number of ethnics is approximately 1.1 million, it is also true that several million others were identified as having "some degree" of native ancestry.[107] Analysts like Joanne Nagel and demographer C. Matthew Snipp have demonstrated rather convincingly that a realistic working estimate would be something on the order of seven million ethnic Indians.[108] Native demographer Jack D. Forbes has also dealt seriously with the question, and his preliminary total comes in at around *fifteen* million.[109]

However many "genuine" ethnic Indians there may be, it is clear that their numbers greatly exceed those of their formally enrolled and recognized relatives. Certainly, there are more than enough to visit a virtually endless rain of lawsuits upon the heads the 400 or so existing tribal councils, should the latter display the effrontery of attempting to employ federal law as a means of suppressing or negating ethnic Indians' sense and expression of indigenous identity. If nothing else, the expense of defending against the potential proliferation of legal actions stands to vastly outstrip any possible financial benefit the councils anticipated as accruing from their support of the Arts and Crafts Act.[110]

ALTERNATIVES

As the internationally acclaimed but unenrolled Mescalero Apache painter John Nieto foresaw in his 1989 testimony before Congress, "the hairsplitting among Indian people invited by efforts to legislate Indianness is both divisive and counterproductive."[111] At present, while it is difficult to name a single bona fide nonindian artist or craftworker whose career has been seriously disrupted by the 1990 Act—or, for that matter, a single native artist whose career has tangibly benefited from it—the toll it has taken on indigenous people is readily apparent.[112] This is true, not only in terms of the severity of the bickering passage of the Act has provoked between and within enrolled and nonenrolled communities, but in the legal/political/financial jeopardy we have incurred in its wake.

Objectively, any law carrying with it the combination of such heavy losses and meager gains as the Arts and Crafts Act is one that Native North America should vigorously and collectively oppose. But, beyond even the possibility of repealing the specific statute at issue, or otherwise effecting its neutralization, there is a compelling need to address the festering complex of attitudes and misunderstandings which led far too many native people to support such legislation in the first place.[113] In the alternative, the problematic outlooks which gave rise to the Act will inevitably linger, continuing to flare up from time to time, always manifesting themselves in concrete forms of self-defeat.

Topping the list of things in need of correction is the binary and simplistic "apples/oranges," "is/is not" construction which uniquely pervades the U.S. discourse on native identity.[114] An expansion of descriptive vernacular to at least the extent evident in Canada, where both "status" and "nonstatus" Indians are officially recognized as being indigenous, albeit occupying different politicolegal niches, would go far in this direction.[115] Adoption of the Canadian classification of "Métis"—that is, of a specific strata of biologically/culturally mixed people—might also prove quite useful, at least in analytical terms.[116]

For any such transition in thinking to occur, however, it is imperative that holdovers from the long discredited tradition of nineteenth-century Euroamerican scientific racism be jettisoned by Indians themselves.[117] Not only does the internalization and adherence by a frightening number of native people to such antiquated racialist myths as "blood quantum" serve to preclude understandings of Indianness in political, cultural, or even genealogical terms, they are already proving suicidal for a number of indigenous nations when used as enrollment criteria.[118]

Put bluntly, American Indians have, overall, long experienced far and away the highest rate of "out marriage" of any "racial" group in North America.[119] The net result, throughout the twentieth century, has been a steady decline in the pool of "pure" or "full-bloods" while the number of native offspring displaying ever more mixed lineage has increased explosively.[120] At this point, the proportion of Fullbloods within most indigenous populations is minimal and declining—among the Minnesota/Wisconsin Chippewa, for example, it is estimated to have dropped to a mere five percent—or already nonexistent.[121] Given this context, "exclusive racial definition of membership will gradually cause a tribe to die out."[122]

Efforts to cope with this harsh reality while nonetheless clinging to conceptions of race have led some tribal councils to venture into the realm of the sublime. Consider the example of the Umatilla, a small people in Washington State. When informed by a consultant that enforcement of enrollment criteria requiring applicants to document "one-quarter degree of Umatilla blood" would result in their virtual extinction within fifty years, they revised their enrollment guidelines to require proof of any degree of Umatilla blood in combination with at least one-quarter degree in some other federally-recognized tribe.[123] As one critic of such maneuvers has observed:

> They've completely lost touch. I'd really like to see them go before a judge—which is exactly what they're going to have to do if they actually try to enforce this thing against people who are demonstrably of Umatilla descent while admitting those with other native pedigrees—and try to explain how being genetically linked to the Lakotas or Mohawks makes a person one whit more Umatilla than being full-blood Irish, Bantu, or Japanese. This has nothing to do with "culture" or "sovereignty." It's a transparently racist construction, no more defensible than any other.[124]

A more tenable approach may be found in that of the Cherokee Nation of Oklahoma, which dropped blood quantum in favor of genealogy as the decisive criterion for enrollment during the 1970s. What the CNO achieved as a result might well serve as an example worthy of replication or adaptation across the continent.

The Oklahoma Cherokee, without a reservation landbase, have been able to survive tribally by an inclusive definition of what it is to be Cherokee. Their definition allowed relatively large numbers of people with Cherokee lineage but relatively small amounts of Cherokee blood into the tribe. This allowed the tribe to reestablish itself after virtual "dissolution" and to achieve political power in Oklahoma. The tribe, in turn, has protected a smaller group of full-blood, more traditional Cherokee from American non-Indian ways of life.[125]

Responding to arguments that the CNO model has led to an "unnecessary degree of acculturation . . . genetic dilution . . . and comparable maladies," historian Mary Young points to a multitude of peoples such as the Yamasee who seem to have gone out of existence altogether while pursuing other, more exclusionary strategies. "The Cherokee people today still have a tribal identity, a living language, and at least [three] tribal government bodies," she says. "That's more than one can say of the Yamasee."[126]

Although no other people has as yet adopted inclusive policies of enrollment to the extent evident among the Cherokees, there are signs that some are considering and in a few cases experimenting with their own variations. Both the Yankton Sioux Tribe of South Dakota and the Oklahoma Tonkawas have, for instance, issued certifications of Indian identity to craftspeople who, although not biologically native, had been adopted and raised by enrolled tribal members from an early age.[127] The Sault Ste. Marie Chippewa in Michigan have also expressed interest in developing guidelines which would allow for the certification of such individuals.[128]

These signs auger the possibility that there may yet be a way to bridge more generally the now widening chasm separating "the core population of American Indians" from a much larger body of "Americans of Indian descent . . . who can recall, legitimately, some amount of Indian ancestry" and those who have, through marriage, adoption, or other forms of naturalization been incorporated into indigenous societies.[129] If so, it seems likely that the threats to native sovereignty posed by the Arts and Crafts Act will prove transitory, as will much of the duplicity, hypocrisy, and sheer maliciousness which has marked the behavior of many of its more outspoken proponents. Thus may the identity police be consigned to their proper place in history's dustbin.

Such would be one of the strongest imaginable reassertions of indigenous tradition because, in the end, "what seems important . . . is that American Indians be allowed to do their own defining, either as individuals or as tribes. This may occur on the individual level through self-identification; it may occur on the tribal level through formal membership. One may object that self-identification allows considerable variation among individuals defined as American Indian, but American Indians have *always* had tremendous variation among themselves, and the variations have in many ways been increased, not reduced, by the events of history, demographic and other. Allowing self-identification and the differences it encompasses is simply to allow American Indians to be American Indians, something done all too infrequently in the short history of the United States."[130]

3

CONFRONTING COLUMBUS DAY

An Argument Based in International Law

♦ ♦ ♦ ♦ ♦ ♦ ♦ ♦ ♦ ♦ ♦ ♦ ♦

> The fact that domestic law does not punish an act which is an international crime does not free the perpetrator of such crime from responsibility under international law.
> —International Law Commission Report of Principles,
> UN Doc. A/1706, Dec. 13, 1950

THE FOLLOWING IS A BRIEF SUPPORTING A MOTION TO DISMISS CHARGES AGAINST the author, Russell Means, Glenn T. Morris, and Cahuilla Red Elk (a.k.a., Margaret Martinez), principal leaders of the American Indian Movement of Colorado, for having halted a Columbus Day celebratory parade near the Colorado State Capitol Building in Denver, on October 12, 1991. Having stopped the parade for approximately forty-five minutes, the defendants—supported by more than three hundred other protestors—refused police directives to remove themselves from the street until we were arrested. The four of us were then charged with refusing to obey a lawful police order, obstructing a public thoroughfare, and disturbing the peace, offenses carrying a combined potential of two years incarceration.

The charges were not dismissed on the basis of the arguments contained herein. At trial, however, we were allowed considerable latitude in presenting them to the jury (which, predictably enough, was composed not of like-minded activists but rather of twelve "average" citizens). In the end, we were not only acquitted on all counts, but the jury foreman read into the record a stinging indictment, concurred in unanimously by his colleagues, of the parade organizers, police and city officials, the local press (which had gone out of its way to cast us as "brown-shirted thugs"), and the whole notion that either Columbus or his legacy are worthy of public commemoration.

In the aftermath, it was decided that I should publish the brief insofar as it stands to be adaptable to other contexts, not only among those who would seek to confront the spectacle of Columbus Day, but others who wish to take comparable positions with regard to the public agitation by the Ku Klux Klan, American Nazi Party, and similar organizations of the racist right. It is also felt that the material may well lend itself, not only to utilization by defendants in criminal proceedings, but to public education and potential litigation against groups which, directly or indirectly, endorse racism, colonialism, genocide, and aggression as acceptable forms of behavior.

THE BRIEF

The defendants contend that we were engaged in entirely lawful conduct on October 12, 1991, and that such charges as are presently lodged against us as a result of our actions on that date are invalid. We anchor this contention in various elements of international law and legal doctrine, most specifically the 1948 Convention on Prevention and Punishment of the Crime of Genocide, to which the United States is by its own assertion(s) and comportment bound.

GENOCIDE AND THE GENOCIDE CONVENTION

The crime of genocide is usually understood in the United States as being more or less exclusively associated with the forms and programs developed by nazi Germany in its drive to physically exterminate such *untermenschen* ("subhuman peoples") as the Slavs, Gypsies, and, especially, the Jews. This is an entirely erroneous view. The meaning of the term, coined by the Polish jurist Raphaël Lemkin in 1944, is something very much broader, both in temporal scope and in terms of the techniques employed. Although the word itself was constructed by combining the Greek *genos* ("race" or "tribe") and the Latin *cidium* ("killing"), according to Lemkin it describes a process considerably more multifaceted and sophisticated than simple mass murder. Indeed, mass murder may or not be present within the genocidal context:

> Generally speaking, genocide does not necessarily mean the immediate destruction of a nation, *except when* accomplished by mass killing of all the members of a nation. It is intended rather to signify a coordinated plan of different actions aimed at destruction of the essential foundations of the life of national groups, with the aim of annihilating the groups themselves. The objective of such a plan would be disintegration of the political and social institutions, of culture, language, national feelings, religion, and the economic existence of national groups, and the destruction of personal security, liberty, health, dignity, and the lives of individuals belonging to such groups. Genocide is the destruction of the national group as an entity, and the actions involved are directed against individuals, not in their individual capacity but as members of the national group (emphasis added).[1]

Reinforcement of the view that genocide often entails methods radically different than the outright murder of large numbers of people is found in Lemkin's observation that, "Genocide has two phases: one, destruction of the national pattern of the oppressed group; the other, the imposition of the national pattern of the oppressor."[2] Clearly, the latter imposition could not occur if it were a definitional requirement that all or even most members of the oppressed group be killed in order for a genocide to have occurred. To the contrary, as it was put by the Lebanese delegate to the United Nations (U.N.) committee which produced the Draft Convention on Punishment and Prevention of the Crime of Genocide in 1947, what is at issue is the "destruction of a [recognizably distinct] human group, *even though the individual members survive* (emphasis added)."[3]

This guiding conceptualization of genocide as the creation of conditions inducing the coerced disappearance of discrete cultural entities (as such) resulted in a formulation within the initial U.N. Draft Convention on Genocide which focused not only upon mass killing, but upon actions and policies which brought about the "disintegration of the political, social or economic structure of a group or nation" and the "systematic moral debasement of a group, people, or nation."[4] In the subsequent Draft Convention produced by the U.N. Secretariat in 1948, genocide was defined in a two-fold way, as "destruction of a group" and as "preventing its preservation and development."[5]

All in all, the construction of international law expressly prohibiting genocidal conduct followed, as the Lebanese delegate put it, the idea that distinct human groups should be treated as "absolute entities . . . which it would be criminal to attack."[6] In the end, Article II of the U.N.'s 1948 Convention on Prevention and Punishment of the Crime of Genocide (UN GAOR Res. 260A (III) 9 Dec. 1948; effective 12 Jan. 1951) specifies five categories of activity, only one of which involves outright killing, to be genocidal when directed against an identified "national, ethnical, racial, or religious group," and therefore criminal under international law.

(a) Killing members of the group;
(b) Causing serious bodily or mental harm to members of the group;
(c) Deliberately inflicting on the group conditions of life calculated to bring about its physical destruction in whole or in part;
(d) Imposing measures intended to prevent births within the group;
(e) Forcibly transferring children of the group to another group.

Under Article III, the Convention makes the following acts punishable under the law:

(a) Genocide;
(b) Conspiracy to commit genocide;
(c) Direct and public incitement to commit genocide;
(d) Attempt to commit genocide;
(e) Complicity in genocide.

Article IV states that all persons shall be held accountable for acts committed under Article III, "whether they are constitutionally responsible rulers, public officials, or private individuals," while Article V calls upon the nations of the world to enact "the necessary legislation to give effect to the present Convention and, in particular, to pro-

vide effective penalties for persons guilty of genocide or any of the other acts enumerated in Article III." Because the Convention was intended to prevent as well as punish
commission of genocide, a broad latitude of meaning, centering in notions of "advocacy," has been associated with the provisions concerning incitement of (Article III(c))
and complicity in (Article III(e)) genocide and/or genocidal processes.[7] In situations
where there is disagreement as to the meaning of such terms, or in which a given government professes confusion concerning the substance of the law, the Convention
provides under Article IX for interpretation and adjudication by the International
Court of Justice (ICJ).

U.S. RESPONSE TO THE GENOCIDE CONVENTION

It is instructive that, although more than one hundred nations rapidly ratified the
Genocide Convention, the United States declined to do so for a period of forty years.
The reason for this extensive delay resides primarily, as revealed in the records of Senate debate of the Genocide Convention after it was referred to that body by President
Truman in 1950, in congressional concern that a broad range of federal policies vis-à-
vis minority populations in the U.S. might be viewed as genocidally criminal under
international law.[8] Considerable anxiety was expressed by various senators and expert
witnesses over the years that certain activities of subordinate (state and local) governments and private parties, each of them sanctioned and/or protected by the federal
government, might well violate the terms of the Convention.

Examples include the persistence of "Jim Crow" laws in various southern states
despite the extreme and well-recognized mental harm such statutes imposed upon
African American and other readily identifiable minority populations.[9] Another illustration is found in official toleration of the organizing activities of the Ku Klux Klan
and comparable groups, despite their advocacy of patently genocidal principles and
frequent resort to physical violence against racially-defined target groups (e.g., more
than 1,000 lynchings of blacks between 1930 and 1960).[10] Other issues specifically
concerning American Indians, such as involuntary sterilization programs and the massive forced transfer of children, will be covered below.

When the United States Senate finally ratified the Genocide Convention during
the closing days of the 100th Congress, it was largely on the basis of a growing belief
that the U.S. was forfeiting "moral leadership" in world affairs as a result of its nonrat-
ification,[11] and on the basis of the Genocide Convention Implementation Act of 1988
(Title 18, Part I, U.S.C., otherwise known as the Proxmire Act), a statute which incorporated certain language designed to narrow the intent of the internationally accepted
convention in its application to the United States.[12] Further, the instrument of treaty
ratification which the Senate instructed President Ronald Reagan to deposit with the
U.N. Secretary General in November of 1988 contained a Resolution of Ratification
(S. Exec. Rep. 2, 99th Cong., 1st Sess. 26-27 (1985), adopted February 19, 1986, and
otherwise referred to as the Lugar-Helms-Hatch Sovereignty Package). The resolution
contained a reservation (Article I (2)) stating:

[N]othing in the Convention requires or authorizes legislation or other action by the United States of America prohibited by the Constitution of the United States as interpreted by the United States.

It is thus plain that the Senate sought, even while enacting legislation to "implement" the Genocide Convention and effecting a corresponding ratification of its terms by treaty, to exempt the U.S. from the implications of international legal custom and convention. In effect, it sought to elevate the U.S. Constitution to a status above that of international law. As has been noted elsewhere, "the acknowledged purpose of the Sovereignty Package was to reduce the convention to nothing more than a mere symbol of opposition to genocide. This fact alone raises the question of whether the United States ratified in good faith."[13] The Package has been described by a Senate Committee as an "embarrassment to the United States" insofar as it clearly suggests that the U.S. formally seeks to retain prerogatives to engage in or sanction policies and activities commonly understood as being genocidal, even while professing to condemn genocide.[14]

LEGAL VALIDITY OF THE U.S. POSTURE ON GENOCIDE

There is abundant evidence that the Senate was aware, even as it advanced its "Sovereignty Package" purporting to subordinate the Genocide Convention to the U.S. Constitution, that the gesture contradicted the requirements of the constitution itself. Not the least indicator of this lies in the testimony of an expert witness, American Bar Association representative George Finch, in his testimony before the Senate Foreign Affairs Committee during its 1950 hearings on the matter. After observing that a formal treaty would be required in order for the U.S. to become a party of record to the Convention, Finch observed that, "By the United States Constitution [Article VI, Section 2] treaties are 'the supreme law of the land, and the judges in every State shall be bound thereby, anything in the Constitution or laws of any State to the contrary notwithstanding.'"[15] In other words, the government would be unable to unilaterally legislate exceptions for itself with regard to the terms, provisions, and understandings of the Genocide Convention if it were ratified by treaty.

On its face, the problem might seem to have been resolved, domestically at least, by a Supreme Court opinion rendered in *Reid v. Covert* (354 U.S. 1 (1957)) that "any treaty provision that is inconsistent with the United States Constitution would simply be invalid under national law." Under Article 27 of the 1969 Vienna Convention on the Law of Treaties, however, no state can invoke the provisions of its internal law as a reason for not abiding by a treaty obligation.[16] Although the United States has not yet ratified the Vienna Convention, it has officially recognized it as being the "definitive" promulgation of international law with regard to treaty relations.[17] Hence, the Senate's attempt to carve out exemptions for itself from the force of international law has no legal integrity, and is subject to protest or renunciation by other parties to the Genocide Convention.

Indeed, a decade before the Senate's Sovereignty Package was submitted to the U.N. Secretariat, the rapporteur of an Economic and Social Council (ECOSOC) working group studying problems in the Genocide Convention's implementation worldwide reviewed the draft language of the various proposed U.S. "reservations" and "understandings," and officially concluded that Article I(2) was invalid insofar as it failed to conform to Vienna Convention standards.[18] The Sovereignty Package was nonetheless submitted in 1988, with the result that by December 1989 nine European allies of the United States—Denmark, Finland, Ireland, Italy, the Netherlands, Norway, Spain, Sweden, and the United Kingdom—had entered formal objections to Article I(2). Three of these nations—Denmark, the Netherlands, and the United Kingdom—also entered strong objections to Article I(1) of the Package, in which the Senate attempted to reserve unto itself the right to determine when and if the ICJ might have authority in dispute resolution involving the U.S. The Netherlands declined to recognize the United States as a party to the Genocide Convention until such time as these "difficulties" are corrected; the other eight nations elected to hold this matter in abeyance, pending "discussions."[19] As has been observed elsewhere:

> [T]he convention has already been ratified by over one hundred states [none of which attached qualifications remotely comparable to those demanded by the United States], and under international rules of treaty law these states have a say in determining whether or not the U.S. conditions are acceptable . . . [B]y insisting on adoption of the Sovereignty Package, the Senate effectively gutted U.S. ratification of the convention.[20]

Moreover, it is legally irrelevant whether or not the United States ever attempted to ratify the Genocide Convention, or whether it manages to accomplish such ratification in a valid fashion in the future. Genocide has come to be seen as a crime within customary law, and the Convention is thus binding upon the U.S. whether or not it chooses to formally acknowledge the fact.[21] This is a matter tacitly recognized by the federal government itself, as is indicated in the authoritative *Restatement of the Foreign Relations Law of the United States* (1987).[22] Further, the Charter of the United Nations, to which the U.S. is a signatory, assumes that the organization can declare principles of international law which are binding, even upon nonmember states.[23]

> The concept of offenses against the [customary] law of nations (*delicti juris gentium*) was recognized by the classical text-writers on international law and has been employed in national constitutions and statutes. It was regarded as sufficiently tangible in the eighteenth century so that United States Federal Courts sustained indictments charging acts as an offense against the law of nations, even if there were no statutes defining the offense. Early in the nineteenth century it was held that criminal jurisdiction of federal courts rested only on statutes though the definition of crimes denounced by statutes might be left largely to international law. Thus "piracy as defined by the law of nations" is an

indictable offense in federal courts and all offenses against the law of nations are indictable at common law in state courts.[24]

Perhaps the clearest U.S. recognition of this principle came during preparation for the trial of nazi criminals at Nuremberg, a process exclusively initiated and subsequently spearheaded by the United States.[25] A U.S. working group chaired by Supreme Court Justice Robert H. Jackson decided that the nazi leadership should be held accountable to the "full measure of international law," despite the fact that much of what was at issue had never seen formal codification, never mind official acceptance by Germany.[26] Following (very loosely) from a passage in the 1907 Hague (IV) Convention, the Jackson group stipulated that:

International law shall be taken to include the principles of the law of nations as they result from usages established among civilized people, from the laws of humanity, and the dictates of public conscience.[27]

This precedent-setting formulation of "customary international law" was "laid before the representatives of Britain, France, and Soviet Russia at the London Conference in June 1945 and served as the foundation of the London Charter," the international agreement which established the juridical predication upon which the nazis were later tried.[28] In an interesting role reversal, Justice Jackson served as Chief U.S. Prosecutor in the trial of the major nazi criminals at Nuremberg during 1945 and 1946, while Attorney General Francis Biddle served as senior U.S. Tribunal member (Judge).[29] Jackson was thus in effect mandated to articulate his government's formal international legal positions through presentations against the defendants, while Biddle was charged with implementing these articulations through his rulings on points of law, votes as to the guilt or innocence of the various defendants on specific charges, and votes concerning imposition(s) of sentence on those convicted.[30]

Both men consistently went on record during the proceedings as rejecting arguments entered by counsel for the defendants that the charges against their clients were invalid because they represented enforcement of *ex post facto* law (*nullem crimen sine lige* or *nulla poena sine lige previa*).[31] The U.S. position devolved upon the principle that customary international law was binding upon all governments. It is worthy of note that neither this posture, nor any other adopted by its representatives during the trial, has ever been renounced by the United States. Rather, a dictum elaborated by Justice Jackson during his opening remarks to the Tribunal—that in order for the standards of legality enunciated at Nuremberg to have integrity, they must be applied as much to the victors as to the vanquished—has seen continuous and approving reiteration by U.S. jurists and officials.[32] The implication is obvious: having articulated international legal doctrine upon which others were tried, convicted, and sentenced, the United States is bound both legally and morally to comply with its strictures.[33]

Hence, the apparent intent of the Senate's Sovereignty Package, to allow "the United States [to] set its own agenda and be accountable to no one" with regard to its comportment on genocide, is quite invalid on both constitutional and a range of international legal grounds.[34] Further, while doing nothing to alter the force or substance of international legality, such a stance carries with it obvious overtones of Hitlerian "diplomacy," compounding the impression abroad, already engendered by the Reagan Administration's 1986 disavowal of ICJ authority vis-à-vis U.S. foreign policy, that the United States is becoming (or has become) an "outlaw" nation.[35] It is, of course, incumbent upon the courts at every level to constrain government to adhere to the rule of law, international no less than any other, rather than to unrestricted prerogatives of power. Any other course of conduct on the part of the judiciary would be repugnant to both the letter and spirit of U.S. juridical doctrine.

THE QUESTION OF FIRST AMENDMENT RIGHTS

Implicit to the charges against the defendants is a contention by the City of Denver that those against whom the accused directed our actions of October 12, 1991, were engaged in lawful activities protected by the First Amendment of the U.S. Constitution. The defendants contest this assumption on the basis that First Amendment guarantees of free speech and peaceful assembly are not absolute or unqualified. Such rights must be balanced against, among other things, the Fourteenth Amendment guarantees of the right to equitable social treatment of all citizens. Other constraints center in the famous dictum that it is illegal for one to falsely shout "Fire!" in a crowded theater. Similarly, it is well established law that it is criminally actionable behavior to make statements which threaten the life of the President of the United States or other officials, and so forth. A range of existing statutes and regulations, long upheld by U.S. courts, concerning "hate speech," harassment, verbal assault, and misrepresentation might also be cited in this regard.[36]

The defendants, all American Indians, maintain that the Columbus Day festivities which were conducted in Denver on October 12, 1991, constituted a celebration of the genocide perpetrated against our people, beginning with the Columbian landfall on October 12, 1492 (details supporting our belief will be provided in the following section). Insofar as this is true, it follows that the Columbus Day celebration constitutes advocacy of (or incitement of) genocide within the meaning of Article III(c) of the Genocide Convention. Further, to the extent that at least some of the elements of the genocidal process initiated by Columbus remain in evidence, the celebration constitutes complicity in genocide within the meaning of Article III(e) of the Convention. Such activities, of course, are unlawful by accepted international definition, binding upon the United States and its various levels of government. Thus, not only did the participants in the Columbus Day celebration lack a lawful right to engage in the activities at issue, the City of Denver lacked legal authority to grant them a permit for this purpose.

It will no doubt be argued by the prosecution that the defendants overreach in these contentions, and that the juridical waters they seek to navigate are in any event uncharted. This is untrue. Precedents, accruing from the first Nuremberg Trial,[37] do exist in which the United States clearly revealed its doctrinal posture with regard to the specific actions (offenses) alleged here. These precedents must be considered binding upon American courts at every level. Three examples will be used as illustration.

- In the case brought by the United States against nazi party ideologist *Alfried Rosenberg* at Nuremberg, Justice Jackson argued at length that the defendant was guilty of "Crimes Against Humanity" on the basis of his articulation during the 1930s of ideological/philosophical theses which "laid the theoretical foundation for" and helped "shape public opinion to accept" a policy of genocide which emerged during the following decade. It is instructive that, although the British, French, and Soviet members of the Tribunal declined to convict Rosenberg on this basis, the U.S. member, Francis Biddle, entered a guilty vote in behalf of his government. Rosenberg was ultimately convicted and hanged for his subsequent role in implementing criminal policies during the nazi occupation of the western USSR in the 1940s.[38]

- A similar case was brought by Jackson against prewar Hitler Youth leader *Baldur von Schirach*, because of his role in indoctrinating German young people to accept the premises which led to genocide and aggressive war; "ideological and emotional preparation . . . was the central issue" of the American case. In this instance, Biddle joined the other Tribunal members in voting to acquit, but only on the basis that the case had not been made (rather than because he felt the charges to be misguided). Von Schirach was ultimately sentenced to twenty years imprisonment because of his wartime role in deporting Jews to extermination facilities while serving as head of the nazi regime in Vienna.[39]

- Jackson made an almost identical Crimes Against Humanity case against propagandist *Julius Streicher*, despite the fact that he was aware Streicher "was never a member of the inner ring" of nazis, and "had nothing to do with the formulation of Nazi policy." The accusations against him consisted solely of his having sometimes penned and often published virulently anti-semitic materials. Insofar as he was found to have participated directly in no aspect of the physical extermination of the Jews, he was convicted (by vote of all four Tribunal members) only of having participated in the "psychological conditioning of the German public" which led to a genocidal outcome. On this basis, he was hanged.[40]

From these three cases, it seems indisputable that the United States government, through participating judicial officials, committed itself firmly to both a conception and implementation of international law which proscribes advocacy of genocide even when the immediate physical implementation of genocidal policies are absent. In part, this can only be attributed to a desire, explained by Justice Jackson in his predication to the Nuremberg Tribunal's creation, not simply to punish those guilty of given offenses, but to establish an international legal "groundwork barring revival of such power" as had led to the nazi genocide.[41] In the latter connection, matters of advocacy become an all-important consideration. For this reason, the United States, along with the other three allied powers, complemented the proceedings at Nuremberg by implementing occupation regulations—subsequently incorporated into German domestic law at the behest of the occupying powers—prohibiting all celebratory demonstrations of nazism (including, most prominently, parades and speeches), the display of nazi symbols and regalia, portraits of Adolf Hitler and other nazi leaders, and so forth. The premise of these laws and regulations was/is that celebration of a perpetrator of genocide can only be construed as advocacy or endorsement of the genocide itself.[42]

COLUMBUS AND THE BEGINNING OF GENOCIDE IN THE NEW WORLD

It has been contended by those who would celebrate Columbus that accusations concerning his perpetration of genocide are distortive "revisions" of history. Whatever the process unleashed by his "discovery" of the "New World," it is said, the discoverer himself cannot be blamed; no matter his defects and offenses, they are surpassed by the luster of his achievements; however "tragic" or "unfortunate" certain dimensions of his legacy may be, they are more than offset by the benefits—even for the victims— of the resulting blossoming of a "superior civilization" in the Americas.[43] It should be noted before continuing that essentially the same arguments might be advanced with regard to Adolf Hitler: Hitler caused the Volkswagen to be created, after all, and the autobahn. His leadership of Germany led to jet propulsion, significant advances in rocket telemetry, laid the foundation for genetic engineering. Why not celebrate his bona fide accomplishments in behalf of humanity rather than "dwelling" so persistently on the genocidal by-products of his policies?

To be fair, Columbus was never a head of state. Comparisons of him to nazi SS leader Heinrich Himmler, rather than Hitler himself, are therefore more accurate and appropriate. It is time to delve into the substance of the defendants' assertion that Columbus and Himmler, nazi *lebensraumpolitik* (conquest of "living space" in eastern Europe) and the "settlement of the New World" bear more than casual resemblance to one another. This has nothing to do with the Columbian "discovery," not that this in itself is completely irrelevant. Columbus did not sally forth upon the Atlantic for reasons of "neutral science" or altruism. He went, as his own diaries, reports, and letters make clear, fully expecting to encounter wealth belonging to others. It was his stated purpose to seize this wealth, by whatever means necessary and available, in order to enrich both his sponsors and himself.[44] Plainly, he prefigured, both in design and by intent, what came next. To this extent, he not only symbolizes the process of conquest and genocide which eventually consumed the indigenous peoples of America, but bears the personal responsibility of having participated in it. Still, if this were all there was to it, the defendants would be inclined to dismiss him as a mere thug along the lines of Al Capone rather than viewing him as a counterpart to Himmler.

The 1492 "voyage of discovery" is, however, hardly all that is at issue. In 1493 Columbus returned with an invasion force of seventeen ships, appointed at his own request by the Spanish Crown as "viceroy and governor of [the Caribbean islands] and the mainland" of America, a position he held until 1500.[45] Setting up shop on the large island he called Española (today Haiti and the Dominican Republic), he promptly instituted policies of slavery (*encomiendo*) and systematic extermination against the native Taino population.[46] Columbus' programs reduced Taino numbers from as many as eight million at the outset of his regime to about three million in 1496.[47] Perhaps 100,000 were left by the time of the governor's departure. His policies, however, remained, with the result that by 1514 the Spanish census of the island showed barely 22,000 Indians remaining alive. In 1542, only two hundred were recorded.[48] Thereafter, they were considered extinct, as were Indians throughout the Caribbean Basin, an aggregate population which totalled at least fourteen million at the point of first contact with the Admiral of the Ocean Sea, as Columbus was known.[49]

This, to be sure, constitutes an attrition of population in real numbers every bit as great as the toll of twelve to fifteen million—about half of them Jewish—most commonly attributed to Himmler's slaughter mills. Moreover, the proportion of indigenous Caribbean population destroyed by the Spanish in a single generation is, no matter how the figures are twisted, far greater than the two-thirds of European Jews usually said to have been exterminated by the nazis.[50] Worst of all, these data apply *only* to the Caribbean Basin; the process of genocide in the Americas was only just beginning at the point such statistics become operant, not ending, as they did upon the fall of the Third Reich. All told, it is probable that more than one hundred million native people were "eliminated" in the course of Europe's ongoing "civilization" of the Western Hemisphere.[51]

It has long been asserted by "responsible scholars" that this decimation of American Indians which accompanied the European invasion resulted primarily from disease rather than direct killing or conscious policy.[52] There is a certain truth to this, although starvation may have proven just as lethal in the end. It must be borne in mind when considering such facts, however, that a considerable portion of those who perished in the nazi death camps died, not as the victims of bullets and gas, but from starvation, as well as epidemics of typhus, dysentery, and the like.

Their keepers, who could not be said to have killed these people directly, were nonetheless found to have been culpable in their deaths by way of deliberately imposing the conditions which led to the proliferation of starvation and disease among them.[53] Certainly, the same can be said of Columbus' régime, under which the original residents were, as a first order of business, permanently dispossessed of their abundant cultivated fields while being converted into chattel, ultimately to be worked to death for the wealth and "glory" of Spain.[54]

Nor should more direct means of extermination be relegated to incidental status. As the matter is framed by Kirkpatrick Sale in his book, *The Conquest of Paradise*:

The tribute system, instituted by [Columbus] sometime in 1495, was a simple and brutal way of fulfilling the Spanish lust for gold while acknowledging the Spanish distaste for labor. Every Taino over the age of fourteen had to supply the rulers with a hawk's bell of gold every three months (or, in gold-deficient areas, twenty-five pounds of spun cotton); those who did were given a token to wear around their necks as proof that they had made their payment; those who did not were, as [Columbus' brother, Fernando] says discreetly, "punished"—by having their hands cut off, as [the priest, Bartolomé de] Las Casas says less discreetly, and left to bleed to death.[55]

It is entirely likely that upwards of 10,000 Indians were killed in this fashion alone, on Española alone, as a matter of policy, during Columbus' tenure as governor. Las Casas' *Brevísima relación*, among other contemporaneous sources,[56] is also replete with accounts of Spanish colonists (*hidalgos*) hanging Tainos en mass, roasting them on spits or burning them at the stake (often a dozen or more at a time), hacking their children into pieces to be used as dog feed and so forth, all of it to instill in the natives a "proper attitude of respect" toward their Spanish "betters."

> [The Spaniards] made bets as to who would slit a man in two, or cut off his head at one blow; or they opened up his bowels. They tore the babes from their mother's breast by their feet and dashed their heads against the rocks . . . They spitted the bodies of other babes, together with their mothers and all who were before them, on their swords.[57]

No SS trooper could be expected to comport himself with a more unrelenting viciousness. And there is more. All of this was coupled to wholesale and persistent massacres:

> A Spaniard . . . suddenly drew his sword. Then the whole hundred drew theirs and began to rip open the bellies, to cut and kill [a group of Tainos assembled for this purpose]—men, women, children and old folk, all of whom were seated, off guard and frightened . . . And within two credos, not a man of them there remains alive. The Spaniards enter the large house nearby, for this was happening at its door, and in the same way, with cuts and stabs, began to kill as many as were found there, so that a stream of blood was running, as if a great number of cows had perished.[58]

Elsewhere, Las Casas went on to recount how:

> In this time, the greatest outrages and slaughterings of people were perpetrated, whole villages being depopulated . . . The Indians saw that without any offense on their part they were despoiled of their kingdoms, their lands and liberties, and of their lives, their wives, and homes. As they saw themselves each day

perishing by the cruel and inhuman treatment of the Spaniards, crushed to earth by the horses, cut in pieces by swords, eaten and torn by dogs, many buried alive and suffering all kinds of exquisite tortures . . . [many surrendered to their fate, while the survivors] fled to the mountains [to starve].[59]

Such descriptions correspond almost perfectly to those of systematic nazi atrocities in the western USSR offered by William Shirer in Chapter 27 of his *The Rise and Fall of the Third Reich*.[60] But, unlike the nazi extermination campaigns of World War II, the Columbian butchery on Española continued until there were no Tainos left to butcher.

EVOLUTION OF THE COLUMBIAN LEGACY

Nor was this by any means the end of it. The genocidal model of conquest and colonization established by Columbus was to a large extent replicated by others such as Cortez (in Mexico) and Pizarro (in Peru) during the following half-century.[61] During the same period, expeditions—such as those of Ponce de Leon in 1513, Coronado in 1540, and de Soto during the same year—were launched with an eye towards effecting the same pattern on the North American continent.[62] In the latter sphere, the Spanish example was followed and in certain ways intensified by the British, beginning at Roanoke in 1607 and Plymouth in 1620.[63] Overall, the process of English colonization along the Atlantic Coast was marked by a series of massacres of native people as relentless and devastating as any perpetrated by the Spaniards. One of the best known illustrations—drawn from among hundreds—was the slaughter of some 800 Pequots at present-day Mystic, Connecticut, on the night of May 26, 1637.[64]

During the latter portion of the seventeenth century, and throughout most of the eighteenth, Great Britain battled France for colonial primacy in North America. The resulting sequence of "French and Indian Wars" greatly accelerated the liquidation of indigenous people as far west as the Ohio River Valley. During the last of these, concluded in 1763, history's first documentable case of bacteriological genocide occurred against Pontiac's Algonkian Confederacy, a powerful military alliance aligned with the French.

Sir Jeffrey Amherst, commander-in-chief of the British forces . . . wrote in a postscript of a letter to Bouquet [a subordinate] that smallpox be sent among the disaffected tribes. Bouquet replied, also in a postscript, "I will try to [contaminate] them . . . with some blankets that may fall into their hands, and take care not to get the disease myself" . . . To Bouquet's postscript Amherst replied, "You will do well to [infect] the Indians by means of blankets as well as to try every other method that can serve to extirpate this execrable race." On June 24, Captain Ecuyer, of the Royal Americans, noted in his journal: ". . . we gave them two blankets and a handkerchief out of the smallpox hospital. I hope it will have the desired effect."[65]

It did. Over the next few months, the disease spread like wildfire among the Mingo, Delaware, Shawnee, and other Ohio River nations, killing perhaps 100,000 people.[66] The example of Amherst's action does much to dispel the myth that the postcontact attrition of Indian people through disease introduced by Europeans was necessarily unintentional and unavoidable. There are a number of earlier instances in which native people felt disease had been deliberately inculcated among them. For example, the so-called "King Philip's War" of 1675–76 was fought largely because the Wampanoag and Narragansett nations believed English traders had consciously contaminated certain of their villages with smallpox.[67] Such tactics were also continued by the United States after the American War of Independence. At Fort Clark on the upper Missouri River, for instance, the U.S. Army distributed smallpox-laden blankets as gifts among the Mandan. The blankets had been gathered from a military infirmary in St. Louis where troops infected with the disease were quarantined. Although the medical practice of the day required the precise opposite procedure, army doctors ordered the Mandans to disperse once they exhibited symptoms of infection. The result was a pandemic among the Plains Indian nations which claimed at least 125,000 lives, and may have reached a toll several times that number.[68]

Contemporaneous with the events at Fort Clark, the U.S. was also engaged in a policy of wholesale "removal" of indigenous nations east of the Mississippi River, "clearing" the land of its native population so that it might be "settled" by "racially superior" Anglo-Saxon "pioneers."[69] This process assumed the form of a series of extended forced marches—some more than a thousand miles in length—in which entire peoples were walked at bayonet-point to locations west of the Mississippi. Rations and medical attention were poor, shelter at times all but nonexistent. Attrition among the victims was correspondingly high. As many as fifty-five percent of all Cherokees, for example, are known to have died during or as an immediate result of that people's "Trail of Tears."[70] The Creeks and Seminoles also lost about half their existing populations as a direct consequence of being "removed."[71] It was the example of nineteenth century U.S. Indian Removal policy upon which Hitler relied for a practical model when articulating and implementing his *lebensraumpolitik* during the 1930s and '40s.[72]

By the 1850s, U.S. policymakers had adopted a popular philosophy called "Manifest Destiny" by which they imagined themselves enjoying a divinely ordained right to possess *all* native property, including everything west of the Mississippi.[73] This was coupled to what has been termed a "rhetoric of extermination" by which governmental and corporate leaders sought to shape public sentiment to embrace the eradication of American Indians.[74] The professed goal of this physical reduction of "inferior" indigenous populations was to open up land for "superior" Euroamerican "pioneers."[75] One outcome of this dual articulation was a series of general massacres perpetrated by the United States military.

A bare sampling of some of the worst must include the 1854 massacre of perhaps 150 Lakotas at Blue River (Nebraska), the 1863 Bear River (Idaho) Massacre of some 500 Western Shoshones, the 1864 Sand Creek (Colorado)

Massacre of as many as 250 Cheyennes and Arapahoes, the 1868 massacre of another 300 Cheyennes at the Washita River (Oklahoma), the 1875 massacre of about 75 Cheyennes along the Sappa Creek (Kansas), the 1878 massacre of still another 100 Cheyennes at Camp Robinson (Nebraska), and the 1890 massacre of more than 300 Lakotas at Wounded Knee (South Dakota).[76]

Related phenomena included the army's internment of the bulk of all Navajos for four years (1864–68) under abysmal conditions at the Bosque Redondo, during which about half the population of this nation is known to have perished of starvation and disease.[77] Even worse in some ways was the unleashing of Euroamerican civilians to kill Indians at whim, and sometimes for profit. In Texas, for example, an official bounty on native scalps—*any* native scalps—was maintained until well into the 1870s. The result was that the indigenous population of this state, once the densest in all of North America, had been reduced to near zero by 1880. As it has been put elsewhere, "The facts of history are plain: Most Texas Indians were exterminated or brought to the brink of oblivion by [civilians] who often had no more regard for the life of an Indian than they had for that of a dog, sometimes less."[78] Similarly, in California, "the enormous decrease [in indigenous population] from about a quarter-million [in 1800] to less than 20,000 is due chiefly to the cruelties and wholesale massacres perpetrated by miners and early settlers."[79]

Much of the killing in California and southern Oregon Territory resulted, directly and indirectly, from the discovery of gold in 1849 and the subsequent influx of miners and settlers. Newspaper accounts document the atrocities, as do oral histories of the California Indians today. It was not uncommon for small groups or villages to be attacked by immigrants . . . and virtually wiped out overnight.[80]

All told, the North American Indian population within the area of the forty-eight contiguous states of the United States, an aggregate group which had probably numbered in excess of twelve million in the year 1500, was reduced by official estimate to barely 237,000 four centuries later.[81] This vast genocide—historically paralleled in its magnitude and degree only by that which occurred in the Caribbean Basin—is the most sustained such process on record. Corresponding almost perfectly with this upper ninetieth percentile erosion of indigenous population by 1900 was the expropriation of about 97.5 percent of native land by 1920.[82] The situation in Canada was/is entirely comparable.[83] Plainly, the naziesque dynamics set in motion by Columbus in 1492 continued, and were not ultimately consummated until the twentieth century.

THE COLUMBIAN LEGACY IN THE UNITED STATES

While it is arguable that the worst of the genocidal programs directed against Native North America had ended by 1900, it seems undeniable that several have been continued into the current period. One obvious illustration is that of the massive compulsory transfer of American Indian children from their families, communities, and societies to Euroamerican families and institutions, a policy which is quite blatant in its disregard for Article II(e) of the 1948 Convention. Effected through such mechanisms as the U.S. Bureau of Indian Affairs (BIA) boarding school system,[84] and a pervasive policy of placing Indian children for adoption (including "blind" adoption) with non-indians, such circumstances have been visited upon as many as three-quarters of all indigenous youth in some generations after 1900.[85] The stated goal motivating such policies has been to bring about the "assimilation" of native people into the value orientations and belief system of their conquerors.[86] Rephrased, the objective has been to bring about the disappearance of indigenous societies as such, a patent violation of the terms, provisions, and intent of the Genocide Convention (Article II(c)).

An even clearer example is that of a program of involuntary sterilization of American Indian women by the BIA's Indian Health Service (IHS) during the 1970s. While the federal government, in announcing that the program had been terminated, acknowledged having performed several thousand such sterilizations, independent researchers have concluded that as many as forty-two percent of all native women of childbearing age in the United States had been sterilized by that point.[87] That the program represented a rather stark—and very recent—violation of Article II(d) of the 1948 Convention seems beyond all reasonable doubt.

More broadly, implications of genocide are quite apparent in the federal government's self-assigned exercise of "plenary power" and concomitant "trust" prerogatives over the residual Indian land base pursuant to the Supreme Court's *"Lone Wolf" v. Hitchcock* opinion (187 U.S. 553 (1903)). This has worked, with rather predictable results, to systematically deny native people the benefit of our remaining material assets. At present, the approximately two million Indians recognized by the government as residing within the U.S., when divided into the fifty million-odd acres nominally reserved for our use and occupancy, remain the continent's largest landholders on a per capita basis.[88] Moreover, the reservation lands have proven to be extraordinarily resource rich, holding an estimated two-thirds of all U.S. "domestic" uranium reserves, about a quarter of the readily accessible low sulfur coal, as much as a fifth of the oil and natural gas, as well as substantial deposits of copper, iron, gold, and zeolites.[89] By any rational definition, the U.S. Indian population should thus be one of the wealthiest—if not *the* wealthiest—population sectors in North America.

Instead, by the federal government's own statistics, we comprise far and away the poorest. As of 1980, American Indians experienced, by a decided margin, the lowest annual and lifetime incomes on a per capita basis of any ethnic or racial group on the continent. Correlated to this are all the standard indices of extreme poverty: the highest rates of infant mortality, death by exposure and malnutrition, incidence of tuberculosis and other plague diseases. Indians experience the highest level of unemployment, year after year, and the lowest level of educational attainment. The overall quality of life is so dismal that alcoholism and other forms of substance abuse are endemic, the rate of teen suicide several times that pertaining to the nation as a whole. The average life expectancy of reservation-based Native American males is less than 45 years; that of reservation-based females less than three years longer.[90]

It's not that reservation resources are not going unexploited, or profits unaccrued. To the contrary, virtually all uranium mining and milling occurred on or immediately adjacent to reservation land during the life of the Atomic Energy Commission's ore-buying program, 1952–81;[91] the largest remaining enclave of traditional Indians in North America is currently undergoing forced relocation in order that coal may be mined on the Navajo Reservation;[92] Alaska native peoples are being converted into landless "village corporations" in order that the oil under their territories be tapped; and so on.[93]

Rather, the BIA has utilized its plenary and trust capacities to arrange contracts "in behalf of" its "Indian wards" with major mining corporations which pay pennies on the dollar of conventional mineral royalty rates.[94] Further, the BIA has typically exempted such corporations from an obligation to reclaim whatever reservation lands have been mined, or even to perform basic environmental cleanup of nuclear and other forms of waste. One outcome has been that the National Institute for Science has recommended that the two locales within the U.S. most heavily populated by native people—the Four Corners Region and the Black Hills Region—be designated as "National Sacrifice Areas."[95] Indians have responded that this would mean their being converted into "national sacrifice *peoples*."[96]

Even such seemingly innocuous federal policies as those concerning Indian identification criteria carry with them an evident genocidal potential. In clinging insistently to a eugenics formulation dubbed "blood-quantum"—ushered in under the 1887 General Allotment Act—while implementing such policies as the Federal Indian Relocation Program (1956–1982), the government has set the stage for a "statistical extermination" of the indigenous population within its borders.[97] As the noted western historian Patricia Nelson Limerick has observed: "Set the blood-quantum at one-quarter, hold to it as a rigid definition of Indians, let intermarriage proceed . . . and eventually Indians will be defined out of existence. When that happens, the federal government will finally be freed from its persistent 'Indian problem'."[98] Ultimately, there is precious little difference, other than matters of style, between this and what was once called the "Final Solution of the Jewish Problem."

CONFRONTING GENOCIDE IN AMERICA

Were the genocide of American Indians initiated by Christopher Columbus and carried on with increasing ferocity by his successors a matter of only historical significance—as with the nazi extermination campaigns—it would be utterly inappropriate, and unlawful, to celebrate it. Insofar as aspects of the genocide at issue are demonstrably ongoing—not just here, but in Central and South America as well—this becomes all the more true.[99] The indigenous people of the Americas have an unquestionable, absolute, and vitally urgent need to alter the physical and political circumstances which have been and continue to be imposed upon us. In the alternative, we face, collectively, a final eradication through a number of means.

Given contemporary demographic disparities between indigenous and nonindigenous populations in the Americas, and the power relations which attend these, it seems self-evident that a crucial aspect of native survival must go to altering the nonindian sensibilities which contribute to—either by affirming the rightness of, or acquiescing in—the continuing genocide against Native America. Very high on any list of those expressions of nonindigenous sensibility which contribute to the perpetuation of genocidal policies against Indians are the annual Columbus Day celebrations, events in which it is baldly asserted that the process, events, and circumstances described above are, at best, either acceptable or unimportant. More often, the sentiments expressed by participants are, quite frankly, that the fate of Native America embodied in Columbus and the Columbian legacy is a matter to be openly and enthusiastically applauded as an unrivaled "boon to all mankind."[100] Undeniably, the situation of American Indians will not—in fact, *cannot*—change for the better so long as such attitudes are deemed socially acceptable by the mainstream populace. Hence, such celebrations as Columbus Day *must* be stopped.

On the basis of the Genocide Convention and other elements of international law, American Indians have a right to expect the support of all levels of governance in the United States, from the federal executive to local mayors, in putting a stop to celebration/advocacy/incitement of our destruction. It follows that we have the same right to expect support from the judiciary, from the Supreme Court to county and municipal courts. Further, we have the same right to expect support from the various law enforcement agencies in this country, from the Federal Bureau of Investigation and U.S. Marshals Service to the Denver Police Department. In other words, under the law, the City of Denver *should* under no circumstances have issued a permit for the conducting of activities celebrating Columbus Day on October 12, 1991. The courts *should* have intervened to enjoin such activities, and the police *should* have enforced the prohibition of such activities against anyone attempting to violate it. Of course, none of these official actions occurred. The executive branch of government, the courts, and the police all defaulted upon their legal responsibilities. The illegal activities of the participants in the public celebration of Columbus Day in Denver, Colorado, were not only allowed, but to all appearances endorsed by those mandated to prevent them.[101]

The rights and responsibilities of individual citizens in such situations are not mysterious. During the course of the Nuremberg proceedings, Justice Jackson and his associates repeatedly queried how it was that "average Germans" had simply "stood by" while their government pursued a policy of Crimes Against Humanity.[102] Given the legitimation of precisely these crimes under then-prevailing German law, one can only conclude that Jackson meant individual German citizens had shirked a binding obligation under a higher (international) law to do whatever was necessary to prevent such crimes from occurring. Such a principle is not inconsistent with U.S. domestic laws concerning the right to effect "citizens' arrests" and so forth.[103] Moreover, it is now universally embodied in covenants relieving all persons, including active duty soldiers and police, of any "responsibility" to comply with unlawful orders, regulations, or statutes.[104] Indeed, it is arguable that, after Nuremberg, a legal requirement was incurred by each individual citizen to vigorously—and, when necessary, *physically*—oppose the commission of a Crime Against Humanity by *any* party, official or otherwise.[105] As Ben Whitaker, senior American diplomat, framed the matter before the United Nations in 1985:

> [S]ince wider public education about this doctrine is highly crucial for the aversion of future genocide . . . explicit wording should be added to the [Genocide] Convention, perhaps at the end of Article III, that "In judging culpability, a plea of superior orders is not an excusing defense." Similarly, wider publicity should be given to the principle in national codes governing armed forces, prison staffs, police officers, doctors, and others, to advise and warn them that it is not only their right to disobey orders violating human rights, such as to carry out genocide or torture, but their legal duty to disobey. Such precepts should be taught in the schools, and the United Nations Educational, Scientific and Cultural Organization might be asked to encourage this internationally.[106]

In essence, then, the defendants cannot be convicted of any crime in the instant case insofar as they comported themselves in an entirely lawful manner. We cannot have refused to obey a lawful order by a police official insofar as the order in question—to allow an illegal activity to proceed unhampered—was itself unlawful. It was therefore our legal *duty* to disobey it. We cannot have obstructed a public thoroughfare insofar as said thoroughfare was already obstructed by an illegal assembly. We merely met the legal requirement of attempting to put a stop to the unlawful activity already occurring. We cannot have disturbed the peace insofar as the peace was already disturbed by the already-mentioned unlawful assembly, which included, among other things, brass bands. Again, we simply met the legal requirement of attempting to halt the commission of a Crime Against Humanity. In addition, we were engaged in a form of the very "educational" activity concerning the Genocide Convention called for by Mr. Whitaker. There being no basis to the charges leveled against the defendants, we collectively demand that all charges be immediately dismissed.

PART II

STRUGGLES FOR LANDS AND LIVES

◆◆◆◆◆◆◆◆◆◆◆◆◆◆

Of course our whole national history has been one of expansion . . . That the barbarians recede or are conquered, with the attendant fact that peace follows their retrogression or conquest, is due solely to the power of the mighty civilized races which have not lost their fighting instinct, and which by their expansion are gradually bringing peace into the red wastes where the barbarian peoples of the world hold sway.

—Theodore Roosevelt
The Strenuous Life, 1901

4

THE EARTH IS OUR MOTHER

Struggles for American Indian Land and Liberation
in the Contemporary United States

♦♦♦♦♦♦♦♦♦♦♦♦♦♦

> The inhabitants of your country districts regard—wrongfully, it is
> true—Indians and forests as natural enemies which must be exter-
> minated by fire and sword and brandy, in order that they may seize
> their territory. They regard themselves, themselves and their poster-
> ity, as collateral heirs to all the magnificent portion of land which
> God has created from Cumberland and Ohio to the Pacific Ocean.
> — Pierre Samuel Du Pont de Nemours
> letter to Thomas Jefferson, December 17, 1801

SINCE THE INCEPTION OF THE AMERICAN REPUBLIC, AND BEFORE, CONTROL OF
land and the resources within it has been the essential source of conflict between the
Euroamerican settler population and indigenous nations. In effect, contentions over
land usage and ownership have served to define the totality of U.S./Indian relationships
from the first moment, shaping not only the historical flow of interactions between
invader and invaded, but the nature of the ongoing domination of native people in areas such as governance and jurisdiction, identification, recognition, and education.[1]

The issue of a proprietary interest of nonindians in the American Indian landbase
has also been and remains the fundament of popular (mis)conceptions of who and
what Indians were and are, whether we continue to exist, and even whether we ever
"really" existed.[2] All indications are that these circumstances will continue to prevail
over the foreseeable future.

As should have become quite evident in reading the essay entitled "The Law Stood
Squarely on Its Head" in this volume, a rather vast amount of intellectual energy has
been expended by Euroamerican legal theorists over the years in an unending effort to
make the armed expropriation of native land on a continental scale seem not only
"natural" and therefore "inevitable," but "right and just," which is to say "lawful."[3] All
questions of jurisprudence aside, the hegemonic function embodied in any such trajectory of legalistic rationalization is unmistakable.[4] Plainly, the exercise has been harnessed not to the task of extending and perfecting the set of humanitarian and
explicitly anti-imperialist principles to which the United States laid claim in 1787, but

rather to a diametrically opposing purpose. Meanwhile, it has been all along insisted that the opposite of this opposite is true. The result can only be described as comprising, at best, an unremitting juridical subterfuge.[5]

While this pattern of prevarication has always worked well enough within what the U.S. has proclaimed as its own domestic sphere, the situation became considerably more complex during the early-to-mid-twentieth century, during the course of the country's emergence as a bona fide world power.[6] In the main, the objective of American foreign policy during this period can be seen as an undermining of the conceptual cornerstones by which the "classic" European mode of external colonialism was purportedly legitimated,[7] thereby creating openings in the former colonies comprising what has become known as the Third World for a more refined form of neo-colonial exploitation at which the United States all along figured to excel.[8] The trick, of course, was to devise some practical means of discrediting Europe's conquest/colonization of peoples abroad that would not simultaneously demolish the inherently self-contradictory justification(s) with which America larded its continuing subjugation of indigenous nations within its "home" territory.[9]

The crunch came in 1945, when the U.S. sought to assert its "moral leadership" on a planetary basis by formulating and forcing upon its allies a plan to prosecute surviving officials responsible for nazi expansionism during World War II.[10] Charged with having committed "Crimes Against Peace," "Waging Aggressive War," and "Crimes Against Humanity" as a result, the Germans initially professed a certain bewilderment, their first line of defense being that they'd done nothing the United States itself hadn't done to American Indians.[11] Although the presiding judges dodged this bullet by accepting at face value the transparently false assertion advanced by U.S. representatives that, unlike Germany's gunpoint expropriations, their own country's territorial acquisitions had occurred mainly by purchase and always with the consent of prior owners (i.e., through treaties of cession),[12] America's vulnerability to allegations that it was in many respects no better than the Third Reich was glaringly apparent.

THE INDIAN CLAIMS COMMISSION

One upshot of this circumstance was the abrupt passage, on August 2, 1946, of an act establishing what was dubbed the "Indian Claims Commission" (ICC), an entity mandated to review all outstanding grievances expressed by native peoples within the U.S. "domestic" sphere concerning wrongful takings of our property.[13] The idea was plainly to put the United States, however belatedly, on precisely the footing it had already announced it stood, thus creating an appearance that the U.S. record was decisively distinct—or at least distinguishable—from that of the nazis it was busily hanging in Nuremberg.[14] As President Harry Truman insisted when he signed the bill into law on August 13, creation of the ICC was intended to make "perfectly clear what many men and women, here *and abroad*, have failed to recognize, that . . . [I]nstead of confiscating Indian lands we have purchased from the tribes that once owned this continent more than 90 percent of our public domain (emphasis added)."[15]

Predictably, all bets attending this international public relations gesture were from the outset carefully hedged.

- First off, the U.S. assigned itself rather than a neutral third party the prerogative of determining whether and to what extent each claim might be "meritorious."

- Secondly, even in the most egregious cases, the ICC was empowered only to award monetary compensation for whatever land had been taken from native claimants; under no circumstances was it authorized to return the land itself.[16]

- Third, the amount of compensation in each case was restricted to whatever amount the U.S., not the indigenous owners, decided was "fair" (the usual procedure was simply to assign awards in amounts equaling the estimated value of lost lands at the time they were taken—often a century or more earlier—irrespective of contemporary land values or the value of minerals extracted in the interim, and without interest of any sort).[17]

- Reducing the amount of awards still further, the government empowered itself to "offset" and deduct from payments whatever amount(s) it had previously expended in providing "services" like police and schools, many of them over the express ojections—and often open resistance—of native recipients.[18]

- Federal authorities also reserved unto themselves the prerogative of determining how any remaining sums should be paid. Although they were sometimes distributed as per capita payments, by far the most frequently employed method was to transfer the funds into a federal account wherein they would be administered not by the Indians whose money it was, but by the government's own Bureau of Indian Affairs (acting out the self-assigned federal "trust authority" over Indian assets articulated in the Supreme Court's 1903 *Lone Wolf* opinion).[19] Once safely nestled in such accounts, the funds were often permanently "misplaced" in federal accounts.[20]

- Finally, it was left to the Indians themselves—most of whom had been long since rendered destitute by the very dispossession they were now supposedly afforded an opportunity to challenge—to come up with the funds necessary to retain the attorneys, historians, and other experts necessary to present their cases.[21]

Under such circumstances, it was expressly anticipated by federal legislators that all outstanding claims would be "remedied" within five years and for a relatively paltry sum.[22] In the process, it was expected that the documentary basis for U.S. title assertions would be clarified, parcel by parcel, once and for all. Any other course of action would have, in the words of Henry M. Jackson, Chair of the Senate Subcommittee on

Indian Affairs, "perpetuated clouds upon white men's title that [might] interfere with development of our public domain."[23]

Viewed in even the most favorable light, then, the 1946 Act had nothing to do with the dispensation of justice, as its apologists have claimed.[24] Rather, it was at best a self-serving "clean-up measure," affording federal authorities an opportunity to reconcile their own ledgers in terms of real estate.[25] More to the point, awards of compensation by the ICC were coupled to what North Dakota Senator Karl Mundt described as America's "permanent solution to the Indian problem,"[26] a procedure wherein, having forced upon them payment of a pittance in exchange for property they never wished to sell, Congress followed up by "terminating" its relationship with more than a hundred native peoples, professing thereafter to consider them "extinct" (see "Like Sand in the Wind," herein).[27]

At that, however, the congressional notion of how quickly the commission's role in "getting the U.S. out of the Indian business" might be wrapped up proved absurdly shortsighted.[28] While legislators had estimated that at most 200 claims would be presented for consideration, a total of 852—implicating well over half the territory of the 48 contiguous states—had been filed with the ICC by the time its original charter expired at the end of 1951.[29] Of these, a mere 26 had been acted upon, and so the ICC was extended for a second five-year period, then a third.[30] Its lifespan was extended several more times, until finally, in 1978, the commission was abruptly dissolved. At that point, there were still 68 cases pending.[31]

There were, to be sure, substantial reasons underlying this interesting development. As early as 1956, Justice Department personnel assigned to refute claims brought before the ICC, were warning that if it were carried through to its conclusion, the process was likely to produce the opposite of its intended result.[32] Unable to discern a legal or documentary basis upon which to defend the federal interest in scores of cases, they had already resorted to a strategy of seeking to delay the whole procedure, requesting some 5,000 extensions of time in which to file their various pleadings between 1951 and 1955.[33] This clearly obstructionist technique had been perfected to such an extent by 1960 that the ICC's chief commissioner—a former senator and staunch terminationist named Arthur Watkins—complained of "U.S. Attorneys obtaining 35 separate continuances in a single case."[34] More than a decade later, in 1971, Watkins' successor, Jerome Kykendahl, noted that "federal lawyers" had sought 6,451 days-worth of extensions in active cases over the preceding eighteen months.[35]

By the mid-1970s, the source of discomfort among the Attorney General's whiz kids had become apparent for all to see. Try as they might, and no matter how many eminent historians and other archivists they enlisted in the effort, they could muster no evidence that the United States had ever enjoyed a legal right to possess about 35 percent of the continental territory over which it professed "lawful jurisdiction" (see Figure 4.1).[36] Overall, as Russel Barsh has summarized:

> The fact is that about half the land area of the country was purchased by treaty or agreement at an average price of less than a dollar an acre; another third of a

FIGURE 4.1. Indian lands judicially recognized as unceded.

[billion] acres, mainly in the West, were confiscated without compensation; another two-thirds of a [billion] acres were claimed by the United States without pretense of [even] a unilateral action extinguishing native title.[37]

Thus, although the aggregate acreage encompassed within reservation boundaries added up to about 2.5 percent of the total comprising the 48 contiguous states, American Indians remain in a rather straightforward sense the rightful owners of about "one-third of the nation's land."[38] This proportion, moreover, does not include areas to which U.S. title is predicated upon fraudulent treaties or agreements,[39] or those into which native peoples entered under extreme coercion.[40] Nor does it address the implications of America's history of noncompliance with reciprocal provisions in treaties of cession which might otherwise be considered valid.[41] Were U.S. title to territory acquired under such circumstances to be considered null—as, legally, it must— then well over half the country's continental holdings would have to be viewed as "Occupied America."[42]

In other words, it was the nazi defendants at Nuremberg—*not* Robert H. Jackson, the Supreme Court Justice who prosecuted them, or Francis Biddle, the former Attorney General who sat in judgment of them in behalf of the U.S.—who had it exactly right.[43] As to Jackson's famous pronouncement, offered in the course of the trial at Nuremberg , that the United States was "not prepared to lay down a rule of criminal conduct against others which we are not willing to have invoked against us," well, some things speak for themselves.[44] No less, Harry Truman's bald 1947 assertion that "it should be perfectly clear . . . that in our transactions with the Indian tribes we have [always] set for ourselves the standard of fair and honorable dealings, pleadging respect for all Indian property rights."[45]

CRACKS IN THE EMPIRE

Well before the ICC process was finally aborted, some American Indians had begun to home in on the vulnerabilities in the U.S. position exposed during the commissioners' efforts to "quiet title" to the country's purported domestic landbase. As was pointed out by Vine Deloria, Jr., all the commission managed to do in most instances was "update the legal parity" of indigenous property rights by "clearing out the underbrush" previously obscuring an accurate appreciation of who actually owned what in the U.S. portion of North America.[46] Seen in this light, the monetary awards made by the ICC assume more nearly the form of "back rent" payments on native lands used by the United States than a "resolution" or "settlement" of indigenous property interests.[47]

Such knowledge fueled a resurgent indigenous national militancy which, with emergence of the American Indian Movement (AIM) during the early 1970s, has led to a series of spectacular extralegal confrontations over land and liberty with federal authorities (several of them are covered in "The Bloody Wake of Alcatraz," herein). These, in turn, have commanded the very sort of international attention to U.S. territorial claims, and Indian policy more generally, that the ICC was supposed to avert.[48] After 1977, Native North Americans—spearheaded for a time by AIM's "diplomatic arm," the International Indian Treaty Council—have been able to escalate this trend by putting their issues before the United Nations, entering annual reports of official misconduct in both the U.S. and Canada towards native peoples and our lands.[49]

In this changing context, the federal government has once again begun to engage in "damage control," allowing a calculated range of concessions in order to bolster what it seeks to project as its image abroad. Notably, in 1974, the U.S. Supreme Court announced for the first time that American Indians have a right to pursue the actual recovery of stolen land through the federal judiciary.[50] Although resort to the courts of the colonizer is hardly an ideal solution to the issues raised by indigenous nations, it does place another tool in the inventory of means by which we can now pursue our rights. It has, moreover, resulted in measurable gains for some of us over the past quarter-century.

Probably the best example of this is the suit, first entered in 1972 under the auspices of a sponsoring organization, of the basically landless Passamaquoddy and Penobscot Nations in present-day Maine to some twelve million acres acknowledged as being theirs in a series of letters dating from the 1790s and signed by George Washington.[51] Since it was demonstrated that no ratified treaty existed by which the Indians had ceded their land, U.S. District Judge Edward T. Gignoux ordered a settlement acceptable to the majority of the native people involved.[52] This resulted in the recovery, in 1980, of some 300,000 acres of land, and payment of $27 million in compensatory damages by the federal government.[53] In a similarly argued case, the Narragansetts of Rhode Island—not previously recognized by the government as still existing—were in 1978 able to win not only recognition of themselves, but to recover 1,800 acres of the remaining 3,200 stripped from them in 1880 by unilateral action of the state.[54]

In another instance, the Mashantucket Pequot people of Connecticut filed suit in

1976 to recover 800 of the 2,000 acres comprising their original reservation, created by the Connecticut Colony in 1686 but reduced to 184 acres by the State of Connecticut after the American War of Independence.[55] Pursuant to a settlement agreement arrived at with the state in 1982, Congress passed an act providing funds to acquire the desired acreage. It was promptly vetoed by Ronald Reagan on April 11, 1983.[56] After the Senate Select Committee on Indian Affairs convened hearings on the matter, however, Reagan agreed to a slight revision of the statute, affixing his signature on October 18 the same year.[57]

Other nations, however, have not fared as well, even in an atmosphere where the U.S. has sometimes proven more than usually willing to compromise as a means to contain questions of native land rights. The Wampanoags of the Mashpee area of Cape Cod, for example, filed suit in 1974 in an attempt to recover about 17,000— later reduced to 11,000—of the 23,000 acres historically acknowledged as theirs. (The Commonwealth of Massachusetts unilaterally declared their reservation a "township" in 1870.) At trial, the all-white jury, each of whom had property interests in the Mashpee area, were asked to determine whether the Wampanoag plaintiffs were "a tribe within the meaning of the law." After deliberating for 21 hours, the jury returned with the absurd finding that they were *not* such an entity in 1790, 1869, and 1870 (the years which were key to the Indians' case), but that they *were* in 1832 and 1834 (years in which it was important they had been "a tribe" for purposes of alienating land to the government). Their claim was then denied by District Judge Walter J. Skinner.[58] An appeal to the U.S. First Circuit Court failed, and the U.S. Supreme Court refused to review the case.[59]

Given such mixed results, it is plain that that justice in native land claims cases cannot ultimately be expected to accrue through the federal court system. Whatever remedial potential resides in judicial and diplomatic venues must therefore be pursued through bodies such as the United Nations Working Group on Indigenous Populations, which is even now engaged in finalizing a "Universal Declaration of the Rights of Indigenous Peoples,"[60] and the International Court of Justice (ICJ, or "World Court"), which must interpret and render opinions based in such law.[61] From there, it can be expected that international scrutiny and pressure, as well as changed sentiments among a growing segment of the U.S. body politic, may serve to force the United States to edge closer to a fair and equitable handling of indigenous rights.[62]

In the meantime, nearly every litigation of land claims within the federal system adds to the weight of evidence supporting the international case presented by native people: when we win, it proves we were entitled to the land all along; when we lose, it proves that the "due process rights" the U.S. insists protect our interests are, at most, inconsistently available to us. Either way, these legalistic endeavors force cracks in the ideological matrix of the American empire. In combination with extralegal efforts such as refusal to leave their homes by native traditionals and physical occupations of contested areas by groups such as AIM, as well as the increasing international work by indigenous delegations, they comprise the core of the ongoing land struggles which represent the future of Native North America.[63]

CONTEMPORARY LAND STRUGGLES

Aside from those already mentioned, there is no shortage of ongoing struggles for land being mounted by native people within the United States today, all of which might be used to illustrate various aspects of the phenomenon. In Florida, the descendants of the Seminole and Miccosukee "recalcitrants" who had managed to avoid forced relocation to Oklahoma during the 1830s by taking refuge in the Everglades, simply "squatted" in their homeland for more than 130 years, never agreeing to a "peace accord" with the U.S. until the mid-sixties. Because of their unswerving resistance to moving, the state finally agreed to create a small reservation for these people in 1982, and Congress concurred by statute in the same year.[64] In Minnesota, there is the struggle of Anishinabe Akeeng (People's Land Organization) to reassert indigenous control over the remaining twenty percent—250,000 acres—of the White Earth Chippewa Reservation, and to recover some portion of the additional million acres reserved as part of White Earth under an 1854 treaty with the U.S. but declared "surplus" through the General Allotment Act in 1906.[65]

In southern Arizona, the Tohono O'Odam (Papago) Nation continues its efforts to secure the entirety of its sacred Baboquivari Mountain Range, acknowledged by the government to be part of the Papago Reservation in 1916, but opened to nonindian "mineral development" interests—especially those concerned with mining copper—both before and since.[66] In the northern portion of the same state, there have been struggles by both the Hopis and Diné (Navajos) to block the U.S. Forest Service's scheme to convert San Francisco Peaks, a site sacred to both peoples, into a ski resort complex.[67] And, of course, there is the grueling and government-instigated land struggle occurring between the tribal councils of these same two peoples within what was called the "Navajo-Hopi Joint Use Area." The matter is bound up in energy development issues—primarily the stripmining of an estimated 24 billion tons of readily accessible low sulphur coal—and entails a program to forcibly relocate as many as 13,500 traditional Diné, a number of whom have refused to leave their land.[68]

In Massachusetts, the Gayhead Wampanoags, proceeding slowly and carefully so as to avoid the pitfalls encountered by their cousins at Mashpee, are pursuing litigation to regain control over ancestral lands.[69] In Alaska, struggles to preserve some measure of sovereign indigenous—American Indian, Aleut, and Inuit—control over some forty million oil-rich acres corporatized by the 1971 Alaska Native Claims Settlement Act are sharpening steadily.[70] In Hawai'i, the native owners of the islands, having rejected a proffered cash settlement for relinquishment of their historic land rights in 1974,[71] are pursuing a legislative remedy which would both pay monetary compensation for loss of use of their territory and restore a portion of it.[72]

The fact is that, wherever there are indigenous people within the U.S., land claims struggles are occurring with increasing frequency and intensity. To convey a sense of the texture of these continuing battles, it will be useful to consider a small selection of examples in depth. For this purpose, the claims of the Iroquois Confederation in upstate New York, the Lakota Black Hills Land Claim, centered in South Dakota, and the Western Shoshone claims, primarily in Nevada, should serve quite well. Although none is especially unique in its overall configuration—to that extent, each is fittingly representative of a broad range of comparable efforts—they number among the most sustained and intensively pursued.

The Iroquois Land Claims

One of the longest fought and more complicated land claims struggles in the U.S. is that of the Haudenosaunee, or "Six Nations" Iroquoian Confederacy. While the 1783 Treaty of Paris ended hostilities between the England and its secessionist subjects in the thirteen colonies, it had no direct effect upon the state of war existing between those subjects and native peoples allied with the Crown. Similarly, while by the treaty George III had quitclaimed his discovery rights to the affected portion of North America, it was the opinion of Thomas Jefferson and others that this had done nothing to vest title to these lands in the newly-born United States.[73]

On both counts, the Continental Congress found it imperative to come to terms with indigenous nations as expeditiously as possible.[74] A very high priority in this regard was accorded the Haudenosaunee, four nations of which—Mohawk, Seneca, Cayuga, and Onondaga—had fought with the British (the remaining two, the Oneidas and Tuscaroras, having remained largely neutral but occasionally providing assistance to the secessionists).[75] Hence, during October of 1784, the U.S. conducted extensive negotiations with representatives of the Six Nations at Fort Stanwix, in the State of New York.

The result was a treaty, reinforced with a second negotiated at Fort Harmar in 1789, by which the Indians relinquished their interest in lands lying west of a north–south line running from Niagara to the border of Pennsylvania—that is to say, their territory within the Ohio River Valley—as well as parcels on which certain mili-

FIGURE 4.2. Iroquis treaty lands in 1794.

tary posts had been built. In exchange, the U.S. guaranteed three of the four hostile nations the bulk of their traditional homelands. The Oneida and Tuscarora were also "secured in the possession of the lands on which they are now settled." Altogether, the Haudenosaunee reserved about six million acres—about half of the present state of New York—as permanent homelands (see Figure 4.2).[76]

This arrangement, while meeting most of the Indians' needs, was also quite useful to the U.S. central government. As has been observed elsewhere:

> First . . . in order to sell [land in the Ohio River area] and settle it, the Conti-nental Congress needed to extinguish Indian title, including any claims by the Iroquois [nations] of New York. Second, the commissioners wanted to punish the . . . Senecas. Thus they forced the Senecas to surrender most of their land in New York [and Pennsylvania] to the United States . . . Third, the United States . . . wanted to secure peace by confirming to the [Haudenosaunee] their remaining lands. Fourth, the United States was anxious to protect its frontier from the British in Canada by securing land for forts and roads along lakes Erie and Ontario.[77]

New York State, needless to say, was rather less enthusiastic about the terms of the treaty. Indeed, it had already attempted, unsuccessfully, to obtain additional land ces-sions from the Iroquois during meetings conducted prior to arrival of the federal dele-gation at Fort Stanwix.[78] Further such efforts were barred by Article IX of the Articles of Confederation, and subsequently by Article I (Section 10) and the Commerce Clause of the Constitution, all of which combined to render treatymaking and out-right purchases of Indian land by states illegal. New York therefore resorted to sub-terfuge, securing a series of twenty-six "leases," many of them for 999 years, on almost all native territory within its purported boundaries.

The Haudenosaunee initially agreed to these transactions because of Governor George Clinton's duplicitous assurances that the leases represented a way for them to *keep* their land, and for his government to "extend its protection over their property against the dealings of unscrupulous white land speculators." The first such arrangement was forged with the Oneidas in a meeting begun at Fort Schuyler on August 28, 1788.

> The New York commissioners . . . led them to believe that they had [already] lost all their land to the New York Genesee Company, and that the commission-ers were there to restore title. The Oneidas expressed confusion over this since they had never signed any instruments to that effect, but Governor Clinton just waved that aside . . . Thus the Oneidas agreed to the lease arrangement with the state because it seemed the only way they could get back their land. The state re-ceived some five million acres for $2,000 in cash, $2,000 in clothing, $1,000 in provisions, and $600 in annual rental. So complete was the deception that Good Peter [an Oneida leader] thanked the governor for his efforts.[79]

Leasing of the Tuscaroras' land occurred the same day by a parallel instrument.[80] On September 12, the Onondagas leased almost all their land to New York under virtually identical conditions.[81] The Cayugas followed suit on February 25, 1789, in exchange for payment of $500 in silver, plus an additional $1,625 the next June and a $500 annuity.[82] New York's flagrant circumvention of constitutional restrictions on non-federal acquisitions of Indian land was a major factor in passage of the first of the so-called Indian Trade and Intercourse Acts in 1790.[83] Clinton, however, simply shifted to a different ruse, avoiding such tightening in the mechanisms of federal control over his state's manipulations by backdating them. In 1791, for example, he announced that New York would honor a 999-year lease negotiated in 1787 by a private speculator named John Livingston. The lease covered 800,000 acres of mainly Mohawk land, but had been declared null and void by the state legislature in 1788.[84]

Concerned that such maneuvers might push the Iroquois, the largely landless Senecas in particular, into joining Shawnee leader Tecumseh's pan-Indian alliance and physically resisting further U.S. expansion into the Ohio Valley, the federal government sent a new commission to meet with the Haudenosaunee leadership at the principal Seneca town of Canandaigua in 1794. In exchange for a pledge from the Six Nations not to bear arms against the United States, their ownership of the lands guaranteed them at Fort Stanwix was reaffirmed, the state's leases notwithstanding, and the bulk of the Seneca territory in Pennsylvania was restored.[85]

Nonetheless, New York officials, obviously undaunted by this turn of events, rapidly parceled out sections of the leased lands in subleases to the very "unscrupulous whites" it had pledged to guard against. On September 15, 1797, the Holland Land Company, in which many members of the state government had invested, assumed control over all but ten tracts of land, totaling 397 square miles, of the Fort Stanwix Treaty area. The leasing instrument purportedly "extinguished" native title to the

FIGURE 4.3. Land grants, purchases, and Indian reservations within the 1794 treaty area.

land, a process which would be repeated many times over in the coming years (see Figure 4.3).[86]

Given the diminishing military importance of the Six Nations after the Shawnees' 1794 defeat at Fallen Timbers and the eventual vanquishment of Tecumseh at Tippecanoe in 1811, federal authorities ultimately did little or nothing to correct the situation despite continuous Iroquois protests.[87] New York, along with others of the individual states, was thus emboldened to proceed with wholesale appropriations of native territory (albeit an appearance of "free enterprise within the private sector" rather than official policy was usually maintained).

In 1810, for instance, the Holland Company "sold" some 200,000 acres of its holdings in Seneca and Tuscarora land to its own accountant, David A. Ogden, at a price of fifty cents per acre. Ogden then issued shares against development of this land, many of them to the very Albany politicians who already held stock in Holland. Thus (re)capitalized, the "Ogden Land Company" was able to push through a deal in 1826 to buy a further 81,000 acres of previously unleased reservation land at fifty-three cents per acre. A federal investigation into the affair was quashed in 1828 by Secretary of War Peter B. Porter, himself a major stockholder in Ogden.[88]

Under such circumstances, most of the Oneidas requested in 1831 that what was left of their New York holdings, which they were sure they would lose anyway, be exchanged for a 500,000-acre parcel purchased from the Menominees in Wisconsin. President Andrew Jackson, at the time pursuing his policy of general Indian Removal to points west of the Mississippi, readily agreed.[89] In the climate created by Jackson's own posturing, an ever-increasing number of federal officials followed Porter's example, actively colluding with their state-level counterparts and private speculators, thereby erasing altogether whatever meager protection of native rights had previously emanated from Washington, D.C.[90]

One outcome was that on January 15, 1838, federal commissioners oversaw the signing of the Treaty of Buffalo Creek, wherein 102,069 acres of Seneca land was "ceded" directly to the Ogden Company. The $202,000 purchase price was divided almost evenly between the government (to be held "in trust" for the Indians) and individual nonindians seeking to buy and "improve" plots in the former reservation area. At the same time, what was left of the Cayuga, Oneida, Onondaga, and Tuscarora holdings were wiped out, at an aggregate cost of $400,000 to Ogden.[91] The Haudenosaunee were told they should relocate en masse to Missouri. Although the Six Nations never consented to the treaty, and it was never properly ratified by the Senate, President Martin Van Buren proclaimed it to be the "law of the land" on April 4, 1840.[92]

By 1841, Iroquois complaints about the Buffalo Creek Treaty were being supplemented by those of increasing numbers of nonindians outraged not so much by the loss of land to Indians it entailed as by the obvious corruption involved in its terms.[93] Consequently, in 1842, a second Treaty of Buffalo Creek was drawn up. Under this new and "better" instrument, the U.S. again acknowledged the Haudenosaunee right to reside in New York and restored small areas such as the Allegheny and Cattaraugus

Seneca reservations. The Onondaga Reservation was also reconstituted on a 7,300-acre landbase, the Tuscarora Reservation on a paltry 2,500 acres. The Ogden Company, for its part, was allowed to keep the rest.[94]

Although the Tonawanda Band of Senecas immediately filed a formal protest of these terms with the Senate, all they received for their efforts was an 1857 "award" of $256,000 of their own money with which to "buy back" a minor portion of their former territory.[95] Ogden, of course, was thus perfectly positioned to reap an extraordinary profit against what it had originally paid the same unwilling "sellers." And so it went, year after year.

So rich were the rewards to be gleaned from peddling Indian land that, beginning in 1855, the Erie Railway Company entered the picture. While the state legislature quickly approved the company's bids to obtain long-term leases on significant portions of both the Cattaraugus and Allegheny Reservations, the state judiciary sensed an even greater opportunity. Playing upon the depth of then-prevailing federal enthusiasm for railroad construction, New York's high court justices engaged in a cynical and rather elaborate ploy meant to "persuade" Congress to open the door of legitimation to the full range of the state's illicit leasing initiatives.

> Though the [railroad] leases were ratified by New York, the state's supreme court in 1875 invalidated them. In recognition of this action, the New York legislature passed a concurrent resolution that state action was not sufficient to ratify leases because "Congress alone possesses the power to deal with and for the Indians." Instead of setting aside the leases, Congress in 1875 passed an act authorizing [them]. The state now made [all] leases renewable for twelve years, and by an amendment in 1890 the years were extended to ninety-nine. Later the Supreme Court of New York deemed them perpetual.[96]

As a result, by 1889 eighty percent of all Iroquois reservation land in New York was under lease to nonindian interests and individuals. The same year, a commission was appointed by Albany to examine the state's "Indian Problem." Rather than "suggesting that the appropriation of four-fifths of their land had deterred Indian welfare, the commission criticized the Indians for not growing enough to feed themselves," thereby placing an "undue burden" on those profiting from their land. Chancellor C. N. Sims of Syracuse University, a commission member, argued strongly that only "obliteration of the tribes, conferral of citizenship, and allotment of lands" would set things right.[97]

Washington duly set out to undertake allotment, but was stunned to discover it was stymied by the "underlying title" to much of the reserved Haudenosaunee land it had allowed the Ogden Company to obtain over the years. In 1895, Congress passed a bill authorizing a buyout of Ogden's interest, again at taxpayer expense, but the company upped its asking price for the desired acreage from $50,000 to $270,000.[98] The plan thereupon collapsed, and the Six Nations were spared the individual/social/political trauma, and the potential of still further land loss, to which they would have been subjected in the allotment process.[99]

Not that the state did not keep trying. In 1900, after uttering a string of bellicosities concerning "backward savages," Governor Theodore Roosevelt created a commission to reexamine the matter. This led to the introduction in 1902 of another bill (HR 12270) aimed at allotting the Seneca reservations—with fifty thousand acres in all, they were by far the largest remaining Iroquois land areas—by paying Ogden $200,000 of the *Indians'* "trust funds" to abandon its claims on Allegheny and Cattaraugus.[100]

The Senecas retained attorney John VanVoorhis to argue that the Ogden claim was invalid because, for more than a hundred years, the company had not been compelled to pay so much as a nickel of tax on the acreage it professed to "own." By this, they contended, both Ogden and the government had all along admitted that, for purposes of federal law, the land was really still the property of "Indians not taxed." Roosevelt's bill was withdrawn in some confusion at this point, and allotment was again averted.[101] In 1905, the Senecas carried the tax issue into court in an attempt to clear their land title once and for all, but the case was dismissed on the premise that Indians held no legal standing upon which to sue nonindians.[102]

Yet a third attempt to allot the Six Nations reservations (HR 18735) foundered in 1914, as did a New York State constitutional amendment, proposed in 1915, to effectively abolish the reservations. Even worse from New York's viewpoint, in 1919 the U.S. Justice Department for the first time acted in behalf of the Haudenosaunee, filing a suit which (re)established a thirty-two acre "reservation" near Syracuse for the Oneidas.[103]

The state legislature responded by creating yet another commission, this one headed by attorney Edward A. Everett, a political conservative, to conduct a comprehensive study of land title questions in New York and to make recommendations as to how they might be cleared up across the board.[104] The fix again seemed to be in. After more than two years of hearings and intensive research, however, Everett arrived at a thoroughly unanticipated conclusion: The Six Nations still possessed legal title to all six million acres of the Fort Stanwix treaty area.

> He cited international law to the effect that there are only two ways to take a country away from a people possessing it—purchase or conquest. The Europeans who came here did recognize that the Indians were in possession and so, in his opinion, thus recognized their status as nations . . . If then, the Indians did hold fee to the land, how did they lose it? . . . [T]he Indians were [again] recognized by George Washington as a nation at the Treaty of 1784. Hence, they were as of 1922 owners of all the land [reserved by] them in that treaty unless they had ceded it by a treaty equally valid and binding.[105]

In his final report, Everett reinforced his basic finding with references to the Treaties of Forts Harmar and Canandaigua, discounted both Buffalo Creek Treaties as fraudulent, and rejected not only the leases taken by entities such as the Holland and Ogden Companies but those of New York itself as lacking any legal validity at all.[106]

The Albany government quickly shelved the document rather than publishing it, but it could not prevent its implications from being discussed throughout the Six Nations.

On August 21, 1922, a council meeting was held at Onondaga for purposes of retaining Mrs. Lulu G. Stillman, Everett's secretary, to do research on the exact boundaries of the Fort Stanwix treaty area.[107] The Iroquois land claim struggle had shifted from dogged resistance to dispossession to the offensive strategy of land recovery, and the first test case, *James Deere v. St. Lawrence River Power Company* (32 F.2d 550), was filed on June 26, 1925, in an attempt to regain a portion of the St. Regis Mohawk Reservation taken by New York. The federal government declined to intervene on the Mohawks' behalf, as it was plainly its "trust responsibility" to do, and the suit was dismissed by a district court judge on October 10, 1927. The dismissal was upheld on appeal in April 1929.[108]

Things remained quiet on the land claims front during the 1930s, as the Haudenosaunee were mainly preoccupied with preventing the supplanting of their traditional Longhouse form of government by "tribal councils" sponsored by the Bureau of Indian Affairs via the Indian Reorganization Act of 1934.[109] Probably as a means of coaxing them into a more favorable view of federal intentions under the IRA, Indian Commissioner John Collier agreed towards the end of the decade that his agency would finally provide at least limited support to Iroquois claims litigation.

This resulted, in 1941, in the Justice Department's filing of *U.S. v. Forness* (125 F.2d 928) on behalf of the Allegheny Senecas. The suit, ostensibly aimed at eviction of an individual who had refused to pay his $4-per-year rent to the Indians for eight years, actually sought to enforce a resolution of the Seneca Nation canceling hundreds of low-cost, 99-year leases taken in the City of Salamanca on the reservation in 1892. Intervening for the defendants was the Salamanca Trust Corporation, a mortgage institution holding much of the paper at issue. Although the case was ultimately unsuccessful in its primary objective, it did force a judicial clarification of the fact that, in and of itself, New York law had no bearing on leasing arrangements pertaining to Indian land.[110]

This was partly "corrected," in the state view, on July 2, 1948, and September 13, 1950, when Congress passed bills placing the Six Nations under New York jurisdiction in first criminal and then civil matters.[111] Federal responsibility to assist Indians in pursuing treaty-based land claims was nonetheless explicitly preserved.[112] Washington, of course, elected to treat this obligation in its usual cavalier fashion, plunging ahead during the 1950s—while the Indians were mired in efforts to prevent termination of their federal recognition altogether—with the flooding of 130 acres of the St. Regis Reservation near Messena (and about 1,300 acres of the Caughnawaga Mohawk Reserve in Canada) as part of the St. Lawrence Seaway Project.[113]

The government also proceeded with plans to flood more than nine thousand acres of the Allegheny Reservation as a byproduct of constructing the Kinzua Dam. Although studies revealed an alternative site for the dam that would not only spare the Seneca land from flooding but better serve "the greater public good" for which it was supposedly intended, Congress pushed ahead.[114] The Senecas protested the project as a clear violation of the Fort Stanwix guarantees, a position with which lower federal courts agreed, but the Supreme Court ultimately declined to decide the question and the Army Corps of Engineers completed the dam in 1967.[115]

Meanwhile, the New York State Power Authority was attempting to seize more than half (1,383 acres) of the Tuscarora Reservation, near Buffalo, as a reservoir for the Niagara Power Project. In April 1958, the Tuscaroras physically blocked access to the site, and several were arrested (charges were later dropped). A federal district judge entered a temporary restraining order against the state, but the appellate court ruled that congressional issuance of a license through the Federal Power Commission constituted sufficient grounds for the state to "exercise eminent domain" over native property.[116] The Supreme Court again refused to hear the resulting Haudenosaunee appeal. A "compromise" was then implemented in which the state flooded "only" 560 acres, or about one-eighth of the remaining Tuscarora land.[117]

By the early 1960s, it had become apparent that the Six Nations, because their territory fell "within the boundaries of one of the original thirteen states," would not be allowed to seek redress through the Indian Claims Commission.[118] The decade was largely devoted to a protracted series of discussions between state officials and various sectors of the Iroquois leadership. Agreements were reached in areas related to education, housing, and revenue sharing, but on the issues of land claims and jurisdiction, the position of Longhouse traditionals was unflinching. In their view, the state holds *no* rights over the Haudenosaunee in either sphere.[119]

The point was punctuated on May 13, 1974, when Mohawks from the St. Regis and Caughnawaga Reservations occupied an area at Ganiekeh (Moss Lake), in the Adirondack Mountains. They proclaimed the site to be sovereign Mohawk territory under the Fort Stanwix Treaty—"[We] represent a cloud of title not only to [this] 612.7 acres in Herkimer County but to all of northeastern" New York—and set out to defend it, and themselves, by force of arms.[120]

After a pair of local vigilantes engaged in shooting at the Indians were wounded by return gunfire in October, the state filed for eviction in federal court. The matter was bounced back on the premise that it was not a federal issue, and the New York attorney general, undoubtedly discomfited at the publicity prospects entailed in an armed confrontation on the scale of the 1973 Wounded Knee siege, let the case die.[121]

The state next dispatched a negotiating team headed by future Governor Mario Cuomo. In May 1977, partially as a result of Cuomo's efforts but more importantly because of the Indians' obvious willingness to slug it out with state authorities if need be, the "Moss Lake Agreement" was reached. Under its provisions, the Mohawks assumed permanent possession of a land parcel at Miner Lake, near the town of Altona, and another in the nearby McComb Reforestation Area.[122] Mohawk possession of the sites remains ongoing in 2002, a circumstance which has prompted others among the Six Nations to pursue land recovery through a broader range of tactics and, perhaps, with greater vigor than they might otherwise have employed (e.g., Mohawk actions taken in Canada concerning a land dispute at the Oka Reserve, near Montréal, during 1990).[123]

As all this was going on, the Oneidas had, in 1970, filed the first of the really significant Iroquois land claims suits. The case, *Oneida Indian Nation of New York v. County of Oneida*, charged that the transfer of 100,000 acres of Oneida land to New York via a 1795 lease engineered by Governor Clinton was fraudulent and invalid on both constitutional grounds and because it violated the 1790 Trade and Intercourse Act. It was dismissed because of the usual "Indians lack legal standing" argument but reinstated by the Supreme Court in 1974.[124] Compelled to actually examine the merits of the case for the first time, the U.S. District Court agreed with the Indians (and the Everett Report) that title still rested with the Oneidas.

> The plaintiffs have established a claim for violation of the Nonintercourse Act. Unless the Act is to be considered nugatory, it must be concluded that the plaintiffs' right of occupancy and possession of the land in question was not alienated. By the deed of 1795, the State acquired no rights against the plaintiffs; consequently, its successors, the defendant counties, are in no better position.[125]

Terming the Oneidas a "legal fiction," and the lower courts' rulings "racist," attorney Allan Van Gestel appealed on behalf of the defendants to the Supreme Court.[126] On October 1, 1984, the high court ruled against Van Gestel and ordered his clients to work out an accommodation, indemnified by the state, including land restoration, compensation, and rent on unrecovered areas.[127] Van Gestel continued to howl that "the common people" of Oneida and Madison Counties were being "held hostage," but as the Oneidas' attorney, Arlinda Locklear, put it in 1986:

> One final word about responsibility for the Oneida claims. It is true that the original sin here was committed by the United States and the state of New York. It is also no doubt true that there are a number of innocent landowners in the area, i.e., individuals who acquired their land with no knowledge of the Oneida claim to it. But those facts alone do not end the inquiry respecting ultimate responsibility. Whatever the knowledge of the claims before then, the landowners have certainly been aware of the Oneida claims since 1970 when the first suit was filed. Since that time, the landowners have done nothing to seek a speedy and just resolution of the claims. Instead, they have as a point of principle denied the validity of the claims and pursued the litigation, determined to prove the claims to be frivolous. Now that the landowners have failed in that effort, they loudly protest their innocence in the entire matter. The Oneidas, on the other hand, have since 1970 repeatedly expressed their preference for an out-of-court resolution of their claims. Had the landowners joined with the Oneidas sixteen years ago in seeking a just resolution, the claims would no doubt be resolved today. For that reason, the landowners share in the responsibility for the situation in which they find themselves today.[128]

Others would do well to heed these words because, as Locklear pointed out, the Oneida case "paved the legal way for other Indian land claims."[129] Not least of these are other suits by the Oneidas themselves. In 1978, the New York Oneidas filed for adjudication of title to the entirety of their Fort Stanwix claim, about 4.5 million acres, in a case affecting not only Oneida and Madison Counties, but Broome, Chenango, Cortland, Herkimer, Jefferson, Lewis, Onondaga, Oswego, St. Lawrence, and Tiago Counties as well. (The matter was shelved, pending final disposition of the first Oneida claims litigation.)[130] Then, in December 1979, the Oneida Nation of Wisconsin and the Thames Band of Southgold, Ontario, joined in an action pursuing rights in the same claim area, but naming the state rather than individual counties as defendant.[131]

The Cayuga Nation, landless throughout the twentieth century, has also filed suit against Cayuga and Seneca Counties for recovery of 64,015 acres taken during Clinton's leasing foray of 1789. (The Cayuga claim may develop into an action overlapping with those of the Oneida; see Figure 4.4.)[132] The latter case, filed on November 19, 1980, resulted from attempts by the Cayugas to negotiate some sort of landbase and compensation for themselves with federal, state, and county officials from the mid-70s onward. By August 1979, they had worked out a tentative agreement that would have provided them with the 1,852-acre Sampson Park in southern Seneca County, the 3,629-acre Hector Land Use Area in the same county, and an $8 million trust account established by the Secretary of the Interior (up to $2.5 million of which would be used to buy additional land).[133]

Although not one square inch of their holdings was threatened by the arrangement, the response of the local nonindian population was rabid. To quote Paul D. Moonan, Sr., president of the local Monroe Title and Abstract Company: "The Cayugas have no moral or legal justification for their claim."[134] Wisner Kinne, a farmer near the town of Ovid, immediately founded the Seneca County Liberation Organization (SCLO), a group defined by nothing so much as its propensity to express the most virulent anti-Indian sentiments. SCLO attracted several hundred highly vocal members from the sparsely populated county.[135]

FIGURE 4.4. Oneida land claim, State of New York, 1984.

A bill to authorize the settlement subsequently failed due to this "white backlash," and so the Cayugas went to court to obtain a much larger area, eviction of 7,000 county residents and $350 million in trespass damages. Attempts by attorneys for SCLO to have the suit dismissed failed in 1982, as did a 1984 compromise offer initiated by Representative Frank Horton. The latter, which might well have been accepted by the Cayugas, would have provided them with the 3,200-acre Howland Game Management Reserve along the Seneca River, a 2,850-acre parcel on Lake Ontario possessed by the Rochester Gas and Electric Company, and a 2,000-acre parcel adjoining Sampson State Park. Additionally, the Cayugas would have received "well in excess" of the $8 million they had originally sought.[136]

While SCLO appears by this point to have decided that acquiescence might well be the better part of valor, the proposal came under heavy attack from nonindian environmentalists and other supposed progressives "concerned about the animals in the Howland Reserve." Ultimately, it was nixed by Ronald Reagan in 1987, not out of concern for local fauna, or even as part of some broader anti-Indian agenda, but because was he angry with Horton for voting against his own proposal to fund the Nicaraguan Contras' low intensity war against that country's Sandinista government.[137]

Meanwhile, in the town of Salamanca, to which the leases expired at the end of 1991, the Allegheny Senecas also undertook decisive action during the second half of the 1980s. Beginning as early as 1986, they stipulated their intent not only to not renew leasing instruments, but to begin eviction proceedings against nonindian lease and mortgage holders in the area unless the terms of any new arrangement were considerably recast in their favor. In substance, they demanded clarification of underlying Seneca title to the township, a shorter leasing period, fair rates for property rental, and preeminent jurisdiction over both the land and income derived from it.[138]

A further precondition to lease renewal was that compensation be made for all nonpayment and underpayment of fair rental values of Seneca property accruing from the then-existing lease. Although these demands unleashed a storm of protest from local whites, who, as usual, argued vociferously that the Indian owners of the land held no rights to it, the Senecas were successful both in court and in Congress.[139] With passage of the Seneca Nation Settlement Act in 1990, the more essential Seneca demands were met. These included an award of $60 million, with costs borne equally by the federal, state, and local governments, to reimburse the Allegheny Band for rental monies they should have received over the past ninety-nine years, but did not.[140]

The limited but real gains posted thus far, in both the Oneida land claims and with regard to renegotiation of the Salamanca leases, point to a viable strategy for a gradual recovery of Haudenosaunee land and jurisdictional rights in upstate New York during the years ahead. As of this writing, the second Oneida suit remains in process, as does the Cayuga suit. Viewed in light of the sort of settlement achieved in the earlier Oneida win, these seem likely to generate, if not a truly fair resolution of the issues raised, then a marked improvement in the circumstances of both peoples.[141]

Also at issue is a longterm lease of Onondaga land upon which the City of Syracuse has been built. Following the pattern evidenced at Salamanca, the Onondagas have been able to secure an agreement in principle with state, local, and federal authorities which would both compensate them for lost rental earnings over the past century and generate a much higher level of income in the future. These monies can, in turn, be invested in the restoration of rural areas adjoining the presently tiny Onondaga Reservation to the nation's use and control.[142]

Overall, it seems probable that such efforts at litigation and negotiation will continue over the next ten to twenty years, and thereby serve to enhance the relative positions of the Tuscarora and Mohawk nations as well as their four confederates. The increasing scope of native jurisdiction in New York, which such a process would necessarily entail, may accomplish a changed sensibility among the state's nonindian residents, as they discover firsthand that a genuine exercise of indigenous rights does not automatically lead to their disenfranchisement or dispossession of personal property.[143]

Indeed, it may be that at least some sectors of New York's nonindian population may learn that coming under Indian jurisdiction can be preferable to remaining under the jurisdiction of the state (which has, among other things, one of the highest tax levies in the country). If so, it may be that the ongoing (re)assertion of Haudenosaunee sovereignty within the 1794 treaty territory may develop peacefully and with a reasonably high degree of Indian/white cooperation over the long run, reversing the unrelenting manifestation of Euroamerican avarice, duplicity, and racism which has marked this relationship over the past two centuries.[144]

In the alternative, when the methods of litigation and negotiation reach the limit of the state's willingness or ability to give ground—as surely they must, absent a profound alteration in the attitudes of the interloping white populace—conflicts of the sort previewed at Ganiekeh and Oka must be the inevitable result.[145] Something of a crossroads is thus at hand in northern New York State; things could go either way. And in the final analysis, the choice is one which resides with the state and its immigrant citizens. The Haudenosaunee own the land there by all conceivable legal, moral, and ethical definitions.[146] They always have, and will continue to until *they* decide otherwise. As a whole, they have demonstrated a remarkable patience with those who have presumed to take what was and is theirs. But such patience cannot last forever.

The Black Hills Land Claim

A much more harshly fought struggle, at least in terms of physical combat, has been the battle waged by the Lakota Nation ("Western" or "Teton Sioux," composed of the Oglala, Hunkpapa, Minneconjou, Sicangu [Brûlé], Bohinunpa [Two Kettles], Ituzipco [Sans Arcs], and Sihasapa [Blackfeet] bands) to retain their spiritual heartland, the Black Hills. In 1851, the United States entered into the first Fort Laramie Treaty with the Lakota, Cheyenne, Arapaho, Crow, and other indigenous nations of the northern and central plains regions. In large part, the treaty was an attempt by the federal government to come to grips with the matter of Indian property rights within the vast "Louisiana Purchase" area it had acquired from France earlier in the century.[147] The Lakota were formally recognized in the 1851 treaty as being entitled to a huge tract centering upon their sacred lands, called Paha Sapa (Black Hills), including virtually all of the present states of South Dakota and Nebraska, as well as appreciable portions of Kansas, North Dakota, Montana, and Wyoming, and a small portion of Colorado. In sum, the U.S. formally recognized Lakota sovereignty over an area totaling between six and seven percent of the lower 48 states.[148]

It was not long, however, before silver was discovered in the Virginia City portion of Montana Territory, and a "short route" to these ore fields began to be considered essential to a U.S. economy beset by the demands of the Civil War. Hence, at least as early as 1864, the government openly violated the 1851 treaty, sending troops to construct a series of forts intended to secure what was called the "Bozeman Trail," directly through the western portion of the Lakota homeland. The Lakota, under the political leadership of Red Cloud, an Oglala, responded by forming an alliance with the Cheyenne and Arapaho, bringing their joint military forces to bear upon the trail during the winter of 1866–67. By early 1868, the United States, having suffered several defeats in the field, and finding its troops trapped within their forts, sued for peace.[149]

This led, that same year, to a second Fort Laramie Treaty in which (in exchange for being allowed to withdraw its remaining soldiers in one piece) the federal government once again recognized Lakota sovereignty and national territoriality, this time establishing a "Great Sioux Reservation" encompassing all of contemporary South Dakota west of the east bank of the Missouri River, and acknowledging that the "Greater Sioux Nation" was entitled to permanent use of "Unceded Indian Territory" involving large portions of Nebraska, Wyoming, Montana, and North Dakota.[150] Further, the new treaty committed U.S. troops to prevent nonindians from trespassing in Lakota territory, specified that it did nothing to "abrogate or annul" Lakota land rights acknowledged in the 1851 treaty,[151] and provided that:

No [subsequent] treaty for cession of any portion of the reservation herein described which may be held in common shall be of any validity or force as against said Indians, unless executed and signed by at least three-fourths of all adult male Indians [the gender provision was a U.S., rather than Lakota, stipulation], occupying or interested in the same.[152]

Again, the United States was unwilling to honor the treaty for long. A priest, Jean de Smet, ventured illegally into the Black Hills and afterwards reported to the *Sioux Falls Times* (South Dakota) that he had discovered gold therein.[153] In short order, this led to the government's reinforcing Lt. Colonel George Armstrong Custer's élite 7th Cavalry Regiment and violating *both* the 1851 and 1868 treaties by sending this heavy military force directly into the Hills on a "fact-finding" mission. Custer's 1874 report that he too had found gold in the Paha Sapa, much ballyhooed in the eastern press, led to another military foray, the Jenny Expedition, during the summer of 1875.[154] The fact that there was gold in the heart of Lakota Territory, in their most sacred of places, was thus confirmed to the satisfaction of Washington officials.

With that, the government sent yet another treaty commission to meet with the Lakota leadership, this time in an effort to negotiate purchase of the Black Hills.[155]

When the Lakotas refused to sell (as was clearly their right, under either or both treaties), Washington responded by transferring its relations with them from the Bureau of Indian Affairs (BIA) to the Department of War. All Lakotas were ordered to gather at their "assigned agencies" within the Great Sioux Reservation by no later than the end of January 1876, although they plainly had every right to be anywhere they chose within their treaty territory; those who failed to comply with this utterly unlawful federal directive were informed that *they* would be viewed as having "broken the peace" and consequently treated as "hostiles." Meanwhile, President Ulysses S. Grant completed the government's raft of treaty violations by secretly instructing his army commanders to disregard U.S. obligations to prevent the wholesale invasion of the Lakota heartland by nonindian miners.[156]

Rather than submitting to federal dictates, the Lakotas gathered in the remote Powder River Country of southeastern Montana, a part of their unceded territory, to discuss how they should respond. In turn, the army used this "gesture of hostility" as a pretext for launching a massive assault upon them, with the express intent of "crushing Sioux resistance completely, once and for all." The U.S. objective in this was, of course, to simply obliterate any Lakota ability to effectively oppose federal expropriation of the Black Hills. The mechanism chosen to accomplish this task was a three-pronged campaign consisting of some 3,000 troops under Major Generals George Crook (coming into the Powder River Country from the south) and Alfred Terry (from the east). Another thousand men under Colonel John Gibbon were to approach from the west, and the Lakotas (as well as their Cheyenne and Arapaho allies) were to be caught between these powerful forces and destroyed.[157]

The army's plan failed completely. On June 17, 1876, Crook's entire column was met by an approximately equal number of Lakotas led by Crazy Horse, an Oglala. The soldiers were quickly defeated and sent into full retreat.[158] This was followed, on June 25, by the decimation of Custer's 7th Cavalry, part of Terry's column, in the valley of the Little Big Horn River.[159] For the second time in a decade, the Lakotas had successfully defended Paha Sapa, militarily defeating the U.S. Army in what has come to be known as the "Great Sioux War."[160]

On this occasion, however, the victory was to prove bitter. Vengefully licking its wounds after having been unable to best the Indians in open combat, the army imported Colonel Ranald Mackenzie, a specialist who had perfected the craft of "total war" in earlier campaigns against the Kiowas and Comanches on the southern plains of present-day Texas and Oklahoma. The new tactician spent the winter of 1876–77 locating individual Lakota and Cheyenne villages which had been rendered immobile by cold and snow. He then used sheer numbers to overpower each village as it was located, slaughtering women, children, and old people as matter of course.[161] By the spring of 1877, in order to spare their noncombatants further butchery at the hands of the army, most Lakotas decided it was time to stop fighting. Sitting Bull and Gall, Hunkpapa leaders, took their followers to sanctuary in Canada, not returning until 1881. Having laid down his arms, Crazy Horse, preeminent among Oglala resistance leaders, was assassinated by the military on September 5, 1877, and the era of Lakota defensive warfare was brought to a close.[162]

Undoubtedly as a result of the military advantage it ultimately gained over the Lakotas during the Great Sioux War, the Congress felt empowered to pass an act on February 28, 1877, taking for itself a large portion of the Great Sioux Reservation containing the Black Hills (the Unceded Indian Territory was taken about the same time; see Figure 4.5).[163] There is strong evidence that the legislators involved were aware that this act was patently illegal, given that they had effected a slightly earlier measure suspending delivery of subsistence rations, to which the Lakota were entitled, both under their treaties *and* under the laws of war, until such time as the Indians "gave up their claim over the Black Hills."[164]

In simplest terms, the United States set out to starve the captive Lakota population into compliance with its plan. Even under these conditions, however, a commission headed by George Manypenny and sent to obtain the Lakota consent was unable to get the job done. While the 1868 treaty required the agreement of 75 percent of all adult male Lakotas to legitimate any "Sioux Land Cession," Manypenny's commission came away with the signatures of only about ten percent of the Lakota men. Nonetheless, Congress enacted its statute "lawfully" expropriating the Hills.[165]

Over the following two decades, erosion of Lakota sovereignty and landbase were

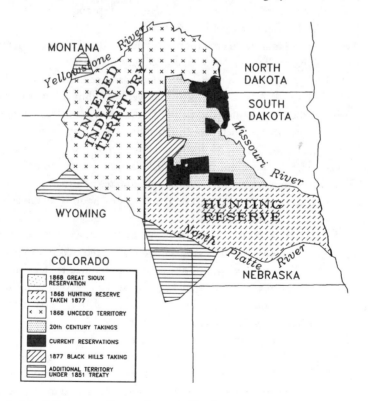

FIGURE 4.5. Lakota Nation reservations and unceded lands.

accelerated by imposition of the Major Crimes and General Allotment Acts.[166] The Lakota economy was thus prostrated, and the political process by which the nation had traditionally governed itself was completely subverted. By 1890, despair at such circumstances had reached a level leading to the widespread adoption of the Ghost Dance religion, a belief that the rigorous performance of certain rituals would lead to a return of things as they had been before the Euroamerican invasion. This phenomenon, dubbed an "incipient uprising" by Indian agents, provided the government an excuse to declare a state of military emergency during which Sitting Bull (last of the great "recalcitrant" leaders) was assassinated at his home near Standing Rock, and some 350 of his followers were massacred along Wounded Knee Creek on what is now the Pine Ridge Reservation.[167] Lakota spiritual practices were then outlawed in general.[168] After that, Washington tended to view the victims as being "thoroughly broken."

During the 1920s and 1930s, Lakota sovereignty was diminished even further through imposition, first of the Indian Citizenship Act, and then the Indian Reorganization Act (IRA).[169] The former did much to confuse Lakota national allegiances, engendering a distorted sort of loyalty to the United States among many younger Indians, especially men, desperate to overcome their sense of personal disempowerment. In practice, such "patriotism," common to most colonial systems, has meant Indians being "allowed" to serve as mercenaries in the military of their oppressors, fighting (usually against other peoples of color) and dying in disproportionate numbers during the Second World War, Korea, and Vietnam.[170]

The IRA was in some ways even more insidious, putting in place a "more democratic and representative" form of "elected council" governance, owing its very existence to federal authority, as a replacement for the popular and consensus-oriented traditional Councils of Elders.[171] As a consequence, divisiveness within Lakota society increased sharply during the 1940s, with "progressives" in the tribal council orbit pitted by Washington directly against the much larger population of grassroots traditionals.[172]

By the mid-1950s, things had deteriorated to such an extent that Congress could seriously consider "termination" (i.e., externally and unilaterally imposed dissolution) of the Lakota Nation altogether.[173] Although, unlike the situation of the Menominees, Klamaths, and a number of other indigenous nations dissolved during the 1950s, the Lakota termination was never ultimately consummated, by 1967 nearly half the "Sioux" population had been removed to city slums—Denver, Minneapolis, Chicago, San Francisco, and Los Angeles were the preferred dumping grounds—through federal relocation programs designed and intended to depopulate the land base of the reservations.[174] The degeneration of social cohesion resulting from this policy-generated diaspora has created for the Lakota and other impacted peoples staggering problems that have never been resolved.

Other effects of advanced colonization were almost as devastating: By the contemporary era, the 1868 treaty territory had been reduced to a meager ten percent of its original area and broken up into a "complex" of reservations geographically separating the bands from one another. Of the residual land base, assertion of BIA leasing prerogatives under a unilaterally assumed federal "trust authority" over Lakota property, a matter accommodated within the U.S. doctrine of exercising "plenary [full] power" over Indian affairs, placed more than two-thirds of the most productive reservation acreage in the hands of nonindian ranchers, farmers, and corporate concerns.[175]

Completely dispossessed of their land and traditional economy, modern Lakotas confront a circumstance on their reservations in which unemployment has hovered in the ninetieth percentile throughout the past half-century and more.[176] The implications of this situation are both predictable and readily apparent. The poorest county in the United States every year since World War II has been Shannon, on the Pine Ridge Reservation. Todd County, on the adjoining Rosebud Reservation, has kept pace, consistently placing among the ten poorest locales in the federal poverty index.[177]

Many Lakotas, of course, never accepted the fact or circumstances of their colonization. Realizing in the wake of the Wounded Knee Massacre that any direct military response to U.S. transgressions would be at best self-defeating, they opted instead to utilize the colonizers' own legal codes—and its pretense of being a "humanitarian power, bound by the laws of civilized conduct"—as a means of recovering what had been stolen from them.[178]

In 1920, a federal law was passed which "authorized" the Lakotas to sue the government "under treaties, or agreements, or laws of Congress, on the misappropriation of any funds or lands of said tribe or band or bands thereof."[179] The law was hardly altruistic. Realizing that there had been "difficulties" with the manner in which Lakota "consent" had been obtained for the 1877 Black Hills land expropriation, the government saw the bill as a handy means to buy the now-impoverished Indians off and "quiet title" to the Paha Sapa. This was amply revealed in 1923 when the Lakotas entered their suit with the federal Court of Claims seeking return of their stolen land rather than the monetary compensation the United States had anticipated would be at issue. Not knowing what to do in the face of this unexpected turn of events, the court stalled for nineteen years, endlessly entertaining motions and countermotions while professing to "study" the matter. Finally, in 1942, when it became absolutely clear the Lakotas would not accept cash in lieu of land, the court dismissed the case, claiming the situation was a "moral issue" rather than a constitutional question over which it held jurisdiction.[180] In 1943, the U.S. Supreme Court refused to even review the claims court decision.[181]

The litigational route appeared to be stalemated, but in 1946 the Indian Claims Commission Act was passed (see above). The Lakotas therefore (re)filed their suit with the ICC in 1950. The Commission, however, opted to view the case as having been "retired" by the 1942 Court of Claims dismissal and subsequent Supreme Court denial of *certiorari*. It likewise dismissed the matter in 1954.[182] The Court of Claims upheld the Commission's decision on appeal from the Lakotas during the same year.[183] Undeterred by this failure of "due process," the Lakotas entered a second (very different) appeal, and in 1958, "[T]he Indian Claims Commission [was] ordered by the Court of Claims to reopen the case on the grounds that the Sioux had previously been represented by inadequate counsel and as a consequence an inadequate record [had] been presented."[184]

In 1961, the U.S. Department of Justice attempted to have the Black Hills case again set aside, requesting a writ of *mandamus* seeking "extraordinary relief" for the government; the Court of Claims rejected this tactic during the same year. The ICC was thereby forced to actually consider the case. After a long hiatus, the commissioners announced that, having "studied the matter," they were reducing the scope of the issue to three elements:

- What land rights were acquired by the U.S. vis-à-vis the Black Hills in 1877?

- What consideration had been given by the U.S. in exchange for these lands?

- If no consideration had been given, had any payment been made by the U.S.?[185]

Proceeding on this basis, the Commission entered a preliminary opinion in 1974 that Congress had been exercising its "power of eminent domain" in 1877, and that it had therefore been "justified" in taking the Black Hills from the Lakotas, although the United States was obligated to pay them "just compensation" for their loss, as provided under the fifth amendment to the U.S. Constitution.[186] The opinion denied any right of the Lakotas to recover the land taken from them, and they therefore objected to it quite strongly.

The federal government also took strong exception to the direction things were moving, given its reluctance to pay any large sum of money as compensation for territory it had always enjoyed free of charge. Hence, in 1975, the Justice Department appealed to the Court of Claims, securing a *res judicata* prohibition against the ICC "reaching the merits" of any proposed Lakota compensation package.[187] What this meant, in simplest terms, was that the Commission was formally constrained to awarding the Lakotas nothing beyond "the value of the land in question at the time of taking." The stipulation resulted in the Commission's assigning an award of $17.5 million for the entire Black Hills area, against which the government sought to "offset" $3,484 in rations issued to the Lakotas in 1877.[188]

The Lakotas attempted to appeal this to the Supreme Court, but the high court of the United States again refused to consider the matter.[189] Meanwhile, arguing that acceptance of compensation would constitute a bona fide land cession, and invoking the consent clause contained in the 1868 Treaty, the Lakotas themselves conducted a referendum to determine whether three-fourths of the people were willing to relinquish title to Paha Sapa. The answer was a resounding "no."[190]

The unexpected referendum results presented the government with yet another dilemma in its continuing quest to legitimize its theft of Lakota territory; in order to make the best of an increasingly bad situation, Congress passed a bill in 1978 enabling the Court of Claims to "review" the nature and extent of Lakota compensation.[191] This the court did, "revising" the proposed award in 1979 to include five percent simple interest, accruing annually since 1877, adding up to a total of $105 million; aggregated with the original $17.5 million principal award, this made the federal offer $122.5 million.[192]

The Justice Department again attempted unsuccessfully to constrict the amount of compensation the government would be obliged to pay by filing an appeal with the Supreme Court. In 1980, the high court upheld the Claims Court's award of interest.[193] The Lakotas, however, remained entirely unsatisfied. Pointing to a second poll of the reservations conducted in 1979 showing that the people were no more willing to accept $122.5 million than $17.5 million in exchange for the Black Hills, and arguing that return of the land itself had always been the object of their suits, they went back to court.[194] On July 18, 1980, the Oglalas entered a claim naming the United States, the State of South Dakota, and a number of counties, towns, and individuals in the U.S. District Court, seeking recovery of the land per se, as well as $11 *billion* in damages. The case was dismissed by the court on September 12, supposedly because "the issue [had] already been resolved."[195]

In 1981, the U.S. Eighth Circuit Court affirmed the District Court's dismissal, and, in 1982, the Supreme Court once again declined to hear the resultant Lakota appeal.[196] These decisions opened the way in 1985 for the Court of Claims to finalize its award of monetary compensation as the "exclusive available remedy" for the Black Hills land claim.[197] In sum, further Lakota recourse in U.S. courts had been extinguished by those courts. The game had always been rigged, and the legal strategy had proven quite unsuccessful in terms of either achieving Lakota objectives or even holding the United States accountable to its own professed system of legality.[198]

On the other hand, the legal route did mark solid achievements in other areas: Pursuing it demonstrably kept alive a strong sense of hope, unity, and fighting spirit among many Lakotas that might otherwise have diminished over time. Further, the more than sixty years of litigation had forced a range of admissions from the federal government concerning the real nature of the Black Hills expropriations; Judge Fred Nichol, for example, had termed the whole affair a "ripe and rank case of dishonorable dealings" and "a national disgrace" in a 1975 opinion written for the Court of Claims.[199] Such admissions went much further toward fostering broad public understanding of Lakota issues than a "one-sided" Indian recounting of the facts could ever have.[200] Cumulatively, then, the Lakota legal strategy set the stage for both an ongoing struggle and for public acceptance of a *meaningful* solution to the Black Hills claim.

It is likely that the limited concessions obtained by the Lakotas from U.S. courts during the 1970s were related to the emergence of strong support for the American Indian Movement (AIM) on the Pine Ridge and Rosebud Reservations during the early part of the decade. At the outset, AIM's involvement on Pine Ridge concerned the provision of assistance to traditional Oglalas attempting to block the illegal transfer of approximately one-eighth of the reservation (the so-called Sheep Mountain Gunnery Range) to the U.S. Forest Service by a corrupt tribal administration headed by Richard Wilson.[201] AIM provided a marked stiffening of the Lakota resolve to pursue land rights by demonstrating a willingness to go toe-to-toe with federal forces on such matters, an attitude largely absent in Indian Country since 1890.[202]

The virulence of the federal response to AIM's "criminal arrogance" in this regard led directly to the dramatic siege of the Wounded Knee hamlet in 1973, a spectacle which riveted international attention on the Black Hills issue for the first time. In turn, this scrutiny resulted in analysis and an increasingly comprehensive understanding of the vast economic interests underlying federal policy in the region (see Figure 5.2, p. 127). This process steadily raised the level of progressive criticism of the government and garnered further nonindian support for the Lakota position. Anxious to reassert its customary juridical control over questions of Indian land rights, the government engaged in what amounted to a counterinsurgency war against AIM and its traditional Pine Ridge supporters from 1973 to 1976.[203]

By the latter year, however, it was a bit too late to effectively contain AIM's application of external pressure to the U.S. judicial system. In 1974, the Lakota elders had convened a treaty conference on the Standing Rock Reservation and charged Oglala Lakota AIM leader Russell Means with taking the 1868 Fort Laramie Treaty "before the family of nations."[204] Means therefore formed AIM's "diplomatic arm," the International Indian Treaty Council (IITC) and set about achieving a presence within the United Nations, not only for the Lakotas, but for all the indigenous peoples of the Western Hemisphere. IITC accomplished this in 1977—largely on the basis of the work of its first director, a Cherokee named Jimmie Durham—when delegations from 98 American Indian nations were allowed to make presentations before a subcommission of the U.N. Commission on Human Rights at the Palace of Nations in Geneva, Switzerland.[205]

In 1981, the United Nations reacted to what it had heard by establishing a Working Group on Indigenous Populations, lodged under the Economic and Social Council (ECOSOC), an entity dedicated to the formulation of international law concerning the rights and status of indigenous nations vis-à-vis the various states by which they'd been subsumed.[206] The regularized series of hearings integral to working group procedure provided an international forum within which American Indians and other indigenous peoples from Australia, New Zealand, Polynesia, and Micronesia could formally articulate the basis of their national rights and the effects of governmental abridgment of these rights.[207]

By the late 1980s, the working group had completed a global study of the conditions under which indigenous peoples were forced to live, and had commissioned a comprehensive study of the treaty relationships existing between U.N. member states and various native nations.[208] The stated objective of the working group has become the eventual promulgation of the earlier mentioned "Universal Declaration of Indigenous Rights" (originally scheduled for submission to the U.N. General Assembly in 1992), holding the same legal and moral force as the Universal Declaration of Human Rights, the 1948 Convention on Prevention and Punishment of the Crime of Genocide, assorted Geneva Conventions, and other elements of international law.[209]

The result of this international approach was to deny the United States the veil of secrecy behind which it had conducted its Indian affairs as a purely "internal matter."

Exposed to the light of international attention, the federal government was repeatedly embarrassed by the realities of its own Indian policies and court decisions. As a consequence, federal courts became somewhat more accommodating in the Black Hills case than they might otherwise have been.

When the Lakotas rejected monetary settlement of their land claim in 1979–80, AIM was instrumental in popularizing the slogan, "The Black Hills Are Not For Sale."[210] This was again coupled with direct extralegal action when Russell Means initiated an occupation in 1981—"the first step in physically reclaiming the Paha Sapa," as he put it—of an 880-acre site near Rapid City in the Black Hills. The AIM action again caused broad public attention to be focused upon the Lakota land claim, and precipitated the potential for another major armed clash with federal forces. The latter possibility was averted at the last moment by a federal district judge who, reflecting the government's concern not to become engaged in another "Wounded Knee-type confrontation," issued an order enjoining the FBI and U.S. Marshals Service from undertaking an assault upon the occupants of what was by then called Yellow Thunder Camp.[211]

Under these conditions, the government was actually placed in the position of having to sue the Indians in order to get them to leave what it claimed was U.S. Forest Service property.[212] AIM countersued on the basis that federal land-use policies in the Black Hills violated not only the 1868 treaty, but also Lakota spiritual freedom under the First Amendment to the U.S. Constitution and the Indian Religious Freedom Act.[213] In 1986, the government was stunned when U.S. District Judge Robert O'Brien ruled in favor of AIM, finding that the Lakotas had every right to the Yellow Thunder site, and that the United States had clearly discriminated against them by suggesting otherwise. The Yellow Thunder ruling was a potential landmark, bearing broad implications for application in other Indian land claims in the United States. However, O'Brien's finding was severely undercut by the Supreme Court's "G-O Road Decision" and was consequently overturned by the Eighth Circuit Court.[214]

Like the Lakota legal strategy, AIM's course of largely extralegal action has proven insufficient in itself to resolve the Black Hills land claim. Nonetheless, it can be seen to have had a positive bearing on the evolution of litigation in the matter, and it has accomplished a great deal in terms of bringing public attention to, and understanding of, the real issues involved. In this sense, the legal and extralegal battles fought by Lakotas for Paha Sapa may be viewed as having been, perhaps inadvertently, mutually reinforcing. And, together, these two efforts may have created the context in which a genuine solution can finally be achieved.

By the mid-1980s, the image of the United States regarding its treatment of the Lakotas had suffered so badly that a New Jersey senator, Bill Bradley, took the unprecedented step of introducing legislation the Indians themselves had proposed.[215] With the goal of finally ending the Black Hills "controversy," the draft bill, S. 1453, was proposed to "re-convey" title to 750,000 acres of the Hills currently held by the federal government, including subsurface (mineral) rights, to the Lakotas. Further, it provided that certain spiritual sites in the area would be similarly retitled. These sites, along with some 50,000 of the re-conveyed acres, would be designated a "Sioux Park"; the balance of the land returned would be designated a "Sioux Forest."

Additionally, considerable water rights within the South Dakota portion of the 1868 treaty territory would be reassigned to the Lakotas. A "Sioux National Council," drawn from all existing Lakota reservations, holding increased jurisdiction within the whole 8.5 million acres of the 1868 Great Sioux Reservation, would also be established. Timbering, grazing permits, and mineral leasing in the Black Hills would be transferred to Lakota control two years after passage of the bill, thus establishing a viable Lakota economic base for the first time in nearly a century. The $122.5 million awarded by the Court of Claims, plus interest accrued since 1980—a total of over $350 million[216]—would be disbursed as compensation for the Lakotas' historic loss of use of their land rather than as payment for the land itself. Finally, the draft bill posited that it would resolve the Black Hills claim *only*, having no effect on "subsisting treaties." In other words, with satisfactory settlement of the Hills issue in hand, the Lakotas would remain free to pursue resolution of their claims to the 1868 Unceded Indian Territory and the 1851 treaty territory.[217]

Although the Bradley Bill was obviously less than perfect—compensation remained very low, considering that the Hearst Corporation's Homestake Mine *alone* has extracted more than $18 *billion* in gold from the Black Hills since 1877,[218] and the United States and its citizens are left with considerable land and rights in the area to which they were never legally entitled—it represented a major potential breakthrough not only with regard to the Black Hills land claim, but to U.S.-Indian relations far more generally. Although the full Lakota agenda was not met by the bill, it probably came close enough that the bulk of the people would have endorsed it. That, more than anything, was a testament to their own perseverance in struggle in the face of astronomical odds. The bill, however, foundered during the late eighties in the wake of a campaign to "improve" upon it advanced by a rather mysterious individual named Phil Stevens.

Throughout his life, Stevens functioned as a nonindian, fashioning for himself a highly profitable defense contracting corporation in Los Angeles. Deciding to retire in 1984, he sold his company for an estimated $60 million. Thereupon, he claimed to have "discovered" he was a direct descendant of a noted Lakota leader and to be consumed with a belated passion to "help" his people. In 1986, he began to approach certain disaffected elements on the reservation, arguing that with his federal contacts and "negotiating expertise," he could better not only the monetary compensation portions of the Bradley Bill, increasing reparations to $3.1 billion, but improve upon its jurisdictional provisions as well.[219] He punctuated his points by spreading relatively small quantities of cash around destitute Lakota communities and stipulated that all he needed was to be designated "Great Chief of All the Sioux" to get the job done.[220]

Resistance to Stevens' posturing was intense in many quarters, especially among those who worked most unstintingly to bring Bradley's initiative into being. Nonetheless, interest in Stevens' ideas had reached sufficient proportions by early 1988 that

Gerald Clifford, chief negotiator and chair of the Black Hills Steering Committee (which had drafted the legislation), was compelled to take him to Washington, D.C., to broach his proposals to various key congresspeople.[221] The timing was most inopportune, given that Bradley had, since introducing his bill for a second time on March 10, 1987, been able to secure support for the legislation even from such notoriously anti-Indian senators as Lloyd Meeds (Washington). The chairs of both the House and Senate Interior Committees—Representative Morris Udall (Arizona) and Senator Daniel Inouye (Hawai'i)—had also agreed to serve as cosponsors.[222]

The baleful consequences of Stevens' Washington tour soon became evident. Bradley had no intention of amending his bill to include Stevens' $3.1 billion compensation package or getting caught in the crossfire between competing Sioux factions. With Clifford's reluctant concurrence, Bradley decided to hold his bill in abeyance until the Lakotas settled their internal dispute.[223] The first significant congressional land return initiative in U.S. history now thoroughly in tatters, Stevens quickly quit the field, withdrawing his flow of funds to the reservation communities as well.

Meanwhile, "liberal" South Dakota Senator Tom Daschle capitalized on the situation, founding what he called the "Open Hills Committee," designed to "counter . . . the long-term campaign . . . by those who seek to replace the 1980 Supreme Court settlement with a massive land and even more massive money transfer."[224] The committee is chaired by Daschle's close friend David Miller, reactionary "revisionist historian" at Black Hills State University in Spearfish, South Dakota.

> The Open Hills Committee [mainly] riled up what Miller himself described as South Dakota's considerable redneck population, people who would "just as soon load up shotguns" as return any portion of the Hills to the Sioux. In a part of the country where many people thought of Indians either as dirty drunks or crazed militants, the Open Hills Committee had no difficulty recruiting.[225]

In a context of mounting tension between Indians and whites in South Dakota during 1989, Daschle had no difficulty in teaming up with his fellow senator from South Dakota, Larry Pressler, in securing an agreement from Inouye, by then chair of the Senate Select Committee on Indian Affairs, that there would be "no hearings, mark-ups, or other action" taken on any Black Hills legislation without the express consent of the "South Dakota senatorial delegation."[226] In 1990, Pressler sought to follow up by introducing a resolution which would have required yet another reservation-by-reservation poll of the increasingly desperate Lakotas with regard to accepting the Supreme Court's 1980 cash award as "final resolution of the Black Hills question."[227]

Small wonder that "Clifford [along with many others who question Stevens' story about his ancestry] view[s] the emergence of Stevens' program as an unmitigated disaster, the work not of a savior but of a 'manipulator and salesman,' a gloryhound whose ties to the tribe were at best attenuated."[228] Russell Means, observing that "no provocateur could have done a better job of screwing up the Black Hills land claim," has openly expressed suspicions that Stevens may have been an outright federal agent of some sort, or at least an individual aligned with the opponents of the Lakota land claims.[229] Uncharacteristically, even arch-conservative editor of the *Lakota Times* Tim Giago agreed with Means, describing Stevens as "a ringer, pure and simple."[230]

In the end, the question becomes whether some version of the Bradley Bill can ever be passed in anything resembling its original form. If so, the Lakotas' long fight for their land, and for their integrity as a nation, will have been significantly advanced. Moreover, a legislative precedent will have been set which could allow other peoples indigenous to what is now the United States to begin the long process of reconstituting themselves. This, in turn, would allow the U.S. itself to begin a corresponding process of reversing some of the worst aspects of its ugly history of colonization and genocide against American Indians. The prospect remains, but it is now only a feeble glimmer of what it was ten years ago. Only a substantial upsurge of nonindian support for the concept—unlikely, given the typical priorities manifested by even the most progressive sectors of Euroamerica—would now serve to salvage the legislative option.

In the alternative, if comparable remedies are rejected, and thus fail to resolve what by any measure is the best known of all Indian land claims in North America, it will be a clear sign that the United States remains unswervingly committed to its long-standing policy of expropriating Indian assets by whatever means are available to it, and to destroying indigenous societies as an incidental cost of "doing business." In that event, the Lakotas will have no real option but to continue their grim struggle for survival, an indication that the future may prove even worse than the past. The crossroads in this sense has already been reached.

The Western Shoshone Land Claim

A differently waged, and lesser known, struggle for land has been conducted by the Newe (Western Shoshone), mainly in the Nevada desert region. In 1863, the United States entered into the Treaty of Ruby Valley, agreeing—in exchange for Newe commitments of peace and friendship, willingness to provide right-of-way through their lands, and the granting of assorted trade licenses—to recognize the boundaries encompassing approximately 24.5 million acres of the traditional Western Shoshone homeland, known in their language as Newe Segobia (see Figure 4.6).[231] The U.S. also agreed to pay $100,000 in restitution for environmental disruptions anticipated as a result of Euroamerican "commerce" in the area.

As concerns the ultimate disposition of territorial rights within the region, researcher Rudolph C. Ryser has observed that, "Nothing in the Treaty of Ruby Valley ever sold, traded or gave away any part of the Newe Country to the United States of America. Nothing in this treaty said that the United States could establish counties or smaller states within Newe Country. Nothing in this treaty said the United States could establish settlements of U.S. citizens who would be engaged in any activity other than mining, agriculture, milling and ranching."[232]

From the signing of the treaty until the mid-twentieth century, no action was taken by either Congress or federal courts to extinguish native title to Newe Segobia.[233] Essentially, the land was an area in which the United States took little interest.

Still, relatively small but steadily growing numbers of nonindians did move into Newe territory, a situation which was generally accommodated by the Indians so long as the newcomers did not become overly presumptuous. By the late 1920s, however, conflicts over land use had begun to sharpen. Things worsened after 1934, when the U.S. installed a tribal council form of government—desired by Washington but rejected by traditional Newes—under provision of the IRA.[234] It was to the IRA council heading one of the Western Shoshone bands, the Temoak, that attorney Ernest Wilkinson went with a proposal in early 1946.

Wilkinson was a senior partner in the Washington-based law firm Wilkinson, Cragen, and Barker, commissioned by Congress toward the end of World War II to draft legislation creating the Indian Claims Commission. The idea he presented to the Temoak council was that his firm be retained to "represent their interests" before the ICC.[235] Ostensibly, his objective was to secure the band's title to its portion of the 1863 treaty area. Much more likely, given subsequent events, is that his purpose was to secure title for nonindian interests in Nevada and to collect the ten percent attorney's fee he and his colleagues had written into the Claims Commission Act as pertaining to any compensation awarded to native clients.[236] In any event, the Temoaks agreed, and a contract between Wilkinson and the council was approved by the Bureau of Indian Affairs in 1947.[237]

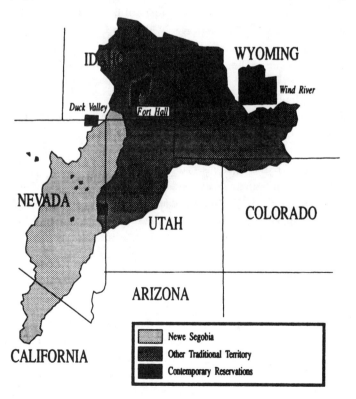

FIGURE 4.6. Traditional Shoshone Territory.

Wilkinson followed up in 1951 with a petition to the ICC arguing that his representation of the Temoaks should be construed as representing the interests of the entire Newe Nation. The commissioners concurred, despite protests from the bulk of the people involved.[238] While such a ruling may seem contrary to popular notions of "American Justice," it is in fact entirely consistent with the form and function not only of the commission, but of federal Indian law more generally. As Dan Bomberry, head of the Seventh Generation Fund, has explained:

> When the U.S. succeeded in forcing the Indian Reorganization Act upon tribes, installing puppet governments, the ultimate U.S. aim was to make Indians a resource colony, like Africa was for Europe. Sometimes the issue is coal or uranium and sometimes it's just open land . . . The role of the Indian Claims Commission is to get the land of tribes who do not have puppet governments, or where the traditional people are leading a fight to keep land and refuse money.[239]

It follows that, from the outset, Wilkinson's pleadings, advanced in hearings by his partner, Robert W. Barker, led directly away from Newe rights over the Ruby Valley Treaty Territory. The Shoshone objectives in agreeing to go to court have been explained by tribal elder Saggie Williams, a resident of Battle Mountain: "All we wanted was for the white men to honor the treaty. [We] believed the lawyers we hired were to work for the Indians and to do what the Indians asked. But they didn't. They did as they pleased and told us we didn't have any land. At the time, we didn't talk about selling our land with the lawyer because we had the treaty, which settled the land question; it protected [our] lands."[240]

As Glenn Holly, a Temoak leader of the contemporary land claims struggle, puts it, "Most of our people never understood that by filing with the Claims Commission, we'd be agreeing we lost our land. They thought we were just clarifying the title question."[241] However, "Barker filed the claim in 1951, asserting that the Western Shoshones had lost not only their treaty lands, but also their aboriginal land extending into Death Valley, California. He put the date of loss at 1872 (only nine years after the Treaty of Ruby Valley), and he included in the twenty-four million acre claim some sixteen million acres that the Shoshones insist were not occupied by anyone but Indian bands, and that were never in question. But the Justice Department agreed with Barker's contention. Since opposing attorneys agreed, the Claims Commission did not investigate or seek other viewpoints."[242]

Clarence Blossom, one of the Newe elders who signed the original contract with Wilkinson, and who supported Barker for a time, points out that "[t]he land claim was never explained to the people. The old people do not even understand English. It was years later that I read that once you accept money, you lose your land. The government pulled the wool over our eyes. If I had known what was going on, I never would have accepted the attorney contract."[243]

As Raymond Yowell, a member of the Temoak Band Council and another original signatory, laid it out in a 1978 issue of the *Native Nevadan*: "A majority of the people present [at a 1965 mass meeting called to confront the attorneys] objected to the way Barker was giving up the remaining rights to our lands and walked out . . . Soon after, at [another such] meeting, about 80 percent of the people showed their opposition by walking out. It is important that at these meetings *Barker insisted we had no choice* as to whether to keep title to some lands or to give them up for claims money. The only choice was whether to approve or disapprove the [compensation package]. And if we disapproved we would get nothing (emphasis added)."[244]

Ultimately, the Wilkinson, Cragen, and Barker firm received a $2.5 million federal subsidy for "services rendered" in its "resolution of the matter" in a fashion which was plainly detrimental to the express interests of its ostensible clients.[245] Shawnee scholar and activist Glenn T. Morris has summarized the matter in what is probably the best article on the Western Shoshone land struggle to date.

In 1962, the commission conceded that it "was unable to discover any formal extinguishment" of Western Shoshone to lands in Nevada, and could not establish a date of taking, but nonetheless ruled that the lands were taken at some point in the past. It did rule that approximately two million acres of Newe land in California was taken on March 3, 1853 [contrary to the Treaty of Ruby Valley, which would have supplanted any such taking], but without documenting what specific Act of Congress extinguished the title. Without the consent of the Western Shoshone Nation, on February 11, 1966, Wilkinson and the U.S. lawyers arbitrarily stipulated that the date of valuation for government extinguishment of Western Shoshone title to over 22 million acres of land in Nevada occurred on July 1, 1872. This lawyers' agreement, entered without the knowledge or consent of the Shoshone people, served as the ultimate loophole through which the U.S. would allege that the Newe had lost their land.[246]

By 1872 prices, the award of compensation to the Newe for the "historic loss" of their territory was calculated, in 1972, at $21,350,000, an amount revised upwards to $26,154,600 (against which the government levied an offset of $9,410.11 for "goods" delivered in the 1870s) and certified on December 19, 1979.[247] In the interim, by 1976, even the Temoaks had joined the other Newe bands in maintaining that Wilkinson and Barker did not represent their interests; they fired them, but the BIA continued to renew the firm's contract "on the Indians' behalf" until the claims commission itself was dissolved in 1979.[248]

Meanwhile, the Newes retained other counsel and filed a motion to suspend commission proceedings with regard to their case. This was denied on August 15, 1977, appealed, but upheld by the U.S. Court of Claims on the basis that if the Newe desired "to avert extinguishment of their land claims, they should go to Congress" rather than the courts for redress. The amount of $26,145,189.89 was then placed in a trust account with the U.S. Treasury Department in order to absolve the U.S. of further responsibility in the matter.[249]

One analyst of the case suggests that if the United States were honest in its valuation date of the taking of Newe land, the date would be December 19, 1979—the date of the ICC award—since the [commission] could point to no other extinguishment date. The U.S. should thus compensate the Shoshone in 1979 land values and not those of 1872. Consequently, the value of the land "that would be more realistic, assuming the Western Shoshone were prepared to ignore violations of the Ruby Valley Treaty, would be in the neighborhood of $40 billion. On a per capita basis of distribution, the United States would be paying each Shoshone roughly $20 million . . . The [U.S.] has already received billions of dollars in resources and use from Newe territory in the past 125 years. Despite this obvious benefit, the U.S. government is only prepared to pay the Shoshone less than a penny of actual value for each acre of Newe territory.[250]

The Newes as a whole have refused to accept payment for their land under the premise articulated by Yowell, now Chair of the Western Shoshone Sacred Lands Association: "We entered into the Treaty of Ruby Valley as co-equal sovereign nations . . . The land to the traditional Shoshone is sacred. It is the basis of our lives. To take away the land is to take away the lives of the people."[251] Glenn Holly concurs. "Nothing happened in 1872," he says. "No land was 'taken' by the government. We never lost that land, we never left that land, and we're not selling it. In our religion, it's forbidden to take money for land. What's really happening is that the U.S. government, through this Claims Commission, is stealing the land from us right now."[252] "We should have listened to our old people," Yowell sums up, "They told us Barker was selling out our lands. It took me years to realize it."[253]

Giving form to this sentiment, were the sisters Mary and Carrie Dann, who not only refused eviction from their homes by the U.S. Interior Department's Bureau of Land Management (BLM)—which claimed at that time to own property that had been in their family for generations—but challenged all U.S. title contentions within the Newe treaty area when the Bureau attempted to enforce its position in court.

In 1974, the Dann sisters were herding cattle near their home (a ranch outside Crescent Valley, Utah) when a BLM ranger stopped them and demanded to see their grazing permit. The Danns replied that they did not need a permit since they were not on U.S. land, but the land of the Western Shoshone Nation. They were charged with trespassing. "I have grazed my cattle and horses on that land all my life," says Carrie Dann, "and my mother did before me and her mother before her. Our people have been on this land for thousands of years. We don't need a permit to graze here."[254]

The trespassing case was filed in the U.S. District Court for Reno, where the sisters invoked aboriginal land rights as a defense. The ensuing litigation has caused federal courts to flounder about in disarray ever since. As John O'Connell, an attorney retained by the Newes to replace Barker, and who has served as lead counsel in defending the Danns, has put it, "We have asked the government over and over again in court to show evidence of how it obtained title to Shoshone land. They start groping around and can't find a damn thing. In fact, the relevant documents show the United

States never wanted the Nevada desert until recently. There's no doubt in my mind that the Western Shoshones still hold legal title to most of their aboriginal territory. The great majority of them still live there and they don't want money for it. They love that desert. But if the Claims Commission has its way, the United States may succeed in finally stealing the land 'legally.'"[255]

In 1977, the district court ruled that the Danns were indeed "trespassers"—fining them $500 each, an amount they have steadfastly refused to pay—because the claims commission had allegedly resolved all title questions. This decision was reversed on appeal to the Ninth Circuit Court in 1978 because, in the higher court's view, the question of land title "had not been litigated, and has not been decided."[256]

On remand, the district court engaged in a conspicuous pattern of stalling, repeatedly delaying its hearing of the case for frivolous reasons. "The judge never wanted [the second] trial," O'Connell recalls. "At one point I accused the government of deliberately delaying the Dann case long enough to get the Indian claims check written, under the theory that once payment was received Indian title would have been extinguished and the Danns would have been prevented from asserting it. The judge admitted on record that he was "sympathetic with the government's strategy" in this regard.[257] In the end, this is exactly what was done.

> In other words, a $26 million payment to Indians who never sought it, tried to stop it, and refused to accept it—payment for lands that were alleged by the payer to have been "taken" in 1872, but which the courts have finally affirmed were never "taken" at all—is now being used as the instrument to extinguish Indian title.[258]

The district court, however, in attempting to reconcile its mutually contradictory determinations on the topic, observed that "Western Shoshone Indians retained unextinguished title to their aboriginal lands *until December of 1979*, when the Indian Claims Commission judgment became final (emphasis added)."[259] This, of course, demolished the articulated basis—that a title transfer had been effected more than a century earlier—for the commission's award amount. It also pointed to the fact that the Commission had comported itself illegally in the Western Shoshone case insofar as the Indian Claims Commission Act explicitly disallowed the commissioners (never mind attorneys representing the Indians) from extinguishing previously unextinguished land titles. Thus armed, the Danns went back to the Ninth Circuit and obtained another reversal of the lower court's decision.[260]

The government appealed the circuit court's ruling to the Supreme Court and, entering yet *another* official (and exceedingly ambiguous) estimation of when Newe title was supposed to have been extinguished, the justices reversed the circuit court's reversal of the district court's last ruling. Having thus served the government's interest on appeal, the high court declined in 1990 to hear an appeal from the Danns concerning the question of whether they might retain individual aboriginal property rights based on continuous occupancy even if the collective rights of the Newe were denied.[261]

Tom Luebben, another of the nonindian attorneys involved in defending Newe rights, has assessed the methods of litigation employed by the U.S. "It is clear that one of the main strategies the government uses in these cases is simply to wear out the Indians over decades of struggle," he observes. "The government has unlimited resources to litigate. If the Indians win one victory in court, the government just loads up its legal guns, adds a new, bigger crew of fresh lawyers, and comes back harder. It is the legal equivalent of what the cavalry did a hundred years ago. There is simply no interest in justice. It is hardball all the way. The government has all the time in the world to achieve its goals. The Indians run out of money, they get tired of fighting; they get old, and finally, after 10 to 20 years, somebody says, 'The hell with it; let's take what we can.' It's really understandable that it worked out that way, but it's disgusting and it's wrong."[262]

Thus far, such tactics have proven unsuccessful against the Newe. "A new [resistance] strategy was hatched [in 1990] to sue the government for mineral and trespass fees from 1872 to 1979," says analyst Jerry Mander. "The logic of the argument was that since the courts now recognize that the Shoshones did have legal title until the Claims Commission took it away in 1979, they are entitled to mineral and trespass fees for 109 years. This would amount to billions of dollars due the Shoshones; it was hoped that this amount [would be] sufficient to cause the government to negotiate. But the [district] court rejected this new intervention on the technical grounds that the specific interveners were not parties to the original claim. This suit may yet - re-emerge."[263]

The need for it was punctuated in November 1992 which the Dann sisters' brother, Clifford, took direct action to block impoundment of wild horses and other livestock by the Bureau of Land Management (BLM). Stating that in "taking away our livelihood and our lands, you are taking away our lives," he doused himself with gasoline and attempted to set set himself afire. Quickly sprayed with fire extinguishers by surrounding BLM rangers, Dann was then arrested and, for reasons never adequately explained, charged with assaulting them. On May 17, 1993, he was sentenced to serve nine months in prison, two years probation and a $5,000 fine.[264]

For their part, Mary and Carrie Dann have announced their intent to go back into court with a new suit of their own, contending that the continuous use and occupancy evidenced by Newes on the contested land "prior to the authority of the Bureau of Land Management" (which began in 1935) affords them tangible rights to pursue their traditional livelihood. "They hope," Mander notes, "to carve a hole in the earlier [judicial] decisions . . . which might open a doorway for the rest of the Western Shoshones" to do much the same thing.[265]

The chances were bolstered on March 6, 1998, when the Inter-American Commission on Human Rights of the Organization of American States issued a formal request to the U.S. government that it stay all further action with respect to evictions, impoundment of livestock, and the like, "pending an investigation by the Commission" into the historical context of the case, the respective rights of the parties involved, and, consequently, the legal validity of current U.S. policies vis-à-vis the Newes.[266]

Perhaps most important, as of this writing, the Dann sisters remain on their land in defiance of federal authority. Their physical resistance, directly supported by most Newes and an increasing number of nonindians, forms the core of whatever will come next. Carrie Dann is unequivocal: "We have to be completely clear. We must not allow them to destroy Mother Earth. We've all been assimilated into white society but now we know it's destroying us. We have to get back to our own ways."[267] Corbin Harney, a resistance leader from the Duckwater Shoshone Community in northern Nevada, reinforces her position: "We don't need their money. We need to keep these lands and protect them."[268]

Federal officials tend to be equally straightforward, at least in what they take to be private conversation. Mander quotes one Interior Department bureaucrat, a reputed "Jimmy Carter liberal" responsible for seeing to it that Indians get a "fair shake," as saying in an interview, "[L]et me tell you one goddamn thing. There's no way we're ever letting any of the Indians have title to their lands. If they don't take the money, they'll get nothing."[269]

The accuracy of this anonymous assertion of federal policy is amply borne out by the fact that an offer of compromise extended by a portion of the Shoshone resistance in 1977—that the Newes would drop their major land claim in exchange for the establishment of a three million-acre reservation, guarantee of perpetual access to specified sacred sites outside the reservation, and payment of cash compensation against the remaining 21 million acres—was peremptorily rejected by then Secretary of the Interior Cecil Andrus. No explanation of this decision was ever offered by the government other than that the secretary felt that being relegated to a landless condition would be in the Indians' "best interests."[270]

Leo Kurlitz, an assistant to Andrus and the Interior Department's chief attorney at the time the compromise offer was rejected, admits that he "didn't give the legal issues much thought."[271] Admitting that he was "uncomfortable" with the very idea that the Shoshones "still seem to possess title" to their land, he acknowledges that "under no circumstances was I going to recommend that we create a reservation . . . I saw my job as assessing the resource needs of the Shoshones, but I couldn't recommend that we establish a reservation."[272]

Mander's unnamed source says much the same thing, observing that, "These Indian cases make me so damned uncomfortable, I wish I didn't have to work on them at all."[273] He professes a certain bewilderment that at least some indigenous nations refuse to be bought off: "I really can't understand what these people want. Their lawyers get them great settlements—the Shoshones were awarded $26 million, and the Sioux may get [more than $300 million] for the Black Hills—and damn if they don't turn around and start talking about land."[274]

Such uniform and undeviating adamance on the part of diverse Interior Department personnel that not so much as a square inch of the Nevada desert, other than the minor reservations already designated as such, will be committed for Newe use and occupancy may seem somewhat baffling on its face. Their collective willingness to lay out not inconsiderable quantities of tax dollars in order to retain absolute control over such barren and lightly populated territory—with interest, the Western Shoshone set-tlement award now exceeds $80 million and is increasing steadily—raises further questions as to their motivations.[275]

Quite possibly, a hallowed U.S. pseudophilosophy, extended from the nineteenth century doctrine of "Manifest Destiny" and holding that Indians are by definition "disentitled" from retaining substantial quantities of real property, has a certain bearing in this connection.[276] Most probably, concern that a significant Newe land recovery might serve to establish a legal precedent upon which other indigenous nations could accomplish similar feats also plays a role.[277] Another part of the answer can probably be glimpsed in the July 1996 purchase of a 48,437-acre ranch in Crescent Valley by the Oro Nevada Mining Company.[278]

Oro Nevada Mining, which also holds mineral rights to an additional 46,606 acres of "public lands" in the area, is a subsidiary of the Canadian transnational, Oro Nevada Resources, Ltd.[279] The parent corporation has been heavily involved in the mining boom which has recently afflicted the Innu and Inuit peoples of Labrador, around Voisy Bay, and in Nitassinan, along the north shore of the St. Lawrence in Québec.[280] Another subsidiary, Bre-X, was created to explore and develop gold deposits for the Suharto régime in Indonesia.[281]

In Crescent Valley, it is believed that Oro is preparing to enter into a collaborative arrangement with Placer Dome/Kennecott subsidiary Cortez Gold, which already operates mines on the Pipeline and Pipeline South gold deposits further north, to extract the mineral from areas immediately adjoining the Dann Ranch.[282] Indeed, there has been talk throughout the mining industry that Crescent Valley may well turn out to be the scene of the next big gold rush. To some extent self-fulfilling prophecies, such rumors have in turn prompted corporations from as far away as Australia to begin acquiring speculative leases.[283]

Even more to the point, however, is the fact that federal usurpation of Newe land rights since 1945 has devolved upon converting their "remote" and "uninhabited" territory into a sprawling complex of nuclear weapons testing facilities. In addition to the experimental detonations conducted in the Marshall Islands during the 1950s, and a handful of tests in the Aleutians a few years later, nearly 1,000 U.S. nuclear test blasts have thus far occurred at the Energy Resource and Development Administration's Nevada Test Site located within the military's huge Nellis Gunnery Range in southern Nevada.[284] At least as recently as July 2, 1997, a "subcritical" plutonium device was detonated there.[285]

This largely secret circumstance has made Newe Segobia an area of vital strategic interest to the United States and, although the Shoshones have never understood themselves to be at war with the United States, it has afforded their homeland the dubious distinction of becoming by a decisive margin "the most bombed country in the world."[286] The devastation and radioactive contamination of an appreciable portion of Newe property has been coupled to construction of a primary permanent storage facility for nuclear waste at Yucca Mountain, a site well within the Ruby Valley treaty area.[287] Moreover, the Pentagon has long since demonstrated a clear desire, evidenced in a series of plans to locate its MX missile system there, for most of the remaining Newe treaty territory, that vast and "vacant" geography lying north of the present testing grounds.

The latter situation, which involved bringing approximately 20,000 additional nonindians onto Newe land, creating another 10,000 miles of paved roads, and drawing down 3.15 billion gallons of water from an already overtaxed water table in order to install a mobile missile system accommodating some two hundred nuclear warheads, provoked what may have been the first concerted Shoshone response to military appropriation of their rights.[288] As Corbin Harney put it at a mass meeting on the matter convened in October 1979 after the Carter administration had made its version of the MX program public, "Now we are witnessing the real reason why we are being forced to accept money for lands."[289]

At the same meeting, Glenn Holley articulated the implications of the MX project to the Newes. "Water is life," he said, "and the MX system will consume our water resources altogether. Another thing the MX will destroy is the natural vegetation: the herbs like the badeba, doza, sagebrush, chaparral, Indian tea . . . [N]ot only the herbs but other medicines like the lizard in the south, which we use to heal the mentally sick and arthritis. There will also be electric fences, nerve gas, and security people all over our lands. It will affect the eagles and the hawks, the rock chuck, ground squirrel, rabbit, deer, sage grouse, and rattlesnake. If this MX goes through, it will mean the total destruction of the Shoshone people, our spiritual beliefs and our ways of life."[290]

On this basis, overt Newe opposition to nuclear militarism became both pronounced and integral to assertion of their land claims. As the matter was framed in a resolution first published by the Sacred Lands Association during the early 1980s, "The Western Shoshone Nation is calling upon citizens of the United States, as well as the world community of nations, to demand that the United States terminate its invasion of our lands for the evil purpose of testing nuclear bombs and other weapons of war."[291]

This stance, in turn, attracted attention and increasing support from various sectors of the nonindian environmental, nuclear freeze, and antiwar movements, all of which are prone to engaging in largescale demonstrations against U.S. nuclear testing and related activities. Organizations such as SANE, Clergy and Laity Concerned, Earth First!, and the Sierra Club were represented at the 1979 mass meeting. Their loose relationship to the Shoshone land claim struggle has been solidified through the work of Newe activists like the late Joe Sanchez, and reinforced by the participation of groups like Friends of the Earth, the Environmental Defense Fund, the Great Basin Greens Alliance, the American Peace Test, and the Global Anti-Nuclear Alliance.[292]

As Mander puts it, "[In this regard], there have been some positive developments. Many of the peace groups have belatedly recognized the Indian issue and now request permission from the Western Shoshone Nation to demonstrate on their land. The Indians, in turn, have been issuing the demonstrators 'safe passage' permits and have agreed to speak at rallies. The Western Shoshone National Council has called the nuclear testing facility 'an absolute violation of the Treaty of Ruby Valley and the laws of the United States' . . . Peace activists are instructed that if they are confronted or arrested by U.S. government officials while on Shoshone land, they should show their Shoshone permits and demand to continue their activities. Furthermore, in case of trial, the defendants should include in their defense that they had legal rights to be on the land, as granted by the landowners."[293]

It is in this last connection that the greatest current potential may be found, not only for the Newes in their struggle to retain (or regain) their homeland, but for (re)assertion of indigenous land rights more generally, and for the struggles of nonindians who seek genuinely positive alternatives to the North American status quo. In the combination of forces presently coalescing in the Nevada desert lie the seeds of a new sort of communication, understanding, respect, and the growing promise of mutually beneficial joint action between native and nonnative peoples in this hemisphere.[294]

For the Shoshones, the attraction of a broad—and broadening—base of popular support for their rights offers far and away the best possibility of bringing to bear the kind and degree of pressure necessary to compel the federal government to restore all, or at least some sizable portion, of their territory. For the nonindian individuals and organizations involved, the incipient unity they have achieved with the Newes represents both a conceptual breakthrough and a seminal practical experience of the fact that active support of native land rights can tangibly further their own interests and agendas.[295] For many American Indians, particularly those of traditionalist persuasion, the emerging collaboration of nonindian groups in the defense of Western Shoshone lands has come to symbolize the possibility that there are elements of the dominant population that have finally arrived at a position in which native rights are not automatically discounted as irrelevancies or presumed to be subordinate to their own.[296] On such bases, bona fide alliances can be built.

Herein lies what may be the most important lesson to be learned by those attempting to forge a truly American radical vision, and what may ultimately translate that vision into concrete reality: Native Americans cannot hope to achieve restoration of the lands and liberty which are legitimately theirs without the support and assistance of nonindians, while nonindian activists cannot hope to effect any transformation of the existing social order which is not fundamentally imperialistic, and thus doomed to replicate some of the most negative aspects of the present system, unless they accept the necessity of liberating indigenous land and lives as a matter of first priority.[297]

Both sides of the equation are at this point bound together in all but symbiotic fashion by virtue of a shared continental habitat, a common oppressor, and an increasingly interactive history. There is thus no viable option but to go forward together, figuratively joining hands to ensure our collective well-being, and that of our children, and our children's children.

MOVING FORWARD

The question which inevitably arises with regard to indigenous land claims, especially in the U.S., is whether they are "realistic." The answer, of course, is "no they aren't."

Further, *no* form of decolonization has *ever* been realistic when viewed within the construct of a colonialist paradigm. It wasn't realistic at the time to expect George Washington's rag-tag militia to defeat the British military during the American independence struggle. Just ask the British. It wasn't realistic, as the French could tell you, that the Vietnamese should be able to defeat U.S.-backed France in 1954,[298] or that the Algerians would shortly be able to follow in their footsteps.[299] Surely, it wasn't reasonable to predict that Fidel Castros's pitiful handful of guerrillas would overcome Batista's regime in Cuba, another U.S. client, after only a few years in the mountains.[300] And the Sandinistas, to be sure, had no prayer of attaining victory over Somoza twenty years later.[301] Henry Kissinger, among others, knew that for a fact.

The point is that in each case, in order to begin their struggles at all, anticolonial fighters around the world have had to abandon orthodox realism in favor of what they knew (and their opponents knew) to be right. To paraphrase Daniel Cohn-Bendit, they accepted as their agenda—the goals, objectives, and demands which guided them—a redefinition of reality in terms deemed quite impossible within the conventional wisdom of their oppressors. And, in each case, they succeeded in their immediate quest for liberation.[302] The fact that all but one (Cuba) of the examples used subsequently turned out to hold colonizing pretensions of its own does not alter the truth of this—or alter the appropriateness of their efforts to decolonize themselves—in the least. It simply means that decolonization has yet to run its course, that much remains to be done.[303]

The battles waged by native nations in North America to free ourselves, and the lands upon which we depend for ongoing existence as discernable peoples, from the grip of U.S. internal colonialism is plainly part of this process of liberation.[304] Given that our very survival depends upon our perseverance in the face of all apparent odds, American Indians have no real alternative but to carry on.[305] We must struggle, and where there is struggle there is always hope. Moreover, the unrealistic or "romantic" dimensions of our aspiration to quite literally dismantle the territorial corpus of the U.S. state begin to erode when one considers that federal domination of Native America is utterly contingent upon maintenance of a perceived confluence of interest between prevailing governmental/corporate elites and common nonindian citizens.[306]

Herein lies the prospect of longterm success. It is entirely possible that the consensus of opinion concerning nonindian "rights" to exploit the land and resources of indigenous nations can be eroded, and that large numbers of nonindians will join in the struggle to decolonize Native North America. Few nonindians wish to identify with or defend the naziesque characteristics of U.S. history. To the contrary, most seek to deny it in rather vociferous fashion.[307] All things being equal, they are uncomfortable with many of the resulting attributes of federal posture and—in substantial numbers—actively oppose one or more of these, so long as such politics do not intrude into a certain range of closely-guarded self-interests. This is where the crunch comes in the realm of Indian rights issues. Most nonindians (of all races and ethnicities, and both genders) have been indoctrinated to believe the officially contrived notion that, in the event "the Indians get their land back," or even if the extent of present federal domination is relaxed, native people will do unto our occupiers exactly as has been done to us; mass dispossession and eviction of nonindians, especially Euroamericans, is expected to ensue.[308]

Hence, even those progressives who are most eloquently inclined to condemn U.S. imperialism abroad and/or the functions of racism and sexism at home tend to deliver a blank stare or profess open "disinterest" when indigenous land rights are mentioned.[309] Instead of attempting to come to grips with this most fundamental of all issues concerning the continent upon which they reside, the more sophisticated among them seek to divert discussion into "higher priority" or "more important" topics like "issues of class and gender equity" in which "justice" becomes synonymous with a redistribution of power and loot deriving from the occupation of Native North America even while the occupation continues (presumably permanently).[310]

Sometimes, Indians are even slated to receive "their fair share" in the division of spoils accruing from expropriation of their resources.[311] Always, such things are couched—and typically seen—in terms of some "greater good" than decolonizing the .6 percent of the U.S. population which is indigenous.[312] Some marxist and environmentalist groups have taken the argument so far as to deny that Indians possess *any* rights distinguishable from those of their conquerors.[313] AIM leader Russell Means snapped the picture into sharp focus when he observed that:

> So-called progressives in the United States claiming that Indians are obligated to give up their rights because a much larger group of non-Indians "need" their resources is exactly the same as Ronald Reagan and Elliot Abrams asserting that the rights of 250 million North Americans outweighs the rights of a couple million Nicaraguans. Colonialist attitudes are colonialist attitudes, and it doesn't make one damn bit of difference whether they come from the left or the right.[314]

Leaving aside the pronounced and pervasive hypocrisy permeating their positions, which add up to a mentality defining "settler state colonialism,"[315] the fact is that the specter driving even most radical nonindians into lockstep with the federal government on questions of native land rights is largely illusory. The alternative *reality* posed by native liberation struggles is actually much different:

- While government propagandists are wont to trumpet—as they did during the Maine and Black Hills land disputes of the 1970s—that an Indian win would mean individual nonindian property owners losing everything, the native position has always been the exact opposite. Overwhelmingly, the lands sought for actual recovery have been governmentally and corporately held. Eviction of small land owners has been suggested only in instances where they have banded together—as they have during certain of the Iroquois claims cases—to prevent Indians from recovering any land at all, and to otherwise deny native rights.[316]

• Official sources contend this is inconsistent with the fact that all nonindian title to any portion of North America *could* be called into question. Once "the dike is breached," they argue, it's just a matter of time before "everybody has to start swimming back to Europe, or Africa, or wherever."[317] Although there is considerable technical accuracy to admissions that all nonindian title to North America is illegitimate, Indians have by and large indicated we would be content to honor the cession agreements entered into by our ancestors even though the U.S. has long since defaulted. This would leave something on the order of half to two-thirds of the continental U.S. in nonindian hands, with the real rather than pretended consent of native people. The remaining one-third-to-one-half, to which the U.S. never acquired title at all, should be recovered by its rightful owners.[318]

• Nonetheless, it is argued, there will still be at least some nonindians "trapped" within such restored areas. Actually, they would not be trapped at all. Federally-imposed genetic criteria of "Indianness" to the contrary notwithstanding, indigenous nations have the same rights as any other to define citizenry by allegiance (naturalization) rather than by race.[319] Nonindians could apply for citizenship, or for some form of landed alien status which would allow them to retain their property until they die. In the event they could not reconcile themselves to living under any jurisdiction other than that of the U.S., they would obviously have the right to leave, and they *should* have the right to compensation from their own government (which got them into the mess in the first place).[320]

• Finally, and one suspects this is the real crux of things from the government/corporate perspective, any such restoration of land and attendant sovereign prerogatives to native nations would result in a truly massive loss of "domestic" resources to the U.S., thereby impairing the country's economic and military capacities.[321] For everyone queued up to wave flags celebrating America's recent imperial adventures in Afghanistan and the Persian Gulf, this prospect may induce a certain psychic trauma. But, for oppositionists at least, it should be precisely the point.

When you think about it like this, the great mass of nonindians in North America *really* have much to gain, and almost nothing to lose, from native people succeeding in struggles to reclaim the land which is rightfully ours. The tangible diminishment of U.S. material power which is integral to our victories in this sphere stands to pave the way for realization of most other agendas—from antiimperialism to environmentalism, from Afroamerican liberation to feminism, from gay rights to the ending of class privilege—pursued by progressives on this continent. Conversely, succeeding with any or even *all* these other agendas would still represent an inherently oppressive situation if their realization is contingent upon an ongoing occupation of Native North America without the consent of Indian people. Any North American revolution which failed to free indigenous territory from nonindian domination would be simply a continuation of colonialism in another form.[322]

Regardless of the angle from which you view the matter, the liberation of Native North America, liberation of the land first and foremost, is *the* key to fundamental and positive social changes of many other sorts. One thing, as they say, leads to another. The question has always been, of course, which "thing" is to be first in the sequence. A preliminary formulation for those serious about achieving (rather than merely theorizing and endlessly debating) radical change in the United States might be "First Priority to First Americans." Put another way, this would mean, "U.S. Out of Indian Country." Inevitably, the logic leads to what we've all been so desperately seeking: The U.S.—at least as we've come to know it—can be permanently banished from the planet. In its stead, surely we can join hands to create something new and infinitely better. That's *our* vision of "impossible realism." Isn't it time we *all* went to work on attaining it?

5

A BREACH OF TRUST

The Radioactive Colonization of Native North America

◆ ◆ ◆ ◆ ◆ ◆ ◆ ◆ ◆ ◆ ◆ ◆ ◆ ◆

> There are whole disciplines, institutions, rubrics in our culture
> which serve as categories of denial.
>
> —Susan Griffin
> *A Chorus of Stones*

IN 1903, THE UNITED STATES SUPREME COURT OPINED THAT, AS A RACIAL GROUP, American Indians, like minor children and those deemed mentally deficient or deranged, should be viewed as legally incompetent to manage our own assets and affairs. Indians were therefore to be understood as perpetual "wards" of the federal government, the high court held, the government our permanent "trustee." With a deft circularity of reasoning, the justices then proceeded to assert that, since it was Indians' intrinsic incompetence which had led to our being placed under trust supervision, we should by the same definition be construed as having no standing from which to challenge the exercise of our trustee's authority over us.[1]

Thus did the U.S. formally and unilaterally assign itself "plenary"—that is, absolute and unchallengeable—power over all native lands, lives, and natural resources within the area of forty-eight contiguous states of North America, as well as Alaska, Hawai'i and other external possessions such as Guam and "American" Samoa. The only curb upon the imagined prerogatives of the United States in this regard was/is an equally self-appointed fiduciary responsibility to act, or at least claim to act, in the "best interests" of those it has subjugated both physically and juridically.[2] Although the basic proposition at issue has undergone almost continuous modification and perfection over the years, it remains very much in effect at present.[3]

The scale and implications of the situation are in some ways staggering. In its 1978 final report, the government's own Indian Claims Commission conceded that after more than thirty years' intensive investigation, it had been unable to find evidence that the U.S. had ever acquired anything resembling legitimate title to about 35 percent of its claimed territoriality, all of which therefore remains native property in a legal sense.[4] The approximately 2.5 percent of U.S. territory currently reserved for Indian use and occupancy—most of it still held in federal trust status—is also extraordinarily rich in mineral resources.[5] As much as two-thirds of the uranium ore the U.S.

claims as its own is situated within reservation boundaries, as is about a quarter of the readily accessible low sulfur coal, up to twenty percent of the oil and natural gas, and substantial deposits of molybdenum, copper, bauxite, and zeolite.[6]

The Bureau of Indian Affairs (BIA), a component of the U.S. Department of Interior, presently administers trust relations with several hundred indigenous peoples and communities encompassing, by official count, some two million individuals.[7] Simple arithmetic reveals that when the fifty million-odd acres of reserved land is divided by the federal tally of Indians, we end up as the largest landholding group in North America on a per capita basis. Divide the estimated dollar value of the mineral assets within the land by the number of Indians and you end up with native people as the wealthiest population aggregate on the continent (again, on a per capita basis).

All of this is, unfortunately, on paper. The practical reality is that American Indians, far from being well off, are today the most impoverished sector of the U.S. population.[8] We experience by far the lowest average annual and lifetime incomes of any group. The poorest locality in the United States for 23 of the past 25 years has been Shannon County, on the Pine Ridge Sioux Reservation in South Dakota, where a recent study found 88 percent of the available housing to be substandard, much of it to the point of virtual uninhabitability. The annual per capita income in Shannon County was barely over $2,000 in 1995, while unemployment hovered in the 90th percentile.[9]

Bad as conditions are on Pine Ridge, they are only marginally worse than those on the adjoining Rosebud Sioux Reservation and a host of others. In many ways, health data convey the costs and consequences of such deep and chronic poverty far better than their financial counterparts. These begin with the facts that, overall, American Indians suffer far and away the highest rates of malnutrition, death from exposure, and infant mortality (14.5 times the national average on some reservations).[10]

> The Indian health level is the lowest and the disease rate the highest of all major population groups in the United States. The incidence of tuberculosis is over 400 percent the national average. Similar statistics show the incidence of strep infections is 1,000 percent, meningitis is 2,000 percent higher, and dysentery is 10,000 percent higher. Death rates from disease are shocking when Indian and non-Indian populations are compared. Influenza and pneumonia are 300 percent greater killers among Indians. Diseases such as hepatitis are at epidemic proportions, with an 800 percent higher chance of death. Diabetes is almost a plague [6.8 times the general population rate].[11]

It should come as no surprise, given the ubiquitousness of such circumstances, that alcoholism and other addictions take an inordinate toll. Although fewer Indians drink than do nonindians, the rate of alcohol-related accidental deaths among native people is ten times that of the general population, while the rate of Fetal Alcohol Syndrome (FAS) among the newborn is 33 times greater.[12] The suicide rate among Indians is ten times the national norm, while, among native youth, it is 10,000 percent higher than among our nonindian counterparts.[13]

All told, the current life expectancy of a reservation-based American Indian male is less than fifty years in a society where the average man lives 71.8 years. Reservation-based Indian women live approximately three years longer than males, but general population women enjoy an average life expectancy seven years longer than nonindian men.[14] Hence, every time an American Indian dies on a reservation—or, conversely, every time a child is born—it can be argued that about one-third of a lifetime is lost. This thirtieth percentile attrition of the native population has prevailed throughout the twentieth century, a situation clearly smacking of genocide.[15]

This last is, of course, a policy-driven phenomenon, not something inadvertent or merely "unfortunate." Here, the BIA's exercise of trust authority over native assets comes into play. While it has orchestrated the increasingly intensive "development" of reservation lands since 1945, a matter which might logically have been expected to alleviate at least the worst of the symptomologies sketched above, the Bureau's role in setting the rates at which land was/is leased and royalties for extracted minerals were/are paid by major corporations has precluded any such result.[16]

Instances in which the BIA has opted to rent out the more productive areas on reservations to nonindian ranchers or agribusiness interests for as little as $1 per acre per year, and for as long as 99 years, are legion and notorious.[17] As to mineral royalties, the Bureau has consistently structured contracts "in behalf of" Indians which require payment of as little as ten percent of market rates while releasing participating corporations from such normal overhead expenses as the maintenance of minimum standards for worker/community safety and environmental safeguards. In fact, most such arrangements have not even provided for a semblance of postoperational clean up of mining and processing sites.[18]

Such "savings" accrue to U.S. corporations in the form of superprofits indistinguishable from those gleaned through their enterprises in the Third World, a matter which has unquestionably facilitated the emergence of the United States as the world's dominant economic power in the post-World War II context.[19] Minerals such as uranium, molybdenum, and zeolite, moreover, are not only commercially valuable but strategically crucial, an important factor in understanding America's present global military ascendancy.[20]

All of this has been obtained, as a matter of policy, at the direct expense of Native North America as well as other underdeveloped regions of the world. As Eduardo Galeano once explained to mainstream Americans, with respect to the impact of their lifestyle(s) on Latin America: "Your wealth is our poverty."[21] The correlation is no less true on American Indian reservations. It holds up even in such superficially more redeemable connections as U.S. efforts to curtail acid rain and other collateral effects of electrical power generation through reliance upon low sulfur bituminous rather than high sulfur anthracite coal.

The largest and most easily extracted deposit of bituminous coal in North America is located at Black Mesa, in northern Arizona, an area occupied almost exclusively by Navajos. Beginning in 1974, the federal government undertook a program of compulsory relocation to remove some 13,500 resident Navajos from the intended mining area, dispersing them into primarily urban areas and completely obliterating their sociocultural existence (until then, they had comprised the largest remaining enclave of traditionally oriented Indians in the lower forty-eight states). The land upon which their subsistence economy was based is itself to be destroyed, a circumstance barring even the possibility of their reconstitution as a viable human group at some future date.[22]

The coal, once mined, is slurried to the Four Corners Power Plant and other generating facilities where it is burned to produce electricity. This "product" is then transported over massive power grids to meet such socially vital needs as keeping the air conditioners humming in the Phoenix Valley and the neon lights lit 24 hours a day at Las Vegas casinos. Meanwhile, 46 percent of the homes on the Navajo Reservation have no electricity at all (54 percent have no indoor plumbing, 82 percent no phone).[23] No more fitting illustration of Galeano's equation seems conceivable.

INTERNAL COLONIALISM

Historically, the term "colonialism" has been employed to describe this sort of relationship between nations. Since ratification of the United Nations Charter in 1945, however, such structural domination/exploitation of any nation or people by another, even (or especially) when it is disguised as the exercise of a perpetual "trust," has been deemed illegal within the canons of international jurisprudence. The principle has been clarified, and has received considerable amplification, in subsequent instruments, most unequivocally in United Nations General Assembly Resolution 1514 (XV), also known as the "Declaration on the Granting of Independence to Colonial Countries and Peoples, 1960."[24]

1. The subjection of peoples to alien subjugation, domination and exploitation constitutes a denial of fundamental human rights, is contrary to the Charter of the United Nations and is an impediment to the promotion of world peace and co-operation.
2. All peoples have the right to self-determination; by virtue of that right they freely determine their political status and freely pursue their economic, social and cultural development.
3. Inadequacy of political, economic, social or educational preparedness should never serve as a pretext for delaying independence.
4. All armed action or repressive measures directed against dependent peoples shall cease in order to enable them to exercise peacefully and freely their right to complete independence, and the integrity of their national territory shall be respected.
5. Immediate steps shall be taken in Trust or Non-Self-Governing Territories or all other territories which have not yet attained independence, to transfer all powers to the peoples of those territories, without any conditions or reservations, in accordance with their freely expressed will and desire, with-

out any distinction as to race, creed or colour, in order to enable them to enjoy complete independence and freedom.

6. Any attempt aimed at the partial or total disruption of the national unity and the territorial integrity of a country is incompatible with the purpose and principles of the Charter of United Nations.

7. All States shall observe faithfully and strictly the provisions in the Charter of the United Nations, the Universal Declaration of Human Rights and the present Declaration on the basis of equality, non-interference in the internal affairs of all States, and respect for the sovereign rights of all peoples and their territorial integrity. [25]

While this would seem straightforward enough, the Declaration's universality was muddied by a follow-up provision—General Assembly Resolution 1541 (XV)—which effectively constrained its applicability to peoples/territories separated from colonizing powers by at least thirty miles of open ocean.[26] This "overseas requirement" has seriously undermined assertions of the right to self-determination by American Indians and other indigenous peoples.[27]

There are decolonization issues in the international system which are not so easily defined, such as the Palestine Question or that of South Africa, while the formation of Pakistan out of greater India and the separation of Bangladesh from Pakistan did not relate to legalisms but to political realities. On the other hand, separation by water is no guarantee of independence, as in the case of Puerto Rico, which is officially the "colony" of the United States under United Nations Trusteeship.[28]

This last could as easily be said of Hawai'i, or such "protectorates" as Guam, "American" Samoa, or the "U.S." Virgin Islands.[29] In any event, the "Blue Water Thesis" institutionalized in Resolution 1541 has afforded the U.S., Canada, and other U.N. member-states a useful pretext upon which to construct the pretense that their ongoing colonization of indigenous nations/peoples is not really colonialism at all. Rather, they contend, they are merely exercising the prerogative, provided in the U.N. Charter, of preserving the integrity of their own respective territories.[30] At present, the U.S. in particular is endeavoring to have native rights (re)defined in international law in a manner conforming to its own practice of maintaining American Indians in a condition of "domestic" subjugation.[31]

While it is true that the "internal" variety of colonialism visited upon native peoples by modern settler states differs in many respects from the "classic" models of external colonization developed by European empires over the past several centuries, it is colonialism nonetheless.[32] Moreover, it is no less genocidal in its implications and effects than were the forms of overseas colonialism analyzed by Jean-Paul Sartre in his famous 1968 essay on the topic.[33] Indeed, given how seamlessly it has been imposed, how imperfectly its existence and functioning are reflected in even the most ostensibly liberatory political discourses, and how committed to attaining its formal legitimation the great majority of states have lately proven themselves, internal colonialism may well prove to be more so.[34]

Predictably, there are a number of ways in which the Sartrian equation of colonialism to genocide can be brought to bear when examining the situation of contemporary Native North America. Several of these were suggested above. Probably the clearest representation will be found, however, in the sorry history of how the United States has wielded its self-assigned trust authority over Indian lands and lives in pursuit of global nuclear supremacy over the past half-century.

RADIOACTIVE COLONIZATION

The origins of U.S. nuclear policy obviously lie in its quest to develop an atomic bomb during World War II. The "Manhattan Project" was conducted mainly at the Los Alamos National Scientific Laboratory, a huge fortified compound created in 1942 on the Pajarito Plateau, northwest of Santa Fe, New Mexico, on land supposedly reserved for the exclusive use and occupancy of the San Ildefonso Pueblo.[35] Uranium, the key material used in the lab's experiments and eventual fabrication of prototype nuclear weapons, was mined and milled exclusively in the Monument Valley area of the nearby Navajo Reservation.[36] Hanford, a uranium enrichment/plutonium manufacturing facility, was added in 1944, near the town of Richland, on Yakima land in eastern Washington.[37] When the first bomb was detonated on July 16, 1945, it was on the Alamogordo Bombing and Gunnery Range, now the White Sands Test Range, adjoining the Mescalero Apache Reservation.[38]

While the official rationale for these site selections has always been that their remoteness from major urban centers was/is essential to protecting the secrecy of the research and production to which they were devoted, this in itself does not account for why they were not situated in such sparsely populated areas as western Kansas.[39] A better explanation would seem to reside in the fact that planners were concerned from the outset that the nuclear program embodied substantial risks to anyone living in proximity to it.[40] Such people as resided in the central plains region by the 1940s were mostly members of the settler society; those at San Ildefonso, Mescalero, and Yakima were almost entirely native. For U.S. policymakers, there appears to have been no real question as to which group was the more readily expendable.

That such an assessment is none too harsh is borne out by even the most cursory review of federal comportment in the immediate postwar period. Already possessed of a nuclear weapons monopoly which it believed would allow it to dictate terms to the planet, the U.S. was unsure exactly how much more uranium it needed to acquire.[41] In such circumstances, it was impossible to entice American corporations to engage in uranium extraction. Beginning in 1947, the government's newly formed Atomic Energy Commission (AEC, now the Department of Energy; DoE) "solved" the problem by arranging for several hundred otherwise destitute Navajos to be underwritten by the Small Business Administration (SBA) in starting up tiny mining operations of their own.[42]

Although it has since been claimed that the AEC was unaware of the dangers attending this occupation, there is ample reason to believe authorities were in possession of sufficient information to realize they were consigning every Navajo they coaxed into going underground to a veritable death sentence.

It is important to realize that uranium mining is unlike most other kinds of mining in that during the course of blasting and digging for ore, radioactive radon-222 gas is released. Radon-222 is a natural decay product of uranium with a half-life of about three and one-half days. Radon gas by itself poses no real danger: as a noble gas, it is chemically inert and is simply exhaled. But its radioactive "daughter products" can settle in the lungs and injure the tissues. The primary hazard comes from polonium-218 and 214, alpha-emitting radionuclides that lodge in the lining of the lung. Uranium miners are also bombarded by gamma radiation, but the primary danger, again, stems from the ingestion and inhalation of alpha emitters . . . Robert J. Roscoe of the National Institute for Occupational Safety and Health has shown that nonsmoking uranium miners followed from 1950 to 1984 were thirteen times more likely to die from lung cancer than a comparable group of nonsmoking U.S. veterans.[43]

Dr. Roscoe's test group included a significant proportion of miners who had worked in relatively large, well-ventilated shafts and even open-air uranium stripping operations. The initial group of Navajos worked in tiny, unventilated shafts where radon concentrations were often hundreds of times higher than average. As a consequence, *all* the AEC/SBA miners were dead or dying of lung cancer and/or other respiratory ailments by the mid-1980s. (In a preview of what by the 1990s would become national policy—and a yuppie fad—an attempt was made to blame cigarette smoking and other personal behaviors for this systemically-induced health catastrophe.)[44]

As early as 1556, Austrian physician Georgius Agricola had described the extraordinary incidence of death by "consumption of the lungs" among Carpathian silver miners digging ores laced with radium.[45] In 1879, F.H. Härting and W. Hesse correctly diagnosed what had by then become known as *Bergkrankheit* (mountain sickness) as lung cancer, and demonstrated that approximately three-quarters of all miners in the Schneeberg region of Saxony died of the disease within twenty years of entering the shafts.[46] By 1924, German researchers P. Ludewig and S. Lorenser had linked the Schneeberg miners' cancers to radon inhalation,[47] a connection explored more fully by American physician Wilhelm C. Hueper, founding director of the American Cancer Institute's Environmental Cancer Section, in his seminal 1942 book, *Occupational Tumors and Allied Diseases.*[48]

Nor was Hueper's study the only one readily available to the AEC. In 1944, Egon Lorenz published an article in the *Journal of the National Cancer Institute* which concluded that "the radioactivity of the ore and the radon content of the air of the mines are generally considered to be the primary cause" of lung cancer among uranium miners.[49] Occupational cancer expert Fred W. Stewart went further in a 1947 issue of the *Bulletin of the New York Academy of Medicine*, predicting that there would likely be epidemic "cases of cancer and leukemia in our newest group of industrialists, workers in the field of fissionable materials."[50] Even Bernard Wolf and Merril Eisenbud, directors of the AEC's own medical division, were warning their superiors of such dangers.[51]

The Navajos, of course, were told none of this. On the contrary, when Wolf and Eisenbud tried to establish minimum safety standards for miners in 1948, they were "told by Washington that the health problems of the mines were not the responsibility of the AEC, and . . . should be left to the jurisdiction of the local authorities."[52]

> The AEC had been assigned by Congress the responsibility for radiation safety in the nuclear program but, according to a bizarre interpretation of the 1946 Atomic Energy Act, the commission was bound only to regulate exposures after the ore had been mined. Responsibility for the health and safety of uranium miners was left up to individual states, a situation that Merril Eisenbud rightly recognized as "absurd," given their lack of equipment and expertise to deal with the expected health problems [not to mention the fact that the states lacked jurisdiction on Indian reservations].[53]

Be that as it may, the AEC plainly went to great lengths to ensure that the general public remained equally uninformed. This was accomplished through a regulation requiring that all scientific papers dealing with radiation prepared under the auspices of the National Institutes of Health (NIH) be cleared by the commission prior to presentation/publication. Thus, when Hueper sought to present a paper at a 1952 meeting of the Colorado State Medical Society, he was instructed by Shields Warren, the AEC's Director of Biology and Medicine, to "delete all references . . . to the hazards of uranium mining."[54]

> Hueper . . . refused on the grounds that he had not joined the [National Cancer Institute (NCI)] to become a "scientific liar" . . . When word got around that he was not silently accepting his censorship, Warren again wrote the director of the NCI, this time asking for Hueper's dismissal. Hueper stayed on but was soon barred from all epidemiological work on occupational cancer. The order came from the surgeon general. Hueper was henceforth allowed to do only experimental work on animals, and was prohibited from further investigations into the causation of cancer in man related to environmental exposure to carcinogenic chemical, physical, or parasitic agents.[55]

Similarly, in 1955 the AEC managed to prevent Nobel laureate H.J. Muller, a geneticist, from speaking at the International Symposium on the Peaceful Uses of Atomic Energy in Geneva because he had concluded that radiation induced mutagenic effects in human organisms.[56] During the early 1960s, the commission was also able to marginalize the work of Ernest J. Sternglass, whose groundbreaking research demonstrated that the proliferation of radioactive contaminants would lead to increased rates of miscarriage, stillbirth, childhood leukemia, and other cancers.[57] A few years later it brought about the dismissal of John W. Gofman, the discoverer of both uranium-233 and the plutonium isolation process, from his position at the Lawrence Livermore Laboratories. Gofman's "offense" was determining that, contrary to the AEC's official posture, there was/is really no "safe" level of exposure to radioactive substances.[58]

While the commission's ability to silence such voices diminished over the years, it never really disappeared altogether. When AEC researcher Thomas F. Mancuso set out in 1977 to publish findings that radiation exposure was causing inordinate rates of cancer among workers at the Hanford Military Complex, he was terminated and his research materials impounded.[59] Much the same fate befell Dr. Rosalie Bertell, albeit indirectly, through the National Cancer Institute, when she began to publish the results of epidemiological research on the effects of nuclear contamination during the late 1970s.[60] And so it went for more than forty years.

Unsurprisingly, given the context, the official stance vis-à-vis uranium miners amounted to little more than quietly tallying up the death toll. Even the Public Health Service (PHS), which called in 1957 for "immediate application of corrective measures" to avert an "impending public health disaster" spawned by radon inhalation among miners, was shortly subordinated to the AEC's demand that the truth be hidden.[61] Victor E. Archer, an epidemiologist with the PHS's National Institute for Occupational Safety and Health (NIOSH), spelled this out in 1977, during his testimony in a suit brought by a group of terminally ill Navajo miners and survivors of those already dead.

> Archer testified that he and his colleagues had caved in to AEC and PHS pressures not to publicize the [radon] hazard: "We did not want to rock the boat . . . [W]e had to take the position that we were neutral scientists trying to find out what the facts were, that we were not going to make any public announcements until the results of our scientific study were completed. Official pressures to "monitor" the disaster without informing those at risk or forcing [mining] companies to reduce the hazard led PHS scientists to characterize their study as a "death watch" or "dead body approach." A federal judge [Aldon Anderson] involved in the Navajo case charged that U.S. atomic authorities had failed to warn the miners in order to guarantee a "constant, uninterrupted and reliable flow" of uranium ore "for national security purposes."[62]

An efficient system for delivering huge quantities of uranium had become an especially high priority for the U.S. military when the Soviet Union, years ahead of expectations, tested a nuclear device of its own on September 23, 1949. This set in motion a mad scramble to amass ever greater numbers of increasingly more powerful and sophisticated atomic weapons, as well as a burgeoning number of nuclear reactors, on both sides of the Atlantic.[63] Thus guaranteed the sustained profitability of such enterprises, and shortly immunized against any liabilities they might entail, America's major corporations entered with a vengeance into uranium mining, milling, and related activities, completely supplanting the first generation of Navajo miners' "mom and pop" operations by the end of 1951.[64]

This sudden and massive corporate tie-in to the expansion of U.S. uranium production did not, however, signal a shifting of the burden of supplying it from the shoulders of Native North America. Rather, such weight was increased dramatically. Although only about sixty percent of uranium deposits in the United States were/are situated on American Indian reservations—most of it in the so-called "Grants Uranium Belt" of northern New Mexico and Arizona—well over ninety percent of all the uranium ever mined in the U.S. had been taken from such sources by the time the AEC's "domestic" ore-buying program was phased out in 1982.[65]

Hence, while the USSR and its satellites relied on slave labor provided by hundreds of thousands of political prisoners in meeting their production quotas, the U.S. utilized its internal, indigenous colonies for the same purpose.[66] Not only did the workforce harnessed to the tasks of uranium mining and milling remain disproportionately native, but the vast majority of extraction and processing facilities were situated in Indian Country as well, conveniently out of sight and mind of the general public, their collateral health impacts concentrated among indigenous populations. Much the same can be said with respect to weapons research, testing, and the disposal of radioactive waste by-products. We will examine each of these components of the nuclear process in turn.

Mining

The first largescale uranium mine in the United States was opened under AEC/BIA sanction by the Kerr-McGee Nuclear Corporation in 1952, on the Navajo Reservation, outside the town of Shiprock, New Mexico. A hundred Navajos were hired to perform the underground labor—at about two-thirds the prevailing off-reservation pay scale for comparable work—in what was ostensibly a ventilated mine shaft.[67] When a federal inspector visited the mine a few months after it opened, however, he discovered the ventilator fans were not functioning. When he returned three years later, in 1955, they were still idle.[68] By 1959, radon levels in the mine shaft were routinely testing at ninety to one hundred times the maximum "safe" levels, a circumstance which remained essentially unchanged until the ore played out and Kerr-McGee closed the mine in 1970.[69]

Of the 150-odd Navajo miners who worked below ground at Shiprock over the years, eighteen had died of radiation-induced lung cancer by 1975; five years later, another twenty were dead of the same disease, while the bulk of the rest had been diagnosed with serious respiratory ailments.[70] Much the same situation pertained with regard to native employees working in the shaft at Kerr-McGee's second mining operation on Navajo, opened at Red Rock in 1953. By 1979, fifteen were dead of lung cancer and dozens of others had been diagnosed with that malady and/or respiratory fibrosis.[71] The same rates prevail among the well over 700 men who worked underground for Kerr-McGee at Grants, New Mexico, the largest uranium shaft mining operation in the world.[72] Of the original 6,000 or so miners of all races employed below ground in the Grants Belt, Victor Archer has estimated 1,000 will eventually die of lung cancer.[73]

Nonetheless, such mines proliferated on the reservation throughout the remainder of the 1950s, as the AEC, with the active complicity of the BIA, entered into a host of additional contracts, not only with Kerr-McGee, but with corporations like Atlantic-Richfield (ARCO), AMEX, Foote Mineral, Utah International, Climax Uranium, United Nuclear, Union Carbide (a chameleon which was formerly known as the Vanadium Corporation of America, and is now called Umetco Minerals Corporation), Gulf, Conoco, Mobil, Exxon, Getty, Sun Oil, Standard Oil of Ohio (Sohio), and Rockwell International.[74] As of 1958, "the Bureau of Indian Affairs reported that more than 900,000 acres of tribal land were leased for uranium exploration and development."[75] From 1946 to 1968, well over thirteen million tons of uranium ore were mined on Navajo—some 2.5 million tons at Shiprock alone—and still the rate of increase increased.[76] By late 1976, the year which turned out to be the very peak of the "uranium frenzy" afflicting the Colorado Plateau, the BIA had approved a total of 303 leases encumbering a quarter-million acres of Navajo land for corporate mining and milling purposes (see Figure 5.1).[77]

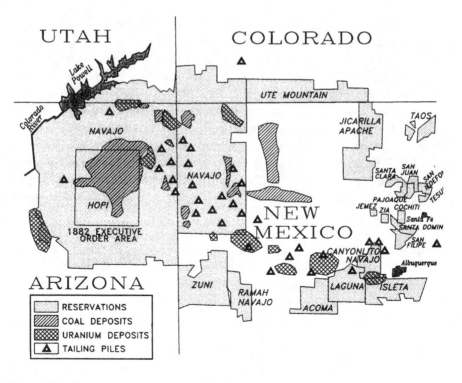

FIGURE 5.1. Four corners area energy exploitation.

Aside from the effects of all this upon those working underground, the shaft mining on Navajo had an increasingly negative impact upon the physical well-being of their families and communities on the surface. One indication of this resides in the fact that, once real ventilation of the mines began to occur during the mid-60s, the vents were often situated right in the middle of residential areas, the inhabitants of which were then forced to breathe the same potent mixtures of radon, thoron, and other toxic substances which were plaguing their husbands, fathers, and neighbors below.[78] There was also the matter of pumping out the groundwater which seeped constantly into scores of the deeper shafts—a process called "dewatering"—all of it heavily contaminated. To appreciate the volume of this outpouring, it should be considered that just one site, Kerr-McGee's Church Rock No. 1 Mine, was pumping more than 80,000 gallons of irradiated effluents per day into the local supply of surface water in 1980.[79]

> The millions of gallons of radioactive water [released in this fashion] carry deadly selenium, cadmium, and lead that are easily absorbed into the local food chain, as well as emitting alpha and beta particles and gamma rays. Human ingestion of radioactive water can result in alpha particles recurrently bombarding human tissue and eventually tearing apart the cells comprising that tissue . . . causing cancer [and/or genetic mutation in offspring].[80]

Small wonder that, by 1981, the Navajo Health Authority (NHA) had documented increasing rates of birth defects—notably cleft palate and Down's Syndrome—among babies born after 1965 in mine-adjacent reservation communities like Shiprock, Red Rock, and Church Rock.[81] At the same time, it was determined that children living in such localities were suffering bone cancers at a rate five times the national average, ovarian cancers at an astonishing seventeen times the norm.[82] Yet another study concluded that, overall, there was "a twofold excess of miscarriages, infant deaths, congenital or genetic abnormalities, and learning disabilities among uranium-area families (compared with Navajo families in nonuranium areas)."[83] Although funding was requested from the Department of Health, Education and Welfare (DHEW) to conduct more extensive epidemiological studies throughout the Grants Belt, the request was promptly denied.

> In fact, in 1983, one agency, the Indian Health Services [a subpart of DHEW, which was by then redesignated the Department of Health and Human Services] sent a report to congress . . . stating that there was "no evidence of adverse health effects on Indians in uranium development areas and there is no need for additional studies or funding for such studies."[84]

Meanwhile, beginning in 1952, an ARCO subsidiary, the Anaconda Copper Corporation, had been operating under AEC/BIA authority on the nearby Laguna Reservation, near Albuquerque. By the early 1970s, the approximately 2,800 acres of

Anaconda's Jackpile-Paguate complex at Laguna—from which 22 million tons of ore and more than 44 million tons of other minerals were removed—was the largest open pit uranium mine in the world.[85] Ultimately, the excavation went so deep that groundwater seepage became as much an issue as in a shaft mine.

> [Anaconda's] mining techniques require "dewatering," i.e., the pumping of water contaminated by radioactive materials to facilitate ore extraction. Since 1972, the Jackpile Mine has wasted more than 119 gallons per minute through this dewatering procedure. Altogether more than 500 million gallons of radioactive water have been discharged [into] a 260-acre tailings pond [from which it] either sinks back into the aquifer, evaporates, or seeps out into the arroyos and drainage channels of the tiny Rio Mequino stream that is fed by a natural spring near the tailings dam.[86]

In 1972, and again in 1977, the Environmental Protection Agency (EPA) notified the Laguna tribal council that both the Río Molino and the nearby Río Paguate, both of which run through the Anaconda leasing area, and which together comprise the pueblo's only source of surface water, were badly contaminated with radium 226 and other heavy metals.[87] This was followed, in 1979, by a General Accounting Office announcement that the aquifer underlying the entire Grants Belt, from which Laguna draws its groundwater, was similarly polluted.[88] The trade-off was, of course, "jobs." But, while most able-bodied Lagunas, and a considerable proportion of neighboring Acomas, were employed by the corporation—a matter touted by the BIA as a "miracle of modernization"—most received poverty-level incomes.[89] And, although the adverse health effects of open pit uranium mining seem somewhat less pronounced than those associated with shaft mining, disproportionately high rates of cancer among long-term miners were being noted by the early 1980s.[90]

All told, about 3,200 underground and 900 open pit miners were employed in uranium operations by 1977, and Kerr-McGee was running a multimillion dollar U.S. Department of Labor-funded job training program in the Navajo community of Church Rock, Arizona, to recruit more.[91] The stated governmental/corporate objective was to create a workforce of 18,400 underground and 4,000 open pit miners to extract ore from approximately 3.5 million acres along the Grants Belt by 1990.[92] Only the collapse of the market for U.S. "domestic" uranium production after 1980—the AEC met its stockpiling quotas in that year, and it quickly became cheaper to acquire commercially-designated supplies mined abroad, first from Namibia, then from Australia, and finally from the native territories of northern Saskatchewan, in Canada—averted realization of this grand plan.[93]

As the dust settled around the Four Corners, the real outcomes of uranium mining began to emerge. The AEC's constellation of corporations had profited mightily as a result, and not just because of their refusal to meet the expense of providing even the most rudimentary forms of worker safety or their having to pay only the artificially depressed wages prevailing within the reservations' colonial economies. The BIA, exercising the government's self-assigned "trust" prerogatives, had written contracts requiring the corporations to pay royalties pegged at an average of only 3.4 percent of market price in an environment where fifteen percent was the normative standard.[94] Moreover, the contracts often included no clauses requiring postmining cleanup of any sort, thus sparing Kerr-McGee and its cohorts what would have been automatic and substantial costs of doing business in off-reservation settings. When lucrative mining was completed, the corporations were thus in a position to simply close up shop and walk away.[95]

The already much-impoverished indigenous nations upon which the uranium extraction enterprise had been imposed in the first place, which seldom if ever made money from the process, and whose prior economies had been demolished into the bargain, were then left holding the bag.[96] On Navajo, this involves the necessity of dealing with hundreds of abandoned mine shafts ranging from fifty to several hundred feet in depth, some subject to caving in and all of them steadily emitting radon and thoron from their gaping maws.[97] At Laguna, conditions are even worse.[98] As Dr. Joseph Wagoner, Director of Epidemiological Research for NIOSH, would later put it, with conspicuous understatement, the situation presents "serious medical and ethical questions about the responsibility [not just of the corporations, but] of the federal government, which was the sole purchaser of uranium during [much of] the period."[99]

Milling

Milling, the separation of pure uranium from its ore, is the first stage of the production process. Ore pockets across the Grants Belt range from .4 to three percent uranium content, yielding an average of about four pounds of "yellowcake" per ton.[100] The remaining 1,996 pounds per ton of waste—reduced to the consistency of course sand called "tailings" during milling—invariably accumulates in huge piles alongside the mills, which, for reasons of cost efficiency, tend to be situated in close proximity to mines. Tailings retain approximately eighty-five percent of the radioactivity of the original ore, have a half-life estimated at 10,000 years, and are a source of continuous radon and thoron gas emissions. They are also subject to wind dispersal and constitute an obvious source of groundwater contamination through leaching.[101]

As with uranium mining, over ninety percent of all milling done in the U.S. occurred on or just outside the boundaries of American Indian reservations.[102] Also, as was the case in the mines, "conditions in the mills were deplorable."[103] Even the most elementary precautions to assure worker protection were ignored as an "unnecessary expense." As Laguna poet Simon J. Ortiz, who was employed in a Kerr-McGee mill during the early 1960s, would later reflect:

> Right out of high school I worked in the mining and milling region of Ambrosia Lake. I was nineteen years old . . . At the mill, I worked in crushing, leaching, and yellowcake, usually at various labor positions . . . I had a job, and for poor people with low education and no skills and high unemployment, that was the important thing: a job . . . In 1960, there was no information about

the dangers of radiation from yellowcake with which I worked . . . In the milling operation at the end of the leaching and settling process, the yellow liquid was drawn into dryers that took the water out. The dryers were screen constructions which revolved slowly in hot air; yellow pellets were extruded and crushed into fine powder. The workers were to keep the machinery operating, which was never smooth, and most of the work was to keep it in free operation; i.e., frequently having to unclog it by hand. There was always a haze of yellow dust flying around, and even though filtered masks were used, the workers breathed in the fine dust. It got in the hair and cuts and scratches and in their eyes. I was nineteen then, and twenty years later I worried about it.[104]

The situation was so acute at Kerr-McGee's first mill on the Navajo Reservation, established at Shiprock in 1953, that after it was abandoned in 1974 inspectors discovered more than $100,000 in uranium dust had settled between two layers of roofing, and former workers recalled having been routinely instructed by their supervisors to stir yellowcake by hand in open, steam-heated floorpans.[105] Needless to say, by 1980, those who'd been lured into the mills with the promise of a small but steady paycheck during the 1950s and '60s were suffering rates of lung cancer and other serious respiratory illnesses rivaling those of their counterparts in the mines.[106]

By far the greater impact of milling, however, has been upon the broader Navajo, Laguna, and Acoma communities. The environmental degradation inflicted by a single mill, the Kerr-McGee plant at Grants—once again, the largest such facility in the world—may equal that of all the shaft mines along the uranium belt combined. At its peak, the monstrosity processed 7,000 tons of ore per day, piling up twenty-three million tons of tailings in a hundred-foot-high mound which covers 265 acres.[107] And this is just one of more than forty mills, several of them not much smaller, operating simultaneously on and around Navajo during the late 1970s.[108] A similar situation prevailed at plants established by Kerr-McGee, Sohio-Reserve, Bokum Minerals, and several other corporations in the immediate vicinity of Laguna and Acoma.[109]

At the Bluewater Mill, eighteen miles west of the Laguna Reservation [on the western boundary of Acoma, a thirty-mile trip by rail from the Jackpile-Paguate complex, with raw ore hauled in open gondolas] near the bed of the San Jose River, Anaconda has added a 107-acre pond and a 159-acre pile comprising 13,500,000 tons of "active" tailings and 765,033 tons of "inactive" residues.[110]

In August 1978, it was discovered that Anaconda, as a means of "holding down costs," had also made massive use of tailings as fill in its "improvement" of the reservation road network at Laguna. At the same time, it was revealed that tailings had constituted the "sand and gravel mix" of concrete with which the corporation had—with much fanfare about the "civic benefits" it was thereby bestowing upon its indigenous "partners"—poured footings for a new tribal council building, community center, and housing complex.[111] All were seriously irradiated as a result, a matter which may well be playing into increasing rates of cancer and birth defects, even among the non-miner sectors of Laguna's population.[112]

Probably the worst single example of mill-related contamination occurred about a year later, on July 16, 1979, at the United Nuclear plant in Church Rock, New Mexico, when a tailings dam gave way, releasing more than a hundred million gallons of highly radioactive water into the nearby Río Puerco.[113] About 1,700 Navajos living downstream were immediately affected, as were their sheep and other livestock, all of whom depended on the river for drinking water.[114] Shortly thereafter, with spill-area cattle exhibiting unacceptably high levels of lead-210, polonium-210, thorium-230, radium-236, and similar substances in their tissues, all commercial sales of meat from such animals was indefinitely prohibited.[115]

Still, even as the ban went into effect, IHS Area Director William Moehler—rather than calling for allocation of federal funds to provide emergency rations to those most directly at risk—approved consumption of the very same mutton and beef by local Navajos.[116] At about the same time, a request by downstream Navajos for United Nuclear to provide them with trucked-in water, at least in quantities sufficient to meet the immediate needs of the afflicted human population, was met with flat refusal.[117] The corporation stonewalled for another five years—until it was revealed by the Southwest Research and Information Center, an Albuquerque-based environmental organization, that it had known about cracks in the dam at least two months before it broke and had failed to repair it—before agreeing to a minimal, state-facilitated "settlement" of $525,000.[118]

By and large, however, it was not outright disasters such as the Church Rock spill, but the huge and rapidly proliferating accumulation of mill tailings throughout the Four Corners region—more than a half-billion tons in 200 locations by 1979, figures which were projected to double by the end of the century—that provoked a team of Los Alamos experts, utterly at a loss as to what to do with such vast quantities of radioactive waste, to recommend the "zon[ing] of uranium mining and milling districts so as to forbid human habitation."[119]

The idea dovetailed perfectly with the conclusions drawn in a contemporaneous study undertaken by the National Institute for Science, that desert lands subjected to stripmining can never be reclaimed.[120] Since the Peabody Coal Company, among others, was/is engaged in ever more massive coal stripping operations on Navajo,[121] the logical outcome of the Los Alamos and NAS studies was the formulation of a secret federal "policy option" declaring the Four Corners, and the Black Hills region of the northern plains as well,[122] "national sacrifice areas in the interests of energy development" (see Figure 5.2).[123]

Not coincidentally, the pair of localities selected contained the largest and second-largest concentrations of reservation-based Indians remaining in the United States: Navajo, with over 120,000 residents in 1980, is by far the biggest reservation both by acreage and by population in the U.S. Also sacrificed in the Four Corners region would be—at a minimum—the Hopi, Zuni, Laguna, Acoma, Isleta, Ramah Navajo, Cañoncito Navajo, Ute Mountain, and Southern Ute reservations. The 50,000-odd residents of the "Sioux Complex" of reservations in North and South Dakota—Pine Ridge, Rosebud, Crow Creek, Cheyenne River, and Standing Rock in particular— make up the second most substantial concentration. Also sacrificed in the Black Hills region would be the Crow and Northern Cheyenne reservations in Montana, and possibly the Wind River Reservation in Wyoming.[124]

As American Indian Movement leader Russell Means observed in 1980, shortly after existence of the plan had been disclosed, to sacrifice the landbase of landbased

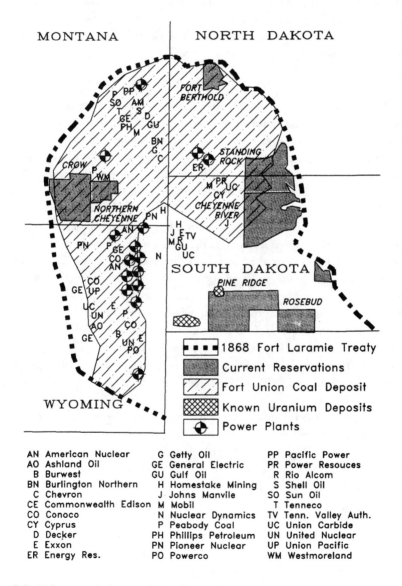

FIGURE 5.2. U.S. corporate interests in the Greater Sioux Nation. Source: The Black Hills "National Sacrifice Area": A Study in U.S. Internal Colonialism.

peoples is tantamount to sacrificing the peoples themselves, a prospect he aptly described as genocide while calling for appropriate modes of resistance.[125]

Although a policy of deliberately creating national sacrifice areas out of American Indian reservations was never formally implemented, the more indirect effect may well be the same. With windblown tailings spread over wide tracts of Navajo, ground and surface water alike contaminated with all manner of radioactive substances, and Navajo children literally using abandoned mounds of tailings as sand piles, it is not unreasonable to suspect that both the land and the people have already been sacrificed on the altar of U.S. armaments development.[126] If so, they and their counterparts at Laguna, Acoma and elsewhere will have become victims of what may be, to date, history's subtlest form of physical extermination.[127]

Weapons Research and Production

The Los Alamos lab might well have extended its zoning recommendations to include not just uranium mining and milling districts but localities in which nuclear weapons research and production have been carried out, beginning with itself. Here again, although the sites at which yellowcake is enriched and/or transformed into plutonium have been scattered across the country in localities not typically associated with indigenous people, the great weight of contamination in this connection has been off-loaded by the dominant society onto Indian Country.[128]

The extent of radioactive contamination at Los Alamos is astonishing. A half-century of nuclear weapons research on the 43-square mile "campus"—which adjoins not only San Ildefonso, but the Santa Clara, San Juan, Jemez, and Zia reservations—has produced some 2,400 irradiated pollution sites containing "plutonium, uranium, strontium-90, tritium, lead, mercury, nitrates, cyanides, pesticides and other lethal leftovers."[129] A single 1950 experiment in which "simulated nuclear devices" were exploded in order to track radioactive fallout patterns was not only kept secret for decades, but left nearby Bayo Canyon heavily contaminated with strontium.[130] The facility also has a long history of secretly and illegally incinerating irradiated wastes—a practice producing significant atmospheric contamination—as was acknowledged by the EPA in 1991.[131]

The greatest concentration of hazardous materials in the Los Alamos compound is situated in what is called "Area G," which "began taking radioactive waste in 1957. Since 1971, 381,000 cubic feet of [lab]-generated transuranic [plutonium-contaminated] waste has been stored there; no one knows how much went in before 1971, since records are scanty. Wastes were "interred without liners or caps, in bulldozed pits [from which] they may be presumed to be leaking."[132]

This, in combination with the lab's chronic release of radioactive substances into the atmosphere is thought to be correlated to dramatic increases in cancers and birth defects among local native populations over the past twenty years.[133] Plutonium contamination of surface water has been found downstream at least as far as the Cochiti Reservation, thirty miles away.[134] At present, Area G is slated for considerable expansion.[135] In the new plan, strongly opposed by area Indians, it "would be able to contain 475,000 cubic yards of mixed-waste in pits 2,000 feet long and divided into 25,000 cubic yard segments."[136]

An even worse situation prevails at Hanford, which was closed in 1990. Despite frequent official denials that it presented any sort of public health hazard during the span of its operation, the complex exhibits an uparalleled record of deliberate environmental contamination, beginning with a secret experimental release of radioactive iodides in 1945, the first of seven, which equaled or surpassed the total quantity of pollutants emitted during the disastrous 1986 Soviet reactor meltdown at Chernobyl.[137] Also in 1945, Hanford officials secretly instructed staff to begin "disposing" of irradiated effluents by the simple expedient of pouring them into unlined "sumps" from which they leached into the underlying aquifer. All told, before the plant was closed something in excess of 440 *billion* gallons of water laced with everything from plutonium to tritium to ruthenium had been dumped in this "cost efficient" manner.[138]

Another 900,000 gallons of even more highly radioactive fluids were stored in a 117-unit underground "tank farm" maintained under contract by ARCO, several components of which were found to be leaking badly.[139] Not only has regional groundwater been severely contaminated, but wastes have been found to have passed into the nearby Columbia River in quantities sufficient to irradiate shellfish at the river's mouth, more than 200 miles distant.[140]

> Not only has the Hanford plant been discharging and leaking radiation into the river for forty-five years, but serious accidents have occurred at the reactors. One could perhaps excuse the accidental release of radiation [if not its cover-up], but on several occasions huge clouds of isotopes were created knowingly and willingly. In December [1952, to provide another example,] about 7,800 curies of radioactive Iodine 131 were deliberately [and secretly] released in an experiment designed to detect military reactors in the Soviet Union (only 15 to 24 curies of Iodine 131 escaped at Three Mile Island in 1979).[141]

The true extent of the ecological holocaust perpetrated at and around Hanford is unknown, and is likely to remain so over the foreseeable future, given that most information about the facility is permanently sealed as a matter of "national security," and DoE/Pentagon/corporate officials claim to have "lost" much of what is supposedly accessible.[142] Such information as has come out, however, tends to speak for itself.

> Abnormally high incidence of thyroid tumors and cancers have been observed in populations living downstream from Hanford. Strontium 90, Cesium 137, and Plutonium 239 have been released in large quantities, as was, between 1952 and 1967, Ruthenium 106. People in adjacent neighborhoods [notably, the Yakimas and nearby Spokanes] were kept uninformed about these releases—before, during and after—and none were warned that they were at

risk for subsequent development of cancer. (Some experts have estimated that downwind farms and families received radiation doses ten times higher than those that reached Soviet people living near Chernobyl in 1986).[143]

In sum, the probability is that Los Alamos, Hanford, and surrounding areas should be added to the extensive geographical sacrifices already discussed with respect to uranium mining and milling. To the extent that this is true—and it is almost certainly the case at Hanford—several more colonized indigenous nations must be added to the roster of those implicitly but officially identified peoples whose sacrifice is deemed necessary, useful, or at least acceptable, in the interests of U.S. nuclear development.

Weapons Testing

Nuclear weapons, once designed, must be tested. During the period immediately following World War II, the U.S. asserted its "trust" authority over the Marshall Islands, gained by its defeat of Japan, for purposes of conducting more than a hundred such tests on the natives' mid-Pacific atolls by 1958.[144] Meanwhile, the search for a more "suitable" continental locality, code-named "Nutmeg," began as early as 1948. Two years later, the AEC/Pentagon combo finally settled on the Las Vegas/Tonopah Bombing and Gunnery Range in Nevada (now called the Nellis Range), an area which it had already decided "really wasn't much good for anything but gunnery practice—you could bomb it into oblivion and never notice the difference."[145]

Of course, nobody bothered to ask the Western Shoshone people, within whose unceded territory the facility was established, whether they felt this was an acceptable use of their land, or whether they were even willing to have it designated as part of the U.S. "public domain" for *any* purpose.[146] Instead, in 1952, having designated 435,000 acres in the Yucca Flats area of Nellis as a "Nevada Test Site"—another 318,000 acres were added in 1961, bringing the total to 753,000—the AEC and its military partners undertook the first of what by now add up to nearly a thousand atmospheric and underground test detonations.[147] In the process, they converted the peaceful and pastoral Shoshones, who had never engaged in an armed conflict with the U.S., into what, by any estimation, is far and away "the most bombed nation on earth."[148]

The deadly atomic sunburst over Hiroshima, in 1945, produced 13 kilotons of murderous heat and radioactive fallout. At least 27 of the 96 above ground bombs detonated between 1951 and 1958 at the Nevada Test Site produced a total of over 620 kilotons of radioactive debris that fell on downwinders. The radioactive isotopes mixed with the scooped-up rocks and earth of the southwestern desert lands and "lay down a swath of radioactive fallout" over Utah, Arizona, and Nevada. In light of the fact that scientific research has now confirmed that *any* radiation exposure is dangerous, the "virtual inhabitants" (more than 100,000 people) residing in the small towns east and south of the test site were placed in . . . jeopardy by the AEC atomic test program (emphasis added).[149]

Those most affected by the estimated twelve billion curies of radioactivity released into the atmosphere over the past 45 years have undoubtedly been the native communities scattered along the periphery of Nellis.[150] These include not only three Shoshone reservations—Duckwater, Yomba, and Timbisha—but the Las Vegas Paiute Colony and the Pahrump Paiute, Goshute, and Moapa reservations as well. Their circumstances have been greatly compounded by the approximately 900 underground test detonations which have, in a region where surface water sources are all but nonexistent, resulted in contamination of groundwater with plutonium, tritium, and other radioactive substances at levels up to 3,000 times the maximum "safe" limits.[151]

Radionuclides released to groundwater include: antimony-125, barium-140, beryllium-7, cadmium-109, cerium-141, cesium-137, cobalt-60, europium-155, iodine-131, iridium-192, krypton, lanthanum-140, plutonium-238, plutonium-239, plutonium-240, rhodium-106, ruthenium-103, sodium-22, strontium-90, and tritium.[152]

Although the government has been steadfast in its refusal to conduct relevant epidemiology studies in Nevada, especially with respect to indigenous peoples, it has been credibly estimated that several hundred people had already died of radiation-induced cancers by 1981.[153] Rather than admit to any aspect of what it was doing, the military simply gobbled up increasingly gigantic chunks of Shoshone land, pushing everyone off and creating ever larger "security areas" that rendered its activities less and less susceptible to any sort of genuine public scrutiny.[154]

Today, in the state of Nevada, in addition to Nellis Air Force Base and Nevada Test Site, we can add the following military reservations: Fallon Navy Training Range Complex with its airspace; the Hawthorne Army Ammunition Depot, with its restricted airspace; the Reno Military Operations Area Airspace; the Hart Military Operations Area Airspace; the Paradise Military Operations Area Airspace; and parts of the Utah Training Range Complex with its airspace. Military ranges in Nevada alone amount to four million acres. Approximately forty percent of Nevada's airspace is designated for military use.[155]

Across the state line in California—it is separated from the gargantuan sprawl of military facilities in Nevada only by the width of the interposed Death Valley National Monument—lies the million-acre China Lake Naval Weapons Center.[156] Butted up against the Army's equally-sized estate at Fort Irwin, and close to both the half-million-acre Edwards Air Force Base and the 800,000-acre Marine Corps Base at Twentynine Palms, China Lake—an oddly-named facility in that it incorporates no lake at all—uses its share of the Mojave Desert in the same manner as White Sands, only more so.[157] Established in November 1943 and expanded steadily thereafter, it was crediting itself by 1968 with being the location in which "over 75% of the airborne weapons of the free world [and] 40% of the world's conventional weapons" had been tested and perfected.[158] As in Nevada, local indigenous communities, both Shoshone and Paiute, have been pushed out while their lands, including sacred sites, have been bombed, strafed, and shelled relentlessly for more than fifty years (see Figure 5.3).[159]

Probably the only "concession" made to native peoples in the region during this entire period has been that the three largest nuclear devices ever detonated underground, culminating in a monstrous five megaton blast in 1971, were exploded not at the Nevada Test Site, but on Amchitka Island, off Alaska. The reason for this change in procedure had nothing to do with concern for the wellbeing of human beings, however. Rather, it was brought on by fears among AEC officials that the shock waves from such large blasts might cause serious damage to casinos and other expensive buildings in downtown Las Vegas, thereby provoking a backlash from segments of the

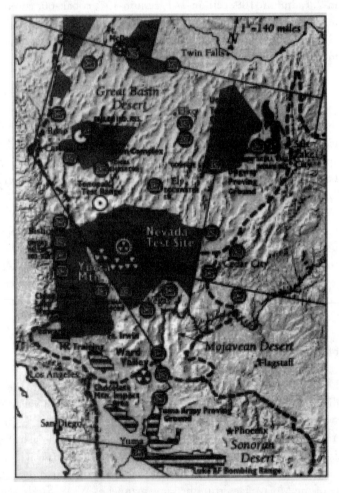

FIGURE 5.3. The Nuclear Landscape. Shaded areas here designate military airspace and military operations areas. Such areas extend the zone of military operations far beyond land holdings. Source: Valerie L. Kuletz, *The Tainted Desert: Environmental and Social Ruin in the American West* (New York, Routledge, 1998).

regional "business community."[160] Hence, the brunt of the environmental/biological consequences wrought by the three biggest "bangs" was shifted from the Indians of Nevada to the Aleuts indigenous to the Aleutian Archipelago.[161]

Exactly how large an area has been sacrificed to nuclear testing and related activities is unknown, but most certainly includes the bulk of southern Nevada and contiguous portions of California.[162] Indications are that it may encompass northern Nevada as well, given the insistence of Reagan era Defense Secretary Casper Weinberger—selected for this position, appropriately enough, on the basis of his credentials as a senior vice president of the Bechtel Corporation, the second largest U.S. nuclear engineering contractor—that the railmounted MX missile system should be sited there, a move which would have effectively precluded human habitation.[163] Given prevailing wind patterns, the sacrifice area likely encompasses northwestern Arizona as well, including three indigenous people—Hualapi, Havasupi, and Kaibab—whose reservations are located there.[164] Also at issue are the more westerly reaches of Utah, a region which includes the small Goshute and Skull Valley reservations in addition to another huge complex of military bases and proving grounds.[165]

Waste "Disposal"

Plutonium, an inevitable byproduct of most reactors and the essential ingredient in nearly all nuclear weapons, has been aptly described as being "the most toxic substance in the universe."[166] Only ten micrograms, a microscopic quantity, is an amount "almost certain to induce cancer, and several grams . . . dispersed in a ventilation system, are enough to cause the death of thousands."[167] Indeed, it has been estimated that a single pound of plutonium, if evenly distributed throughout the earth's atmosphere, would be sufficient to kill every human being on the planet.[168] Viewed from this perspective, the quantity of this material created by the United States during the course of its arms race with the Soviet Union—as of 1989, the U.S. alone had amassed some 21,000 nuclear weapons—is virtually incomprehensible.[169]

> By 1995, military weapons-grade plutonium, in the form of active and dismantled bombs, amounted to 270 metric *tons*. The commercial stockpile of plutonium in nuclear-reactor wastes and isolates from spent fuel amounts to 930 metric tons and will double to 2,130 tons by 2005, . . . "Every four or five years we're [now] making about as much plutonium in the civil sector as we did during the whole Cold War." And this is only plutonium. Fission reactors create eighty radionuclides that are releasing "ionizing radiation," which causes harm to human beings in the form of genetic mutations, cancer, and birth defects.[170]

Leaving aside the proliferation of commercial reactors and other such facilities, as well as the mining and milling zones, there are 132 sites in thirty states where one or another facet of nuclear weapons production has left radioactive contamination of varying orders of magnitude, all of them unacceptable.[171] The DoE currently estimates that it will cost about $500 billion to return these to habitable condition, an absurdly low figure in view of the department's admission that neither concepts nor technologies presently exist with which to even begin the clean-up of "large contaminated river systems like the Columbia, Clinch, and Savannah [as well as] most groundwater [and] nuclear test areas on the Nevada Test Site."[172]

It is also conceded that there is no known method of actually "disposing" of—i.e., decontaminating—plutonium and other radioactive wastes after they've been cleaned from the broader environment.[173] Instead, such materials, once collected, can only be sealed under the dubious premise that they can be somehow safely stored for the next 250,000 years.[174] The sheer volume is staggering: "Hanford [alone] stores 8,200,000 cubic feet of high-level waste and 500,000 cubic feet of transuranic waste. Hanford buried 18,000,000 cubic feet of 'low-level' waste and 3,900,000 cubic feet of transuranic waste."[175] And, daunting as they are, these numbers—associated exclusively with weapons, weapons production, and commercial reactors—don't begin to include the millions of tons of accumulated mill tailings and similar byproducts of "front end" nuclear processing.[176]

Such facilities as now exist to accommodate warhead and reactor wastes are all temporary installations designed to last a century or less, even under ideal conditions which seem never to prevail.[177] The steadily escalating rate of waste proliferation has led to the burning of plutonium and other substances—a practice which certainly reduces the bulk of the offending materials, but also risks sending clouds of radioactivity into the atmosphere[178]—and an increasingly urgent quest for safer interim facilities, called "monitored retrievable storage" (MRS) sites, and permanent "repositories" into which their contents could eventually be moved.[179] Here, as always, emphasis has been on off-loading the problem onto captive indigenous nations.[180]

The reason, predictably enough, is that despite a chorus of official assurances that neither an MRS nor a repository would present a health hazard, the precise opposite is true. John Gofman has calculated that if only 0.01 percent of the plutonium now in storage were to escape into the environment—a record of efficiency never remotely approximated by the nuclear establishment—some 25 million people could be expected to die of resulting cancers over the following half-century.[181] Those most proximate to any dump site can of course expect to suffer the worst impact. Consequently, only one county in the United States has proven amenable to accepting an MRS within its boundaries, and its willingness to do so was quickly overridden by the state.[182]

Federal authorities have therefore concentrated all but exclusively on siting the dumps in Indian Country. As longtime indigenous rights activist Grace Thorpe has observed:

> The U.S. government targeted Native Americans for several reasons: their lands are some of the most isolated in North America, they are some of the most impoverished and, consequently, most politically vulnerable and, perhaps most important, tribal sovereignty can be used to bypass state environmental

laws . . . How ironic that, after centuries of attempting to destroy it, the U.S. government is suddenly interested in promoting Native American sovereignty—just to dump its lethal garbage.[183]

There can be little doubt that during the early 1990s DoE negotiators played heavily upon the colonially-imposed destitution of indigenous peoples in peddling their wares.

[Sixteen] tribes initially applied for $100,000 grants from DOE to study the MRS option on Native lands. The lucrative DOE offer included up to $3 million to actually identify a site for an MRS and as much as $5 million per year for any tribe to accept the deal. The government also offered to build roads, hospitals, schools, railroads, airports, and recreation facilities [most of which the Indians should have been receiving anyway].[184]

Another $100,000 was passed along in 1992 to the federally-oriented National Congress of American Indians (NCAI) to garner its assistance in selling the proposition to its constituents, while a whopping $1.2 million—eighty percent of the DoE's budget for such purposes—was lavished on the Council of Energy Resource Tribes (CERT), a federally/corporately-funded entity created for the sole purpose of systematizing the wholesale brokering of native mineral rights.[185] Despite the best efforts of both organizations—CERT in particular went beyond the MRS concept to promote acceptance of a repository at Hanford by the Yakimas, Nez Percé, and Umatillas—the campaign was largely a failure.[186] By 1995, only three reservations—Mescalero, Skull Valley, and Ft. McDermitt in northern Nevada—indicated any degree of willingness to accept a dump, regardless of the material incentives offered.

The reasoning which led to this result is instructive. At Skull Valley, the feeling expressed by many residents was that they and their land may already have been sacrificed, in part to radiation blown in over the years from the not far distant Nevada Test Site, in part to a host of nuclear, chemical, and bacteriological contaminants emanating from military bases closer to home. Even the specific area committed as an MRS site has long been leased to several corporations as a rocket testing range.[187] As tribal member Leon Bear observes:

People need to understand that this whole area has already been deemed a waste zone by the federal government, the state of Utah, and the country . . . Tooele Depot, a military site, stores 40% of the nation's nerve gas and other hazardous gas only 40 miles away from us. Dugway Proving Grounds, an experimental life sciences center, is only 14 miles away, and it experiments with viruses like plague and tuberculosis. Within a 40 mile radius there are three hazardous waste dumps and a "low-level" radioactive waste dump. From all directions, north, south, east, and west we're surrounded by the waste of Tooele County, the state of Utah, and U.S. society.[188]

The sentiment at Skull Valley, that it is better to at least charge for one's demise than endure the suffering free of charge, is shared by an appreciable segment of the Mescalero population. As one reservation resident noted, the feeling of many people is that "since they are getting impacted by nuclear waste [anyway] they should have a chance to benefit economically."[189] Or, as another put it, "The federal government has forced us to choose between being environmentally conscious [and] starving."[190] Such perspectives notwithstanding, local activists like Rufina Laws were able to engineer a "no-acceptance" vote on an MRS proposal at Mescalero during the winter of 1995. It seems that only a policy of outright bribery by pro-nuclear Tribal Chairman Wendell Chino—reputedly the payment of $2,000 per "yes" vote—was sufficient to reverse the outcome by a narrow margin in a second referendum conducted a few months later.[191]

More important than such subsidies, however, may be the fact that many Mescaleros are now experiencing an overwhelming sense of hopelessness, based on the knowledge that not only are they just downwind from White Sands, but that—over their strong objections—the first U.S. nuclear repository has been sited in the Carlsbad Caverns area, immediately to their east.[192] This is the so-called "Waste Isolation Pilot Plant" (WIPP), a facility intended to house virtually all military transuranics produced after 1970—57,359 cubic meters of it—in a subsurface salt bed already fissured by underground nuclear detonations.[193]

> The disposal area will exceed 100 acres, although the site's surface area covers more than 10,000 acres . . . The repository's design calls for "creeping" salt to seal the wastes [2,150 feet below ground]—a process that is supposed to isolate the substances for tens of thousands of years. Controversy over the WIPP focuses on potential ground water contamination, gases which would be generated by the decomposing wastes, and the hazards posed by transporting approximately 30,000 truckloads of waste to the site, among other things.[194]

It now appears that the deep salt beds below Carlsbad are not so dry as was once believed by the National Institute for Sciences, a matter which could lead to relatively rapid corrosion of the storage canisters in which the repository's plutonium is to be contained, and correspondingly massive contamination of the underlying Rustler Aquifer.[195] Serious questions have also arisen as to whether the mass of materials stored in such close quarters—after accommodating its present allocation of transuranics, the WIPP will still retain some seventy percent of its space availability to meet "future requirements," official shorthand for continuing nuclear weapons production—might not "go critical" and thereby set off an incalculably large atomic explosion.[196]

Even worse problems are evident at Yucca Mountain, located on the southwestern boundary of the Nevada Test Site, where a $15 billion repository to accommodate 70,000 tons of mostly civilian high-level waste is being imposed on the long-suffering Western Shoshones and Paiutes.[197] Not only is "spontaneous detonation" just as much a threat as at the WIPP, but Yucca Mountain, located in a volcanically active region, is undercut by no less than 32 geological fault lines.[198] Needless to say, no amount of engineering brilliance can ensure the repository's contents will remain undisturbed through a quarter-million years of earthquakes interspersed with volcanic eruptions. Once again, however, the project is being moved forward as rapidly as possible.

As if this were not enough, it was announced in 1993 by the Southwestern Compact, a consortium of state governments, that it had "decided to keep the option" of siting a huge low-level waste dump in the Mojave Desert's Ward Valley, near the small town of Needles on the California/Arizona boundary.[199] Envisioned as being large enough to accept the contents of all six existing—and failed—low-level facilities in the U.S. with room to spare for the next thirty years, the proposed site is less than eighteen miles from the Colorado River and directly above an aquifer.[200] It is also very close to the Fort Mojave, Chemehuavi Valley, and Colorado River Indian Tribes reservations, and upstream from those of the Cocopahs and Quechanis around Yuma, Arizona.

Taken as a whole, the pattern of using "deserts as dumps" which has emerged in nuclear waste disposal practices over the past decade serves to confirm suspicions, already well founded, that creation of sacrificial geographies within the U.S. has been an integral aspect of Cold War policies and planning for nearly fifty years.[201] In many ways, the siting of repositories in particular, since they are explicitly intended to remain in place "forever," may be seen as a sort of capstone gesture in this regard. The collateral genocide of those indigenous peoples whose lands lie within the boundaries of the sacrifice zones, nations whose ultimate negation has always been implicitly bound up in the very nature and depth of their colonization, is thus, finally and irrevocably, to be consummated.[202]

FREEING THE MINER'S CANARY

The radioactive colonization of Native North America has involved fundamental miscalculations at a number of levels. In retrospect, the very idea that environmental contamination and consequent epidemiologies could be contained within U.S. internal colonies, hidden from polite society and afflicting only those deemed most expendable by federal policymakers, seems ludicrous. Windblown uranium tailings have never known that they were supposed to end their ongoing dispersal at reservation boundaries, no more than irradiated surface water has realized it was meant to stop flowing before it reached the domain of settler society, or polluted groundwater that it was intended to concentrate itself exclusively beneath Indian wellheads. Still less have clouds of radioactive iodides and strontium-impregnated fallout been aware that they were scripted to remain exclusively within Yakima or Shoshone or Puebloan territories.

As Felix S. Cohen once observed, American Indians serve as the proverbial "miner's canary" of U.S. social, political, and economic policies. Whatever is done to Indians, he said, invariably serves as a prototype for things intended by America's élites for application to others, often to society as a whole. The effects of policy implementation upon Indians can thus be viewed as an "early warning" device for the costs and consequences of policy formation upon the broader society. In paying attention to what is happening to Indians, Cohen concluded, nonindians equip themselves to act in their own self-interest; in the alternative, they will inevitably find themselves sharing the Indians' fate.[203]

Cohen's premise plainly holds in the present connection, and not simply in the more obvious ways. If the citizens of Troy, New York, which became an unanticipated "hot spot" for fallout from atmospheric testing during the early 1950s, can now advance the same claims concerning health impacts as can the residents of Nevada (see Figure 5.4),[204] so too can everyone within a fifty mile radius of any of the more than one hundred nuclear reactors in the United States, all of them made possible by the uranium mined and milled on native land.[205] As well, there are scores of nuclear weapons manufacturing centers, storage facilities, and the more than four *tons* of plutonium and comparable materials missing from U.S. inventories by 1977.[206]

If the disposal of mountainous accumulations of transuranic and other wastes has become a problem admitting to no easy solution, its existence essentially accrues from the fact that even the most progressive and enlightened sectors of the settler society have busied themselves for forty years with the protesting of nuclear proliferation at its tail end rather than at its point(s) of origin. For all the mass actions they have organized at reactors and missile bases over the years, not one has ever been conducted at a mining/milling site like Church Rock, Shiprock, or Laguna.[207] Had things been otherwise, it might have been possible to choke off the flow of fissionable materials at their source rather than attempting to combat them in their most proliferate and dispersed state(s).

The opposition, however, has for the most part proven itself as willing to relegate

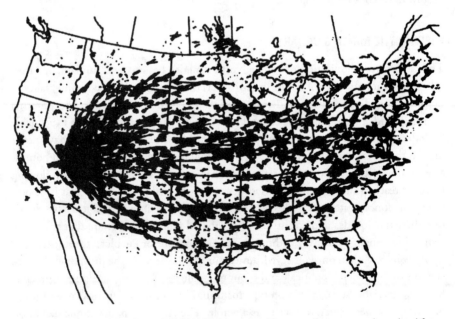

FIGURE 5.4. Areas of continental United States crossed by more than one nuclear cloud from above-ground detonations. Source: Jay M. Gould, *The Enemy Within: The High Cost of Living Near Nuclear Reactors* (New York: Four Walls, Eight Windows, 1996).

native people to stations of marginality, even irrelevancy, as has the order it ostensibly opposes. And here, to borrow from Malcolm X, it can be said that the chickens have truly come home to roost.[208] This takes the form of the increasingly ubiquitous cancers that have made their appearance across the spectrum of American society since World War II, and the spiraling rates of congenital birth defects and suppressed immune systems evident among those whose lives began during the 1940s or later.[209]

Plastering "no smoking" signs on every flat surface in North America will have absolutely no effect in preventing or curing these and myriad other radiation-induced maladies.[210] Wherein lies the cure? In a technical sense, it must be admitted that no one knows. We are very far down the road. The wages of radioactive colonialism are by and large being visited upon the colonizing society itself, and will likely continue to be in what is, in human terms, a permanent fashion. Such effects as have already obtained may well prove irreversible.[211]

Whether or not this is true, one thing is clear: any effort to counter the effects of nuclear contamination must begin by halting its continuing proliferation. Unavoidably, then, success devolves first and foremost upon devising means of stopping still more uranium from coming out of the ground. Until that is accomplished, struggles to shut down individual reactors, to clean up specific mill-sites and production facilities, to reduce the number of nuclear warheads in military inventories or even to figure out how to dispose of the existing accumulation of wastes will prove futile.[212]

The principle of course is as time-honored as it is true: to correct a problem it is necessary to confront its source rather than its symptoms. In and of itself, however, uranium mining is not the source of the affliction at hand. Underlying the mining process is the nature of the relationship imposed by the United States upon indigenous peoples within its borders, that of internal colonization, without which such things could never have happened in the first place. And underlying *that* is a mentality shared by the North American settler population as a veritable whole: a core belief that it is somehow inherently, singularly, even mystically, entitled to dominate all it encounters, possessing or at least benefiting from that which belongs to others, regardless of the costs and consequences visited upon those thereby subjugated and dispossessed.[213]

It can thus be said with certainty that if the dominant society is to have the least prospect of addressing the steadily mounting crisis of nuclear pollution it has no real option but to end the radioactive colonization of Native North America. This can happen only if U.S. élites are forced to abandon their ongoing pretense of holding legitimate and perpetual "trust authority" over native peoples, thus facilitating the genuine exercise of indigenous self-determination and our more general decolonization.[214] In turn, this can happen only to the extent that there is a wholesale alteration in the "genocidal mentality" which marks the settler population.[215]

The key in this regard is a breaking down of the codes of denial, both individual and institutional, by which the settler society has always shielded itself from the implications of its own values and resulting actions.[216] The process is in part simply a matter of insisting that things be called by their right names rather than the noble-sounding euphemisms behind which reality has been so carefully hidden: terms like "discovery" and "settlement" do not reflect the actualities of invasion and conquest they are used to disguise; colonialism is not a matter of "trust," it is colonialism, a crime under international law; genocide isn't an "inadvertent" outcome of "progress," it is genocide, an *always* avoidable crime against humanity; ecocide is not "development," it is ecocide, the most blatant and irremediable form of environmental destruction; mere possession constitutes "nine-tenths of the law" only among thugs devoted to enjoying the fruits of an organized system of theft.[217]

Thus accurately described, many of the measures heretofore accepted by the American public in the name of forging and defending its "way of life" become viscerally repulsive, to average Americans no less than to anyone else. Unlike a society based on discovery and settlement, progress and trust, there are few who would queue up to argue the defensibility of a way of life predicated in/sustained by invasion, conquest, genocide, ecocide, colonization, and other modes of systemic theft. This is all the more true when it can be demonstrated, as it can in the present connection, that the process of intergroup victimization is bound to subject victims and victimizers alike to an identically ugly destiny. In sum, it is not unreasonable to expect an increasing proportion of the settler population to move towards the position sketched above, if not from a sense of altruism (i.e., "doing the right thing"), then on the basis of newly perceived self-interest.[218]

It is worth observing that the ensuing decolonization of Native North America would offer benefits to humanity extending far beyond itself. Every inch of territory and attendant resources withdrawn from U.S. "domestic" hegemony diminishes the relative capacity of America's corporate managers to project themselves outward via multilateral trade agreements and the like, consummating a "New World Order" in which most of the globe is to be subordinated and exploited in accordance with models already developed, tested, and refined through their applications to Indian Country.[219] Overall, elimination of this threat yields the promise of an across-the-board recasting of relations between human beings, and of humans with the rest of nature, which is infinitely more equitable and balanced than anything witnessed since the beginnings of European expansionism more than 500 years ago.[220]

In the alternative, if the current psychopolitical/socioeconomic status quo prevails, things are bound to run their deadly course. Felix Cohen's figurative miners will inevitably share the fate of their canary, the genocide they so smugly allow as an "acceptable cost of doing business" blending perfectly into their own autogenocide until the grim prospect of species extinction has at last been realized. There is, to be sure, a certain unmistakable justice attending the symmetry of this scenario ("What goes around, comes around," as Charlie Manson liked to say).[221] But, surely, we—all of us, settlers as well as natives—owe more to our future generations than to bequeath them a planet so thoroughly irradiated as to deny the possibility of life itself.

6

LIKE SAND IN THE WIND

The Making of an American Indian Diaspora
in the United States

◆◆◆◆◆◆◆◆◆◆◆◆◆

We told them that we would rather die than leave our lands; but we could not help ourselves. They took us down. Many died on the road. Two of my children died. After we reached the new land, all my horses died. The water was very bad. All our cattle died; not one was left. I stayed till one hundred and fifty-eight of my people had died. Then I ran away . . .

—Standing Bear, January 1876

WITHIN THE ARENA OF DIASPORA STUDIES, THE QUESTION OF WHETHER THE field's analytical techniques might be usefully applied to the indigenous population of the United States is seldom raised. In large part, this appears to be due to an unstated presumption on the part of diaspora scholars that because the vast bulk of the native people of the U.S. remain inside the borders of that country, no population dispersal comparable to that experienced by Afroamericans, Asian Americans, Latinos—or, for that matter, Euroamericans—is at issue. Upon even minimal reflection, however, the fallacy imbedded at the core of any such premise is quickly revealed.

To say that a Cherokee remains essentially "at home" so long as s/he resides within the continental territoriality claimed by the U.S. is equivalent to arguing that a Swede displaced to Italy, or a Vietnamese refugee in Korea, would be at home simply because they remain in Europe or Asia. Native Americans, no less than other peoples, can and should be understood as identified with the specific geographical settings by which we came to identify ourselves as peoples.

Mohawks are native to the upstate New York/southern Québec region, not Florida or California. Chiricahua Apaches are indigenous to southern Arizona and northern Sonora, not Oklahoma or Oregon. The matter is not only cultural, although the dimension of culture is crucially important, but political and economic as well.

Struggles by native peoples to retain use and occupancy rights over our traditional territories, and Euroamerican efforts to supplant us, comprise the virtual entirety of U.S./Indian relations since the inception of the republic. All forty of the so-called "Indian Wars" recorded by the federal government were fought over land.[1] On some 400 separate occasions between 1778 and 1871, the Senate of the United States ratified treaties with one or more indigenous peoples by which the latter ceded portions of their landbase to the U.S. In every instance, a fundamental quid pro quo was arrived at: Each indigenous nation formally recognized as such through a treaty ratification was simultaneously acknowledged as retaining a clearly demarcated national homeland within which it might maintain its sociopolitical cohesion and from which it could draw perpetual sustenance, both spiritually and materially.[2]

At least five succeeding generations of American Indians fought, suffered, and died to preserve their peoples' residency in the portions of North America which had been theirs since "time immemorial." In this sense, the fundamental importance they attached to continuing their links to these areas seems unquestionable. By the same token, the extent to which their descendants have been dislocated from these defined, or definable, landbases is the extent to which it can be observed that the conditions of diaspora have been imposed upon the population of Native North America. In this respect, the situation is so unequivocal that a mere sample of statistics deriving from recent census data will suffice to tell the tale:

- By 1980, nearly half of all federally recognized American Indians lived in off-reservation locales, mostly cities. The largest concentration of indigenous people in the country—90,689—was in the Los Angeles metropolitan area.[3] By 1990, the proportion of urban-based Indians is estimated to have swelled to over fifty-five percent.[4]

- All federally unrecognized Indians—a figure which may run several times that of the approximately two million the U.S. officially admits still exist within its borders—are effectively landless and scattered everywhere across the country.[5]

- Texas, the coast of which was once one of the more populous locales for indigenous people, reported a reservation-based Native American population of 859 in 1980.[6] The total Indian population of Texas was reported as being 39,740.[7] Even if this number included only members of peoples native to the area (which it does not), it would still represent an upper 90th percentile reduction from an estimated 1.5 million human beings residing there at the point of first contact with Europeans.[8]

- A veritable vacuum in terms of American Indian reservations and population is now evidenced in most of the area east of the Mississippi River, another region once densely populated by indigenous people. Delaware, Illinois, Indiana, Kentucky, Maryland, New Hampshire, New Jersey, Ohio, Pennsylvania, Rhode Island, Tennessee, Vermont, Virginia, West Virginia show no reservations at all.[9] The total Indian population reported in Vermont in 1980 was 968. In New Hampshire, the figure was 1,297. In Delaware, it was 1,307; in West Virginia, 1,555. The reality is that a greater number of persons indigenous to the North American mainland now live in Hawai'i, far out in the Pacific Ocean, than in any of these easterly states.[10]

The ways in which such deformities in the distribution of indigenous population in the U.S. have come to pass were anything but natural. To the contrary, the major causal factors have consistently derived from a series of official policies implemented over more than two centuries by the federal government of the United States. These have ranged from forced removal during the 1830s to concentration and compulsory assimilation during the 1880s to coerced relocation beginning in the late 1940s. Interspersed through it all have been periods of outright liquidation and dissolution, continuing into the present moment. The purpose of this essay is to explore these policies and their effects on the peoples targeted for such exercises in "social engineering."

THE FORMATIVE PERIOD

During the period immediately following the American War of Independence, the newly formed United States was in a "desperate financial plight [and] saw its salvation in the sale to settlers and land companies of western lands" lying outside the original thirteen colonies.[11] Indeed, the war had been fought in significant part to negate George III's Proclamation of 1763, an edict restricting land acquisition by British subjects to the area east of the Appalachian Mountains and thereby voiding certain speculative real estate interests held by the U.S. Founding Fathers. During the war, loyalty of rank and file soldiers, as well as major creditors, had been maintained through warrants advanced by the Continental Congress with the promise that rebel debts would be retired through issuance of deeds to parcels of Indian land once independence had been attained.[12] A substantial problem for the fledgling republic was that, in the immediate aftermath, it possessed neither the legal nor the physical means to carry through on such commitments.

In the Treaty of Paris, signed on September 3, 1783, England quitclaimed its rights to all present U.S. territory east of the Mississippi. Contrary to subsequent Americana, this action conveyed no bona fide title to any of the Indian lands lying west of the mountains.[13] Rather, it opened the way for the United States to replace Great Britain as the sole entity entitled under prevailing international law to *acquire* Indian land in the region through negotiation and purchase.[14] The U.S.—already an outlaw state by virtue of its armed rejection of lawful Crown authority—appears to have been prepared to seize native property through main force, thereby continuing its initial posture of gross illegality.[15] Confronted by the incipient indigenous alliance advocated by Tecumseh in the Ohio River Valley (known at the time as the "Northwest Territory") and to the south by the powerful Creek and Cherokee confederations, however, the U.S. found itself militarily stalemated all along its western frontier.[16]

The Indian position was considerably reinforced when England went back on certain provisions of the Treaty of Paris, refusing to abandon a line of military installations along the Ohio until the U.S. showed itself willing to comply with minimum standards of international legality, "acknowledging the Indian right in the soil" long since recognized under the Doctrine of Discovery.[17] To the south, Spanish Florida also aligned itself with native nations as a means of holding the rapacious settler population of neighboring Georgia in check.[18] Frustrated, federal authorities had to content themselves with the final dispossession and banishment of such peoples as the Wyandots and Lenni Lenapes (Delawares)—whose homelands fell within the original colonies, and who had been much weakened by more than a century of warfare—to points beyond the 1763 demarcation line. There, these early elements of a U.S.-precipitated indigenous diaspora were taken in by stronger nations such as the Ottawa and Shawnee.[19]

Meanwhile, George Washington's initial vision of a rapid and wholesale expulsion of all Indians east of the Mississippi, expressed in June 1783,[20] was tempered to reflect a more sophisticated process of gradual encroachment explained by General Philip Schuyler of New York in a letter to Congress the following month:

> As our settlements approach their country, [the Indians] must, from the scarcity of game, which that approach will induce, retire farther back, and dispose of their lands, unless they dwindle to nothing, as all savages have done . . . when compelled to live in the vicinity of civilized people, and thus leave us the country without the expense of purchase, trifling as that will probably be.[21]

As Washington himself was to put it a short time later, "[P]olicy and economy point very strongly to the expediency of being on good terms with the Indians, and the propriety of purchasing their Lands in preference to attempting to drive them by force of arms out of their Country . . . The gradual extension of our Settlements will certainly cause the Savage as the Wolf to retire . . . In a word there is nothing to be gained by an Indian War but the Soil they live on and this can be had by purchase at less expense."[22] By 1787, the strategy had become so well accepted that the U.S. was prepared to enact the Northwest Ordinance, codifying a formal renunciation of what it had been calling its "Rights of Conquest" with respect to native peoples: "The utmost good faith shall always be observed towards the Indian; their land shall never be taken from them without their consent; and in their property, rights, and liberty, they shall never be invaded or disturbed—but laws founded in justice and humanity shall from time to time be made, for wrongs done to them, and for preserving peace and friendship with them."[23]

THE ERA OF REMOVAL

By the early years of the nineteenth century, the balance of power in North America had begun to shift. To a certain extent, this was due to a burgeoning of the Angloamerican population, a circumstance actively fostered by government policy. In other respects, it was because of an increasing consolidation of the U.S. state and a generation-long erosion of indigenous strength resulting from the factors delineated in Schuyler's policy of gradual expansion.[24] By 1810, the government was ready to resume what Congress described as the "speedy provision of the extension of the territories of the United States" through means of outright force.[25] Already, in 1803, provision had been made through the Louisiana Purchase for the massive displacement of all eastern Indian nations into what was perceived as the "vast wasteland" west of the Mississippi.[26] The juridical groundwork was laid by the Supreme Court with Chief Justice John Marshall's opinion in *Fletcher v. Peck*, a decision holding that the title of U.S. citizens to parcels of Indian property might be considered valid even though no Indian consent to cede the land had been obtained.[27]

With the defeat of Great Britain in the War of 1812, the defeat of Tecumseh's confederation in 1811, and General Andrew Jackson's defeat of the Creek Red Sticks in 1814, the "clearing" of the east began in earnest.[28] By 1819, the U.S. had wrested eastern Florida from Spain, consummating a process begun in 1810 with assaults upon the western ("panhandle") portion of the territory.[29] Simultaneously, the first of three "Seminole Wars" was begun on the Florida peninsula to subdue an amalgamation of resident Miccosukees, "recalcitrant" Creek refugees, and runaway chattel slaves naturalized as free citizens of the indigenous nations.[30] In 1823, John Marshall reinforced the embryonic position articulated in *Peck* with *Johnson v. McIntosh*, an opinion inverting conventional understandings of indigenous status in international law by holding that U.S. sovereignty superseded that of native nations, even within their own territories.[31] During the same year, President James Monroe promulgated his doctrine professing a unilateral U.S. "right" to circumscribe the sovereignty all other nations in the hemisphere.[32]

In this environment, a tentative policy of Indian "removal" was already underway by 1824, although not codified as law until the Indian Removal Act was passed in 1830. This was followed by John Marshall's opinions, rendered in *Cherokee v. Georgia* and *Worcester v. Georgia*, that Indians comprised "domestic dependent nations," the sovereignty of which was subject to the "higher authority" of the federal government.[33] At that point, the federal program of physically relocating entire nations of people from their eastern homelands to what was then called the "Permanent Indian Territory of Oklahoma" west of the Mississippi became full-fledged and forcible.[34] The primary targets were the prosperous "Five Civilized Tribes" of the Southeast: the Cherokee, Creek, Chickasaw, Choctaw, and Seminole nations. They were rounded up and interned by troops, concentrated in camps until their numbers were sufficient to make efficient their being force-marched at bayonet point, typically without adequate food, shelter, or medical attention, often in the dead of winter, as much as 1,500 miles to their new "homelands."[35]

There were, of course, still those who attempted to mount a military resistance to what was happening. Some, like the Sauk and Fox nations of Illinois, who fought what has come to be known as the "Black Hawk War" against those dispossessing them in 1832, were simply slaughtered en masse.[36] Others, such as the "hard core" of Seminoles who mounted the second war bearing their name in 1835, were forced from the terrain associated with their normal way of life. Once ensconced in forbidding locales like the Everglades, they became for all practical intents and purposes invincible—one group refused to make peace with the U.S. until the early 1960s—but progressively smaller and more diffuse in their demography.[37]

In any event, by 1840 removal had been mostly accomplished (although it lingered as a policy until 1855), with only "the smallest, least offensive, and most thoroughly integrated tribes escaping the pressure to clear the eastern half of the continent from its original inhabitants."[38] The results of the policy were always catastrophic for the victims. For instance, of the approximately 17,000 Cherokees subjected to the removal process, about 8,000 died of disease, exposure and malnutrition along what they called the "Trail of Tears."[39] Additionally:

> The Choctaws are said to have lost fifteen percent of their population, 6,000 out of 40,000; and the Chickasaw . . . surely suffered severe losses as well. By contrast the Creeks and Seminoles are said to have suffered about 50 percent mortality. For the Creeks, this came primarily in the period immediately after removal: for example, "of the 10,000 or more who were resettled in 1836–37. . . an incredible 3,500 died of 'bilious fevers.'"[40]

Nor was this the only cost. Like the Seminoles, portions of each of the targeted peoples managed through various means to avoid removal, remaining in their original territories until their existence was once again recognized by the U.S. during the twentieth century. One consequence was a permanent sociocultural and geographic fragmentation of formerly cohesive groups; while the bulk of the identified populations of these nations now live in and around Oklahoma, smaller segments reside on the tiny "Eastern Cherokee" Reservation in North Carolina (1980 population 4,844); "Mississippi Choctaw" Reservation in Mississippi (population 2,756); the Miccosukee and "Big Cypress," "Hollywood," and "Brighton" Seminole Reservations in Florida (populations 213; 351; 416; and 323, respectively).[41]

An unknown but significant number of Cherokees also went beyond Oklahoma, following their leader, Sequoia, into Mexico in order to escape the reach of the U.S. altogether.[42] This established something of a precedent for other peoples, such as the Kickapoos, a small Mexican "colony" of whom persists to this day.[43] Such dispersal was compounded by the fact that throughout the removal process varying numbers of Indians escaped at various points along the route of march, blending into the surrounding territory and later intermarrying with the incoming settler population. By and large, these people have simply slipped from the historical record, their descendants today inhabiting a long arc of mixed-blood communities extending from northern Georgia and Alabama, through Tennessee and Kentucky, and into the southernmost areas of Illinois and Missouri.[44]

Worse was to come. At the outset of the removal era proper, Andrew Jackson—a leading proponent of the policy, who had ridden into the White House on the public acclaim deriving from his role as commander of the 1814 massacre of the Red Sticks at Horseshoe Bend and a subsequent slaughter of noncombatants during the First

Seminole War—offered a carrot as well as the stick he used to compel tribal "cooperation."[45] In 1829, he promised the Creeks that:

> Your father has provided a country large enough for all of you, and he advises
> you to remove to it. There your white brothers will not trouble you; they will
> have no claim to the land, and you can live upon it, you and all your children,
> as long as the grass grows or the water runs, in peace and plenty. It will be yours
> forever.[46]

Jackson was, to put it bluntly, lying through his teeth. Even as he spoke, he was
aware that the Mississippi, that ostensible border between the U.S. and Permanent Indian Territory proclaimed by Thomas Jefferson and others, had already been breached
by the rapidly consolidating states of Louisiana, Arkansas, and Missouri in the south,
Iowa, Wisconsin, and Minnesota in the north.[47] Nor could Jackson not have known
that his close friend, Senator Thomas Hart Benton of Missouri, had stipulated as early
as 1825 that the Rocky Mountains rather than the Mississippi should serve as an
"everlasting boundary" of the U.S.[48] By the time the bulk of removal was completed a
decade later, Angloamerican settlement was reaching well into Kansas. Their cousins
who had infiltrated the Mexican province of Texas had revolted, proclaimed themselves an independent republic, and were negotiating for statehood. The eyes of empire had also settled on all of Mexico north of the Río Grande, and the British portion
of Oregon as well.[49]

Peoples such as the Shawnee and Potawatomi, Lenni Lenape and Wyandot, Peoria,
Kickapoo, Sac, and Fox, already removed from their eastern homelands, were again
compulsorily relocated as the western Indian Territory was steadily reduced in size.[50]
This time, they were mostly shifted southward into an area eventually conforming to
the boundaries of the present state of Oklahoma. Ultimately, sixty-seven separate nations (or parts of nations), only six of them truly indigenous to the land at issue, were
forced into this relatively small dumping ground.[51] When Oklahoma, too, became a
state in 1907, most of the territorial compartments reserved for the various Indian
groups were simply dissolved. Today, although Oklahoma continues to report the second largest native population of any state, only the Osage retain a reserved landbase
which is nominally their own.[52]

SUBJUGATION IN THE WEST

The U.S. "Winning of the West" which began around 1850—that is, immediately after the northern half of Mexico was taken in a brief war of conquest—was, if anything, more brutal than the clearing of the east.[53] Most of the U.S. wars against native
people were waged during the following thirty-five years, under what has been termed
an official "rhetoric of extermination."[54]

The means employed in militarily subjugating the indigenous nations of California and southern Oregon, the Great Plains, Great Basin, and northern region of the Sonora Desert devolved upon a lengthy series of wholesale massacres. Representative of these are the slaughter of about 150 Lakotas at Blue River (Nebraska) in 1854, some five hundred Shoshones at Bear River (Idaho) in 1863, as many as 250 Cheyennes and Arapahos at Sand Creek (Colorado) in 1864, perhaps two hundred Cheyennes on the Washita River (Oklahoma) in 1868, 175 Piegans at the Marias River (Montana) in 1870, and at least a hundred Cheyennes at Camp Robinson (Nebraska) in 1878. The parade of official atrocities was capped by the butchery of more than three hundred unarmed Lakotas at Wounded Knee (South Dakota) in 1890.[55]

Other means employed by the government to reduce its native opponents to a state of what it hoped would be abject subordination included the four-year internment of the entire Navajo (Diné) Nation in a concentration camp at the Bosque Redondo, outside Fort Sumner, New Mexico, beginning in 1864. The Diné, who had been force-marched in what they called the "Long Walk," a three-hundred-mile trek from their Arizona homeland, were held under abysmal conditions, with neither adequate food nor shelter, and died like flies. Approximately half perished before their release in 1868.[56] Similarly, if less dramatically, food supplies to the Lakotas were cut off in 1877—militarily defeated the year before, they were being held under army guard at the time—until starvation compelled their leaders to "cede" the Black Hills area to the U.S.[57] The assassination of resistance leaders such as the Lakotas Crazy Horse (1877) and Sitting Bull (1890) was also a commonly used technique.[58] Other recalcitrant figures like Geronimo (Chiricahua Apache) and Satanta (Kiowa) were separated from their people by being imprisoned in remote facilities like Fort Marion, Florida.[59]

In addition to these official actions, which the U.S. Census Bureau acknowledged in an 1894 summary as having caused a minimum of 45,000 native deaths, there was a far greater attrition resulting from what were described as "individual affairs."[60] These took the form of Angloamerican citizens at large killing Indians, often systematically, under a variety of quasiofficial circumstances. In Dakota Territory, for example, a $200 bounty for Indian scalps was paid in the territorial capital of Yankton during the 1860s; the local military commander, General Alfred Sully, is known to have privately contracted for a pair of Lakota skulls with which to adorn the city.[61] In Texas, first as a republic and then as a state, authorities also "placed a bounty upon the scalp of any Indian brought in to a government office—man, woman, or child, no matter what 'tribe'—no questions asked."[62] In California and Oregon, "the enormous decrease [in the native population of 1800] from about a quarter-million to less than 20,000 [in 1870 was] due chiefly to the cruelties and wholesale massacres perpetrated by the miners and early settlers."[63]

Much of the killing in California and southern Oregon Territory resulted, directly and indirectly, from the discovery of gold in 1848 and the subsequent influx of miners and settlers. Newspaper accounts document the atrocities, as do oral histories of the California Indians today. It was not uncommon for small groups or villages to be attacked by immigrants . . . and virtually wiped out overnight.[64]

It has been estimated that Indian deaths resulting from this sort of direct violence may have run as high as a half-million by 1890.[65] All told, the indigenous population of the continental United States, which may still have been as great as two million when the country was founded, had been reduced to well under 250,000 by 1890.[66] As the noted demographer Sherburn F. Cook has observed, "The record speaks for itself. No further commentary is necessary."[67]

Under these conditions, the U.S. was able to shuffle native peoples around at will. The Northern Cheyennes and closely allied Arapahos, for instance, were shipped from their traditional territory in Montana's Powder River watershed to the reservation of their southern cousins in Oklahoma in 1877. After the Cheyenne remnants, more than a third of whom had died within a year of malaria and other diseases endemic to this alien environment, made a desperate attempt to return home in 1878, they were granted a reservation in the north country, but not before the bulk of them had been killed by army troops. Moreover, they were permanently separated from the Arapahos, who were "temporarily" assigned to the Wind River Reservation of their hereditary enemies, the Shoshones, in Wyoming.[68]

A faction of the Chiricahua Apaches who showed signs of continued "hostility" to U.S. domination in the 1880s were yanked from their habitat in southern Arizona and "resettled" around Fort Sill, Oklahoma.[69] Hinmaton Yalatkit (Chief Joseph) of the Nez Percé and other leaders of that people's legendary attempt to escape the army and flee to Canada were also deposited in Oklahoma, far from the Idaho valley they'd fought to retain.[70] Most of the Santee Dakotas of Minnesota's woodlands ended up on the windswept plains of Nebraska, while a handful of their relatives remained behind on tiny plots which are now called the "Upper" and "Lower Sioux" reservations.[71] A portion of the Oneidas, who had fought on the side of the rebels during their war for independence, were moved to a small reservation near Green Bay, Wisconsin.[72] An even smaller reserve was provided in the same area for residual elements of Connecticut's Mahegans, Mohegans, and other peoples, all of them lumped together under the heading "Stockbridge-Munsee Indians."[73] On and on it went.

ALLOTMENT AND ASSIMILATION

With the native ability to militarily resist U.S. territorial ambitions finally quelled, the government moved first to structurally negate any meaningful residue of national status on the part of indigenous peoples, and then to dissolve them altogether. The opening round of this drive came in 1871, with the attachment of a rider to the annual congressional appropriations act suspending any further treatymaking with Indians. This was followed, in 1885, with passage of the Major Crimes Act, extending U.S. jurisdiction directly over reserved Indian territories for the first time. Beginning with seven felonies delineated in the initial statutory language, and combined with the

Supreme Court's opinion in *U.S. v. Kagama* that Congress possessed a unilateral and "incontrovertible right" to exercise its authority over Indians as it saw fit, the 1885 act opened the door to subsequent enactment of the more than five thousand federal laws presently regulating every aspect of reservation life and affairs.[74]

In 1887, Congress passed the General Allotment Act, a measure designed expressly to destroy what was left of the basic indigenous socioeconomic cohesion by eradicating traditional systems of collective landholding. Under provision of the statute, each Indian identified as such by demonstrating "one-half or more degree of Indian blood" was to be issued an individual deed to a specific parcel of land—160 acres per family head, eighty acres per orphan or single person over eighteen years of age, and forty acres per dependent child—within existing reservation boundaries. Each Indian was required to accept U.S. citizenship in order to receive his or her allotment. Those who refused, such as a substantial segment of the Cherokee "full-blood" population, were left landless.[75]

Generally speaking, those of mixed ancestry whose "blood quantum" fell below the the required level were summarily excluded from receiving allotments. In many cases, the requirement was construed by officials as meaning that an applicant's "blood" had to have accrued from a single people; persons whose cumulative blood quantum derived from intermarriage between several native peoples were thus often excluded as well. In other instances, arbitrary geographic criteria were also employed; all Cherokees, Creeks, and Choctaws living in Arkansas, for example, were not only excluded from allotment, but permanently denied recognition as members of their respective nations as well.[76] Once all eligible Indians had been assigned their allotments within a given reservation—usually from the worst land available therein—the remainder of the reserved territory was declared "surplus" and opened to nonindian homesteaders, corporate acquisition, and conversion into federal or state parks and forests.[77]

Under the various allotment programs, the most valuable land was the first to go. Settlers went after the rich grasslands of Kansas, Nebraska, and the Dakotas; the dense black-soil forests of Minnesota and Wisconsin; and the wealthy oil and gas lands of Oklahoma. In 1887, for example, the Sisseton Sioux of South Dakota owned 918,000 acres of rich virgin land on their reservation. But since there were only two thousand of them, allotment left more than 600,000 acres for European American settlers . . . The Chippewas of Minnesota lost their rich timber lands; once each member had claimed his [or her] land, the government leased the rest to timber corporations. The Colvilles of northeastern Washington lost their lands to cattlemen, who fraudulently claimed mineral rights there. In Montana and Wyoming the Crows lost more than two million acres, and the Nez Percés had to cede communal grazing ranges in Idaho. All sixty-seven of the tribes in Indian Territory underwent allotment . . . On the Flathead Reservation [in Montana]—which included Flatheads, Pend Oreilles, Kutenais, and Spokanes . . . the federal government opened 1.1 million acres to settlers. A similar story prevailed throughout the country.[78]

By the time the allotment process had run its course in 1934, the residue of native land holdings in the U.S. had been reduced from approximately 150 million acres to less than fifty million.[79] Of this, more than two-thirds consisted of arid or semiarid terrain deemed useless for agriculture, gazing, or other productive purposes. The remaining one-third had been leased at extraordinarily low rates to nonindian farmers and ranchers by local Indian agents exercising "almost dictatorial powers" over remaining reservation property.[80]

Indians across the country were left in a state of extreme destitution as a result of allotment and attendant leasing practices. Worse, the situation was guaranteed to be exacerbated over succeeding generations insofar as what was left of the reservation landbase, already insufficient to support its occupants at a level of mere subsistence, could be foreseen to become steadily more so as the native population recovered from the genocide perpetrated against it.[81] A concomitant of allotment was thus an absolute certainty that ever increasing numbers of Indians would be forced from what remained nominally their own land during the twentieth century, dispersed into the vastly more numerous American society at large. There, it was predictable (and often predicted) that they would be "digested," disappearing once and for all as anything distinctly Indian in terms of sociocultural, political, or even racial identity.[82] The record shows that such outcomes were anything but unintentional.

> The purpose of all this was "assimilation," as federal policymakers described their purpose, or—to put the matter more unabashedly—to bring about the destruction and disappearance of American Indian peoples as such. In the words of Francis E. Leupp, Commissioner of Indian Affairs from 1905 through 1909, the Allotment Act in particular should be viewed as a "mighty pulverizing engine for breaking up the tribal mass" which stood in the way of complete Euroamerican hegemony in North America. Or, to quote Indian Commissioner Charles Burke a decade later, "[I]t is not desirable or consistent with the general welfare to promote tribal characteristics and organization."[83]

The official stance was consecrated in the Supreme Court's determination in the 1903 *Lone Wolf v. Hitchcock* opinion—extended from John Marshall's "domestic dependent nation thesis of the early 1830s—that the U.S. possessed "plenary" (full) power over all matters involving Indian affairs. In part, this meant the federal government was unilaterally assigning itself perpetual "trust" prerogatives to administer or dispose of native assets, whether these were vested in land, minerals, cash, or any other medium, regardless of Indian needs or desires.[84] Congress then consolidated its position with passage of the 1906 Burke Act, designating the Secretary of the Interior as permanent trustee over Indian Country. In 1924, a number of loose ends were cleaned up with passage of the Indian Citizenship Act, imposing U.S. citizenship upon all native people who had not otherwise been naturalized. The law was applied across the board to all Indians, whether they desired citizenship or not, and thus included those who had forgone allotments rather than accept it.[85]

Meanwhile, the more physical dimensions of assimilationist policy were coupled to a process of ideological conditioning designed to render native children susceptible to dislocation and absorption by the dominant society. In the main, this assumed the form of a compulsory boarding school system administered by the Interior Department's Bureau of Indian Affairs (BIA) wherein large numbers of indigenous children were taken, often forcibly, to facilities remote from their families and communities. Once there, the youngsters were prevented from speaking their languages, practicing their religions, wearing their customary clothing or their hair in traditional fashion, or in any other way overtly associating themselves with their own cultures and traditions. Instead, they were indoctrinated—typically for a decade or more—in Christian doctrine and European values such as the "work ethic." During the summers, they were frequently "farmed out" to Euroamerican "foster homes" where they were further steeped in the dominant society's views of their peoples and themselves.[86]

> Attendance was made compulsory [for all native children, aged five to eighteen] and the agent was made responsible for keeping the schools filled, by persuasion if possible, by withholding rations and annuities from the parents, and by other means if necessary . . . [Students] who were guilty of misbehavior might either receive corporal punishment or be imprisoned in the guardhouse [a special "reform school" established to handle "incorrigible" students who clung to their traditions] . . . A sincere effort was made to develop the type of school that would destroy tribal ways.[87]

The intention of this was, according to federal policymakers and many of its victims alike, to create generations of American Indian youth who functioned intellectually as "little white people," facilitating the rapid dissolution of traditional native cultures desired by federal policymakers.[88] In combination with a program in which native children were put out for wholesale adoption by Euroamerican families, the effect upon indigenous peoples was devastating.[89] This systematic transfer of children not only served to accelerate the outflow of Indians from reservation and reservation-adjacent settings, but the return of individuals mentally conditioned to conduct themselves as nonindians escalated the rate at which many native societies unraveled within the reservation contexts themselves.[90]

The effects of the government's allotment and assimilation programs are reflected in the demographic shifts evidenced throughout Indian Country from 1910 through 1950. In the former year, only 0.4 percent of all identified Indians lived in urban locales. By 1930, the total had grown to 9.9 percent. As of 1950, the total had grown to 13.4 percent. Simultaneously, the displacement of native people from reservations to off-reservation rural areas was continuing apace.[91] In 1900, this involved only about 3.5 percent of all Indians. By 1930, the total had swelled to around 12.5 percent and, by 1950, it had reached nearly eighteen percent.[92] Hence, in the latter year, nearly one-third of the federally recognized Indians in the United States had been dispersed to locales other than those government officials had defined as being "theirs."

REORGANIZATION AND COLONIZATION

It is likely, all things being equal, that the Indian policies with which the United States ushered in the twentieth century would have led inexorably to a complete eradication of the reservation system and the corresponding disappearance of American Indians as distinct peoples by some point around 1950. There can be no question but that such a final consolidation of its internal landbase would have complemented the phase of transoceanic expansionism into which the U.S. entered quite unabashedly during the 1890s.[93] That things did not follow this course seems mainly due to a pair of ironies, one geological and the other unwittingly embedded in the bizarre status of "quasi-sovereignty" increasingly imposed upon native nations by federal jurists and policy-makers over the preceding hundred years.

As regards the first of these twin twists of fate, authorities were becoming increasingly aware by the late 1920s that the "worthless" residue of territory to which indigenous people were consigned was turning out to be extraordinarily endowed with mineral wealth. Already, in 1921, an exploratory team from Standard Oil had come upon what it took to be substantial fossil fuel deposits on the Navajo Reservation.[94] During the next three decades, it would be discovered just how great a proportion of U.S. "domestic" resources lay within American Indian reservations. For example:

> Western reservations in particular . . . possess vast amounts of coal, oil, shale oil, natural gas, timber, and uranium. More than 40 percent of the national reserves of low sulfur, strippable coal, 80 percent of the nation's uranium reserves, and billions of barrels of shale oil exist on reservation land. On the 15-million-acre Navajo Reservation, there are approximately 100 million barrels of oil, 25 trillion cubic feet of natural gas, 80 million pounds of uranium, and 50 billion tons of coal. The 440,000-acre Northern Cheyenne Reservation in Montana sits atop a 60-foot-thick layer of coal. In New Mexico, geologists estimate that the Jicarilla Apache Reservation possesses 2 trillion cubic feet of natural gas and as much as 154 million barrels of oil.[95]

This led directly to the second quirk. The more sophisticated federal officials, even then experiencing the results of opening up Oklahoma's lush oil fields to unrestrained corporate competition, realized the extent of the disequilibriums and inefficiencies involved in this line of action when weighed against the longer-term needs of U.S. industrial development.[96] Only by retaining its "trust authority" over reservation assets would the government continue to be in a position to dictate which resources would be exploited, in what quantities, by whom, at what cost, and for what purpose, allowing the North American political economy to evolve in ways preferred by the country's financial élite.[97] Consequently, it was quickly perceived as necessary that both Indians and Indian Country be preserved, at least to some extent, as a facade behind which the "socialistic" process of central economic planning might occur.

For the scenario to work in practice, it was vital that the reservation-based indigenous nations be made to appear "self-governing" enough to be exempt from the usual requirements of the U.S. "free market" system whenever this might be convenient to their federal "guardians." On the other hand, they could never become independent or autonomous enough to assume control over their own economic destinies, asserting demands that equitable royalty rates be paid for the extraction of their ores, for example, or that profiting corporations underwrite the expense of environmental cleanup once mining operations had been concluded.[98] In effect, the idea was that many indigenous nations should be maintained as outright internal colonies of the United States rather than being liquidated out of hand.[99] All that was needed to accomplish this was the creation of a mechanism through which the illusion of limited Indian self-rule might be extended.

The vehicle for this purpose materialized in 1934, with passage of the Indian Reorganization Act, or "IRA," as it is commonly known. Under provision of this statute, the traditional governing bodies of most indigenous nations were supplanted by "Tribal Councils," the structure of which was devised in Washington, D.C., functioning within parameters of formal constitutions written by BIA officials.[100] A democratic veneer was maintained by staging a referendum on each reservation prior to its being reorganized, but federal authorities simply manipulated the outcomes to achieve the desired results.[101] The newly installed IRA councils were patterned much more closely upon the model of corporate boards than of governments, and possessed little power other than to sign-off on business agreements. Even at that, they were completely and "voluntarily" subordinated to U.S. interests: "All decisions of any consequence (in thirty-three separate areas of consideration) rendered by these 'tribal councils' were made 'subject to the approval of the Secretary of the Interior or his delegate,' the Commissioner of Indian Affairs."[102]

One entirely predictable result of this arrangement has been that an inordinate amount of mining, particularly that related to "energy development," has occurred on Indian reservations since the mid-to-late 1940s. Virtually *all* uranium mining and milling during the life of the U.S. Atomic Energy Commission (AEC) ore-buying program (1954–81) occurred on reservation land; Anaconda's Jackpile Mine, located at the Laguna Pueblo in New Mexico, was the largest open pit uranium extraction operation in the world until it was phased out in 1979.[103] Every year, enough power is generated by Arizona's Four Corners Power Plant alone—every bit of it from coal mined at Black Mesa, on the Navajo Reservation—to light the lights of Tucson and Phoenix for two decades, and present plans include a four-fold expansion of Navajo coal extraction.[104] Throughout the West, the story is the same.

On the face of it, the sheer volume of resource "development" in Indian Country over the past half-century should—even under disadvantageous terms—have translated into *some* sort of "material improvement" in the lot of indigenous people. Yet the mining leases offered to selected corporations by the BIA "in behalf of" their native "wards"—and duly endorsed by the IRA councils—have consistently paid such a meager fraction of prevailing market royalty rates that no such advancement has been discernable. Probably the best terms were those obtained by the Navajo Nation in 1976, a contract paying a royalty of fifty-five cents per ton for coal; this amounted to eight percent of market price at a time when Interior Secretary Cecil Andrus admitted the *minimum* rate paid for coal mined in off-reservation settings was 12.5 percent (more typically, it was upwards of fifteen percent).[105] Simultaneously, a 17.5 cents per ton royalty was being paid for coal on the Crow Reservation in Montana, a figure which was raised to forty cents—less than half the market rate—only after years of haggling.[106] At issue are not profits, but the sort of "super-profits" usually associated with U.S. domination of economies elsewhere in the world.[107]

Nor has the federally coordinated corporate exploitation of the reservations translated into wage income for Indians. As of 1989, the government's own data indicated that reservation unemployment nationwide still hovered in the mid-sixtieth percentile, with some locales running persistently in the ninetieth.[108] Most steady jobs involved administering or enforcing the federal order, reservation by reservation. Such "business-related" employment as existed tended to be temporary, menial, and paid the minimum wage, a matter quite reflective of the sort of transient, extractive industry—which brings its cadre of permanent, skilled labor with it—the BIA had encouraged in Indian Country.[109] Additionally, the impact of extensive mining and associated activities had done much to disrupt the basis for possible continuation of traditional self-sufficiency, destroying considerable acreage which held potential as grazing or subsistence garden plots.[110] In this sense, U.S. governmental and corporate activities have "underdeveloped" Native North America in classic fashion.[111]

Overall, according to a federal study completed in 1988, reservation-based Indians experienced every indicia of extreme impoverishment: by far the lowest annual and lifetime incomes of any North American population group, highest rate of infant mortality (up to 14.5 times the national average), highest rates of death from plague disease, malnutrition, and exposure, highest rate of teen suicide, and so on. The average life expectancy of reservation-based Native American males is 44.6 years, that of females about three years longer.[112] The situation is much more indicative of a Third World context than of rural areas in a country that claims to be the world's "most advanced industrial state." Indeed, the poignant observation of many Latinos regarding their relationship to the U.S., that "your wealth is our poverty," is as appropriate to the archipelago of Indian reservations in North America itself as it is to the South American continent. By any estimation, the "open veins of Native America" created by the IRA have been an incalculable boon to the maturation of the U.S. economy, while Indians continue to pay the price by living in the most grinding sort of poverty.[113]

And there is worse. One of the means used by the government to maximize corporate profits in Indian Country over the years—again rubber-stamped by the IRA councils—has been to omit clauses requiring corporate reclamation of mined lands from leasing instruments. Similarly, the cost of doing business on reservations has been pared to the bone (and profitability driven up) by simply waiving environmental protection standards in most instances.[114] Such practices have spawned ecological catastrophe in many locales. As the impact of the Four Corners plant, one of a dozen coal-fired electrical generation facilities currently "on-line" on the Navajo reservation, has been described elsewhere:

> The five units of the 2,075 megawatt power plant have been churning out city-bound electricity and local pollution since 1969. The plant burns ten tons of coal per minute—five million tons per year—spewing three hundred tons of fly-ash and other waste particulates into the air each day. The black cloud hangs over ten thousand acres of the once-pristine San Juan River Valley. The deadly plume was the only visible evidence of human enterprise seen from the Gemini-12 satellite which photographed the earth from 150 miles in space. Less visible, but equally devastating is the fact that since 1968 the coal mining operations and power plant requirements have been extracting 2,700 gallons from the Black Mesa water table each minute—60 million gallons per year—causing extreme desertification of the area, and even the sinking of some ground by as much as twelve feet.[115]

Corporations engaged in uranium mining and milling on the Navajo Reservation and at Laguna were also absolved by the BIA of responsibility for cleaning up upon completion of their endeavors, with the result that hundreds of tailings piles were simply abandoned during the 1970s and '80s.[116] A fine sand retaining about eighty-five percent of the radioactive content of the original ore, the tailings constitute a massive source of wind-blown carcinogenic/mutagenic contaminants affecting all persons and livestock residing within a wide radius of each pile.[117] Both ground and surface water have also been heavily contaminated with radioactive byproducts throughout the Four Corners region.[118] In the Black Hills region, the situation is much the same.[119] At its Hanford Nuclear Weapons Facility, located near the Yakima Reservation in Washington State, the AEC itself secretly discharged some 440 billion gallons of plutonium, strontium, celsium, tritium, and other high-level radioactive contaminants into the local aquifer between 1955 and 1989.[120]

Given that the half-life of the substances involved is as long as 250,000 years, the magnitude of the disaster inflicted upon Native North America by IRA colonialism should not be underestimated. The Los Alamos National Scientific laboratory observed in its February 1978 *Mini-Report* that the only "solution" its staff could conceive of to the problems presented by wind-blown radioactive contaminants would be "to zone the land into uranium mining and milling districts so as to forbid human habitation." Similarly:

> A National Academy of Sciences (NAS) report states bluntly that [reclamation after any sort of mining] cannot be done in areas with less than 10 inches of rainfall a year; the rainfall over most of the Navajo Nation [and many other western reservations] ranges from six to ten inches a year. The NAS suggests that such areas be spared development or honestly labeled "national sacrifice areas."[121]

Tellingly, the two areas considered most appropriate by the NAS for designation as "national sacrifices"—the Four Corners and Black Hills regions—are those containing the Navajo and "Sioux Complex" of reservations, the largest remaining blocks of acknowledged Indian land and concentrations of landbased indigenous population in the U.S. For this reason, many American Indian activists have denounced both the NAS scheme and the process of environmental destruction which led up to it, as involving not only National Sacrifice Areas, but "National Sacrifice Peoples" as well.[122] At the very least, having the last of their territory zoned "so as to forbid human habitation" would precipitate an ultimate dispersal of each impacted people, causing its disappearance as a "human group" per se.[123] As American Indian Movement leader Russell Means has put it, "It's genocide . . . no more, no less."[124]

Regardless of whether a policy of national sacrifice is ever implemented in the manner envisioned by the NAS, it seems fair to observe that the conditions of dire poverty and environmental degradation fostered on Indian reservations have contributed heavily to the making of the contemporary native diaspora in the United States. In combination with the constriction of the indigenous landbase brought about through earlier policies of removal, concentration, allotment, and assimilation, they have created a strong and ever-increasing pressure upon reservation residents to "cooperate" with other modern federal programs meant to facilitate the outflow and dispersal of Indians from their residual landbase. Chief among these have been termination and relocation.

TERMINATION AND RELOCATION

As the IRA method of administering Indian Country took hold, the government returned to such tasks as "trimming the fat" from federal expenditures allocated to support Indians, largely through manipulation of the size and disposition of the recognized indigenous population.

> By 1940, the . . . system of colonial governance on American Indian reservations was largely in place. Only the outbreak of World War II slowed the pace of corporate exploitation, a matter that retarded initiation of maximal "development" activities until the early 1950s. By then, the questions concerning federal and corporate planners had become somewhat technical: what to do with those indigenous nations which had refused reorganization? How to remove the portion of Indian population on even the reorganized reservations, whose sheer physical presence served as a barrier to wholesale strip mining and other profitable enterprises anticipated by the U.S. business community?[125]

The first means to this end was found in a partial resumption of nineteenth century assimilationist policies, focused this time on specific peoples, or parts of peoples, rather than upon Indians as a whole. On August 1, 1953, Congress approved House Resolution 108, a measure by which the federal legislature empowered itself to enact statutes "terminating" (i.e., withdrawing recognition from, and thus unilaterally dissolving) selected native peoples, typically those who had rejected reorganization, or lacked the kind of resources necessitating their maintenance under the IRA.[126]

> Among the [nations] involved were the comparatively large and wealthy Menominee of Wisconsin and the Klamath of Oregon—both owners of extensive timber resources. Also passed were acts to terminate . . . the Indians of western Oregon, small Paiute bands in Utah, and the mixed-bloods of the Uintah and Ouray Reservations. Approved, too, was legislation to transfer administrative responsibility for the Alabama and Coushatta Indians to the state of Texas . . . Early in the first session of the Eighty-Fourth Congress, bills were submitted to [terminate the] Wyandotte, Ottawa, and Peoria [nations] of Oklahoma. These were enacted early in August of 1956, a month after passage of legislation directing the Colville Confederated Tribes of Washington to come up with a termination plan of their own . . . During the second administration of President Dwight D. Eisenhower, Congress enacted three termination bills relating to . . . the Choctaw of Oklahoma, for whom the termination process was never completed, the Catawba of South Carolina, and the Indians of the southern California rancherias.[127]

It is instructive that the man chosen to implement the policy was Dillon S. Myer, an Indian Commissioner whose only apparent "job qualification" was having headed up the internment program targeting Japanese Americans during the Second World War.[128] In all, 109 indigenous nations encompassing more than 35,000 people were terminated before the liquidation process had run its course during the early 1960s.[129] Only a handful, like the Menominee and the Siletz of Oregon, were ever "reinstated."[130] Suddenly landless, mostly poor, and largely unemployed, the others were scattered like sand in the wind.[131] In this, they were joined by a rapidly swelling exodus of people from unterminated reservations, a circumstance fostered by yet another federal program.

Passed in 1956, the "Relocation Act" (P.L. 959) followed a steady diminishment throughout the first half of the decade of federal allocations to provide assistance to people living on reservations. The statute provided funding to underwrite the expenses of any Indian agreeing to move to an urban area, establish a residence, and undergo a brief period of job training. The *quid pro quo* was that each person applying for such relocation was required to sign an agreement that s/he would never return to his or her reservation to live. It was also specified that all federal support would be withdrawn after relocatees had spent a short period—often no more than six weeks— "adjusting" to city life.[132] Under the conditions of near-starvation on many reservations, there were many takers; nearly 35,000 people signed up to move to places like Los Angeles, Minneapolis, San Francisco, Chicago, Denver, Phoenix, Seattle, and Boston during the period 1957–59 alone.[133]

Although there was ample early indication that relocation was bearing disastrous fruit for those who underwent it—all that was happening was that relocatees were ex-changing the familiar squalor of reservation life for that of the alien Indian ghettos that shortly emerged in most major cities—the government accelerated the program during the 1960s. As a result of termination and relocation during the fifties, the pro-portion of native people who had been "urbanized" rose dramatically, from 13.5 per-cent at the beginning of the decade to 27.9 percent at the end. During the sixties, relocation alone drove the figure upwards to 44.5 percent. During the 1970s, as the program began to be phased out, the rate of Indian urbanization decreased sharply, with the result that the proportion had risen to "only" forty-nine percent by 1980.[134] Even without a formal federal relocation effort on a national scale, the momentum of what had been set in motion over an entire generation carried the number into the mid-fiftieth percentile by 1990, and there is no firm indication the trend is abating.[135]

Despite much protest to the contrary, those who "migrated" to the cities under the auspices of termination and relocation have already begun to join the legions of others, no longer recognized as Indians even by other Indians, who were previously discarded and forgotten along the tortuous route from 1776 to the present.[136] Cut off irrevocably from the centers of their sociocultural existence, they have increasingly adopted arbi-trary and abstract methods to signify their "Indianness." Federally-sanctioned "Certifi-cates of Tribal Enrollment" have come to replace tangible participation in the political life of their nations as emblems of membership. Federally issued "Certificates of Degree of Indian Blood" have replaced discernible commitment to Indian interests as the ulti-mate determinant of identity.[137] In the end, by embracing such "standards," Indians are left knowing no more of being Indian than do nonindians. The process is a cultural form of what, in the physical arena, has been termed "autogenocide."[138]

LOOKING AHEAD

The Indian policies undertaken by the United States during the two centuries since its inception appear on the surface to have been varied, even at times contradictory. Openly genocidal at times, they have more often been garbed, however thinly, in the attire of "humanitarianism." In fact, as the matter was put by Alexis de Tocqueville, the great French commentator on the early American experience, it would occasionally have been "impossible to destroy men with more respect to the laws of humanity."[139] Always, however, there was an underlying consistency in the sentiments which begat policy: to bring about the total dispossession and disappearance of North America's indigenous population. It was this fundamental coherence in U.S. aims, invariably de-nied by responsible scholars and officials alike, which caused Adolf Hitler to ground his own notions of *lebensraumpolitik* ("politics of living space") in the U.S. example.[140]

> Neither Spain nor Britain should be the models of German expansion, but the Nordics of North America, who had ruthlessly pushed aside an inferior race to win for themselves soil and territory for the future. To undertake this essential

task, sometimes difficult, always cruel—this was Hitler's version of the White Man's Burden.[141]

As early as 1784, A British observer remarked that the intent of the fledgling United States with regard to American Indians was that of "extirpating them totally from the face of the earth, men, women and children."[142] In 1825, Secretary of State Henry Clay opined that U.S. Indian policy should be predicated on a presumption that the "Indian race" was "destined to extinction" in the face of persistent expansion by "superior" Anglo-Saxon "civilization."[143] During the 1870s, General Phil Sheridan is known to have called repeatedly the for "complete extermination" of targeted native groups as a means of making the West safe for repopulation by Euroamericans.[144] Subsequent assimilationists demanded the disappearance of any survivors through cultural and genetic absorption by their conquerors.[145] Well into the twentieth century, Euroamerica as a whole typically referred—often hopefully—to indigenous people as "the vanishing race," decimated and ultimately subsumed by the far greater number of invaders who had moved in upon their land.[146]

Many of the worst U.S. practices associated with these sensibilities have long since been suspended (arguably, because their goals were accomplished). Yet, largescale and deliberate dislocation of native people from their land is anything but an historical relic. Probably the most prominent current example is that of the Big Mountain Diné, perhaps the largest remaining enclave of traditionally oriented Indians in the United States. Situated astride an estimated twenty-four billion tons of the most accessible low sulfur coal in North America, the entire 13,500 person population of the Big Mountain area is even now being forcibly expelled to make way for the Peabody corporation's massive shovels. There being no place left on the remainder of the Navajo Reservation to accommodate their sheepherding way of life, the refugees, many of them elderly, are being "resettled" in off-reservation towns like Flagstaff, Arizona.[147] Some have been sent to Phoenix, Denver, and Los Angeles. All suffer extreme trauma and other maladies resulting from the destruction of their community and consequent "transition."[148]

Another salient illustration is that of the Western Shoshone. Mostly resident to a vast expanse of the Nevada desert secured by their ancestors in the 1863 Treaty of Ruby Valley, the Shoshones have suffered the fate of becoming the "most bombed nation on earth" by virtue of the U.S. having located the majority of its nuclear weapons testing facilities in the southern portion of their homeland since 1950. During the late seventies, despite being unable to demonstrate that it had ever acquired valid title to the territory the Shoshones call Newe Segobia, the government began to move into the northern area as well, stating an intent to construct the MX missile system there. While the MX plan has been dropped, the Shoshones are still being pushed off their land, "freeing" it for use in such endeavors as nuclear waste dumps like the one at Yucca Mountain.[149]

In Alaska, where nearly two hundred indigenous peoples were instantly converted into "village corporations" by the 1971 Alaska Native Claims Settlement Act, there is a distinct possibility that the entire native population of about 22,000 will be displaced by the demands of tourism, North Slope oil extraction, and other "developmental" enterprises by some point early in the twenty-first century. Already, their landbase has been constricted to a complex of tiny "townships" and their traditional economy mostly eradicated by the impacts of commercial fishing, whaling, and sealing, as well as the effects of increasing Arctic industrialization on regional caribou herds and other game animals.[150] Moreover, there is a plan—apparently conceived in all seriousness—to divert the waterflow of the Yukon River southward all the way to the Río Grande, an expedient to supporting continued nonindian population growth in the arid regions of the "lower forty-eight" states and creating the agribusiness complex in the northern Mexican provinces of Sonora and Chihuahua envisioned in the North American Free Trade Agreement.[151] It seems certain that no traditional indigenous society can be expected to stand up against such an environmental onslaught.

Eventually, if such processes are allowed to run their course, the probability is that a "Final Solution of the Indian Question" will be achieved.[152] The key to this will rest, not in an official return to the pattern of nineteenth-century massacres or the emergence of some Auschwitz-style extermination program, but in the erosion of sociocultural integrity and confusion of identity afflicting any people subjected to conditions of diaspora. Like water flowing from a leaking bucket, the last self-consciously Indian people will pass into oblivion silently, unnoticed and unremarked. The deaths of cultures destroyed by such means usually occur in this fashion, with a faint whimper rather than resistance and screams of agony.[153]

There are, perhaps, glimmers of hope flickering upon the horizon. One of the more promising is the incipient International Convention on the Rights of Indigenous Peoples. Drafted over the past decade by the United Nations Working Group on Indigenous Populations, the instrument is due for submission to the General Assembly at some point in the near future. When it is ratified, the Convention could at last extend to native peoples the essential international legal protections enjoyed by their colonizers the world over.[154] Should it be adhered to by this "nation of laws," the instrument will effectively bar the United States from completing its quietly ongoing drive to obliterate the remains of Native North America. If not—and the U.S. has historically demonstrated a truly remarkable tendency to simply ignore those elements of international legality it finds inconvenient—the future of American Indians looks exceedingly grim.[155]

7

THE BLOODY WAKE OF ALCATRAZ
Repression of the American Indian Movement during the 1970s

◆ ◆ ◆ ◆ ◆ ◆ ◆ ◆ ◆ ◆ ◆ ◆ ◆ ◆

The reality is a continuum which connects Indian flesh sizzling over Puritan fires and Vietnamese flesh roasting under American napalm. The reality is the compulsion of a sick society to rid itself of men like Nat Turner and Crazy Horse, George Jackson and Richard Oaks, whose defiance uncovers the hypocrisy of a declaration affirming everyone's right to liberty and life. The reality is an overwhelming greed which began with the theft of a continent and continues with the merciless looting of every country on the face of the earth which lacks the strength to defend itself.

—Richard Lundstrom

IN COMBINATION WITH THE FISHING RIGHTS STRUGGLES OF THE PUYALLUP, Nisqually, Muckleshoot, and other nations in the Pacific Northwest from 1965 to 1970, the 1969–71 occupation of Alcatraz Island by the San Francisco Bay Area's Indians of All Tribes coalition ushered in a decade-long period of uncompromising and intensely confrontational American Indian political activism.[1] Unprecedented in modern U.S. history, the phenomenon represented by Alcatraz also marked the inception of a process of official repression of indigenous activists without contemporary North American parallel in its virulence and lethal effects.[2]

The nature of the post-Alcatraz federal response to organized agitation for native rights was such that by 1979 researchers were describing it as a manifestation of the U.S. government's "continuing Indian Wars."[3] For its part, in secret internal documents, the Federal Bureau of Investigation (FBI)—the primary instrument by which the government's policy of anti-Indian repression was implemented—concurred with such assessments, abandoning its customary counterintelligence vernacular in favor of the terminology of outright counterinsurgency warfare.[4] The result, as the U.S. Commission on Civil Rights officially conceded at the time, was the imposition of a virtual "reign of terror" upon certain of the less compliant sectors of indigenous society in the United States.[5]

In retrospect, it may be seen that the locus of both activism and repression in Indian Country throughout the 1970s centered squarely upon one group, the American Indian Movement (AIM). Moreover, the crux of AIM activism during the '70s, and thus of the FBI's campaign to "neutralize" it,[6] can be found in a single locality: the Pine Ridge (Oglala Lakota) Reservation, in South Dakota. The purpose of the present essay, then, is to provide an overview of the federal counterinsurgency program against AIM on and around Pine Ridge, using it as a lens through which to explore the broader motives and outcomes attending it. Finally, conclusions will be drawn as to its implications, not only with respect to American Indians, but concerning non-indigenous Americans as well.

BACKGROUND

AIM was founded in 1968 in Minneapolis, by a group of urban Anishinabes (Chippewas) including Dennis Banks, Pat Ballanger, Clyde Bellecourt, Eddie Benton Benai, and George Mitchell. Modeled loosely after the Black Panther Party for Self-Defense, established by Huey P. Newton and Bobby Seale in Oakland, California, two years previously, the group took as its first tasks the protection of the city's sizable native community from a pattern of rampant police abuse, and the creation of programs for jobs, housing and education.[7] Within three years, the organization had grown to include chapters in several other cities, and had begun to shift its focus from civil rights issues to an agenda more specifically attuned to the conditions afflicting Native North America.

What AIM discerned as the basis of the latter was not so much a matter of socioeconomic discrimination against Indians as it was our internal colonization by the United States.[8] This perception accrued from the fact that, by 1871, when federal treatymaking with native peoples was permanently suspended, the rights of indigenous nations to distinct, self-governing territories had been recognized by the U.S. more than 370 times through treaties duly ratified by its Senate.[9] Yet, during the intervening century, more than ninety percent of treaty-reserved native land had been expropriated by the federal government, in defiance of both its own constitution and international custom and convention.[10] One consequence of this was creation of the urban diaspora from which AIM itself had emerged; by 1970, about half of all Indians in the U.S. had been pushed off their land altogether.[11]

Within the residual archipelago of reservations, an aggregation of about fifty million acres, or roughly 2.5 percent of the forty-eight contiguous states, indigenous forms of governance had been thoroughly usurped through the imposition of U.S. jurisdiction under the federal government's self-assigned prerogative of exercising "plenary [full and absolute] power over Indian affairs."[12] Correspondingly, Indian control over what had turned out to be rather vast mineral resources within reservation boundaries—an estimated two-thirds of all U.S. "domestic" uranium deposits, a quarter of the low-sulfur coal, twenty percent of the oil and natural gas, and so on—was essentially nonexistent.[13]

It followed that royalty rates set by the U.S. Bureau of Indian Affairs (BIA), in its exercise of federal "trust" prerogatives vis-à-vis corporate extraction of Indian mineral assets, amounted to only a fraction of what the same corporations would have paid had they undertaken the same mining operations in nonreservation localities.[14] The same principle of underpayment to Indians, with resulting "super-profit" accrual to nonindian business entities, prevailed with regard to other areas of economic activity handled by the Indian Bureau, from the leasing of reservation grazing land to various ranching interests to the harvesting of reservation timber by corporations such as Weyerhauser and Boise-Cascade.[15] Small wonder that, by the late 1960s, Indian radicals like Robert K. Thomas had begun to refer to the BIA as "the Colonial Office of the United States."[16]

In human terms, the consequence was that, overall, American Indians—who, on the basis of known resources, comprised what should have been the single wealthiest population group in North America—constituted by far the most impoverished sector of U.S. society. According to the federal government's own data, Indians suffered, by a decisive margin, the highest rate of unemployment in the country, a matter correlated to our receiving by far the lowest annual and lifetime incomes of any group in the country.[17] It also corresponded well with virtually every other statistical indicator of extreme poverty: a truly catastrophic rate of infant mortality and the highest rates of death from malnutrition, exposure, plague disease, teen suicide, and accidents related to alcohol abuse. The average life expectancy of a reservation-based Indian male in 1970 was less than 45 years; reservation-based Indian females could expect to live less than three years longer than their male counterparts; urban Indians of either gender were living only about five years longer on average than their relatives on the reservations.[18]

AIM's response to its growing apprehension of this squalid panorama was to initiate a campaign consciously intended to bring about the decolonization of Native North America: "Only by reestablishing our rights as sovereign nations, including our right to control our own territories and resources, and our right to genuine self-governance," as Dennis Banks put it in 1971, "can we hope to successfully address the conditions currently experienced by our people."[19]

Extrapolating largely from the example of Alcatraz, the Movement undertook a multifaceted political strategy combining a variety of tactics. On the one hand, it engaged in activities designed primarily to focus media attention, and thus the attention of the general public, on Indian rights issues, especially those pertaining to treaty rights. On the other hand, it pursued the sort of direct confrontation meant to affirm those rights in practice. It also began to systematically reassert native cultural/spiritual traditions.[20] Eventually, it added a component wherein the full range of indigenous rights to decolonization/self-determination were pursued through the United Nations venue of international law.[21]

In mounting this comprehensive effort, AIM made of itself a bona fide National Liberation Movement, at least for a while.[22] Its members consisted of "the shock troops of Indian sovereignty," to quote non-AIM Oglala Lakota activist Birgil Kills Straight.[23] They essentially reframed the paradigm by which U.S.-Indian relations are understood in the late twentieth century.[24] They also suffered the worst physical repression at the hands of the United States of any "domestic" group since the 1890 massacre of Big Foot's Minneconjous by the 7th Cavalry at Wounded Knee.[25]

PRELUDE

AIM's seizure of the public consciousness may in many ways be said to have begun at the point in 1969 when Dennis Banks recruited a young Oglala named Russell Means to join the Movement. Instinctively imbued with what one critic described as a "bizarre knack for staging demonstrations that attracted the sort of press coverage Indians had been looking for,"[26] Means was instrumental in AIM's achieving several of its earliest and most important media coups: painting Plymouth Rock red before capturing the Mayflower replica on Thanksgiving Day 1970, for example, and staging a "4th of July Countercelebration" by occupying the Mt. Rushmore National Monument in 1971.[27]

Perhaps more important, Means proved to be the bridge which allowed the Movement to establish its credibility on a reservation for the first time. In part, this was because when he joined AIM he brought along virtually an entire generation of his family—brothers Ted, Bill, and Dale, cousin Madonna Gilbert, and others—each of whom possessed a web of friends and acquaintances on the Pine Ridge Reservation. It was therefore rather natural that AIM was called upon to "set things right" concerning the torture-murder of a middle-aged Oglala in the off-reservation town of Gordon, Nebraska, in late February 1972.[28] As Bill Means would later recall:

> When Raymond Yellow Thunder was killed, his relatives went first to the BIA, then to the FBI, and to the local police, but they got no response. Severt Young Bear [Yellow Thunder's nephew and a friend of Ted Means] then . . . asked AIM to come help clear up the case.[29]

Shortly afterwards, Russell Means led a caravan of some 1,300 Indians into the small town, announcing from the steps of the courthouse that, "We've come here today to put Gordon on the map . . . and if justice is not immediately forthcoming, we're going to take Gordon *off* the map." The killers, brothers named Melvin and Leslie Hare, were quickly arrested, and a police officer who had covered up for them suspended. The Hares soon became the first whites in Nebraska history sent to prison for killing an Indian and "AIM's reputation soared among reservation Indians. What tribal leaders had dared not do to protect their people, AIM had done."[30]

By fall, things had progressed to the point that AIM could collaborate with several other native rights organizations to stage the "Trail of Broken Treaties" caravan, bringing more than 2,000 Indians from reservations and urban areas across the country to Washington, D.C., on the eve of the 1972 presidential election. The idea was to present the incumbent chief executive, Richard M. Nixon, with a twenty-point program redefining the nature of U.S.-Indian relations. Publicity attending the critical timing

and location of the action, as well as the large number of Indians involved, were calculated to force serious responses by the administration to each point.[31]

In the event, Interior Department officials who had earlier pledged logistical support to caravan participants once they arrived in the capital reneged on their promises,
apparently in the belief that this would cause the group to meekly disperse. Instead,
angry Indians promptly took over the BIA headquarters building on November 2,
evicted its staff, and held it for several days. Russell Means, in fine form, captured the
front page of the nation's newspapers and the *Six O'Clock News* by conducting a press
conference in front of the building while adorned with a makeshift "war club" and a
"shield" fashioned from a portrait of Nixon himself.[32]

Desperate to end what had become a major media embarrassment, the Administration publicly agreed to formally reply to the twenty-point program within a month,
and to immediately provide $66,600 in transportation money, in exchange for a
peaceful end to the occupation.[33] AIM honored its part of the bargain, leaving the
BIA building on November 9. But, explaining that "Indians have every right to
known the details of what's being done to us and to our property," it took with it a
vast number of "confidential" files concerning BIA leasing practices, operation of the
Indian Health Service (IHS), and so forth. The originals were returned as rapidly as
they could be xeroxed, a process that required nearly two years to complete.[34]

Technically speaking, the government also honored its end of the deal, providing
official—and exclusively negative—responses to the twenty points within the specified timeframe.[35] At the same time, however, it initiated a campaign utilizing federally
subsidized Indian "leaders" in an effort to discredit AIM members as "irresponsi-
ble . . . renegades, terrorists and self-styled revolutionaries."[36] There is also strong indication that it was at this point that the Federal Bureau of Investigation was
instructed to launch a secret program of its own, one in which AIM's capacity to engage in further political activities of the kind and effectiveness displayed in Washington was to be, in the vernacular of FBI counterintelligence specialists, "neutralized."[37]

Even as this was going on, AIM's focus had shifted back to the Pine Ridge area. At
issue was the January 23, 1973, murder of a young Oglala named Wesley Bad Heart
Bull by a white man, Darld Schmitz, in the off-reservation village of Buffalo Gap,
South Dakota. As in the Yellow Thunder case, local authorities had made no move to
press appropriate charges against the killer.[38] At the request of the victim's mother,
Sarah, Russell Means called for a demonstration at the Custer County Courthouse,
the jurisdiction in which the crime occurred. Terming western South Dakota "the
Mississippi of the North,"[39] Dennis Banks simultaneously announced a longer-term
effort to force abandonment "of the anti-Indian attitudes which result in Indian-
killing being treated as a sort of local sport."[40]

When the Custer demonstration occurred on February 6, it followed a very different course than that of the protest in Gordon a year earlier. An anonymous call had
been placed to the main regional newspaper, the *Rapid City Journal*, on the evening of
February 5. The caller, saying he was "with AIM," asked that a notice canceling the ac-

tion "because of bad weather" be prominently displayed in the paper the following morning. Consequently, relatively few Indians turned out for the protest.[41] Those who did were met by an amalgamated force of police, sheriff's deputies, state troopers, and FBI personnel when they arrived in Custer.[42]

For a while, there was a tense standoff. Then, a sheriff's deputy manhandled Sarah Bad Heart Bull when she attempted to enter the courthouse. In the melée that followed, the courthouse was set ablaze—reportedly, by a police tear gas canister—and the local Chamber of Commerce building burned to the ground. Banks, Means, and other AIM members, along with Mrs. Bad Heart Bull, were arrested and charged with riot. Banks was eventually convicted, sentenced to three years imprisonment, and became a fugitive; Sarah Bad Heart Bull herself served five months of a one-to-five-year sentence. Her son's killer never served a day in jail.[43]

WOUNDED KNEE

Meanwhile, on Pine Ridge, tensions were running extraordinarily high. The point of contention was an escalating conflict between the tribal administration headed by Richard "Dickie" Wilson, installed on the reservation with federal support in 1972, and a large body of reservation traditionals who objected to Wilson's nepotism and other abuses of his position.[44] Initially, Wilson's opponents had sought redress of their grievances through the BIA. The BIA responded by providing a $62,000 grant to Wilson for purposes of establishing a "Tribal Ranger Group"—a paramilitary entity reporting exclusively to Wilson which soon began calling itself "Guardians Of the Oglala Nation" (GOONs)—with which to physically intimidate the opposition.[45] The reason underlying this federal largesse appears to have been the government's desire that Wilson sign an instrument transferring title over a portion of the reservation known as the Sheep Mountain Gunnery Range—secretly known to be rich in uranium and molybdenum—to the U.S. Forest Service.[46]

In any event, forming what was called the Oglala Sioux Civil Rights Organization (OSCRO), the traditionals next attempted to obtain relief through the Justice Department and FBI. When this too failed to bring results, they set out to impeach Wilson, obtaining more signatures of eligible voters on their petitions than had cast ballots for him in the first place. The BIA countered by naming Wilson himself to chair the impeachment proceedings, and the Justice Department dispatched a sixty-five member "Special Operations Group" (SOG; a large SWAT unit) of U.S. Marshals to ensure that "order" was maintained during the travesty. Then, on the eve of the hearing, Wilson ordered the arrest and jailing of several members of the tribal council he felt might vote for his removal. Predictably, when the impeachment tally was taken on February 23, 1973, the tribal president was retained in office. Immediately thereafter, he announced a reservation-wide ban on political meetings.[47]

Defying the ban, the traditionals convened a round-the-clock emergency meeting at the Calico Hall, near the village of Oglala, in an effort to determine their next move. On February 26, a messenger was sent to the newly-established AIM headquarters in nearby Rapid City to request that Russell Means meet with the Oglala elders. As one of them, Ellen Moves Camp, later put it:

> We decided we needed the American Indian Movement in here . . . All of our older people from the reservation helped make that decision . . . This is what we needed, a little more push. Most of the reservation believes in AIM, and we're proud to have them with us.[48]

Means came on the morning of the 27th, then drove on to the village of Pine Ridge, seat of the reservation government, to try and negotiate some sort of resolution with Wilson. For his trouble, he was physically assaulted by GOONs in the parking lot of the tribal administration building.[49] By then, Dennis Banks and a number of other AIM members had arrived at the Calico Hall. During subsequent meetings, it was decided by the elders that what was necessary was to draw public attention to the situation on the reservation. For this purpose, a 200-person AIM contingent was sent to the symbolic site of Wounded Knee to prepare for an early morning press conference; a much smaller group was sent back to Rapid City to notify the media, and to guide reporters to Wounded Knee at the appropriate time.[50]

The intended press conference never occurred because by dawn Wilson's GOONs had established roadblocks on all four routes leading into (or out of) the tiny hamlet. During the morning, these positions were reinforced by uniformed BIA police, then by elements of the Marshals' SOG unit, and then by FBI "observers." As this was going on, the AIM members in Wounded Knee began the process of arming themselves from the stores of the local Gildersleeve Trading Post and building defensive positions.[51] By afternoon, General Alexander Haig, military liaison to the Nixon White House, had dispatched two special warfare experts—Colonel Volney Warner of the 82nd Airborne Division, and Colonel Jack Potter of the Sixth Army—to the scene.[52]

> Documents later subpoenaed from the Pentagon revealed Colonel Potter directed the employment of 17 APCs [tanklike armored personnel carriers], 130,000 rounds of M-16 ammunition, 41,000 rounds of M-40 high explosive [for the M-79 grenade launchers he also provided], as well as helicopters, Phantom jets, and personnel. Military officers, supply sergeants, maintenance technicians, chemical officers, and medical teams [were provided on site]. Three hundred miles to the south, at Fort Carson, Colorado, the Army had billeted a fully uniformed assault unit on twenty-four hour alert.[53]

Over the next seventy-one days, the AIM perimeter at Wounded Knee was placed under siege. The ground cover was burned away for roughly a quarter-mile around the AIM position as part of the federal attempt to staunch the flow of supplies—food, medicine, and ammunition—backpacked in to the Wounded Knee defenders at night; at one point such material had to be air-dropped by a group of supporting pilots.[54] More than 500,000 rounds of military ammunition were fired into AIM's jerry-rigged "bunkers" by federal forces, killing two Indians—an Apache named Frank Clearwater and Buddy Lamont, an Oglala—and wounding several others.[55] As many as thirteen more people may have been killed by roving GOON patrols, their bodies secretly buried in remote locations around the reservation, while they were trying to carry supplies through federal lines.[56]

At first, the authorities sought to justify what was happening by claiming that AIM had "occupied" Wounded Knee, and that the Movement had taken several hostages in the process.[57] When the latter allegation was proven to be false, a press ban was imposed, and official spokespersons argued that the use of massive force was needed to "quell insurrection." Much was made of two federal casualties who were supposed to have been seriously injured by AIM gunfire.[58] In the end, it was Dickie Wilson who perhaps expressed matters most candidly when he informed reporters that the purpose of the entire exercise was to see to it that "AIM dies at Wounded Knee."[59]

Despite Wilson's sentiments—and those of FBI senior counterintelligence specialist Richard G. Held, expressed in a secret report prepared at the request of his superiors early in the siege[60]—an end to the standoff was finally negotiated for May 7, 1973. AIM's major condition, entered in behalf of the Pine Ridge traditionals and agreed to by government representatives, was that a federal commission would meet with the chiefs to review U.S. compliance with the terms of the 1868 Fort Laramie Treaty with the Lakota, Cheyenne, and Arapaho Nations.[61] The idea was to generate policy recommendations as to how the United States might bring itself into line with its treaty obligations. A White House delegation did in fact meet with the elders at the home of Chief Frank Fools Crow, near the reservation town of Manderson, on May 17. The delegates' mission, however, was to stonewall all efforts at meaningful discussion.[62] They promised a follow-up meeting on May 30, but never returned.[63]

On other fronts, the authorities were demonstrating no comparable lack of vigor. Before the first meeting at Fools Crow's, the FBI had made 562 arrests of those who had been involved in defending Wounded Knee.[64] Russell Means was in jail awaiting release on $150,000 bond; OSCRO leader Pedro Bissonette was held against $152,000; AIM leaders Stan Holder and Leonard Crow Dog against $32,000 and $35,000 respectively. Scores of others were being held pending the posting of lesser sums.[65] By the fall of 1973, agents had amassed some 316,000 separate investigative file classifications on those who had been inside Wounded Knee.[66]

This allowed federal prosecutors to obtain 185 indictments over the next several months. (Means alone was charged with thirty-seven felonies and three misdemeanors.)[67] Although in 1974 AIM and the traditionals used the 1868 Treaty as a basis upon which to challenge in federal court the U.S. government's jurisdiction over Pine Ridge, the trials of the "Wounded Knee Leadership" went forward.[68] Even after the FBI's and prosecution's willingness to subvert the judicial process became so blatantly obvious that U.S. District Judge Fred Nichol was compelled to dismiss all charges against Banks and Means, cases were still pressed against Crow Dog, Holder, Carter Camp, Madonna Gilbert, Lorelei DeCora, and Phyllis Young.[69]

The whole charade resulted in a meager fifteen convictions, all of them on such paltry offenses as trespass and "interference with postal inspectors in performance of their lawful duties."[70] Still, in the interim, the virtual entirety of AIM's leadership was tied up in a seemingly endless series of arrests, incarcerations, hearings, and trials. Similarly, the great bulk of the Movement's fundraising and organizing capacity was diverted into posting bonds and mounting legal defenses for those indicted.[71]

On balance, the record suggests a distinct probability that the post-Wounded Knee prosecutions were never seriously intended to result in convictions at all. Instead, they were designed mainly to serve the time-honored—and utterly illegal—expedient of "disrupting, misdirecting, destabilizing or otherwise neutralizing" a politically objectionable group.[72] There is official concurrence with this view: As army counterinsurgency specialist Volney Warner framed matters at the time, "AIM's best leaders and most militant members are under indictment, in jail, or warrants are out for their arrest . . . [Under these conditions] the government can win, even if nobody goes to [prison]."[73]

THE REIGN OF TERROR

While AIM's "notables" were being forced to slog their way through the courts, a very different form of repression was being visited upon the Movement's rank and file membership and the grassroots traditionals of Pine Ridge. During the three-year period beginning with the Siege of Wounded Knee, at least sixty-nine members and supporters of AIM died violently on the reservation.[74] During the same period, nearly 350 others suffered serious physical assault. Overall, the situation on Pine Ridge was such that, by 1976, the U.S. Commission on Civil Rights was led to describe it as a "reign of terror."[75]

> Using only documented political deaths, the yearly murder rate on the Pine Ridge Reservation between March 1, 1973, and March 1, 1976, was 170 per 100,000. By comparison, Detroit, the reputed "murder capital of the United States," had a rate of 20.2 per 100,000 in 1974. The U.S. average was 9.7 per 100,000 . . . In a nation of 200 million persons, a murder rate comparable with that on Pine Ridge between 1973 and 1976 would have left 340,000 persons dead for political reasons alone in one year; 1.32 million in three . . . The political murder rate at Pine Ridge was almost equivalent to that in Chile during the three years after a military coup supported by the United States killed President Salvador Allende.[76]

Despite the fact that eyewitnesses identified the assailants in twenty-one of these homicides, the FBI—which maintains preeminent jurisdiction over major crimes on all American Indian reservations—was responsible for ensuring that not one of the killers was ever convicted of murder.[77] In many cases, no active investigation of the murder of an AIM member or supporter was undertaken by the Bureau.[78] In others, those associated with the victims were falsely arrested as "perpetrators."[79]

When queried by reporters in 1975 as to the reason for his office's abysmal record of investigating murders on Pine Ridge, George O'Clock, agent in charge of the FBI's Rapid City Resident Agency—which has operational authority over the reservation—replied that he was "too short of manpower" to assign agents to such tasks.[80] O'Clock omitted to mention that, at the time, he had at his disposal the highest sustained ratio of agents to citizens enjoyed by any FBI office in the history of the Bureau.[81] He also neglected the fact that the same agents who were too busy to look into the murders of AIM people appear to have had unlimited time to undertake the investigative activities covered in the preceding section. O'Clock's pat "explanation" was and remains implausible.

A far more likely scenario begins to take shape when it is considered that in each instance where there were eyewitness identifications of the individuals who had killed an AIM member or supporter, those identified were known GOONs.[82] The FBI's conspicuous inability to apprehend murderers on Pine Ridge may thus be located, not in the incompetence of its personnel, but in the nature of its relationship to the killers. In effect, the GOONs seem to have functioned under a more or less blanket immunity from prosecution provided by the FBI so long as they focused their lethal attentions upon targets selected by the Bureau. Put another way, the appearance is that the FBI used the GOONs as a surrogate force against AIM on Pine Ridge in precisely the same manner that Latin American death squads have been utilized by the CIA to destroy the opposition in countries like Guatemala, El Salvador, and Chile.[83]

The roots of the FBI/GOON connection can be traced back at least as far as April 23, 1973, when U.S. Marshals Service Director Wayne Colburn, driving from Pine Ridge village to Wounded Knee, was stopped at what the Wilsonites referred to as "The Residents' Roadblock." One of the GOONs manning the position, vocally disgruntled with what he called the "soft line" taken by the Justice Department in dealing with AIM, leveled a shotgun at the head of Colburn's passenger, Solicitor General Kent Frizzell. Colburn was forced to draw his own weapon before the man would desist. Angered, Colburn drove back to Pine Ridge and dispatched a group of his men to arrest everyone at the roadblock. When the marshals arrived at the Pennington County Jail in Rapid City with those arrested, however, they found an FBI man waiting with instructions to release the GOONs immediately.[84]

By this point, Dickie Wilson himself had reestablished the roadblock, using a fresh crew of GOONs. Thoroughly enraged at this defiance, Colburn assembled another group of marshals and prepared to make arrests. Things had progressed to the point of a "High Noon"-style showdown when a helicopter appeared, quickly landing on the blacktop road near the would-be combatants. In it was FBI counterintelligence ace Richard G. Held, who informed Colburn that he had received instructions "from the highest level" to ensure that no arrests would be made and that "the roadblock stays where it is."[85]

Humiliated, and increasingly concerned for the safety of his own personnel in a situation where the FBI was openly siding with a group hostile to them, Colburn ordered his men to disarm GOONs whenever possible.[86] Strikingly, as the marshals impounded the sort of weaponry the Wilsonites had up until then been using—conventional deer rifles, World War II surplus M-1s, shotguns, and other firearms normally found in a rural locality—the same GOONs Colburn's men had disarmed began to reappear, well-stocked with ammunition and sporting fully-automatic military-issue M-16s.[87]

The Brewer Revelations

It has always been the supposition of those aligned with AIM that the FBI provided such hardware to Wilson's GOONs. The Bureau and its apologists, meanwhile, pointing to the absence of concrete evidence with which to confirm the allegation, have consistently denied any such connection, charging those referring to its probability with journalistic or scholarly "irresponsibility."[88] Not until the early 1990s, with publication of extracts from an interview with former GOON commander Duane Brewer, was AIM's premise borne out.[89]

Not only does the one-time death squad leader make it clear that the FBI provided him and his men with weaponry, but with ample supplies of armor-piercing ammunition, hand grenades, "det cord" and other explosives, communications gear and additional paraphernalia.[90] Agents would drop by his house, Brewer maintains, to provide key bits of field intelligence which allowed the GOONs to function in a more efficient manner than might otherwise have been the case. And, perhaps most important, agents conveyed the plain message that members of the death squad would enjoy virtual immunity from federal prosecution for anything they did, so long as it fell within the realm of repressing dissidents on the reservation.[91]

Among other murders which Brewer clarifies in his interview is that of Jeanette Bissonette, a young woman shot to death in her car as she sat at a stop sign in Pine Ridge village at about one o'clock in the morning of March 27, 1975. The FBI has all along insisted, for reasons which remain mysterious, that it is "probable" Bissonette was assassinated by AIM members.[92] Brewer, on the other hand, explains on the basis of first-hand knowledge that the killing was "a mistake" on the part of his execution team, which mistook Bissonette's vehicle for that of area resistance leader Ellen Moves Camp.[93]

It is important to note, before moving ahead, that at the time he functioned as a GOON leader, Duane Brewer also served as second-in-command of the BIA police on Pine Ridge. His boss as a policeman, Delmar Eastman—primary liaison between the police and the FBI—was simultaneously in charge of all GOON operations on the reservation.[94] In total, it is reliably estimated that somewhere between one-third and one-half of all BIA police personnel on Pine Ridge between 1972 and 1976 moonlighted as GOONs. Those who didn't become directly involved, actively covered for their colleagues who did, or at least kept their mouths shut about the situation.[95]

Obviously, whatever meager hope for relief AIM and the Oglala traditionals might have extended to the workings of local law enforcement quickly disappeared under such circumstances.[96] In effect, the police were the killers, their crimes not only condoned, but for all practical intents and purposes commanded and controlled by the

FBI. Other federal agencies did no more than issue largely uncirculated reports confirming that the bloodbath was in fact occurring.[97] "Due process" on Pine Ridge during the crucial period was effectively nonexistent.

The Oglala Firefight

By the spring of 1975, with more than forty of their number already dead, it had become apparent to the Pine Ridge resisters that they had been handed a choice of either acquiescing to the federal agenda or being annihilated. All other alternatives, including a 1974 electoral effort to replace Dickie Wilson with AIM leader Russell Means, had been met by fraud, force, and unremitting violence.[98] Those who wished to continue the struggle and survive were therefore compelled to adopt a posture of armed self-defense. Given that many of the traditionals were elderly, and thus could not reasonably hope to accomplish the latter on their own, AIM was asked to provide physical security for them. Defensive encampments were quickly established at several key locations around the reservation.[99]

For its part, the FBI seems to have become increasingly frustrated at the capacity of the dissidents to absorb punishment, and the consequent failure of the Bureau's counterinsurgency campaign to force submission. Internal FBI documents suggest that the coordinators of the Pine Ridge operation had come to greatly desire some sensational event which might serve to justify in the public mind a sudden introduction to the reservation of the kind of overwhelming force which might break the back of the resistance once and for all.[100]

Apparently selected for this purpose was a security camp set up by the Northwest AIM Group at the request of traditional elders Harry and Cecelia Jumping Bull on their property, along Highway 18, a few miles south of the village of Oglala. During the early evening of June 25, 1975, two agents, Ron Williams and Jack Coler, escorted by a BIA policeman (and known GOON) named Bob Ecoffey, entered the Jumping Bull Compound. They claimed to be attempting to serve an arrest warrant on a seventeen-year-old Lakota and AIM supporter named Jimmy Eagle on spurious charges of kidnapping and aggravated assault.[101]

Told by residents that Eagle was not there and had not been seen for weeks, the agents and their escort left. On Highway 18, however, the agents accosted three young AIM members—Mike Anderson, Norman Charles, and Wilfred "Wish" Draper—who were walking back to camp after taking showers in Oglala, drove them to the police headquarters in Pine Ridge village, and interrogated them for more than two hours. As the young men reported when they finally returned to the Jumping Bulls', no questions had been asked about Jimmy Eagle. Instead, the agents had wanted to know how many men of fighting age were in the camp, what sort of weapons they possessed, and so on. Thus alerted that something bad was about to happen, the Northwest AIM contingent put out an urgent call for support from the local AIM community.[102]

At about 11:00 a.m. the following morning, June 26, Williams and Coler returned to the Jumping Bull property. Driving past the compound of residences, they moved down into a shallow valley, stopped and exited their cars in an open area, and began to fire in the general direction of the AIM encampment in a treeline along White Clay Creek.[103] Shortly thereafter, they began to take a steadily growing return fire, not only from the treeline, but from the houses above. At about this point, agent J. Gary Adams and BIA police officer/GOON Glenn Two Birds attempted to come to Williams' and Coler's aid. Unexpectedly taking fire from the direction of the houses, they retreated to the ditch beside Highway 18.[104]

Some 150 SWAT-trained BIA police and FBI personnel were prepositioned in the immediate locale when the firefight began. This, especially when taken in combination with the fact that more than 200 additional FBI SWAT personnel were on alert awaiting word to proceed *post haste* to Pine Ridge from Minneapolis, Milwaukee, and Quantico, Virginia, raises the probability that Williams and Coler were actually assigned to provoke an exchange of gunfire with the AIM members on the Jumping Bull land.[105] The plan seems to have been that they would then be immediately supported by the introduction of overwhelming force, the Northwest AIM Group destroyed, and the FBI afforded the pretext necessary to launch an outright invasion of Pine Ridge.[106]

A number of local AIM members had rallied to the call to come to the Jumping Bulls'. Hence, instead of encountering the eight AIM "shooters" they anticipated, there were about thirty, and the two agents were cut off from their erstwhile supporters.[107] While the BIA police, reinforced by GOONs put up roadblocks to seal off the area, and the FBI agents on hand were deployed as snipers, no one made a serious effort to get to Williams and Coler until 5:50 p.m. By that point, they'd been dead for some time, along with a young Coeur d'Alene AIM member, Joe Stuntz Killsright, killed by FBI sniper Gerard Waring as he attempted to depart the compound.[108] Aside from Killsright, all AIM participants had escaped across country.

By nightfall, hundreds of agents equipped with everything from APCs to Vietnam-style Huey helicopters had begun arriving on the reservation.[109] The next morning, Tom Coll, an FBI "Public Information Specialist" imported for the purpose, convened a press conference in Oglala—the media was barred from the firefight site itself—in which he reported that the dead agents had been "lured into an ambush" by AIM, attacked with automatic weapons from a "sophisticated bunker complex," dragged wounded from their cars, stripped of their clothing, and then executed in cold blood while one of them pleaded with his killer(s) to spare him because he had a wife and children. Each agent, Coll asserted, had been "riddled with 15–20 bullets."[110]

Every word of this was false, as Coll well knew—the FBI had been in possession of both the agents' bodies and the ground on which they were killed for nearly a eighteen hours before he made his statements—and the report was retracted in full by FBI Director Clarence Kelley at a press conference conducted in Los Angeles a week later.[111] By then, however, a barrage of sensational media coverage had "sensitized" the public to the need for a virtually unrestricted application of force against the "mad dogs of AIM." Correspondingly, the Bureau was free to run air assaults and massive sweeping operations on Pine Ridge—complete with the wholesale use of no-knock searches and John Doe warrants—for the next three months.[112] By the end of that period, its mission had largely been accomplished.[113] In the interim, on July 27, 1975, it was finally felt, given the preoccupation of all concerned parties with the FBI's literal invasion of Pine Ridge, that the time was right for Dickie Wilson to sign a memorandum transferring the Gunnery Range to the federal government; on January 2, 1976, a more formal instrument was signed and, in the spring, Congress passed a Public Law assuming U.S. title over this portion of Oglala territory.[114]

THE CASE OF LEONARD PELTIER

It is unlikely that the FBI intended that its two agents be killed during the Oglala Firefight. Once Coler and Williams were dead, however, the Bureau capitalized upon their fate, not only as the medium through which to pursue its anti-AIM campaign with full ferocity, but as a mechanism with which to block an incipient congressional probe into what the FBI had been doing on Pine Ridge. This last took the form of a sympathy play: Bureau officials pleaded that the "natural" emotional volatility engendered among their agents' by the deaths made it "inopportune" to proceed with the investigation "at the present time." Congress responded, on July 3, 1975, by postponing the scheduling of preliminary interviews, a delay which has become permanent.[115]

Still, with two dead agents, it was crucial for the Bureau's image that someone be brought directly to account. To fill this bill, four names were selected from the list of thirty "shooters" field investigators had concluded were participants in the exchange. Targeted were a pair of Anishinabe/Lakota cousins, Leonard Peltier and Bob Robideau, and Darrelle "Dino" Butler, a Tuni, the heads of Northwest AIM. Also included was Jimmy Eagle, whose name seems to have appeared of expediency, since the Bureau claimed Williams and Coler were looking for him in the first place (all charges against him were later simply dropped, without investiture of discernible prosecutorial effort).[116]

Butler and Robideau, captured early on, were to be tried first, as codefendants, separate from Peltier.[117] The latter, having managed to avoid arrest in a trap set for him in Oregon, had found sanctuary in the remote encampment of Cree leader Robert Smallboy in northern Alberta.[118] By the time he could be apprehended, extradited via a thoroughly fraudulent proceeding involving the presentation of an "eyewitness" affidavit from a psychotic Lakota woman named Myrtle Poor Bear to a Canadian court, and docketed in the U.S., the proceedings against Peltier's cohorts were ready to begin.[119] He was thus scheduled to be tried later and alone.

At the Butler/Robideau trial, conducted in Cedar Rapids, Iowa, during the summer of 1976, the government's plan to turn the defendants—and AIM itself—into examples of the price of resistance began to unravel. Despite the calculated ostentation with which the FBI prepared to secure the judge and jurors from "AIM's potential for violence," and another media blitz designed to convince the public that Butler and Robideau were part of a vast "terrorist conspiracy," the carefully selected all-white Midwestern panel of jurors was unconvinced.[120] After William Muldrow of the U.S. Commission on Civil Rights was called by the defense to testify regarding the FBI-fostered reign of terror on Pine Ridge, and Director Kelley himself was forced to admit under oath that he knew of nothing which might support many of the Bureau's harsher characterizations of AIM, the jury voted to acquit on July 16, 1976.[121]

The "not guilty" verdict was based in the panel-members' assessment that—although both defendants acknowledged firing at the agents, Robideau that he had in fact hit them both[122]—they had acted in self-defense. Under the conditions described by credible witnesses, jury foreman Robert Bolin later recounted, "We felt that any reasonable person would have reacted the same way when the agents came in there shooting." Besides, Bolin continued, their personal observations of the behavior of governmental representatives during the trial had convinced most jury members that "it was the government, not the defendants or their movement, which was dangerous."[123]

Although the Cedar Rapids jury had essentially determined that Coler and Williams had not been murdered, the FBI and federal prosecutors opted to proceed against Peltier. In a pretrial conference they analyzed what had "gone wrong" in the Butler/Robideau case and, in a report dated July 20, 1976, concluded that among the problems encountered was the fact that the defendants had been allowed to present a self-defense argument, their lawyers allowed "to call and question witnesses" and subpoena government documents.[124] They then removed the Peltier trial from the docket of the judge at Cedar Rapids, Edward McManus, and reassigned it to another, Paul Benson, whom they felt would be more amenable to their view.[125]

When Peltier was brought to trial in Fargo, North Dakota, on March 21, 1977, Benson ruled virtually everything presented by the defense at Cedar Rapids, including the Butler/Robideau trial transcript itself, inadmissible.[126] Prosecutors then presented a case against Peltier which was precisely the opposite of what they—and their FBI witnesses—professed to believe was true in the earlier trial.[127] A chain of circumstantial evidence was constructed, often through resort to fabricated physical evidence,[128] perjury,[129] and the use of demonstrably suborned testimony,[130] to create a plausible impression among jurors—again all white Midwesterners—that the defendant was guilty.

Following a highly emotional closing presentation by Assistant Prosecutor Lynn Crooks, in which he waved color photos of the agents' bloody bodies under the jury's collective nose and graphically described the "cold-bloodedness" with which "Leonard Peltier executed these two wounded and helpless human beings," they voted on April 18, after only six hours of deliberation, to convict on both counts of first degree murder.[131] Benson then sentenced Peltier to serve two consecutive life terms in prison and he was transported straight away to the federal "supermaximum" facility at Marion, Illinois.[132]

Almost immediately, an appeal was filed on the basis of FBI misconduct and multiple judicial errors on Benson's part. The matter was considered by a three-member panel of the Eighth Circuit Court—composed of judges William Webster, Donald Ross, and Gerald Heaney—during the spring of 1978. Judge Webster wrote the opinion on behalf of his colleagues, finding that although the record revealed numerous reversible errors on the part of the trial judge, and many "unfortunate misjudgments" by the FBI, the conviction would be allowed to stand.[133] By the time the document was released, Webster was no longer there to answer for it. He had moved on to a new position as Director of the FBI. On February 12, 1979, the U.S. Supreme Court declined, without stating a reason, to review the lower court's decision.[134]

Undeterred, Peltier's attorneys had already filed a suit under the Freedom of Information Act (FOIA) to force disclosure of FBI documents withheld from the defense at trial. When the paperwork, more than 12,000 pages of investigative material, was finally produced in 1981, they began the tedious process of indexing and reviewing it.[135] Finding that the Bureau had suppressed ballistics reports which directly contradicted what had been presented at trial, they filed a second appeal in 1982.[136] This led to an evidentiary hearing and oral arguments in 1984 during which the FBI's chief ballistics expert, Evan Hodge, was caught in the act of perjuring himself,[137] and Lynn Crooks was forced to admit that the government "really has no idea who shot those agents."[138]

Crooks then attempted to argue that it didn't matter anyway, because Peltier had been convicted of "aiding and abetting in the murders rather than of the murders themselves."[139] This time, the circuit court panel—now composed of judges Heaney and Ross, as well as John Gibson—took nearly a year to deliberate. On October 11, 1986, they finally delivered an opinion holding that the content of Crooks' own closing argument to the jury, among many other factors precluded the notion that Peltier had been tried for aiding and abetting. They also concluded that the circumstantial ballistics case presented by the prosecution at trial was hopelessly undermined by evidence even then available to the FBI.[140]

Still, they refused to reverse Peltier's conviction because, "We recognize that there is evidence in this record of improper conduct on the part of some FBI agents, but we are reluctant to impute even further improprieties to them" by remanding the matter to trial.[141] On October 5, 1987, the Supreme Court once again refused to review the lower court's decision.[142] Most recently, a third appeal, argued on the basis of *habeas corpus*—if Peltier was never tried for aiding and abetting, and if the original case against him no longer really exists, then why is he in prison?—was filed. In November 1992, the Eighth Circuit, without ever really answering such questions, allowed his "conviction" to stand.[143] Eight years later, although he'd repeatedly insinuated that a pardon was in the offing, President Bill Clinton knuckled under to extreme pressure from the FBI by declining to commute Peltier's sentence.[144]

AFTERMATH

The government repression of AIM during the mid-70s had the intended effect of blunting the movement's cutting edge. After 1977, things occurred in fits and starts rather than a sustained drive. AIM's core membership, those who were not dead or in prison, scattered to the winds, many, like Wounded Knee security head Stan Holder, seeking other avenues along which to channel their activism.[145] Others, exhausted and intimidated by the massive violence directed against them, "retired" altogether from active politics.[146] Among the remainder, personal, political, and intertribal antagonisms, often exacerbated by the rumors spread by federal *provocateurs*, instilled a deep and lasting factional fragmentation.[147]

In 1978, Dennis Banks, occupying the unique status in California of having been officially granted sanctuary by one state of the union against the extradition demands of another, sought to bring things back together by organizing what he called the "Longest Walk."[148] To some extent replicating on foot the Trail of Broken Treaties caravan of 1972, the Walk succeeded in its immediate objective; the walkers made it from Alcatraz Island—selected as a point of departure because of the importance of the 1969–71 occupation in forging AIM—to Washington, D.C., presenting a powerful manifesto to the Carter Administration in July.[149] But there was no follow-up, and the momentum was quickly lost.

Much hope was placed in the formation of the Leonard Peltier Defense Committee (LPDC) the same year, and, for a time it seemed as though it might serve as a kind of sparkplug reenergizing the movement as a whole.[150] However, with the February 12, 1979, murder of AIM Chair John Trudell's entire family on the Duck Valley Reservation in Nevada, apparently as a deterrent to the effectiveness of Trudell's fiery oratory, things took an opposite tack.[151] The result was the abolition of all national officer positions in AIM; "These titles do nothing but provide a ready-made list of priority targets for the feds," as Trudell put it at the time.[152] The gesture consummated a trend against centralization which began with the dissolution of AIM's national office at the time Banks had gone underground in 1975, a fugitive from sentencing after his conviction on charges stemming from the Custer Courthouse confrontation.[153]

In 1979 and '80, largescale "Survival Gatherings" were held outside Rapid City in an attempt to bring together Indian and nonindian activists in collaborative opposition to uranium mining and other corporate "development" of the Black Hills.[154] An ensuing organization, the Black Hills Alliance (BHA), achieved momentary national prominence, but petered out after the demise of domestic uranium production in the early-80s dissolved several of the more pressing issues it confronted.[155]

Meanwhile, Russell Means, fresh out of prison, launched a related effort in 1981, occupying an 880-acre site in the Black Hills to establish a "sustainable, alternative, demonstration community" and "to initiate the physical reoccupation of Paha Sapa by the Lakota people and our allies." The occupation of what was dubbed *Wincanyan Zi Tiospaye* (Yellow Thunder Camp) in memory of Raymond Yellow Thunder lasted until 1985.[156] By that point, its organizers had obtained what on its face was landmark judicial opinion from a federal district judge; not only did the Yellow Thunder occupiers have every right to do what they were doing, the judge decreed, but the Lakota—and other Indians as well—are entitled to view entire geographic areas such as the Black Hills, rather than merely specific sites within them, to be of sacred significance.[157] The emergent victory was gutted, however, by the Supreme Court's controversial "G-O Road Decision" in 1988.[158]

Elsewhere, an AIM security camp was established on Navajo land near Big Mountain, Arizona, during the mid-80s, to support the traditional Diné elders of that area in their resistance to forced relocation.[159] It is maintained through the present, and, somewhat comparably, AIM contingents began to become involved in the early '90s in providing physical security to Western Shoshone resisters to forced removal from their land in Nevada.[160] Similar scenarios have been played out in places as diverse as northern Minnesota and Wisconsin, Oregon, California, Oklahoma, Illinois, Florida, Georgia, Nebraska, Alaska, and upstate New York. The issues confronted have been as wide-ranging as the localities in which they've been confronted.

Another potential bright spot which was ultimately eclipsed was the International Indian Treaty Council (IITC). Formed at the request of the Lakota elders in 1974 to "carry the message of indigenous people into the community of nations" and to serve more generally as "AIM's international diplomatic arm," it had by August 1977 gotten off to a brilliant start, playing a key role in bringing representatives of 98 native peoples throughout the Americas together in an unprecedented convocation before the United Nations Commission on Human Rights. This led directly to the establishment of a formal Working Group on Indigenous Populations—mandated to draft a Universal Declaration of the Rights of Indigenous Peoples for incorporation into international law—under the U.N. Economic and Social Council.[161]

Despite this remarkable early success, with the 1981 departure of its original director, Cherokee activist Jimmie Durham, IITC began to unravel.[162] By 1986, his successors were widely perceived as using the organization's reputation as a vehicle for personal profit and prestige, aligning themselves for a fee with various state governments against indigenous interests. Allegations that they were also using their *de facto* diplomatic status as a medium in which to engage in drug trafficking also abounded. Whether or not such suspicions were well founded, IITC today has reduced itself to the stature of a small sectarian corporation, completely divorced from AIM and the traditional milieu which legitimated it, subsisting mainly on donations from the very entities it was created to oppose.[163]

The early '90s, with the imminence of the Columbian Quincentennial Celebration, presented opportunities for the revitalization of AIM. Indeed, the period witnessed a more or less spontaneous regeneration of autonomous AIM chapters in at least sixteen localities around the country.[164] In Colorado, an escalating series of confrontations with Columbus Day celebrants organized by the local AIM chapter beginning in 1989 led to the galvanizing of a coalition of some fifty progressive organizations, Indian and nonindian alike, by 1992.[165] In Denver, the city where Columbus Day was first proclaimed an official holiday, Quincentennial activities were stopped in their tracks. A similar process was evident in San Francisco and, to a lesser extent, other locales.

Perhaps ironically, the most vicious reaction to the prospect of a resurgent movement came, not from the government per se, but from a small group in Minneapolis professing itself to be AIM's "legitimate leadership." How exactly it imagined it had attained this exalted position was a bit murky, there not having been an AIM general membership conference to sanction the exercise of such authority since 1975. Nonetheless, in July 1993, the clique constituted itself under the laws of the State of

Minnesota as "National-AIM, Inc.," announced formation of a "National Board" and "Central Committee," and provided the address to what it described as the "AIM National Office."[166] Among the very first acts of this interesting amalgam—which proudly reported it was receiving $4 million per year in federal funding, and more than $3 million annually from corporations like Honeywell—was the issuance of letters "expelling" most of the rest of the movement from itself.[167]

A LEGACY

It may be, as John Trudell has said, that "AIM died years ago. It's just that some people don't know it yet."[168] Certainly, as a viable organization, the evidence exhibits every indication of bearing him out. And yet there is another level to this reality, one which has more to do with the spirit of resistance than with its tangible form. Whatever else may be said about what AIM was (or is), it must be acknowledged that, as Russell Means contends:

> Before AIM, Indians were dispirited, defeated and culturally dissolving. People were *ashamed* to be Indian. You didn't see the young people wearing braids or chokers or ribbon shirts in those days. Hell, *I* didn't wear 'em. People didn't Sun Dance, they didn't Sweat, they were losing their languages. Then there was that spark at Alcatraz, and we took off. Man, we took a *ride* across this country. We put Indians and Indian rights smack dab in the middle of the public consciousness for the first time since the so-called Indian Wars. And, of course, we paid a heavy price for that. Some of us are still paying it. But now you see braids on our young people. There are dozens of Sun Dances every summer. You hear our languages spoken again in places they had almost died out. Most important, you find young Indians all over the place who understand that they don't have to accept whatever sort of bullshit the dominant society wants to hand them, that they have the right to fight, to struggle for their rights, that in fact they have an obligation to stand up on their hind legs and fight for their future generations, the way our ancestors did. Now, I don't know about you, but I call that pride in being Indian. And I think that's a very positive change. And I think—no, I *know*—AIM had a lot to do with bringing that change about. We laid the groundwork for the next stage in regaining our sovereignty and self-determination as nations, and I'm proud to have been a part of that.[169]

To the degree this is true, and much of it seems very accurate, AIM may be said to have succeeded in fulfilling its original agenda.[170] The impulse of Alcatraz was carried forward into dimensions its participants could not yet envision. And that legacy is even now being refashioned and extended by a new generation, as it will be by the next, and the next. The continuity of Native North America's traditional resistance to domination was reasserted by AIM in no uncertain terms.

There are other aspects of the AIM legacy, to be sure. Perhaps the most crucial should be placed under the heading of "Lessons Learned." These go to defining the nature of the society we now inhabit, the lengths to which its government will go to maintain the kinds of domination AIM fought to cast off, and the techniques it uses in doing so. The experience of the American Indian Movement, especially in the mid-1970s, provides what amounts to a textbook exposition of these things. It teaches what to expect, and, if properly understood, how to overcome many of these methodologies of repression. The lessons are applicable, not simply to American Indians, but to anyone whose lot in life is to be oppressed within the American conception of business as usual.[171]

Ultimately, the gift bestowed by AIM is in part an apprehension of the fact that the Third World is not something "out there." It is everywhere, behind the facade of liberal democracy masking the substance of the United States as much as anywhere else.[172] It is there on every reservation in the country, in the teeming ghettos of Brownsville, Detroit, and Compton, in the barrios and migrant fields and share cropping farms of the Deep South.[173] It is there in the desolation of the Appalachian coal regions. It is there in the burgeoning prison industry of America, warehousing what is proportionally the largest incarcerated population on the planet.[174]

The Third World is there in the nation's ever more proliferate and militarized police apparatus. And it is there in the piles of corpses of those—not just AIM members, but Black Panthers, Brown Berets, Puerto Rican *independentistas*, labor organizers, civil rights workers, and many others—who tried to say "no" and make it stick.[175] It is there in the fate of Malcolm X and Fred Hampton, Mark Clark and Ché Payne, Geronimo ji Jaga Pratt and Alejandrina Torres, Susan Rosenberg and Martin Luther King, George Jackson and Ray Luc Lavasseur, Rob Paxton and Reyes Tijerina, Mutulu Shakur and Marilyn Buck, and so many others.[176]

To win, it is said, one must know one's enemy. Winning the sorts of struggles engaged in by the individuals and organizations just mentioned is unequivocally necessary if we are to effect a constructive change in the conditions they faced, and that we continue to face. In this, there are still many lessons to be drawn from the crucible of AIM experience. These must be learned by all of us. They must be learned well. And soon.

PART III

CULTURE WARS

◆◆◆◆◆◆◆◆◆◆◆◆◆◆

One should not speak lightly of "cultural genocide," as if it were a fanciful invention. The consequence in real life is far too grim to speak of cultural genocide as if it were a rhetorical device to beat the drums for "human rights." The cultural mode of group extermination is genocide, a crime. Nor should "cultural genocide" be used in the game: "Which is more horrible, to kill and torture; or, remove the reason and will to live?" Both are horrible.

—Robert Davis and Mark Zannis
The Genocide Machine in Canada, 1973

8

FANTASIES OF THE MASTER RACE
The Cinematic Colonization of American Indians

◆◆◆◆◆◆◆◆◆◆◆◆◆

Now those movie Indians wearing all those feathers can't come out
as human beings. They're not expected to come out as human beings because I think the American people do not regard them as
wholly human. We must remember that many, many American
children believe that feathers grow out of Indian heads.

—Stephan Feraca
Motion Picture Director, 1964

THE CINEMATIC DEPICTION OF INDIGENOUS PEOPLES IN AMERICA IS OBJECTIVELY
racist at all levels. This observation encompasses not only the more than 2,000 Hollywood movies featuring or at least touching upon such subject matters over the years,
but the even greater number of titles made for television.[1] In this, film is linked closely
to literature of both the fictional and ostensibly nonfictional varieties, upon which
most scripts are based. It is thus both fair and accurate to observe that all modes of
projecting images and attendant conceptualizations of native people to the "mainstream" public fit the same mold.[2] Moreover, it is readily observable that within the
confines of this mold are included only the narrowest and most negative range of
graphic/thematic possibilities.[3]

While the same points might undoubtedly be made with respect to the celluloid
portrayals accorded any/all "primitive" peoples, or even people of color per se, the vast
weight, more than 4,500 productions in all, has fallen upon American Indians.[4] On
balance, it seems no overstatement to suggest that throughout the twentieth century
mass audiences have been quite literally saturated with very specific and repetitive dramatic characterizations of Indians. It follows, as with anything pursued with such intensity, that these characterizations themselves have been carefully contrived to serve
certain ends.[5]

It would be well, then, to come to grips with the manner in which Indians have
been displayed on both tube and silver screen, as well as the stimulus underlying it.
And, since the former may be easily divided into several distinct but related categories of
stereotyping—indeed, it virtually divides itself in this way—it seems appropriate to take
each in turn, using the whole as a basis upon which to explore the question of motive(s).

INDIANS AS CREATURES OF A PARTICULAR TIME

Nothing, perhaps, is more emblematic of Hollywood's visual pageantry than scenes of Plains Indian warriors astride their galloping ponies, many of them trailing a flowing headdress in the wind, thundering into battle against the blue-coated troops of the United States. By now, more than 500 feature films and half again as many television productions have included representations of this sort.[6] We have been served such fare along with that of the tipi and the buffalo hunt, the attack upon the wagon train and the ambush of the stagecoach, until they have become so indelibly imprinted upon the American consciousness as to be synonymous with Indians as a whole (to nonindians at any rate and, unfortunately, to many native people as well).[7]

It's not the technical inaccuracies in such representations that are most problematic, although these are usually many and often extreme. Rather, it is the fact that the period embodied in such depictions spans barely the three decades running from 1850 to 1880, the interval of warfare between the various Plains peoples and the ever-encroaching soldiers and settlers of the United States.[8] There is no "before" to the story, and there is no "after." Cinematic Indians have no history before Euroamericans come along to momentarily imbue them with it, and then, mysteriously, they seem to pass out of existence altogether.[9]

So it has been since the earliest experimental flickers like *Buck Dancer* and *Serving Rations to the Indians* in 1898. Never, with the exception of the sublimely ridiculous *Windwalker* (1980), has an effort been made to produce a movie centering on the life of Native North Americans a thousand years before Columbus, a timeframe corresponding rather favorably to that portrayed in such eurocentric epics as Robert Wise's 1955 *Helen of Troy*, or Cecil B. DeMille's extravagant remake of his 1924 *The Ten Commandments* in 1956. Nowhere will one find a Native American counterpart to *Quo Vadis?* (1912; 1951), *The Robe* (1953), *Ben Hur* (1907; 1926; 1959), *Spartacus* (1960), *Cleopatra* (1917; 1934; 1963) or any of scores of less noteworthy releases set deep in what Euroamerica takes to be its own heritage.[10]

Much the same vacuum pertains to depictions of things Indian after conclusion of the so-called "Indian Wars" (they were actually settlers' wars throughout).[11] While a relative few films have been devoted to, or at least include, twentieth-century Native Americans, they have largely served to trivialize and degrade us through "humor." These include such "classics" as Busby Berkeley's *Whoopee!* (1930), the Marx Brothers' *Go West* (1940) and the W.C. Fields/Mae West hit *My Little Chickadee* (1940), as well as Abbott and Costello's *Ride 'Em Cowboy* (1942).[12] Other heavy hitters include the Bowery Boys' *Bowery Buckaroo* (1947), Bob Hope's *Paleface* (1948), *Son of Paleface* (1952) and *Cancel My Reservation* (1972), not to mention Lewis and Martin's *Hollywood or Bust* (1956).[13]

As Daniel Francis comments, Euroamericans "did not expect Indians to adapt to the modern world. Their only hope was to assimilate, to become White, to cease to be Indians. In this view, a modern Indian is a contradiction in terms: Whites could not imagine such a thing. Any Indian was by definition a traditional Indian, a relic of the past."[14] To find "real" or "serious" Indians, then, it was necessary to look back upon the "vanishing" species of the nineteenth century, a theme diligently pursued in early documentaries like Edward Sheriff Curtis' perversely titled *In the Land of the Head-hunters* (1913–14) and Robert Flaherty's *Nanook of the North* (1922), and subsequently picked up in commercial movies like *The Vanishing American* (1925), *Eskimo* (1930), *The Last of the Redman* (1947), *Last of the Comanches* (1953), *The Last Frontier* (1955), *The Last Hunt* (1956), *The Apache's Last Battle* (1966) and, most recently, the Academy Award-winning *Dances With Wolves* (1990), *The Last of the Mohicans* (1992), and *Last of His Tribe* (1995).[15] All the while, untold thousands of doomed savages have been marched off to the oblivion of their reservations at the end of literally hundreds of lesser films.

In its most virulent form, Hollywood's "famous disappearing Indian" trick was backdated onto the nineteenth century's "crimsoned prairie" itself, rendering native people invisible even there. One will look in vain for any sign of an indigenous presence, even as backdrop, in such noteworthy westerns as *High Noon* (1952), *Shane* (1953), *Gunfight at the OK Corral* (1957), *Warlock* (1959), *Pat Garrett and Billy the Kid* (1973), *Heaven's Gate* (1981), and *Tombstone* (1994). It's as if, observes Cherokee artist/aesthetician/cultural theorist Jimmie Durham, at "some point late at night, by the campfire, presumably, the Lone Ranger ate Tonto. By the time Alan Ladd becomes the lone ranger in *Shane*, his Indian companion has been consumed."[16]

In the alternative, when not being depicted as drunken buffoons, as in *Flap* (1970), or simply as buffoons, as in the 1989 "road" movie *Powwow Highway*, modern Indians have been mostly portrayed in a manner deriving directly from the straightjacket of temporal stereotype.[17] The ways in which this has been accomplished are somewhat varied, ranging from 1950s war stories like *Battle Cry* and *Never So Few* to monster flicks like *Predator* (1987) and 1998's *Deep Rising*, and they have sometimes been relatively subtle, as in *One Flew Over the Cuckoo's Nest* (1975), but the rule nonetheless applies.

CREATURES OF A PARTICULAR PLACE

Constricting the window of Native America's celluloid existence to the mid-nineteenth century, simply because it was then the locus of Indian/white warfare, has had the collateral effect of confining natives to the geographic region known generically as the "West." In truth, the area is itself subdivided into several distinct bioregional locales, of which Hollywood selected two, the Plains and the Upper Sonoran Desert region of New Mexico and Arizona (often referred to as the "Southwest"), as being representative. It follows that the bulk of tinseltown's filmstock would be expended in setting forth images of the peoples indigenous to its chosen domain(s).[18]

The Plains of Filmdom are shown to be inhabited primarily by "Sioux" (Lakotas) to the north, Cheyennes in the center, and Comanches to the south. Not infrequently, smaller peoples like the Arapahos and Kiowas (or "Kee-oo-wahs," as it was often mispronounced) make appearances, and, every now and again, Pawnees and Crows as well (usually as scouts for the army).[19] Leaving aside a host of glaring inaccuracies otherwise conveyed by filmmakers about each of these cultures, it can be said that they at least managed (or bothered) to get the demographic distribution right.

Not so the Southwest. Although the "empty desert" was/is filled with a host of peoples running the gamut from the Hopi, Zuni, and other "Puebloans" to the Pima, Maricopa, Cocopah, Yuma, Yaqui, and Navajo, anyone taking their ethnographic cues from the movies would be led rapidly to the conclusion that there was but one: The Apaches.[20] In fact, more films have been dedicated to supposedly depicting Apacheria than the domain of any other native people, the "mighty Sioux" included.[21]

The roster began with silent movies like *Apache Gold* (1910; remade in 1965), *The Curse of the Red Man* (1911), *On the Warpath* (1912), and *A Prisoner of the Apaches* (1913), was continued with talkies like *Bad Lands* and *Stagecoach* in the 1930s, and has most recently included Cherokee actor Wes Studi playing the title role in the third remake of *Geronimo* (1990; earlier versions appeared in 1939 and 1962). Along the way, there have been *Apache Trail* (1942) and *Apache Chief* (1949), *Apache Warrior* (1957), and *Apache Woman* (1955), *Apache War Smoke* (1952) and *Apache Uprising* (1965), *Apache Country* (1953), and *Apache Territory* (1958), *Apache Rifles* (1965) and *Fury of the Apaches* (1965), *The Battle at Apache Pass* (1952), *Stand at Apache River* (1953), *Rampage at Apache Wells* (1966), and *40 Guns to Apache Pass* (1966). On and on and on. The count at this point is nearly 600 titles and rising, plus an untold number of skits made for TV. [22]

The reasoning here is true to form. The people of Victorio and Geronimo, Mangus and Cochise, sustained their resistance to Euroamerican invasion longer, and in a proportionately more effective fashion, than any group other than the Seminoles (who, fortunately or unfortunately for them, depending on one's point of view, did their fighting in the wrong place/time to fall much within the bounds of proper cinematography).[23] Give the duration and intensity of their martial interaction with whites, Apaches could be seen as "consequential," and therefore worthy of an equal intensity of cinematic attention.

There is a certain consistency to this prioritization, albeit a patently objectionable one. Things really become confusing, however, when one considers the approach taken by John Ford, perhaps the most esteemed director of the entire western movie genre. Simultaneously fixated on the beadwork, buckskins, and feather heraldry of Plains Indians and the breathtaking desert geography of the Southwest's Monument Valley, both for what he described as "aesthetic reasons," Ford exercised his "artistic license" by simply combining the two. Still, he and his publicists proudly, loudly, and persistently proclaimed his "unparalleled achievement" in capturing an ultimately "authentic" flavor in visually evoking the "Old West."[24]

Ford won Academy Award nominations for two of the seven pictures he shot in Monument Valley between 1939 and 1964, all of which received substantial critical acclaim.[25] Meanwhile, in *Stagecoach* (1939), *The Searchers* (1956), and *Cheyenne Autumn* (1964), two generations of American moviegoers were brought to understand that western Kansas looks just like northern Arizona, and, consequently, the environments of the Comanches and Cheyennes were indistinguishable from that of the Apaches. As Lakota scholar Vine Deloria, Jr., explains, "It's the same as if Hollywood were claiming to have made the most realistic movie ever about the Cossacks, and it turned out to have been filmed in fishing villages along the Irish coast, or with the Matterhorn as a backdrop. It makes a difference, because culture and environment are pretty intimately connected."[26]

The situation was even more muddled by the fact that before 1965, an era in which location shooting was beyond the budgets of all but the most prestigious directors, the very same Plains topography was represented in literally hundreds of B-movies and TV segments via the Spahn Movie Ranch and similar sets scattered across southern California.[27] By the seventies, when increasing attention began to be paid to the idea that films might be "validated" by way of the technical accuracy inhering in their physical details, the damage had long since been done. American Indians, already denied any sort of genuinely autochthanous history in the movies, had been thoroughly divorced from material reality as well.

SEEN ONE INDIAN, SEEN 'EM ALL

The space/time compression imposed by Hollywood upon Native America has generated other effects, to be sure. "You would think," writes Cherokee law professor Rennard Strickland, "if you relied on the Indian films, that there were no [peoples] east of the Mississippi, none but the Plains Indians [and Apaches], except possibly the Mohawks, and that the country was unoccupied throughout the entire Great Lakes and central region except for an occasional savage remnant, perhaps a stray Yaqui or two who wandered in from the Southwest. We almost never have a Chippewa or a Winnebago or a . . . Hopi or even a Navajo on the screen."[28]

In the few instances filmmakers decided, for whatever reason, to make a movie about native people in the East, the results have usually been bizarre. A prime example, pointed out by Strickland, is that of *Seminole Uprising* (1955), in which we "see Florida Everglades-dwelling Seminoles wearing Plains feathered bonnets and battling bluecoated cavalry on desert buttes."[29] The same principle pertains in somewhat less blatant form to the attire displayed in four other films—*Distant Drums* (1951), *Seminole* (1953), *War Arrow* (1954), and *Yellowneck* (1957)—made about the Seminoles during the same period.[30]

Nor is the displacement of Plains Indian attributes onto other peoples the end of it. The Plains cultures themselves have become distorted in the popular conception, often wildly so, by virtue of a succession of cinematographers' obsessions with conjuring up "great images" out of whatever strikes their fancy. Perhaps the best (or worst) example will be found in *A Man Called Horse* (1970), a movie prefaced with a scrolled testimonial from the Smithsonian Institution's chief "ethnohistorian," Wilcomb Washburn, that it was "the most authentic description of American Indian life ever filmed."[31]

In actuality, borrowing its imagery willy-nilly from the full body of George Catlin's graphic survey of northern Plains cultures during the 1830s,[32] director Eliott Silver-stein's staff had decided that the "Lakotas" depicted in the film should wear an array of hairstyles ranging those typical of the Assiniboin to those of their mortal enemies, the Crows. Their tipi design and decoration is also of a sort unique to Crows. About the only thing genuinely "Sioux" about these supposed Sioux is the name, and even then there is absolutely no indication as to which Sioux they are supposed to be. Oglalas? Hunkpapas? Minneconjous? Sicangus (Brûlés)? Bohinunpas (Two Kettles)? Ituzipcos (Sans Arcs)? Sihasapas (Blackfeet; not to be confused with the indigenous nation of the same name)? The Lakotas, after all, were/are a populous people, divided into seven distinct bands, at least as different from one another as Maine Yankees are from Geor-gia Crackers.[33]

Probably the most repugnant instance of transference in *A Man Called Horse* occurs when Silverstein has his "Sioux" prepare to conduct a Sun Dance, their central spiritual ceremony, in a domed below-ground structure of the sort unknown to Lakota culture but habituated by Mandans along the Missouri River. The ritual itself is then per-formed in a manner more or less corresponding to Catlin's description of the Mandan, *not* the Lakota practice of it.[34] Finally, the meaning of the ceremony, sublimely reveren-tial for both peoples, is explained as being something akin to medieval Europe's macho tests of courage, thence "manhood," by the ability to unflinchingly absorb pain.

Surveying the ubiquitousness of such cinematic travesties as "Delawares dressed as Sioux" and "Indians of Manhattan Island . . . dwelling in tipis," even an establish-mentarian like Alanson Skinner, curator of the Department of Anthropology at the American Museum of Natural History, prefigured Deloria. Condemning such things as "ethnographically grotesque farces" in the pages of the *New York Times*, he posed the obvious question: "If Indians should stage a white man's play, and dress the char-acters in Rumanian, Swiss, Turkish, English, Norwegian and Russian costumes, and place the setting in Ireland, would their pleas that they thought all Europeans alike save them from arousing our ridicule?"[35]

Skinner might also have inquired as to the likely response had Indians portrayed High Mass as a Protestant Communion, interpreted the wine and wafers as symbolic cannibalism, and then implied that the whole affair was synonymous with Satanism. It matters little, however, since until very recently no Indians—with the momentary exception during the 1930s of Will Rogers, a Cherokee—have ever been in a position to make either "plays" or films in which they could personify themselves more accu-rately, much less parody their white tormentors.[36]

A major reason the "seen one Indian, seen 'em all" attitude had become quite firmly entrenched among the public by the end of the fifties was that the public was literally seeing no Indians of any sort in Hollywood's endless renderings of things na-tive. Aside from Molly Spotted Elk, a Penobscot cast as the lead in *Silent Enemy* (1930), and Rogers, who filled the same bill in several comedies during the thirties, no Indian appeared in a substantial film role prior to 1970.[37] The same can be said with respect to directors and scriptwriters.[38]

Instead, pleading all along that it just couldn't find Indians capable of playing

themselves on screen "convincingly," Hollywood consistently hired whites to impersonate native people in a more "believable" manner. As a consequence, the history of
American cinema is replete with such gems as the 6'4" blond, blue-eyed former professional baseball pitcher Chuck Connors being cast as the swarthy, 5'3", obsidian-
eyed title character in *Geronimo* (1962). And, if this "makes about as much sense as
casting Wilt Chamberlain to play J. Edgar Hoover," as one native actor lately put it,
there are plenty of equally egregious examples.[39]

Take Victor Mature being cast as the great Lakota leader in *Chief Crazy Horse*
(1955). Or Gilbert Roland and Ricardo Montalban as the no less illustrious Dull Knife
and Little Wolf in *Cheyenne Autumn* (1946). Or Jeff Chandler cast as Cochise, an
Apache of comparable stature, in *Broken Arrow* (1950). Or Rock Hudson cast in the title role of *Taza, Son of Cochise* (1954). Or Burt Lancaster as the Sac and Fox super-ath-
lete in *Jim Thorpe—All American* (1951).[40] Or J. Carol Naish as *Sitting Bull* (1954). Or
Tony Curtis cast as Pima war hero Ira Hayes in *The Outsider* (1961). Or Robert Blake
in the title role of *Tell Them Willie Boy Is Here* (1969). Or how about Robbie Benson
(no less) playing Lakota Olympic gold medalist Billy Mills in *Running Brave* (1983)?
The list could obviously be extended to include thousands of such illustrations.[41]

Women? Try Debra Paget as Cochise's daughter in *Broken Arrow*. How about Mary
Pickford as "the little Indian maiden [who] Paid Her Debt of Gratitude" to the White
Man with sex in *Iola's Promise* (1912)? Or Delores Del Rio in the title role of *Ramona*
(1928)? Or Linda Darnell as the "Indian" female lead in *Buffalo Bill* (1944)? Or Jennifer Jones as the sultry "half-breed" in *Duel in the Sun* (1946)? May Wynn as a nameless "Indian maiden" in *They Rode West* (1954)? Donna Reed as Sacajawea in *The Far
Horizon* (1955)? And then there's Julie Newmar, complete with a pair of designer
slacks, as the indigenous sex symbol in *McKenna's Gold* (1969)? Again, the list might
go on for pages.[42]

We should perhaps be grateful that John Wayne was never selected to play Red
Cloud, or Madonna Pocahontas, but given Hollywood's overall record—Wayne *was*
cast as the Mongol leader Genghis Khan in a 1956 release entitled *The Conqueror*—
such things seem more a matter of oversight than of design.[43]

Even when Indians were deployed on-screen, usually as extras—a job Oneida ac-
tor/comedian Charley Hill likens to serving as a "prop" or, more accurately, "a pop-up
target to be shot full of holes by cowboys and cavalrymen"[44]—little concern was ever
given to accuracy. John Ford, for instance, habitually hired Navajos to impersonate the
peoples of the Plains with no apparent qualms about the groups being as physically dis-
similar as Swedes and Sicilians.[45] Cumulatively, Hill describes the results of Hollywood's and the television industry's imaging as the creation of "a weird sort of Indian
stew" rather than anything resembling a valid apprehension of indigenous realities.[46]

PEOPLES WITHOUT CULTURE

The emulsification of native cultural content embodied in Hollywood's handling of it
amounted, in essence, to its negation. As Rennard Strickland points out, "In the thou-

sands of individual films and the millions of frames in those films, we have few, if any, real Indians . . . who have individuality or humanity. We see little, if any, of home or village life, of the day-to-day world of Native Americans or their families."[47] Creation of this vacuum has, in turn, allowed filmmakers to figuratively reconstruct native culture(s) in accordance with their own biases, preconceptions, or senses of expediency and convenience.

Mostly, they elected to follow the quasi-official script traditionally advanced by the Smithsonian Institution, that Native North Americans were, until Euroamericans came along to "civilize" us, typically brutish Stone Age savages, maybe a million primitives wandering nomadically about the landscape, perpetually hunting and gathering our way along the bare margins of subsistence, devoid of all that might be called true culture.[48] An astonishing example of such (mis)perceptions at play will be found in the 1954 film *Apache*, in which the sullen southwesterners are taught to cultivate corn by a group of displaced southeasterners, Cherokees, who supposedly picked up the "art" from their benevolent white neighbors in Georgia.[49]

Never mind that it is an established fact that corn was hybridized from grass by indigenous Americans centuries before an Italian seaman, now revered as a "Great Navigator," washed up on a Caribbean beach half a world away from where he thought he was. Never mind that, like corn, two-thirds of the vegetal foodstuffs now commonly consumed by humanity were undeniably under cultivation in the Americas and *nowhere else* at the time of the "Columbian landfall."[50] Never mind that, as a matter of record, American military commanders from John Sullivan to Anthony Wayne, even Kit Carson, had to burn off miles of native croplands in order to starve Indians onto reservations where we could be "taught to farm."[51]

Agriculture is indicative of civilization, not savagery, and so, ipso facto, Indians could not have engaged in it, no matter how self-evident the fact that we did, or how extensively so.[52] In its stead, the Smithsonian, and therefore Hollywood, bestowed upon us an all-consuming and wholly imaginary "warrior mystique," that is to say, a certain propensity to use force in stealing from others that which we had, in their telling, never learned to do or make for ourselves. Thus were the relational roles of Indian and white in American history quite neatly and completely reversed so that those who stole a continent might be consistently portrayed as the victims of their victims' wanton and relentless "aggression."[53]

Such themes have always been exceedingly difficult to apply to the East where it had taken Europe fully two centuries of armed conflict with masses of native people to "win the day." How to explain that we who were supposedly so few had managed, generation after generation, to field so many in the course of our resistance? And how, once our real numbers were to some extent admitted, to explain either where we went, or how we'd been able to sustain ourselves for all those thousands of years before "the coming of the white man" supposedly endowed us with the miracle of growing our own food?[54]

To be fair, Hollywood *has* tried to incorporate such matters into its master narrative, especially during its formative years. From 1908 to 1920, not less than 28 feature films and perhaps a hundred one-reel shorts purported to deal with Indian/white relations during the sixteenth, seventeenth, and eighteenth centuries.[55] Without substantially altering the structure of narrative itself, however, the task proved impossible, or nearly so, and thereafter the number of such pictures declined steadily, centering mainly in the above-mentioned "Seminole" movies and periodic remakes of James Fenimore Cooper's "Leatherstocking" fables.[56]

Thus, by 1935 movieland had locked in all but monolithically upon the final round of wars in the West as its interpretive vehicle. The choice carried obvious advantages in that it placed Indians entirely within a geography remote from, and thus alien to, the vast majority of nonindians residing east of the Mississippi (and, later, along the west coast). From there, it seemed reasonable to expect that the people inhabiting the area might seem equally alien and remote. Also helpful was the fact that western lands did/do not appear suitable for farming, and that the events ostensibly depicted occurred at the very point when the native population, already reduced by some ninety percent and suffering severe dislocation from its traditional ways of life, was fighting most frantically to stave off being liquidated altogether.[57]

Having attained such utter decontextualization, filmmakers were free to indulge themselves—and their audiences—almost exclusively in fantasies of Indians as warriors. Not just any warriors, mind you, but those of a most hideously bestial variety. This is exemplified in John Ford's *Stagecoach*, where the director uses techniques common to monster movies of the era, and which would later be employed to great effect in the sci-fi flicks of the fifties, in building among his viewers a tremendous sense of dread long before any Indian is allowed to appear. Then, late in the movie, when the "Apaches" finally materialize, they are portrayed in an entirely dimensionless and inhuman fashion.[58]

Some directors went Ford one better, hiring actors known mostly for their portrayals of actual cinematic monsters to play native people. Bela Lugosi, for instance, who would later gain fame as the vampire in *Dracula*, was cast as Uncas in a 1922 German-made version of *Last of the Mohicans* which was received quite well in the U.S.[59] Cecil B. DeMille selected Boris Karloff, already famous as the creature in *Frankenstein*, to play an Indian in his 1947 movie *Unconquered*.[60] "Wolfman" Lon Chaney was also cast repeatedly in such roles, most notably in *The Pathfinder and the Mohican* (1956), *Along the Mohawk Trail* (1956), and *The Long Rifle* (1964), a ghastly trilogy pasted together from episodes of the *Hawkeye and the Last of the Mohicans* TV series (CBS; 1957–58).[61]

In other instances—Robert Mulligan's *The Stalking Moon* (1968) comes to mind—things are put even more straightforwardly. Here, a fictional Apache named "Salvaje," is withheld from view for most of the movie (à la *Stagecoach*) as he tracks a terrified Gregory Peck and Eva Marie Sainte across two states. Towards the end of the film Salvaje is finally revealed, but always from a distance and garbed in a strange and very un-Apachean set of "cave man" furs conveying the distinct impression that he is actually a dangerous form of animal life.[62]

Hundreds of movies and television segments follow more or less the same formula.

Those that don't revolve around the notion of individual Indians being caught up in the full-time job of "menacing" unoffending whites most often have us far too busy *attacking* the same victims in "swarms," howling like "wolves," slaughtering and mutilating the innocent or carrying them away as captives upon whom we can work our animalistic wills at leisure.[63] And believe it or not, those, for Hollywood, are our *good* points.

The "down" side is that, even as warriors, we are in the end abysmally incompetent. Witness how gratuitously we expend ourselves while riding our ponies around and around the circled wagons of our foes (time after time after time). Watch as we squander our strength in pointless frontal assaults upon the enemy's most strongly fortified positions (again and again and again).[64] Worst of all, observe that we don't even know how to use our weapons properly, a matter brought forth most clearly in *A Man Called Horse*, when scriptwriter Jack DeWitt and director Silverstein team up to have an Englishman, played by Richard Harris, teaching his "Sioux" captors how best to employ their bows and arrows when repelling an attack by other Indians.[65]

Small wonder, given our continuous bombardment with such malignant trash, that by the 1950s, probably earlier, American Indian children had often become as prone as anyone else to "root for the cavalry" in its cinematic extermination of their ancestors (and, symbolically, themselves).[66] "After all," asked a native student in one of my recent film classes (by way of trying to explain the phenomenon to her nonindian peers), "who wants to identify with such a bunch of losers?" Yes, who indeed?

THE ONLY GOOD INDIAN . . .

"The only good Indians I ever saw," General Phil Sheridan famously observed in 1869, "were dead."[67] Filmmakers, for their part, brought such sentiments to life on the screen with a vengeance, beginning at least as early as D.W. Griffith's *The Battle of Elderbush Gulch* in 1913.[68] By the mid-30s, native people were being symbolically eradicated in the movies at a truly astounding rate, often with five or six of us falling every time a single bullet was fired by gallant white men equipped with what were apparently fifty-shot six-shooters.[69] The celluloid bloodbath by no means abated until a general decline of public interest in westerns during the mid-to-late 1960s.[70]

So fixated was Hollywood upon images of largescale Indian killing by the military during the late nineteenth century that it transplanted them to some extent into western Canada, where nothing of the sort occurred. Apparently preoccupied with the possibility that the red coats of the North West Mounted Police (NWMP; now the Royal Canadian Mounted Police, RCMP) might look better on screen than U.S. army blue, directors simply shifted the Mounties into the role traditionally filled by the cavalry and cranked away.[71]

The first such epic, *The Flaming Forest*, appeared in 1926 and has the NWMP putting down the first Métis rebellion (1868) five years before the Mounties actually appeared on the scene. In 1940, DeMille made a picture entitled *North West Mounted Police*, about the second Métis rebellion (1885). Three features—*Fort Vengeance*

(1953), *Saskatchewan* (1954), and *The Canadians* (1961)—were then produced on the theme of Mounties battling Sitting Bull's Lakota refugees during their brief Canadian sojourn in the late 1870s.[72]

In the style of the shoot-'em-up western, Indians in the Mountie movies attacked wagon trains, burned settlers' cabins and roasted captives at the stake, all things that never took place in the Canadian West. The Canadian frontier had its problems: the illicit trade in alcohol, the disappearance of the buffalo, the spread of disease. But these were not the problems moviegoers saw. Rather the Mountie movie provided another opportunity for the Hollywood dream machine to act out its melodramatic fantasies about the American Wild West.[73]

Meanwhile, another sort of "good" Indian was being cultivated. Based archetypally on Fenimore Cooper's Chingachgook and/or Daniel Defoe's Friday in *Robinson Crusoe*, the character is exemplified by "Tonto"—the word literally means "fool, dunce, or dolt" in Spanish—"faithful Indian companion" of *The Lone Ranger* radio program's masked white hero from 1933 onward.[74] By 1938, the formula had proven so popular that it was serialized by moviemakers as Saturday matinee fare. The serial was condensed into a 1940 feature entitled *Hi-Ho Silver* before mutating into a longrunning ABC TV series in 1948.[75] Back in theater venues with *The Lone Ranger* in 1956 and *The Lone Ranger and the City of Gold* in 1958, the Masked Man and Tonto did not make their final big screen appearance (to date) until a 1979 remake of the 1956 film.[76]

As Cherokee analyst Rayna Green explains, the "good Indian [embodied in Tonto] acts as a friend to the white man, offering . . . aid, rescue, and spiritual and physical comfort even at the cost of his own life or status and comfort in his own [nation] to do so. He saves white men from 'bad' Indians, and thus becomes a 'good' Indian."[77] Or, to quote Canadian author Daniel Francis, the "Good Indian is one who stands shoulder to shoulder" with whites in their "settlement" of the continent, serving as "loyal friends and allies" to the invaders who were committing genocide to fulfill their self-assigned "Manifest Destiny" of possessing *all* native land and resources.[78] It is "their antiquated, stoic acceptance" of their own inherent inferiority to Euroamericans and, consequently, "their individual fate and the ultimate demise of their people that endeared these noble savages to white [audiences]."[79]

By 1950, the stereotype had been perfected to a point that director Delmer Daves was prepared to deploy it as the centerpiece of his *Broken Arrow*, usually considered to be the first major motion picture to attempt a "sympathetic" depiction of Indians.[80] Based loosely on the real life interaction during the 1870s between Cochise, a principal Chiricahua Apache leader, and a white scout named Tom Jeffords, the entire story is presented through the voice-over narrative of the latter while the former is reduced in the end to a Kiplingesque parody of himself.[81] So edifying was Daves' treatment to mainstream viewers that the film received a special award from the thoroughly nonindian Association of American Indian Affairs and Jeff Chandler, the then-unknown white actor cast as Cochise, was nominated for an Academy Award. Television quickly cashed in when NBC cloned a *Broken Arrow* TV series which ran for several seasons.[82]

Every cinematic good guy must, of course, be counterbalanced by a "heavy."[83] In *Broken Arrow*, the requirement is met by the film's handling of Geronimo, another important Chiricahua leader. Where Cochise's "virtue" is manifested in the lengths to which he is prepared to go in achieving not just peace but cordiality with whites—at one point Daves even has him executing another Apache to ensure the safety of his friend Jeffords—Geronimo's "badness" is embodied in the adamance of his refusal to do the same. In essence, capitulation/accommodation to aggression is defined as "good," resistance as "evil."[84] As S. Elizabeth Bird has framed the matter, wherever plot lines devolve upon "constructive" figures like *Broken Arrow*'s fictionalized Cochise:

> [T]he brutal savage is still present in the recurring image of the rene-gade . . . These Indians have not accepted White control, refuse to stay on the reservation, and use violent means to combat White people, raiding farms and destroying White property. Although occasional lip service is paid to the just-ness of their anger, the message is clear that these warriors are misguided. [En-lightened whites] are frequently seen trying to persuade the friendly Indians to curb the ["hostiles'"] excesses. The renegades are clearly defined as deviant, out of control, and a challenge to the ["Good Indian"] who suffers all indignities with a stoic smile and acknowledgment that really there are many good, kind White people who wish this had never happened.[85]

The dichotomy of indigenous good and evil thus concretized in Daves' historically distortive juxtaposing of Cochise and Geronimo was almost immediately hammered home in *Taza, Son of Cochise*, another vaguely historical film in which one of the long-suffering Apache's two sons, Tahzay, who followed his father onto the San Carlos Reservation and ultimately succeeded him as principal Chiricahua leader, is employed as the vehicle for depicting native virtue. He is framed in harsh contrast to his brother, Naiche, a "recalcitrant" who was a noted figure in Geronimo's protracted resistance struggle. [86]

From there, such scenarios became something of an industry standard. As early as 1951, in *Across the Wide Missouri*, MGM cast Clark Gable in a role quite similar to James Stewart's portrayal of Tom Jeffords in *Broken Arrow*.[87] In 1952, the same studio had a youthful Charlton Heston playing an oddly Cochise-like Sioux in *The Savage*. In *Drum Beat* (1954), it was Alan Ladd's turn to emulate Stewart's performance, although no suitable counterpart to Cochise materialized. Other period films attempting more or less the same thematics included *The Big Sky* (1952), *The Great Sioux Uprising* (1953), *The Last Wagon* (1956), *Walk the Proud Land* (1956), *The Redmen and the Renegades* (1956), *The Oregon Trail* (1959), *The Unforgiven* (1960), *The Long Rifle and the Tomahawk* (1964), *Last of the Renegades* (1966), and *Frontier Hellcat* (1966).[88]

Although the drop in the number of westerns produced after the latter years has re-sulted in a corresponding diminishment in the number of such "statements" by Hollywood, there is ample evidence that the Good Indian genre remains alive, well, and firmly entrenched. Prime examples will be found in the parts assigned Squamish actor Dan George in such acclaimed films as *Little Big Man* (1970) and *The Outlaw Josey Wales* (1976), Lakota AIM leader *cum* actor Russell Means in the latest version of *Last of the Mohicans*, Graham Greene, an Oneida, in *Thunderheart* (1991), Eric Schweig as *Squanto* (1994), and, most recently, the character portrayed by Cree actor Gordon Tootoosis in *Legends of the Fall* (1996).[89]

Television also followed up on the early success enjoyed by ABC's *Broken Arrow* with a CBS effort, *Brave Eagle* (1955–56) and NBC's dismal *Hawkeye* series. In 1957, ABC weighed in again with *Cheyenne*, staring *Yellowstone Kelly*'s Clint Walker as a part-Indian cowboy/scout obviously inclined towards his "better" genetics (the series was highly popular and ran until 1963). NBC finally scored in 1959 with *Law of the Plainsman*, an utterly incongruous saga in which a fourteen-year-old Apache boy "about to scalp a wounded army captain, inexplicably relents and nurses the soldier back to health. The captain adopts the supposedly nameless boy, christening him Sam Buckhart. Sam eventually goes to Harvard, then becomes a lawman in New Mexico [serving] the larger society in trying to calm angry natives."[90]

So well was the latter theme received that ABC countered in 1966 with *Hawk*, a series starring part-Seminole actor Burt Reynolds as a contemporary New York police lieutenant of mixed ancestry. There being no Indian uprisings to quell in the Big Apple, the program folded after only three months, only to be replaced in 1974 with *Nakia*, a series focused on a Navajo, played by stock Indian stand-in Robert Forster, who hires on as a rural New Mexico deputy sheriff in furtherance of his struggle to "bridge" himself from the anachronism of his own society to the "modern world" of Euroamerica.[91]

The latest in television's seemingly endless variations on the "Good Indian" theme came with CBS's *Dr. Quinn, Medicine Woman* in 1992. A transparent genuflection to the "postmodern" mainstream sensibilities of the nineties, the series' predominantly white cast is peopled by "several strong, independent women; a male population of bigots and weaklings, who receive their comeuppance from Dr. Quinn on a weekly basis; and one African-American couple, who provide opportunities for Dr. Quinn to display her progressive fervor."[92] An interesting setting is provided by a nearby "Cheyenne village" whose mostly anonymous inhabitants engage themselves for the most part in looking perfectly serene and "natural," although the show is set in Colorado during the very period when the territorial government was waging what it called a "campaign of extermination" against them.[93]

The main Indian character is "Cloud Dancing," a supposed traditional healer played by Larry Sellers who spends most of his time alternately passing his secrets to and trying to learn from the *real* "Medicine Woman"—who is of course a white M.D.—all the while looking sad and, most of all, being "friendly." He is "a calm, noble person who never fights back and is grateful for the attentions of heroic White individuals."[94] As the series progresses, Cloud Dancing loses an unborn child because of his wife's malnutrition (caused by white buffalo hunters' killing off the Cheyennes' main food supply); his adult son is killed while saving Dr. Quinn's life; 45 members of his village die hideous deaths due to the whites' distribution of typhus-infested blankets; finally, he suffers the butchery of the remainder of his people, including his wife, first during the 3rd Colorado Volunteers' infamous Sand Creek Massacre of 1864 and then at the at the at the hands of Custer's cavalry during the 1868 Washita Massacre. The handling of the last incident is indicative of the rest.

> While Sand Creek has received only passing mention, [the] Washita was finally addressed in an episode broadcast late in the 1994–95 season. The episode was revealing in the characteristic way in which it showed the massacre—not as a catastrophe for the Cheyenne, but as a trauma for Michaela Quinn. She fails to talk Custer out of attacking and she and Sully [her boyfriend], along with Cloud Dancing, come upon the village, completely wiped out, with everyone dead. Cloud Dancing's wife, Snowbird, dies in his arms. Everything from then on continues from Michaela's point of view. She withdraws from her family, blames herself for the massacre, and goes into a depression. Finally, Cloud Dancing comes to her and assures her that it was not her fault, then spends several days passing on his medical skills to her, before leaving for South Dakota. Michaela returns to her family, and happiness reigns again.[95]

At another point, after Sully professes to being "sorry for everything my people are doing to yours," Cloud Dancing replies that the "spirits tell me anger is good [but] hate is not. There are good men, there are bad men. You're a good man, Sully. You're still my brother."[96] Every Indian-focused segment of *Dr. Quinn* is salted with comparable gestures of absolution and forgiveness from victim to victimizer. The "role of the Cheyenne is to provide an exotic, attractive backdrop for the heroes and, subtly, to suggest that they are willing to fade away in the face of White [superiority]. Part of that role is to die, sometimes in great numbers, in order to move the plot along [while] showcasing Michaela and Sully. The show has a knack for touching on some of the most horrific episodes in the history of Indian-White relations, yet nevertheless suggesting that everything really came out all right."[97]

What a wonderful tonic for a body politic beset during the Great Columbus Quincentennial Controversy of the early '90s by flickerings of doubt about the honor and even the legitimacy of "The American Heritage."[98] Small wonder, all things considered, that *Dr. Quinn* became the most popular new TV series of the 1992–93 season.[99] Someone out there has clearly found it expedient to ignore the response of a character played by Creek actor Will Sampson after being made the butt of Tonto jokes one too many times by his white partner in the 1977 CBS television movie *Relentless*: "Hey . . . Buck," sighs Sampson. "That's enough . . . No more."[100]

VOICES OF THE VOICELESS

All of this is, to be sure, pure nonsense. Real Indians—as opposed to Reel Indians— even of the Tonto variety, would never actually have said/done what Hollywood has needed us to say and do. Occasional snatches of autonomous dialogue such as that of Sampson quoted above make this abundantly clear. Hence, it has been necessary to render us either literally voiceless, as with the "Chief Broom" character Sampson played in *One Flew Over the Cuckoo's Nest*, or effectively so.

A standard means to the latter end ties directly to the more general nullification of indigenous culture addressed earlier. This takes the form of a pretense that native "tongues," despite their typically being just as intellectually refined and expressive as European languages, often more so—Micmac, for instance, evidences much more semantic precision and contains five times as many words as English[101]—are extraordinarily crude or "primitive." A classic example of how this is accomplished will be found in *The Way West* (1967), where director Andrew McLaglen has a "Sioux chief" wearing a Mohawk haircut and a woman's shawl address a group of whites with a string of Lakota terms selected seemingly at random (translated, they make up a meaningless word salad).[102]

One director went further, presenting his audiences with English language recordings played in reverse to signify the exotic sounds of spoken "Indian." Most often, however, filmmakers have simply followed historian Francis Parkman's notoriously ignorant comment that the word "How!" constitutes "a monosyllable by which an Indian contrives to express half the emotions of which he is susceptible."[103] Or, in fairness, they have elected to enrich Parkman's vocabulary by adding "Ugh," "Ho," and a smattering of guttural grunts. To this has been added a weird sort of pidgin English best described by Ralph Stedman as comprising a "Tonto School of Communication."[104] Consider as sufficient illustration the following four consecutive lines delivered by the faithful Indian companion during a *Lone Ranger* program aired on June 30, 1939.

> Who you?
> Ugh.
> You see-um him?
> Me want-um him.[105]

With Indians thus rendered functionally mute in our own right, however, it remained nonetheless necessary that audiences often be informed as to exactly how they should understand many of the celluloid savages' otherwise inexplicable on-screen actions. This problem was solved when, early in *Broken Arrow*, Delmer Daves has James Stewart peremptorily announce that "when the Apaches speak, it will be in our language."[106] From that point on, everything is explained "through the eyes of"—which is to say, from the point of view and *in the voice of*—Stewart's white character.

The same can be said of Audie Murphy's John Clum in *Walk the Proud Land*, the Britton Davis character in the latest remake of *Geronimo*, or any of a host of other real-life soldiers, settlers, and frontiersmen whose memoirs, letters, and diaries have been used as the basis for scripts purportedly telling "Indian" stories.[107] Completely fictional variants of the same device have also been used with such regularity over the past fifty years as to establish a cinematic convention. Sometimes it is adhered to in unorthodox ways, as when John Ford gratuitously appended a white female school-teacher to the body of fleeing Indians in *Cheyenne Autumn*, but inevitably there is a central white character to "tell the story of the Indians" in a manner familiar and ultimately comfortable to Euroamerican audiences.[108]

This is as true of *Soldier Blue* and *Little Big Man*, the so-called "revisionist" or "protest" flicks of 1970, and such successors as *Dances With Wolves*, as it is of the most blatantly reactionary John Wayne western.[109] Indeed, it may well be more so. John Wayne movies, after all, don't pretend to be *about* Indians, or even sympathetic to us. Rather, they are for the most part unabashed celebrations of our "conquest" and, in that sense at least, they are honest enough.[110]

The subgenre of "protest" or "progressive" films *do*, on the other hand, purport to be about native people, and sympathetically so. To this extent, they are fundamentally *dis*honest, if for no other reason than because the whole purpose of their persistent in-jection of nonindian narrators into indigenous contexts amounts to nothing so much as a way of creating the illusion of sympathetic *white* alternatives to Wayne's tri-umphalist status quo.

The most topical examples undoubtedly reside among the ever so enlightened and sensitive Euroamerican leads of *Dr. Quinn*. In fact, as S. Elizabeth Bird has observed with regard to the male character in particular, "Sully's ongoing role is to stand in for the Cheyennes, so that their culture can be represented, while they as a people can be pushed into the background. After all, he is a better Indian than the Cheyenne, as is made abundantly clear in the opening scene of one episode, when he beats Cloud Dancing at a tomahawk-throwing contest."[111] The principle applies equally to all such figures, from Dustin Hoffman's Jack Crabbe in *Little Big Man* to Richard Harris' Lord Morgan in *A Man Called Horse* to Kevin Costner's Lieutenant Dunbar in *Dances With Wolves* to Daniel Day-Lewis' Hawkeye in the most recent iteration of *Last of the Mohicans*.

Having thus contrived to substitute whites for Indians both verbally and to some extent physically as well, filmmakers have positioned themselves perfectly, not just to spin their yarns in whatever manner strikes their fancy at a given moment but to make them appear to have been embraced by all sides, native and nonnative alike. Hence, white story or Indian story, they become indistinguishable in the end, following as they do a mutual trajectory to the same destination within the master narrative of an overarching "American Story."[112]

THOSE CAVALIERS IN BUCKSKIN

The ways in which this has been accomplished have plainly undergone a significant metamorphosis through the years. In the "bad old days" of unadulterated triumphal-ism, plot lines invariably orbited around the personas of noble and heroic white fig-ures, whether ostensibly real or admittedly invented, with whom it was intended that audiences identify. Such projections were never as easily achieved as it may seem in retrospect, entailing for the most part a wholesale rewriting of history.

Irrespective of the false and degrading manner in which native people were depicted, it was still vitally important that cinematic whites be portrayed in ways which posed them as embodying some diametrically opposite set of "traits." This was no mean feat when it came to things like the 1890 Wounded Knee Massacre, still a vividly current event during the movies' early days, where U.S. troops had slaughtered more than 300 disarmed Lakota prisoners, overwhelmingly composed of women, children, and old men.[113]

The problem of how such behavior might come to be perceived was addressed, experimentally, by a group calling itself the Colonel W.F. Cody (Buffalo Bill) Historical Picture Company in 1914. Retaining General Nelson A. Miles, renowned as an expert Indian fighter, to verify the accuracy of their endeavor in much the same fashion Wilcomb Washburn would authenticate *A Man Called Horse* more than a half-century later, they produced a film entitled *The Indian Wars Refought*. In it, the "Battle of Wounded Knee" was reenacted in such a way as to show how the defenseless Lakotas had themselves "picked a fight" with the hundreds of well-armed soldiers surrounding them. The Indians had thus brought their fate upon themselves, so the story went, the troopers having "had no choice" but to defend themselves with Hotchkiss guns.[114]

Heavily promoted by its makers for use in, and widely adopted by, the nation's schools as a medium of "truth," the film set the "standard" for much of what would follow.[115] Within a few years, the reversal of reality was complete: the massacre at Wounded Knee was popularly understood to have been a "battle" while the 1876 annihilation of a portion of "General" (actually Lt. Colonel) George Armstrong Custer's 7th Cavalry Regiment in open combat was habitually described as a "massacre."[116] Indians were "killed" by whites while whites were always "murdered" by Indians; Indians "committed depredations" while whites "defended themselves" and "won victories."[117]

The same sort of systematic historical falsification was of course brought to bear on the records of individual whites, notably Custer himself. This was epitomized in director Raoul Walsh's casting of Hollywood's premier swashbuckling glamour boy, Errol Flynn, to play "the boy general" in *They Died With Their Boots On* (1941). Here, Custer, whose pedigree included the documented cowardice and desertion for which he was court-martialed and at one point relieved of his command, and whose main claim to fame as an Indian fighter rested in having perpetrated the Washita Massacre, is presented in an altogether different light.[118]

Actually, Walsh saw to it that neither the court martial nor the Washita were so much as mentioned, while Flynn's Custer was quite literally backlit with a Christ-like halo at various points in the film. Meanwhile, the man who broke the 1868 Fort Laramie Treaty with the Lakotas, Cheyennes, and Arapahos by leading an 1874 expedition into the Black Hills, the very heart of their homeland, was presented as its staunchest defender.[119] Similarly, although Custer personally instigated the war of conquest against these same peoples in which he was killed two years later—a gambit meant to further his presidential ambitions[120]—he is depicted as having gallantly sacrificed himself and his men to prevent just such a war.

And so it went, from Edward Sedgwick's *The Flaming Frontier* (1926) to DeMille's *The Plainsman* (1936), from Michael Curtiz's *The Santa Fe Trail* (1941) to Charles Marquiz Warren's *Little Big Horn* (1951), from Ernest Haycox's *Bugles in the Afternoon* (1952) to Joseph H. Lewis's *Seventh Cavalry* (1956), from Lewis R. Foster's *Tonka* (1958) to Sidney Salkow's *The Great Sioux Massacre* (1965). As late as 1967, director Robert Siodmak cast the dashing Irish actor Robert Shaw in the lead role when making his conspicuously Walsh-style *Custer of the West*.[121]

Although paleohistorians like Robert Utley persist to this day in describing the wretched Custer as a "cavalier in buckskins,"[122] the preferences of an appreciable portion of the U.S. viewing public had begun to undergo a sea change by the time Siodmak released his movie. Horrified at the prospect of being conscripted to serve as fodder in Vietnam, and taking their cue from the military's own references to enemy-held territory there as "Indian Country," millions of young whites began, increasingly, as a part of their own resistance, to analogize the ongoing carnage in Southeast Asia to that of the Indian Wars and to revile the leaders presiding over both processes.[123]

Sensing that the potential for a vast audience/market was bound up in the desire of America's baby boomers to emotionally/figuratively distance themselves from the status quo, hip directors like Arthur Penn and Ralph Nelson were quick to cash in. In catering to the new "countercultural" sensibility, Penn opted to display the Custer of *They Died With Their Boots On* in virtual reverse image. Where the Walsh/Flynn approach decreed Custer's intrinsic nobility, hence that of the tradition he was mustered to represent, the characterization offered in *Little Big Man* was that of a vulgarly egotistical psychopath.[124] Nelson followed suit in *Soldier Blue*, albeit using a somewhat amorphous representation of Colonel John Chivington, the already infamous commander at Sand Creek, to make his point.[125]

Chivington had previously received such cinematic packaging under the name "Colonel Templeton" in a somewhat innovative Arthur Hiller movie, *Massacre at Sand Creek* (1956), and he would again, as "Colonel Schemmerhorne," in a TV miniseries made from James Michener's *Centennial* during the late '70s. As for Custer, he has continued to be portrayed primarily in accordance with the negative model established by Penn, most recently in 1995, in the episode of *Dr. Quinn* discussed earlier.

While *Little Big Man* and *Soldier Blue* certainly punched large holes in the triumphalist stereotype, as critics Ralph and Natasha Friar observed shortly after the films were released, this merely signified that Hollywood had shifted from glorifying the extermination of native people to "excusing genocide by attributing it to the whims of a few unbalanced people, i.e., General Custer."[126] More precisely, by making such attribution filmmakers were both acknowledging the obvious—admitting, that is, that genocidal events had occurred in the course of American history and that they were wrong—and presenting it as something abnormal and therefore exceptional.

When this was combined with sympathetic white characters like Hoffman's Jack Crabbe in *Little Big Man*, Candice Bergen's Christa Lee and Peter Strauss's Honis

Gant in *Soldier Blue*, Costner's Dunbar in *Dances With Wolves*, or Michaela Quinn and Sully in *Dr. Quinn*, the appearance of a fundamental polarity within Euroamerican society itself is created. This serves a very useful purpose, especially when stirred in with the Good Indian (friendly)/Bad Indian (hostile) stereotypes already discussed. As Elisabeth Bird explains:

> [While] *Dr. Quinn* goes along with notions of White guilt, it equally clearly allows White audiences to see the destruction of Indian culture as both inevitable and as somehow accidental. The show holds on to the "renegade" image, for example, because it helps assuage guilt: After all, some of the Indians drove us to it, helping to bring about their own destruction. Thus there were good and bad guys on both sides, and the bad things happened because of bad guys like Custer and the renegades, but good guys like Michaela and Sully are who *we* are [emphasis added].[127]

Thus, psychologically at least, genuinely sympathetic white figures, who did exist but who were historically anomalous at best, are rendered normative in terms of audience identification.[128] Conversely, men like Custer and Chivington, who were in fact normatively expressive of public sentiment—virtually the entire citizenry of Denver *did* turn out to cheer when the "Bloody Third" returned from Sand Creek, parading its scalps, genitalia, and other anatomical "trophies"; Custer *was* an extraordinarily popular public figure after the Washita; bounties on Indian scalps *were* proclaimed in *every* state and territory of the continental U.S. at one time or another—become the anomalies.[129]

The result is in no sense a transformation but instead a much more potent reconfiguring of the Euroamerican status quo. What Penn, Nelson, and their colleagues accomplished was to find a means to let the "protest generation" of the 1960s off the hook of its own professed dissidence. What they provided was/is a convenient surrogate reality allowing whites to symbolically disassociate themselves from the intolerable ugliness of "Custerism" (whether in the Wild West or Vietnam), thereby "feeling good about themselves" even while continuing to participate in and benefit from the very socioeconomic order Custerism has produced.[130]

This "reconstitution of imperial ideology" as a "friendlier" form of fascism has been expressed in a variety of ways, both on-screen and in the real world, but nowhere more clearly than in an exchange between Sully and Michaela's young son, Brian, during a special two-hour episode of *Dr. Quinn* broadcast during the 1993–94 season.[131] Toward the end, having just listened to a thoroughly triumphalist explanation of why the Cheyennes were being exterminated, the boy asks whether these weren't lies. Sully, the "White Indian," responds: "I'm afraid so, Brian; they lie to themselves. But this is still the best country in the world. . . . "[132]

Although the style of delivery is obviously different, such lines might easily have been uttered by John Wayne at the conclusion of any John Ford western. In fact, it seems no stretch at all to suggest that The Duke would have been proud to pronounce them. So much for the alleged "critical distinctions" between films like *Little Big Man* or *Dances With Wolves* on the one hand, and *They Died With Their Boots On* or *Custer of the West* on the other. "Meet the new boss," as Pete Townsend of The Who once put it with admirable succinctness, "same as the old boss."[133]

RAVAGES BY SAVAGES

As Eldridge Cleaver brilliantly explained in *Soul on Ice*, the structure of sexual relations imposed by Euroamerica upon African Americans can be understood as a metaphor for the broader relational matrix of domination and subjugation defining the social positions of whites and blacks respectively. In this formulation, white men are accorded a self-assigned status as "Omnipotent Administrators," primarily cerebral beings who, by presuming to monopolize the realm of thought itself, have assigned black men the subordinate status of mindless "Ultramasculine Menials."[134]

To complete the figurative disempowerment of the latter, and thus to signify their own station of unimpeachable supremacy, the Administrators proceed first to constrain and then to preempt the Menials in that most crucial of all physical arenas, their sexuality. Black men are, by white male ordination, categorically denied sexual access to white women ("Ultrafeminine Females") while, concomitantly, white men grant themselves unrestricted rights to the black female "Booty" deriving from their posture of domination. Black men are thereby reduced to a degraded status as "social eunuchs" while black women, transformed into sexual commodities, are dehumanized altogether, and white women, consigned to serve as desexualized objects adorning the omnipotence of their men, fare little better.[135]

The great fear for the Administrators, according to Cleaver, is that the Menials might somehow discover a means of breaking the psychic bounds of their oppression, that is, of liberating themselves from their state of emasculated debasement by allegorically turning the tables and violating the "purity" of white womanhood.[136] So deep seated was this dread that it assumed the form of an outright cultural psychosis leading, among other things, to the ubiquitousness of a myth that black men are imbued, innately and insatiably, with a "need" to rape the Ultrafeminine Female. Several thousand lynchings were carried out in the U.S. between 1889 and 1930, mainly to deter black men from acting upon this supposed compulsion.[137]

With only minor transpositions, the paradigm can be as readily applied to Euroamerica's perception of its relationship to native people as to imported African chattel. Indeed, the evidence strongly suggests that transposition occurred in reverse order; the model was developed with respect to Indians, then modified to some extent for application to blacks. In any event, preoccupation with the idea that native men were animated by the "darkest" desires vis-à-vis white women can be traced back to the earliest writings of the New England Puritans.[138] By the end of the nineteenth century, the theme had long been a staple of American literature and drama, both high-brow and low.[139]

Once movies became a factor, the situation was exacerbated substantially. In *The*

Battle at Elderbush Gulch, for example, only the timely arrival of the cavalry saved a trembling Lillian Gish from a "mercy slaying" meant to save her from a "fate worse than death" at the hands of surrounding savages.[140] The scene was repeated with some regularity over the next forty years, most prominently in Ford's *Stagecoach*. By the early fifties, white women were accorded a bit more autonomy, as when director Anthony Mann has James Stewart hand actress Shelley Winters a weapon in *Winchester '73* (1953) so that she may participate in their mutual defense. "Don't worry," she assures him, "I understand about the last [bullet]."[141] Better death than "suffering ravage by a savage," as Charley Hill puts it.[142] In *Fort Massacre* (1969), Joel McCrea's wife goes everybody one better by killing not only herself but her two children rather than allow any of them to be taken captive by Apaches.

Despite a veritable mountain of evidence that rape was practiced in few if any native societies, a diametrically opposed "truth" was presented in hundreds of Hollywood westerns.[143] "Did you ever see what Indians do when they get a *white* woman?" asks a seasoned scout portrayed by James Whitmore in *Chato's Land* (1972). "Comanches," another scout explains to an army captain trying to figure out whether it was they or the Apaches who had perpetrated a massacre, in *A Thunder of Drums* (1961), "rape their own women" rather than whites, "so it was likely Apaches." "If we stop now," one beleaguered cavalry officer tells another in *The Gatling Gun* (1971), "all those women have to look forward to is rape and murder."[144]

"You *know* what Indians do to women," declaims a trooper at the beginning of *Soldier Blue*. "They're going to rape me, Soldier Blue, and then they're going to kill you," Candice Bergen clarifies to a horrified Peter Strauss after the pair are captured by Kiowas later in the same film. "They're going to rape me, Jack," explains Crabbe's older sister in *Little Big Man*, shortly after they'd been taken home by a Cheyenne who'd happened upon the two children after their family had been massacred by Pawnees.[145] Most recently, in a 1994 episode of *Dr. Quinn*, Cloud Dancing's son proves that he, like his father, is a "Good Indian" by sacrificing himself to save the white heroine from being raped and murdered by "Dog Soldier renegades."[146]

In both *The Searchers* and *Ulzana's Raid* (1972), white women are depicted as having been "raped into insanity" by Indians.[147] In *Land Raiders* (1969), Apaches attack a town and, despite the ferocity of the fighting and the severity of their casualties, still find time to rape white women. In *The Deserter* (1970), the hero's wife is not only raped but skinned alive and left for her husband to kill.[148] Who could blame white men for having responded to such unrelenting horror by exterminating those responsible?

Often the rescue of white women taken by Indians comprises the entire plot of a movie, or a substantial part of it. Such is the case with *Iona, the White Squaw* (1909), *The Peril of the Plains* (1911), *The Pale-Face Squaw* and *The White Squaw* (both 1913), *Winning of the West* (1922), *Northwest Passage* (1940), *Ambush* (1950), *Flaming Feather* (1951), *Fort Ti* (1953), *The Charge at Feather River* (1953), *Comanche* (1956), *Comanche Station* (1960), *The Last Tomahawk* (1965), and *Duel at Diablo* (1966), among scores of others.[149] Sometimes, as in *Two Rode Together* (1961), the idea is handled with at least a semblance of sensitivity.[150] The worst of the lot is Ford's *The Searchers*, in which John Wayne is scripted to track down his abducted niece so he can kill her because she's been so irredeemably "soiled" by her experience.[151]

Even where the intended fate of the "rescued" is not so grim, it is often made plain that the purpose of their recovery is not so much to save *them* as it is to deny Indians the "spoils" they represent. Just as the effrontery of having "known" a white woman constitutes a death sentence for a native man and frequently his entire people, so too does the fact of her "fall from grace" license punishment of the woman herself. The scorn of townspeople visited upon the former "Indian's woman" portrayed by Barbara Stanwyck in *Trooper Hook* (1957), for example, forces her to live outside *any* society, white *or* native. Much the same principle applies to Linda Cristal's character in *Two Rode Together*, that of Eva Marie Sainte in *The Stalking Moon*, and many others.[152]

The only occasion prior to 1975's *Winterhawk* in which the American cinema had a native male actually marrying a white female was in the 1909 short, *An Indian's Bride*. The reasons for this glaring bias were none too subtle.

> Zane Grey originally published his novel, *The Vanishing American* (1925), as a magazine serial in 1922 in *The Ladies Home Journal*, a Curtis publication . . . At the conclusion, Grey had his heroine, a blonde-haired, blue-eyed school-teacher marry his full-blood Navajo hero. This set off such an outraged reaction among the magazine's readers that, henceforth, Curtis publications made it a stipulation that Indian characters were never again to be characterized and *Harper's* refused to publish the novel until Grey agreed to have the Navajo die at the end.[153]

The second ending, of course, was the one used in the movie. Probably the most ridiculous contortion undertaken with respect to this squalid convention came in Lambert Hillyer's *White Eagle* (1932). In this oat-burner, the hero, played by Buck Jones, is supposedly a full-blooded Bannock pony express rider who falls head over heels for a white woman. Just before the movie ends, "Buck's father tells him the truth: he is white! He was stolen from his family as a child. This permits Buck, without violating the color line, to embrace the heroine."[154]

Native women, of course, are another matter entirely. Not uncommonly they are depicted as appropriate objects of Euroamerican sexual aggression; the James Whitmore line quoted above was uttered to justify the fact that two white men were busily raping an Indian woman just off screen.[155] Apache actress Sacheen Littlefeather was able to fashion something of a cinematic career for herself only by her willingness to portray indigenous rape victims, as she did in *Winterhawk*, in one movie after another.[156] The same pertained, albeit to a lesser extent, to her contemporaries, women like Dawn Little Sky, Princess Lois Red Elk, and Pablita Verde Hardin.[157]

At the same time, Indian women have been consistently limned as suffering a hopeless, usually fatal, attraction to the omnipotence of white men. It's a story as old as the legend of *Pocahontas* (1908) coined by John Smith in 1624,[158] and has been repeated on the big screen hundreds of times, beginning with films like *An Indian Maiden's Choice* and *The Indian Girl's Romance* (both 1910), *Love in a Tepee* (1911), *Broncho Billy and the Navajo Maid* (1912) and *The Fate of the Squaw* (1914), and continuing right up to the present moment with such fare as *Captain John Smith and Pocahontas* (1953), *Fort Yuma* (1955), *Fort Bowie* (1958), *Oklahoma Territory* (1960), *Wild Women* (1970) and, of course, Disney's 1995 animated version of *Pocahontas*.[159]

Such romantic yearnings were doomed from the outset, or, more properly, the female characters who expressed them were. It was one thing for white men to gratify themselves sexually at the expense of native women, not only by raping them but, sometimes more tenderly, by cohabiting; it was quite another for "mere squaws" to be accorded the dignity of actually marrying one of their racial/cultural "betters." The consequence of Pocahontas's wedding an Englishman was, after all, her death by smallpox.[160]

Fenimore Cooper made it even plainer: the *only* possible outcome of such romantic entanglements was/is death.[161] Although the theme was first explored in *The Indian Maiden's Sacrifice* (1910), it is *The Squaw Man* (1913, 1918, 1931) which really serves as the cinematic prototype for all that would follow.

Based on Edwin Milton Royce's very successful stage play of 1905, the film concerns an English noble, falsely accused of a crime his brother actually committed, who ventures into the American west in an effort to clear his name. He falls in love with an Indian maiden of the Pocahontas stereotype variety and they have a child. Years pass and his brother, on his death bed, makes a confession exonerating the hero . . . The hero, now able to return to England and claim his title, accidentally shoots the Indian maiden (in the play she is a suicide); she dies in his arms, happy, because, as she tells him, she knows white culture to be superior and their child need not be held back because of her primitive ways.[162]

And so it went. Debra Paget, as James Stewart's Apache bride in *Broken Arrow*, dies tragically, the victim of an ambush by "Bad Whites." In *Drum Beat*, "Marisa Pavan, among the noble savages, has a crush on the white hero, Alan Ladd. Ladd sets her straight: she must marry within her own people. Then he pays court to the white heroine while Pavan, apparently in despair, loses her life trying to save his."[163] Linda Darnell does herself in when she can't ride off into the sunset with *Buffalo Bill;* Marie Elena Marques does pretty much the same in *Across the Wide Missouri*. Even Donna Reed's Sacajawea considers it when she realizes she'll never fit into the world of Charlton Heston's William Clark in *The Far Horizon*.[164]

All told, then, the panorama of Indian/white sexuality presented in movies has always been far more akin to what one might have expected from the Marquis de Sade's sick pen than from anything socially constructive or redeemable.[165] Foundationally, there is little to distinguish even the best of Hollywood's productions from *Jungle Blue*

(1978), *Sweet Savage* (1979), *Kate and the Indians* (1979), *Deep Roots* (1980), and other such X-rated, Indian-themed filth spewing from America's thriving porn-video industry.[166]

LUST IN THE DUST

Carnality, whether packaged as rape or love, "true" or unrequited, inevitably results in offspring. When the progenitors are of different races, such progeny will obviously be endowed with an interracial admixture of "blood" and thence, presumably, of culture as well. Hollywood, as much as the dominant society of which it is part, has from the first exhibited an abiding confusion as to how it should respond to the existence of such creatures, especially since their numbers have tended to swell at rates much greater than those of any "purer breeding stock" throughout the course of American history.[167]

At one level, it might be argued, as it has been by American thinkers like Thomas Jefferson and Henry Lewis Morgan, that a "touch of Indian" in the country's then preponderantly Caucasian makeup might serve to create a hybrid superior to the original strain (even as it diluted native gene stocks to the point of extinction and beyond).[168] On another level, it has been argued, and vociferously, that any such process of "mongrelization" results only in a dilution and consequent degradation of the "white race" itself.[169]

The best of both worlds or the worst? That is the question, never resolved. Typically, filmmakers have followed the lead set by D.W. Griffith in *Birth of a Nation* (1914), his aesthetically groundbreaking cinematic exaltation of the Ku Klux Klan.[170] By and large, children of mixed parentage have been consigned either to their mother's society rather than their father's—movies figuring upon the spawn of unions between native men and white women having for reasons discussed above been exceedingly rare—or to drift in anguish through an existential netherworld located somewhere between.

Such has been the case, certainly, with films like *The Halfbreed*, first released in 1916, and then remade as *The Half Breed* in 1922 and *The Half-Breed* in 1952. And so it has been with *The Dumb Half-Breed's Defense* (1910), *The Half-Breed's Atonement* (1911), *Breed of the North* and *Bred in the Bone* (both 1913), *Indian Blood* (1914), *The Ancient Blood* and *The Quarter Breed* (1916), *The Great Alone* and *One Eighth Apache* (both 1922), *Call Her Savage* (1932), *Wagon Wheels* (1934), *Daughter of the West* and *Colorado Territory* (both 1949), *The Hawk of Wild River* (1952), *The Proud and the Profane* (1956), *Nevada Smith* (1966), and well over a hundred others.[171]

Most frequently, those of mixed heritage have been depicted as a sort of antimiscegenist's incarnation of evil, as in *The Halfbreed*, *The Half Breed*, and *The Half-Breed*. Films produced using this motif have included *Half Breed's Treachery* (1909, 1912), *The Half-Breed's Way* (1912), *Bring Him In* (1921), *The Heritage of the Desert* (1924), *The Verdict of the Desert* (1925), *Hawk of the Hills* (1927), *Pony Soldier* (1952), *Reprisal* (1956), *War Drums* (1957), and *Last Train from Gun Hill* (1959). Sometimes the "breeds" turn out wrong because of the influence of dubious white men, as in *Broken Lance* (1954). On other occasions, our malignity is even explained as having been precipitated by white atrocities, as in the *Centennial* miniseries' (mis)representation of Charlie Bent and his brothers.[172] But the resulting impression is essentially the same.

Breeds are bad, as is explained in *The Barrier of Blood* (1913) and *The Apache Way* (1914), because we "naturally" incline towards our "Indian side." Nowhere is this brought out more clearly than in the "wholesome family entertainment" provided by cinematic adaptations of Mark Twain's *Tom Sawyer* and *The Adventures of Huckleberry Finn*, books in which the most malevolent character, a half-breed called Injun Joe, readily explains that his evil deeds are due to the fact that his "Injun blood ain't in me for nothing."[173]

The Unforgiven, a film that remains arguably the most venomously racist of all Hollywood's treatments of native people, was anchored by this premise. A few lines from the 1957 Alan LeMay novel upon which it was based should prove sufficient to carry the point.

> This is one thing I know. The red niggers are no human men. Nor are they beasts, nor any kind of earthly varmint, for all natural critters act like God made them to do. Devil-spirits, demons out of red kill, these be, that somehow, on some evil day, found a way to clothe themselves in flesh. I say to you, they must be cleansed from the face of this earth! Wherever one drop of their blood is found, it must be destroyed! For that is man's most sacred trust, before Almighty God.[174]

This transparently Hitlerian statement is made to a young woman played by Audrey Hepburn, presumably a child captive brought up by the Kiowas and then recovered by whites, who is mortally afraid that she might in fact be of mixed ancestry. Her self-protective response is to try and sound even worse. At one point, when queried by her adoptive white mother about the people in the village where she was raised, she replies, "There weren't any *people* there, Mama. Those were Indians."[175]

Ironically, it is this very same DNA structure, deemed so dangerous by D. W. Griffith and his ilk, which has been seized upon by more "progressive" filmmakers to project mixed-bloods as being good, or at least better than native "fullbloods," simply by way of inclining us towards our "white side."[176] This countering interpretation was manifested in all four versions of *Ramona* (1910, 1914 [reissue], 1916, 1928, 1936), as well as such early releases as *Red Wing's Constancy* and *Red Wing's Loyalty* (both 1910), *An Indian Hero* (1911), *The Half-Breed's Sacrifice* (1912), *The Half-Breed Parson*, and *The Half-Breed Sheriff* (both 1913).[177]

By the 1960s, Hollywood was even prepared to cast actual mixed-bloods like Elvis Presley in such roles, once in the passable *Flaming Star* (1960) and again in *Stay Away Joe* (1968), a movie "so bad that one is tempted to shout: 'John Wayne, where are you now that we need you?'"[178] Things have improved little in portrayals of mixed-bloods in the 1990s, as is witnessed by Val Kilmer's role in the idiotic *Thunderheart* and the even more recent characterization offered in the *Walker, Texas Ranger* TV series.[179]

Regardless of whether they've been oriented towards the notion of "breeds" as good, or convinced that we're inherently bad, however, one thing most directors seem to have been able to agree upon is that, as the fruit of illicit matings, we're somehow sexy.

> The screen almost burst into flames with Jennifer Jones as half-breed Pearl Chavez. Her sultry walk captured the eye of Gregory Peck in *Duel in the Sun* (1946), a film one sharp-tongued critic called "Lust in the Dust" . . . Dimitri Tiomkin recalls creating the musical score . . . He rewrote and rewrote it. Finally, in a meeting with [David O.] Selznik he said he had done all he could or would do. In desperation, he asked the producer what he really wanted. "I want it to sound like an orgasm," [Selznik replied].[180]

And it's not just women. As Peter van Lent has lately pointed out, "In current popular culture the exoticism of the Native male is always carefully controlled. For example, most of the heroes of the Indian romance novels are of mixed blood—'half-breeds.' This convention provides a safety net against several sexual pitfalls. First, it checks the exotic image from being too alien and keeps it within the bounds of 'tall, dark and handsome.' Second, it avoids any sqeamishness about miscegenation on the part of the reader. Since the hero is half-white, the romantic-sexual bond is not truly interracial and . . . 'the half-breed's' appearance can be quite comfortably Caucasian. In the words of one romance author: 'Bronson could pass as a white man.'"[181]

Van Lent, while correct in the main, is wrong about mixed-bloodedness quelling qualms among Euroamerican readers about miscegenation. In the same novel he quotes—Fabio's *Comanche*—the plot line devolves upon a white wife's rejection of her husband once she discovers the truth of his gene code.[182] The book is a bestseller in its niche, likely to be made into a movie, at least for TV consumption. Moreover, it is but one among scores of comparable tracts lining bookstore shelves and grocery store checkout lanes across the country.[183] The more things "change," the more they stay the same.

COWBOYS AND . . .

"From 1913 to the present, Hollywood has produced thousands of feature films on cowboys and Indians," wrote native documentary producer Phil Lucas in 1980. "These films, coupled with a preponderance of supportive literature (dime novels, poems, books, essays, journals, and plays), art, and more recently, television and advertising erase the varied cultural and ethnic identities of over 400 distinct . . . nations of the original inhabitants of the Americas, and have successfully replaced them with a fictional identity . . . the Hollywood Indian."[184]

The process began much earlier than either cinema or the twentieth century. Robert Berkhofer, for one, dates its inception from the earliest writings by Europeans about Indians.[185] Daniel Francis, a more visually oriented analyst, finds the point of origin somewhere among the renderings of George Catlin, Karl Bird King, Karl Bodmer, and Canadian counterparts like Paul Kane.[186] Extending Susan Sontag's observation that "to photograph is to appropriate the thing photographed" to cover painting, drawing and, ultimately, cinema, Francis concludes that when "they drew the Indians or took their photographs, artists . . . were taking possession of the Indian image. It was [then] theirs to manipulate and display in any way they wanted."[187]

> When . . . cultures meet, especially cultures as different as those of western Europe and indigenous North America, they inevitably interpret each other in terms of stereotypes. At its best, in a situation of equality, this might be seen as a phase in a longer process of familiarization. But if one side in the encounter enjoys advantages of wealth or power or technology, then it will usually try to impose its stereotypes on the other. That is what occurred in the case of the North American encounter between European and aboriginal. We have been living with the consequences ever since.[188]

"Images have consequences in the real world," Francis sums up, "ideas have results. The Imaginary Indian does not exist in a void. In their relations with Native people over the years, non-Native[s] have put their image of the Indian into practice."[189] This is true, whether the image is that of Cassily Adams' famously howling hordes in Budweiser's "Custer's Last Stand" poster or the nobly vanishing savage of James Fraser's equally famed 1914 sculpture, "The End of the Trail."[190] Both are false, and have the effect of dehumanizing those thus depicted, one no less than the other.

A consequence has been that, while Native North Americans have today been consigned to a degree of material destitution and attendant physical degradation comparable to that evident in most areas of the Third World, hardly a glimmer of concern emanates from the vast settler population benefiting from both our historical decimation/dispossession and the current régime of impoverishment imposed upon us. Why, after all, should those conditioned to see us as less or other than human, or even at some level to believe us nonexistent, care *what* happens to us?[191]

Euroamerican cinema's defending aestheticians have typically sought to skirt such issues by asserting, as Robin Wood did in 1971, that however erroneous and "unpleasant" the dominant society's portrayals of Indians, they are nonetheless defensible in "mythic terms."[192] On this score, one can do no better than to quote John Tuska's rejoinder that, "To put it bluntly, what apologists mean by a 'mythic' dimension in a western film is that part of it which they know to be a lie but which, for whatever reason, they still wish to embrace."[193]

Other comers have tried to varnish such polemics with a patina of belated "balance" or "equity," as when John H. Lenihan attempted to justify Delmer Daves' extravagantly inaccurate and anti-Indian *Drum Beat* on the basis that since the director had already "presented the Indian's point of view in *Broken Arrow*," it was necessary for him "to offer the settler's side of the story" in the later film (as if a couple of thousand movies already doing exactly that weren't enough to "offset" Daves' single "pro-Indian" picture).[194]

Somewhat more sophisticated have been the superficially critical arguments advanced by Jack Nachbar and others, holding that it is time for Hollywood to transcend the "appealing but shallow concepts of right and wrong" altogether, offering instead "a new synthesis of understanding" in which, historically speaking, Indian or white, "ain't none of us right."[195] While such suggestions undoubtedly resonate quite favorably with social élites increasingly desirous of decontextualized "I'm okay/you're okay" historical constructions,[196] and a mainstream saturated with cinematic dramatizations of how the disempowered poor tend to victimize the rich and powerful, they plainly beg more than a few significant points.

Foremost in this regard is the fact that if Wood/Lenihan/Nachbar-style prescriptions were to be applied equally to all sets of historical relations, it would be "necessary" that the Holocaust, for example, be depicted in such a way as to show that nobody was right, nobody wrong. The SS, as much as the inmates at Auschwitz, would be as cast victims; the Jews and Gypsies as much aggressors as the SS.[197] Having told "the Jewish side of the story" for so long, Hollywood would "need" at last to "balance" its record by representing "the nazi side."[198] In such an endeavor, filmmakers could reply in the "mythic terms" advanced by Julius Streicher and others of Germany's more noteworthy antisemitic publicists as plot devices.[199]

Then, perhaps, as Navajo activist John Redhouse once recommended, instead of being restricted merely to playing "Cowboys and Indians," American children could with as much gusto play "Nazis and Jews."[200] In addition to dressing their third graders up in greasepaint and turkey feathers on "Indian Day" each "Thanksgiving," maybe the country's public school teachers could also observe "Jewish Day" on Yom Kippur each year by adorning their more Nordic-looking pupils in construction paper yarmulkes and fake beards; an annual "Himmler Day" could be celebrated along with "Columbus Day"; professional athletics could franchise "Rabbis" and "Kikes" sports teams to compliment the already existing "Chiefs," "Braves," and "Redskins"; the automotive industry could add models like the "Yid," the "Hebe," and the "Jew" to the "Cherokees," "Cheyennes," and "Apaches" rolling with such regularity off its assembly lines.[201]

Contra Nachbar and his colleagues, it should "be required of filmmakers, if they expect their films [not to be] classed as a form of racist propaganda, to be truthful not only to the period and the place [they depict] but to the people as well."[202] Nothing of the least positive value "will become possible until screenwriters and filmmakers generally are willing to present audiences with historical reconstructions, until there is a legitimate historical reality informing both the structure and the characters in a western film."[203]

"If 'Indians' are not to be considered as victims of colonial aggression," Jimmie Durham once queried, "how are we to be considered" at all?[204] And since, as Sartre insisted, the meaning of colonial aggression can only be fully understood as genocide,[205] American Indians must be viewed as being on the receiving end of both. There are to be sure clearcut dimensions of right and wrong in any realistic appraisal of both historical and topical circumstance, dimensions which are not ultimately reducible to the superficialities of good guys and bad.

As more than one native analyst has commented in this connection, "you can look at somebody like Custer as an evil person, but the fact [is] that it was a deliberate policy . . . these things were [and remain] institutional."[206] As Indians have heretofore been portrayed by Hollywood, and as we would continue to be portrayed in Nachbar's "new synthesis," we serve as the simulacrum by which Euroamerica has been best able to hide the truth of itself *from* itself in order to continue to pretend that it can do what it does in "all good conscience."[207]

THE SONG REMAINS THE SAME

One of the very few genuinely poignant and meaningful Hollywood movies ever made about modern Indian life is *Geronimo Jones* (1970), the story of an Indian youngster agonizing over whether to keep an old Indian medal, his only inheritance from his grandfather, or to trade it for a new TV. Decision made, he lugs the tube home, gathers his family and turns it on. The first image appearing on the screen is that of a savage "redskin" in an old Hollywood western.[208]

There have been a few other such efforts, as with the superbly well-intentioned *Journey Through Rosebud* (1972) and the Canadian *Fish Hawk* (1980), but, overwhelmingly, nonindian filmmakers have opted to pursue the formula advanced in *Indian in the Cupboard* (1995), a children's movie, implying that to be an Indian man even in the contemporary era is still "naturally" to be a warrior. This is the case, obviously, with the fictional native characters, invariably dubbed "Chief," routinely included in the World War II All-American platoons of films like *Battle Cry* (1955) and *Never So Few* (1959), and with Tony Curtis's supposedly more factual Ira Hayes in *The Outsider.*[209] Figuratively, the rule might also be applied to Burt Lancaster's *Jim Thorpe* and Jack Palance's boxer in *Requiem for a Heavyweight* (1962).

Most assuredly, it finds another resonance in the mixed-blood former Green Beret karate expert turned ersatz native traditionalist/friend of flower power central to Tom Laughlin's moronic but initially very popular series of countercultural ditties: *Billy Jack* (1971), *The Trial of Billy Jack* (1974), and *Billy Jack Goes to Washington* (1977).[210] The same can be said of the Indians cast more recently as members of élite military units, Sonny Landham's "Billy" in *Predator* being a case in point. Wes Studi's character in *Deep Rising*, although technically a civilian, fits very much the same mold. Probably the clearest, and most asinine, example of such thematics will be found in director Franc Roddams' *War Party* (1989), in which three young Blackfeet get themselves killed in the best John Ford manner while trying to "become" their nineteenth-century ancestors.[211]

Other nonindian-made pictures have gone in the already discussed direction embodied in 1990s releases like *Dances With Wolves, Last of the Mohicans, Geronimo,* and TV's *Dr. Quinn.* These include several somewhat more sensitive and marginally more accurate—but aesthetically very flimsy—Turner Network Television productions like *Son of the Morning Star* (1991), *The Broken Chain* (1993), *Lakota Woman* (1994), and *Crazy Horse* (1996),[212] as well as such quincentennial epics as *Christopher Columbus— The Discovery* and *1492: The Conquest of Paradise* (both 1992).[213]

Television did much better than most big screen filmmakers with its *Northern Exposure* series (1990–97), the ensemble cast of which included two native actors, Elaine Miles and Darren E. Burrows, who portrayed contemporary indigenous Alaskans as fully dimensional human beings. Nonetheless, the show was a disaster in terms of its cultural characterizations.

> Despite the variances among real Alaskan Natives, *Northern Exposure* dilutes native identity to one generic form. Marilyn [Miles] comes simply from "Marilyn's tribe," and Ed [Burrows] comes from "Ed's tribe," which for four years remained anonymous. Although refusing to name the cultural base for Cicely [the town in which it is set], *Northern Exposure* has nevertheless progressively appropriated a Tlingit culture. Since the premier episode, the town has featured totem poles, which are found only among the Tlingits and the Haidas, and various artwork and artifacts in the Tlingit black, form-line style. However . . . all geographic references since the premier have put Cicely north of Anchorage . . . in the Alaskan interior, home primarily to Athabascans in real life . . . By the 1994–1995 season, Cicely had shifted west and seemed very close to being in an Inupiat Eskimo area. Creating a Tlingit identity for an Alaska interior village is akin to fabricating a Canadian town in Mexico or identifying New Yorkers as the majority population of Louisiana: It is ridiculous.[214]

Hence, while it can be said that Geronimo Jones might do somewhat better at the beginning of the new millennium than he did during the early 1970s, tuning his new TV to *Northern Exposure* or its superior Canadian counterpart, *North of 60*, rather than watching endless reruns of *The Searchers* and *The Stalking Moon*, the improvement is hardly sufficient to warrant the metaphorical exchange of his heritage for access to popular culture any such swap implies.

FROM REEL TO REAL

Probably the only white-constructed cinema to date which represents a genuine break with convention in its handling of Indian themes has been that of such offbeat writer/directors as Sam Shepard, whose independently produced *Silent Tongue* (1994) is at points too surreal to allow coherent analysis. Somewhat better was Frank Perry's *Rancho Deluxe* (1975), which features Sam Waterston as a young mixed-blood prone to parodying Hollywood stereotypes with sardonic suggestions that he and his cattle rustler partner go out to "rape and pillage" during moments of boredom. Television has also had its avant-garde moments in this connection during the 1980s, each time Michael Horse put in an appearance as the enigmatic Deputy Hawk in David Lynch's eccentric series, *Twin Peaks*.[215]

The most promising efforts have come from Canada, as with Richard Bugajski's *Clearcut* (1991), a deliberately ambiguous tale tracing the desublimation of the guilt-ridden understandings of a white liberal lawyer presuming to help his native clients obtain a modicum of justice in modern Euroamerican society.[216] Best of all is undoubtedly Jim Jarmusch's *Dead Man* (1997), featuring Gary Farmer and Johnny Depp in a well-crafted and accessibly surrealistic black and white travelogue across late-nineteenth-century North America, replete with biting literary metaphors and analogies to contemporary circumstance.[217]

While such examples demonstrate that at least some Euroamericans are capable of producing worthwhile films on the theme of Indian/white relations, a greater potential would seem to reside in a still embryonic native filmmaking scene, pioneered by actors like Will Sampson and Chief Dan George, which has been slowly gathering steam since 1970. Although the truly accomplished acting of men like Graham Greene and Gary Farmer, and to a somewhat lesser extent women like Tantoo Cardinal, Sheila Tsoosie, and Irene Bedard, remains definitive of the milieu, indigenous documentarists, scriptwriters, producers, and directors have recently asserted an increasing presence.[218]

Evidence of this came as early as 1969 with Duke Redbird's *Charley Squash Goes to Town*, a breakthrough followed by George Burdeau's *Buffalo, Blood, Salmon and Roots* (1976). In 1982, Creek director Bob Hicks came out with *Return of the Country*, a film produced through the American Film Institute in Los Angeles which hoists Hollywood on its own petard by satirizing "almost every cliché of the Indian in film, from the over-heated love sequence by wig-bedecked white actors to the elaborate musical dance sequences and the late-night talk-show promotion."[219]

A brilliant, ironic perspective dominates the sequences, done as if in a dream. *Return of the Country* turns the tables, with an Indian President of the United States and the formation of a Bureau of Caucasian Affairs, which is instructed to enforce policies to help little Anglo boys and girls into the mainstream of Indian culture. The performances of Native American actors offset the old Hollywood stereotype of emotionless players incapable of deep, varied, and mature performances. Actor Woodrow Haney, a Seminole-Creek musician and tribal elder, infuses his role as a Native American leader with both humanity and dignity.[220]

Hicks's comedy followed close behind a five-part series put together by Choctaw director Phil Lucas for Seattle television station KCTS/9 in 1980 and covering much of the same ground in documentary fashion. Entitled *Images of Indians* and narrated by Will Sampson, the series' segments include "The Great Movie Massacre," "Heathen Indians and the Hollywood Gospel," "How Hollywood Wins the West," "The Movie Reel Indians," and "War Paint and Wigs." To call it a devastating indictment is to substantially understate the case.[221]

Another such short film, Chippewa novelist/postmodern critic-writer Gerald Vizenor's *Harold of Orange* (1984), with Charly Hill cast in the lead role, gores the ox of the federal funding agencies upon which Indians have been rendered dependent. Still another, Chris Spotted Elk's *Do Indians Shave?* (1974), "uses the man-on-the-street-interview technique to probe the depth of stereotypes about Native Americans; of what one reviewer called the 'potpourri of inane myths, gross inaccuracies, and inadvertent slander . . . used to justify genocide, and the mindless indifference . . . that makes possible the continuing oppression of Indian people."[222]

More serious still was Spotted Elk's *The Great Spirit in the Hole* (1983), a compelling look at "the efficacy of Native American religious practices in rebuilding the lives of a group of Indian [prison] inmates. This is a significant film that shows how cinema can be used as a powerful tool for displacing negative stereotypes. A number of courts and prison boards have been persuaded by this film to allow religious . . . freedom to Native [prisoners] in using their traditional sweatlodges."[223] Other fine work has been done by individuals like George Horse Capture (*I'd Rather Be Powwowing*, 1981); Arlene Bowman (*Navajo Talking Picture*, 1986) and Victor Massayesva, Jr. (*Hopiit*, 1982; *Itam Hakim, Hopiit*, 1985; *Hopi Ritual Clowns*, 1988; and others), as well as collectively: the Creek Nation's *Green Corn Festival* (1982), for example, and the American Indian Theater Company's *Black Elk Speaks* (1984).[224]

Strong as some of these films are, however, they are of the sort shown mainly at indigenous confabs like Oklahoma City's Red Earth Festival, in film and native studies courses, and occasionally on the Discovery Channel or PBS. They thus have little or no possibility of attracting and influencing a mass audience. To do that, it is necessary for native filmmakers to penetrate the cost-intensive venue of commercial feature films, a realm from which a combination of Hollywood's history of anti-Indian bias and their own community's endemic poverty have always served to exclude them.

This has been understood all along, of course, and attempts have been made to address the issue. In 1972, for instance, Kiowa author N. Scott Momaday managed to organize the filming of his Pulitzer Prize-winning novel, *A House Made of Dawn*, casting Harold Littlebird as the lead. Completed on a veritable shoestring budget, the film "captured a real sense of Indianness. Unfortunately, it did not receive the support and promotion necessary to reach the audiences that the quality of production warranted."[225] The same could be said for Will Sampson's independently produced *Pieces of Dreams* (1970) and others.

It was not until 1996 that Indians finally got on the commercial feature map, albeit through the side door, when the Home Box Office (HBO) cable channel came out with *Grand Avenue*, a beautifully constructed picture, the screenplay for which was adapted by Pomo/Miwok writer/UCLA professor Greg Sarris from a volume of his own short stories bearing the same title.[226] Coproduced by Sarris along with Paul Aaron of the Sundance Institute—Robert Redford served as executive producer—*Grand Avenue* featured uniformly excellent performances by native actors like Sheila Tsoosie and Irene Bedard, received the highest viewer ratings of any HBO program for the season, and was described in the *New York Times* as "a giant step toward offering a gritty and unsparing depiction of urban Indian life."[227]

In 1998, this auspicious beginning was followed by Chris Eyre's *Smoke Signals*, released by Miramax, the first major motion picture since Edwin Carewe's *Ramona* (1928) to be directed by an American Indian.[228] Eyre, an Arapaho, coproduced the film with Spokane author Sherman Alexie, who developed the screenplay from the short stories contained in his *The Lone Ranger and Tonto Fistfight in Heaven*.[229] Although hardly as challenging as *Grand Avenue*, *Smoke Signals* is a nonetheless well-crafted film, highlighted by the solid lead acting of Adam Beach and Evan Adams, both slotted in such roles for the first time, as well as fine support work by Tantoo Cardinal, Irene Bedard, and Gary Farmer.

At present, *Smoke Signals* appears to be as well received as *Grand Avenue*, perhaps better, a matter heartening the prospect of other such productions in the future. This is all the more true in that these movies' success has attracted the attention of the Mashantucket Pequots, a small but suddenly very wealthy people in Connecticut—their revenues derive from a casino operation established during the mid-1980s—who have expressed interest in underwriting big screen ventures by other native filmmakers.[230] The degree of indigenous autonomy embodied in such a proposition tends to speak for itself.

Given these current developments, it may be that things may yet be turned around, that, to borrow a phrase from African American critic bell hooks, people like Chris Eyre and Greg Sarris can still transform Indians from "reel to real" in the popular imagination.[231] It's true that the thousands of films already devoted to creating the opposite impression constitute a tremendous barrier to overcome, but maybe, just maybe, like Chief Broom in *Cuckoo's Nest*, the sleeping giant of Native North America can still reawaken, crushing Hollywood's time-honored fantasies of the master race beneath the heel of a different future. But, as they say in tinseltown, that's another story. . . .

9

LET'S SPREAD THE "FUN" AROUND
The Issue of Sports Team Names and Mascots

◆◆◆◆◆◆◆◆◆◆◆◆◆◆

If people are genuinely interested in honoring Indians, try getting
your government to live up to the more than 400 treaties it signed
with our nations. Try respecting our religious freedom which has
been repeatedly denied in federal courts. Try stopping the ongoing
theft of Indian water and other natural resources. Try reversing
your colonial process that relegates us to the most impoverished,
polluted, and desperate conditions in this country . . . Try understanding that the mascot issue is only the tip of a very huge problem of continuing racism against American Indians. Then maybe
your ["honors"] will mean something. Until then, it's just so much
superficial, hypocritical puffery. People should remember that an
honor isn't born when it parts the honorer's lips, it is born when it
is accepted in the honoree's ear.

—Glenn T. Morris
Colorado AIM, 1992

DURING THE PAST TWENTY SEASONS, THERE HAS BEEN AN INCREASING CONTRO-
versy regarding the names of professional sports teams like the Atlanta "Braves,"
Cleveland "Indians," Washington "Redskins," and Kansas City "Chiefs." The issue extends to the names of college teams like the Florida State University "Seminoles,"
University of Illinois "Fighting Illini," and so on, right on down to high school out-
fights like the Lamar (Colorado) "Savages." Also involved have been team adoptions
of "mascots," replete with feathers, buckskins, beads, spears, and "warpaint" (some
fans have opted to adorn themselves in the same fashion), and nifty little "pep" gestures like the "Indian Chant" and "Tomahawk Chop."

A substantial number of American Indians have protested that use of native names,
images, and symbols as sports team mascots and the like is, by definition, a virulently
racist practice. Given the historical relationship between Indians and nonindians during what has been called the "Conquest of America," American Indian Movement
leader (and American Indian Anti-Defamation Council founder) Russell Means has
compared the practice to contemporary Germans naming their soccer teams the

"Jews," "Hebrews," and "Yids," while adorning their uniforms with grotesque carica-
tures of Jewish faces taken from the nazis' antisemitic propaganda of the 1930s. Numerous demonstrations have occurred in conjunction with games—notably during
the November 15, 1992, match-up between the Chiefs and Redskins in Kansas
City—by angry Indians and their supporters.

In response, a number of players—especially African Americans and other minority athletes—have been trotted out by professional team owners like Ted Turner, as
well as university and public school officials, to announce that they mean not to insult, but instead to "honor," native people. They have been joined by the television
networks and most major newspapers, all of which have editorialized that Indian discomfort with the situation is "no big deal," insisting that the whole thing is just "good,
clean fun." The country needs more such fun, they've argued, and "a few disgruntled
Native Americans" have no right to undermine the nation's enjoyment of its leisure
time by complaining. This is especially the case, some have contended, "in hard times
like these." It has even been contended that Indian outrage at being systematically degraded—rather than the degradation itself—creates "a serious barrier to the sort of intergroup communication so necessary in a multicultural society such as ours."

Okay, let's communicate. We may be frankly dubious that those advancing such
positions really believe in their own rhetoric, but, just for the sake of argument, let's
accept the premise that they are sincere. If what they are saying is true in any way at
all, then isn't it time we spread such "inoffensiveness" and "good cheer" around among
all groups so that *everybody* can participate *equally* in fostering the round of national
laughs they call for? Sure it is—the country can't have too *much* fun or "intergroup involvement"—so the more, the merrier. Simple consistency demands that anyone who
thinks the Tomahawk Chop is a swell pastime must be just as hearty in their endorsement of the following ideas, which—by the "logic" used to defend the defamation of
American Indians—should help us all start *really* yukking it up.

First, as a counterpart to the Redskins, we need an NFL team called the "Niggers"
to "honor" Afroamerica. Halftime festivities for fans might include a simulated stew-
ing of the opposing coach in a large pot while players and cheerleaders dance around
it, garbed in leopard skins and wearing fake bones in their noses. This concept obviously goes along with the kind of gaiety attending the Chop, but also the actions of
the Kansas City Chiefs, whose team members—prominently including black team
members—lately appeared on a poster looking "fierce" and "savage" by way of wearing
Indian regalia. Just a bit of harmless "morale boosting," says the Chiefs' front office.
You bet.

So that the newly-formed Niggers sports club won't end up too out of sync while
expressing the "spirit" and "identity" of Afroamericans in the above fashion, a baseball
franchise—let's call this one the "Sambos"—should be formed. How about a basket-
ball team called the "Spearchuckers?" A hockey team called the "Jungle Bunnies?"
Maybe the "essence" of these teams could be depicted by images of tiny black faces
adorned with huge pairs of lips. The players could appear on TV every week or so

gnawing on chicken legs and spitting watermelon seeds at one another. Catchy, eh? Well, there's "nothing to be upset about," according to those who love wearing "war bonnets" to the Super Bowl or having "Chief Illiniwik" dance around the sports arenas of Urbana, Illinois.

And why stop there? There are plenty of other groups to include. "Hispanics?" They can be "represented" by the Galveston "Greasers" and San Diego "Spics," at least until the Wisconsin "Wetbacks" and Baltimore "Beaners" get off the ground. Asian Americans? How about the "Slopes," "Dinks," Gooks," and "Zipperheads"? Owners of the latter teams might get their logo ideas from editorial page cartoons printed in the nation's newspapers during World War II: slant-eyes, buck teeth, big glasses, but nothing racially insulting or derogatory, according to the editors and artists involved at the time. Indeed, this Second World War-vintage stuff can be seen as just another barrel of laughs, at least by what current editors say are their "local standards" concerning American Indians.

Let's see. Who's been left out? Teams like the Kansas City "Kikes," Hanover "Honkies," San Leandro "Shylocks," Daytona "Dagos," and Pittsburgh "Polacks" will fill a certain social void among white folk. Have a religious belief? Let's all go for the gusto and gear up the Milwaukee "Mackerel Snappers" and Hollywood "Holy Rollers." The Fighting Irish of Notre Dame can be rechristened the "Drunken Irish" or "Papist Pigs." Issues of gender and sexual preference can be addressed through creation of teams like the St. Louis "Sluts," Boston "Bimbos," Detroit "Dykes," and the Fresno "Faggots." How about the Gainesville "Gimps" and Richmond "Retards," so the physically and mentally impaired won't be excluded from our fun and games?

Now, don't go getting "overly sensitive" out there. *None* of this is demeaning or insulting, at least not when it's being done to Indians. Just ask the folks who are doing it, or their apologists like Andy Rooney in the national media. They'll tell you—as in fact they *have* been telling you—that there's been no harm done, regardless of what their victims think, feel, or say. The situation is exactly the same as when those with precisely the same mentality used to insist that Step'n' Fetchit was okay, or Rochester on the *Jack Benny Show*, or Amos and Andy, Charlie Chan, the Frito Bandito, or any of the other cutsey symbols making up the lexicon of American racism. Have we communicated yet?

Let's get just a little bit real here. The notion of "fun" embodied in rituals like the Tomahawk Chop must be understood for what it is. There's not a single nonindian example deployed above which can be considered socially acceptable in even the most marginal sense. The reasons are obvious enough. So why is it different where American Indians are concerned? One can only conclude that, in contrast to the other groups at issue, Indians are (falsely) perceived as being too few, and therefore too weak, to defend themselves effectively against racist and otherwise offensive behavior. The sensibilities of those who take pleasure in things like the Chop are thus akin to those of schoolyard bullies and those twisted individuals who like to torture cats. At another level, their perspectives have much in common with those manifested more literally—

and therefore more honestly—by groups like the nazis, aryan nations, and ku klux klan. Those who suggest this is "okay" should be treated accordingly by anyone who opposes nazism and comparable belief systems.

Fortunately, there are glimmers of hope that this may become the case. A few teams and their fans have gotten the message and have responded appropriately. One illustration is Stanford University, which opted to drop the name "Indians" with regard to its sports teams (and, contrary to the myth perpetrated by those who enjoy insulting Native Americans, Stanford has experienced *no* resulting drop-off in attendance at its games). Meanwhile, the local newspaper in Portland, Oregon, has decided its longstanding editorial policy prohibiting use of racial epithets should include derogatory sports team names. The Redskins, for instance, are now simply referred to as being "the Washington team," and will continue to be described in this way until the franchise adopts an inoffensive moniker. (Newspaper sales in Portland have suffered no decline as a result.)

Such examples are to be applauded and encouraged. They stand as figurative beacons in the night, proving beyond all doubt that it is—and has always been—quite possible to indulge in the pleasure of athletics without accepting blatant racism into the bargain. The extent to which Stanford and Portland remain atypical is exactly the extent to which America remains afflicted with an ugly reality far different from the noble and enlightened "moral leadership" it professes to show the world. Clearly, the United States has a very long way to go before it measures up to such an image of itself.

ADDITIONAL READINGS

Carol Spindel, *Dancing at Halftime: Sports and the Controversy over American Indian Mascots* (New York: New York University Press, 2000).

C. Richard King and Charles Fruehling Springwood, eds., *Team Spirits: The Native American Mascots Controversy* (Lincoln: University of Nebraska Press, 2001).

10

INDIANS 'R' US

Reflections on the "Men's Movement"

◆◆◆◆◆◆◆◆◆◆◆◆◆◆

We are living at an important and fruitful moment, now, for it is clear to men that the images of adult manhood given by the popular culture are worn out; a man can no longer depend on them. By the time a man is thirty-five he knows that the images of the right man, the tough man, the true man he received in high school do not work in life. Such a man is open to new visions of what a man is supposed to be.

—Robert Bly, 1990

THERE ARE FEW THINGS IN THIS WORLD I CAN CONCEIVE AS BEING MORE INSTANTLY ludicrous than a prosperously middle-aged lump of pudgy Euroamerican versemonger, an apparition looking uncannily like some weird cross between the Malt-O-Milk Marshmallow Man and Pillsbury's Doughboy, suited up in a grotesque mismatch combining pleated Scottish tweeds with a striped Brooks Brothers shirt and Southwest Indian print vest, peering myopically along his nose through coke-bottle steel-rim specs while holding forth in stilted and somewhat nasal tonalities on the essential virtues of virility, of masculinity, of being or becoming a "warrior." The intrinsic absurdity of such a scene is, moreover, compounded by a factor of five when it is witnessed by an audience—all male, virtually all white, and on the whole obviously well accustomed to enjoying a certain pleasant standard of material comfort—which sits as if spellbound, rapt in its attention to every nuance of the speaker, altogether fawning in its collective nods and murmurs of devout agreement with each detail of his discourse.

At first glance, the image might seem to be the most vicious sort of parody, a satire offered in the worst of taste, perhaps an hallucinatory fragment of a cartoon or skit offered by the likes of *National Lampoon* or *Saturday Night Live*. Certainly, in a reasonable universe we would be entitled (perhaps required) to assume that no group of allegedly functional adults would take such a farce seriously, never mind line up to pay money for the privilege of participating in it. Yet, as we know, or should by now, the universe we are forced to inhabit has been transformed long since—notably by the very group so prominent in its representation among those constituting our warrior/mystic/wordsmith's assemblage—into something in which reasonable behavior and comportment play only the smallest of parts. And so the whole travesty is advanced with the utmost seriousness, at least by its proponents and a growing body of adherents who subsidize and otherwise support them.

The founder and reigning Grand Pooh-Bah of that variant of the "New Age" usually referred to as the "Men's Movement" is Robert Bly, a rather owlish butterball of a minor poet who seems to have set out at fifty-something to finally garner unto himself some smidgin of the macho self-esteem his physique and life of letters had conspired to deny him up to that point.[1] Writerly even in this pursuit, however, Bly has contented himself mainly with devising a vague theory of "masculinism" designed or at least intended to counter prevailing feminist dogma concerning "The Patriarchy," rising interest in "multicultural" interpretations of how things work, and an accompanying sense among middle- to upper-middle-class males that they are "losing influence" in contemporary society.[2]

A strange brew consisting of roughly equal parts Arthurian, Norse, and Celtic legend, occasional adaptations of fairy tales by the brothers Grimm, a scattering of his own and assorted dead white males' verse and prose, a dash of environmentalism, and, for spice, bits and pieces of Judaic, Islamic, East Asian, and American Indian spiritualism, Bly's message of "male liberation" has been delivered via an unending series of increasingly well-paid podium performances beginning in the mid-80s. Presented in a manner falling somewhere between mystic parable and pop psychology, Bly's lectures are frequently tedious, often pedantic, pathetically pretentious in both content and elocution. Still, they find a powerful emotional resonance among those attracted to the central themes announced in his interviews and advertising circulars, especially when his verbiage focuses upon the ideas of "reclaiming the primitive within us . . . attaining freedom through use of appropriate ritual . . . [and] the rights of all men to transcend cultural boundaries in redeeming their warrior souls."[3]

By 1990, the master had perfected his pitch to the point of committing it to print in a turgid but rapidly-selling tome entitled *Iron John*.[4] He had also established something like a franchise system, training cadres in various localities to provide "male empowerment rituals" for a fee (a "Wild Man Weekend" goes at $250 a pop; individual ceremonies are usually pro-rated).

Meanwhile, the rising popularity and consequent profit potential of Bly's endeavor had spawned a number of imitators—Patrick M. Arnold, Asa Baber, Tom Daly, Robert Moore, Douglas Gillette, R.J. Stewart, Kenneth Wetcher, Art Barker, F.W. McCaughtry, John Matthews, and Christopher Harding among them—literary and otherwise.[5] Three years later, the Men's Movement had become pervasive enough to be viewed as a tangible and growing social force rather than merely as a peculiar fringe group; active chapters are listed in 43 of the 50 major U.S. cities (plus four in Canada) in the movement's "selected" address list; 25 periodicals are listed in the same directory.[6]

AN INTERLUDE WITH COLUMBUS IN COLORADO

The ability of a male to shout and be fierce does not imply domination, treating people as if they were objects, demanding land or empire, holding on to the Cold War—the whole model of machismo . . . The Wild Man here amounts to an invisible presence, the companionship of the ancestors and the great artists among the dead . . . The native Americans believe in that healthful male power.

—Robert Bly, 1990

At first glance, none of this may seem particularly threatening. Indeed, the sheer silliness inherent to Bly's routine at many levels is painfully obvious, a matter driven home to me one spring morning when, out looking for some early sage, I came upon a group of young Euroamerican males cavorting stark naked in a meadow near Lyons, Colorado. Several had wildflowers braided into their hair. Some were attempting a chant I failed to recognize. I noticed an early growth of poison oak near where I was standing, but determined it was probably best not to disrupt whatever rite was being conducted with anything so mundane as a warning about the presence of discomforting types of plant life. As discreetly as possible, I turned around and headed the other way, both puzzled and somewhat amused by what I'd witnessed.

A few days later, I encountered one of the participants, whom I knew slightly, and who kept scratching at his left thigh. Seizing the opportunity, I inquired what it was they'd been doing. He responded that since he and the others had attended a workshop conducted by Robert Bly earlier in the year, they'd become active in the Men's Movement and "made a commitment to recover the Druidic rituals which are part of our heritage" (the man, an anthropology student at the University of Colorado, is of Slavic descent, making Druidism about as distant from his own cultural tradition as Sufism or Zen Buddhism). Interest piqued, I asked where they'd learned the ritual form involved and its meaning. He replied that, while they'd attempted to research the matter, "it turns out there's not really a lot known about exactly how the Druids conducted their rituals."

"It's mostly guesswork," he went on. "We're just kind of making it up as we go along." When I asked why, if that were the case, they described their ritual as being Druidic, he shrugged. "It just sort of feels good, I guess," he said. "We're trying to get in touch with something primal in ourselves."

Harmless? Maybe. But then again, maybe not. The Druids, after all, have reputedly been dead and gone for centuries. They are thus immune to whatever culturally destructive effects might attend such blatant appropriation, trivialization, and deformation of their sacred rites by non-Druidic feel-gooders. Before departing the meadow, however, I'd noticed that a couple of the men gamboling about in the grass were adorned with facepaint and feathers. So I queried my respondent as to whether in the view of his group such things comprised a part of Druid ritual life. "Well, no," he confessed. "A couple of the guys are really into American Indian stuff. Actually, we all are.

Wallace Black Elk is our teacher.[7] We run sweats on the weekends, and most of us have been on the hill [insider slang for the undertaking of a Vision Quest]. I myself carry a Sacred Pipe and am studying herbal healing, Lakota Way. Three of us went to the Sun Dance at Crow Dog's place last summer. We've made vows, and are planning to dance when we're ready."[8] Intermingled with these remarks, he extended glowing bits of commentary on his and the others' abiding interest in a diversity of cultural/ spiritual elements ranging from Balinese mask-making to Andean flute music, from Japanese scent/time orientation to the deities of the Assyrians, Polynesian water gods, and the clitoral circumcision of Somali women.

I thought about protesting that spiritual traditions cannot be used as some sort of Whitman's Sampler of ceremonial form, mixed and matched—here a little Druid, there a touch of Nordic mythology, followed by a regimen of Hindu vegetarianism, a mishmash of American Indian rituals somewhere else—at the whim of people who are part of none of them. I knew I should say that to play at ritual potluck is to debase all spiritual traditions, voiding their internal coherence and leaving nothing usably sacrosanct as a cultural anchor for the peoples who conceived and developed them, and who have consequently organized their societies around them. But, then, in consideration of who it was I was talking to, I abruptly ended the conversation instead. I doubted he would have understood what I was trying to explain to him. More important, I had the distinct impression he wouldn't have cared even if he had. Such observations on my part would most likely have only set loose "the warrior in him," a flow of logorrhea in which he asserted his and his peers' "inalienable right" to take anything they found of value in the intellectual property of others, converting it to whatever use suited their purposes at the moment. I was a bit tired, having just come from a meeting with a white environmental group where I'd attempted unsuccessfully to explain how support of native land rights might bear some positive relationship to their announced ecological concerns, and felt it just wasn't my night to deal with the ghost of Christopher Columbus for a second time, head on.

That's an excuse, to be sure. Probably, I failed in my duty. Perhaps, regardless of the odds against success, I should have tried reasoning with him. More likely, I should've done what my ancestors should have done to Columbus himself when the "Great Discoverer" first brought his embryo of the Men's Movement to this hemisphere. But the amount of prison time assigned these days to that sort of response to aggression is daunting, to say the least. And I really do lack the wallspace to properly display his tanned hide after skinning him alive. So I did nothing more than walk out of the coffee shop in which we'd been seated, leaving him to wonder what it was that had upset me. Not that he's likely to have gotten the message. The result of my inaction is that, so far as I know, the man is still out there cruising the cerebral seas in search of "spiritual landscapes" to explore and pillage. Worse, he's still sending his booty back to his buddies in hopes of their casting some "new synthesis of paganism"—read, "advancement of civilization as we know it"—in which they will be able to continue their occupancy of a presumed position at the center of the universe.

INDIANS 'R' US

> We must get out of ourselves, or, more accurately, the selves we have been
> conned into believing are "us." We must break out of the cage of artificial "self"
> in which we have been entrapped as "men" by today's society. We must get in
> touch with our true selves, recapturing the Wild Man, the animal, the primitive
> warrior being which exists in the core of every man. We must rediscover the
> meaning of maleness, the art of being male, the way of the warrior priest. In do-
> ing so, we free ourselves from the alienating tyranny of being what it is we're told
> we are, or what it is we should be. We free ourselves to redefine the meaning of
> "man," to be who and what we can be, and what it is we ultimately must be. I
> speak here, of course, of genuine liberation from society's false expectations and
> thus from the false selves these expectations have instilled in each and every one
> of us here in this room. Let the Wild Man loose, I say! Free our warrior spirit!
>
> —Robert Bly, 1991

In retrospect, it seems entirely predictable that, amidst Robert Bly's welter of babble
concerning the value of assorted strains of imagined primitivism and warrior spirit, a
substantial segment of his following—and he himself in the workshops he offers on
"practical ritual"—would end up gravitating most heavily toward things Indian. After
all, Native Americans and our ceremonial life constitute living, ongoing entities. We
are therefore far more accessible in terms of both time and space than the Druids or
the old Norse Odinists. Further, our traditions offer the distinct advantage of seeming
satisfyingly exotic to the average Euroamerican yuppie male, while not forcing them
to clank about in the suits of chain mail and heavy steel armor which would be required if they they were to opt to act out their leader's hyperliterate Arthurian fantasies. I mean, really . . . Jousting, anyone? A warrior-type fella could get seriously
hurt that way.[9]

A main sticking point, of course, rests precisely in the fact that the cultures indigenous to America *are* living, ongoing entities. Unlike the Druids or the ancient Greek
man-cults who celebrated Hector and Achilles, Native American societies *can* and *do*
suffer the socioculturally debilitating effects of spiritual trivialization and appropriation at the hands of the massively larger Euro-immigrant population which has come
to to dominate literally every other aspect of our existence. As Margo Thunderbird, an
activist of the Shinnecock Nation, has put it, "They came for our land, for what grew
or could be grown on it, for the resources in it, and for our our clean air and pure water. They stole these things from us, and in the taking they also stole our free ways and
the best of our leaders, killed in battle or assassinated. And now, after all that, they've
come for the very last of our possessions; now they want our pride, our history, our
spiritual traditions. They want to rewrite and remake these things, to claim them for
themselves. The lies and thefts just never end."[10] Or, as the Oneida scholar Pam Colorado frames the matter:

The process is ultimately intended to supplant Indians, even in areas of their own culture and spirituality. In the end, non-Indians will have complete power to define what is and what is not Indian, even for Indians. We are talking here about a complete ideological/conceptual subordination of Indian people in addition to the total physical subordination they already experience. When this happens, the last vestiges of real Indian society and Indian rights will disappear. Non-Indians will then claim to "own" our heritage and ideas as thoroughly as they now claim to own our land and resources.[11]

From this perspective, the American Indian Movement passed a resolution at its 1984 Southwest Leadership Conference condemning the laissez-faire use of native ceremonies and/or ceremonial objects by anyone not sanctioned by traditional indigenous spiritual leaders.[12] The AIM position also echoed an earlier resolution taken by the Traditional Elders Circle in 1980, condemning even Indians who engage in "use of [our] spiritual ceremonies with non-Indian people for profit."[13] Another such condemnation had been issued during the First American Indian Tribunal at D-Q University in 1982.[14] In June 1993, the Lakota Nation enacted a similar resolution denouncing non-Lakotas who presume to "adopt" their rituals, and censoring those Lakotas who have chosen to facilitate such cultural appropriation.[15] Several other indigenous nations and national organizations have already taken comparable positions, or are preparing to.[16]

This may seem an exaggerated and overly harsh response to what the Spokane/Coeur d'Alene writer Sherman Alexie has laughingly dismissed as being little more than a "Society for Confused White Men."[17] But the hard edges of Euroamerican hubris and assertion of proprietary interest in native assets which has always marked Indian/white relations are abundantly manifested in the organizational literature of the Men's Movement itself. Of even greater concern is the fact that the sort of appropriation evidenced in these periodicals is no longer restricted simply to claiming "ownership" of Indian ceremonies and spiritual objects, as in a passage in a recent issue of the *Men's Council Journal* explaining that "sweats, drumming, dancing, [and] four direction-calling [are] once-indigenous now-ours rituals."[18] Rather, participants have increasingly assumed a stance of expropriating native identity altogether, as when, in the same journal, it is repeatedly asserted that "we . . . are all Lakota" and that members of the Men's Movement are now displacing actual Lakotas from their "previous" role as "warrior protectors" (of what, is left unclear).[19]

The indigenous response to such presumption was perhaps best expressed by AIM leader Russell Means, himself an Oglala Lakota, when he stated that, "This is the ultimate degradation of our people, even worse than what's been done to us by Hollywood and the publishing industry, or the sports teams who portray us as mascots and pets. What these people are doing is like Adolf Eichmann claiming during his trial that, at heart, he was really a zionist, or members of the Aryan Nations in Idaho claiming to be 'True Jews'."[20] Elsewhere, Means has observed that:

What's at issue here is the same old question that Europeans have always posed with regard to American Indians, whether what's ours isn't somehow theirs. And, of course, they've always answered the question in the affirmative . . . We are resisting this because spirituality is the basis of our culture. If our culture is dissolved [via the expedients of spiritual appropriation/expropriation], Indian people as such will cease to exist. By definition, the causing of any culture to cease to exist is an act of genocide.[21]

Noted author Vine Deloria, Jr., agrees in principle, finding that as a result of the presumption of groups like the Men's Movement, as well as academic anthropology, "the realities of Indian belief and existence have become so misunderstood and distorted at this point that when a real Indian stands up and speaks the truth at any given moment, he or she is is not only unlikely to be believed, but will probably be publicly contradicted and 'corrected' by the citation of some non-Indian and totally inaccurate 'expert'."[22]

Moreover, young Indians in [cities and] universities are now being trained to view themselves and their cultures in the terms prescribed by such experts *rather than* in the traditional terms of the tribal elders. The process automatically sets the members of Indian communities at odds with one another, while outsiders run around picking up the pieces for themselves. In this way [groups like the Men's Movement] are perfecting a system of self-validation in which all semblance of honesty and accuracy are lost. This is . . . absolutely devastating to Indian societies.[23]

Even Sherman Alexie, while choosing to treat the Men's Movement phenomenon with scorn and ridicule rather than open hostility, is compelled to acknowledge that there is a serious problem with the direction taken by Bly's disciples. "Peyote is not just an excuse to get high," Alexie points out. "A Vision Quest cannot be completed in a convention room rented for that purpose . . . [T]he sweat lodge is a church, not a free clinic or something . . . A warrior does not have to scream to release the animal that is supposed to reside inside every man. A warrior does not necessarily have an animal inside him at all. If there happens to be an animal, it can be a parakeet or a mouse just as easily as it can be a bear or a wolf. When a white man adopts an animal, he [seems inevitably to choose] the largest animal possible. Whether this is because of possible phallic connotations or a kind of spiritual steroid abuse is debatable, [but] I can imagine a friend of mine, John, who is white, telling me that his spirit animal is the Tyrannosaurus Rex."[24]

The men's movement seems designed to appropriate and mutate so many aspects of native traditions. I worry about the possibilities: men's movement chain stores specializing in portable sweat lodges; the "Indians 'R' Us" commodification of ritual and artifact; white men who continue to show up at powwows in full regalia and dance.[25]

Plainly, despite sharp differences in their respective temperaments and resultant stylistic approaches to dealing with problems, Alexie and many other Indians share Russell Means' overall conclusion that the "culture vultures" of the Men's Movement are "not innocent or innocuous . . . cute, groovy, hip, enlightened or any of the rest of the things they want to project themselves as being. No, what they're about is cultural genocide. And genocide is genocide, no matter how you want to 'qualify' it. So some of us are starting to react to these folks accordingly."[26]

VIEW FROM A FOREIGN SHORE

Western man's connection to the Wild Man has been disturbed for centuries now, and a lot of fear has been built up [but] Wild Man is part of a company or a community in a man's psyche. The Wild Man lives in complicated inter-changes with other interior beings. A whole community of beings is what is called a grown man . . . Moreover, when we develop the inner Wild Man, he keeps track of the wild animals inside us, and warns when they are liable to be-come extinct. The Wild One in you is the one which is willing to leave the busy life, and able to be called away.

—Robert Bly, 1990

In many ways, the salient questions which present themselves with regard to the Men's Movement center on motivation. Why, in this day and age, would any group of well-educated and self-proclaimedly sensitive men, the vast majority of whom may be ex-pected to exhibit genuine outrage at my earlier comparison of them to Columbus, elect to engage in activities which can plausibly be categorized as culturally genocidal? Assuming initial ignorance in this regard, why do they choose to persist in these activ-ities, often escalating their behavior after its implications have been explained by its victims repeatedly and in no uncertain terms? And, perhaps most of all, why would such extraordinarily privileged individuals as those who've flocked to Robert Bly—a group marked by nothing so much as the kind of ego-driven self-absorption required to insist upon its "right" to impose itself on a tiny minority even to the point of cul-turally exterminating it—opt to do so in a manner which makes them appear not only repugnant, but utterly ridiculous to anyone outside their ranks?

Sometimes it is necessary to step away from a given setting in order to better un-derstand it. For me, the answers to these seemingly inexplicable questions were to a large extent clarified during a political speaking tour of Germany, during which I was repeatedly confronted by the spectacle of Indian "hobbyists," all of them men resplen-dently attired in quillwork and bangles, beaded moccasins, chokers, amulets, medicine bags, and so on.[27] Some of them sported feathers and buckskin shirts or jackets; a few wore their blond hair braided with rawhide in what they imagined to be high plains style (in reality, they looked much more like Vikings than Cheyennes or Shoshones). When queried, many professed to have handcrafted much of their own regalia.[28] A number also made mention of having fashioned their own pipestone pipes, or to have been presented with one, usually after making a hefty monetary contribution, by one of a gaggle of Indian or pretended-Indian hucksters.[29]

Among those falling into this classification, belonging to what Christian Feest has branded the "Faculty of Medicine" plying a lucrative "Greater Europa Medicine Man Circuit,"[30] are Wallace Black Elk, "Brooke Medicine Eagle" (a bogus Cherokee; real name unknown), "John Redtail Freesoul" (a purported Cheyenne-Arapaho; real name unknown), Archie Fire Lamedeer (Northern Cheyenne), "Dhyani Ywahoo" (supposedly a 27th generation member of the nonexistent "Etowah" band of the Eastern Cherokees; real name unknown), "Eagle Walking Turtle" (Gary McClain, an alleged Choctaw), "Eagle Man" (Ed McGaa, Oglala Lakota), "Beautiful Painted Arrow" (a supposed Shoshone; real name unknown).[31] Although the success of such people "is completely independent of traditional knowledge, just so long as they can impress a public impressed by the books of Carlos Castaneda,"[32] most of the hobbyists I talked to noted they'd "received instruction" from one or more of these "Indian spiritual teachers" and had now adopted various deformed fragments of Native American ritual life as being both authentic and their own.

Everyone felt they had been "trained" to run sweats. Most had been provided similar tutelage in conducting Medicine Wheel Ceremonies and Vision Quests. Several were pursuing what they thought were Navajo crystal-healing techniques, and/or herbal healing (where they figured to gather herbs not native to their habitat was left unaddressed). Two mentioned they'd participated in a "sun dance" conducted several years ago in the Black Forest by an unspecified "Lakota medicine man" (they displayed chest scars verifying that they had indeed done something of the sort), and said they were now considering launching their own version on an annual basis. Half a dozen more inquired as to whether I could provide them entree to the Sun Dances conducted each summer on stateside reservations (of special interest are those of the "Sioux").[33] One poor soul, a Swiss national as it turned out, proudly observed that he'd somehow managed to survive living in an Alpine tipi for the past several years.[34] All of them maintained that they actually considered themselves to *be* Indians, at least "in spirit."[35]

These "Indians of Europe," as Feest has termed them, were uniformly quite candid as to why they felt this way.[36] Bluntly put—and the majority were precisely this harsh in their own articulations—they absolutely *hated* the idea of being Europeans, especially Germans. Abundant mention was made of their collective revulsion to the European heritage of colonization and genocide, particularly the ravages of nazism. Some went deeper, addressing what they felt to be the intrinsically unacceptable character of European civilization's relationship to the natural order in its entirety. Their response, as a group, was to try and disassociate themselves from what it was/is they object to by announcing their personal identities in terms as diametrically opposed to it as they could conceive. "Becoming" American Indians in their own minds apparently fulfilled this deep-seated need in a most gratifying fashion.[37]

Yet, when I delved deeper, virtually all of them ultimately admitted they were little more than weekend warriors, or "cultural transvestites," to borrow another of Feest's descriptors.[38] They typically engaged in their Indianist preoccupations only during their off hours while maintaining regular jobs—mainly quite responsible and well-paying positions, at that—squarely within the very system of Germanic business-as-usual they claimed so heatedly to have disavowed, root and branch. The most candid respondents were even willing to admit, when pushed, that were it not for the income accruing from their daily roles as "Good Germans," they'd not be able to afford their hobby of imagining themselves to be something else . . . or to pay the fees charged by imported Native American "spirit leaders" to validate this impression. Further, without exception, when I inquired as to what they might be doing to challenge and transform the fundamental nature of the German culture, society, and state they professed to detest so deeply, they observed that they had become "spiritual people" and therefore "apolitical." Queries concerning whether they might be willing to engage in activities to physically defend the rights and territories of indigenous peoples in North America drew much the same reply.

The upshot of German hobbyism, then, is that, far from constituting the sort of radical divorce from Germanic context its adherents assert, part-time impersonation of American Indians represents a means through which they can psychologically reconcile themselves to it. By pretending to be what they are not—and in fact can never be, because the objects of their fantasies have never existed in real life—the hobbyists are freed to be what they are (but deny), and to "feel good about themselves" in the process.[39] And, since this sophistry allows them to contend in all apparent seriousness that they are somehow entirely separate from the oppressive status quo upon which they depend, and which their "real world" occupations do so much to make possible, they thereby absolve themselves of any obligation whatsoever to materially confront it (and thence themselves). Voilà! "Wildmen" and "primitives" carrying out the most refined functions of the German corporate state; "warriors" relieved of the necessity of doing battle other than in the most metaphorical of senses, and then always (and only) in service to the very structures and traditions they claim—and may even have convinced themselves to *believe* at some level or another—their perverse posturing negates.[40]

THE DYNAMICS OF DENIAL

Contemporary business life allows competitive relationships only, in which the major emotions are anxiety, tension, loneliness, rivalry, and fear . . . Zeus energy has been steadily disintegrating decade after decade in the United States. Popular culture has been determined to destroy respect for it, beginning with the "Maggie and Jiggs" and "Dagwood and Blondie" comics of the 1920s and 1930s, in which the man is always weak and foolish . . . The recovery of some form of [powerful rituals of male] initiation is essential to the culture. The

United States has undergone an unmistakable decline since 1950, and I believe
if we do not find [these kinds of male ritual] the decline will continue.

—Robert Bly, 1990

Obviously, the liberatory potential of all this for actual American Indians is considerably less than zero. Instead, hobbyism is a decidedly parasitical enterprise, devoted exclusively to the emotional edification of individuals integrally and instrumentally
involved in perpetuating and perfecting the system of global domination from which
the genocidal colonization of Native America stemmed and by which it is continued.
Equally, there is a strikingly close, if somewhat antecedent, correspondence between
German hobbyism on the one hand, and the North American Men's Movement on
the other. The class and ethnic compositions are virtually identical, as are the resulting
social functions, internal dynamics, and external impacts.[41] So close is the match, not
only demographically, but motivationally and behaviorally, that Robert Bly himself
scheduled a tour of Germany during the summer of 1993 to bring the Old World's
Teutonic sector into his burgeoning fold.[42]

Perhaps the only significant difference between the Men's Movement at home and
hobbyism abroad is just that: the hobbyists at least are "over there," but the Men's
Movement is right here, where we live. Hobbyism in Germany may contribute to what
both Adolf Hitler and George Bush called the "New World Order," and thus yield a
negative but somewhat indirect effect upon native people in North America, but the
Men's Movement is quite *directly* connected to the ever more efficient imposition of
that order upon Indian lands and lives in the U.S. and Canada. The mining engineer
who joins the Men's Movement and thereafter spends his weekends "communing with
nature in the manner of an Indian" does so—in precisely the same fashion as his German colleagues—in order to exempt himself from either literal or emotional responsibility for the fact that, to be who he is and live at the standard he does, he will spend
the rest of his week making wholesale destruction of the environment an operant reality. Not infrequently, the land being stripmined under his supervision belongs to the
very Indians whose spiritual traditions he appropriates and reifies in the process of
"finding inner peace" (i.e., empowering himself to do what he does).[43]

By the same token, the corporate lawyer, the Wall Street broker and the commercial banker who accompany the engineer into a sweat lodge do so because, intellectually, they understand quite well that, without them, his vocation would be impossible.
The same can be said for the government bureaucrat, the corporate executive, and the
marketing consultant who keep Sacred Pipes on the walls of their respective offices.
All of them are engaged, to a greater or lesser degree—although, if asked, most will
adamantly reject the slightest hint that they are involved at all—in the systematic destruction of the residue of territory upon which prospects of native life itself are balanced. The charade by which they cloak themselves in the identity of their victims is
their best and ultimately most compulsive hedge against the psychic consequences of
acknowledging who and what they really are.[44]

Self-evidently, then, New Age-style rhetoric to the contrary notwithstanding, this pattern of emotional/psychological avoidance embedded in the ritual role-playing of Indians by a relatively privileged stratum of Euroamerican men represents no alternative to the status quo. To the contrary, it has become a steadily more crucial ingredient in an emergent complex of psychosocial mechanisms allowing North American business-as-usual to sustain, stabilize, and reenergize itself. Put another way, had the Men's Movement not come into being complements of Robert Bly and his clones, it would have been necessary—just as the nazis found it useful to do so in their day—for North America's governmental-corporate élite to have created it on their own.[45] On second thought, it's not altogether clear they didn't.[46]

ALTERNATIVES

The ancient societies believed that a boy becomes a man only through ritual and effort—only through the "active intervention of the older men." It's becoming clear to us that manhood doesn't happen by itself; it doesn't just happen because we eat Wheaties. The active intervention of the older men means the older men welcome the younger man into the ancient, mythologized, instinctive male world.

—Robert Bly, 1990

With all this said, it still must be admitted that there is a scent of undeniably real human desperation—an all but obsessive desire to find some avenue of alternative cultural expression different from that sketched above—clinging to the Men's Movement and its New Age and hobbyist equivalents. The palpable anguish this entails allows for, or requires, a somewhat more sympathetic construction of the motives prodding a segment of the movement's membership, and an illative obligation on the part of anyone not themselves experiencing it to respond in a firm, but helpful rather than antagonistic manner.

Perhaps more accurately, it should be said that the sense of despair at issue evidences itself not so much in the ranks of the Men's Movement and related phenomena themselves, but within the milieu from which these manifestations have arisen: white, mostly urban, affluent or affluently reared, well-schooled, young (or youngish) people of both genders who, in one or another dimension, are thoroughly dis-eased by the socioeconomic order into which they were born and their seemingly predestined roles within it.[47] Many of them openly seek, some through serious attempts at political resistance, a viable option with which they may not only alter their own individual fates, but transform the overall systemic realities they correctly perceive as having generated these fates in the first place.[48] As a whole, they seem sincerely baffled by the prospect of having to define for themselves the central aspect of this alternative.

They cannot put a name to it, and so they perpetually spin their wheels, waging continuous theoretical and sometimes practical battles against each "hierarchical" and "patriarchal" fragment of the whole they oppose: capitalism and fascism, colonialism, neocolonialism and imperialism, racism and sexism, ageism, consumerism, the entire vast plethora of "isms" and "ologies" making up the "modern" (or "postmodern") society they inhabit.[49] Frustrated and stymied in their efforts to come up with a new or different conceptualization by which to guide their oppositional project, many of the most alienated—and therefore most committed to achieving fundamental social change—eventually opt for the intellectual/emotional reassurance of prepackaged "radical solutions." Typically, these assume the form of yet another battery of "isms" based in all the same core assumptions as the system being opposed. This is especially true of that galaxy of doctrinal tendencies falling within the general rubric of "marxism"—Bernsteinian revisionism, council communism, marxism-leninism, stalinism, maoism, etc.—but it is also an actuality pervading most variants of feminism, environmentalism, and anarchism/anti-authoritarianism as well.[50]

Others, burned out by an endless diet of increasingly sterile polemical chatter and symbolic political action, defect from the resistance altogether, deforming what German New Left theorist Rudi Dutschke[51] once advocated as "a long march through the institutions" into an outright embrace of the false and reactionary "security" found in statism and bureaucratic corporatism (a tendency exemplified in the U.S. by such 1960s radical figures as Tom Hayden, Jerry Rubin, Eldridge Cleaver, David Horowitz, and Rennie Davis).[52] A mainstay occupation of this coterie has been academia, wherein they typically maintain an increasingly irrelevant and detached "critical" discourse, calculated mainly to negate whatever transformative value or utility might be lodged in the concrete oppositional political engagement they formerly pursued.[53]

Some members of each group—formula radicals and sellouts—end up glossing over the psychic void left by their default in arriving at a genuinely alternative vision, immersing themselves either in some formalized religion (Catholicism, for example, or, somewhat less frequently, denominations of Islam or Buddhism), or the polyglot "spiritualism" offered by the New Age/Men's Movement/Hobbyism syndrome.[54] This futile cycle is now in its third successive generation of repetition among European and Euroamerican activists since the so-called "new student movement" was born only thirty years ago. At one level or another, almost all of those currently involved, and quite a large proportion of those who once were, are figuratively screaming for a workable means of breaking the cycle, some way of foundationing themselves for a sustained and successful effort to effect societal change rather than the series of dead ends they've encountered up till now. Yet a functional alternative exists, and has always existed.

The German Tour Revisited

This was brought home to me most dramatically during my earlier-mentioned speaking tour of Germany.[55] The question most frequently asked by those who turned out to hear me speak on the struggle for liberation in Native North America was, "What can we do to help?" Quite uniformly, the answer I provided to this query was that, strategically, the most important assistance the people in the audience could render American Indians would be to win their own struggle for liberation in Germany. In effect, I reiterated time after time, this would eliminate the German corporate state as a linchpin of the global politicoeconomic order in which the United States (along with its Canadian satellite) serves as the hub.

"You must understand," I stated each time the question arose, "that I really mean it when I say we are all related. Consequently, I see the mechanisms of our oppression as being equally interrelated. Given this perspective, I cannot help but see a victory for you as being simultaneously a victory for American Indians, and vice versa; that a weakening of your enemy here in Germany necessarily weakens ours there, in North America; that your liberation is inseparably linked to our own, and that you should see ours as advancing yours. Perhaps, then, the question should be reversed: what is it that we can best do to help *you* succeed?"

As an expression of solidarity, these sentiments were on every occasion roundly applauded. Invariably, however, they also produced a set of rejoinders intended to qualify the implications of what I'd said to the point of negation. The usual drift of these responses was that the German and American Indian situations and resulting struggles are entirely different, and thus not to be compared in the manner I'd attempted. This is true, those making this point argued, because Indians are colonized peoples while the Germans are colonizers. Indians, they went on, must therefore fight to free our occupied and underdeveloped landbase(s) while the German opposition, effectively landless, struggles to rearrange social and economic relations within an advanced industrial society. Most importantly, they concluded, native people in America hold the advantage of possessing cultures separate and distinct from that which we oppose, while the German opposition, by contrast, must contend with the circumstance of being essentially "cultureless" and disoriented.[56]

After every presentation, I was forced to take strong exception to such notions. "As longterm participants in the national liberation struggle of American Indians," I said, "we have been forced into knowing the nature of colonialism very well. Along with you, we understand that the colonization we experience finds its origin in the matrix of European culture. But, apparently unlike you, we also understand that in order for Europe to do what it has done to us—in fact, for Europe to become 'Europe' at all—it first had to do the same thing to all of you. In other words, to become a colonizing culture, Europe had first to colonize *itself*.[57] To the extent that this is true, I find it fair to say that if our struggle must be explicitly anticolonial in its form, content and aspirations, yours must be even more so. You have, after all, been colonized far longer than we, and therefore much more completely. In fact, your colonization has by now been consolidated to such an extent that—with certain notable exceptions, like the Irish and Euskadi (Basque) nationalists—you no longer even see yourselves as having been colonized.[58] The result is that you've become self-colonizing, conditioned to be so self-identified with your own oppression that you've lost your ability to see it for what it is, much less to resist it in any coherent way.

"You seem to feel that you are either completely disconnected from your own heritage of having been conquered and colonized, or that you can and should disconnect yourselves from it as a means of destroying that which oppresses you. I believe, on the other hand, that your internalization of this self-hating outlook is exactly what your oppressors want most to see you do. Such a posture on your part simply perfects and completes the structure of your domination. It is inherently self-defeating because in denying yourselves the meaning of your own history and traditions, you leave yourselves with neither an established point of departure from which to launch your own struggle for liberation, nor any set of goals and objectives to guide that struggle other than abstractions. You are thereby left effectively anchorless and rudderless, adrift on a stormy sea. You have lost your maps and compass, so you have no idea where you are or where to turn for help. Worst of all, you sense that the ship on which you find yourselves trapped is rapidly sinking. I can imagine no more terrifying situation to be in, and, as relatives, we would like to throw you a life preserver.

"So here it is," I went on. "It takes the form of an insight offered by our elders: 'To understand where you are are, you must know where you've been, and you must know where you are to understand where you are going.'[59] For Indians, you see, the past, present and future are all equally important parts of the same indivisible whole. And I believe this is as true for you as it is for us. In other words, you must set yourselves to reclaiming your own indigenous past. You must come to know it in its own terms— the terms of its internal values and understandings, and the way these were applied to living in this world—not the terms imposed upon it by the order which set out to destroy it. You must learn to put your knowledge of this heritage to use as a lens through which you can clarify your present circumstance, to 'know where you are,' so to speak. And, from this, you can begin to chart the course of your struggle into the future. Put still another way, you, no less than we, must forge the conceptual tools that will allow you to carefully and consciously orient your struggle to regaining what it is that has been taken from you rather than presuming a unique ability to invent it all anew. You must begin with the decolonization of your own minds, with a restoration of your understanding of who you are, where you come from, what it is that has been done to you to take you to the place in which you now find yourselves. Then, and *only* then, it seems to us, will you be able to free yourselves from your present dilemma.

"*Look* at us, and really *hear* what we're saying," I demanded. "We are not unique in being indigenous people. *Everyone* is indigenous somewhere. *You* are indigenous here. You, no more than we, are landless; your land is occupied by an alien force, just like ours. You, just like us, have an overriding obligation to liberate your homeland. You, no less than we, have models in your own traditions upon which to base your alternatives to the social, political, and economic structures now imposed upon you. It is your responsibility to put yourselves in direct communication with these traditions, just as it is our responsibility to remain in contact with ours. We cannot fulfill this responsibility for you any more than you can fulfill ours for us.

"You say that the knowledge we speak of was taken from you too long ago, at the time of Charlemagne, more than a thousand years in the past. Because of this, you say, the gulf of time separating then from now is too great, that what was taken then is now lost and gone. We know better. We know, and so do you, that right up into the 1700s your 'European' colonizers were still busily burning 'witches' at the stake. We know, and you know too, that these women (and some men) were the leaders of your own indigenous cultures.[60] The span of time separating you from a still-flourishing practice of your native ways is thus not so great as you would have us—and yourselves—believe. It's been 200 years, no more. And we also know that there are still those among your people who retain the knowledge of your past, knowledge handed down from one generation to the next, century after century. We can give you directions to some of them if you like, but we think you know they are there.[61] You *can* begin to draw appropriate lessons and instruction from these faithkeepers, if you want to.

"Indians have said that 'for the world to live, Europe must die.'[62] We meant it when we said it, and we still do. But do not be confused. The statement was never intended to exclude you or consign you, as people, to oblivion. We believe the idea underlying that statement holds just as true for you as it does for anyone else. You *do* have a choice, because you are *not* who you've been convinced to believe you are. Or, at least not necessarily. You are not necessarily a part of the colonizing, predatory reality of 'Europe.' You are not even necessarily 'Germans,' with all that that implies. You are, or can be, who your ancestors were and who the faith-keepers of your cultures remain: Angles, Saxons, Huns, Goths, Visigoths. The choice is yours, but in order for it to have meaning you must meet the responsibilities which come with it."

Objections and Responses

Such reasoning provoked considerable consternation among listeners. "But," more than one exclaimed with unpretended horror, "*think* of who you're speaking to! These are very dangerous ideas you are advocating. You are in Germany, among people raised to see themselves as Germans, and yet, at least in part, you are telling us we should do exactly what the nazis did! We Germans, at least those of us who are consciously antifascist and antiracist, renounce such excavations of our heritage precisely because of our country's own recent experiences with them. We *know* where Hitler's politics of 'blood and soil' led not just us but the world. We *know* the outcome of Himmler's reassertion of 'Germanic paganism.' Right now, we are being forced to confront a resurgence of nazism in this country. Surely you can't be arguing that we should *join* in the resurrection of all that."

"Of course not!" I retorted. "We, as American Indians, have at least as much reason to hate nazism as any people on earth. Not much of anything done by the nazis to people here had not already been done to us, for centuries, and some of the things the nazis did during their twelve years in power are *still* being done to us today. Much of what has been done to us in North America was done, and continues to be done, on the basis of philosophical rationalizations indistinguishable from those used by the nazis to justify their policies. If you want to look at it that way, you could say that antinazism is part of the absolute bedrock upon which our struggle is based. So, don't even *hint* that any part of our perspective is somehow 'pro-nazi.'

"I am aware that this is a highly emotional issue for you. But try and bear in mind that the world isn't one-dimensional. Everything is multidimensional, possessed of positive as well as negative polarities. It should be obvious that the nazis didn't represent or crystallize your indigenous traditions. Instead, they perverted your heritage for their own purposes, using your ancestral traditions against themselves in a fashion meant to supplant and destroy them. The European predator has always done this, whenever it was not simply trying to suppress the indigenous host upon which it feeds. Perhaps the nazis were the most overt, and in some ways the most successful, in doing this in recent times. And for that reason some of us view them as being a sort of culmination of all that is European. But, the point is, they very deliberately tapped the negative rather than the positive potential of what we are discussing.

"Now, polarities aside," I continued, "the magnitude of favorable response accorded by the mass of Germans to the themes taken up by the nazis during the 1930s illustrates perfectly the importance of the question we are raising.[63] There is unquestionably a tremendous yearning among all peoples, including your own—and you yourselves, for that matter—for a sense of connectedness to their roots. This yearning, although often sublimated, translates quite readily into transformative power whenever (and however) it is effectively addressed.[64] Hence, part of what we are arguing is that you must consciously establish the positive polarity of your heritage as a counter to the negative impulse created by the nazis. If you don't, it's likely we're going to witness German officials walking around in black death's head uniforms all over again. The signs are there, you must admit.[65] And you must also admit there's a certain logic involved, since you yourselves seem bent upon abandoning the power of your indigenous traditions to nazism. Suffice it to say we'd not give *our* traditions over to the uncontested use of nazis. Maybe you shouldn't either."

Such remarks usually engendered commentary about how the audience had "never viewed the matter in this light," followed by questions as to how a positive expression of German indigenism might be fostered. "Actually," I said, "it seems to me you're already doing this. It's all in how you look at things and how you go about explaining them to others. Try this: You have currently, as a collective response to perceived problems of centralization within the German left, atomized into what you call *autonomen*. These can be understood as a panorama of autonomous affinity groups bound together in certain lines of thought and action by a definable range of issues and aspirations.[66] Correct? So, instead of trying to explain this development to yourselves and everyone else as some 'new and revolutionary tendency'—which it certainly is not— how about conceiving of it as an effort to recreate the kinds of social organization and political consensus marking your ancient 'tribal' cultures (adapted of course to the contemporary context)?

"Making such an effort to connect what you are doing to what was done quite successfully by your ancestors, and using that connection as a mode through which to prefigure what you wish to accomplish in the future, would serve to (re)contextualize your efforts in a way you've never before attempted. It would allow you to obtain a sense of your own cultural continuity which, at present, appears to be conspicuously absent in your struggle. It would allow you to experience the sense of empowerment which comes with reaching into your own history at the deepest level and altering outcomes you've quite correctly decided are unacceptable. This is as opposed to your trying to invent some entirely different history for yourselves. A project of this sort, if approached carefully and with considerable flexibility from the outset, could revitalize your struggle in ways which will astound you.

"Here's another possibility: You are at the moment seriously engaged in efforts to redefine power relations between men and women, and in finding ways to actualize these redefined relationships. Instead of trying to reinvent the wheel in this respect, why not see it as an attempt to reconstitute in the modern setting the kind of gender balance that prevailed among your ancestors? Surely this makes as much sense as attempting to fabricate a whole new set of relations. And, quite possibly, it would enable you to explain your intentions in this regard to a range of people who are frankly skeptical right now, in a manner which would attract them rather than repelling them.

"Again: You are primarily an urban-based movement in which 'squatting' plays a very prominent role.[67] Why not frame this in terms of liberating your space in very much the same way we approach the liberation of our land? The particulars are very different, but the principle involved seems to me to be quite similar. And it's likely that thinking of squatting in this way would lead you right back toward your traditional relationship to land/space. This seems even more probable when squatting is considered in combination with the experiments in collectivism and communalism which are its integral aspects. A lot of translation is required to make these connections, but that too is exactly the point. Translation between the concrete and the theoretical is *always* necessary in the formation of praxis. What I'm recommending is no different from any other approach in this respect. The question is whether these translations will serve to link political activity to reassertion of indigenous traditions, or to force an even further disjuncture in that regard. That's true in any setting, whether it's yours or ours. As I said, there are choices to be made.

"These are merely a few preliminary possibilities I've been able to observe during the short time I've been here," I concluded. "I'm sure there are many others. What's important, however, is that we can and must *all* begin wherever we find ourselves. Start with what already exists in terms of resistance, link this resistance directly to your own native traditions, and build from there. The sequence is a bit different, but that's basically what we in the American Indian Movement have had to do. And we can testify that the process works. You end up with a truly organic and internally sustainable framework within which to engage in liberatory struggle. Plainly, this is something very different from Adolf Hitler's conducting of 'blood rituals' on the playing fields of Nuremberg,[68] or Heinrich Himmler's convening of some kind of 'Mystic Order of the SS' in a castle at Wewelsburg,[69] just as it's something very different from tripped-out hippies prancing about in the grass every spring pretending they're 'rediscovering' the literal ceremonial forms of the ancient Celts, or a bunch of yuppies spending their off-hours playing at being American Indians. All of these are facets of the negative polarity you so rightly reject. I am arguing, not that you should drop your rejection of the negative, but that you should intensify your pursuit of its positive alternative. Let's not confuse the two. And let's not throw the baby out with the bath water. Okay?"

APPLICATIONS TO NORTH AMERICA

It is not necessary for crows to become eagles.

—Sitting Bull, 1888

Much of what has been said with regard to Germany can be transposed for application in North America, albeit there can be no suggestion that Euroamericans are in any way indigenous to this land (cutesy bumper stickers reading "Colorado Native" displayed by blond suburbanites notwithstanding). What is meant is that the imperative of reconnecting to their own traditional roots pertains as much, and in some ways more, to this dislocated segment of the European population as it does to their cousins who have remained in the Old World. By extension, the same point can be made with regard to the descendants of those groups of European invaders who washed up on the beach in other quarters of the planet over these past five hundred years: in various locales of South and Central America, for instance, and in Australia, New Zealand, South Africa, and much of Polynesia and Micronesia. In effect, the rule would apply wherever settler state colonialism has come into existence.[70]

Likely, it will be much more difficult for those caught up in Europe's far-flung diaspora to accomplish this than it may be for those still within the confines of their native geography. The latter plainly enjoy a much greater proximity to the sources of their indigenous traditions, while the former have undergone several generations of continuous indoctrination to see themselves as "new peoples" forging entirely new cultures.[71] The sheer impossibility of this last has inflicted upon the Eurodiaspora an additional dimension of identity confusion largely absent among even the most conspicuously deculturated elements of the subcontinent itself. Rather than serving as a deterrent, however, this circumstance should be understood as heightening the urgency assigned the reconstructive task facing Euroamericans and others, elsewhere, who find themselves in similar situations.

By and large, the Germans have at least come to understand, and to accept, what nazism was and is. This has allowed the best among them to seek to distance themselves from it by undertaking whatever political action is required to destroy it once and for all.[72] Their posture in this respect provides them a necessary foundation for resumption of cultural/spiritual traditions among themselves which constitute a direct and fully internalized antidote to the nazi impulse. In affecting this reconnection to their own indigenous heritage, the German dissidents will at last be able to see nazism—that logical culmination of so much of the predatory synthesis which is "Europe"—as being not something born of their own traditions, but something as alien and antithetical to those traditions as it was/is to the traditions of any other people in the world. In this way, by reintegrating themselves with their indigenous selves, they simultaneously reintegrate themselves with the rest of humanity.

In North America, by contrast, no such cognition can be said to have taken hold, even among the most politically developed sectors of the Euroamerican population. Instead, denial remains the norm. Otherwise progressive whites still seek at all costs to evade even the most obvious correlations between their own history in the New World and that of the nazis in the Old. A favorite intellectual parlor game remains the debate over whether genocide is "really" an "appropriate" term to describe the physical eradication of some 98 percent of the continent's native population between 1500 and 1900.[73] "Concern" is usually expressed that comparisons between the U.S. government's assertion of its "Manifest Destiny" to expropriate through armed force about 97.5 percent of all native land, and the nazis' subsequent effort to implement what they called "*lebensraumpolitik*"—the expropriation through conquest of territory belonging to the Slavs, and other "inferior" peoples only a couple of generations later—might be "misleading" or "oversimplified."[74]

The logical contortions through which Euroamericans persist in putting themselves in order to avoid reality are sometimes truly amazing. A salient example is that of James Axtell, a white "revisionist" historian prone to announcing his "sympathies" with Indians, who has repeatedly gone on record arguing in the most vociferous fashion that it is both "unfair" and "contrary to sound historiography" to compare European invaders and settlers in the Americas to nazis. His reasoning? Because, he says, the former were, "after all, human beings. They were husbands, fathers, brothers, uncles, sons, and lovers. And we must try to reach back in time to understand them as such."[75] Exactly what he thinks the nazis were if not human beings fulfilling identical roles in their society, is left unstated. For that matter, Axtell fails to address how he ever arrived at the novel conclusion that either the nazis or European invaders and Euroamerican settlers in the New World consisted only of men.

A more sophisticated ploy is the ready concession on the part of white activists/ theorists that what was done to America's indigenous peoples was "tragic," even while raising carefully loaded questions suggesting that things are working out "for the best" in any event.[76] "Didn't Indians fight wars with one another?" the question goes, implying that the native practice of engaging in rough intergroup skirmishing—a matter more akin to full-contact sports like football, hockey, and rugby than anything else—somehow equates to Europe's wars of conquest and annihilation, and that traditional indigenous societies therefore stand to gain as much from Euroamerican conceptions of pacifism as anyone else.[77] (You bet, boss. Left to our own devices, we'd undoubtedly have exterminated ourselves. Praise the Lord that y'all came along to save us from ourselves.)

Marxist organizations like the Revolutionary Communist Party USA express deep concern that native people's economies might have been so unrefined that we were commonly forced to eat our own excrement to survive, a premise clearly implying that Euroamerica's industrial devastation of our homelands has ultimately worked to our advantage, ensuring our "material security" whether we're gracious enough to admit it or not.[78] (Thanks, boss. We were tired of eating shit anyway. Glad you came and taught us to farm.[79]) The "cutting edge" ecologists of Earth First! have conjured up queries as to whether Indians weren't "the continent's first environmental pillagers"— they claim we beat all the woolly mammoths to death with sticks, among other things—meaning we were always sorely in need of Euroamerica's much more advanced views on preserving the natural order.[80]

White male anarchists fret over possible "authoritarian" aspects of our societies—"You had *leaders*, didn't you? That's hierarchy!"[81]—while their feminist sisters worry that our societies may have been "sexist" in their functioning.[82] (Oh no, boss. We too managed to think our way through to a position in which women did the heavy lifting and men bore the children. Besides, hadn't you heard? We were all "queer," in the old days, so your concerns about our being patriarchal have always been unwarranted.[83]) Even the animal rights movement chimes in from time to time, discomfited that we were traditionally so unkind to "non-human members of our sacred natural order" as to eat their flesh.[84] (Hey, no sweat boss. We'll jump right on your no-meat bandwagon. But don't forget the sacred Cherokee Clan of the Carrot. You'll have to reciprocate our gesture of solidarity by not eating any more fruits and vegetables either. Or had you forgotten that plants are non-human members of the natural order as well? Have a nice fast, buckaroo.)

Not until such apologist and ultimately white supremacist attitudes begin to be dispelled within at least that sector of Euroamerican society which claims to represent an alternative to U.S./Canadian business-as-usual can there be hope of *any* genuinely positive social transformation in North America. And only in acknowledging the real rather than invented nature of their history, as the German opposition has done long since, can they begin to come to grips with such things.[85] From there, they too will be able to to position themselves—psychologically, intellectually, and eventually in practical terms—to step outside that history, not in a manner which continues it by presuming to appropriate the histories and cultural identities of its victims, but in ways allowing them to recapture its antecedent meanings and values. Restated, Euroamericans, like their European counterparts, will then be able to start reconnecting themselves to their indigenous traditions and identities in ways which instill pride rather than guilt, empowering themselves to join in the negation of the construct of "Europe" which has temporarily suppressed their cultures as well as ours.

At base, the same principle applies here that pertains "over there." As our delegation put it repeatedly to the Germans in our closing remarks, "The indigenous peoples of the Americas can, have, and will continue to join hands with the indigenous peoples of this land, just as we do with those of any other. We are reaching out to you by our very act of being here, and of saying what we are saying to you. We have faith in you, a faith that you will be able to rejoin the family of humanity as peoples interacting respectfully and harmoniously—on the basis of your own ancestral ways—with the traditions of all other peoples. We are at this time expressing a faith in you that you perhaps lack in yourselves. But, and make no mistake about this, we *cannot* and *will not* join hands with those who default on this responsibility, who instead insist upon wielding an imagined right to stand as part of Europe's synthetic and predatory tradition, the tradition of colonization, genocide, racism, and ecocide. The choice, as we've said over and over again, is yours to make. It cannot be made for you. You alone must make your choice and act on it, just as we have had to make and act upon ours."

In North America, there will be an indication that affirmative choices along these lines have begun to emerge among self-proclaimed progressives, not when figures like Robert Bly are simply dismissed as being ridiculous kooks, or condoned as harmless irrelevancies,[86] but when they come to be treated by "their own" as signifying the kind of menace they actually entail. Only when white males themselves start to display the sort of profound outrage at the activities of groups like the Men's Movement as is manifested by its victims—when they rather than we begin to shut down the movement's meetings, burn its sweat lodges, impound and return the sacred objects it desecrates, and otherwise make its functioning impossible—will we be able to say with confidence that Euroamerica has finally accepted that Indians are Indians, not toys to be played with by whoever can afford the price of the game. Only then will we be able to say that the "Indians 'R' Us" brand of cultural appropriation and genocide has passed, or at least is passing, and that Euroamericans are finally coming to terms with who they've been and, much more important, who and what it is they can become. Then, finally, these immigrants can at last be accepted among us upon our shores, fulfilling the speculation of the Duwamish leader Seattle in 1854: "We may be brothers after all." As he said then, "We shall see."[87]

PART IV

THE INDIGENIST ALTERNATIVE

♦ ♦ ♦ ♦ ♦ ♦ ♦ ♦ ♦ ♦ ♦ ♦ ♦ ♦

Philosophers have only *interpreted* the world, in various ways; the point is to *change* it.

—Karl Marx
"Theses on Feuerbach (IX)," 1845

11

FALSE PROMISES

An Indigenist Examination of Marxist Theory and Practice

◆ ◆ ◆ ◆ ◆ ◆ ◆ ◆ ◆ ◆ ◆ ◆ ◆

> Sure, I'm a Marxist. But I've never been able to decide which one of them I like best: Groucho, Harpo, Chico, or Karl.
> —American Indian Movement joke, *circa* 1975

HAU, METAKUYEAYASI. THE GREETING I HAVE JUST GIVEN IS A LAKOTA PHRASE meaning, "Hello, my relatives." Now, I'm not a Lakota, and I'm not particularly fluent in the Lakota language, but I ask those of you who are to bear with me for a moment while I explore the meaning of the greeting because I think it is an important point of departure for our topic: the relationship, real and potential, existing between the marxist tradition on the one hand, and that of indigenous peoples such as American Indians on the other.

DIALECTICS

The operant words here are "relatives," "relationship," and, by minor extension, "relations." I have come to understand that when Lakota people use the word Metakuyeayasi, they are not simply referring to their mothers and fathers, grandparents, aunts and uncles, ancestors, nieces and nephews, children, grandchildren, cousins, future generations, and all the rest of humankind. Oh, these relatives are certainly included, but things don't stop there. Also involved is reference to the ground we stand on, the sky above us, the light from the sun and water in the oceans, lakes, rivers, and streams. The plants who populate our environment are included, as are the four-legged creatures around us, those who hop and crawl, the birds who fly, the fish who swim, the insects, the worms. Everything. These are all understood in the Lakota way as being relatives. What is conveyed in this Lakota concept is the notion of the universe as a relational whole, a single interactive organism in which all things, all beings, are active and essential parts; the whole can never be understood without a knowledge of the function and meaning of each of the parts, while the parts cannot be understood other than in the context of the whole.[1]

This essay began its evolution as a Phyllis Burger Memorial Lecture at Montana State University in March 1988.

The formation of knowledge is, in such a construct, entirely dependent upon the active maintenance of a fully symbiotic, relational—or, more appropriately, *inter*relational—approach to understanding. This fundamental appreciation of things, the predicate upon which worldview is established, is, I would argue, common not only to the Lakota but to all American Indian cultural systems.[2] Further, it seems inherent to indigenous cultures the world over. At least I can say with certainty that I've looked in vain for a single concrete example to the contrary.

The ancient Greeks had a term, *dialitikos*, the idea for which was borrowed from an Egyptian concept, and which, I'm told, the civilization of the Nile had itself appropriated from the people of what is now called Ethiopia, describing such a way of viewing things.[3] The Greeks held this to be the superior mode of thinking. In modern parlance, the word at issue has become "dialectics," popularized in this form by the German posttheological philosopher Friedrich Hegel.[4] As has so often happened in the history of European intellectuality, Hegel's notable career spawned a bevy of philosophical groupies. Among the more illustrious, or at least more industrious, of these "Young Hegelians" was a doctoral student named Karl Marx.[5]

Indeed, Marx was always clear in his student work—much of which can now be read in a volume titled *The Economic and Philosophic Manuscripts of 1844*—and forever after that it was the structure of "dialectical reasoning" he'd absorbed from Hegel that formed the fundament of his entire theoretical enterprise.[6] He insisted to his dying day that this remained true despite his famous "inversion" of Hegel, that is: the reversal of Hegel's emphasis upon such "mystical" categories as "the spirit" in favor of more "pragmatic" categories like "substance" and "material."[7]

Let us be clear at this point. The dialectical theoretical method adopted by Marx stands—at least in principle—in as stark an oppositional contrast, and for all the same reasons, to the predominant and predominating tradition of linear and nonrelational European logic exemplified by Bacon, Locke, Descartes, Feuerbach, and Newton as do indigenous systems of knowledge.[8] It follows from this that there should be a solid conceptual intersection between Marx, marxism, and indigenous peoples. Indeed, I myself have suggested such a possibility in an essay collected in my book, *From a Native Son*.[9]

At an entirely abstract level, I remain convinced that this is in fact the case. There is, however, a decisive defect in such a thesis in any less rarefied sense. The most lucid articulation of the problem was perhaps offered by Michael Albert and Robin Hahnel in their *Unorthodox Marxism*:

> [Marxist] dialecticians have never been able to indicate exactly how they see dialectical relations as different from any of the more complicated combinations of simple cause/effect relations such as co-causation, cumulative causation, or simultaneous determination of a many variable system where no variables are identified as dependent or independent in advance . . . for orthodox practitioners [of marxian dialectics] there is only the word and a lot of "hand waving" about its importance.[10]

A substantial case can be made that this confusion within marxism began with Marx himself. Having philosophically accepted and described a conceptual framework which allowed for a holistic and fully relational apprehension of the universe, Marx promptly abandoned it at the level of his applied intellectual practice. His impetus in this regard appears to have been his desire to see his theoretical endeavors used, not simply as a tool of understanding, but as a proactive agent for societal transformation, a matter bound up in his famous dictum that "the purpose of philosophy is not merely to understand history, but to change it."[11]

Thus Marx, a priori and without apparent qualms, proceeded to anchor the totality of his elaboration in the presumed primacy of a given relation—that sole entity which can be said to hold the capability of active and conscious pursuit of change, i.e., humanity—over any and all other relations.[12] The marxian "dialectic" was thus unbalanced from the outset, skewed as a matter of faith in favor of humans. Such a disequilibrium is, of course, not dialectical at all. It *is*, however, quite specifically eurocentric in its attributes, springing as it does from the late Roman interpretation of the Judeochristian assertion of "man's" supposed responsibility to "exercise dominion over nature,"[13] a tradition which Marx claimed oft, loudly and rather paradoxically, to have "voided" in his rush to materialism.[14]

All of this must be contrasted to the typical indigenous practice of dialectics, a worldview recognizing the human entity as being merely one relation among the myriad, each of which is entirely dependent upon all others for its continued existence. Far from engendering some sense of "natural" human dominion over other relations, the indigenous view virtually requires a human behavior geared to keeping humanity *within* nature, maintaining relational balance and integrity—a condition often referred to as "harmony"—rather than attempting to harness and subordinate the universe.[15]

The crux of this distinction may be discovered in the Judeochristian assertion that "man was created in God's image," a notion which leads to the elevation of humans as a sort of surrogate deity, (self-)empowered to transform the universe at whim.[16] Indigenous tradition, on the other hand, in keeping with its truly dialectical understandings, attributes the inherent ordering of things, not to any given relation, but to another force often described as constituting a "Great Mystery," far beyond the realm of mere human comprehension.[17]

We may take this differentiation to a somewhat more tangible level for purposes of clarity. The culmination of European tradition has been a honing in on rationality, the innate characteristic of the human mind lending humanity the capacity to disrupt the order and composition of the universe. Rationality is held by those of European intellectual inclination—marxist and antimarxist alike—to be the most important ("superior") relation of all; humans, being the only entity possessing it, are thus held ipso facto to be *the* superior beings of the universe; manifestations of rationality, whether cerebral or physical, are therefore held to be the cardinal signifiers of virtue.[18]

Within indigenous traditions, meanwhile, rationality is more often viewed as being something of a "curse," a facet of humanity which must be consistently leashed and controlled in order for it not to generate *precisely* this disruption.[19] The dichotomy between outlooks could not be more pronounced. All of this is emphatically *not* to suggest that indigenous cultures are, to employ a pet epithet hurled against challengers by the eurosupremacists of American academia, somehow "irrational" in our makeup.[20] Rather, it is to observe that, as consummate dialecticians, we have long since developed functional and functioning methods of keeping our own rationality meshed with the rest of the natural order. And this, in my view, is the most rational exercise of all.

DIALECTICAL MATERIALISM

In any event, having wholeheartedly accepted the European mainstream's antidialectical premise that the human relation is paramount over all others in what are termed "external relations," Marx inevitably set out to discover that which occupied the same preeminence among "internal relations" (that is, those relations comprising the nature of the human project itself).[21] With perhaps equal inevitability, his inverted hegelianism—which he dubbed "dialectical materialism"[22]—led him to locate this in the need of humans to *consciously* transform one aspect of nature into another, a process he designated by the term "production."[23] It is important to note in this regard that Marx focused upon what is arguably the most rationalized, and therefore most unique, characteristic of human behavior, thus establishing a mutually reinforcing interlock between the relation which he advanced as being most important externally, and that to which he assigned the same position internally.[24]

So interwoven have these two relations become in the marxian mind that today we find marxists utilizing the terms "rationality" and "productivity" almost interchangeably, and with a virtually biblical circularity of reasoning.[25] It goes like this: The ability to produce demonstrates human rationality, thereby distinguishing humans as superior to all other external relations, while rationality (left unchecked) leads unerringly to proliferate productivity, thereby establishing the latter as more important than any other a activity among humans (internally). The record, of course, can be played in reverse with equally satisfying results.

From here, Marx was in a position to launch his general theory, laid out in the thousands of pages of his major published works—*Introduction to the Critique of Political Economy*, and the three volumes of *Capital*—in which he attempted to explain the full range of implications attendant to what he described as "the relations of production." Initially, he was preoccupied with applying his concepts temporally, a project he tagged as "historical materialism," in order to assess and articulate the nature of the development of society through time.[26] Here, he theorized that the various relations of society—ways of holding land, kinship structures, systems of governance, spiritual beliefs, and so on—represented, not a unified whole, but a complex of "contradictions" (in varying degrees) to the central, productive relation.[27]

All history, for Marx, became a stream of conflict within which these contradictions were increasingly "reconciled with"—that is, subordinated to—production. As such reconciliation occurred over time, he argued, various transformations in socio-cultural relations correspondingly took place. Hence, he sketched history as a grand "progression," beginning with the "prehistory" of the "Stone Age" (the most "primi-tive" level of truly human existence) and "advancing" to the emergent capitalism of his own day.[28] "Productive relations," in such a schema, determine all and everything.

One of Marx's theoretical heirs, the late-twentieth-century French structuralist Louis Althusser, summed up historical materialism quite succinctly when he defined production as the "overdetermined contradiction of all human history," and observed that from a marxian standpoint society would not, in fact *could not* exist as a unified whole until the process had worked its way through to culmination, a point at which all other social relations stood properly reconciled to the "productive mission" of hu-manity.[29] In a more critical vein, we might note another summation offered by Albert and Hahnel:

> [O]rthodox [marxism] doesn't stop at downgrading the importance of the cre-ative aspect of human consciousness and the role it plays in historical develop-ment. According to the orthodox materialists, of all the different objective material conditions, those having to do with production are always the most critical. Production is the prerequisite to human existence. Productive activity is the basis for all other activity. Therefore, consciousness rests primarily on the nature of objective production relations. Cut to the bone, this is the essence of the orthodox materialist [marxist] argument.[30]

It is difficult to conceive of a more economistic or deterministic ideological con-struction than this. Indeed, as then-poststructuralist/now-postmodernist French theo-retician Jean Baudrillard pointed out in his book, *The Mirror of Production*, Marx never so much offered a critique or alternative to the capitalist mode of political econ-omy he claimed to oppose as he *completed* it, plugging its theoretical loopholes.[31] This, in turn, has caused indigenous liberationists such as Russell Means to view marxism not as a potential revolutionary transformation of world capitalism but as a *continuation* of all of capitalism's worst vices "in a more efficient form."[32]

There are numerous aspects of marxian general theory—concepts such as surplus value, alienation, and domination among them—that might be useful to explore at this juncture. It seems to me, however, the most fruitful avenue of pursuit lies in what Marx termed "the labor theory of value."[33] By this, he meant that value can be assigned to anything *only* by virtue of the quantity and quality of human labor—i.e., productive, transformative effort—put into it. This idea carries with it several interesting subprop-erties, most strikingly that the natural world holds no intrinsic value of its own. A mountain is worth nothing as a mountain; it only accrues value by being "developed" into its raw productive materials such as ores, or even gravel. It can hold a certain spec-ulative value, and thus be bought and sold, but only with such developmental ends in view. Similarly, a forest holds value only in the sense that it can be converted into a product known as lumber; otherwise, it is merely an obstacle to valuable, productive use of land through agriculture or stock raising, etc. (an interesting commentary on the marxian view of the land itself). Again, other species hold value only in terms of their utility to productive processes (e.g., meat, fur, leather, various body oils, eggs, milk, transportation in some instances, even fertilizer); otherwise they may, indeed *must* be preempted and supplanted by the more productive use of the habitat by humans. [34]

The preceding is no doubt an extreme formulation. There have been a number of "mediations" of this particular trajectory by twentieth-century marxian theorists. Still, at base, the difference they offer lies more in the degree of virulence with which they express the thesis than in any essential break with it. All self-professing marxists, in order to be marxists at all, must share in the fundamental premise involved, and this goes for sophisticated phenomenological marxists like Merleau-Ponty,[35] existential marxists such as Sartre,[36] critical theorists of the Frankfurt School like Adorno and Marcuse,[37] as well as Habermas (among other heirs apparent),[38] right along with "mechanistic vulgarians" of the leninist persuasion (a term I use to encompass all those who trace their theoretical foundations directly to Lenin: stalinists, maoists, castroites, althusserian structuralists, and so on).[39] To put a cap on this particular point, I would offer the observation that the labor theory of value is the underpinning of a perspective which is about as contrary to the indigenous worldview as it is possible to define.[40]

It goes without saying that there are other implications in this connection, as concerns indigenous cultures and people. Marx's concept of value ties directly to his notion of history, wherein progress is defined in terms of the evolution of production. From this juxtaposition we may discern that agricultural society is viewed as an "advance" over hunting and gathering society, feudalism is an advance over simple agriculture, mercantilism is seen as an advance over feudalism, and capitalism over mercantilism.[41] Marx's supposed "revolutionary" content comes from his projection that socialism will "inevitably" be the next advance over capitalism and that it, in turn, will give way to communism.[42] The first key is that each advance represents not only a quantitative/qualitative step "forward" in terms of productivity, but also a corresponding rearrangement of other social relations, with both factors assigned a greater degree of *value* than their "predecessors." In other words, agricultural society is seen by marxists as being more valuable than hunting and gathering society, feudalism as more valuable than mere agriculture, and so on.[43] The picture should be becoming clear.

Now, there is a second facet. Marx was very straightforward in acknowledging that the sole cultural model upon which he was basing his theses on history and value was his own, that is to say European (or, more accurately, northwestern European) context. He even committed to paper several provisos stipulating that it would be inappropriate and misleading to attempt to apply the principles deriving from his examination of the dominant matrix in Europe to other, noneuropean contexts, each of which he correctly pointed out would have to be understood on its own terms before it could be properly understood in comparison to Europe.[44] This said, however, he promptly violated his own professed method in this regard, offering a number of noneuropean examples—of which he admittedly knew little—to illustrate various points he wished to make in his elaboration on the historical development of Europe.

Chinese society, to offer a prominent example, was cast—really *mis*-cast—by Marx as "Oriental despotism" and/or "Asiatic feudalism," thus supposedly shedding a certain light on the feudal stage of European history (and vice versa).[45] "Red Indian" cultures, about which Marx knew even less than he did about China, became examples of "primitive society," illustrating what he wanted to say about Europe's Stone Age.[46] In this fashion, he universalized what he claimed were the primary ingredients of Germanic history, extending the de facto contention that *all* cultures are subject to the same essential dynamics and, therefore, follow essentially the same historical progression.[47]

Insofar as all cultures were identified as corresponding materially to one or another moment in European history, and given that only Europe exhibited a "capitalist mode of production" and social organization—which Marx held to be the "highest form of social advancement" as of the point he was writing[48]—it follows that all noneuropean cultures could be seen as objectively lagging behind Europe. We are presented here with a sort of "universal Euro yardstick" by which we can measure with considerable precision the relative ("dialectical") degree of retardation shown by each and every culture on the planet, vis-à-vis Europe.[49] Simultaneously, we are able to assign, again with reasonable precision, a relatively ("dialectically") lesser value to each of these cultures as compared to that of Europe.

We are dealing here with the internal relations of humanity, but in order to understand the import of such thinking we must bear in mind the fate assigned "inferior" (less valuable) *external* relations—mountains, trees, deer—within the marxian vision. In plainest terms, marxism holds as "an immutable law of history" that all noneuropean cultures must be subsumed in what is now called "Europeanization."[50] It is our inevitable destiny, a matter to be accomplished in the name of progress and "for our own good." Again, one detects echoes of the Jesuits within Marx's "antispiritualist" construct.[51]

Those who would reject such an assessment should consider the matter more carefully. Do not such terms as "preindustrial" and "precapitalist" infest the marxian vernacular whenever analysis of noneuropean—that is, "undeveloped," "backward," or "primitive"—societies is at hand?[52] What possible purpose does the qualifier "pre"—as opposed to, say, "non"—serve in this connection other than to argue that such societies are *in the process of becoming* capitalist? And is this not simply another way of stating that we are lagging behind those societies which have *already become* industrialized?[53] Or, to take another example, to what end do marxists habitually refer to those societies which have "failed" (refused) to enter a productive progression as being "ahistorical" or "outside of history"? Is this to suggest that such cultures have *no* history, or is it to say that they have the wrong *kind* of history, that only a certain (marxian) sort of history can be "real"?[54]

Again: Do marxists not hold that achieving communism will embody an historical culmination for *all* humanity?[55] Is there another sense in which we can understand the term "*world* revolution"?[56] Did Marx himself not proclaim in no uncertain terms that the attainment of the "capitalist stage of development" is an absolute prerequisite for the social transformation he envisioned when he spoke of "revolution"?[57] I suggest that, given the only honest answers to these questions, there really are no other conclusions to be drawn from the corpus of marxist theory than those I'm drawing. The punchline is that marxism as a worldview is not only diametrically opposed to that held by indigenous peoples, it quite literally precludes our right to a continued existence as functioning sociocultural entities. This, I submit, will remain true despite the fact that we may legitimately disagree on the nuance and detail of precisely how it happens to be true.

THE NATIONAL QUESTION

Up to this point, our discussion has been restricted to the consideration of marxist theory. It is one thing to say that there are problems with a set of ideas, and that those ideas carry unacceptable implications if they were to be put into practice. The "proof," however, is in the practice, or "praxis" if you follow the marxian conception that theory and practice are a unified whole and must consequently be maintained in a dialectically-reciprocal and interactive state at all times.[58] Hence, it is quite another matter to assert that the negative implications of doctrine and ideology have in fact been actualized in "the real world" and are thereby subject to concrete examination. Yet marxism offers us exactly this means of substantiating our theoretical conclusions.

To be fair, when we move into this area we are no longer concerned with the totality of marxism. Rather, we must focus upon that stream which owes a special allegiance to the legacy of Lenin. The reason for this is that *all* marxist revolutions, beginning with the one in the Soviet Union, have been carried out under the mantle of Lenin's interpretation, expansion, and revision of Marx. This has been true of the revolutionary processes in China, Vietnam, Cuba, Algeria, Cambodia, Laos, Mozambique, Angola, and Nicaragua.[59] Arguably, it is also true for Zimbabwe (formerly Rhodesia),[60] and it is certainly true for those countries brought into a marxian orbit through "Great Power negotiations" and/or exertions of main force: Latvia, Lithuania, Estonia, Poland, East Germany, Czechoslovakia, Hungary, Rumania, Albania, Bulgaria, North Korea, Tibet, and Afghanistan, among them.[61]

Yugoslavia represents a special case,[62] as did Chile during the Allende period,[63] but the "deviations" involved seem largely due to capitalist influences rather than to some discernibly marxian subtext. One might go on to say that those self-proclaimed revolutionary marxist formations worldwide which seem capable of effecting a seizure of state power at any point in the foreseeable future—that in Namibia, for example,[64] and perhaps those in Columbia and Peru[65]—are all decisively leninist in orientation. They certainly have disagreements among themselves, but this does not change the nature of their foundations. There have been no nonleninist marxian revolutions to date, nor does it seem likely there will be in the coming decades. Be this as it may, there are again a number of aspects of marxist-leninist postrevolutionary practice which we might consider, e.g., the application of Lenin's concept of "the dictatorship of the proletariat," centralized state economic planning and the issue of forced labor, the imposition of rigid state parameters upon political discourse of all types, and so forth.[66] Each of these holds obvious and direct consequences for the populations involved, including whatever indigenous peoples happen to become encapsulated within one or another (sometimes more than one) revolutionary state. It seems appropriate, nonetheless, that we follow the lead of Albert and Hahnel in "cutting to the bone." We will therefore take up that aspect of marxist-leninist praxis which has led to indigenous peoples being encompassed by revolutionary states at all. This centers upon what is called the "national question" (or "nationalities question").[67]

At issue is "the right to self-determination of all peoples," a concept codified in international law by the United Nations from 1945 onward,[68] but originally espoused by Marx and his colleague, Friedrich Engels, during the London Conference of the First International in 1865.[69] In essence, the right to self-determination has come to mean that each people, identifiable as such through the sharing of a common language and cultural understandings, system of governance and social regulation, and a definable territoriality within which to maintain a viable economy, is inherently entitled to decide for itself whether or not and to what extent it wishes to merge itself culturally, politically, territorially, and economically with any other (usually larger) group.[70]

The right to self-determination thus accords to each people on the planet a bedrock entitlement to (re)establish and/or continue itself as a culturally distinct, territorially and economically autonomous, and politically sovereign entity: as a *nation*, in other words.[71] Correspondingly, no nation holds a legitimate prerogative to preempt the exercise of such rights by another. For these reasons, the right of self-determination has been linked closely with the movement toward global decolonization, and the resultant body of international law.[72] All this, to be sure, is very much in line with the stated aspirations of American Indians and other indigenous peoples around the world.[73]

But marxism's handling of the right to self-determination has not followed the general development of the concept. Having opened the door, Marx and Engels quickly adopted what— superficially, at least—seems to be a very curious posture, arguing that self-determining rights pertained only to *some* peoples. They were quite strong, for instance, in asserting that the Irish, who were even then waging a serious struggle to rid themselves of their British colonizers, should be supported.[74] Similarly, Marx came out in favor of the right of the Poles to break free from the yoke of both Russian and German colonialism.[75] On the other hand, Engels argued vociferously that "questions as to the right of independent national existence of those small relics of peoples" such as the Highland Scots (Celts), Welsh, Manxmen, Serbs, Croats, Ruthenes, Slovaks, and Czechs constitute "an absurdity."[76] Marx concurred, and proceeded to openly advocate the imposition of European colonialism upon the "backward peoples" of Africa, Asia, and elsewhere.[77]

Such positioning may initially seem confusing, even contradictory. Upon closer examination, however, an underlying consistency with Marx's broader and more philosophical pronouncements is revealed. The Irish and Poles had been, over the course of several centuries of English and Russo-German colonization (respectively), sufficiently "advanced" by the experience (i.e., reformed in the image of their conquerors) to be "ready" in Marx's mind to assume control over their own future in conformity to the "iron laws" of historical materialism.[78] The other peoples in question, especially the "tribal" peoples of Africa and Asia—and one may safely assume that American Indians fell into the same category—had not yet been comparably "developed." A continuing dose of colonization—subjugation by superior beings, from superior cultures—was thus prescribed to help us overcome our "problem."[79]

A second level of consideration also entered into Marx's and Engels' calculations in such matters. This concerns the notion of "economies of scale." Marx held that the larger an "economic unit" became, the more rational and efficient it could be rendered. Conversely, smaller economic units were deemed inefficient by virtue of being "irrationally" duplicative ("redundant").[80] The Irish and Poles were not only populous enough to be considered among Engels' "great peoples," but—viewed as economic units—large enough to be worthy of support in their own right, at least during a transitional phase en route to the ultimate achievement of "world communism." Conversely, indigenous peoples were seen as being not only too "backward," but too *small* to warrant the least solidarity in our quest(s) to survive, much less to assert our independence;[81] our only real destiny, from a marxist perspective, was to be consigned to what León Trotsky would later call "the dustbin of history," totally and irrevocably subsumed by larger and more efficient economic units. [82]

The national question thus emerged for marxists as a problem in determining precisely which peoples were entitled to even a transient national existence along the way to the "true internationalism" of global communism, and which should have such rights foreclosed out of hand as a means of expediting the process. This in itself became quite a controversial discussion when marxists faced the issue of adopting tactics with which to wage their own revolutionary struggles, rather than simply tendering or denying endorsement to the struggles of others.[83] At that point, things become truly cynical and mercenary.

While marxism has all along been conceptually opposed to the nationalistic aspirations of "marginal" peoples, it has been perceived by many marxists that a certain advantage might accrue to marxian revolutionaries if they were to *pretend* that things were otherwise. The struggles of even the smallest and least developed nationalities might be counted upon to sap the strength of the capitalist status quo while marxist cadres went about the real business of overthrowing it;[84] in certain instances, "national minorities" might even be counted upon to absorb the brunt of the fighting, thus sparing marxism an unnecessary loss of highly trained personnel.[85]

After the revolution, it was reasoned, the marxist leadership could simply utilize their political acumen to consolidate state power in their own hands and revoke as "unrealistic"—even "counterrevolutionary"—the aspirations to national integrity for which those of the minority nationalities had fought and died.[86] Once in power, they could also accomplish the desired abrogation of independent national minority existence either rapidly or more gradually, depending upon the vagaries of what are usually called "objective conditions." As Walker Connor put it in his magisterial study, *The National Question in Marxist-Leninist Theory and Strategy*, "Grand strategy was . . . to take precedence over ideological purity and consistency" where the right to self-determination was concerned.[87]

It is not that all this was agreed upon in anything resembling a harmonious or unanimous fashion. To the contrary, during the period leading up to the Russian Revolution, the national question was the topic of an extremely contentious debate within the Second International. On one side was Rosa Luxemburg and the bulk of all delegates, arguing a "purist" line that the right to self-determination does not exist in and of itself and should thus be renounced by marxism.[88] On the other side was a rather smaller group clustered around Lenin. They insisted not only that marxism should view with favor *any* struggle against the status quo prior to the revolution, but that the International should extend guarantees which might serve to stir national minorities into action.[89]

Towards this end, Lenin wrote that from the bolshevik perspective all nations have an *absolute* right to self-determination, including the right to total secession and independence from any marxist revolutionary state.[90] He also endorsed, as the official party position on the national question, a formulation put forth by Joseph Stalin:

> The right to self-determination means that a nation can arrange its life according to its own will. It has the right to arrange its life on the basis of autonomy. It has the right to enter into federal relations with other nations. It has the right to complete secession. Nations are sovereign and all nations are equal.[91]

Of course, as Connor points out, "Lenin . . . made a distinction between the abstract right of self-determination, which is enjoyed by all nations, and the right to exercise that right, which evidently is not."[92] Thus, shortly after the bolshevik attainment of power came the pronouncement that, "The principle of self-determination must be subordinated to the principles of socialism."[93] The result, predictably, was that of the more than 300 distinct nationalities readily observable in what had been the czarist Russian empire, only twenty-eight—consisting primarily of substantial and relatively europeanized population blocks such as the Ukrainians, Armenians, Moldavians, Byelorussians, and so on—were accorded even the gesture of being designated as "republics," and this only after the matter of secession had been foreclosed.[94]

The supposed "right to enter into federal relations with other nations" was also immediately circumscribed to mean only with each other and with the central government which, of course, was seated in the former czarist citadel at Moscow. Those, such as the Ukrainians, who persisted in pursuing a broader definition of self-determination were first branded as counterrevolutionary, and then radically undercut through liquidation of their sociocultural and political leadership during the stalinist purges of the 1920s and '30s.[95] There is simply no other way in which to describe the Soviet marxist process of state consolidation other than as the ruthlessly forcible incorporation of all the various peoples conquered by the czars into a single, seamless economic polity. As Marx once completed the capitalist model of political economy, so too did the Bolsheviks complete the unification of the Great Russian empire.[96]

In China, the practical reality was much the same. During the so-called "Long March" of the mid-1930s, Mao Zedung's army of marxist insurgents traversed nearly the whole of the country. In the midst of this undertaking, they "successfully communicated the party's public position [favoring] self-determination to the minorities they encountered," virtually all of whom were well known to be yearning for freedom from the domination of the Han empire.[97] The marxists gained considerable, perhaps decisive, support as a result of this tactic, but, to quote Connor:

> While thus engaged in parlaying its intermittent offers of national independence into necessary support for its cause, the party never fell prey to its own rhetoric but continued to differentiate between its propaganda and its more privately held commitment to maintaining the territorial integrity of the Chinese state.[98]

As had been the case in the USSR, the immediate wake of the Chinese revolution in 1949 saw marxist language suddenly shift, abandoning terms such as secession and self-determination altogether. Instead, the new Chinese constitution was written to decry "nationalism and national chauvinism," and "the peoples who, during the revolution, were promised the right of political independence were subsequently reincorporated by force and offered the diminished prospect of regional autonomy."[99] Only Outer Mongolia was accorded the status of existing even in the truncated Soviet sense of being a republic.

In Vietnam and Laos, leaving aside the lowland ethnic Nungs (Chinese), the only peoples holding the requisites of national identity apart from the Vietnamese and Lao themselves are the tribal cultures of the Anamese Cordillera—often referred to as "Montagnards"—such as the Rhadé, Krak, Sedand, Hré, Bru, Bahnar, Je, Ma, and Hmong.[100] Insofar as they are neither populous nor "advanced" enough to comprise promising marxian-style economic units, they were never offered so much as the "courtesy" of being lied to before the revolution; national self-determination for the mountain people was never mentioned in Ho Chi Minh's agenda.[101] Consequently, the "Yards"—as they were dubbed by U.S. military personnel—formed their own political independence organization called the Front Unifé pour la Liberation des Races Opprimées (Unified Front for the Liberation of Oppressed Peoples) or, acronymically, FULRO during the early 1960s.[102]

The purpose of FULRO was/is to resist Vietnamese encroachments upon Montagnard national rights. Consequently, U.S. Special Forces troopers were able to utilize the FULRO consortium to good advantage as a highland mobile force interdicting the supply routes and attacking the staging areas of both the National Liberation Front's main force guerrilla units and units of the regular People's Army of Vietnam (North Vietnamese Army or "NVA," in American parlance), both of which were viewed by the Montagnards as threats to their sovereign way of life.[103] Much to the surprise of U.S. military advisers, however, beginning in 1964 FULRO also began to use its military training and equipment to fight the troops of the American-backed Saigon régime, whenever *they* entered the mountains.[104]

The message was plain enough: The mountain people rejected incorporation into *any* Vietnamese state, whether "capitalist" or "communist." In postrevolutionary Vietnam, FULRO continued to exist until at least the late 1980s, and to conduct armed resistance against the imposition of Vietnamese suzerainty within the Montagnards' traditional homelands. For its part, the Hanoi government has refused to acknowledge either the fact of such resistance or its basis.[105] The rather better known example of the Hmong in Laos follows very much the same contours as the struggles of their cousins to the southeast, albeit on a larger scale.[106]

One would of course like to report that there is at least one exception to the rule, if for no better reason than to establish a model for potential emulation. Right through the 1990s, however, an undeviating consistency has been exhibited by marxist-leninist régimes in every locale where they've taken root. Nowhere was this more apparent than in Nicaragua during the 1980s. There, three native peoples—the Miskitos, Sumus, and Ramas—were forced into a protracted armed resistance to being forcibly incorporated into a revolutionary state proclaimed in 1979 after the victory of the country's Sandinista insurgents over a right-wing dictatorship headed by Anastasio Somoza.[107]

It is important to note that the indigenous nations in question had each and mutually maintained a high degree of insularity and autonomy vis-à-vis Nicaragua's dominant Latino society, and that they had remained economically self-sufficient within their own territories on the Atlantic Coast. Their sole requirement of the Sandinista revolution was that it allow them to continue to do so within their traditional territory, known as Yapti Tasba, which they wished to have declared an "autonomous zone."[108] The response of the régime in Managua was that this would be impossible because allowing the Indians to retain such self-determining prerogatives would create a veritable "state within a state" (i.e., precisely the sort of situation supposedly guaranteed by leninist doctrine). As interior minister Tomas Borgé Martinez put it in 1985, the Sandinistas were "unswervingly dedicated" to the principle that, "There [can be] no whites, blacks, Miskitos, or Creoles. Here there are only revolutionary and counterrevolutionary Nicaraguans, regardless of the color of their skin. The only thing that differentiates us is the attitude we assume" towards the state.[109]

In substance, it was thereby demanded that the Miskitos, Sumus, and Ramas *as such* simply cease to exist. To punctuate his point, Borgé sent substantial numbers of troops into Indian territory, ordered the relocation of much of the native population into what in a comparable maneuver in Vietnam the United States had called "strategic hamlets," imposed blatantly assimilative "education" upon indigenous children, and set about integrating the resources of the Atlantic Coast region into the overall Nicaraguan economy.[110] Ironically, it was their own eurosupremacist arrogance in this regard that led to the Sandinistas' eventual demise. So committed were they to exercising their presumed "right" to usurp and expunge indigenous peoples that even when it became obvious that the resulting conflict was undermining their ability to defend themselves against U.S. aggression, they persisted in trying to enforce their anti-Indian policies.[111]

The bottom line is that in *no* marxist-leninist setting have the national rights of *any* small nations been respected, most especially those of landbased, indigenous ("tribal") peoples.[112] Our very right to exist in a national sense, and usually as distinct cultures as well, has instead been denied *as such*. Always and everywhere, marxism-leninism has assigned itself a practical priority leading directly to the incorporation, subordination, and dissolution of native societies *as such*. This is quite revealing, considering that the term "genocide" was coined to describe not only policies leading to the outright physical liquidation of "ethnical, racial, religious or national" aggregates, but also policies designed to bring about the dissolution, destruction, and disappearance of these "identified human groups, *as such*," by other means.[113] Viewed in this way, it is impossible to avoid the conclusion that marxism-leninism is and has always been a genocidal doctrine, wherever indigenous nationalities/cultures are concerned.[114]

CONCLUSION

None of what has been said herein should be taken as an apology or defense, direct or implied, of U.S. (or other capitalist) state policies. American Indians, first and foremost, know what the U.S. has done and what it's about. We experienced the meaning of the United States since long before there were marxists around to "explain" it to us. And we've continued to experience it in ways which leave little room for confusion on the matter. That's why we seek change. That's why we demand sovereignty and self-determination. That's why we cast about for allies and alternatives of the sort marxists have often claimed to be.

In considering any alliance, however, it is necessary—indeed, essential—that we first interrogate it in terms of our own best interests. This is no less true of marxism than of anything else. Thus, we *must* ask—only fools would not—whether marxism offers the vision of a bona fide alternative to that which capitalism has already imposed upon us. From the answer(s) to this query we can discern whether marxists can really be the sort of allies who would, or even *could*, actually guarantee us a positive change "come the revolution." Here, we need to *know* exactly what is meant when marxist "friends" like Bob Avakian and David Muga assures us, as they have, that the solutions to our present problems lie in the models offered by the USSR, China, Vietnam, and revolutionary Nicaragua.[115] And this, it seems to me, is rather painfully evident in what has been discussed above. Marxism, in its present form at least, offers us far worse than nothing. With friends such as these, we will be truly doomed.

So it is. But must it be? I think not. An increasing number of thoughtful marxists have broken with at least the worst of marxian economism, determinism, and human chauvinism. Salient examples such as Albert, Hahnel, and the early Baudrillard have been mentioned or quoted herein. The German Green Movement, involving a number of marxists or former marxists like Rudi Dutschke and Rudolph Bahro, has been in some ways a hopeful phenomenon (albeit, less so in North America).[116] All in all, there is sufficient basis to suggest that at least some elements of the marxian tradition are capable of transcending dogma to the extent that they may possess the potential to forge mutually fruitful alliances with American Indians and other indigenous peoples (although, at the point where this becomes true, one has reason to ask whether they may be rightly viewed as marxists any longer).[117]

The key for us, as Indians, is, I think, to remain both clear and firm in the values and insights of our own traditions. We must hold true to the dialectical understanding embodied in the word Metakuyeayasi and reject anything less as an unbalanced and imperfect view, even a mutilation of reality. We must continue to pursue our traditional vision of a humanity *within* rather than apart from and above the natural order. We must continue to insist, as a fundamental principle, upon the right of *all* peoples—each and every one, no matter how small and "primitive"—to freely select the fact and form of their ongoing national existence. Concomitantly, we must reject *all* contentions by *any* state that it holds license—for *any* reason—to dissolve the inherent rights of *any* other nation.[118] Perhaps most important of all, we must choose our friends and allies accordingly. I submit that there's nothing in this game-plan which contradicts any aspect of what we've come to describe as "the Indian way."[119]

In conclusion, I must say that I believe such an agenda, which I call "indigenist," can and will attract real friends, real allies, and offer real alternatives to *both* marxism and capitalism. What will result, in my view, is the emergence of a movement predicated on the principles of what are termed "deep ecology,"[120] "soft-path technology,"[121] "green anarchism,"[122] and global "balkanization."[123] But we are now entering into the topic of a whole different discussion. So, with that, allow me to close.

12

THE NEW FACE OF LIBERATION

Indigenous Rebellion, State Repression,
and the Reality of the Fourth World

◆ ◆ ◆ ◆ ◆ ◆ ◆ ◆ ◆ ◆ ◆ ◆ ◆ ◆

> The 4th World is the name given to indigenous peoples descended
> from a country's aboriginal population and who today are com-
> pletely or partly deprived of their own territory and its riches. . .
> The peoples to whom we refer are the Indians of North and South
> America, the Inuit (Eskimos), the Sami people [of northern Scan-
> dinavia], the Australian aborigines, as well as the various indige-
> nous populations of Africa, Asia and Oceania.
>
> —George Manuel, 1974

THERE HAS BEEN CONSIDERABLE DISCUSSION AT THIS CONFERENCE,* AND I THINK
appropriately so, of the modes of state repression which have been created within or
directed against the Third World. The latter term has been employed, appropriately
enough, in conformity with Mao Zedung's famous observation that the planet has
been divided essentially into three spheres: the industrialized, capitalist "First World";
the industrialized, socialist "Second World"; and a colonially underdeveloped "Third
World" which may be either socialist or capitalist in its orientation, but which is in either event industrializing.[1]

Afroamerica and other peoples or communities of color in this country have by-
and-large been classified by conference presenters as "Third Worlders," a matter I again
find to be generally accurate and therefore appropriate. The black population of the
United States to my mind constitutes an internal colony, as does the Latino population,
most especially its Chicano and Puertorriqueño segments. The Asian American population, or at least appreciable portions of it, also fall into this category and, I would argue,
so do certain sectors of the Euroamerican population itself, perhaps most notably the
Scotch-Irish transplants who are now referred to as "Appalachian Whites."[2]

I am here, however, as may have been gleaned from my opening quotation of
George Manuel, to discuss a reality left unmentioned not only by Mao, but by analysts

---

*An earlier version of this essay was presented at the Unfinished Liberation conference at the Univer-
sity of Colorado/Boulder, March 14, 1998.

of almost every ideological persuasion. This is the existence of yet another world, a world composed of a plethora of indigenous peoples, several thousand of us, each of whom constitutes a nation in our own right.³ Taken together, these nations comprise a nonindustrial "Fourth World," a "Host World" upon whose territories and with whose natural resources each of the other three, the worlds of modern statist sociopolitical and economic organization, have been constructed.⁴

In substance, the very existence of any state—and it doesn't matter a bit whether it is fascist, liberal democratic, or marxist in orientation—is absolutely contingent upon usurpation of the material and political rights of every indigenous nation within its boundaries. To put it another way, the denial of indigenous rights, both national and individual, is integral to the creation and functioning of the world order which has evolved over the past thousand years or so, and which is even now projecting itself in an ever more totalizing manner into our collective future.⁵

We say, and I believe this includes all of us here, that we oppose this prospect, that we oppose what was once pronounced by the papacy to be the "Divine Order" of things, what England's Queen Victoria asserted was the world's "Natural Order," what George Bush, following Adolf Hitler, described as a "New World Order," what Bill Clinton and Newt Gingrich have sought to consummate behind alphabet soup banalities like GATT and NAFTA and the MAI. In other words, we are opposed to the entire system presently "coordinated" by bodies like the World Bank and the International Monetary Fund and the Trilateral Commission.⁶

We say we oppose all of this, and, with at least equal vehemence, we announce our opposition to more particularized byproducts of the trajectory of increasingly consolidated corporate statism, or statist corporatism, or whatever else it might be more properly called, that we as a species are presently locked into. The litany is all too familiar: an increasingly rampant homogenization and commodification of our cultures and communities; the ever more wanton devastation and toxification of our environment; an already overburdening, highly militarized and steadily expanding police apparatus, both public and private, attended by an historically unparalleled degree of social regimentation and an astonishingly rapid growth in the prison-industrial complex; conversion of our academic institutions into veritable "votechs" churning out little more than military/corporate fodder; unprecedented concentration of wealth and power. . . .

We say we oppose it all, root and branch, and of course we are, each of us in our own way, entirely sincere in the statement of our opposition. But, with that said, and in many cases even acted upon, what do we *mean*? Most of us here identify ourselves as "progressives," so let's start with the term "progressivism" itself. We don't really have time available to go into this very deeply, but I'll just observe that it comes from the word "progress," and that the progression involved is basically to start with what's already here and carry it forward.

The underlying premise is that the social order we were born into results from the working of "iron laws" of evolution and, however unpalatable, is therefore both necessary and inevitable. By the same token, these same deterministic forces make it equally unavoidable that what we've inherited can and will be improved upon.⁷ The task of progressives, having apprehended the nature of the progression, is to use their insights to hurry things along.

This isn't a "liberal" articulation. It's what's been passing itself off as a *radical* left alternative to the status quo for well over a century. It forms the very core of Marx's notion of historical materialism, as when he observes that feudalism was the social precondition for the emergence of capitalism and that capitalism is itself the essential precondition for what he conceives as socialism. Each historical phase creates the conditions for the next; that's the crux of the progressive proposition.[8]

Now you tell me, how is that fundamentally different from what Bush and Clinton have been advocating? Oh, I see. *You* want to "move forward" in pursuance of another set of goals and objectives than those espoused by these self-styled "centrists." Alright. I'll accept that that's true. Let me also state that I tend to find the goals and objectives advanced by progressives *immensely* preferable to anything advocated by Bush or Clinton. Fair enough?

However, I must go on to observe that the differences at issue are *not* fundamental. They are not, as Marx would have put it, of "the base." Instead, they are superstructural. They represent remedies to symptoms rather than causes. In other words, they do not derive from a genuinely *radical* critique of our situation—remember, radical means to go to the *root* of any phenomenon in order to understand it[9]—and thus cannot offer a genuinely radical solution. This will remain true regardless of the fervor with which progressive goals and objectives are embraced, or the extremity with which they are pursued. Radicalism and extremism are, after all, not really synonyms.

Maybe I can explain what I'm getting at here by way of indulging in a sort of grand fantasy. Close your eyes for a moment and dream along with me that the current progressive agenda has been realized. Never mind how, let's just dream that it's been fulfilled. Things like racism, sexism, ageism, militarism, classism, and the sorts of corporatism with which we are now afflicted have been abolished. The police have been leashed and the prison-industrial complex dismantled. Income disparities have been eliminated across the board, decent housing and healthcare are available to all, an amply endowed educational system is actually devoted to teaching rather than indoctrinating our children. The whole nine yards.

Sound good? You bet. Nonetheless, there's still a very basic—and I daresay uncomfortable—question which must be posed: In this seemingly rosy scenario, what, exactly, happens to the rights of native peoples? Face it, to envision the progressive transformation of "American society" is to presuppose that "America"—that is, the United States—will continue to exist. And, self-evidently, the existence of the United States is, as it has always been and *must always be*, predicated first and foremost on denial of the right of self-determining existence to every indigenous nation within its purported borders.

Absent this denial, the very society progressives seek to transform would never have had a landbase upon which to constitute itself in any form at all. So, it would have had no resources with which to actualize a mode of production, and there would be no basis for arranging or rearranging the relations of production. All the dominoes fall from there, don't they? In effect, the progressive agenda is no less contingent upon the continuing internal colonial domination of indigenous nations than that advanced by Bill Clinton.[10]

Perhaps we can agree to a truism on this score: Insofar as progressivism shares with the status quo a need to maintain the structure of colonial dominance over native peoples, it is *at base* no more than a variation on a common theme, intrinsically a part of the very order it claims to oppose. As Vine Deloria once observed in a related connection, "these guys just keep right on circling the same old rock while calling it by different names."[11]

Since, for all its liberatory rhetoric and sentiment, even the self-sacrifice of its proponents, progressivism replicates the bedrock relations with indigenous nations marking the present status quo, its agenda can be seen as serving mainly to increase the degree of comfort experienced by those who benefit from such relations. Any such outcome represents a continuation and reinforcement of the existing order, *not* its repeal. Progressivism is thus one possible means of consummating that which is, *not* its negation.[12]

It's time to stop fantasizing and confront what this consummation might look like. To put it bluntly, colonialism is colonialism, no matter what its trappings. You can't end classism in a colonial system, since the colonized by definition comprise a class lower than that of their colonizers.[13] You can't end racism in a colonial system because the imposed "inferiority" of the colonized must inevitably be "explained" (justified) by their colonizers through contrived classifications of racial hierarchy.[14] You can't end sexism in a colonial system, since it functions—again by definition—on the basis of one party imposing itself upon the other in the most intimate of dimensions for purposes of obtaining gratification.[15]

If rape is violence, as feminists correctly insist,[16] then so too is the interculture analogue of rape: colonial domination. As a consequence, it is impossible to end social violence in a colonialist system. Read Fanon and Memmi. They long ago analyzed that fact rather thoroughly and exceedingly well.[17] Better yet, read Sartre, who flatly equated colonialism with genocide.[18] Then ask yourself how you maintain a system incorporating domination and genocidal violence as integral aspects of itself *without* military, police, and penal establishments? The answer is that you can't.

Go right down the list of progressive aspirations and what you'll discover, if you're honest with yourself, is that none of them can really be achieved outside the context of Fourth World liberation. So long as indigenous nations are subsumed against our will within "broader" statist entities—and this applies as much to Canada as to the United States, as much to China as to Canada, as much to Mexico and Brazil as to China, as much to Ghana as to any of the rest; the problem is truly global—colonialism will be alive and well.[19]

So long as this is the case, all efforts at positive social transformation, no matter how "revolutionary" the terms in which they are couched, will be self-nullifying, simply leading us right back into the groove we're in today. Actually, we'll probably be worse off after each iteration since such outcomes generate a steadily growing popular disenchantment with the idea that meaningful change can ever be possible. This isn't a zero-sum game we're involved in. As Gramsci pointed out, every failure of supposed alternatives to the status quo serves to significantly reinforce its hegemony.[20]

When a strategy or, more important, a way of looking at things, proves itself bankrupt or counterproductive, it must be replaced with something more viable. Such, is the situation with progressivism, both as a method and as an outlook. After a full century of failed revolutions and derailed social movements, it has long since reached the point where, as Sartre once commented, it "no longer knows anything."[21] The question, then, comes down to where to look for a replacement.

There are a lot of ways I could try and answer that one. Given the emphasis I've already placed on the Fourth World, I suppose I could take a "New Age" approach and say you should all go sit at the feet of the tribal elders and learn all about the native worldview. But, I'll tell you instead that the last thing the old people need is to be inundated beneath a wave of wannabe "tribalists" seeking "spiritual insights."[22] This is not to deny there's a lot in the indigenous way of seeing the world that could be usefully learned by others and put to work in the forging of new sets of relationships between humans both as individuals and as societies, as well as between humans and the rest of nature.

Such information is plainly essential. There are, however, serious considerations as to when and how it is to be shared. As things stand, we lack the intellectual context which, alone, might allow a constructive transfer of knowledge to take place. For the people here, or your counterparts throughout the progressive milieu, to run right out and try to pick up on what the Naropa Institute likes to market under the heading of "indigenous wisdom" would be an act of appropriation just as surely as if you were to go after Indian land. There *is* such a thing as intellectual property, and, therefore, intellectual imperialism.[23]

The point is that the right of the Fourth World to decolonize itself exists independently of any direct benefit this might impart to colonizing societies or any of their subparts, progressivism included. More strongly, the right of the Fourth World to decolonization exists *undiminished* even if it can be shown that this is tangibly *dis*advantageous to our colonizers. The principle is not especially mysterious, having been brought to bear in Third World liberation struggles for the past half-century and more.[24] Yet, where indigenous nations are concerned, nearly everyone—Third World liberationists, not least—professes confusion concerning its applicability.[25]

To connect this point to that on New Age dynamics I was making a few moments ago, it's as if Simone de Beauvoir had demanded she be made privy to the "folk wisdom" of the Berber elders as a quid pro quo for supporting the Algerian liberation struggle against France. But of course she didn't. De Beauvoir, her colleague Sartre, and a relative handful of others broke ranks with the mainstream of French progressivism—it's worth noting that the French communist party actually *opposed* the decolonization of Algeria—by embracing Algerian independence unequivocally, unconditionally, and in its own right.[26]

Let's be clear on this. De Beauvoir and Sartre did not take the position they did on the basis of altruism. Although they gained no direct personal benefit from their stance, they *did* perceive an *indirect* advantage accruing from any success attained by the Algerian liberationists. This came in the form of a material weakening of the French state to which they, apparently unlike French progressivism more generally, were genuinely and seriously opposed. Converting such an externally generated weakness into something more directly beneficial to the liberation of French domestic polity was seen as being their own task.[27]

De Beauvoir and Sartre displayed an exemplary posture, one worthy of emulation by those members of colonizing societies who reject not just colonialism but the statist forms of sociopolitical and economic organization that beget colonialism. The transition from taking this position vis-à-vis the Third World to taking it with respect to the Fourth seems straightforward enough.

The trick is for members of colonizing societies who wish to support Fourth World liberation struggles to figure out how to convert the indirect advantages gained thereby into something more direct and concrete. This, they must obviously draw from their own tradition; it cannot simply be lifted from another culture. And here is precisely where progressivism, most especially historical materialism, which by its very nature consigns all things "primitive" to Trotsky's "dustbin of history," proves itself worse than useless.[28]

Fortunately, an alternative is conveniently at hand. It will be found in what is usually referred to as the "Foucauldian method," actually an approach to historical interpretation and resulting praxis developed by Nietzsche during the 1870s and adapted by Michel Foucault a century later.[29] Without getting bogged down in a lot of theory, let's just say the method stands historical materialism squarely on its head. Rather than interrogating institutions and other phenomena in such a way as to explain how they can/must "carry us forward into the future," the Nietzschean *cum* Foucauldian approach is to define what is objectionable in a given institution and then trace is "lineage" backwards in time to discover how it went wrong and, thus, how it can be "fixed."[30]

In effect, where Lenin asked, "What is to be done?," Foucault asks, "What is to be *un*done?"[31]

I can hear mental gears grinding out there: "This guy can't possibly mean we should all 'go back to the past!'" Well, yes and no. The method I've suggested is not to try and effect a kind of across the board rollback. It's to determine with some exactitude *which* historical factors have led to objectionable contemporary outcomes and undo *them.* You might say that Foucault provided a kind of analytical filter which allows you to pick, choose, and prioritize what needs working on. What I've called for are lines of action that materially erode the power concentrated in centralized entities like the state, major corporations, and financial institutions, things like that.

The ways of going at this, at least initially, really aren't so alien. Consumer boycotts are a useful tool, especially when combined with the creation of co-ops and collectives producing wares to offset reliance upon corporate manufacturers in the future. Barter systems, labor exchanges, a whole infrastructure allowing people to opt out of the existing system in varying degrees can be created. Something of the sort was beginning to emerge in the U.S. during the late 1960s, as it had in the '30s.[32]

Most of all, it's imperative to remember that the first element of oppositional power projection lies in refusal. That means, in the context at hand, that we must rid ourselves of the progressive notion that we can "get laws passed" to fix things. You can hardly set out to undermine the authority of the state while endeavoring to put still more legislation, *any* kind of legislation, on the books. The only legitimate form of activity in the legislative arena is to pursue repeal of the tremendous weight of laws, ordinances, rules, and regulations that already exist. Meanwhile, at least some of them can be nullified by our conscious and deliberate refusal to comply with them.

You've got to break "The Law"—*whose* law?—to get anywhere at all. To cop a line from Bob Dylan back in the days when he still had something to say, "To live outside the law, you must be honest." The flip side of the coin is that if you choose to "live *inside* the law you must be *dis*honest." Worse, you end up being the moral equivalent of a "Good German." Not a very lofty stature, that.

Let me put it to you this way. If I were to say that our mutual goal is ultimately to achieve "freedom," everyone here would immediately agree. But then we'd become mired in some long philosophical debate about what we mean by that, because freedom is typically presented as a sort of abstract concept. Well, it's not really so abstract, and most assuredly not "intangible." In fact, I think it can be quantified and measured. Try this: Freedom may be defined as absence of regulation. The more regulated you are, the less free, and vice versa.

I'm not sure at this point that it matters much which laws you defy, there's such a vast proliferation to choose from, and in some ways *any* of them will do for purposes of initiating a process of transforming the prevailing individual and mass psychologies from that of "going along" to that of refusal. Use your imagination, pick a point of departure, it doesn't matter how small or in what connection, and get on with it. Once a particular bit of "unruliness" takes hold, it can be used as the fulcrum for prying open the next level, and so on. This is what Marcuse meant when he said that false consciousness is always breached at some "infinitesimally small spot," but that any such breach might serve as an "Archimedean point for a broader emancipation."[33]

Can application of this principle actually produce results at higher levels? You bet. Look at Prohibition, the Eighteenth Amendment to the U.S. Constitution, to find an example. It was rescinded for one reason and one reason only: People refused to obey. It didn't matter what penalties the state assigned to violating it, or what quantity of resources were pumped into the apparatus of enforcement, Prohibition was met with a curiously ubiquitous "culture of resistance" in all quarters of American society. Eventually, it was determined by those who make such decisions that attempts to enforce it were becoming so socially disruptive as to destabilize the state itself, and so the law was withdrawn.[34]

The so-called "War on Drugs" currently being waged by the state offers the prospect of a similar outcome over the long run, albeit at a statutory rather than constitutional level, particularly if we were astute enough to try and translate the rather substantial resistance to it into a coherent opposition politics.[35] The Black Panther Party's strategy of focusing its recruitment on "lumpen proletarians"—street gang members, in plain English—made a lot of sense and is another idea that might be usefully resuscitated.[36]

The primary purpose of everything we do must be to make this society increasingly unmanageable. That's key. The more unmanageable the society becomes, the more of its resources the state must expend in efforts to maintain order "at home." The more this is true, the less the state's capacity to project itself outwardly, both geographically and temporally. Eventually, a point of stasis will be reached, and, in a system such as this one, anchored as it is in the notion of perpetual growth, this amounts to a sort of "Doomsday Scenario" because, from there, things start moving in the other direction—"falling apart," as it were—and *that* creates the conditions of flux in which alternative social forms can really begin to take root and flourish.

This is kind of a crude sketch, but its easy enough to follow. And, you know what? The rewards of following it don't have to be deferred until the aftermath of a cataclysmic "revolutionary moment" or, worse, the progressive actualization of some far-distant Bernsteinian utopia (which would only turn out to be dystopic, anyway).[37] No, in the sense that every rule and regulation rejected represents a tangibly liberating experience, the rewards begin immediately and just keep on getting better. You will in effect feel freer right from the get-go.

Alright, let's follow things out a bit further. The more disrupted, disorganized, and destabilized the system becomes, the less its ability to expand, extend, or even maintain itself. The greater the degree to which this is so, the greater the likelihood that Fourth World nations struggling to free ourselves from systemic domination will succeed. And the more frequently we of the Fourth World succeed, the less the ability of the system to utilize our resources in the process of dominating *you*.

At this point, we've arrived at an understanding of a confluence of interest that utterly transcends the old "three worlds" paradigm, harkening an entirely different praxical symbiosis, one which is not so much revolutionary as it is *de*volutionary. We don't want China out of Tibet so much as we want China out of China. We don't just want the U.S. out of Southeast Asia or Southern Africa or Central America, we want it out of North America, off the planet, out of existence altogether. This is to say that we want the U.S. out of our own lives and *thereby* everyone else's. The pieces dovetail rather well, don't they? Indeed, they can't really be separated and only a false analysis might ever have concluded that they could.

Hence, we must seek nothing less than the dismemberment and dissolution of every statist/corporate entity in the world. All of them. No exceptions. In their stead, we seek reconstitution of that entire galaxy of *nations* upon which the states have imposed themselves. All of *them*, and, again, no exceptions. We are in effect the staunchest and most prideful of all "irridentists."

Here, a certain structure of priorities presents itself, and it does so in two ways. First, methodologically, any process of "undoing" such as I've recommended must commence with the "fixing" of that which is most proximate or recent. Unquestionably, the colonization of those peoples who are still indigenous is the most recent aspect or dimension of the phenomenon we've been considering. It follows that decolonization of what I've been calling the Fourth World must assume a clear primacy of importance within *everybody's* liberatory agenda.

This is not to say that it is of exclusive importance—I've been trying to show how a very wide range of struggles can be made to interact constructively when properly framed—but that, to reiterate, no other liberatory objective can ever be truly fulfilled until this one is.

The second aspect of prioritization is closely related to the first and concerns the fact that Fourth Worlders still retain the codes of knowledge which allow us to practice our traditional forms of ecologically balanced socioeconomic and political organization. Our expedient decolonization therefore serves to establish working models for adaptation by others.

Doubling back for a moment to what I said earlier about New Agers and cultural imperialism, it seems important to observe that what was just mentioned is precisely the sort of intercultural dialogue I was calling for instead. Note that it represents a sharing of information born in the crucible of mutual struggle and resultant political consciousness, *not* from the structure of domination prevailing today. Note also that it consists of an informational sharing dedicated to the furtherance of the struggle, *not* to the self-indulgent collector's desire to acquire the inside scoop on ritual forms and the like. Learning the size, number, and placement of rocks used in a sweat lodge is about as relevant to the process of liberation as finding out the particular type of wine used when the IRA takes communion.

If your preoccupation is with the "teachings" of hucksters like Carlos Castaneda, Ed McGaa, Brooke Medicine Ego, Sun Bear, Mary Summer Rain, Dhyani Ywahoo, or all of the above, you're engaged in something that is at best a form of dilettantism.[38] Unless your aspiration is to *be* a dilettante, to enjoy "quality time" masturbating in the woods along with the rest of Robert Bly's "men's movement," or making perpetual tithes to Lynne Andrews' women's equivalent, it would behoove you to hook into something else.[39]

That "something else" is of course what I've been advocating here tonight, and it's time we put a name to it. "Anarchism" might be a good one, since quite a lot of what I've had to say overlaps with anarchist thinking. I see a lot of commonality between anarchist ideas of social organization and political economy on the one hand, and indigenous ways of seeing and doing on the other, and so I push people to explore anarchism as their first and most immediate alternative to progressivism.

Check me out on this. Do your homework. Cruise through some classical anarchist material: Lassalle, Proudhon, Bakunin, Kropotkin, Rudolph Rocker. Take a gander at Goldman and Berkman and some of the newer stuff.[40] I recommend Kirkpatrick Sale's *Dwellers in the Land* and John Zerzan's *Future Primitive*, even though Zerzan eventually goes off the deep end and starts demanding the decolonization of carrots.[41]

What's left hanging in such readings, however, is both the emphasis I've placed on

Fourth World liberation and the exemplary value I've claimed in behalf of self-determining indigenous societies. Anarchism as it is presently configured does not encompass, nor necessarily even accommodate, such a stance. The position I've been outlining is thus readily distinguishable from anarchism, per se, and, to that extent at least, requires another descriptor. The term I use is "indigenism."[42]

You'll recall that I opened with a quote from George Manuel. His book, *The Fourth World*, would be worthwhile reading for anyone interested in pursuing the idea of indigenism in more depth.[43] Roxanne Dunbar Ortiz offers a pretty good survey of indigenist literature in her *Indians of the Americas*, although it's not been updated since 1984 and omitted a few things like John Mohawk's *A Basic Call to Consciousness* even then.[44] Other titles you may find useful are Haunani-Kay Trask's *From a Native Daughter* and Jimmie Durham's *A Certain Lack of Coherence*.[45] Oh yeah, and my own *Struggle for the Land*.[46]

Now, by way of closing, I'd like to take up the question of whether the indigenist vision is "unrealistic." All I have to say on the matter is that if you are colonized or otherwise oppressed, you must *never* allow your oppressor to define what's "realistic" for you. If you do, you'll just end up reinforcing the terms of your own colonization. That's because your oppression *is* reality to your colonizer. Anything else will always and inevitably be dismissed as "unrealistic"—or "impossible," to put it less politely—by those who benefit from the oppressive relationship.

The best reply to this I've ever heard came from the 1968 student/worker revolt in France. To "be realistic," the insurgents announced, it was essential that they "demand the impossible."[47]

One thing that confirms my conviction that indigenism is the correct recipe for the contemporary setting will be found in the sheer virulence of state efforts to repress it. A decade ago, Bernard Neitschmann did a global survey of armed conflicts then occurring. The results were remarkable. Of the more than 100 wars he catalogued, fully 85 percent were between indigenous nations and one or more states presuming an authority to subordinate them.[48] The situation has not abated in the 1990s. If anything, it's intensified. Chiapas is sufficient evidence of that.[49]

Right here in the U.S. a "low intensity" war was waged during the mid-1970s against the American Indian Movement, an unabashedly indigenist organization. Put simply, a counterinsurgency campaign was conducted to quell AIM's efforts to decolonize the Pine Ridge Reservation in South Dakota. At least 69 AIM members and supporters were killed on Pine Ridge between March 1973 and March 1976, while another 350-odd people suffered severe physical assaults during the same period. Another casualty was Leonard Peltier, the details and implications of whose case have been dealt with elsewhere in this conference.[50]

Let's pause for a moment to consider the number of dead I just mentioned. It may not seem great when compared to the body counts racked up elsewhere. But you have to realize that there were never more than a few hundred AIM members and that the population of Pine Ridge was only about 10,000 in 1975. Proportionately, the rate of AIM fatalities was identical to that incurred by the Chilean left during the three years following Pinochet's overthrow of the Allende government.[51] *Nobody* questions the severity of what happened in Chile.

I can't say for sure what happened to the Chilean left as a result of its repression—I suspect it dissipated, because I've not heard much of it for a long time now—but I *do* know what's happened with AIM. We've absorbed the body blows, evolved, decentralized and reappeared all over the continent in different guises. During the armed confrontation at Oka, near Montréal, in 1990, AIM was called the Mohawk Warrior Society.[52] At the armed confrontation at Gustafsen Lake, British Columbia, a couple of years later, AIM was called something else.[53] Whatever the name, whatever the location—James Bay, Big Mountain, Lubicon Lake, Western Shoshone, it doesn't matter—it's all the same thing and it's all indigenist to the core.[54]

The same can be said of the native sovereignty movements in Hawai'i and elsewhere across the Pacific, of the struggles for a "Karin free state" in Burma and for the independence of Nagaland in India, of the Kurdish secessionist movement in the Middle East, the Polisario in the Western Sahara, the Basques and Catalans in Spain, the Irish in Ulster, even the Scots and Welsh on the main British isle.[55] Anywhere you look, on every continent save Antarctica, you'll find Fourth World liberation struggles. Indigenism, not communism, is the "specter haunting Europe" and the rest of the world these days.[56]

It seems obvious than anything considered threatening enough by the world's ruling élites that they'd wage ninety simultaneous wars to suppress it is something to be taken seriously. Assessing what he'd discovered, Neitschmann described it as amounting to a "Third World War," and in many ways he was right.[57] World War III, the war for the most fundamental forms of human liberation and against what Noam Chomsky has called "world orders, old and new," is going on right now, as I speak.[58]

Because of it, the world as we all know it is changing rapidly and irrevocably for the better. The only choice to be made in seeking to come to grips with this new face of liberation is whether, like Sartre and Simone, you wish to stand on the "right side of history." If so, the possibilities which present themselves are limitless.

13

I AM INDIGENIST

Notes on the Ideology of the Fourth World

◆◆◆◆◆◆◆◆◆◆◆◆◆

The growth of ethnic consciousness and the consequent mobilization of Indian communities in the Western hemisphere since the
early 1960s have been welcomed neither by government forces nor
by opposition parties and revolutionary movements. The "Indian
Question" has been an almost forbidden subject of debate throughout the entire political spectrum, although racism, discrimination
and exploitation are roundly denounced on all sides.

—Roxanne Dunbar Ortiz
Indians of the Americas

VERY OFTEN IN MY WRITINGS AND LECTURES, I HAVE IDENTIFIED MYSELF AS BEING
"indigenist" in outlook. By this, I mean that I am one who not only takes the rights of
indigenous peoples as the highest priority of my political life, but who draws upon the
traditions—the bodies of knowledge and corresponding codes of value—evolved over
many thousands of years by native peoples the world over. This is the basis upon
which I not only advance critiques of, but conceptualize alternatives to the present social, political, economic, and philosophical status quo. In turn, this gives shape not
only to the sorts of goals and objectives I pursue, but the kinds of strategy and tactics I
advocate, the variety of struggles I tend to support, the nature of the alliances I'm inclined to enter into, and so on.

Let me say, before I go any further, that I am hardly unique or alone in adopting this
perspective. It is a complex of ideas, sentiments, and understandings which motivate the
whole of the American Indian Movement, broadly defined, here in North America. This
is true whether you call it AIM, or Indians of All Tribes (as was done during the 1969
occupation of Alcatraz), the Warriors Society (as was the case with the Mohawk rebellion at Oka in 1990), Women of All Red Nations, or whatever.[1] It is the spirit of resistance which shapes the struggles of traditional Indian people on the land, whether the
struggle is down at Big Mountain, in the Black Hills, or up at James Bay, in the Nevada
desert or out along the Columbia River in what is now called Washington State.[2] In the

---

This essay is based on the transcripts of talks delivered at Alfred University, the University of Vermont
and Cal Poly State University at San Luis Obispo during the early 1990s.

sense that I use the term, indigenism is also, I think, the outlook which guided our great leaders of the past: King Philip and Pontiac, Tecumseh and Creek Mary and Osceola, Black Hawk and Big Bear, Nancy Ward, and Satanta, Little Wolf and Red Cloud, Satank and Quannah Parker, Left Hand and Crazy Horse, Dull Knife and Chief Joseph, Sitting Bull, Roman Nose, and Captain Jack, Louis Ríel and Poundmaker and Geronimo, Cochise and Mangus, Victorio, Chief Seattle, and on and on.[3]

In my view, those—Indian and nonindian alike—who do not recognize these names and what they represent have no sense of the true history, the reality, of North America. They have no sense of where they've come from or where they are, and thus can have no genuine sense of who or what they they are. By not looking at where they've come from, they cannot know where they're going, or where it is they should go. It follows that they cannot understand what it is they are to do, how to do it, or why.[4] In their confusion, they identify with the wrong people, the wrong things, the wrong traditions. They therefore inevitably pursue the wrong goals and objectives, putting last things first and often forgetting the first things altogether, perpetuating the very structures of oppression and degradation they think they oppose.[5] Obviously, if things are to be changed for the better in this world, then this particular problem must itself be changed as a matter of first priority.

In any event, all this is not to say that I think I'm one of the people I have named, or the host of others, equally worthy, who've gone unnamed. I have no "New Age" conception of myself as the reincarnation of someone who has come before. But it *is* to say that I take these ancestors as my inspiration, as the only historical examples of proper attitude and comportment on this continent, this place, this land on which I live and of which I am a part. I embrace them as my heritage, my role models, the standard by which I must measure myself. I try always to be worthy of the battles they fought, the sacrifices they made. For the record, I've always found myself wanting in this regard, but I subscribe to the notion that one is obligated to speak the truth, even if one cannot live up to or fully practice it. As Chief Dan George once put it, I "endeavor to persevere,"[6] and I suppose this is a circumstance which is shared more or less equally by everyone presently involved in what I refer to as "indigenism."

Others whose writings and speeches and actions may be familiar, and who fit the definition of indigenist—or "Fourth Worlder," as we are sometimes called[7]—include Winona LaDuke and John Trudell, Simon Ortiz, Russell Means and Dennis Banks and Leonard Peltier, and Glenn Morris and Leslie Silko, Jimmie Durham, John Mohawk and Oren Lyons, Bob Robideau and Dino Butler, Vine Deloria, Ingrid Washinawatok and Dagmar Thorpe. There are scholars and attorneys like Don Grinde, Pam Colorado, Sharon Venne, George Tinker, Bob Thomas, Jack Forbes, Rob Williams, and Hank Adams. There are poets like Wendy Rose, Adrian Louis, Dian Million, Chrystos, Elizabeth Woody, and Barnie Bush. There are grassroots contemporary warriors, people like Bobby Castillo, Rob Chanate and Regina Brave, Chief Bernard Ominayak, Art Montour and Buddy Lamont, Madonna Thunderhawk, Anna Mae Aquash, Kenny Kane and Joe Stuntz, Minnie Garrow and Bobby Garcia, Dallas Thundershield, Phyllis Young, Andrea Smith and Richard Oaks, Margo Thunderbird, Tina Trudell, and

Roque Duenas. And, of course, there are the elders, those who have given, and continue to give, continuity and direction to indigenist expression; I'm referring to people like Chief Fools Crow and Matthew King, Henry Crow Dog and Grampa David Sohappy, David Monongye and Janet McCloud and Thomas Banyacya, Roberta Blackgoat and Katherine Smith and Pauline Whitesinger, Marie Leggo and Philip Deer and Ellen Moves Camp, Raymond Yowell, and Nellie Red Owl.[8]

Like the historical figures I mentioned earlier, these are names representing positions, struggles and aspirations which should be well known to every socially conscious person in North America. They embody the absolute antithesis of the order represented by the "Four Georges"—George Washington, George Custer, George Patton, and George Bush—emblemizing the sweep of "American" history as it is conventionally taught in that system of indoctrination the United States passes off as "education." They also stand as the negation of a long stream of "Vichy Indians" spawned and deemed "respectable" by the process of predation, colonialism, and genocide the Four Georges signify.[9]

The names I've named cannot be associated with the legacy of the "Hang Around the Forts," Indians broken, disempowered, and intimidated by their conquerors, the sellouts who undermined the integrity of their own cultures, appointed by the United States to sign away their peoples' homelands in exchange for trinkets, sugar, and alcohol.[10] They are not the figurative descendants of those who participated in the assassination of men like Crazy Horse and Sitting Bull, and who filled the ranks of the colonial police to enforce an illegitimate and alien order against their own.[11] They are not among those who have queued up to roster the régimes installed by the U.S. to administer Indian Country from the 1930s onward, the craven puppets who to this day cling to and promote the "lawful authority" of federal force as a means of protecting their positions of petty privilege, imagined prestige, and often their very identities as native people.[12] No, indigenists and indigenism have nothing to do with the sorts of quisling impulses driving the Ross Swimmers, Dickie Wilsons, Webster Two Hawks, Peter McDonalds, and David Bradleys of this world.[13]

Instead, indigenism offers an antidote to all that, a vision of how things might be which is based in how things have been since time immemorial, and how things must be once again if the human species, and perhaps the planet itself, is to survive much longer. Predicated in a synthesis of the wisdom attained over thousands of years by indigenous, landbased peoples around the globe—the Fourth World or, as Winona LaDuke puts it, "The Host World upon which the first, second and third worlds all sit at the present time"—indigenism stands in diametrical opposition to the totality of what might be termed "Eurocentric business as usual."[14]

INDIGENISM

The manifestation of indigenism in North America has much in common with the articulation of what in Latin America is called *indigenismo*. One of the major proponents of this, the Mexican anthropologist/activist Guillermo Bonfil Batalla, has framed its precepts this way: "[I]n America there exists only one unitary Indian civilization. All the Indian peoples participate in this civilization. The diversity of cultures and languages is not an obstacle to affirmation of the unity of this civilization. It is a fact that all civilizations, including Western civilization, have these sorts of internal differences. But the level of unity—the civilization—is more profound than the level of of specificity (the cultures, the languages, the communities). The civilizing dimension transcends the concrete diversity."[15]

> The differences between the diverse peoples (or ethnic groups) have been accentuated by the colonizers as part of the strategy of domination. There have been attempts by some to fragment the Indian peoples . . . by establishing frontiers, deepening differences and provoking rivalries. This strategy follows a principal objective: domination, to which end it is attempted ideologically to demonstrate that in America, Western civilization is confronted by a magnitude of atomized peoples, differing from one another (every day more and more languages are "discovered"). Thus, in consequence, such peoples are believed incapable of forging a future of their own. In contrast to this, the Indian thinking affirms the existence of one—a unique and different—Indian civilization, from which extend as particular expressions the cultures of diverse peoples. Thus, the identification and solidarity among Indians. Their "Indianness" is not a simple tactic postulated, but rather the necessary expression of an historical unity, based in common civilization, which the colonizer has wanted to hide. Their Indianness, furthermore, is reinforced by the common experience of almost five centuries of [Eurocentric] domination.[16]

"The past is also unifying," Bonfil Batalla continues. "The achievements of the classic Mayas, for instance, can be reclaimed as part of the Quechua foundation [in present-day Guatemala], much the same as the French affirm their Greek past. And even beyond the remote past which is shared, and beyond the colonial experience that makes all Indians similar, Indian peoples also have a common historic project for the future. The legitimacy of that project rests precisely in the existence of an Indian civilization, within which framework it could be realized, once the 'chapter of colonialism ends.' One's own civilization signifies the right and the possibility to create one's own future, a different future, not Western."[17]

As has been noted elsewhere, the "new" indigenous movement Bonfil describes equates "colonialism/imperialism with the West; in opposing the West, [adherents] view themselves as anti-imperialist. Socialism, or Marxism, is viewed as just another Western manifestation."[18] A query is thus posed:

> What, then, distinguishes Indian from Western civilization? Fundamentally, the difference can be summed up in terms of [humanity's] relationship with the natural world. For the West . . . the concept of nature is that of an enemy to be overcome, with man as boss on a cosmic scale. Man in the West believes he

must dominate everything, including other [people around him] and other peoples. The converse is true in Indian civilization, where [humans are] part of an indivisible cosmos and fully aware of [their] harmonious relationship with the universal order of nature. [S]he neither dominates nor tries to dominate. On the contrary, she exists within nature as a moment of it . . . Traditionalism thus constitutes a potent weapon in the [indigenous] civilization's struggle for survival against colonial domination.[19]

Bonfil contends that the nature of the indigenist impulse is essentially socialist, insofar as socialism—or what Karl Marx described as "primitive communism"—was and remains the primary mode of indigenous social organization in the Americas.[20] Within this framework, he remarks that there are "six fundamental demands identified with the Indian movement," all of them associated with sociopolitical, cultural, and economic autonomy (or sovereignty) and self-determination:

First there is land. There are demands for occupied ancestral territories . . . demands for control of the use of the land and subsoil; and struggles against the invasion of . . . commercial interests. Defense of land held and recuperation of land lost are the central demands. Second, the demand for recognition of the ethnic and cultural specificity of the Indian is identified. All [indigenist] organizations reaffirm the right to be distinct in culture, language and institutions, and to increase the value of their own technological, social and ideological practices. Third is the demand for [parity] of political rights in relation to the state . . . Fourth, there is a call for the end of repression and violence, particularly that against the leaders, activists and followers of the Indians' new political organizations. Fifth, Indians demand the end of family planning programmes which have brought widespread sterilization of Indian women and men. Finally, tourism and folklore are rejected, and there is a demand for true Indian cultural expression to be respected. The commercialization of Indian music and dance are often mentioned . . . and there is a particular dislike for the exploitation of those that have sacred content and purpose for Indians. An end to the exploitation of Indian culture in general is [demanded].[21]

In North America, these indigenista demands have been adopted virtually intact, and have been conceived as encompassing basic needs of native peoples wherever they have been subsumed by the sweep of Western expansionism. This is the idea of the Fourth World, explained by Cree author George Manuel, founding president of the World Council of Indigenous Peoples:

The 4th World is the name given to indigenous peoples descended from a country's aboriginal population and who today are completely or partly deprived of their own territory and its riches. The peoples of the 4th World have only limited influence or none at all in the nation state [in which they are now encapsulated]. The peoples to whom we refer are the Indians of North and South America, the Inuit (Eskimos), the Sami people [of northern Scandinavia], the Australian aborigines, as well as the various indigenous populations of Africa, Asia and Oceana.[22]

Manuel might well have included segments of the European population itself, as is evidenced by the ongoing struggles of the Irish, Welsh, Basques, and others to free themselves from the yoke of settler state oppression imposed upon them as long as 800 years ago.[23] In such areas of Europe, as well as in "the Americas and [large portions of] Africa, the goal is not the creation of a state, but the expulsion of alien rule and the reconstruction of societies."[24]

That such efforts are entirely serious is readily evidenced in the fact that, in a global survey conducted by University of California cultural geographer Bernard Neitschmann, it was discovered that of the more than one hundred armed conflicts then underway, some eighty-five percent were being waged by indigenous peoples against the state or states which had laid claim to and occupied their territories.[25] As Theo van Boven, former director of the United Nations Division (now Center) for Human Rights, put it in 1981: the circumstances precipitating armed struggle "may be seen with particular poignancy in relation to the indigenous peoples of the world, who have been described somewhat imaginatively—and perhaps not without justification—as representing the fourth world: the world on the margin, on the periphery."[26]

THE ISSUE OF LAND IN NORTH AMERICA

What must be understood about the context of the Americas north of the Río Grande is that neither of the states, the U.S. and Canada, which claim sovereignty over the territoriality involved has any legitimate basis at all in which to anchor its absorption of huge portions of that territory. I'm going to restrict my remarks in this connection mostly to the U.S., mainly because that's what I know best, but also because both the U.S. and Canada have evolved on the basis of the Anglo-Saxon common law tradition.[27] So, I think much of what can be said about the U.S. bears utility in terms of understanding the situation in Canada. Certain of the principles, of course, also extend to the situation in Latin America, but there you have an evolution of states based in the Spanish legal tradition, so a greater transposition in terms is required.[28] Let's just say that the shape of things down south was summarized eloquently enough by the Qechuan freedom fighter Hugo Blanco with his slogan, "Land or Death!"[29]

Anyway, during the first ninety-odd years of its existence, the United States entered into and ratified some 400 separate treaties with the peoples indigenous to the area now known as the 48 contiguous states.[30] There are a number of important dimensions to this, but two aspects will do for our purposes here. First, by customary international law and provision of the U.S. Constitution itself, each treaty ratification represented a formal recognition by the federal government that the other parties to the treaties—the native people(s) involved—were fully sovereign nations in our own right.[31] Second, the purpose of the treaties, from the U.S. point of view, was to serve as real estate documents through which it acquired legal title to specified portions of North American geography from the indigenous nations it was thereby acknowledging already owned it. From the viewpoint of the indigenous nations, of course, the treaties served other purposes: the securing of permanently guaranteed borders to what remained of our national territories, assurance of the continuation of our ongoing self-governance, trade and military alliances, and so forth. The treaty relationships were invariably reciprocal in nature: Indians ceded certain portions of their land to the U.S., and the U.S. incurred certain obligations in exchange.[32]

Even at that, there were seldom any outright sales of land by Indian nations to the U.S. Rather, the federal obligations incurred were usually couched in terms of perpetuity. The arrangements were set up by the Indians so that, as long as the U.S. honored its end of the bargains struck, it would have the right to occupy and use defined portions of Indian land. In this sense, the treaties more resemble rental or leasing agreements than actual deeds. And you know what happens under Anglo-Saxon common law when a tenant violates the provisions of a rental agreement, eh?[33] The point here is that the U.S. has long since defaulted on its responsibilities under every single treaty obligation it ever incurred with regard to Indians.

There is really no dispute about this. In fact, there's even a Supreme Court opinion—the 1903 *"Lone Wolf"* case—in which the good "justices" held that the U.S. enjoyed a "right" to disregard any treaty obligation to Indians it found inconvenient, but that the remaining treaty provisions continued to be binding upon the Indians. This was, the high court said, because the U.S. was the stronger of the nations involved, and thus wielded "plenary" power—this simply means *full* power—over the affairs of the weaker indigenous nations. Therefore, the court felt itself free to unilaterally "interpret" each treaty as being a bill of sale rather than as a rental agreement.[34]

Stripped of its fancy legal language, the Supreme Court's position was (and remains) astonishingly crude. There's an old adage that "possession is nine-tenths of the law." Well, in this case the court went a bit further, arguing that possession was *all* of the law. Further, the highest court in the land went on record arguing bold-faced that, where Indian property rights are concerned, might, and might alone, makes right. The U.S. held the power to simply take Indian land, they said, and therefore it had the "right" to do so.[35] If you think about it, that's precisely what the nazis argued only thirty years later, while the United States displayed the unmitigated audacity to profess outrage and shock that Germany so blatantly transgressed elementary standards of international law and the most basic requirements of human decency.[36] It's not that the United States was wrong in its attitude towards the nazis, it's just that it was a clear case of the pot calling the kettle black.

An almost identical reasoning, that power equals rights, appears to have been at the heart of Sadam Hussein's decision to take Kuwait in 1990—actually, Iraq had a far stronger claim to rights over Kuwait than the U.S. has ever had with regard to Indian Country—with the result that President George Bush the 41st immediately began babbling about being "legally required" to wage a "just war" for purposes of "roll[ing] back naked aggression wherever it occurs . . . freeing occupied territory [and] rein-stating legitimate government[s]" that have been "usurped." If he was in any way sincere about *that* proposition, of course, he'd have had to call air strikes in on himself instead of ordering the bombing of Baghdad.[37] Any American Indian could tell you that much, obviously, and the double standard is once again glaring.

Be that as it may, there are a couple of other significant problems with the treaty constructions by which the U.S. allegedly assumed title over its landbase. On the one hand, a number of the ratified treaties can be shown to be fraudulent or coerced, and thus invalid. The nature of the coercion is fairly well known, so let's just say that perhaps a third of the ratified treaties involved direct coercion and shift over to the matter of fraud. This assumes the form of everything from the deliberate misinterpretation of proposed treaty provisions to Indian representatives during negotiations to the Senate's alteration of treaty language after the fact and without the knowledge of the Indian signatories. On a number of occasions, the U.S. appointed its own preferred Indian "leaders" to represent their nations in treaty negotiations.[38] In at least one instance—the 1861 Treaty of Fort Wise—U.S. negotiators appear to have forged the signatures of various Cheyenne and Arapaho leaders.[39] Additionally, there are about 400 treaties which were never ratified by the Senate, and were therefore never legally binding, but upon which the U.S. now asserts its claims concerning lawful use and occupancy rights to, and jurisdiction over, appreciable portions of North America.[40]

When all is said and done, however, even these extremely dubious bases for U.S. title are insufficient to cover the gross territoriality at issue. The federal government itself has tacitly admitted as much during the late 1970s, in the findings of the so-called Indian Claims Commission, an entity created in 1946 to "quiet" title to all illegally taken Indian land within the Lower 48.[41] What the commission did over the ensuing thirty-five years was in significant part to research the ostensible documentary basis for U.S. title to literally every square foot of its claimed territory. It found, among other things, that the U.S. had no legal basis whatsoever—no treaty, no agreement, not even an arbitrary act of Congress—to fully one-third of the area within its boundaries.[42] At the same time, the data revealed that the reserved areas still nominally possessed by Indians had been reduced to about 2.5 percent of the same area.[43]

What this means in plain English is that the United States cannot pretend to even a shred of legitimacy in its occupancy and control of upwards of thirty percent of its "home" territory. And, lest such matters be totally lost in the shuffle, I should note that it has even less legal basis for its claims to the land in Alaska and Hawai'i.[44] Beyond that, its "right" to assert dominion over Puerto Rico, the "U.S." Virgin Islands, "American" Samoa, Guam, and the Marshall Islands, tends to speak for itself, don't you think?[45]

INDIAN LAND RECOVERY IN THE U.S.?

Leaving aside questions concerning the validity of various treaties, the beginning point for any indigenist endeavor in the United States centers, logically enough, in efforts to restore direct Indian control over the huge portion of the continental U.S. which was plainly never ceded by native nations. Upon the bedrock of this foundation, a number of other problems integral to the present configuration of power and privilege in North American society can be resolved, not just for Indians, but for everyone else as well.[46] It's probably impossible to solve, or even to begin meaningfully addressing, certain of these problems in any other way. Still, it is, as they say, "no easy sell" to convince anyone outside the more conscious sectors of the American Indian population itself of the truth of this very simple fact.

In part, uncomfortable as it may be to admit, this is because even the most progressive elements of the North American immigrant population share a perceived commonality of interest with the more reactionary segments.[47] This takes the form of a mutual insistence upon an imagined "right" to possess native property, merely because they are here, and because they desire it. The Great Fear is, within any settler state, that if indigenous land rights are ever openly acknowledged, and native people therefore begin to recover some significant portion of their land, that the settlers will correspondingly be dispossessed of that—most notably, individually held homes, small farms and ranches, and the like—which they've come to consider "theirs."[48] Tellingly, every major Indian land recovery initiative in the U.S. during the second half of the twentieth century—those in Maine, the Black Hills, the Oneida claims in New York State, and Western Shoshone land claim are prime examples—has been met by a propaganda barrage from right-wing organizations ranging from the Ku Klux Klan to the Republican Party warning individual nonindian property holders of exactly this "peril."[49]

I'll debunk some of this nonsense in a moment, but first I want to take up the posture of self-proclaimed left radicals in the same connection. And I'll do so on the basis of principle, because justice is supposed to matter more to progressives than to right-wing hacks. Allow me to observe that the pervasive and near-total silence of the left in this respect has been quite illuminating. Nonindian activists, with only a handful of exceptions, persistently plead that they can't really take a coherent position on the matter of Indian land rights because, "unfortunately," they're "not really conversant with the issues" (as if these were tremendously complex). Meanwhile, they do virtually nothing, generation after generation, to inform themselves on the topic of who actually owns the ground they're standing on.[50]

Listen up folks: The record can be played only so many times before it wears out and becomes just another variation of "hear no evil, see no evil." At this point, it doesn't take Einstein to figure out that the left doesn't know much about such things because it's never *wanted* to know, or that this is so because it has always had its own plans for utilizing land it has no more right to than does the status quo it claims to oppose.[51]

The usual technique for explaining this away has always been a sort of pro forma acknowledgement that Indian land rights are of course "really important" (yawn), but that one "really doesn't have a lot of time" to get into it. (I'll buy your book, though, and keep it on my shelf even if I never read it.) Reason? Well, one is just "too busy" working on "other issues" (meaning, things that are considered to *actually* be important). Typically enumerated are sexism, racism, homophobia, class inequities, militarism, the environment, or some combination thereof. It's a pretty good evasion, all in all. Certainly, there's no denying any of these issues their due; they *are* all important, obviously so. But more important than the question of whose land we're standing on? There are some serious problems of primacy and priority embedded in the orthodox script.[52]

To frame things clearly in this regard, let's hypothesize for a moment that all of the various nonindian movements concentrating on each of the above-mentioned issues were suddenly successful in accomplishing their objectives. Let's imagine that the United States as a whole were somehow transformed into an entity defined by the parity of its race, class, and gender relations, its embrace of unrestricted sexual preference, its rejection of militarism in all forms, and its abiding concern with environmental protection. (I know, I know, this is a sheer impossibility, but that's my point.) When all is said and done, the society resulting from this scenario is still, first and foremost, a colonialist society, an imperialist society in the most fundamental possible sense, with all that that implies.[53]

This is true because the scenario does nothing at all to address the fact that whatever is happening happens on someone else's land, not only without their consent, but through an adamant disregard for their rights to the land. Hence, all it means is that the invader population has rearranged its affairs in such a way as to make itself more comfortable at the continuing expense of indigenous people. The colonial equation remains intact and may even be reinforced by a greater degree of participation and vested interest in maintenance of the colonial order among the settler population at large.[54]

The dynamic here is not very different from that evident in the American "Revolution" of the late eighteenth century, is it?[55] And we all know very well where that led, don't we? Should we therefore begin to refer to socialist imperialism, feminist imperialism, gay and lesbian imperialism, environmentalist imperialism, Afroamerican and *la Raza* imperialism? I hope not. I hope instead that this is mostly just a matter of confusion, of muddled priorities among people who really do mean well and would like to do better.[56] If so, then all that is necessary to correct the situation is a basic rethinking of what it is that must be done, and in what order. Here, I'll advance the straightforward premise that the land rights of "First Americans" should serve as a first priority for attainment of everyone seriously committed to accomplishing positive change in North America.[57]

But before I suggest everyone jump up and adopt this priority, I suppose it's only fair that I interrogate the converse of the proposition: if making things like class inequity and sexism the preeminent focus of progressive action in North America inevitably perpetuates the internal colonial structure of the U.S., does the reverse hold true? I'll state unequivocally that it does not. There is no indication whatsoever that a restoration of indigenous sovereignty in Indian Country would foster class stratification anywhere, least of all in Indian Country. In fact, all indications are that when left to our own devices, indigenous peoples have consistently organized our societies in the most class-free manner.[58] Look to the example of the Haudenosaunee (Six Nations Iroquois Confederacy).[59] Look to the Muscogee (Creek) Confederacy.[60] Look to the confederations of the Yaquis and the Lakotas,[61] as well as those pursued and nearly perfected by Pontiac and Tecumseh.[62] They represent the very essence of enlightened egalitarianism and democracy. Every imagined example to the contrary brought forth by even the most arcane anthropologist can be readily offset by a couple of dozen other illustrations along the lines of those I just mentioned.[63]

Would sexism be perpetuated? Ask one of the Haudenosaunee clan mothers, who continue to assert political leadership in their societies through the present day.[64] Ask Wilma Mankiller, recent head of the Cherokee Nation, a people traditionally led by what were called "Beloved Women."[65] Ask a Lakota woman—or man, for that matter—about who it was that owned all real property in traditional society, and what that meant in terms of parity in gender relations.[66] Ask a traditional Navajo grandmother about her social and political role among her people.[67] Women in most traditional native societies not only enjoyed political, social, and economic parity with men, they often held a preponderance of power in one or more of these spheres.[68]

Homophobia? Homosexuals of both genders were (and in many settings still are) deeply revered as special or extraordinary, and therefore spiritually significant, within most indigenous North American cultures. The extent to which these realities do not now pertain in native societies is exactly the extent to which Indians have been subordinated to the morés of the invading, dominating culture. Insofar as restoration of Indian land rights is tied directly to reconstitution of traditional indigenous social, political, and economic modes, you can see where this leads; the relations of sex and sexuality accord rather well with the aspirations of feminism and gay rights activism.[69]

How about a restoration of native land rights precipitating some sort of "environmental holocaust?" Let's get at least a little bit real here. If you're not addicted to the fabrications of Smithsonian anthropologists about how Indians lived,[70] or to George Weurthner's eurosupremicist *Earth First!* fantasies about how we beat all the woolly mammoths and sabertoothed cats to death with sticks,[71] then this question isn't even on the board. I know it's become fashionable among *Washington Post* editorialists to make snide references to native people "strewing refuse in their wake" as they "wandered nomadically" about the "prehistoric" North American landscape.[72] What is that supposed to imply? That we, who were mostly "sedentary agriculturalists" in any event, were dropping plastic and aluminum cans as we went? Like I said, let's get real. Read the accounts of early European invaders about what they encountered: North America was invariably described as being a "pristine wilderness" at the point of European arrival, despite the fact that it had been occupied by fifteen or twenty million people enjoying a remarkably high standard of living for nobody knows how long: 40,000 years? 50,000 years? Longer?[73] Now contrast that reality to what's been done to this continent over the past couple of hundred years by the culture Weurthner, the Smithsonian, and the *Post* represent, and you tell *me* about environmental devastation.[74]

That leaves militarism and racism. Taking the last first, there really is no indication of racism in traditional Indian societies. To the contrary, the record reveals that

Indians habitually intermarried between groups, and frequently adopted both children and adults from other groups. This occurred in precontact times between Indians, and the practice was broadened to include persons of both African and European origin—and ultimately Asian origin as well—once contact occurred. Those who were naturalized by marriage or adoption were considered members of the group, pure and simple. This was always the Indian view.[75] The Europeans and subsequent Euroamerican settlers viewed things rather differently, however, and foisted off the notion that Indian identity should be determined primarily by "blood quantum," an outright eugenics code similar to those developed in places like nazi Germany and apartheid South Africa. Now, *that's* a racist construction if there ever was one. Unfortunately, a lot of Indians have been conned into buying into this anti-Indian absurdity, and that's something to be overcome. But there's also solid indication that quite a number of native people continue to strongly resist such things as the quantum system.[76]

As to militarism, no one will deny that Indians fought wars among themselves both before and after the European invasion began. Probably half of all indigenous peoples in North America maintained permanent "warrior" societies. This could perhaps be reasonably construed as "militarism." But not, I think, with the sense the term conveys within the European/Euroamerican tradition. There were never, so far as anyone can demonstrate, wars of annihilation fought in this hemisphere prior to the Columbian arrival. None.[77] In fact, it seems that it was a more or less firm principle of indigenous warfare *not* to kill, the object being to demonstrate personal bravery, something which could be done only against a *live* opponent. There's no honor to be had in killing another person, because a dead person can't hurt you. There's no risk. This is not to say that nobody ever died or was seriously injured in the fighting. They were, just as they are in full contact contemporary sports like football and boxing. Actually, these kinds of Euroamerican games are what I would take to be the closest modern parallels to traditional interindian warfare. For Indians, it was a way of burning excess testosterone out of young males, and not much more. So, militarism in the way the term is used today is as alien to native tradition as smallpox and atomic bombs.[78]

Not only is it perfectly reasonable to assert that a restoration of native control over unceded lands within the U.S. would do nothing to perpetuate such problems as sexism and classism, but the reconstitution of indigenous societies this would entail stands to free the affected portions of North America from such maladies altogether. Moreover, it can be said that the process should have a tangible impact in terms of diminishing such things elsewhere. The principle is this: sexism, racism, and all the rest arose here as concomitants to the emergence and consolidation of the eurocentric state form of sociopolitical and economic organization.[79] Everything the state does, everything it *can* do, is entirely contingent upon its maintaining its internal cohesion, a cohesion signified above all by its pretended territorial integrity, its ongoing domination of Indian Country.[80] Given this, it seems obvious that the literal dismemberment of the state inherent to Indian land recovery correspondingly reduces the ability of the state to sustain the imposition of objectionable relations within itself. It follows that realization of indigenous land rights serves to undermine or destroy the ability of the status quo to continue imposing a racist, sexist, classist, homophobic, militaristic order upon *non*indians.[81]

A brief aside: anyone with doubts as to whether it's possible to bring about the dismemberment from within of a superpower state in this day and age ought to sit down and have a long talk with a guy named Mikhail Gorbachev. It would be better yet if you could chew the fat with Leonid Brezhnev, a man who we can be sure would have replied in all sincerity—only three decades ago—that this was the most outlandish idea he'd ever heard. Well, look on a map today, and see if you can find the Union of Soviet Socialist Republics. It ain't there, my friends.[82] Instead, you're seeing, and you're seeing it more and more, the reemergence of the very nations Léon Trotsky and his colleagues consigned to the "dustbin of history" clear back at the beginning of the century.[83] These megastates are not immutable. They *can* be taken apart. They *can* be destroyed. But first we have to decide that we can do it, and that we *will* do it.

So, all things considered, when indigenist movements like AIM advance slogans like "U.S. Out of North America," nonindian radicals shouldn't react defensively.[84] They should cheer. They should see what they might do to help. When they respond defensively to sentiments like those expressed by AIM, what they are ultimately defending is the very government, the very order they claim to oppose so resolutely.[85] And if they manifest this contradiction often enough, consistently enough, pathologically enough, then we have no alternative but to take them at their word, that they really are at some deep level or other aligned—all protestations to the contrary notwithstanding—with the mentality which endorses our permanent dispossession and disenfranchisement, our continuing oppression, our ultimate genocidal obliteration as self-defining and self-determining peoples.[86] In other words, they make themselves part of the problem rather than becoming part of the solution.

THE THRUST OF INDIAN LAND RESTORATION

There are certain implications to Indian control over Indian land which need to be clarified, beginning with a debunking of the "Great Fear," the reactionary myth that any substantive native land recovery would automatically lead to the mass dispossession and eviction of individual nonindian homeowners.[87] Maybe in the process I can reassure a couple of radicals that it's okay to be on the right side of this issue, that they won't have to give something up in order to part company with George Bush on this. It's hard, frankly, to take this up without giggling, because of some of the images it inspires. I mean, what *are* people worried about here? Did somebody really believe Vine Deloria's old joke about Indians standing out on the piers of Boston and New York City, issuing sets of waterwings to long lines of nonindians so they can all swim back to the Old World?[88] Gimme a break.

Seriously, you can search high and low, and you'll never find an instance in which Indians have advocated that small property owners be pushed off the land in order to satisfy land claims. The thrust in every single case has been to recover land within national and state parks and forests, grasslands, military reservations, and the like. In some instances, major corporate holdings have been targeted. A couple of times, as in the Black Hills, a sort of joint jurisdiction between Indians and the existing nonindian government has been discussed with regard to an entire treaty area.[89] But even in the most hard line of the indigenous positions concerning the Black Hills, that advanced by Russell Means in his TREATY Program, where resumption of exclusively Lakota jurisdiction is demanded, there is no mention of dispossessing or evicting nonindians.[90] Instead, other alternatives—which I'll take up later—were carefully spelled out.

In the meantime, though, I'd like to share with you something the right-wing propagandists never mention when they're busily whipping up nonindian sentiment against Indian rights. You'll recall that I said the quantity of unceded land within the continental U.S. makes up about one-third of the overall landmass? Now juxtapose that total to the approximately 35 percent of the same landmass the federal government presently holds in various kinds of trust status. Add the ten or twelve percent of the land the 48 contiguous states hold in trust. You end up with a 35 percent Indian claim against a 45–47 percent *governmental* holding.[91] Never mind the percentage of the land held by major corporations. Conclusion? It is, and always has been, quite possible to accomplish the return of every square inch of unceded Indian Country in the United States without tossing a single nonindian homeowner off the land on which they live.

"Critics"—that's the amazingly charitable term for themselves employed by those who ultimately oppose indigenous rights in *any* form as a matter of principle—are always quick to point out that the problem with this arithmetic is that the boundaries of the government trust areas do not necessarily conform in all cases to the boundaries of unceded areas. That's true enough, although I'd just as quickly observe that more often than not they *do* correspond. This "problem" is nowhere near as big as it's made out to be. And there's nothing intrinsic to the boundary question which couldn't be negotiated, once nonindian America acknowledges that Indians have an absolute moral and legal right to the quantity of territory which was never ceded. Boundaries can be adjusted, often in ways which can be beneficial to both sides of the negotiation.[92]

Let me give you an example. Along about 1980, a couple of Rutgers University professors, Frank and Deborah Popper, undertook a comprehensive study of land-use patterns and economy on the Great Plains.[93] What they discovered is that 110 counties—a quarter of all the counties in the entire Plains region, falling within the western portions of the states of North and South Dakota, Nebraska, Kansas, Oklahoma, and Texas, as well as eastern Montana, Wyoming, Colorado, and New Mexico—have been fiscally insolvent since the moment they were taken from native people a century and more ago.[94] This is an area of about 140,000 square miles, inhabited by a widely dispersed nonindian population of only around 400,000, attempting to maintain school districts, police and fire departments, roadbeds, and all the other basic accouterments of "modern life" on the negligible incomes which can be eked from cattle grazing and wheat farming on land which is patently unsuited for both enterprises. The Poppers found that, without considerable federal subsidy each and every year, none of these counties would ever have been viable. Nor, on the face of it, will any of them *ever* be.

Put bluntly, the pretense of bringing Euroamerican "civilization" to the Plains represents nothing more than a massive economic burden on the rest of the United States.[95]

What the Poppers proposed on the basis of these findings is that the government cut its perpetual losses, buying out the individual landholdings within the target counties, and converting them into open space wildlife sanctuaries known as the "Buffalo Commons" (see Figure 13.1). The whole area would in effect be turned back to the bison, which were very nearly exterminated by Phil Sheridan's buffalo hunters

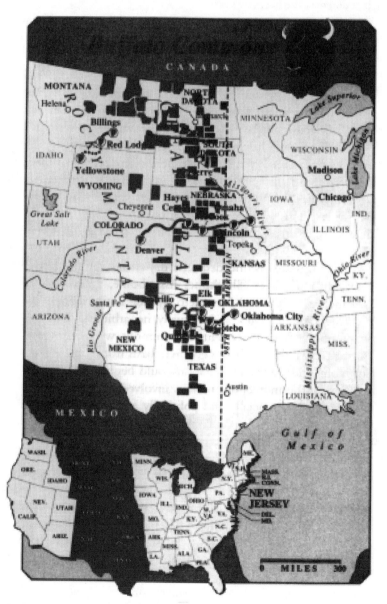

FIGURE 13.1. Anne Mathews, *Where the Buffalo Roam.*

back in the nineteenth century as a means of starving "recalcitrant" Indians into surrendering.[96] The result would, they argue, be both environmentally and economically beneficial to the nation as a whole. It is instructive that their thinking has gained increasing credibility and support from Indians and nonindians alike since the late '80s. Another chuckle here: Indians have been trying to tell nonindians that this would be the outcome of fencing in the Plains ever since 1850 or so, but some folks have a real hard time catching on. Anyway, it is entirely possible that we'll see some actual motion in this direction over the next few years.[97]

So, let's take the Poppers' idea to its next logical step. There are another hundred or so counties which have always been economically marginal adjoining the "perpetual red ink" counties they've identified. These don't represent an actual drain on the U.S. economy, but they don't contribute much either. They could be "written off" and included into the Buffalo Commons with no one feeling any ill effects whatsoever. Now add in adjacent areas like the national grasslands in Wyoming, the national forest and parklands in the Black Hills, extraneous military reservations like Ellsworth Air Force Base, and existing Indian reservations. What you end up with is a huge territory lying east of Denver, west of Kansas City, and extending from the Canadian border to southern Texas, all of it "outside the loop" of U.S. business-as-usual. The bulk of this area is unceded territory owned by the Lakota, Pawnee, Arikara, Hidatsa, Mandan, Crow, Shoshone, Assiniboin, Cheyenne, Arapaho, Kiowa, Comanche, Jicarilla and Mescalero Apache nations.[98] There would be little cost to the United States, and virtually no arbitrary dispossession/dislocation of nonindians, if the entire Commons were restored to these peoples. Further, it would establish a concrete basis from which genuine expressions of indigenous self-determination could begin to (re)emerge on this continent, allowing the indigenous nations involved to begin the process of reconstituting themselves socially and politically, and to begin to recreate their traditional economies in ways which make contemporary sense.[99] This would provide alternative socioeconomic models for possible adaptation by nonindians, and alleviate a range of not inconsiderable costs to the public treasury incurred by keeping the Indians in question in a state of abject and permanent dependency.[100]

Alright, as critics will undoubtedly be quick to point out, an appreciable portion of the Buffalo Commons area I've sketched out—several million acres, perhaps—lies outside the boundaries of unceded territory. That's the basis for the sort of multilateral negotiations between the U.S. and indigenous nations I mentioned earlier. This land will need to be "charged off" in some fashion against unceded land elsewhere, and in such a way as to bring other native peoples into the mix.[101] The Ponca, Omaha, and Osage, whose traditional territories fall within the area at issue, come immediately to mind; but this would extend as well to all native peoples willing to exchange land claims somewhere else for actual acreage within this locale. The idea is to consolidate a distinct indigenous territoriality while providing a definable landbase to as many different Indian nations as possible in the process (see Figure 13.2).

From there, the principle of the Buffalo Commons *cum* Indian Territory could be

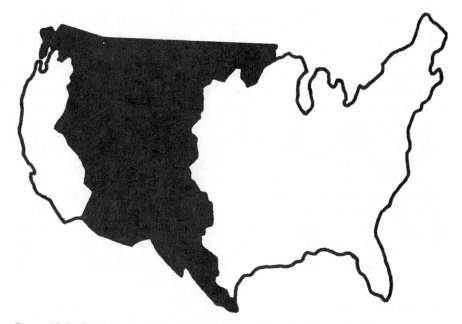

FIGURE 13.2. Possible Boundaries: North American Union of Indigenous Nations.

extended westwards into areas which adjoin or are at least immediately proximate to the Commons area itself. The fact is that vast areas of the Great Basin and Sonoran Desert regions of the U.S. are even more sparsely populated and economically insolvent than the Plains. A great deal of the area is also held in federal trust.[102] Hence, it is reasonable—in my view at least—to expand the Commons territory to include most of Utah and Nevada, northern Montana and Idaho, quite a lot of eastern Washington and Oregon, most of the rest of New Mexico, and the lion's share of Arizona. This would encompass the unceded lands of the Blackfeet and Gros Ventre, Salish, Kootenai, Nez Percé, Yakima, Western Shoshone, Goshutes and Utes, Paiutes, Navajo, Hopi and other Pueblos, Mescalero and Chiricahua Apache, Havasupi, Yavapai, and Tohono O'odam.[103] It would also set the stage for further exchange negotiations, in order to consolidate this additional territory, which would serve to establish a landbase for a number of other indigenous nations.

At this point, we've arrived at an area comprising roughly one third of the continental U.S., a territory which—regardless of the internal political and geographical subdivisions effected by the multiplicity of native peoples within it—could be defined as a sort of "North American Union of Indigenous Nations."[104] Such an entity would be in a position to assist other indigenous nations outside its borders, but still within the remaining territorial corpus of the U.S., to resolve land claim issues accruing from fraudulent or coerced treaties of cession (another fifteen or twenty percent of the present 48 states). It would also be in a position to facilitate an accommodation of the needs of untreated peoples within the U.S., the Abenaki of Vermont, for example, and the Native Hawaiians and Alaskan natives.[105] Similarly, it would be able to help secure the self-determination of U.S. colonies like Puerto Rico.[106] You can see the direction the dominoes begin to fall.

Nor does this end with the United States. Any sort of indigenous union of the kind I've described would be as eligible for admission as a fully participating member of the United Nations as, say, Croatia, the Ukraine, and Uzbekistan have recently become.[107] This would set a very important precedent, insofar as there has never been an American Indian entity of any sort accorded such political status on the world stage. The precedent could serve to pave the way for comparable recognition and attainments by other Native American nations, notably the confederation of Incan peoples of the Andean highlands and the Mayans of present-day Guatemala and southern Mexico (Indians are the majority population, decisively so, in both locales). And, from there, other indigenous nations, elsewhere around the world.[108] Again, you can see the direction the dominoes fall. If we're going to have a "New World Order," let's make it something just a bit different from what George Bush and friends have in mind. Right?[109]

SHARING THE LAND

There are several closely related matters which should be touched upon before wrapping this up. One has to do with the idea of self-determination. What is meant when indigenists demand an unrestricted exercise of self-determining rights by native peoples? Most nonindians, and even a lot of Indians, seem confused by this and want to know whether it's not the same as complete separation from the U.S., Canada, or whatever the colonizing power may be. The answer is, "not necessarily." The unqualified acknowledgement by the colonizer of the right of the colonized to total separation ("secession") is the necessary point of departure for any exercise of self-determination. Decolonization means the colonized exercise the right as we see fit, in accordance with our own customs, traditions, and appreciations of our needs. We decide for ourselves what degree of autonomy we wish to enjoy, and thus the nature of our political and economic relationship(s), not only with our former colonizers, but with all other nations as well.[110]

My own inclination, which is in some ways an emotional preference, tends to run toward complete sovereign independence, but that's not the point. I have no more right to impose my preferences on indigenous nations than do the colonizing powers; each indigenous nation will choose for itself the exact manner and extent to which it expresses its autonomy, its sovereignty.[111] To be honest, I suspect very few would be inclined to adopt my sort of "go it alone" approach (and, actually, I must admit that part of my own insistence upon it often has more to do with forcing concession of the right from those who seek to deny it than it does with putting it into practice). In the event, I expect you'd see the hammering out of a number of sets of international relations in the "free association" vein, a welter of variations of commonwealth and home rule governance.[112]

The intent here is not, no matter how much it may be deserved in an abstract sense, to visit some sort of retribution, real or symbolic, upon the colonizing or former colonizing powers. It is to arrive at new sets of relationships between peoples which effectively put an end to the era of international domination. The need is to gradually replace the existing world order with one which is predicated in collaboration and cooperation between nations.[113] The only way to ever really accomplish that is to physically disassemble the gigantic state structures which evolved from the imperialist era, structures which are literally predicated in systematic intergroup domination and cannot in any sense exist without it.[114] A concomitant of this disassembly is the inculcation of voluntary, consensual interdependence between formerly dominated and dominating nations, and a redefinition of the word "nation" itself to conform to its original meaning: bodies of people bound together by their bioregional and other natural cultural affinities.[115]

This last point is, it seems to me, crucially important. Partly, that's because of the persistent question of who it is who gets to remain in Indian Country once land restoration and consolidation has occurred. The answer, I think, is anyone who wants to, up to a point. By "anyone who wants to," I mean anyone who wishes to apply for formal citizenship within an indigenous nation, thereby accepting the idea that s/he is placing him/herself under unrestricted Indian jurisdiction and will thus be required to abide by native law.[116] Funny thing; I hear a lot of nonindians asserting that they reject nearly every aspect of U.S. law, but the idea of placing themselves under anyone else's jurisdiction seems to leave them pretty queasy. I have no idea how many nonindians might actually opt for citizenship in an indigenous nation when push comes to shove, but I expect there will be some. And I suspect some Indians have been so indoctrinated by the dominant society that they'll elect to remain within it rather than availing themselves of their own citizenship. So there'll be a bit of a trade-off in this respect.

Now, there's the matter of the process working only "up to a point." That point is very real. It is defined, not by political or racial considerations, but by the carrying capacity of the land. The population of indigenous nations everywhere has always been determined by the number of people who could be sustained in a given environment or bioregion without overpowering and thereby destroying that environment.[117] A very carefully calculated balance—one which was calibrated to the fact that in order to enjoy certain sorts of material comfort, human population had to be kept at some level below saturation—was always maintained between the number of humans and the rest of the habitat. In order to accomplish this, native peoples have always incorporated into the very core of our spiritual traditions the concept that all life forms and the earth itself possess rights equal to those enjoyed by humans.[118]

Rephrased, this means it would be a violation of a fundament of traditional indigenous law to supplant or eradicate another species, whether animal or plant, in order to make way for some greater number of humans, or to increase the level of material comfort available to those who already exist. Conversely, it is a fundamental requirement of traditional law that each human accept his or her primary responsibility, that of maintaining the balance and harmony of the natural order *as it is encountered*.[119] One is essentially free to do anything one wants in an indigenous society so long as this cardinal rule is adhered to. The bottom line with regard to the maximum population limit of Indian Country as it has been sketched in this presentation is some very finite number. My best guess is that five million people would be pushing things right to the limit.[120] Whatever. Citizens can be admitted until that point has been reached, and no more. And the population cannot increase beyond that number over time, no matter at what rate. Carrying capacity is a fairly constant reality; it tends to change over thousands of years, when it changes at all.

POPULATION AND ENVIRONMENT

What I'm going to say next will probably startle a few people (as if what's been said already hasn't). I think this principle of population restraint is the single most important example Native North America can set for the rest of humanity. It is *the* thing which it is most crucial for others to emulate. Check it out. I recently heard that Japan, a small island nation which has so many people that they're literally tumbling into the sea, and which has exported about half again as many people as live on the home islands, is expressing "official concern" that its birth rate has declined very slightly over the last few years. The worry is that in thirty years there'll be fewer workers available to "produce," and thus to "consume" whatever it is that's produced.[121]

Ever ask yourself what it is that's used in "producing" something? Or what it is that's being "consumed"? Yeah. You got it. Nature is being consumed, and with it the ingredients which allow ongoing human existence. It's true that nature can replenish some of what's consumed, but only at a certain rate. That rate has been vastly exceeded, and the extent of excess is increasing by the moment. An overburgeoning humanity is killing the natural world, and thus itself. It's no more complicated than that.[122]

Here we are in the midst of a rapidly worsening environmental crisis of truly global proportions, every last bit of it attributable to a wildly accelerating human consumption of the planetary habitat, and you have one of the world's major offenders expressing grave concern that the rate at which it is able to consume might actually drop a notch or two. *Think* about it. I suggest that this attitude signifies nothing so much as stark, staring madness. It is insane: suicidally, homicidally, ecocidally, *omnicidally* insane. No, I'm not being rhetorical. I meant what I've just said in the most literal way possible,[123] but I don't want to convey the misimpression that I see the Japanese as being in this respect unique. Rather, I intend them to serve as merely an illustration of a far broader and quite virulent pathology called "industrialism"—or, lately, "postindustrialism"—a sickness centered in an utterly obsessive drive to dominate and destroy the natural order. (Words like "production," "consumption," "development," and "progress" are mere code words masking this reality.)[124]

It's not only the industrialized countries which are afflicted with this dis-ease. One byproduct of the past five centuries of European expansionism and the resulting hegemony of eurocentric ideology is that the latter has been drummed into the consciousness of *most* peoples to the point where it is now subconsciously internalized. Everywhere, you find people thinking it "natural" to view themselves as the incarnation of God on earth—i.e., "created in the image of God"—and thus duty-bound to "exercise dominion over nature" in order that they can "multiply, grow plentiful, and populate the land" in ever increasing "abundance."[125]

The legacy of the forced labor of the latifundia and inculcation of Catholicism in Latin America is a tremendous overburden of population devoutly believing that "wealth" can be achieved (or is defined) by having ever *more* children.[126] The legacy of Mao's implementation of "reverse technology" policy—the official encouragement of breakneck childbearing rates in his already overpopulated country, solely as a means to deploy massive labor power to offset capitalism's "technological advantage" in production—resulted in a tripling of China's population in only two generations.[127] And then there is India. . . .

Make absolutely no mistake about it. The planet was never designed to accommodate five billion human beings, much less the *ten* billion predicted to be here a mere forty years hence.[128] If we are to be about turning power relations around between people, and between groups of people, we must also be about turning around the relationship between people and the rest of the natural order. If we don't, we'll die out as a species, just like any other species which irrevocably overshoots its habitat. The sheer numbers of humans on this planet needs to come down to about a quarter of what they are today, or maybe less, and the plain fact is that the bulk of these numbers are in the Third World.[129] So, I'll say this clearly: not only must the birth rate in the Third World come down, but the population levels of Asia, Latin America, and Africa *must* be reduced over the next few generations. The numbers must start to come down dramatically, beginning right now.

Of course, there's another dimension to the population issue, one which is in some ways even more important, and I want to get into it in a minute. But first I have to say something else. This is that I don't want a bunch of Third Worlders jumping up in my face screaming that I'm advocating "genocide." Get *off* that bullshit. It's genocide when some centralized state, or some colonizing power, imposes sterilization or abortion on target groups.[130] It's not genocide at all when we recognize that *we* have a problem, and take the logical steps *ourselves* to solve them. Voluntary sterilization is not a part of genocide. Voluntary abortion is not a part of genocide. And, most important, educating ourselves and our respective peoples to bring our birth rates under control through conscious resort to birth control measures is not a part of genocide.[131] What it *is*, is part of taking responsibility for ourselves again, of taking responsibility for our destiny and our children's destiny. It's about rooting the ghost of the Vatican out of our collective psyches, and the ghosts of Adam Smith and Karl Marx. It's about getting back in touch with our *own* ways, our *own* traditions, our *own* knowledge, and it's long past time we got out of our own way in this respect. We've got an awful lot to unlearn, and an awful lot to relearn, not much time in which we can afford the luxury of avoidance, and we need to get on with it.

The other aspect of population I wanted to take up is that there's another way of counting. One way, the way I just did it, and the way it's conventionally done, is to simply point to the number of bodies, or "people units." That's valid enough as far as it goes, so we have to look at it and act upon what we see, but it doesn't really go far enough. This brings up the second method, which is to count by differential rates of resource consumption—that is to say, the proportional degree of environmental impact per individual—and to extrapolate that into people units. Using this method, which is actually more accurate in ecological terms, we arrive at conclusions that are a little different from the usual notion that the most overpopulated regions on earth are in the Third World. The average resident of the United States, for example, consumes about thirty times the resources of the average Ugandan or Laotian. Since a lot of poor folk reside in the U.S., this translates into the average yuppie consuming about seventy times the resources of an average Third Worlder.[132]

Every yuppie born has the same impact on the environment as another seventy Chinese. Lay *that* one on the next Polo-clad geek who approaches you with a baby stroller and an outraged look, demanding that you put your cigarette out, eh?[133] Tell 'em you'll snuff the smoke when they snuff the kid, and not a moment before. Better yet, tell 'em they need to get busy snuffing *themselves*, along with the kid, and do the planet a *real* favor. Just "kidding" (heh-heh).

Returning to the topic at hand, you have to multiply the U.S. population by a factor of thirty—a noticeably higher ratio than either Western Europe or Japan—in order to figure out how many Third Worlders it would take to have the same environmental impact. I make that 7.5 *billion* U.S. people units. I think I can thus safely say the most overpopulated portion of the globe is the United States. Either the consumption rates really have to be cut in this country, most especially in the more privileged social sectors, or the number of people must be drastically reduced, or both. I advocate both. How much? That's a bit subjective, but I'll tentatively accept the calculations of William Catton, a respected ecological demographer. He estimated that North America was thoroughly saturated with humans by 1840.[134] So we need to get both population and consumption levels down to what they were in that year, or preferably a little earlier. Alternatively, we need to bring population down to an even lower level in order to sustain a correspondingly higher level of consumption.

Here's where I think the reconstitution of indigenous territoriality and sovereignty in the west can be useful with regard to population. Land isn't just land, you see; it's also the resources within the land, things like coal, oil, natural gas, uranium, and maybe most important, water. How does that bear on U.S. overpopulation? Simple. Much of the population expansion in this country over the past quarter-century has been into the southwestern desert region. How many people have they got living in the valley down there at Phoenix, a place which might be reasonably expected to support 500?[135] Look at L.A.: twenty million people where there ought to be maybe a few thousand.[136] How do they accomplish this? Well, for one thing, they've diverted the entire Colorado River from its natural purposes. They're siphoning off the Columbia River and piping it south.[137] They've even got a project underway to divert the Yukon River all the way down from Alaska to support southwestern urban growth, and to provide irrigate for the agribusiness penetration of northern Sonora and Chihuahua called for by NAFTA.[138] Whole regions of our ecosphere are being destabilized in the process.

Okay, in the scenario I've described, the whole Colorado watershed will be in Indian Country, under Indian control. So will the source of the Columbia. And diversion of the Yukon would have to go right through Indian Country. Now, here's the deal. No more use of water to fill swimming pools and sprinkle golf courses in Phoenix and L.A. No more watering Kentucky bluegrass lawns out on the yucca flats. No more drive-thru car washes in Tucumcari. No more "Big Surf" amusement parks in the middle of the desert. Drinking water and such for the whole population, yes, Indians should deliver that. But water for this other insanity? No way. I guarantee that'll stop the inflow of population cold. Hell, I'll guarantee it'll start a pretty substantial *out*flow. Most of these folks never wanted to live in the desert anyway. That's why they keep trying to make it look like Florida (another delicate environment which is buckling under the weight of population increases).[139]

And we can help move things along in other ways as well. Virtually all the electrical power for the southwestern urban sprawls comes from a combination of hydroelectric and coal-fired generation in the Four Corners area. This is smack dab in the middle of Indian Country, along with all the uranium with which a "friendly atom" alternative might be attempted,[140] and most of the low sulfur coal. Goodbye, the neon glitter of Reno and Las Vegas. Adios to air conditioners in every room. Sorry about your hundred-mile expanses of formerly street-lit expressway. Basic needs will be met, and that's it. Which means we can also start saying goodbye to western rivers being backed up like so many sewage lagoons behind massive dams. The Glen Canyon and Hoover dams are coming down, boys and girls.[141] And we can begin to experience things like a reduction in the acidity of southwestern rainwater as facilities like the Four Corners Power Plant are cut back in generating time, and eventually eliminated altogether.[142]

What I'm saying probably sounds extraordinarily cruel to a lot of people, particularly those imbued with the belief that they hold a "God-given right" to play a round of golf on the well-watered green beneath the imported palm trees outside an air-conditioned casino at the base of the Superstition Mountains. Tough. Those days can be ended with neither hesitation nor apology. A much more legitimate concern rests in the fact that many people who've drifted into the Southwest have nowhere else to go to. The places they came from are crammed. In many cases, that's why they left.[143] To them, I say there's no need to panic; no one will abruptly pull the plug on you, or leave you to die of thirst. Nothing like that. But quantities of both water and power will be set at minimal levels. In order to have a surplus, you'll have to bring your number down to a more reasonable level over the next generation or two. As you do so, water and power availability will be steadily reduced, necessitating an ongoing population reduction. Arrival at a genuinely sustainable number of regional residents can thus be phased in over an extended period, several generations, if need be.[144]

Provision of key items such as western water and coal should probably be negotiated on the basis of reductions in population/consumption by the U.S. as a whole rather than simply the region served—much the way the U.S.-controlled World Bank and International Monetary Fund now dictate sweeping terms to Third World countries in exchange for relatively paltry investments, but for opposite reasons[145]—in order to prevent population shifts being substituted for actual reductions. Any such negotiated arrangement should also include an agreement by the U.S. to alter its distribution of food surpluses and the like, so as to ease the transition to lower population and correspondingly greater self-sufficiency in destitute Third World areas.[146]

The objective inherent to every aspect of this process should be, and can be, to let everyone down as gently as possible from the long and intoxicating high that has beset so much of the human species in its hallucination that it, and it alone, holds value and importance in the universe. In doing so, and I believe *only* in doing so, can we fulfill our obligation to bequeath our grandchildren, and our grandchildren's grandchildren, a world which is fit (or even possible) to live in.[147]

I AM INDIGENIST

There are any number of other matters which by rights should be discussed, but they will of necessity have to await another occasion. What has been presented has been only the barest outline, a glimpse of what might be called an "indigenist vision." Hopefully, it provides enough shape and clarity to allow anyone who wishes to pursue the thinking further, to fill in at least some of the gaps I've not had time to address, and to arrive at insights and conclusions of their own. Once the main tenets have been advanced, and I think to some extent that's been accomplished, the perspective of indigenism is neither mystical nor mysterious.

In closing, I would like to turn again to the critics, the skeptics, those who will decry what has been said here as being "unrealistic," or even "crazy." On the former score, my reply is that so long as we define realism, or reality itself, in conventional terms, the terms imposed by the order of understanding in which we now live, we will be locked forever into the trajectory in which we presently find ourselves.[148] We will never break free, because any order, any structure, defines reality only in terms of itself. Consequently, allow me to echo the sentiments expressed in the French student revolt of 1968: "Be realistic, demand the impossible!"[149] If you read through a volume of American Indian oratory, and there are several available, you'll find that native people have been saying the same thing all along.[150]

As to my being crazy, I'd like to say, "Thanks for the compliment." Again, I follow my elders and my ancestors—and R.D. Laing, for that matter—in believing that when confronted with a society as obviously insane as this one, the only sane posture one can adopt is what that society would automatically designate as crazy.[151] I mean, it wasn't *Indians* who turned birthing into a religious fetish while butchering a couple hundred million people with weapons of mass destruction and systematically starving another billion or so to death. Indians never had a Grand Inquisition, and we never came up with a plumbing plan to reroute the water flow on an entire continent. Nor did we ever produce "leaders" of the caliber of Ronald Reagan, Madeleine Albright, and Pat Buchanan. Hell, we never even figured out that turning prison construction into a major growth industry was an indication of social progress and enlightenment.[152] Maybe we were never so much crazy as we were congenitally retarded.

Whatever the reason, and you'll excuse me for suspecting it might be something other than craziness or retardation, I'm indescribably thankful that our cultures turned out to be so different, no matter how much abuse and sacrifice it's entailed. I'm proud to stand inside the heritage of native struggle. I'm proud to say I'm an unreconstructable indigenist. For me, there's no other reasonable or realistic way to look at the world. And I invite anyone who shares that viewpoint to come aboard, regardless of your race, creed, or national origin. Maybe Chief Seattle said it best back in 1854: "Tribe follows tribe, and nation follows nation, like the waves of the sea. Your time of decay may be distant, but it will surely come, for even the white man whose god walked with him and talked with him as friend with friend, cannot be exempt from the common destiny. We may be brothers after all. We will see."[153]

PERMISSIONS AND ACKNOWLEDGMENTS

"The Law Stood Squarely on Its Head" is a major expansion of an essay entitled "Subverting the Law of Nations," published in Donald A. Grinde, Jr., ed., *A Political History of Native Americans* (Washington, D.C.: CQ Press, 2002).

"Bringing the Law Home" was first published in my *Indians Are Us? Culture and Genocide in Native North America* (Monroe, ME: Common Courage Press, 1994).

A much different version of "The Earth Is Our Mother" appeared in my *From a Native Son: Essays in Indigenism, 1985–1995* (Boston: South End Press, 1996).

"A Breach of Trust" was originally published in *American Indian Culture and Research Journal*, Vol. 23, No. 4, Winter 1999.

"Like Sand in the Wind" made its first appearance in my *Since Predator Came: Notes from the Struggle for American Indian Liberation* (Littleton, CO: Aigis, 1995).

"The Bloody Wake of Alcatraz" was initially published in *American Indian Culture and Research Journal*, Vol. 18, No. 4, Fall 1995.

"Fantasies of the Master Race," in its present form, was written as the title essay for my *Fantasies of the Master Race: Literature, Cinema and the Colonization of American Indians* (San Francisco: City Lights, [2nd ed.] 1998).

"Let's Spread the 'Fun' Around" has been collected in a number of anthologies and readers including Robert Atwan's and John Roberts's coedited *Left, Right and Center: Voices from Across the Political Spectrum* (New York: Bedford Books/St. Martin's Press, 1996), a volume in the publishers' "Best American Essays Series."

"Indians 'R' Us" was written as the title essay for *Indians Are Us?*

An earlier version of "False Promises" is included in *From A Native Son.*

A somewhat different version of "I Am Indigenist" appears in my *Struggle for the Land: Native North American Resistance to Genocide, Ecocide and Colonization* (Winnipeg: Arbeiter Ring, [2nd] 1999).

NOTES

INTRODUCTION

1. Nationals from 86 different countries are reported to have been killed; U.S. Attorney General John Ashcroft, press briefing carried on CNBC, Nov. 29, 2001. The total number of dead is a bit mysterious, however. The official estimate of overall fatalities was initially 4,500, a number shortly ratcheted up to 5,000. By Dec. 11, the tally of those killed in the WTC attacks, as reported on Fox News, had declined 3,040. Adding the 300-odd dead consistently attributed to the Pentagon attack produces a total of under 3,400. The same evening as the Fox News report, however, Senator Orin Hatch, appearing on CNN's *Larry King Live*, stated that "7,000 innocent Americans" had been killed. Since adding foreign nationals to Hatch's count would produce a CNN total more than double that simultaneously announced on Fox, it is easy to see why people elsewhere in the world tend to consider U.S. sources a bit less than credible.

2. *Time*, special issue, Sept. 14, 2001.

3. Yonah Alexander and Michael S. Swetman, *Usama bin Laden's al-Qaida: Profile of a Terrorist Network* (Ardsley, NY: Transnational, 2001). For context, see John Prados, *Presidents' Secret Wars: CIA and Pentagon Covert Operations Since World War II* (New York: William Morrow, 1986).

4. Bin-Laden's reasoning was so compelling, in fact, that officials immediately demanded—under the ludicrous pretext that he might use the tapes as a means of "sending coded instructions to his followers"—that no more of them be broadcast in the U.S. America's "free press," of course, meekly complied.

5. According to 1995 U.N. estimates, 567,000 children under 12 years of age had already died as a result of U.S. sanctions against Iraq; cited in Noam Chomsky, "Rogue State," in Noam Chomsky and Edward Said, *Acts of Aggression: Policing "Rogue" States* (New York: Steven Stories Press, 1999) p. 42. Also see Ramsey Clark, *The Impact of Sanctions on Iraq: The Children are Dying* (Washington, D.C.: Maisonneuve Press, 1996).

6. For a sampling of Halliday's actions and statements, see Ramsey Clark and Others, *Challenge to Genocide: Let Iraq Live* (Washington, D.C.: International Action Center, 1998); see esp. pp. 79, 127, 191.

7. The interview first aired on May 12, 1996.

8. This is a condition clinically described as an "empathic wall"; Donald L. Nathanson, "Denial, Projection and the Empathic Wall," in E.L. Edelstein, Donald L. Nathanson and Andrew Stone, eds., *Denial: A Clarification of Concepts and Research* (New York: Plenum, 1989) esp. 43–44.

9. Noam Chomsky, interviewed by David Barsamian, "The United States is a Leading Terrorist State," *Monthly Review*, Vol. 53, No. 6, 2001, pp. 14–15.

10. For a fairly comprehensive itemization of the many international conventions, declarations, and covenants the U.S. has refused to accept over the past three decades, see William Blum, *Rogue State: A Guide to the World's Only Superpower* (Monroe, ME: Common Courage Press, 2000) pp.187–97.

11. "U.S. Terminates Acceptance of ICJ Compulsory Jurisdiction," *Department of State Bulletin*, No. 86, Jan. 1986.

12. The U.S. refused to join 120 other states voting to affirm the ICC Charter in 1998, and continues to insist it will never do so until the Charter is revised to grant Americans "100 percent protection" against—that is, blanket immunity from—indictment and prosecution; Blum, *Rogue State*, p. 7; Geoffrey Robertson, *Crimes Against Humanity: The Struggle for Global Justice* (New York: Free Press, 2000) pp. 327–28.

13. Blum, *Rogue State*; Chomsky and Said, *Acts of Aggression*; Noam Chomsky, *Rogue States: The Rule of Force in World Affairs* (Cambridge, MA: South End Press, 2000).

14. Suffice it here to observe that the "unilateralist" policy pursued by the U.S. in international af-

fairs draws much of its inspiration from the theory of a "prerogative state"—a "governmental system which exercises unlimited arbitrariness and violence unchecked by any legal guarantees" other than those it elects on the basis of expedience or transient self-interest to observe—described by legal philosopher Ernst Fraenkel, in his *The Dual State: A Contribution to the Theory of Dictatorship* (New York: Oxford University Press, 1941) p. xiii.

15. Chomsky (note 9) posits as a "precedent" for "how to go about [obtaining] justice" the 1985 *Nicaragua v. U.S.* case. This involves a people "subjected to violent assault by the U.S. [and therefore] went to the World Court, which issued a judgment in their favor condemning the U.S. for what it called 'unlawful use of force,' which means international terrorism, ordering the U.S. to desist and pay substantial reparations." As Chomsky goes on to observe, however, "the U.S. dismissed the court judgment with contempt, responding with an immediate escalation of the attack [in which] tens of thousands of people died. The country was substantially destroyed, it may never recover." For background, see Holly Sklar, *Washington's War on Nicaragua* (Boston: South End Press, 1988).

16. Articles 41 and 42 of the United Nations Charter spell out these "measures not involving the use of armed force." Article 51 specifically states that unilateral resort to warfare is illegal other than in cases requiring "self-defense against armed attack," until 9-1-1 a circumstance not directly suffered by Americans since its own Civil War (Pearl Harbor is dubious, occurring as it did in a colony illegally occupied by the U.S. from 1898 onward; Rich Budnick, *Stolen Kingdom: An American Conspiracy* (Honolulu: Aloha Press, 1992)). Where armed attack is at issue, unilateral military prerogatives are lawful only until the Security Council can mount what it, collectively, considers an intervention appropriate to "maintain[ing] international peace and security." In all other instances, U.N. member states are required "to refrain in their international relations from the threat or use of force."

17. "The record of the superpower veto, as exercised inconsistently and cynically [by the U.S.] in crisis after crisis, deprives the Security Council of that moral authority which is necessary for 'law' of any kind, national or international"; Robertson, *Crimes Against Humanity*, pp. 443–44. "Rendering the U.N. 'utterly ineffective' has [become] routine procedure . . . One index is Security Council vetoes, covering a wide range of issues: from the 1960s, the U.S. has been far in the lead, Britain second, France a distant third. General Assembly votes are similar. The more general principle is that if an international organization does not serve the interests that govern U.S. policy, there is little reason to allow it to survive"; Noam Chomsky, "Rogues Gallery: Who Qualifies?" in his *Rogue States*, p. 3.

18. Quincy Wright, "The Law of the Nuremberg Trials," *American Journal of International Law*, No. 41, Jan. 1947. For adaptations of the principle to the U.S. context, see Malcolm X, *By Any Means Necessary* (New York: Pathfinder Press, 1992); Peter Stansill and David Zain Mairowitz, eds., *BAMN [by any means necessary]: Outlaw Manifestos and Ephemera, 1965-1970* (New York: Autonomedia, 1999).

19. "We are not prepared to lay down a [legal principle] against others which we are not willing to have invoked against us"; U.S. Supreme Court Justice Robert H. Jackson, opening statement before the Nuremberg Tribunal, Nov. 21, 1945," quoted in Bertrand Russell, *War Crimes in Vietnam* (New York: Monthly Review Press, 1967) p. 125.

20. Those deluded enough to believe the sorts of measures set forth in the recent "Patriot Act" (Office of Homeland Security Act of 2001 (H.R. 3026, Oct. 4, 2001)) will stop seriously committed persons from accomplishing their retaliatory missions should ask the Israelis how well such policies have worked for *them* over the past 30 years.

21. Noam Chomsky, Znet Commentaries, Sept. 17, 2001.

22. Georgia State University law professor Natsu Saito, interview on NPR's *Powerpoint*, broadcast on Atlanta radio station WCLK, Nov. 4, 2001.

23. I am by no means alone in this; see, e.g., Christopher Hitchens, *The Trial of Henry Kissinger* (London: Verso, 2001).

24. Karl Jaspers, *The Question of German Guilt* (New York: Fordham University Press, 2001).

25. Daniel Jonah Goldhagen, "*Modell Bundesrepublik*: National History, Democracy, and Internationalization in Germany," in Robert R. Shandley, *Unwilling Germans? The Goldhagen Debate* (Minneapolis: University of Minnesota Press, 2000) pp. 275–76.

26. For explication of the phrase used, see Wilhelm Reich, *The Mass Psychology of Fascism* (New York: Farrar, Straus & Giroux, 1970).

27. Robertson, *Crimes Against Humanity*, p. 249. Also see Diane F. Orentlicher, "Settling Accounts: The Duty to Prosecute Human Rights Violations of a Prior Regime," *Yale Law Journal*, No. 258, 1991.

28. Beginning in 1949, "Germany has enacted a number of laws providing compensation for people who suffered persecution at the hands of the Nazis. Over the course of its forty year-plus compensation program, these laws have resulted in billions of dollars being paid to hundreds of thousands of individuals"; United States Department of Justice, Foreign Claims Settlement Commission, "German Compensation for National Socialist Crimes: March 8, 1996," in Roy L. Brooks, ed., *When Sorry Isn't Enough: The Controversy over Apologies for Human Injustice* (New York: New York University Press, 1999) pp. 61–67. On problems, see Hubert Kim, "German Reparations: Industrialized Insufficiency," in Brooks, *Sorry Isn't Enough*, pp. 77–80.

29. Aside from the German trials mentioned in conjunction with note 27, the sole example of a domestic court evoking international law in the prosecution of its own officials occurred with Romania's 1991 trial of former dictator Nicolae Ceausescu and his wife, Elena, on the charge of genocide (several members of the Ceausescu regime were also convicted of complicity in the crime). Unfortunately, the procedures used in adjudicating these cases left much to be desired; Robertson, *Crimes Against Humanity*, p. 277.

30. See Jonathan B. Tucker, ed., *Toxic Terror: Assessing Terrorist Use of Chemical and Biological Weapons* (Cambridge, MA: MIT Press, 2000).

31. The best overview is provided in Noam Chomsky's *The Fateful Triangle: The United States, Israel and the Palestinians* (Cambridge, MA: South End Press, [classics ed.] 1999).

32. Noam Chomsky, "East Timor Retrospective," in his *Rogue States*, pp. 51–61.

33. Stephen Schlesinger and Stephen Kinzer, *Bitter Fruit: The Untold Story of the American Coup in Guatemala* (Garden City, NY: Doubleday, 1982); Ricardo Falla, *Massacres in the Jungle: Ixcán, Guatemala, 1975-1982* (Boulder, CO: Westview Press, 1994).

34. This concerns the extermination of up to a million "communists" in the wake of Suharto's U.S.-supported 1965 coup; Noam Chomsky and Edward S. Herman, *The Political Economy of Human Rights, Vol. 1: The Washington Connection and Third World Fascism* (Boston: South End Press, 1979) pp. 205–9.

35. Ibid. Also see A.J. Languuth, *Hidden Terrors: The Truth About U.S. Police Operations in Latin America* (New York: Pantheon, 1978); Martha K. Huggins, *Political Policing: The United States and Latin America* (Durham, NC: Duke University Press, 1998).

36. About 3 million dead; H. Bruce Franklin, *Vietnam and Other American Fantasies* (Amherst: University of Massachusetts Press, 2000) p. 111.

37. I.F. Stone, *The Hidden History of the Korean War, 1950–51* (Boston: Little, Brown, [2nd ed.] 1988); Charles J. Hanley, Sang-Hun Choe and Martha Mendoza, *The Bridge at No Gun Ri: A Hidden Nightmare from the Korean War* (New York: Henry Holt, 2001).

38. Against Germany, with the exception of its participation in the notorious 1945 incendiary attack on Dresden, the U.S. restricted itself to daylight "precision" bombing raids using high explosives, its stated objective being to avoid unnecessary civilian deaths. Against Japan—about which U.S. officials openly announced their desire to precipitate "extermination of the Japanese people in toto"—the preferred method was nocturnal saturation bombing by masses of aircraft dropping incendiaries to create "firestorms" in which vast numbers of noncombatants were deliberately cremated. During the great Tokyo fire raid of March 9–10, 1945, to give but one example, more than 267,000 buildings were destroyed, a million people rendered homeless, and upwards of 100,000 burned alive. Under such conditions, more "innocent civilians"—to use the currently popular American catch-phrase— were killed in only six months than among all branches of the Japanese military during the entirety of World War II; H. Bruce Franklin, *Star Wars: The Superweapon and the American Imagination* (New York: Oxford University Press, 1988) pp. 107–11. The public statement by U.S. War Manpower

Commissioner Paul V. McNutt is quoted by John W. Dower, *War Without Mercy: Race and Power in the Pacific* (New York: Pantheon, 1986) p. 55.

39. Stuart Creighton Miller, *"Benevolent Assimilation": The American Conquest of the Philippines, 1899–1903* (New Haven, CT: Yale University Press, 1982).

40. David Eltis and David Richardson, eds., *Routes to Slavery: Direction, Ethnicity and Mortality in the Transatlantic Slave Trade* (London: Frank Cass, 1997).

41. Matthew J. Mancini, *One Dies, Get Another: Convict Leasing in the American South, 1866–1928* (Columbia: University of South Carolina Press, 1996); David M. Oshinsky, *"Worse Than Slavery": Parchman Farm and the Ordeal of Jim Crow Justice* (New York: Free Press, 1996); Alex Lichtenstein, *Twice the Work of Free Labor: The Political Economy of Convict Labor in the New South* (London: Verso, 1996).

42. Stewart Emory Tolnay, *A Festival of Violence: An Analysis of the Lynching of African Americans in the American South, 1882–1930* (Urbana: University of Illinois Press, 1995); Ralph Ginzberg, *100 Years of Lynchings* (Baltimore: Black Classics Press, 1997).

43. Ronald Takaki, *Strangers from a Different Shore: A History of Asian Americans* (Boston: Little, Brown, 1989), pp. 80–87, 130, 240; Suchen Chan, *Asian Americans: An Interpretive History* (New York: Twayne, 1991) pp. 28–32.

44. Rodolfo Acuña, *Occupied America: A History of the Chicanos* (New York: Longman, 2000) esp. pp. 350–55, 400–10.

45. "Our wealth has always generated our poverty by nourishing the prosperity of others—the empires and their native overseers"; Eduardo Galeano, *Open Veins of Latin America: Five Centuries of the Pillage of a Continent* (New York: Monthly Review Press, 1973) p. 12. More broadly, see Paul Harrison, *Inside the Third World: The Anatomy of Poverty* (New York: Penguin, 1993); Peter L. Hahn and Mary Ann Heiss, eds., *Empire and Revolution: The United States and the Third World since 1945* (Columbus: Ohio State University Press, 2001).

46. For insights, see Michel-Rolph Trouillot, *Silencing the Past: Power and the Production of History* (Boston: Beacon Press, 1995). Also see Léon Wurmser, "Cultural Paradigms of Denial," and Rafael Moses, "Denial in Political Process," in Edelstein, Nathanson and Stone, *Denial*, pp. 277–86, 287–97.

47. Since 9-1-1, the two words have become so fused in the public discourse that the pairing is routinely employed to describe even fatalities among U.S. combat personnel. Although extreme, the situation is hardly new; see the chapter entitled "The Triumph of American Innocence" in Creighton-Miller, *"Benevolent Assimilation"*, pp. 253–67. Suffice it here to observe that relatively few of those killed on 9-1-1 itself could by any reasonable definition be thus described; for explication, see Hannah Arendt, *Eichmann in Jerusalem: A Report on the Banality of Evil* (New York: Viking, 1963); Bernard J. Bergen, *The Banality of Evil* (Lanham, MD: Rowman & Littlefield, 1998). Given the terms of engagement the U.S. has imposed upon the world, moreover, there is very little basis for *American* complaint even with respect to those who *could be* considered innocent.

48. See, e.g., Frederick Merk *Manifest Destiny and Mission in American History: A Reinterpretation* (New York: Alfred A. Knopf, 1963); Frank Parella, *Lebensraum and Manifest Destiny: A Comparative Study in the Justification of Expansionism* (Washington, D.C.: M.A. Thesis, Dept. of International Affairs, Georgetown University, 1950).

49. On U.S. presumptions of "world leadership," see Phyllis Bennis, *Calling the Shots: How Washington Dominates Today's U.N.* (New York: Olive Branch Press, 2000).

50. The phrase is taken from the title of James McGregor Burns' *The American Experiment*, 3 vols. (New York: Alfred A. Knopf, 1983–86).

51. With only minor modification, this is the question posed by Sartre in his *Search for a Method* (New York: Alfred A. Knopf, 1963). He was of course following upon Marx's famous observation that the point of philosophy is not simply to interpret the world but to change it; Karl Marx, *The German Ideology* (New York: New World, 1963) p. 197.

52. Howard Zinn, *A People's History of the United States* (New York: HarperPerennial, 1980);

Samuel Eliot Morison, *The Oxford History of the American People* (New York: Oxford University Press, 1965).

53. This is the classical marxist approach to historiography; see Perry Anderson, *In the Tracks of Historical Materialism* (Chicago: University of Chicago Press, 1984).

54. A neomarxian approach, the principles are set forth in Max Weber's *Economy and Society: An Outline of Interpretive Sociology* (New York: Bedminister, 1968). The term achieved its greatest prominence in the "intentionalist/functionalist debate" during the so-called *Historikerstreit* (historians' conflict) during the 1980s in Germany; Charles S. Maier, *The Unmasterable Past: History, Holocaust, and German National Identity* (Cambridge, MA: Harvard University Press, 1988) esp. p. 95.

55. Another marxist adaptation, the leading proponent of structuralist historiography was Louis Althusser, who proclaimed Marx to have discovered the "continent" of history; Louis Althusser, "Lenin and Philosophy," in his *Lenin and Philosophy* (New York: Monthly Review Press, 1971) esp. pp. 23–70. For further background, see Richard De George and Fernand De George, *The Structuralists: From Marx to Lévi-Strauss* (New York: Anchor Books, 1972).

56. See, e.g., Fredric Jameson's "aggressive reassertion of hermeneutics as an allegorical act of textual rewriting which reorganizes texts and their social histories within the unity of a narrative form that recuperates the 'truth' of the historical past," in his *Political Unconscious: Narrative as Socially Symbolic Act* (Ithaca, NY: Cornell University Press, 1981) pp. 19–49. Also see Paul Ricouer, *The Reality of the Historical Past* (Milwaukee: Marquette University Press, 1984).

57. Christopher Norris, *Deconstruction: Theory and Practice* (London: Methuen, 1982); Derek Attridge, Geoff Bennington and Robert Young, eds., *Post-Structuralism: The Question of History* (Cambridge, U.K.: Cambridge University Press, 1987).

58. Gayatri Chakravorty Spivak and Ranagit Guha, eds., *Selected Subaltern Studies* (New York: Oxford University Press, 1988). More broadly, see Bart Moore-Gilbert, *Postcolonial Theory: Contexts, Practices, Politics* (London: Verso, 1997).

59. For an excellent survey of the thinking of leading practitioners in most of the areas mentioned, see Henry Ablove, Betsy Blackmar, Peter Dimock and Jonathan Schneer, eds., *Visions of History: Interviews with E.P. Thompson, Eric Hobsbaum, Sheila Robothom, Linda Gordon, Natalie Zemon Davis, William Appleman Williams, Staughton Lynd, David Montgomery, Herbert Gutman, Vincent Harding, John Womack, C.L.R. James and Moshe Lewin* (New York: Pantheon, 1983).

60. See the chapter entitled "Histories" in Terry Eagleton's *The Illusions of Postmodernism* (Oxford, U.K.: Blackwell, 1996) pp. 45–68. Also see Arif Dirlik, *The Postcolonial Aura: Third World Criticism in the Age of Global Capitalism* (Boulder, CO: Westview Press, 1997) esp. pp. 165–71.

61. For background, see Hayden V. White, *Metahistory: The Historical Imagination in Nineteenth Century Europe* (Baltimore: Johns Hopkins University Press, 1973). For critique, see the chapter entitled "W(h)ither History" in Julian Pefanis' *Heterology and the Postmodern: Bataille, Baudrillard, and Lyotard* (Durham, NC: Duke University Press, 1991) pp. 9–20.

62. Michel Foucault, *The Archaeology of Knowledge* (New York: Pantheon, 1971). For explication of Foucault's reliance upon Nietzsche's notion of "genealogy," see Mark Poster, *Foucault, Marxism, History: Mode of Production versus Mode of Information* (Cambridge, U.K.: Polity Press, 1984) pp. 8–9, 64–65, 159.

63. Friedrich Nietzsche, *The Use and Abuse of History* (New York: Bobbs-Merrill, 1957); *The Genealogy of Morals* (New York: Vintage, 1967).

64. Poster, *Foucault, Marxism and History*, p. 96.

65. Ibid., p. 159.

66. The method here is "to confront the existent, in its historical context, with the claim of its historical principles, in order to realize the relationship between the two and transcend them"; Max Horkheimer, *The Eclipse of Reason*, quoted in Paul Z. Simmons, "Afterword: Commentary on Form and Content in *Elements of Refusal*," in John Zerzan, *Elements of Refusal* (New York: C.A.L. Press/Paleo Editions, [2nd ed.] 1999) p. 266.

67. Poster, *Foucault, Marxism and History*, p. 159. Although his method is quite different from

Gramsci's, Foucault's goals are categorically counterhegemonic in a Gramscian sense; see Walter L. Adamson, *Hegemony and Revolution: A Study of Antonio Gramsci's Political and Cultural Theory* (Berkeley: University of California Press, 1980) pp. 170–79.

68. See generally, Francis Jennings, *The Invasion of America: Indians, Colonialism and the Cant of Conquest* (New York: W.W. Norton, 1975); Ian K. Steele, *Warpaths: Invasions of North America* (New York: Oxford University Press, 1994).

69. The matter is put very well by Vine Deloria, Jr., in his "Foreword: American Fantasy," in Gretchen M. Bataille and Charles L.P. Silet, eds., *The Pretend Indians: Images of Native Americans in the Movies* (Ames: Iowa State University Press, 1980) pp. ix–xvi.

70. This theme is developed by Tzvetan Todorov in his *The Conquest of America: The Question of the Other* (New York: Harper & Row, 1984).

71. To do otherwise is either to pretend that Others do not exist—not, for the most part, a viable option—or to interpret them as inferior/exotic versions of one's self. Not only does the latter serve as a pretext for discounting their humanity, and thus as a justification of their ill-treatment, it necessarily precipitates distortions in the interpreter's self-concept. "Just as a people that oppresses another cannot be free, so a culture that is mistaken about another must also be mistaken about itself"; Jean Baudrillard, *The Mirror of Production* (St. Louis: Telos Press, 1975), p. 107. Also see Deborah Gewertz and Frederick Errington, "We Think, Therefore They Are? On Occidentalizing the World," in Amy Kaplan and Donald Pease, eds., *Cultures of United States Imperialism* (Durham, NC: Duke University Press, 1993) pp. 635–55.

72. For a partial view of what is intended here, see Robert Jay Lifton and Eric Markusen, *The Genocidal Mentality: Nazi Holocaust and Nuclear Threat* (New York: Basic Books, 1990).

73. Jaspers, *Question of German Guilt*, pp. 28, 64.

74. "Let's Spread the Fun Around" was originally prepared for the *Rocky Mountain News*, in Denver, but rejected by editor of the editorial page Vincent Carroll on the grounds that it did not meet that paper's lofty standards. It has since become the most reprinted piece on its topic ever written and was selected as one of the best short nonfiction expositions produced in the U.S. during the 1990s; see Ward Churchill, "The Indian Chant and the Tomahawk Chop," in Rise B. Axelrod and Charles R. Cooper, eds., *The St. Martin's Guide to Writing* (New York: St. Martin's Press, 1997).

75. Having said this, it should be noted that I absolutely reject Homi K. Bhabha's "exorbitation of discourse" at the expense of other modes of liberatory struggle; Moore-Gilbert, *Postcolonial Theory*, p. 138. At issue is Bhabha's (mis)reading of Frantz Fanon, most notably in his "Interrogating identity: Frantz Fanon and the postcolonial prerogative," in his *The Location of Culture* (New York: Routledge, 1994) pp. 40–65; "Remembering Fanon: Self, Psyche, and the Colonial Condition," Nigel Gibson, *Rethinking Fanon: The Continuing Dialogue* (New York: Humanity Books, 1999) pp. 179–98.

76. Chief Justice of the Supreme Court John Marshall, following John Adams, enshrined this bit of nonsense in U.S. jurisprudence in his 1803 *Marbury* opinion (1 Cranch. (5 U.S.) 137). For analysis, see the chapter entitled "It's the Law" in Rodolfo Acuña's *Sometimes There Is No Other Side: Chicanos and the Myth of Equality* (Notre Dame, IN: Notre Dame University Press, 1998) pp. 33–56.

77. See, e.g., Bruce Wright, *Black Robes, White Justice: Why Our Legal System Doesn't Work for Blacks* (New York: Lyle Stuart, 1990).

78. At the level of high theory, see James L. Marsh, *Unjust Legality: A Critique of Habermas's Law* (Lanham, MD: Rowman & Littlefield, 2001).

79. For a wealth of information in these connections, see Robert Justin Goldstein, *Political Repression in Modern America, 1870 to the Present* (Cambridge/New York: Schenkman/Two Continents, 1978).

80. Streicher was charged only as an "anti-Semitic agitator," and that the "core of the case against [him] came down to a question of whether he had advocated and encouraged extermination of the Jews while knowing, or having reason to believe, that such extermination was the settled policy of the Nazi government"; Bradley F. Smith, *Reaching Judgment at Nuremberg* (New York: Basic Books, 1977) pp. 200–1.

81. For analysis, see Richard Delgado and Jean Stefancic, *Must We Defend Nazis? Hate Speech, Pornography, and the New First Amendment* (New York: New York University Press, 1997).

1. "THE LAW STOOD SQUARELY ON ITS HEAD"

1. The texts of 371 ratified treaties are compiled by Charles J. Kappler in his *Indian Treaties, 1778–1885* (New York: Interland, 1973). Another 30 ratified treaty texts, as well as the texts of 400 additional treaties, all of them unratified but many purportedly forming the basis for U.S. assertions of title to particular chunks of territory, will be found in Vine Deloria, Jr., and Raymond J. DeMallie, eds., *Documents of American Indian Diplomacy: Treaties, Agreements and Conventions, 1775–1979*, 2 vols. (Norman: University of Oklahoma Press, 1999). On the pattern of U.S. treaty violations, see Vine Deloria, Jr., *Behind the Trail of Broken Treaties: An Indian Declaration of Independence* (Austin: University of Texas Press, [2nd. ed.] 1984).

2. The customary law from which this principle is adduced is codified in the Vienna Convention on the Law of Treaties (U.N. Doc. A/CONF.39/27 at 289 (1969), 1155 U.N.T.S. 331, reprinted in 8 I.L.M. 679 (1969)); the full text is included in Burns H. Weston, Richard A. Falk and Anthony D'Amato, eds., *Basic Documents in International Law and World Order* (St. Paul, MN: West, 1990) pp. 93–107. For analysis, see Sir Ian Sinclair, *The Vienna Convention on the Law of Treaties* (Manchester, U.K.: Manchester University Press, 1984) pp. 1–21. For further amplification of the fact that the customary principles set forth in the Vienna Convention were very much in effect at the time U.S. Indian treaties were negotiated, see Samuel Benjamin Crandell, *Treaties: Their Making and Enforcement* (New York: Columbia University Press, [2nd. ed.] 1916).

3. For background on Garment, see Paul Chaat Smith and Robert Allen Warrior, *Like a Hurricane: The American Indian Movement from Alcatraz to Wounded Knee* (New York: Free Press, 1996) pp. 164–65, 174.

4. For a succinct overview of the series of opinions involved, see Jill Norgren, *The Cherokee Cases: The Confrontation of Law and Politics* (New York: McGraw-Hill, 1996).

5. *Marbury v. Madison* (1 Cranch 137 (1803)). For analysis, see Jean Edward Smith, *John Marshall: Defender of a Nation* (New York: Henry Holt, 1996) pp. 309–26, quote at p. 325.

6. A prime example of this thesis will be found in Wilcomb E. Washburn's *Red Man's Land, White Man's Law: The Past and Present Status of the American Indian* (Norman: University of Oklahoma Press, [2nd ed.] 1995).

7. For use of the phrase employed here, see William Blum, *Rogue State: A Guide to the World's Only Superpower* (Monroe, ME: Common Courage Press, 2000).

8. One prefiguration came in 1066, when Pope Alexander II recognized the conquest of Saxon England, vesting underlying fee title to English land in the Norman King William; Carl Erdmann, *The Origin of the Idea of the Crusade* (Princeton, NJ: Princeton University Press, 1977) pp. 150–60. On the Innocentian Bulls, see Robert A. Williams, Jr., *The American Indian in Western Legal Thought: The Discourses of Conquest* (New York: Oxford University Press, 1990) pp. 43–49, 59–60, 64–67, 69–72.

9. Robert A. Williams, Jr., "The Medieval and Renaissance Origins of the Status of American Indians in Western Legal Thought," *Southern California Law Review*, Vol. 57, No. 1, 1983. Also see the opening chapter of Alfred Nussbaum's *A Concise History of the Laws of Nations* (New York: Macmillan, [rev. ed.] 1954); Herbert Andrew Deane, *The Political and Social Ideals of St. Augustine* (New York: Columbia University Press, 1963).

10. See, e.g., Tzvetan Todorov, *The Conquest of America: The Question of the Other* (New York: Harper & Row, 1984) pp. 146–67.

11. Probably the best and most detailed analysis of the debate will be found in Lewis Hanke's *Aristotle and the American Indian: A Study in Race Prejudice in the Modern World* (Chicago: Henry Regnery, 1959).

12. See generally, James Muldoon, *Popes, Lawyers and Infidels: The Church and the Non-Christian World, 1250–1550* (Philadelphia: University of Pennsylvania Press, 1979). Also see Lewis Hanke, *The*

Spanish Struggle for Justice in the Conquest of America (Philadelphia: University of Pennsylvania Press, 1947); Etienne Grisel, "The Beginnings of International Law and General Public Law Doctrine: Francisco de Vitoria's *De Indis prior,*" in Fredi Chiapelli, ed., *First Images of America,* 2 vols. (Berkeley: University of California Press, 1976) Vol. 1; John Taylor, *Spanish Law Concerning Discoveries, Pacifications, and Settlements Among the Indians* (Salt Lake City: University of Utah Press, 1980); L.C. Green and Olive P. Dickason, *The Law of Nations and the New World* (Edmonton: University of Alberta Press, 1989).

13. The original conception is covered in Antonio Truyol y Serra, "The Discovery of the New World and International Law," *University of Toledo Law Review,* No. 43, 1971.

14. See, Felix S. Cohen, "The Spanish Origin of Indian Rights in the United States," *Georgetown Law Journal,* Vol. 31, No. 1, 1942, and "Original Indian Title," *Minnesota Law Review,* No. 32, 1947. Also see Nell Jessup Newton, "At the Whim of the Sovereign: Aboriginal Title Reconsidered," *Hastings Law Journal,* No. 31, 1980; Brian Slattery, *Ancestral Lands, Alien Laws: Judicial Perspectives on Aboriginal Title* (Saskatoon: University of Saskatchewan Native Law Centre, 1983).

15. At least one scholar has contended that the arrangement was designed *only* to regulate relations between European states and carried no negative connotations vis-à-vis native standing at all; Milner S. Ball, "Constitution, Court, Indian Tribes," *American Bar Foundation Research Journal,* No. 1, 1987.

16. Editors, "United States Denial of Indian Property Rights: A Study of Lawless Power and Racial Discrimination," in National Lawyers Guild, Committee on Native American Struggles, *Rethinking Indian Law* (New Haven, CT: Advocate Press, 1982) p. 16. Such divvying up of turf amounted to a universalization of the principle expounded by Pope Alexander VI in his Bull *Inter Caetera* of May 4, 1493, dividing interests in the southern hemisphere of the New World between Spain and Portugal; Paul Gottschalk, *The Earliest Diplomatic Documents of America* (Albany: New York State Historical Society, 1978) p. 21.

17. Andrew A. Lipscomb and Albert Ellery Bergh, eds., *The Writings of Thomas Jefferson,* 20 vols. (Washington, D.C.: Thomas Jefferson Memorial Association, 1903–1904) Vol. VII, pp. 467–69.

18. Abundant examples will be found in Alden T. Vaughan, ed., *Early American Indian Documents: Treaties and Laws, 1607–1789* (Washington, D.C.: University Publications of America, 1979). For further analysis, see Dorothy V. Jones, *License for Empire: Colonialism by Treaty in North America* (Chicago: University of Chicago Press, 1982).

19. As the matter is put in the Vienna Convention on the Law of Treaties, "'treaty' means an international agreement concluded between States in written form and governed by international law"; Weston, Falk and D'Amato, *Basic Documents,* p. 93.

20. Quoted in Francis Paul Prucha, *American Indian Policy in the Formative Years: The Trade and Intercourse Acts, 1790–1834* (Lincoln: University of Nebraska Press, 1970) p. 141.

21. *Opinions of the Attorney General* (Washington, D.C.: U.S. GPO, 1828) pp. 613–18, 623–33. Later theorists, mainly positivists like Westlake and Hyde, argued that treaties with Indians and other "backward" peoples did not carry the same force and effect as treaties between "civilized" states; see, as examples, John Westlake, *Chapters on the Principles of International Law* (Cambridge, U.K.: Cambridge University Press, 1894) pp. 143–45; Charles C. Hyde, *International Law Chiefly as Interpreted by the United States* (Boston: Little, Brown, 1922) pp. 163–64. There is nothing in the interpretation of customary law codified in the Vienna Convention on the Law of Treaties to support such views, however.

22. In substance, where the English sought ultimately to displace or supplant indigenous peoples altogether, the French ambition was to harness modified versions of existing native economies to their own profit; see Hugh Edward Edgerton, *A Short History of British Colonial Policy* (London: Metheun, 1920) pp. 164–65; Klaus E. Knorr, *British Colonial Theories, 1570–1850* (London: Frank Cass, 1963) pp. 63–104. Also see Charles J. Balesi, *The Time of the French at the Heart of North America* (Chicago: Alliance Française, 1992).

23. Williams, *Western Legal Thought,* pp. 233–80. For broader philosophical applications, see

Crawford Brough Macpherson, *The Political Theory of Possessive Individualism: Hobbes to Locke* (Oxford, U.K.: Clarendon Press, 1962).

24. The idea has yielded a still-lingering effect. Its basic premise plainly underlay the 1862 Homestead Act (*U.S. Statutes at Large*, Vol. XII, at p. 392) by which any U.S. citizen could claim a quarter-section (160 acres) of "undeveloped" land, merely by paying a nominal "patent fee" to offset the expense of registering it. S/he then had a specified period of time, usually five years, to fell trees, build a house, plow fields, etc. If these requirements were met within the time allowed, the homesteader was issued a deed to the property. While it remains "on the books," claims under the Act were last pressed to a significant extent in Alaska during the 1960s and early 1970s.

25. Such reasoning formed a portion of the legal basis upon which England waged four wars— King William's War (1689–1697), Queen Anne's War (1702–1713), King George's War (1744–1748) and the "Seven Years' War," which actually lasted 14 years (1749–1763)—against the French in North America; Albert Marrin, *Struggle for a Continent: The French and Indian Wars, 1690–1760* (New York: Atheneum, 1987).

26. Alden T. Vaughan, *The New England Frontier* (Boston: Little, Brown, 1965) pp. 113–21.

27. Letter from the Massachusetts Bay Company to Governor John Endicott, Apr. 17, 1629, in N. Shurtleff, ed., *Records of the Governor and the Company of the Massachusetts Bay in New England* (Boston: William White, 1853) p. 231.

28. Rennard Strickland and Charles F. Wilkinson, eds., *Felix S. Cohen's Handbook on Federal Indian Law* (Charlottesville, VA: Michie, 1982) p. 55.

29. See James Thomas Flexner, *Lord of the Mohawks: A Biography of Sir William Johnson* (Boston: Little, Brown, 1979).

30. This was following England's final victory over France in the last of the so-called French and Indian Wars (see note 25). On the proclamation (RSC 1970, App. II, No. 1, at 127) and subsequent legislation, Jack Stagg, *Anglo-Indian Relations in North America to 1763 and an Analysis of the Royal Proclamation of 7 October 1763* (Ottawa: Carlton University Press, 1981). Also see Bruce Clark, *Native Liberty, Crown Sovereignty: The Existing Aboriginal Right of Self-Government in Canada* (Montréal: McGill-Queens University Press, 1990) pp. 134–46.

31. Thomas Perkins Abernathy, *Western Lands and the American Revolution* (New York: Russell and Russell, 1959).

32. The complete text of the Treaty of Paris (Sept. 3, 1783) is included in Ruhl J. Bartlett, ed., *The Record of American Diplomacy: Documents and Readings in the History of U.S. Foreign Relations* (New York: Alfred A. Knopf, [4th ed.] 1964) pp. 39–42.

33. For the text of the Treaty Between the United States and France for the Cession of Louisiana (Apr. 30, 1803), see Bartlett, *American Diplomacy*, pp. 116–17. On similar acquisitions, see generally, David M. Pelcher, *The Diplomacy of Annexation: Texas, Oregon and the Mexican War* (Columbia: University of Missouri Press, 1973).

34. Merrill D. Peterson, *Thomas Jefferson and the New Nation: A Biography* (New York: Oxford University Press, 1970) p. 300.

35. Vine Deloria, Jr., "Self-Determination and the Concept of Sovereignty," in Roxanne Dunbar Ortiz and Larry Emerson, eds., *Economic Development in American Indian Reservations* (Albuquerque: University of New Mexico Native American Studies Center, 1979) pp. 22–28. See note 5 and accompanying text for an example of hyperlegal posturing.

36. This concerns a written plan submitted to the Congress in which the "Father of His Country" recommended using treaties with Indians in much the same fashion Hitler would later employ them against his adversaries at Munich and elsewhere (i.e., to lull them into a false sense of security or complacency which placed them at a distinct military disadvantage when it came time to confront them with a war of aggression). "Apart from the fact that it was immoral, unethical and actually criminal, this plan placed before Congress by Washington was so logical and well laid out that it was immediately accepted practically without opposition and immediately put into action. There might be— certainly *would* be—further strife with the Indians, new battles and new wars, but the end result was,

with the adoption of Washington's plan, inevitable: Without even realizing it had occurred, the fate of all the Indians in the country was sealed. They had lost virtually everything"; Allan W. Eckert, *That Dark and Bloody River: Chronicles of the Ohio River Valley* (New York: Bantam, 1995) p. 440.

37. 1 Stat. 50. (1789). For background, see Francis Paul Prucha, *American Indian Policy in the Formative Years: The Trade and Intercourse Acts, 1790–1834* (Lincoln: University of Nebraska Press, 1970).

38. As the indigenous population was steadily eroded by disease and ad hoc attritional warfare all along the frontier, plummeting to only a few hundred thousand by 1812, the U.S. population had swelled to 7.5 million. While the U.S. could field 12,000 regulars and at least 4 times as many militiamen, even the broad alliance attempted by Tecumseh figured to muster fewer than 5,000 fighters in response. For U.S. population data, see *Niles Register*, No. 1, Nov. 30, 1811. On native population size, see Henry F. Dobyns, *Their Numbers Become Thinned: Native American Population Dynamics in Eastern North America* (Knoxville: University of Tennessee Press, 1983). On U.S. troop strength, see J.C.A. Stagg, "Enlisted Men in the United States Army, 1812–1815: A Preliminary Survey," *William and Mary Quarterly*, 3rd Ser., No. 43, 1986. On Tecumseh's alliance, see Allan W. Eckert, *A Sorrow in Our Heart: The Life of Tecumseh* (Boston: Little, Brown, 1992).

39. 10 U.S. (6 Cranch.) 87 (1810). To all appearances, the opinion was an expedient meant to facilitate redemption of scrip issued to troops during the American independence struggle in lieu of cash. These vouchers were to be exchanged for land parcels in Indian Country once victory had been achieved. (Marshall and his father received instruments entitling them to 10,000 acres apiece in what is now Kentucky, part of the more than 200,000 acres they jointly amassed there.) On the Marshalls' Kentucky land transactions, see Jean Edward Smith, *John Marshall: Definer of a Nation* (New York: Henry Holt, 1996) pp. 74–75. On the case itself, see C. Peter McGrath, *Yazoo: The Case of Fletcher v. Peck* (New York: W.W. Norton, 1966).

40. Robert A. Williams, Jr., "Jefferson, the Norman Yoke, and American Indian Lands," *Arizona Law Review*, Vol. 29, No. 3, 1987. The notion that the concept of *terra nullius* might ever have been applied in any legitimate sense to inhabited areas was firmly repudiated by the International Court of Justice ("World Court") in its 1975 *Advisory Opinion on Western Sahara*. For analysis, see Robert Vance, "Questions Concerning Western Sahara: Advisory Opinion of the International Court of Justice, October 16, 1975," *International Lawyer*, No. 10, 1976; "Sovereignty Over Unoccupied Territories: The Western Sahara Decision," *Case Western Reserve Journal of International Law*, No. 9, 1977.

41. See generally, Reginald Horsman, *Expansion and American Policy, 1783–1812* (Lansing: Michigan State University Press, 1967).

42. *Johnson & Graham's Lessee v. McIntosh* (21 U.S. (8 Wheat.) 543 (1823)). For background, see Norgren, *Cherokee Cases*, pp. 92–95; David E. Wilkins, *American Indian Sovereignty and the U.S. Supreme Court* (Austin: University of Texas Press, 1997) pp. 27–35.

43. "The United States . . . maintain, as all others have maintained, that discovery gave an exclusive right to extinguish the Indian title of occupancy, either by purchase or by conquest; and gave also a right to such degree of sovereignty as the circumstances of [the U.S. itself] allow [it] to exercise"; *Johnson v. McIntosh* at 587.

44. "It has never been contended that the Indian title amounted to nothing. Their right of possession has never been questioned. The claim of government extends [however] to the complete ultimate [or absolute] title . . . An absolute [title] must be an exclusive title, a title which excludes all others not compatible with it. All our institutions recognize the absolute title of the crown [now held by the U.S.], subject only to the Indian right of occupancy, [a matter] incompatible with an absolute and complete title in the Indians"; *Johnson v. McIntosh* at 588, 603.

45. *Johnson v. McIntosh* at 573, 587, 591.

46. *Johnson v. McIntosh* at 591. For further analyses, see Howard R. Berman, "The Concept of Aboriginal Rights in the Early History of the United States," *Buffalo Law Review*, No. 27, 1978; Robert A. Williams, Jr., "The Algebra of Federal Indian Law: The Hard Trail of Decolonizing the White Man's Jurisprudence," *Wisconsin Law Review*, No. 31, 1986; David E. Wilkins, "*Johnson v.*

McIntosh Revisited: Through the Eyes of *Mitchell v. United States*," *American Indian Law Review*, No. 19, 1994.

47. Williams, *Western Legal Thought*, p. 317.

48. *Cherokee Nation v. The State of Georgia* (30 U.S. (5 Pet.) 1 (1831)) and *Worcester v. The State of Georgia* 31 U.S. (6 Pet.) 551 (1832). For background, see Norgren, *Cherokee Cases*, pp. 98–111, 114–22.

49. *Cherokee v. Georgia* at 16.

50. Ibid., at 17.

51. Ibid.

52. *Worcester v. Georgia* at 560–61.

53. There are numerous examples of this being so; see Vine Deloria, Jr., "The Size and Status of Nations," in Susan Lobo and Steve Talbot, eds., *Native American Voices: A Reader* (New York: Longman, 1998) pp. 457–65.

54. *Cherokee v. Georgia* at 16.

55. Joining Marshall was Justice John McLean; Norgren, *Cherokee Cases*, p. 100.

56. Ibid., pp. 106–7.

57. Thompson wrote the dissent, Story endorsing it; Joseph C. Burke, "The Cherokee Cases: A Study in Law, Politics, and Morality," *Stanford Law Review*, No. 21, 1969, pp. 516–18.

58. *Cherokee v. Georgia* at 55.

58. Norgren, *Cherokee Cases*, pp. 117, 120–21.

60. *Worcester v. Georgia* at 553–54.

61. Ibid., at 551–56.

62. "Indian tribes are still recognized as sovereigns by the United States, but they are deprived of the one power all sovereigns must have in order to function effectively—the power to say 'no' to other sovereigns"; Vine Deloria, Jr., and David E. Wilkins, *Tribes, Treaties, and Constitutional Tribulations* (Austin: University of Texas Press, 1999) p. 70.

63. Ibid., p. 29.

64. This was carried out under provision of the 1887 General Allotment Act (ch. 119, 24 Stat. 362, 385, now codified at 18 U.S.C. 331 *et seq.*). For historical overview, see Janet A. McDonnell, *The Dispossession of the American Indian, 1887–1934* (Bloomington: Indiana University Press, 1991). For legal background, see Sidney L. Harring, *Crow Dog's Case: American Indian Sovereignty, Tribal Law, and United States Law in the Nineteenth Century* (Cambridge, U.K.: Cambridge University Press, 1994) pp. 142–74.

65. "The sun-dance, and all other similar dances and so-called religious ceremonies are considered 'Indian Offenses' under existing regulations, and corrective penalties are provided"; U.S. Department of Interior, Office of Indian Affairs Circular 1665, Apr. 26, 1921.

66. See generally, David Wallace Adams, *Education for Extinction: American Indians and the Boarding School Experience, 1875–1928* (Lawrence: University Press of Kansas, 1995).

67. Article II(c) of the 1948 Convention on Prevention and Punishment of the Crime of Genocide (78 U.N.T.S. 277), outlaws as genocidal any policy leading to the "destruction . . . in whole or in part, [of] a national, ethnical, racial or religious group, as such." Article II(e) specifically prohibits any policy devolving upon the "forced transfer of children"; Weston, Falk and D'Amato, *Basic Documents*, p. 297.

68. For details, see Charles C. Royce, *Indian Land Cessions in the United States: 18th Annual Report, 1896–97*, 2 vols. (Washington, D.C.: Bureau of American Ethnography, Smithsonian Institution, 1899).

69. The implications of the term, first employed by the Marshall Court in *Gibbons v. Ogden* (22 U.S. (9 Wheat.) 1 (1824), were set forth more fully in *U.S. v. Kagama* (118 U.S. 375 (1886)), and finalized in *"Lone Wolf" v. Hitchcock* (187 U.S. 553 (1903)). In the latter case, Justice Edward D. White opined that "Congress possesse[s] full power over Indian affairs, and the judiciary cannot question or inquire into its motives . . . If injury [is] occasioned . . . by the use made by Congress of

its power, relief must be sought by an appeal to that body for redress and not to the courts"; *"Lone Wolf" v. Hitchcock* at 568. By 1942, the courts were even more blunt, stating that Congress wielded "full, entire, complete, absolute, perfect, and unqualified" power over indigenous nations within its borders; *Mashunkasky v. Mashunkasky* (134 P.2d 976 (1942)). For background, see Nell Jessup Newton, "Federal Power over Indians: Its Sources, Scope, and Limitations," *University of Pennsylvania Law Review*, No. 132, 1984; Rachel San Kronowitz, Joanne Lichtman, Stephen P. McSloy and Matthew G. Olsen, "Toward Consent and Cooperation: Reconsidering the Political Status of Indian Nations," *Harvard Civil Rights-Civil Liberties Law Review*, No. 22, 1987; David E. Wilkins, "The Supreme Court's Explication of 'Federal Plenary Power': An Analysis of Case Law Affecting Tribal Sovereignty, 1886–1914," *American Indian Quarterly*, Vol. 18, No. 3, 1994.

70. A territorial title deriving from discovery cannot prevail over a title based in a prior and continuing display of sovereignty; *American Journal of International Law*, No. 22, 1928, reporting the *Island of Palmas* case (*U.S. v. Netherlands*, Perm. Ct. Arb., Hague, 1928).

71. Chapter XI of the U.N. Charter (59 Stat. 1031, T.S. No. 993, 3 Bevans 1153, Y.B.U.N. 1043 (1945)), and the full text of the Declaration (U.N.G.A. Res. 1514 (XV), 15 U.N. GAOR, Supp. (No. 16) 66, U.N. Doc. A/4684 (1961)); Weston, Falk and D'Amato, *Basic Documents*, pp. 27, 343–44.

72. See generally, Alpheus Snow, *The Question of Aborigines in the Law and Practice of Nations* (Northbrook, IL: Metro Books, 1972 reprint of 1918 original); Mark Frank Lindley, *The Acquisition and Government of Backward Territory in International Law: A Treatise on the Law and Practice Related to Colonial Expansion* (London: Longmans, Green, 1926). On the material process leading to repudiation, see Stewart C. Easton, *The Rise and Fall of Western Colonialism: A Historical Survey from the Early Nineteenth Century to the Present* (New York: Praeger, 1964); Franz Ansprenger, *The Dissolution of Colonial Empires* (New York: Routledge, 1981).

73. For a broad exploration of the concept, see Michael Walzer, *Just and Unjust Wars: A Moral Argument with Historical Illustrations* (London: Allen Lane, 1978).

74. See note 37.

75. Franciscus de Vitoria, "De Indis Recenter Inventis," in his *De Indis et de Jure Belli Reflectiones* (Washington, D.C.: Carnegie Institution of Washington, 1917), esp. pp. 151–55; Jorge Díaz, "Los Doctrinas de Palacios Rubios y Matías de Paz ante la Conquista America," in *Memoria de El Colegio Nacional* (Burgos, Spain: Colegio Nacional, 1950). For background, see Williams, *Western Legal Thought*, pp. 85–108.

76. Matthew M. McMahon, *Conquest and Modern International Law: The Legal Limitations on the Acquisition of Territory by Conquest* (Washington, D.C.: Catholic University of America Press, 1940), p. 35; Sharon Korman, *The Right of Conquest: The Acquisition by Force in International Law and Practice* (Oxford, U.K.: Clarendon Press, 1996) pp. 52–56.

77. On the present disposition of "federally recognized tribes," see Francis Paul Prucha, *Atlas of American Indian Affairs* (Lincoln: University of Nebraska Press, 1990). For the official count of "Indian Wars," see U.S. Department of Commerce, Bureau of the Census, *Report on Indians Taxed and Not Taxed (1890)* (Washington, D.C.: U.S. GPO, 1894) pp. 637–38. For details on the wars themselves, see Alan Axelrod, *Chronicle of the Indian Wars from Colonial Times to Wounded Knee* (New York: Prentice-Hall, 1993).

78. *Tee-Hit-Ton v. United States* (348 U.S.273 (1955)) at 291. "The Alaska natives [who had pressed a land claim in *Tee-Hit-Ton*] had never fought a skirmish with Russia [which claimed their territories before the U.S.] or the United States . . . To say that the Alaska natives were subjugated by conquest stretches the imagination too far. The only sovereign act that can be said to have conquered the Alaska native was the *Tee-Hit-Ton* opinion itself"; Jessup Newton, "Whim of the Sovereign," pp. 1215, 1244.

79. *Martin v. Waddell*, 41 U.S. (6 Pet.) 367 (1842) at 409; *Johnson v. McIntosh* at 591.

80. Samuel Pufendorf, *Elementorum Jurisprudentiae Universalis* (Oxford, U.K.: Clarendon Press, 1931 trans. of 1672 original); *De Officio Hominis et Civis Juxta Legem Naturalem* (Oxford, U.K.:

Clarendon Press, 1927 trans. of 1682 original); *De Jure Naturae et Gentium* (Oxford, U.K.: Clarendon Press, 1934 trans. of 1688 original).

81. See esp., Hugo Grotius, *De Jure Belli ac Pacis* (Oxford, U.K.: Clarendon Press, 1925 trans. of 1625 original); Emmerich de Vattel, *The Law of Nations* (Philadelphia: T. & J.W. Johnson, 1863 trans. of 1758 original); William Edward Hall, *A Treatise on International Law* (Oxford, U.K.: Clarendon Press, 1884); John Westlake, "The Nature and Extent of the Title by Conquest," *Legal Quarterly Review*, No. 17, 1901.

82. See generally, Julius W. Pratt, *The Imperialists of 1898: The Acquisition of Hawaii and the Spanish Islands* (Baltimore: Johns Hopkins University Press, 1936); Stuart Creighton Miller, *"Benevolent Assimilation": The American Conquest of the Philippines, 1899–1903* (New Haven, CT: Yale University Press, 1982); Noel J. Kent, *Hawaii: Islands Under the Influence* (Honolulu: University of Hawaii Press, [2nd ed.] 1993).

83. On Wilson's role and Senate obstruction, see Francis Anthony Boyle, *Foundations of World Order: The Legalist Approach to International Relations, 1898–1922* (Durham, NC: Duke University Press, 1999) pp. 47–48, 53–54.

84. For context, see Lothar Kotzsch, *The Concept of War in Contemporary History and International Law* (Geneva: Droz, 1956); Ian Brownlie, *International Law and the Use of Force by States* (Oxford, U.K.: Clarendon Press, 1963).

85. Korman, *Right of Conquest*, p. 192.

86. Stimson's statement will be found in U.S. Department of State, *Documents on International Affairs* (Washington, D.C.: U.S. GPO, 1932) p. 262. For discussion, see Robert Langer, *Seizure of Territory: The Stimson Doctrine and Related Principles in Legal Theory and Diplomatic Practice* (Princeton, NJ: Princeton University Press, 1947).

87. U.S. Dept. of State Press Release, No. 136 (7 May 1932), quoted in Henry W. Briggs, "Non-Recognition of Title by Conquest and Limitations of the Doctrine," *Papers of the American Society for International Law*, No. 34, 1940, p. 73. Also see Langer, *Seizure of Territory*.

88. Stimson, letter to Senator W.E. Borah (23 Feb. 1932), quoted in Briggs, "Non-Recognition," p. 73.

89. League Assembly Resolution (Mar. 11, 1932); Chaco Declaration (Aug. 3, 1932); Saaverda Lamas Pact (Oct. 10, 1933); Montevideo Convention (Dec. 26, 1933). For background, see Briggs, "Non-Recognition," esp. p. 74; Korman, *Right of Conquest*, pp. 240–41.

90. Quoted in Langer, *Seizure of Territory*, p. 78.

91. Quoted in Korman, *Right of Conquest*, pp. 241–42. Korman goes on to note that, in its 1945 Act of Chapultepec, the Inter-American Conference on Problems of War and Peace not only asserted non-recognition of conquest rights as customary law but declared that the principle of "non-recognition had been incorporated into the [black letter] international law of American States since 1890."

92. Bradley F. Smith, *The Road to Nuremberg* (New York: Basic Books, 1981); Arnold C. Brackman, *The Other Nuremberg: The Untold Story of the Tokyo War Crimes Trials* (New York: Quill/Morrow, 1987).

93. On the U.S. role in founding the United Nations, see Phyllis Bennis, *Calling the Shots: How Washington Controls Today's U.N.* (New York: Olive Branch Press, [2nd ed.] 2000) pp. 1–13. On the OAS, see Boyle, *World Order*, pp. 119–22. On the League, see F.P. Walters, *A History of the League of Nations* (New York: Oxford University Press, 1960).

94. As stated in Article 1(1) and (2) of the U.N. Charter, "The Purposes of the United Nations are [t]o maintain international peace and security [by] adjustment and settlement of international disputes or situations which might lead to a breach of the peace," mainly by developing "friendly relations among nations based on respect for the principle of equal rights and self-determination of peoples." Reference to "the principles of equal rights and self-determination of all peoples" is made in the earlier cited Declaration on the Granting of Independence to Colonial Countries and Peoples. Elsewhere, it is simply stated that "All peoples have the right to self-determination." See, as examples, Article 1(1) of the International Covenant on Economic, Social and Cultural Rights (U.N.G.A. Res. 2200 (XXI), 21

U.N. GAOR, Supp. (No. 16) 49, U.N. Doc. A/6316 (1967)) and Article 1(1) of the International Covenant on Civil and Political Rights (U.N.G.A. Res. 2200 (XXI), 21 U.N. GAOR, Supp. (No. 16) 52, U.N. Doc. A/6316 (1967)). Article 1 of the OAS Charter (2 U.S.T. 2394, T.I.A.S. No. 2361, 119 U.N.T.S. 3 (1948)), declares the organization to be "a regional agency" subject to provisions of the U.N. Charter, while Article 3(a) declares the elements of law promulgated by the U.N. to be binding upon all OAS member states; Weston, Falk and D'Amato, *Basic Documents*, pp. 16, 50, 343, 371, 376.

95. Hitler, for one, was quite clear that the nazi *lebensraumpolitik* was based, theoretically, practically, and quite directly, on the preexisting model embodied in the U.S. realization of its "manifest destiny" vis-à-vis American Indians and other racial/cultural "inferiors"; Adolf Hitler, *Mein Kampf* (New York: Reynal and Hitchcock, 1939) pp. 403, 591; *Hitler's Secret Book* (New York: Grove Press, 1961) pp. 46–52. Another iteration will be found in a memorandum prepared by an aide, Col. Friedrich Hössbach, summarizing Hitler's statements during a high-level "Führer Conference" conducted shortly before Germany's 1939 invasion of Poland; *Trial of the Major Nazi War Criminals Before the International Military Tribunal*, 42 vols. (Nuremberg: International Military Tribunal, 1947–49) Vol. 25, pp. 402–13. The relationship between nazi and U.S. theory/practice is closely examined in Frank Parella, *Lebensraum and Manifest Destiny: A Comparative Study in the Justification of Expansionism* (Washington, D.C.: Master's Thesis, School of International Relations, Georgetown University, 1950). Also see Norman Rich, *Hitler's War Aims: Ideology, the Nazi State, and the Course of Expansion* (New York: W.W. Norton, 1973) p. 8; John Toland, *Adolf Hitler* (New York: Doubleday, 1976) p. 802.

96. The most detailed overview of the ICC will be found in Harvey D. Rosenthal's *Their Day in Court: A History of the Indian Claims Commission* (New York: Garland, 1990). Also see pp. 66–69 of "The Earth Is Our Mother," herein.

97. *Public Papers of the Presidents of the United States: Harry S. Truman, 1946* (Washington, D.C.: U.S. GPO, 1962) p. 414.

98. All the ICC accomplished was to "clear out the underbrush" obscuring an accurate view of who actually owns what in North America; Deloria, *Broken Treaties*, p. 227. Also see my "Charades Anyone? The Indian Claims Commission in Context," *American Indian Culture and Research Journal*, Vol. 24, No. 1, Spring 2000.

99. U.S. House of Representatives, Committee on Indian Affairs, *Hearings on H.R. 1198 and 1341 to Create an Indian Claims Commission* (Washington, D.C.: 79th Cong., 1st Sess., March and June 1945) pp. 81–84.

100. Thomas LeDuc, "The Work of the Indian Claims Commission Under the Act of 1946," *Pacific Historical Review*, Vol. 26, No. 1, Feb. 1957; John T. Vance, "The Congressional Mandate and the Indian Claims Commission," *North Dakota Law Review*, No. 45, Spring 1969; Wilcomb E. Washburn, "Land Claims in the Mainstream of Indian/White Relations," in Imre Sutton, ed., *Irredeemable America: The Indians' Estate and Land Claims* (Albuquerque: University of New Mexico Press, 1985) pp. 21–34.

101. U.S. House of Representatives, Subcommittee of the Committee on Appropriations, *Hearings on the Independent Office Appropriations for 1952* (Washington, D.C.: 82nd Cong., 1st Sess., 1951) pp. 28–37.

102. U.S. Senate, Committee on Interior and Insular Affairs, *Amending the Indian Claims Commission Act of 1946 as Amended* (Washington, D.C.: 92nd Cong., 2nd Sess., Rpt. 682, Mar. 2, 1972).

103. The remaining 68 dockets were turned over to the U.S. Court of Claims; Russel Barsh, "Behind Land Claims: Rationalizing Dispossession in Anglo-American Law," *Law and Anthropology*, No. 1, 1986.

104. Howard Friedman, "Interest on Indian Land Claims: Judicial Protection of the Fisc," *Valparaiso University Law Review*, No. 5, Fall 1970; Robert F. Heizer and Alfred L. Kroeber, "For Sale: California at 47¢ Per Acre," *Journal of California Anthropology*, No. 3, 1976; M. Annette Jaimes, "The Pit River Indian Land Claim Dispute in Northern California," *Journal of Ethnic Studies*, Vol. 4, No. 4, Winter 1987.

105. Indian Claims Commission, *Final Report* (Washington, D.C.: U.S. GPO, 1978); Public Lands Law Review Commission, *One Third of the Nation's Land* (Washington, D.C.: U.S. GPO, 1970).

106. Russel Barsh, "Indian Land Claims Policy in the United States," *North Dakota Law Review*, No. 58, 1982.

107. The territorial integrity of all member states is guaranteed in Chapter I, Article 2(4) of the U.N. Charter. The guarantee presupposes, however, that there was a degree of basic *legal* integrity involved in the territorial acquisitions by which member states composed themselves in the first place. In cases where this is not so, the rights to self-determination of involuntarily subordinated or usurped peoples *always* outweigh the right to preserve territorial integrity; see Lee C. Buchheit, *Secession: The Legitimacy of Self-Determination* (New Haven: Yale University Press, 1978); Ved Nanda, "Self-Determination Under International Law: Validity of Claims to Secede," *Case Western Journal of International Law*, No. 13, 1981.

108. On international torts, see Eduardo Jiminez de Arechaga, "International Responsibility," in M. Sorenson, ed., *Manual of Public International Law* (New York: St. Martin's Press, 1968) pp. 564–72.

109. Treaty fraud, which is specifically prohibited under Article 49 of the Convention as a matter of *jus cogens*, has been defined by the International Law Commission (ILC) as including "any false statements, misrepresentations or other deceitful proceedings by which a State is induced to give consent to a treaty which it would not otherwise have given." Coercion, which is prohibited under Articles 51–52, also as a matter of *jus cogens*, involves "acts or threats" directed by one nation involved in a treaty negotiation against another (or its representative[s]). The ILC has concluded that "the invalidity of a treaty procured by the illegal threat or use of force is a principle which is *lex lata* in . . . international law," and that the nullity of treaties invalidated on this basis is absolute; Sinclair, *Vienna Convention*, pp. 14–16, 169–81.

110. Treaty with the Cheyennes and Arapahos (12 Stat. 1163; proc., Dec. 5, 1861); for text, see Kappler, *Indian Treaties*, pp. 807–11. For background, see Stan Hoig, *The Sand Creek Massacre* (Norman: University of Oklahoma Press, 1961) pp. 13–17.

111. The full text of the Treaty with the Sioux—Brulé, Oglala, Miniconjou, Yanktonai, Hunkpapa, Blackfeet, Cuthead, Two Kettle, Sans Arcs, and Santee—and Arapaho, 1868 (15 Stat. 635; proc., Feb. 24, 1869); for text, see Kappler, *Indian Treaties*, pp. 998-1007. On the "negotiation" process at issue, see the chapter entitled "Sell or Starve" in Edward Lazarus, *Black Hills, White Justice: The Sioux Nation versus the United States, 1775 to the Present* (New York: HarperCollins, 1991) pp. 71–95. Also see "The Earth Is Our Mother," herein, p. 87.

112. U.S. title was formally asserted in an Act (19 Stat. 254) passed by Congress on Feb. 28, 1877. It should be noted that while the express consent of three-quarters of all adult male Lakotas was required under Article 12 of the 1868 treaty for any future land alienations by that people to be legal, the signatures of barely 15 percent were obtained on the Black Hills cession agreement.

113. Also see the preliminary sketch included in my *Struggle for the Land: Native North American Resistance to Genocide, Ecocide and Colonization* (Winnipeg: Arbeiter Ring, [2nd ed.] 1999) p. 10.

114. For a related development of the thesis, see Rodolfo Acuña, *Occupied America: The Chicano's Struggle for Liberation* (San Francisco: Canfield Press, 1972).

115. See Robert K. Thomas, "Colonialism: Classic and Internal," *New University Thought*, Vol. 4, No. 4, Winter 1966–67; my own "Indigenous Peoples of the United States: A Struggle Against Internal Colonialism," *Black Scholar*, Vol. 16, No. 1, Feb. 1985; and Leah Renae Kelly's "The Open Veins of Native America: A Question of Internal Colonialism," in her *In My Own Voice: Essays in the Sociopolitical Context of Art and Cinema* (Winnipeg: Arbeiter Ring, 2001) pp. 112–15.

116. See Blum, *Rogue State*; Noam Chomsky, *Rogue States: The Rule of Force in World Affairs* (Cambridge, MA: South End Press, 2000).

117. As Justice Robert H. Jackson put it while serving as lead U.S. prosecutor at Nuremberg, "We are not prepared to lay down a rule of criminal conduct against others which we are not willing to

have invoked against us"; "Opening Statement for the United States before the International Military Tribunal, November 21, 1945," in Jay W. Baird, ed., *From Nuremberg to My Lai* (Lexington, MA: D.C. Heath, 1972) p. 28; also quoted in Bertrand Russell, *War Crimes in Vietnam* (New York: Monthly Review Press, 1967) p. 125. As concerns U.S. replication of the major offenses of which the nazis were convicted, see Quincy Wright, "Legal Aspects of the Vietnam Situation," in Richard Falk, ed., *The Vietnam War and International Law* (Princeton, NJ: Princeton University Press, 1968) pp. 271–91; Ralph Stavins, Richard J. Barnet and Marcus G. Raskin, *Washington Plans an Aggressive War* (New York: Random House, 1971).

118. Bush is quoted at length in George Cheney's "'Talking War': Symbols, Strategies and Images," *New Studies on the Left*, Vol. XIV, No. 3, Winter 1990–91. On the human toll ultimately extracted by the U.S. in its "roll back" of Iraq's "naked aggression"—which had, at most, resulted in the deaths of "several hundred" Kuwaitis—see Ramsey Clark, et al., *War Crimes: A Report on United States War Crimes Against Iraq* (Washington, D.C.: Maisonneuve Press, 1992); *The Impact of Sanctions on Iraq: The Children are Dying* (Washington, D.C.: Maisonneuve Press, 1996); *Challenge to Genocide: Let Iraq Live* (Washington, D.C.: International Action Center, 1998).

119. Noam Chomsky, "'What We Say Goes': The Middle East in the New World Order," in Cynthia Peters, ed., *Collateral Damage: The "New World Order" at Home and Abroad* (Boston: South End Press, 1992) pp. 49–92; *World Orders, Old and New* (New York: Columbia University Press, 1994). Also see the essays collected by Phyllis Bennis and Michael Moushabeck in their coedited volume, *Altered States: A Reader in the New World Order* (New York: Olive Branch Press/Interlink, 1993).

120. The U.S. formally repudiated the jurisdiction of the International Court of Justice in 1986, when the ICJ ruled against it in *Nicaragua v. U.S.*; Abraham Sofaer, "The United States and the World Court," *Current Affairs*, No. 769, Dec. 1985; "U.S. Terminates Acceptance of ICJ Compulsory Jurisdiction," *Department of State Bulletin*, No. 86, Jan. 1986. It has subsequently refused to accept jurisdiction of the newly established International Criminal Court (ICC), unless its policymakers and military personnel are specifically exempted from prosecution; Geoffrey Robertson, *Crimes Against Humanity: The Struggle for Global Justice* (New York: Free Press, 1999) pp. 446–48, 450. On the U.S. refusal of international law, per se, see Blum, *Rogue State*, pp. 184–99; Bennis, *Calling the Shots*, esp. pp. 279–82.

121. An in-depth study of this process at work will be found in Lawrence J. LeBlanc's *The United States and the Genocide Convention* (Durham, NC: Duke University Press, 1991).

122. Article I(2) of the so-called Sovereignty Package (S. Exec. Rep. 2, 99th Cong., 1st Sess., 1985) attached to its much-belated 1988 "ratification" of the 1948 Genocide Convention pledges the U.S. to comply only insofar as "nothing in the Convention requires legislation or other action by the United States of America prohibited by the Constitution of the United States as interpreted by the United States"; reproduced in LeBlanc, *Genocide Convention*, pp. 253–54. Such comportment has become so routine that otherwise establishmentarian analysts have begun to remark upon "the traditional Washington stance that the US is above international law"; Robertson, *Crimes Against Humanity*, p. 327.

123. Isabelle Schulte-Tenckhoff, "The Irresistible Ascension of the U.N. Declaration of the Rights of Indigenous Peoples: Stopped Dead in Its Tracks?" *European Review of Native American Studies*, Vol. 9, No. 2, 1995; Glenn T. Morris, "Further Motion by the State Department to Railroad Indigenous Rights," *Fourth World Bulletin*, No. 6, Summer 1998.

124. National Security Council cable dated Jan. 18, 2001; reproduced as Appendix B in my *Perversions of Justice: Indigenous Peoples and Angloamerican Law* (San Francisco: City Lights, 2002). For background on U.S. posturing at the U.N. with its "Indian Self-Determination Act" (88 Stat. 2203 (1975), codified at 25 U.S.C. 405a and elsewhere in titles 25, 42 and 50, U.S.C.A.), see S. James Anaya, *Indigenous Peoples in International Law* (New York: Oxford University Press, 1996) pp. 86–87, 157.

125. National Security Council cable, Jan. 18, 2001.

126. Leonard Garment (see note 3 and accompanying text). The NSC cable cited in the note above also refers to the U.N. Charter's guarantee of the territorial integrity of states addressed in note 107.

127. Lassa Oppenheim, *International Law* (London: Longman's, Green, [8th ed.] 1955) p. 120.

128. Robert T. Coulter, "Contemporary Indian Sovereignty," in Committee on Native Struggles, *Rethinking Indian Law*, p. 117; citing M. Whitman, *Digest of International Law* § 1 at 2 (1963).

129. As U.S. Ambassador to the United Nations, later Secretary of State, Madeleine Albright put it in the mid-1990s, "the U.N. is [merely] a tool of American foreign policy"; quoted by Catherine Toups in the *Washington Times*, Dec. 15, 1995. Overall, see the chapter entitled "The Laws of Empire" in Bennis, *Calling the Shots*, pp. 245–312.

130. As the matter was recently framed by French Foreign Minister Lionel Jospin, "the predominant weight of the United States and the absence for the moment of a counterweight . . . leads it to hegemony"; John Vinoceur, "Going It Alone: The U.S. Upsets France So Paris Begins a Campaign to Strengthen Multilateral Institutions," *International Herald-Tribune*, Feb. 3, 1999. Also see Jan Morris, "Mankind Stirs Uneasily at American Dominance," *Los Angeles Times*, Feb. 10, 2000.

131. For an early—and rather prescient—assessment of this prospect, see Sandy Vogelsang, *American Dream, Global Nightmare: The Dilemma of U.S. Human Rights Policy* (New York: W.W. Norton, 1980).

132. See the chapter entitled "The Contemporary Structure of Plunder" in Eduardo Galeano's *The Open Veins of Latin America: Five Centuries of the Pillage of a Continent* (New York: Monthly Review Press, 1973) pp. 225–83. More broadly, the essays collected by Peter L. Hahn and Mary Ann Heiss in their coedited volume, *Empire and Revolution: The United States and the Third World Since 1945* (Columbus: Ohio State University Press, 2001).

133. Bennis, *Calling the Shots*, pp. 262–63.

134. Ibid., p. 263. Also see note 117.

135. See note 101. For further information, see Florence Connolly Shipeck, *Pushed into the Rocks: Southern California Indian Land Tenure, 1769–1986* (Lincoln: University of Nebraska Press, 1988).

136. See note 69. For additional discussion of the peculiarly one-sided—and legally unfounded— notion of treaty abrogation implicit to the opinion, see Blue Clark, *"Lone Wolf" v. Hitchcock: Treaty Rights and Indian Law at the End of the Nineteenth Century* (Lincoln: University of Nebraska Press, 1999) esp. pp. 4–5, 70–74, 110.

137. During the 1997 conference in Ottawa which resulted in promulgation of the Convention on Prohibition of the Use, Stockpiling, Production and Transfer of Anti-Personnel Mines and on Their Destruction, to cite one notorious example, U.S. representatives argued straightforwardly that the treaty should bind *every* country in the world *except* theirs. When the 129 signatory states in attendance refused to accept the premise that the U.S. should be uniquely exempted from compliance, the U.S. delegation withdrew in a huff; Robertson, *Crimes Against Humanity*, pp. 198–99; Bennis, *Calling the Shots*, pp. 279–80. As of this writing (Feb. 2002), the U.S. has still not endorsed the Convention, although it went into force in March 1999. Instead, it has indulged in a flagrant violation by dropping thousands of cluster bombs—outlawed under the treaty—on Afghanistan since October 2001.

138. Upon even cursory examination, it becomes evident that virtually every one of the multitudinous post–World War II U.S. military/paramilitary interventions abroad has been harnessed to these ends; see, e.g., Noam Chomsky, *Deterring Democracy* (New York: Hill and Wang, 1992); *Year 501: The Conquest Continues* (Boston: South End Press, 1994). It should be noted that, according to no less authoritative a figure than Secretary of State Colin Powell, the U.S., having employed criminal means to replace Afghanistan's Taliban régime with a government of its own choosing in late 2001, is now gearing up to do the same in Iraq (Iran and North Korea have been named as likely follow-ups). It should also be noted that military force has not been the only means employed to accomplish the subordination of other countries, nor have the victims necessarily been confined to the Third World; see, e.g., Stephen McBride and John Shields, *Dismantling a Nation: The Transition to Corporate Rule in Canada* (Halifax, N.S.: Fernwood, [2nd ed.] 1997).

139. Felix S. Cohen, "The Erosion of Indian Rights, 1950–53: A Case-Study in Bureaucracy," *Yale Law Journal*, No. 62, 1953, p. 390.

140. Despite our retention of the largest landholdings on a per capita basis of any North Ameri-

can population group, and despite that land's being some of the most mineral-rich in the world, internal colonial exploitation of our resources by the U.S. has left American Indians in a material circumstance so degraded that by the late 1990s our average lifespan was one-third less than that of the settler population. For reasons, see Rennard Strickland, *Tonto's Revenge: Reflections on American Indian Culture and Policy* (Albuquerque: University of New Mexico Press, 1997) p. 53. Entirely comparable data applies to the Kanaka Maoli (Native Hawaiians); see H. Barringer and H.P. O'Hagan, *Socioeconomic Characteristics of Native Hawaiians* (Honolulu: Alu Like, 1989); Papa Ola Lokahi, *State of Hawai'i Native Hawaiian Health Data Book* (Honolulu: Office of Hawaiian Affairs, 1990).

141. The term employed originates with Jürgen Habermas; see James L. Marsh, *Unjust Legality: A Critique of Habermas's Law* (Lanham, MD: Rowman & Littlefield, 2001).

142. Several of the themes sketched in this section are developed more fully in "The New Face of Liberation" and "I Am Indigenist," herein.

143. The U.S. Congress actually issued a statutory apology to the Kanaka Maoli on the 100th anniversary of its admittedly illegal participation in the armed overthrow of Hawai'i's constitutional monarchy. Signed by President Bill Clinton on Nov. 23, 1993, Public Law 103–150 made no offer to restore the native people's property and other sovereign rights, however. Nor did it mention that Hawai'i's being declared a U.S. state in1959 was accomplished in a manner violating the requirements of Chapter IX of the U.N. Charter, and was thus simply another illegality; see Haunani-Kay Trask, *From a Native Daughter: Colonialism and Sovereignty in Hawai'i* (Honolulu: University of Hawai'i Press, [2nd ed.] 1999) pp. 27–32. On Guam, see Robert Underwood and Laura Souder, eds., *Chamorro Self-Determination* (Agana, Guam: Micronesia Area Research Center, 1987). On Puerto Rico, see Ronald Fernandez, *Prisoners of Colonialism: The Struggle for Justice in Puerto Rico* (Monroe, ME: Common Courage Press, 1994); Christina Duffy Burnett and Burke Marshall, eds., *Foreign in a Domestic Sense: Puerto Rico, American Expansion, and the Constitution* (Durham, NC: Duke University Press, 2001). By far the best overview of federal holdings, including such little-considered places as "American" Samoa and the "U.S." Virgin Islands, will be found in Arnold H. Leibowitz, *Defining Status: A Comprehensive Overview of United States Territorial Relations* (Norwell, MA: Kluwer Law International, 1989).

144. Ronald L. Trosper, "Appendix I: Indian Minerals," in American Indian Policy Review Commission, *Task Force 7 Final Report: Reservation and Resource Development and Protection* (Washington, D.C.: U.S. GPO, 1977); U.S. Department of Interior, Bureau of Indian Affairs, *Indian Lands Map: Oil, Gas and Minerals on Indian Reservations* (Washington, D.C.: U.S. GPO, 1978); Louis R. Moore, *Mineral Development on Indian Lands: Cooperation and Conflict* (Denver: Rocky Mountain Mineral Law Foundation, 1983); Presidential Commission on Indian Reservation Economies, *Report and Recommendation to the President of the United States* (Washington, D.C.: U.S. GPO, Nov. 1984).

145. My use of the word "serious" here is intended in opposition to the liberal notion that solutions to the kinds of intractable socioeconomic, political, and environmental problems generated by the existing system can somehow be obtained through recourse to the system itself. Regardless of the rhetorical reinforcing of systemic hegemony. For further elaboration, see Ernesto Laclau and Chantal Mouffe, *Hegemony and Socialist Strategy: Towards a Radical Democratic Politics* (London: Verso, [2nd ed.] 2001).

146. For some of the better descriptions of the statist system, see Boyle, *World Order*; Hedley Bull, *The Anarchical Society: A Study of Order in World Politics* (New York: Columbia University Press, 1977); Fritz Kratochwil, *Foreign Policy and International Order* (Boulder, CO: Westview Press, 1978).

147. Immanuel Wallerstein, *The Modern World-System*, 3 vols. (New York: Academic Press, 1974–1988). For further discussion, see Andre Gunder Frank and Barry K. Ellis, eds., *The World System: Five Hundred Years of Five Thousand?* (New York: Routledge, 1993).

148. Russell Means, remarks at the Four Winds Community Center, Denver, Oct. 7, 1996 (notes on file). Concerning the distinction at issue, see Hugh Seton-Watson, *Nations and States: An Inquiry into the Origins of Nations and the Politics of Nationalism* (Boulder, CO: Westview Press, 1977). More sharply, see Bernard Neitschmann, "The Fourth World: Nations versus States," in George J. Demko and William B. Wood, eds., *Reordering the World: Geopolitical Perspectives on the 21st Century* (Boul-

der, CO: Westview Press, 1994) pp. 225–42.

149. *Calder v. Attorney General of British Columbia* (SCR 313 1973) at 380. In concluding that the federal government of Canada enjoys a unilateral prerogative to extinguish indigenous rights, the court noted that it had been "unable to find a Canadian case dealing with precisely the same subject" and that it would therefore rely on a U.S. judicial interpretation found in *State of Idaho v. Coffee* (56 P.2d 1185 (1976)); 68 OR (2d) 353 (HC) at 412–43. The first example of this sort will be found in the 1867 Québec case *Connolly v. Woolrich* (11 LCJ 197), in which the court, considering the validity of a marriage effected under native tradition for purposes of determining inheritance rights, repeated verbatim a lengthy passage from Marshall's *Worcester* opinion. See John Hurley, "Aboriginal Rights, the Constitution and the Marshall Court," *Revue Juridique Themis*, No. 17, 1983; Stan Persky, *Delgamuukw: The Supreme Court of Canada Decision on Aboriginal Title* (Vancouver: Douglas & McIntyre, 1998).

150. At the Berlin Conference of 1884–85, the European powers partitioned Africa in accordance with their own interests on the continent. The resulting demarcation of colonial boundaries conforms rather precisely to borders claimed by most "postcolonial" African states today; see the map delineating the 1885 colonial boundaries included in J.M. MacKenzie, *The Partition of Africa, 1880–1900* (London: Metheun, 1983) p. 28. For background on the Berlin Conference, see Thomas Pakenham, *The Scramble for Africa: The White Man's Conquest of the Dark Continent from 1876 to 1912* (New York: Random House, 1991). For observations on the outcome(s), see Anthony D. Smith, *State and Nation in the Third World: The Western State and African Nationalism* (New York: St. Martin's, 1983) esp. pp. 124–35; Basil Davidson, *The Black Man's Burden: Africa and the Curse of the Nation-State* (New York: Times Books, 1992).

151. The "Belgian Thesis," as it was called, had been articulated for more than a decade prior to the U.N. debate; see, e.g., Foreign Ministry of Belgium, *The Sacred Mission of Civilization: To Which Peoples Should the Benefit be Extended?* (Brussels: Belgium Government Information Center, 1953).

152. On the Blue Water Principle itself, see Roxanne Dunbar Ortiz, "Protection of American Indian Territories in the United States: Applicability of International Law," in Sutton, *Irredeemable America*, pp. 260–61. For insights on the eurocentrism of the logic guiding Lumumba and his counterparts, see Partha Chatterjee, *Nationalist Thought and the Colonial World: A Derivative Discourse* (London: Zed Books, 1986), pp. 1–35.

153. Indeed, some Third Worlders felt that both the principle and its OAU endorsers did not go far enough. Rather than simply preserving the individuated-state structure inherited from European colonialism, Pan-Africanists like Kwame Nkrumah sought to forge a single continental "megastate" along the lines of the U.S. or the USSR; see Kwame Nkrumah, *Neo-Colonialism: The Last Stage of Imperialism* (New York: International, 1965); Elenga M'buyinga, *Pan-Africanism or Neo-Colonialism: The Bankruptcy of the O.A.U.* (London: Zed Books, 1982).

154. For a good survey, see Norman Miller and Roderick Aya, eds., *National Liberation: Revolution in the Third World* (New York: Free Press, 1971). More theoretically, see "False Promises," herein.

155. Neitschmann, "Fourth World"; George Manuel and Michael Posluns, *The Fourth World: An Indian Reality* (New York: Free Press, 1974). At least one writer has referred to the Fourth World as being a "Host World" upon which the other three have been constructed; Winona LaDuke, "Preface: Natural to Synthetic and Back Again," in my *Marxism and Native Americans* (Boston: South End Press, 1983) pp. i–viii.

156. See Franz Shurmann, *The Logic of World Power* (New York: Pantheon, 1974); Jacqueline Stevens, *Reproducing the State* (Princeton, NJ: Princeton University Press, 1999).

157. Neitschmann, "Fourth World," p. 240.

158. Ibid. For background, see Greg Urban and Joel Sherzer, *Nation States and Indians in Latin America* (Austin: University of Texas Press, 1991).

159. For a partial overview, see the map of China's "minority nationalities" in Walker Connor, *The National Question in Marxist-Leninist Theory and Strategy* (Princeton, NJ: Princeton University Press, 1984) p. 70.

160. Ibid., p. 116. For more on the Montagnards, see "False Promises," herein.

161. For background, see Glenn T. Morris, and my "Between a Rock and a Hard Place: Left-Wing Revolution, Right-Wing Reaction, and the Destruction of Indigenous Peoples," *Cultural Survival Quarterly*, Vol. 11, No. 3, Fall 1988.

162. On Chechnya, see Bradford L. Thomas, "International Boundaries: Lines in the Sand (and Sea)," in George J. Demko and William B. Wood, eds., *Reordering the World: Geopolitical Perspectives on the 21st Century* (Boulder, CO: Westview Press, [2nd ed.] 1999) p. 72. With respect to the smaller peoples, see *Indigenous Peoples of the Soviet North* (Copenhagen: IWGIA Doc. 67, 1990) esp. the map on pp. 6–7. On the nations which gained a measure of genuine independence as a result of the Soviet breakup, see Hélène Carrère d'Encausse, *The End of the Soviet Empire: Triumph of the Nations* (New York: Basic Books, 1992); Alexander J. Motyl, ed., *The Post-Soviet Nations: Perspectives on the Demise of the USSR* (New York: Columbia University Press, 1992).

163. Gerard Chaliand, ed., *People Without a Country: The Kurds and Kurdistan* (New York: Olive Branch).

164. Jonathan Bearman, *Qadhafi's Libya* (London: Zed Books, 1986); Tony Hodges, *Western Sahara: Roots of a Desert War* (Westport, CT: Lawrence Hill, 1983).

165. See the special-focus issue of *Cultural Survival Quarterly* (Vol. 9, No. 3, 1985) entitled "Nation, Tribe and Ethnic Group in Africa." Also see Malcolm N. Shaw, *Title to Territory in Africa: International League Issues* (Oxford, U.K.: Clarendon Press, 1986).

166. Julian Burger, *Report from the Frontier: The State of the World's Indigenous Peoples* (London: Zed Books, 1987); Sadruddin Aga Khan and Hassan bin Talal, *Indigenous Peoples: A Global Quest for Justice* (London: Zed Books, 1987).

167. See Richard Falk, *Predatory Globalization: A Critique* (Cambridge, U.K.: Polity Press, 1999). Also see James H. Mittleman, ed., *Globalization: Critical Reflections* (Boulder, CO: Lynne Rienner, 1997), esp. Mittleman's own essay, "How Does Globalization Really Work?" pp. 229–41.

168. Frank Furedi, *The New Ideology of Imperialism: Renewing the Moral Imperative* (London: Pluto Press, 1994); Ash Narain Roy, *The Third World in the Age of Globalization: Requiem or New Agenda?* (London: Zed Books, 1999); James Petras and Henry Veltmeyer, *Globalization Unmasked: Imperialism in the 21st Century* (London/Halifax, N.S.: Zed Books/Fernwood, 2001). For further theoretical background, see Albert Szymanski, *The Logic of Imperialism* (New York: Praeger, 1981) esp. the chapters entitled "The Dynamic of Imperialism" and "The State and Military Intervention," pp. 123–216.

169. For an interesting iteration of more or less the same perception, see Gustavo Esteva and Madhu Suri Prakash, *Grassroots Postmodernism: Remaking the Soil of Cultures* (London: Zed Books, 1998). Also see John Zerzan, *Elements of Refusal* (Columbia, MO: C.A.L. Paleo Editions, [2nd ed.] 1999).

170. Jules Gerard-Libois, *Katanga Secession* (Madison: University of Wisconsin Press, 1966); Peter Schwab, ed. *Biafra* (New York: Facts on File, 1971).

171. Bernard Nietschmann, "The Third World War," *Cultural Survival Quarterly*, Vol. 11, No. 2, 1987.

172. Isak Chisi Swu and Th. Muiva, *Free Nagaland Manifesto* (Oking: National Socialist Council of Nagaland, 1993). Much more broadly, see the special-focus issue of *Cultural Survival Quarterly* (Vol. 13, No. 2, 1989) entitled "India: Cultures in Crisis."

173. Edith T. Mirante, "Ethnic Minorities of the Burma Frontiers and Their Resistance Organizations," in *Southeast Asian Tribal Groups and Ethnic Minorities* (Cambridge, MA: Cultural Survival Report No. 22, 1987) pp. 59–71. Also see the special-focus issue of *Cultural Survival Quarterly* (Vol. 13, No. 4) devoted to the situation in Burma.

174. Democratic Peoples' Liberation Front, "The Tamils in Sri Lanka," *IWGIA Newsletter*, No. 58, Aug. 1989.

175. David Robie, *Blood on Their Banner: Nationalist Struggles in the South Pacific* (London: Zed Books, 1989).

176. Joseph Collins, *The Philippines: Fire on the Rim* (San Francisco: Food First Books, 1989) pp. 129–202.

177. John G. Taylor, *Indonesia's Forgotten War: The Hidden History of East Timor* (London/Sidney: Zed Books/Pluto Press, 1991).

178. Bernard Nietschmann, *The Unknown War: The Miskito Nation, Nicaragua, and the United States* (Lanham, MD: Freedom House, 1989). Also see Morris' and my "Rock and a Hard Place."

179. A good overview is provided in John K. Cooley's *Unholy Wars: Afghanistan, America and International Terrorism* (London: Pluto Press, [2nd ed.] 2000) pp. 174–84.

180. John Ross, *The War Against Oblivion: The Zapatista Chronicles* (Monroe, ME: Common Courage Press, 2000).

181. Cyrus Ernesto Zirakzadeh, *A Rebellious People: Basques, Protests, and Politics* (Reno: University of Nevada Press, 1991); Joseba Zulaika, *Basque Violence: Metaphor and Sacrament* (Reno: University of Nevada Press, 1988); Robert P. Clark, *Negotiating with ETA: Obstacles to Peace in the Basque Country, 1975–1988* (Reno: University of Nevada Press, 1990); John Sullivan, *ETA and Basque Nationalism* (London: Routledge, 1988).

182. On the "French Basques," see Paddy Woodworth, *Dirty War, Clean Hands: ETA, the GAL and Spanish Democracy* (Cork, Eire: Cork University Press, 2001) esp. pp. 87–99. On the Bretons, Peter Berresford Ellis, *The Celtic Revolution: A Study in Anti-Imperialism* (Talybont, Wales: Y Lofta, 1985) pp. 54–75.

183. Padraig O'Malley, *The Uncivil Wars: Ireland Today* (Boston: Beacon Press, 1990); Ciaran de Baroid, *Ballymurphy and the Irish War* (London: Pluto Press, [2nd ed.] 2000).

184. On the construction of the English domain, see Michael Hector, *Internal Colonialism: The Celtic Fringe in British National Development, 1526–1966* (Berkeley: University of California Press, 1975). On the liberation struggle, see Ellis, *Celtic Revolution*, pp. 28–53, 76–97, 134–48. Also see H.J. Hanham, *Scottish Nationalism* (London: Faber & Faber, 1969); Gwynfor Evans, *Fighting for Wales* (Talybont, Wales: Y Lofta, 1991).

185. Ellis, *Celtic Revolution*, pp.139–64.

186. See the map of Saamiland included in *IWGIA Newsletter*, No. 51/52, Oct./Dec. 1987, p. 84.

187. Jens Dahl, "Greenland: General election supports continuing decolonization," *IWGIA Newsletter*, No. 51/52, Oct./Dec. 1987. For background, see Gudmunder Alfredsson, "Greenland and the Law of Political Decolonization," *German Yearbook on International Law*, No. 25, 1982.

188. Geoffrey York and Linda Pindera, *People of the Pines: The Warriors and the Legacy of Oka* (Boston: Little, Brown, 1991); Janice G.A.E. Switlow, *Gustafson Lake: Under Siege* (Peachland, B.C.: TIAC Communications, 1997); Olive Patricia Dickason, *Canada's First Nations: A History of Founding Peoples from Earliest Times* (Norman: University of Oklahoma Press, 1992) pp. 414–15.

189. Leopold Kohr, *The Breakdown of Nations* (London: Routledge & Kegan Paul, 1957).

190. Robert D. Kaplan, *The Coming Anarchy: Shattering the Dreams of the Post Cold War* (New York: Random House, 2000). Kaplan and others of his ilk delight in pointing to the bloodbath in the former Yugoslavia as previewing far worse to come, were the statist system to disintegrate; see, e.g., Bogdan Denitch, *Ethnic Nationalism: The Tragic Death of Yugoslavia* (Minneapolis: University of Minnesota Press, 1994). Ignored altogether in such analyses are the facts that the animus provoking such bloodletting is a legacy of statist imposition on the one hand, and efforts to reimpose centralized state authority on the other.

191. Bennis, *Calling the Shots*, p. 274.

192. Leopold Kohr, *The Overdeveloped Nations: The Diseconomies of Scale* (New York: Schocken Books, 1978); James D. Cockcroft, Andre Gunder Frank and Dale L. Johnson, *Dependence and Underdevelopment: Latin America's Political Economy* (New York: Anchor, 1970); Neil Smith, *Uneven Development: Nature, Capital and the Production of Space* (Oxford, U.K.: Basil Blackwell, 1984); Samir Amin, *Maldevelopment: Anatomy of a Global Failure* (London: Zed Books, 1990). Overall, see Ian Roxborough, *Theories of Underdevelopment* (New York: Macmillan, 1979).

193. Frank Harrison, *The Modern State: An Anarchist Analysis* (Montréal: Black Rose Books, 1983);

Robert Paul Wolff, *In Defense of Anarchism* (Berkeley: University of California Press, [2nd ed.] 1998); Christian Parenti, *Lockdown America: Police and Prisons in the Age of Crisis* (London: Verso, 1999).

194. As Antonio de Nebrija famously put it in 1492, language might be seen as "a perfect companion to empire" in the sense that the colonizer's imposition of his own tongue upon the colonized would serve to undermine the latter's cultural integrity and concomitant capacity to resist subordination; Patricia Seed, *Ceremonies of Possession in Europe's Conquest of the New World, 1492–1640* (Cambridge, U.K.: Cambridge University Press, 1995) p. 8. By the 1880s, linguistic imposition had progressed to a program of systematically supplanting indigenous languages; Martin Carnoy, *Education as Cultural Imperialism* (New York: David McKay, 1974) esp. pp. 69–72; David Wallace Adams, *Education for Extinction: American Indians and the Boarding School Experience, 1875-1928* (Lawrence: University Press of Kansas, 1995) esp. pp. 137–42. Today, it is estimated that fully half the world's 6,000-odd languages are in danger of disappearance within the next few years, and half the remainder over the coming generation.

195. Michael Albert and Robin Hahnel, *Unorthodox Marxism: An Essay on Capitalism, Socialism and Revolution* (Boston: South End Press, 1978) pp. 14–16.

196. Glenn T. Morris, lecture at Alfred University, Oct. 14, 1990 (tape on file). This is the same talk from which the epigraph used in this essay was taken.

197. On the concept of "Master Narratives"—also known as "Great" or "Grand" Narratives, as well as "metanarratives"—see Fredric Jameson, *Political Unconscious: Narrative as Socially Symbolic Act* (Ithaca, NY: Cornell University Press, 1981). In the sense the term is used here, it figures into the Gramscian notion of hegemony; see Walter Adamson, *Hegemony and Revolution: A Study of Antonio Gramsci's Political and Cultural Theory* (Berkeley: University of California Press, 1980) esp. pp. 170–79; Judith Butler, "Restaging the Universal: Hegemony and the Limits of Formalism," in Judith Butler, Ernesto Laclau and Slajov Zizek, *Contingency, Hegemony, Universality: Contemporary Dialogues on the Left* (London: Verso, 2000) pp. 11–43.

198. Jürgen Habermas, *Legitimation Crisis* (Boston: Beacon Press, 1973).

199. Richard Falk, *The End of World Order: Essays in Normative International Relations* (New York: Holmes & Meier, 1983); esp. the essay entitled "Political Prospects, Cultural Choices, Anthropological Horizons," pp. 315–36.

200. See, e.g., David Knight, "People Together, Yet Apart: Rethinking Territory, Sovereignty, and Identities," in Demko and Wood, *Reordering the World* (2nd ed.), pp. 209–26.

201. Louis Snyder, *Global Mini-Nationalisms: Autonomy or Independence?* (Westport, CT: Greenwood, 1982).

202. Janet L. Abu-Lughod, *Before European Hegemony: The World System, A.D. 1250–1350* (New York: Oxford University Press, 1989). For an overview of the transition to the current world system, see Wallerstein, *Modern World-System*; Mark Greenglass, ed., *Conquest and Coalescence: The Shaping of the State in Early Modern Europe* (London: Edward Arnold, 1991).

203. Kirkpatrick Sale, *Human Scale* (New York: Coward, McCann & Geoghegan, 1980); *Dwellers in the Land: The Bioregional Vision* (Philadelphia: New Society, 1991).

204. See Roger Moody, ed., *The Indigenous Voice: Visions and Realities*, 2 vols. (London: Zed Books, 1988). Also see "The New Face of Liberation" and "I Am Indigenist," herein.

205. See Richard Falk, "Anarchy and World Order," in his *End of World Order*, pp. 277–98. Also see Harvey Starr, *Anarchy, Order, and Integration: How to Manage Interdependence* (Ann Arbor: University of Michigan Press, 1999). For a more concrete exploration of how an anarchist arrangement of international relations might look in practice, see Juan Gómez Casas, *Anarchist Organization: The History of the F.A.I.* (Montréal: Black Rose Books, 1986).

2. THE NULLIFICATION OF NATIVE AMERICA?

1. In draft form, the law was listed as HR 2006 and sponsored by Colorado's Representative (later Senator) Ben Nighthorse Campbell, a Democrat (later Republican). Campbell's Senate cosponsor

was Arizona Republican John Henry Kyl. Congressional passage occurred on Oct. 27. The 1990 Act radically expands the authority vested in the American Indian Arts and Crafts Board, established under the Act of Aug. 27, 1935 (25 U.S.C. § 305 and 18 U.S.C. §§ 1158 and 1159). On the latter, see generally, Robert Fay Schrader, *The Indian Arts & Crafts Board: An Aspect of New Deal Indian Policy* (Albuquerque: University of New Mexico Press, 1983).

2. The Native American Artists Association (NAAA) is a mainstay of enforcement with respect to arts and crafts production in the conventional sense. Ava Hamilton, President of the Native American Film Producers Association, makes it clear in public presentations that tribal enrollment—though not necessarily producing anything—is the "fundamental qualification" for membership. At its 1993 annual meeting in Phoenix, the Association of American Indian and Alaska Native University Professors passed a resolution on "ethnic fraud" demanding that institutions of higher learning "require documentation of enrollment in a state or federally recognized nation/tribe" of all native faculty. The same year, a panel presentation conducted during a meeting of the American Council on Education in Houston was geared to imposing the same criteria upon the admission of college students.

3. Norbert S. Hill, Jr., former Executive Director of the American Indian Science and Engineering Society (AISES) confirms that such discussions have occurred "for years," but that the organization has not adopted a firm policy on the matter. Other organizations at issue here include the Native American Journalists Association and American Indian Education Association.

4. Suzan Shown Harjo, talk at the Biannual Atlatl Conference, Minneapolis, Oct. 24, 1992 (tape on file). The position is entirely consistent with Harjo's advocacy during the 1980s, the period in which she served as executive director of the National Congress of American Indians, of a "Native American Cultural Rights Act" which would have banned virtually *any* "unauthorized" identification by individuals as Indians; Gail K. Sheffield, *The Arbitrary Indian: The Indian Arts and Crafts Act of 1990* (Norman: University of Oklahoma Press, 1997) p. 52. Similarly, Mohawk painter Richard Glazer Danay, who doubles as U/Cal Riverside instructor and member of the federal Indian Arts and Crafts Board, has argued vehemently that the law should be applied "to anyone who calls themselves Indian without any sort of proof or documentation"; Jonathan Tilove, "Who's an Indian Artist?" Newhouse News Service, Mar. 25, 1993. Ironically, since his lineage traces to the Caughnawaga Reserve in Canada, Danay himself cannot enroll in conformity with the 1990 Act. Whether he actually believes this makes him a "nonindian" has gone somewhat conveniently unaddressed.

5. The argument is well made in "Federal Indian Identification Policy: A Usurpation of Indigenous Sovereignty in North America," M. Annette Jaimes' contribution to her *The State of Native America: Genocide, Colonization and Resistance* (Boston: South End Press, 1992) pp. 123–38. A comparable position was articulated by Seneca photographer Jolene Ricard in a telephone interview conducted in Nov. 1997.

6. Panel discussion, Biannual Conference of Atlatl, Minneapolis, Oct. 23, 1992 (tape on file). According to federal census data and Department of Labor statistics, American Indians comprise the single most impoverished population aggregate in the U.S.; for a good overview, see Teresa L. Amott and Julie A. Matthaei, *Race, Gender and Work: A Multicultural History of Women in the United States* (Boston: South End Press, 1991) Chap. 3.

7. See, e.g., the angry exchanges published in *News From Indian Country* during 1994 and '95.

8. The Five Civilized Tribes Museum in Muskogee was also forced to close; Lyn Nichols, "New Indian Art Regulations Shut Down Muskogee Museum," *San Francisco Chronicle*, Dec. 3, 1990. See also, "Congress' Help Hurts Indians," *McAlester News-Capital & Democrat* (Okla.), Dec. 21, 1990.

9. On the tradition of resistance among Cherokees, see Robert K. Thomas, "The Redbird Smith Movement," in W.N. Fenton and John Gulick, eds., *Symposium on Cherokee and Iroquois Cultures* (Washington, D.C.: Bureau of American Ethnology Bulletin 180, 1960); Albert L. and Jane Lukans Wahrhaftig, "New Militants or Resurrected State? The Five County Northeastern Cherokee Organization," in Duane King, ed., *The Cherokee Nation, A Troubled History* (Knoxville: University of Tennessee Press, 1979); Janey B. Hendrix, *RedBird Smith and the NightHawk Cherokees* (Park Hill, OK: Cross-Cultural Education Center, 1983).

10. As then-Cherokee Principal Chief Wilma Mankiller put it at the time, the Dawes Rolls, upon which the current rolls of the Cherokee Nation of Oklahoma (CNO) are explicitly based, could be viewed quite reasonably as having been a federal "tool of oppression." This has been generally understood by all Cherokees, including those who enrolled, and means of accommodating resisters were quickly developed. "An Indian is an Indian," Mankiller concluded, "regardless of the degree of Indian blood or which little government card they do or do not possess"; quoted in Donna Hales, "Selling Bogus Indian Art is Illegal," *Muskogee Daily Phoenix* (Okla.), Sept. 3, 1990. Aside from enrollment, posthumous or otherwise, one means by which the CNO sought to circumvent the 1990 law's constraints upon their own traditionally inclusive manner of acknowledging Cherokee identity was by issuing letters on the Nation's official stationery vouching for the ethnic bona fides of those unable or unwilling to enroll; Wilma Mankiller, "Buyers Have Final Say on Indian Art," *Muskogee Daily Phoenix*, Dec. 21, 1990.

11. To quote Rorex, "Both my mother and father are descended from two of the many Indian families who refused the mark of the government. The legacy I received from my ancestors was not denial of my heritage, but distrust of 'government aid.' I almost have to thank this new bill for truly opening my eyes. I now have a better understanding of what my people gave me—they gave me independence"; quoted in Sheffield, *Arbitrary Indian*, pp. 111–12.

12. Several other Cherokee Master Artists are also unenrolled; Donna Hales, "Tribe Touts Unregistered Artists," *Muskogee Daily Phoenix* (Okla.), Sept. 3, 1990.

13. On Durham's art, see Lucy R. Lippard, "Jimmie Durham: Postmodernist 'Savage'," *Art in America*, Feb. 1993; Laura Mulvey, Dirk Snauwaert and Mark Alice Durant, *Jimmie Durham* (London: Phaidon, 1996). For a good selection of his theoretical work, see Jimmie Durham, *A Certain Lack of Coherence: Writings on Art and Cultural Politics* (London: Kala Press, 1993).

14. Ultimately, Durham was prompted to prepare a sardonic "Artist's Disclaimer" with which he attended his exhibitions: "I hereby swear to the truth of the following statement: I am a full-blood contemporary artist, of the sub-group (or clan) called sculptors. I am not an American Indian, nor have I ever seen or sworn loyalty to India. I am not a 'Native American,' nor do I feel America has any right to name or un-name me. I have previously stated that I should be considered mixed blood: that is, I claim to be a male but in fact only one of my parents was male."

15. The nature of the process leading to the "alternative exhibition" was described by Dennis Jennings, one of the key organizers, on his KPFA radio program "Living on Indian Time" during the fall of 1991 (tape on file).

16. Coinage of the terms "identity police" and "purity police" has been claimed by one of the group's primary leaders, Carole Standing Elk, putative head of a Bay Area entity dubbed "Center for the SPIRIT" and board member of a federally subsidized Minnesota-chartered corporation calling itself "National American Indian Movement, Inc."; Vince Bielski, "Trail of Blood: Activists and Artists Under Attack as American Indian Movement Splits in Bitter Ancestry Dispute," *San Francisco Weekly*, Oct. 6, 1993.

17. Because of the severity and persistence of their disruptions, Standing Elk and her colleagues were at one point simultaneously enjoined by separate court orders from either setting foot on the San Francisco State campus or attending further meetings of the school district's Title-V Parents Committee. A firm sense of what transpired has been obtained through conversations and interviews with Dr. Betty Parent, former chair of Native American Studies at the university, KPFA programmer Cathy Chapman, KPFA fundraiser Bob Baldock, former Leonard Peltier Defense Committee International Spokesperson Bobby Castillo, community organizers George Martin and Paul Schultz, local speakers bureau coordinator Jean Caiani, and others.

18. The group had announced that it would not allow the clinic to reopen until such time as a list of demands concerning the enrollment status of staff and advisory board members was met. One client, when turned away during an attempt to see his counselor, promptly went home and resolved his sense of deep depression by committing suicide; Castillo interview.

19. The source of this statement, fearing that she herself will be targeted if her name is used, has asked that her confidentiality be protected.

20. The same criteria apply as in note 19.

21. Unlike the Phoenix-based Atlatl and other associations of indigenous artists, which were formed for networking and other constructive purposes, the NAAA's mission statement makes it clear that the organization was created solely for the purpose of "investigating fraudulent misrepresentation by artists claiming to be Indians"; Sheffield, *Arbitrary Indian,* pp. 51, 94.

22. "Who the fuck are these people that I should have to show them anything at all?" demands Guerrero, still incensed by what he describes as the "arrogance and stupidity" displayed by Bradley and other NAAA members. "And what the hell is a Chicano if not an Indian? What are these fools thinking, that everybody south of the Río Grande came from Spain? I am who I am, and who I am is an indigenous person. That would still be just as true, even if I didn't have this silly little identity card from the government 'confirming' it."

23. The incident is recounted by Peltier's cousin, Bob Robideau, an enrolled Turtle Mountain Chippewa, who was attending the Institute at the time; Robideau interview, Dec. 1994 (notes on file).

24. Gerald R. McMaster, "Border Zones: The 'Injun-uity' of Aesthetic Tricks," *Cultural Studies,* Vol. 9, No. 1, 1995, p. 75. The demand that Durham not only be removed from the show, but that he be replaced by someone from NAAA's own ranks seems to be a standard objective, and a matter belying the organization's frequent profession of more altruistic motives.

25. E-mail correspondence from Alfred Young Man, also known as "Eagle Chief," Jan. 1997 (copies on file).

26. See the three-part series by *ICT* staff writer Jerry Reynolds, "Indian writers: the good, the bad and the could be," run in *Indian Country Today,* Sept.–Oct. 1993.

27. See various of the items published under the general heading of "AIM Paper Wars" in *News From Indian Country* during the years in question.

28. E.g., Tim Giago, "Colorado Indian leaders clash with national AIM," *Boulder Daily Camera,* Mar. 4, 1994; the column ran in 54 papers nationally during the same week.

29. See my "Nobody's Pet Poodle: Jimmie Durham, an Artist for Native North America," *Indigenous Thought,* Vol. 1, Nos. 4–5, Oct. 1991; the essay was subsequently reprinted in *Crazy Horse Spirit* and *Z Magazine* (Jan. 1992), and is included in my 1994 collection, *Indians Are Us? Culture and Genocide in North America* (Monroe, ME: Common Courage Press). It is from the latter source that subsequent references will be made.

30. For background, see Scott B. Vickers, *Native American Identities: From Archetype to Stereotype in Art and Literature* (Albuquerque: University of New Mexico Press, 1998) pp. 164–65. Although Vickers is correct in his conclusions, he errs in several matters of fact. Among them is the idea that I share my Keetoowah enrollment status with Bill Clinton. For the record, I am enrolled as a Associate Member of the Band, meaning that I am a "certified" Cherokee who, as a nonresident, neither votes nor holds office. Clinton, on the other hand, has been awarded an honorary membership, meaning that he is a non-Cherokee friend of the Band.

31. The precipitating article in Boulder was publication of Jodi Rave's "Few who know Churchill are indifferent: Some critics question CU prof's 'Indianness'" in a local paper, the *Colorado Daily,* on Nov. 23, 1993. This triggered a veritable avalanche letters to the editor from around the country over the following three months, prominently including Carole Standing Elk, David Bradley, and other key supporters of the 1990 Act (tellingly, locally-originating letters of response were overwhelmingly supportive of me). Impressions that this was a well-orchestrated campaign rather than a "spontaneous" outpouring of sentiment were strongly reinforced when it was learned that Ms. Rave's presence at the University of Colorado had been made possible in part by a grant from Suzan Harjo's Morningstar Foundation.

32. Written statements of Gregg Bates, Common Courage Press, Mar. 1994; Cynthia Peters, South End Press, Mar. 1994.

33. Written statement of Jean Caiani, Speak Out!, Oct. 1993; letter from Ellie Deegan, K&S Speakers, Mar. 13, 1994. There have been four instances in which my speaking engagements have been canceled. First, at the University of New Hampshire in 1994, the institution caved in to pressure and replaced me with Clyde Bellecourt, whose presentation was so weak that, to my knowledge, the university has never invited another indigenous speaker. Second, at Bowling Green State University in 1995, I was replaced by a relatively unknown and inexperienced—and by that definition, "non-controversial"—native woman from Wisconsin. That was fine in and of itself, except that the event at which she spoke was a twentieth anniversary celebration of the founding of the Ethnic Studies Department on that campus. The other minorities were bringing in heavy hitters like Cornell West for the occasion and in that juxtaposition she was completely overshadowed. So, there was effectively no native voice at all. In the third example, at Florida State in 1997, a student organization was persuaded not to bring me in. The result was that a Euroamerican speaker, Michael Albert, was invited instead. And finally, there's the university up at Sault Ste. Marie, Michigan, where I was first invited, then disinvited and never replaced. Hence, a demonstrable loss was suffered by native people in each and every instance where the identity cops were successful.

34. Giago, "Colorado Indian leaders"; Reynolds, "Indian Writers."

35. It is impossible to provide anything resembling adequate citation in this connection. *Dark Night field notes*, a Chicago publication, maintains a voluminous but decidedly incomplete hard copy file on these internet postings. See generally, Glen Martin, "Internet Indian Wars," *Wired*, No. 3, 1995.

36. The group consisted of Vernon Bellecourt, CEO of Minneapolis-based "National AIM, Inc."; Margaret Martinez (aka, "Cahuilla Red Elk"), National AIM's delegate in Colorado Springs; and one unidentified student from the Colorado Springs campus of the University of Colorado who claimed to be "uncomfortable" with the fact that I was on the Boulder faculty, 100 miles away. Instructively, no representative from my own campus accompanied the group despite the meeting's highly confidential nature. By his own account, then-Chancellor James Corbridge, previously and currently professor of law, explained that "ethnic fraud" did not constitute an actionable category of behavior; Churchill investigation file.

37. According to Dr. Evelyn Hu-DeHart, who was assigned to coordinate the investigation, "it rapidly became obvious that there was no basis whatsoever for the charges. Far from misappropriating funds, either directly or by misuse of institutional resources, it turned out that Ward consumed the least of any faculty member on campus. The rating of his performance by students in his courses, which occurs at the end of every semester, had been in the top five percent of all faculty for five solid years. It's important to note that very nearly a thousand students were involved in submitting these evaluations, which are anonymous, and there was not so much as a hint of complaint about 'physical intimidation.' The only concrete allegation in this respect was submitted, not by a student, but by Suzan Harjo, and it turned out to have no basis according to Vine Deloria, Jr., and other witnesses. What can I say? We not only exonerated Churchill, but I recommended him for promotion to full professor, based upon what we'd found"; Hu-DeHart, Oct. 1997.

38. Carole Standing Elk, for one, played to the hilt the fact that I was under investigation—a circumstance the investigative file reveals she secretly helped precipitate via a communication to the university administration accusing me of "financial malfeasance"—in her public statements. In her memorandum concluding the university's scrutiny of my activities, Hu-DeHart observed that the entire affair appeared to have been "carefully orchestrated" by a "relatively small group of individuals," all "loosely affiliated with one another" and "united in this instance by a common desire to discredit Professor Churchill because of personal or political disagreements with him." She went on to question whether an investigation had been warranted in the first place, insofar as "it would have seemed entirely reasonable to doubt that persons residing in locations as remote from the university as San Francisco, Minneapolis, Santa Fe, Oklahoma and Washington, D.C., might have been in a position to have had any factual basis for the allegations at issue." She concluded by recommending that the institution take steps to protect its personnel from the effects of such "gratuitous allegations" in the future; Churchill investigation file.

39. The new books have included *Since Predator Came: Notes from the Struggle for American Indian Liberation* (Littleton, CO: Aigis, 1995); *From a Native Son: Essays in Indigenism, 1985–1995* (Boston: South End Press, 1996); *A Little Matter of Genocide: Holocaust and Denial in the Americas, 1492 to the Present* (San Francisco: City Lights, 1997); *Pacifism as Pathology: Reflections on the Role of Armed Struggle in North America* (Winnipeg: Arbeiter Ring, 1998); *Islands in Captivity: Findings of the International Tribunal on the Rights of Indigenous Hawaiians*, 3 vols. (Cambridge, MA: South End Press, 2002), and *Indians Are Us?* A new, revised and expanded edition of my 1993 *Fantasies of the Master Race* was published by City Lights in 1998; Arbeiter Ring did the same with *Struggle for the Land* in 1999. In 1996, *Indians Are Us?* was translated into French and published under the title *Que Sont les Indiens Devenues?* by Editions du Rocher (Monaco). A new English language edition of *Indians*, revised and expanded, is among those currently in press.

40. It is true that the rate at which I've delivered public lectures has fallen off dramatically since 1992. It should also be noted, however, that before that I was very much involved in the debate concerning the proposed Columbian Quincentennial Celebration. In 1991, I spent more than 200 days on the road speaking in opposition to it. Such a pace could not be sustained, nor did I desire to try. My present schedule of delivering no more than three invited lectures per month during the academic year is about right, given my other responsibilities.

41. Any such outcome would simply exacerbate the chronic and oft-bemoaned underrepresentation of both Indians and Indian-oriented content in most U.S. educational institutions. See generally, Jorge Noriega, "American Indian Education in the United States: Indoctrination for Subordination to Colonialism," Jaimes, *State of Native America*, pp. 371–402.

42 . Cited and analyzed in Sheffield, *Arbitrary Indian*, pp. 21–22.

43. 19 U.S.C.A. § 1304. Although native craftspeople have long requested that the Tariff Act be revised to require that import labels be affixed in some permanent fashion, and an Omnibus Trade Act passed in 1988 did in fact mandate such revisions, federal regulations *still* allow easily removable stick-on labels to be used on such things as "Indian" jewelry and beadwork. This is undoubtedly because of strong opposition to implementation expressed by the National Jewelers Association and several other interested groups.

44. Quoted in Sheffield, *Arbitrary Indian*, p. 93. For solid elaboration and analysis of the dynamics underlying such statements, see Joanne Nagel, "Resource Competition Theories of Ethnicity," *American Behavioral Scientist*, No. 38, 1995.

45. Sheffield, *Arbitrary Indian*, p. 93.

46. Rep. Ben Nighthorse Campbell, "The Ken Hanlon Show," radio station KOA, Denver, Feb. 1990 (tape on file). How many millions "a few" might be is of course open to interpretation. My own best guess in this regard is that Campbell meant less than ten.

47. Among other things, "Freesoul," who heads something called the "Redtail Intertribal Society," claims to be the "official pipe maker of the Cheyenne-Arapaho Tribe in Oklahoma" (which has no such position). The case is profiled by Susan D. Atchison in her "Who Is an Indian, and Why Are They Asking?" *Business Week*, Dec. 26, 1988, p. 71.

48. Pletka is of eastern European descent and has always openly identified himself as such.

49. See, e.g., Joan Frederick, *T.C. Cannon: He Stood in the Sun* (Flagstaff, AZ: Northland, 1995); Joshua C. Taylor, et al., *Fritz Scholder* (New York: Rizzoli, 1982); Doris Monthan, *R.C. Gorman: A Retrospective* (Flagstaff, AZ: Northland, 1990).

50. This is a point made by Mankiller in her "Buyers Have Final Say on Indian Art." It is also a lesson learned the hard way by none other than the NAAA's David Bradley, who spent considerable time and energy during the early-90s attacking the "ethnic credentials" of Randy Lee White, an unenrolled mixed-blood Comanche artist with whom he shared space in Santa Fe's Elaine Horwitch Gallery, and whose thematically native work outsold Bradley's by a considerable margin. Finally successful in driving his only Indian competitor out of the gallery, Bradley was forced to watch White relocate to Los Angeles and resume his highly successful career—this time without reference to his heritage, and absent indigenous thematics—while Bradley's own sales actually declined.

51. Interview, conducted in Tahlequah, Okla., Oct. 1997; name withheld at the artist's request. "I've got work to do," he says, "and if my name gets printed in this connection, I'm going to end up spending all my time dodging snipers. I really don't need the headache."

52. A more extensive list of such individuals is provided in my "Spiritual Hucksterism: The Rise of the Plastic Medicine Men," in *From a Native Son*, pp. 355–66. It should be noted that this short essay, first published in a 1990 issue of *Z Magazine*, includes as attachments the texts of a 1980 resolution of the Traditional Elders Circle and a 1984 AIM resolution condemning such practices.

53. Instead, they typically claim to be the "medium" through which some indigenous "spirit" has elected to speak and/or the "messenger" through which a "traditional native shaman," usually invented, has decided to communicate with the "outside world" of nonindians; see, e.g., Richard de Mille, *Castaneda's Journey: The Power and the Allegory* (Santa Barbara, CA: Capra Press, 1976); *The Don Juan Papers: Further Castaneda Controversies* (Santa Barbara, CA: Ross-Erikson, 1980).

54. A major exception to this rule is "Jamake Highwater," a purported "Blackfoot/Cherokee" whose books on native art and "the primal mind" of indigenous people became bestsellers. Highwater eventually admitted that in a previous incarnation he'd been "J. Marks," a nonindian dance choreographer and biographer of Mick Jagger. Ultimately, it was revealed by Assiniboin/Sioux researcher Hank Adams that Marks himself was in fact Gregory Markopoulis, a Greek immigrant and failed cinematic follower of avant garde filmmaker Kenneth Anger. Fittingly, in light of his true origins, it was also demonstrated that his expositions on "native philosophy" were merely repackagings of Greek mythology; Hank Adams, *Cannibal Green*, unpublished manuscript © 1984 (full copy on file; excerpts published in *Akwesasne Notes* during 1984–85). For Markopoulis/Marks/Highwater's own view, see his "Second Class Indians," *American Indian Journal*, No. 6, 1980.

55. My own case has already been discussed. Primarily at issue in the present connection is the credibilty of my *Fantasies of the Master Race* and *Indians Are Us?*, books containing what are arguably some of the strongest critiques yet published with respect to the New Age and plastic medicine man phenomena. (It is noteworthy that even Carole Standing Elk's Center for the SPIRIT saw fit to "borrow" from me when preparing its own 1993 position paper on such matters; *Indians Are Us?*, pp. 279–81.) Rayna Green's "The Tribe Called Wannabe," published in *Folklore* (Vol. 9, No. 1, 1988), fits very much the same mold. Nonetheless, and despite having been issued a letter certifying her Cherokee identity by Chief Mankiller (see note 10), Green was herself publicly branded as a "wannabe" by Suzan Harjo in 1991. Most astonishingly, Harjo's blatant override of Cherokee sovereignty was couched in terms of "upholding Indian sovereignty" more generally.

56. Stephen Harrod Buhner, *one spirit, many peoples: a manifesto for earth spirituality* (Niwot, CO: Roberts, Rinehart, 1997).

57. James J. Kilpatrick, "Government Playing the Indian Game," syndicated column © 1992, distributed by the Thomas Jefferson Center, Charlottesville, VA.

58. Mankiller, "Buyers Have Final Say."

59. Ibid.

60. Herman J. Viola, *Ben Nighthorse Campbell: An American Warrior* (New York: Orion Books, 1993) p. 191. It should be noted that this is Campbell's approved biography, used by his campaign committee to promote his candidacy during his last race; David Brinkley, "Campbell to throw his book at the public," *Rocky Mountain News*, Dec. 10, 1993.

61. Viola, *Ben Nighthorse Campbell*, pp. 169–70. Instructively, although he now claims to believe such activities are so wrong as to warrant million dollar fines and years of imprisonment, he has never offered to divest himself of his own "ill-gotten gains." On the contrary, he is paving the way for his two children, Colin and Shanan—neither of whom is enrolled, nor even enrollable as things stand—to carry on the family business; ibid., p. 193.

61. Ibid., p. 191.

62. As official biographer Viola admits at p. 104, as of 1993 the "only documentary genealogical evidence in Campbell's possession is a badly tattered [and altered] copy of his father's Army discharge." There follows 25 pages of "what if's" and "maybe so's," culminating in an observation at

p. 125 that, in the end, "Campbell himself has no way of knowing" whether he's really related to the Cheyennes he posits as relatives. Whatever else may be said of Ben Campbell's saga—and there's actually much with which to redeem it—it's most certainly *not* evidence that "tracing [one's] background" should be "no problem" for many or even most diasporic native people. Quite the reverse.

64. Al Knight, "The government has no business deciding the purity of Indian art," *Denver Post*, Mar. 28, 1991. It should be noted that earlier press statements from Campbell's office had stated he was "three-eighths Indian."

65. Leah Renae Kelly, unpublished research paper, citing Viola, *Ben Nighthorse Campbell*, pp. 108, 112–14, 128–29.

66. Viola, *Ben Nighthorse Campbell*, p. 123.

67. Ibid., pp. 128, 139, 142.

68. Ibid., p. 141.

69. According to Smithsonian Institution employee Rayna Green, Harjo was enrolled at Southern Cheyenne during the mid-1980s at the behest of tribal official Richard West, with whom she was collaborating on a project to relocate the Museum of the American Indian from New York to Washington, D.C.; Churchill interview. For characterization of Harjo as a "prime mover," see Tilove, "Who's an Indian Artist?" Also see Steven Rosen, "Airport 'Tribute' Art Project Takes Heat on Indian Entrants," *Denver Post*, Mar. 28, 1993.

70. The denial was made in a letter to *Indian Country Today* published on Dec. 8, 1993.

71. Suzan Shown Harjo, "Legislation Stiffens Art Authenticity Laws," *Lakota Times*, Sept. 11, 1991.

72. It has recently been revealed, for instance, that National AIM CEO Vernon Bellecourt and his brother Clyde are "essentially Frenchmen, possessing only 1/32 degree of Indian blood"; Joe Geshick, "Integrity of Bellecourt Brothers called into question again," *Ojibwe News*, Feb. 18, 1994. Tim Giago, publisher of *Indian Country Today*, to take another prominent example, has long been accused by many on the Pine Ridge Reservation of being "a Chicano who snuck onto our roll." For Giago's response when he himself has been the target of his own techniques, see "Blood Quantum is a Measure of Discrimination," in his *Notes From Indian Country* (Pierre, SD: State Publishing Co., 1984), p. 337.

73. See, e.g., the quotes deployed in Sheffield, *Arbitrary Indian*, pp. 93–94.

74. Quoted in Viola, *Ben Nighthorse Campbell*, pp. 182–83, 193.

75. J.J. Brody, "The Creative Consumer: Survival, Revival and Invention in Southwest Indian Arts," in Nelson H.H. Graburn, ed., *Ethnic and Tourist Arts* (Berkeley: University of California Press, 1976), pp. 82–83. For a fuller exposition of the thesis, see Brody's *Indian Artists, White Patrons* (Albuquerque: University of New Mexico Press, 1971). It should be noted that Brody's analysis is entirely consistent with Luisaño artist Fritz Scholder' observation that, as he himself attained prominence, "everybody started to call me an Indian Artist—which I have never called myself . . . To tell the truth, I don't know what Indian Art is." Scholder considers the major influences upon his painting, including his acclaimed depictions of American Indians, to be the Euroamericans Wayne Thiebaud and Richard Diebenkorn, as well as English painter Francis Bacon; Clinton Adams, *Fritz Scholder: The Lithographs* (Boston: New York Graphic Society, 1975), pp. 13, 19.

76. As with Campbell, one is inclined to sympathize with Bradley's plight, signifying as it does the experience of all too many "detribalized" Indians in North America. However, as is also the case with Campbell, Bradley's blatant propensity to seek to compensate for his own resulting sense of insecurity by deliberately compounding the suffering of those in comparable circumstances simply cannot be justified or excused.

77. Quoted in Sheffield, *Arbitrary Indian*, p. 51. How Bradley manages in his own mind to make the leap from a plurality of indigenous "nations" to the singularity of an indigenous "nation" is mysterious, to say the least. It is, however, quite consistent with the totalizing federal impulse to arrive at handy "one definition fits all" formulations concerning Indians.

78. Ibid., pp. 51–52. To put it more succinctly, as Tim Giago did in an editorial in the Mar. 12, 1991 issue of his *Lakota Times*, "before you can truly be considered an Indian you must become an

enrolled member of a tribe." He then goes on to complete the circle by offering his belief that "most Indians"—whom he's already defined as consisting exclusively as enrollees—"would agree that this is the only way you can truly be accepted as Indian." In actuality, however, a significant portion of the enrolled population don't agree at all.

79. Sheffield, *Arbitrary Indian*, p. 51.

80. For analysis, see my "Naming Our Destiny: Toward a Language of American Indian Liberation," in *Indians Are Us?*, pp. 291–355.

81. See my "Subterfuge and 'Self-Determination': Suppression of Indigenous Sovereignty in the 20th Century United States," *Z Magazine*, May 1997.

82. Under Article I, Section 10, the U.S. Constitution both reserves treatymaking as an exclusively federal prerogative, and constrains the federal government itself from entering into treaty relations with any entity below its own level of political sovereignty. In effect, the U.S. government is authorized to treat *only* with the governing authorities of other nations, never with individuals, corporations, community organizations, local or provincial governments, racial/ethnic/gender groups or "tribes."

83. 430 U.S. 641, 645–47 (1977). For clarification, see Rennard Strickland and Charles Wilkinson, eds., *Felix S. Cohen's Handbook on Federal Indian Law* (Charlottesville, VA: Michie Bobbs Merrill, 1982) p. 654.

84. Sheffield, *Arbitrary Indian*, p. 134.

85. For a good overview of why this is so, the reader is referred to the voluminous compilation of extracts edited by John Hutchinson and Anthony D. Smith and published under the title *Ethnicity* (New York: Oxford University Press, 1996). With specific regard to Indians, see Joanne Nagel, *American Indian Ethnic Renewal: Red Power and the Resurgence of Identity and Culture* (New York: Oxford University Press, 1996).

86. This is a point made by Cherokee painter and Cornell University professor Kay Walkingstick, who contends that while a certain range of rights, benefits and entitlements should—and do—accrue exclusively to those on the rolls of indigenous nations by virtue of their status, monopolization of the terms of native identity is by no means one of them; quoted in Tilove, "Who's an Indian artist?"

87. For a poignant exposition on this theme, see Patricia Penn Hilden, *When Nickels Were Indians: An Urban Mixed-Blood Story* (Washington, D.C.: Smithsonian Institution Press, 1995).

88. Kimberly Craven, former aide to Campbell and staunch defender of the Act, explicitly described it as an "intellectual property law" during a "Sovereignty Symposium" conducted in the Oklahoma State Senate chambers on Jan. 15, 1991; video recording, Oklahoma Historical Society Archives, Oklahoma City, OK. The term "marketable commodity" was used several times during the earlier-mentioned Atlatl panel discussion (note 6).

89. Sheffield, *Arbitrary Indian*, p. 130.

90. Ibid., p. 138.

91. *Santa Clara Pueblo v. Martinez* (436 U.S. 49, 98 S. Ct. 1670 (1978)). In this case, an enrolled Santa Clara woman who married an enrolled Navajo sued in federal court after the Pueblo's government denied enrollment to her children on the basis of her "out marriage." Ms. Martinez argued that since the tribal government duly enrolled offspring of out-married Santa Clara men, it stood in violation of the Equal Protection provision of the Indian Civil Rights Act of 1968 (P.L. 90-284, 25 U.S.C.A. §§ 1301-41). The court ruled that, since determination of its membership was "the internal prerogative of each Indian tribe," the inequitable conduct of the tribal government was in this instance protected by the doctrine of sovereign immunity. Kimberly Craven, for one, has stated flatly that the 1990 Act was drafted with the *Martinez* precedent in mind ("Sovereignty Symposium").

92. A tidy survey of enrollment criteria is offered by Russell Thornton in his *American Indian Holocaust and Survival: A Population History Since 1492* (Norman: University of Oklahoma Press, 1987) Chap. 8. More broadly, but less accessibly, see Thornton's "Tribal History, Tribal Population and Tribal Membership Requirements" (Chicago: Newberry Library Research Conf. Rpt. No. 8,

1987). C. Matthew Snipp also includes considerable information as Appendix 1 in his *American Indians: The First of This Land* (New York: Russell Sage Foundation, 1989). Snipp's data is extracted from an unpublished table prepared by Edgar Lister for the Indian Health Service under the title "Tribal Membership Rates and Requirements" (Washington, D.C.: U.S. Dept. of Health and Human Services, 1987).

93. Jerome A. Barrons and C. Thomas Dienes, *Constitutional Law in a Nutshell* (St. Paul, MN: West, [2d ed.] 1991) p. 218.

94. Sheffield, *Arbitrary Indian,* p. 158.

95. See generally, Janet A. McDonnell, *The Dispossession of the American Indian, 1887–1934* (Bloomington: Indiana University Press, 1991).

96. Sen. Jeff Bingaman, "Address to the Senate on the Arts and Crafts Act of 1990," *Congressional Record,* Vol. 137, Pt. 1, Nov. 26, 1991, pp. S.18150–3.

97. Ibid., p. S.18152.

98. Ibid., p. S.18153.

99. Quoted in Sheffield, *Arbitrary Indian,* p. 113. Cornsilk habitually identifies himself in this fashion, and, in 1993, was described in print as a "genealogist for the Cherokee Nation of Oklahoma"; Rave, "Few who know Churchill." According to the CNO enrollment office, however, he "does not now, nor has he ever held such a position." In reality, he was at the time an admissions assistant at Bacone College; Nagel, *Ethnic Renewal,* p. 239. As was mentioned earlier, fraud can assume many forms.

100. Cornsilk is at least straightforward. "I don't believe in the right to self-identification" under any circumstances, he says flatly; quoted in Nagel, *Ethnic Renewal,* p. 239. He is also prone to spewing blanket disparagements of the ancestors of those currently unenrolled. They "were ashamed," he asserts, without offering the least substantiation, "hid among the whites and participated in the oppression of the tribal Indians"; quoted in Sheffield, *Arbitrary Indian,* p. 113.

101. Ibid., p. 100. Along with Sheffield (p. 153), and *Webster's Third New International Dictionary,* I take "arbitrary" to mean a "random or convenient selection or choice . . . arising from unrestrained exercise of will, caprice, or personal preference . . . rather than reason or nature."

102. U.S. Senate, Select Committee on Indian Affairs, *Hearings on an Act to Transfer Administrative Consideration of Applications for Federal Recognition of an Indian Tribe to an Independent Commission* (Washington, D.C.: 102d Cong., 1st Sess., Oct. 22, 1991) p. 105.

103. See, e.g., Calvin L. Beale, "An Overview of the Phenomenon of Mixed Racial Isolates in the United States," *American Anthropologist,* Vol. 74, No. 3, 1972; Susan Greenbaum, "What's in a Label? Identity Problems of Southern Indian Tribes," *Journal of Ethnic Studies,* Vol. 19, No. 2, 1991.

104. See generally, Donald L. Fixico, *Termination and Relocation: Federal Indian Policy, 1945–1960* (Albuquerque: University of New Mexico Press, 1986). On treaty rights, see *Menominee Tribe v. U.S.* (388 F.2d 988, 1000 [Ct. CL. 1967], aff'd, 391 U.S. 404 (1968)).

105. See, e.g., David L. Ghere, "The 'Disappearance' of the Abenaki in Western Maine: Political Organization and Ethnocentric Assumptions," *American Indian Quarterly,* Vol. 17, No. 2, 1993. As of March 1996, there were 179 pending applications for federal recognition; U.S. Department of Interior, "Summary Statement of Acknowledgment Cases" Washington, D.C.: Bureau of Indian Affairs, Branch of Acknowledgment and Research, Mar. 22, 1996). This is consistent with earlier estimates that only about half of all potentially eligible groups had even bothered to apply; Frank W. Porter III, "An Historical Perspective on Non-Recognized American Indian Tribes," in his *Non-Recognized American Indian Tribes: An Historical and Legal Perspective* (Chicago: Newberry Library Occasional Papers No. 7, 1983) p. ii. It should be noted that the federal courts have held that absence of formal political recognition by the U.S. is not to be taken as evidence that a native people "is not a tribe in the ordinary sense" of culture and ethnicity; *Joint Tribal Council of the Passamaquoddy Tribe v. Morton,* 528 F.2d 370 (1st Cir. (1975)).

106. U.S. Department of Commerce, Bureau of the Census, Economics and Statistics Division,

U.S. Census of Population: General Population Characteristics, United States (Washington, D.C.: U.S. GPO, 1990) p. 3; *Census Bureau Releases: 1990 Census Counts on Specific Racial Groups* (Washington, D.C.: U.S. GPO, 1992) Table I; Lister, "Tribal Membership Data."

107. U.S. Department of Commerce, Bureau of the Census, Economics and Statistics Division, *1990 Census of the Population and Housing: Public Use Microdata A* (Washington, D.C.: U.S. GPO, 1991).

108. Nagel, *Ethnic Renewal*, pp. 95–101; Snipp, *American Indians*, pp. 51–56.

109. Jack D. Forbes, "Undercounting Native Americans: The 1980 Census and the Manipulation of Racial Identity in the United States," *Wicazo Sa Review*, Vol. VI, No. 1, 1990; "The Manipulation of Race, Caste and Identity: Classifying Afroamericans, Native Americans and Red-Black People," *Journal of Ethnic Studies*, Vol. 17, No. 3, 1990. Thornton and other native demographers have analyzed and commented upon the inadequacies of census data without venturing estimates as to the number of persons excluded from ethnic/racial classification as Indians.

110. Walter Echohawk, an attorney with the Native American Rights Fund, an entity devoted more or less exclusively to pursuing litigation in behalf of federally recognized tribal councils, describes the costs associated with defending such cases as being "very high"; telephone interview, May 12, 1997 (notes on file).

111. U.S. House of Representatives, Committee on Interior and Insular Affairs, *Hearings on an Act to Expand the Powers of the Indian Arts and Crafts Board* (Washington, D.C.: 101st Cong., 1st Sess., Aug. 17, 1989) p. 48.

112. David Bradley would no doubt like to point to Randy Lee White as an example of the successful exposure of a big time "ethnic fraud." However, as was mentioned in note 50, White—who may well *be* of native descent—continued to work and sell paintings at essentially the same rate and for the same prices after the "controversy" as he had before. His career was eventually truncated not by the identity police, but by an automobile accident. Meanwhile, Bradley's own artistic career, already languishing, has virtually collapsed.

113. Even Ben Campbell has conceded at this point that there "may be" problems with the Act, and that he is therefore willing to see it amended; Sheffield, *Arbitrary Indian*, p. 126.

114. As Judith Toland has observed, the "concept that one cannot understand the meaning of what something is, unless the meaning of what something is not is articulated" may be in some ways methodologically sound, but, where group definitions are concerned, "it is still the dynamic [of] the cultural hegemony" in statist forms of political organization. She recommends instead the more holistic approach of multivariant analysis in understanding ethnic identity; Judith D. Toland, *Ethnicity and the State* (New Brunswick, NJ: Transaction, 1993) p. 7.

115. Bill Wilson, "Aboriginal Rights: The Non-Status Indian Perspective," in Menno Boldt and J. Anthony Long, eds., *The Quest for Justice: Aboriginal Peoples and Aboriginal Rights* (Toronto: University of Toronto Press, 1985) pp. 62–70.

116. Clem Chartier, "Aboriginal Rights: The Métis Perspective," in Bolt and Long, *Quest for Justice*, pp. 54–61.

117. The whole idea is a throwback to the bizarre idea that "blood" is somehow the vehicle by which "culture" itself is transmitted. For a solid analysis of the "enormous conceptual and practical problems" attending the "use of blood quantum to define the modern Indian population" see Snipp, *American Indian*, pp. 32–44. More broadly, see William Stanton, *The Leopard's Spots: Scientific Attitudes Towards Race in America, 1815–1859* (Chicago: University of Chicago Press, 1960); Stephen Jay Gould, *The Mismeasure of Man* (New York: W.W. Norton, 1981).

118. As Native Hawaiian scholar/activist Haunani-Kay Trask has observed while explaining traditional indigenous methods of fixing identity through kinship, "race and genealogy are not interchangeable ideas and should never be confused. If you are part of my family, you are part of my family, regardless of your race"; Trask interview/discussion, Nov. 1996 (notes on file).

119. By 1980, fewer than half of all American Indians were marrying other native people, while

upwards of 95 percent of all whites, blacks, and persons of Asian descent married within their respective groups; Gary D. Sandefur and Trudy McKinnell, "American Indian Intermarriage," *Social Science Research*, No. 15, 1986.

120. Russell Thornton, Gary D. Sandefur and C. Matthew Snipp, "American Indian Fertility Patterns: 1910 and 1940 to 1980," *American Indian Quarterly*, No. 15, 1991.

121. Lenore Stiffarm and Phil Lane, Jr., "The Demography of Native North America: A Question of American Indian Survival," in Jaimes, *State of Native America*, p. 45.

122. Ronald Trosper, "Native American Boundary Maintenance: The Flathead Indian Reservation, Montana, 1869–1970," *Ethnicity*, No. 3, 1976, p. 257.

123. See my "The Crucible of American Indian Identity: Native Tradition versus Colonial Imposition in Postconquest North America," *American Indian Culture and Research Journal*, Vol. 23, No. 1, Spring 1999.

124. Electronic posting by "Nighthawk," Feb. 19, 1997.

125. Thornton, *Holocaust and Survival*, pp. 142–43.

126. Mary Young, "Pagans, Converts, and Backsliders, All: A Secular View of the Metaphysics of Indian-White Relations," in Calvin Martin, ed., *The American Indian and the Problem of History* (New York: Oxford University Press, 1987) p. 81. The Cherokees' recognized governments included those of the CNO and the United Keetoowah Band in Oklahoma, as well as that of the Eastern Band in North Carolina.

127. Resolution 92-68, passed by the Yankton Sioux Tribal Council, June 4, 1992; Resolution T-SR-02-2, passed by the Tribal Business Committee, Tonkawa Tribe of Oklahoma, Dec. 18, 1992. Both are covered in Sheffield, *Arbitrary Indian*, pp. 103–4.

128. Ibid., p. 104. It should be noted that, despite almost continuous assertions by Suzan Harjo and other identity policers that the 1990 Act is "about sovereignty, not race," such self-determining certification procedures have been ruled out of order by the federal government. In a memorandum written on April 23, 1993, the Solicitor-Indian Affairs of the U.S. Interior Department held that while, technically, it is within the rights of an indigenous nation to "certify any, irrespective of Indian blood, as an Indian artisan," the intent of Congress in passing the Act was plainly "to limit certification to those of that tribe's lineage." Hence, "a tribe may only certify persons of Indian blood as Indian artisans."

129. Snipp, *American Indian*, pp. 310–11.

130. Thornton, *Holocaust and Survival*, p. 224.

3. CONFRONTING COLUMBUS DAY

1. Raphaël Lemkin, *Axis Rule in Occupied Europe* (Washington, D.C.: Carnegie Institution, 1944) p. 79.

2. Ibid.

3. U.N. Doc. E/A.C. 25/S.R. 1–28.

4. Report of the United Nations Economic and Social Council, 1947, 6th Part; quoted in Robert Davis and Mark Zannis, *The Genocide Machine in Canada: The Pacification of the North* (Montréal: Black Rose Books, 1973) p. 19.

5. U.N. Doc. A/36, 1948.

6. U.N. Doc. E/A.C. 25/S.R. 1–28.

7. "[B]ecause Canadian Law already forbids most substantive aspects of genocide in that it prohibits homicide or murder vis-à-vis individuals, and because it may be undesirable to have the same acts forbidden under two different legal categories, we deem it advisable that the Canadian legislation [on genocide], which we urge as a symbol of our country's dedication to the rights set out in the Convention should be confined to 'advocating and promoting genocide,' acts which are not forbidden at present by the Criminal Code"; Maxwell Cohen, *Brief to the Senate Standing Committee on Legal and*

Constitutional Affairs on Hate Propaganda (Ottawa: Canada Civil Liberties Assoc., Apr. 22, 1969) p. 3.

8. Analysis of these debates will be found in Lawrence J. LeBlanc, *The United States and the Genocide Convention* (Durham, NC: Duke University Press, 1991).

9. Ibid., pp. 99–115. Also see C. Vann Woodward, *The Strange Career of Jim Crow* (New York: Oxford University Press, [3rd ed.] 1974); William L. Patterson, ed., *We Charge Genocide: The Crime of Government Against the Negro People* (New York: International, 1970).

10. Again, a broad literature exists. Perhaps the most focused for purposes of this presentation is Wyn Craig Wade, *The Fiery Cross: The Ku Klux Klan in America* (New York: Simon and Schuster, 1987). Also see Leonard Zeskind, *The Christian Identity Movement: A Theological Justification for Racist and Anti-Semitic Violence* (New York: Division of Church and Society of the National Council of Churches of Christ in the U.S., 1986).

11. *Congressional Record*, Feb. 18, 1986, p. 132. Also see U.S. Senate, *Hearings on the Genocide Convention Before the Senate Committee on Foreign Relations* (Washington, D.C.: 97th Cong., 1st Sess., 1985).

12. U.S. Senate, *Hearing on Legislation to Implement the Genocide Convention Before the Senate Committee on the Judiciary: S. 1851*, (Washington, D.C.: 100th Cong., 2d Sess., 1989).

13. LeBlanc, *Genocide Convention*, p. 98.

14. As the matter was framed during Senate debates, "a question arises as to what the United States is really seeking to accomplish by attaching this understanding. The language suggests the United States fears it has something to hide"; *S. Exec. Rep. No. 2* (Washington, D.C.: 99th Cong., 1st Sess., 1987) p. 32

15. U.S. Senate, *Hearings on the Genocide Convention Before a Subcommittee of the Senate Committee on Foreign Relations* (Washington, D.C.: 81st Cong., 2d Sess., 1955) p. 217.

16. The text of the Vienna Convention may be found in L. Henkin, et al., *International Law: Cases and Materials, Basic Documents Supplement*, (Charlottesville, VA: Michie, 1980) p. 264.

17. See Michla Pomerance, *The Advisory Function of the International Court in the League and U.N. Eras* (The Hague: Martinus Nijhoff, 1973) pp. 115–25.

18. U.N. Economic and Social Council, *Study of the Question of the Prevention and Punishment of the Crime of Genocide* (U.N. Doc. E/CN.4/Sub.2/416 (1978)) Note 9 at pp. 46–47. For interpretation of the 1969 Convention itself, see Sir Ian Sinclair, *The Vienna Convention on the Law of Treaties* (Manchester, U.K.: Manchester University Press, [2nd ed.] 1984).

19. U.N. Secretariat, *Multilateral Treaties Deposited with the Secretary-General: Status as of 31 December 1989* (St/Leg/Ser. E/8, 1990) Note 2 at pp. 102–4. Also see Leich, "Contemporary Practice of the United States Relating to International Law," *American Journal of International Law*, No. 82, 1988, pp. 337–40.

20. LeBlanc, *Genocide Convention*, pp. 7–8.

21. International Court of Justice, *Advisory Opinions and Orders*, "Reservations to the Convention on Prevention and Punishment of the Crime of Genocide," 1951, pp. 15–69.

22. According to Section 701, the United States is bound by the international customary law of human rights (p. 153). In Section 702, genocide is recognized as a violation of customary international human rights law (pp. 161–63).

23. The text of the U.N. Charter may be found in Ian Brownlie, ed., *Basic Documents on Human Rights* (Oxford, U.K.: Clarendon Press, 1971).

24. Quincy Wright, "The Law of the Nuremberg Trial," in Jay W. Baird, ed., *From Nuremberg to My Lai* (Lexington, MA: D.C. Heath, 1972) p. 37.

25. An exhaustive analysis of the decisively central role played by the U.S. in creating what became known as the "Nuremberg Doctrine" may be found in Bradley F. Smith, *The Road to Nuremberg* (New York: Basic Books, 1981).

26. Secretary of War Henry L. Stimson, "The Nuremberg Trial, Landmark in Law," *Foreign Affairs*, Vol. XXV, Jan. 1947, pp. 179–89. Also see U.N. War Crimes Commission, *History of the United*

Nations War Crimes Commission and the Development of the Laws of War (London: His Majesty's Stationery Office, 1948).

27. Quoted in Smith, *Reaching Judgment*, p. 241.

28. The London Charter assumed the force of international law by virtue of its endorsement and subsequent ratification by twenty-three nations pursuant to the London Conference. For the official interpretation of the extent of the U.S. role in this connection, see U.S. Department of State, *Report of Robert H. Jackson, United States Representative to the International Conference on Military Trials, London, 1945* (Washington, D.C.: Department of State Pub. 3080, 1949); the text of the Charter is included therein.

29. Eugene C. Gerhart, *America's Advocate: Robert H. Jackson* (Indianapolis: Bobbs-Merrill, 1958); Francis Biddle, *In Brief Authority* (New York: Alfred A. Knopf, 1962).

30. For a thorough examination of the structure of U.S. participation during the trial, see Bradley F. Smith, *Reaching Judgment at Nuremberg* (New York: Basic Books, 1977).

31. For the German arguments, see International Military Tribunal, *Trial of the Major War Criminals before the International Military Tribunal*, 42 vols. (Nuremberg: IMT, 1949) Vol. 1, pp. 168–70, 458–94.

32. Jackson's opening remarks are contained in *Trial of the Major War Criminals*, Vol. 2, pp. 98–155.

33. It should be noted that the same principles pertain to the prosecution of major Japanese criminals following World War II. See Arnold C. Brackman, *The Other Nuremberg: The Untold Story of the Tokyo War Crimes Trials* (New York: Quill/Morrow, 1987); Philip Piccagallo, *The Japanese on Trial* (Austin: University of Texas Press, 1979).

34. LeBlanc, *Genocide Convention*, p. 55.

35. In October 1985, President Ronald Reagan withdrew a 1946 U.S. declaration accepting ICJ jurisdiction in all matters of "international dispute." The withdrawal took effect in April 1986. This was in response to the ICJ determination in *Nicaragua v. United States*, the first substantive case ever brought before it to which the U.S. was a party. The ICJ ruled the U.S. action of mining Nicaraguan harbors in times of peace to be unlawful. The Reagan Administration formally rejected the authority of the ICJ to decide the matter (but removed the mines). It is undoubtedly significant that the Reagan instrument contained a clause accepting continued ICJ jurisdiction over matters pertaining to "international commercial relationships," thus attempting to convert the world court into a mechanism for mere trade arbitration. See U.S. Department of State, *U.S. Terminates Acceptance of ICJ Compulsory Jurisdiction* (Washington, D.C.: Department of State Bulletin No. 86, Jan. 1986).

36. For the best analysis of the issues involved here, see Richard Delgado and Jean Stefanic, *Must We Defend Nazis? Hate Speech, Pornography, and the New First Amendment* (New York: New York University Press, 1997) esp. pp. 149–62.

37. There were actually a series of "Nuremberg Trials" conducted from 1945–49, beginning with the trial of the nazi leadership, in which we are most interested here. For summaries of the others, including those of the German industrialists and judiciary, nazi doctors, etc., see John Alan Appleman, *Military Tribunals and International Crimes* (Greenwood, CT: Greenwood Press, 1954).

38. As Smith puts it at p. 192 of *Reaching Judgment*, "The American prosecution spent endless hours asserting . . . that Rosenberg's theoretical writings had been significant in the nazi rise to power and that his work in education had played a vital role in preparing German youth for [the crimes which were to follow]." For further detail, see International Military Tribunal, *Trial of the Major War Criminals before the International Military Tribunal*, 42 vols. (Nuremberg: IMT, 1949) Vols. 4–5.

39. The quote is from Smith, *Reaching Judgment*, p. 236. At p. 233, Smith observes that, "[Von Schirach's prewar] position required him to perform two main tasks: to undermine and finally eliminate all independent youth groups, and to gather the overwhelming majority of young Germans into the Hitler Youth and related organizations, where they could receive massive doses of Nazi indoctrination . . . The [American] prosecution made a vigorous effort to [implicate the defendant in]

Hitler's general plans by stressing the importance the Führer attached to the indoctrination of youth and by showing that the . . . ideological training that Schirach had provided in the Hitler Youth fitted in with the Nazi 'blueprint' for aggression."

40. The description of Streicher's place (or lack of it) within the nazi hierarchy is taken from a defense memorandum prepared by staff member Robert Stewart for Justice Jackson during the summer of 1946. It is quoted in Smith, *Reaching Judgment*, p. 200. At p. 201, Smith observes that Streicher was charged only as an "anti-Semitic agitator," and that the "core of the case against [him] came down to a question of whether he had advocated and encouraged extermination of the Jews while knowing, or having reason to believe, that such extermination was the settled policy of the Nazi government."

41. Quoted in Smith, *Reaching Judgment*, p. 47.

42. John Gimble, *The American Occupation of Germany* (Stanford, CA: Stanford University Press, 1968). Also see John J. McCloy, "The Present Order of German Government" (*Department of State Bulletin*, June 11, 1951), and General Lucius D. Clay, "The Present State of Denazification, 1950," reprinted in Constantine Fitzgibbon, ed., *Denazification* (New York: W.W. Norton, 1969). These proscriptions were, under U.S. "tutelage," built into the constitution and statutory code of the German Republic during the early 1950s as an expedient to "attaining true democracy." Surely, this performance bespeaks something of an official posture of the United States with regard to "First Amendment Guarantees" where celebration/advocacy/incitement of genocide is concerned.

43. A survey of opinion pieces from *Time* and *Newsweek* magazines, June through Aug. 1991, will abundantly illustrate this point.

44. Samuel Eliot Morrison, ed., *Journals and Other Documents on the Life and Voyages of Christopher Columbus* (New York: Heritage, 1963).

45. The letter of appointment to these positions, signed by Ferdinand and Isabella, and dated May 28, 1493, is quoted in full in Benjamin Keen, *The Life of the Admiral Christopher Columbus by His Son Ferdinand* (New Brunswick, NJ: Rutgers University Press, 1959) pp. 105–6.

46. Among the better sources on Columbus' policies are Troy Floyd's *The Columbus Dynasty in the Caribbean, 1492–1526* (Albuquerque: University of New Mexico Press, 1973), and Stuart B. Schwartz's *The Iberian Mediterranean and Atlantic Traditions in the Formation of Columbus as a Colonizer* (Minneapolis: University of Minnesota Press, 1986).

47. Regarding the eight million figure, see Sherburn F. Cook and Woodrow Borah, *Essays in Population History, Vol. I* (Berkeley: University of California Press, 1971) esp. Chap. VI. The three million estimate pertaining to the year 1496 derives from a survey conducted by Bartolomé de Las Casas in that year, covered in J.B. Thatcher, *Christopher Columbus*, 2 vols. (New York: Putnam's, 1903–1904) Vol. 2, p. 348ff.

48. For summaries of the Spanish census records, see Lewis Hanke, *The Spanish Struggle for Justice in the Conquest of America* (Philadelphia: University of Pennsylvania Press, 1947), p. 200ff.

49. Aggregate estimates of the precontact indigenous population of the Caribbean Basin will be found in William Denevan, ed., *The Native Population of the Americas in 1492* (Madison: University of Wisconsin Press, 1976); Henry F. Dobyns, *Their Numbers Become Thinned: Native American Population Dynamics in Eastern North America* (Knoxville: University of Tennessee Press, 1983); and Russell Thornton, *American Indian Holocaust and Survival: A Population History Since 1492* (Norman: University of Oklahoma Press, 1987). For additional information, see Dobyns' bibliographic *Native American Historical Demography* (Bloomington/Indianapolis: Indiana University Press, 1976).

50. These figures are utilized in numerous studies. One of the more immediately accessible is Leo Kuper's *Genocide: Its Political Use in the Twentieth Century* (New Haven, CT: Yale University Press, 1981).

51. See Henry F. Dobyns, "Estimating American Aboriginal Population: An Appraisal of Techniques with a New Hemispheric Estimate," *Current Anthropology*, No. 7, 1981, pp. 395–416.

52. An overall pursuit of this theme will be found in P.M. Ashburn, *The Ranks of Death* (New York: Coward, 1947). Also see John Duffy, *Epidemics in Colonial America* (Baton Rouge: Louisiana State University Press, 1953). Broader and more sophisticated articulations of the same idea are em-

bodied in Alfred W. Crosby, Jr., *The Columbian Exchange: Biological and Cultural Consequences of 1492* (Greenwood, CT: Greenwood Press,1972) and *Ecological Imperialism: The Biological Expansion of Europe, 900–1900* (Cambridge, U.K.: Cambridge University Press, 1986).

53. Among the more thoughtful elaborations of this theme are Smith's *Reaching Judgment* and Eugene Davidson's *The Trial of the Germans, 1945–1946* (New York: Macmillan, 1966).

54. See Tzvetan Todorov, *The Conquest of America: The Question of the Other* (New York: Harper & Row, 1984).

55. Kirkpatrick Sale, *The Conquest of Paradise: Christopher Columbus and the Columbian Legacy* (New York: Alfred A. Knopf, 1990) p. 155.

56. Far from the "revisionist historian" he was described as being in the July 15, 1991 edition of *Newsweek*, las Casas was the *first* historian of the New World. There was no one for him to revise. Consequently, those who seek to counter or deny his accounts—"mainstream" historians all—are the actual revisionists, seeking to maintain a "politically correct interpretation" of events.

57. Bartolomé de Las Casas, *The Spanish Colonie: Brevísima revacíon* (New York: University Microfilms Reprint, 1966).

58. Bartolomé de Las Casas, *Historia de las Indias, Vol. 3*, (Mexico City: Fondo de Cultura Económica, 1951), esp. Chap. 29.

59. Las Casas, quoted in Thatcher, *Columbus*, p. 348ff.

60. For instance, quoting an affidavit by SS *Obergruppenführer* Otto Ohlendorf: "The Einsatz 'special action' unit would enter a village or town and order the prominent Jewish citizens to call together all Jews . . . Then they were shot, kneeling or standing, by firing squads in a military manner"; quoted in William Shirer, *The Rise and Fall of the Third Reich: A History of Nazi Germany* (New York: Simon and Schuster, 1960) p. 959.

61. Todorov, *Conquest*.

62. See Charles Gibson, ed., *The Spanish Tradition in America* (New York: Harper & Row, 1968).

63. For detailed examination of the conceptual linkages and differentiations between Spanish and English practices in the New World, see Robert A. Williams, *The American Indian in Western Legal Thought: The Discourses of Conquest* (New York: Oxford University Press, 1990).

64. The estimate of Pequot casualties—most of them women, children, and old people—accrues from a conservative source; Robert M. Utley and Wilcomb E. Washburn, *Indian Wars* (Boston: Houghton-Mifflin, 1977) p. 42.

65. E. Wagner Stearn and Allen E. Stearn, *The Effects of Smallpox on the Destiny of the Amerindian* (Boston: Bruce Humphries, 1945) pp. 44–45.

66. Ibid.

67. Sherburn F. Cook, "The Significance of Disease in the Extinction of the New England Indians," *Human Biology*, No. 45, 1973, pp. 485–508.

68. The Fort Clark incident is covered in Thornton, *American Indian Holocaust*, pp. 94–96.

69. Donald E. Green, *The Politics of Indian Removal: Creek Government and Society in Crisis* (Lincoln: University of Nebraska Press, 1977).

70. Russell Thornton, "Cherokee Population Losses During the Trail of Tears: A New Perspective and a New Estimate," *Ethnohistory*, No. 31, 1984, pp. 289–300.

71. Ibid., p. 293. Also see Grant Foreman, *Indian Removal: The Immigration of the Five Civilized Tribes* (Norman: University of Oklahoma Press, 1953).

72. On the template for nazi *lebensraumpolitik* provided by U.S. removal and extermination policies vis-à-vis Indians, see Adolf Hitler, *Mein Kampf* (New York: Reynal and Hitchcock, 1939) pp. 403, 501; *Hitler's Secret Book* (New York: Grove Press, 1961) pp. 46–52. Another iteration will be found in a lengthy memorandum prepared by an aide, Col. Freidrich Hössbach, summarizing Hitler's statements during a "Führer Conference" conducted on Nov. 5, 1937; *Trial of the Major War Criminals*, Vol. 25, pp. 402–13.

73. This too played directly into the nazi formulation of *lebensraumpolitik*; Frank Parrella, *Lebensraum and Manifest Destiny: A Comparative Study in the Justification of Expansionism* (Washington,

D.C.: M.A. Thesis, Dept. of International Affairs, Georgetown University, 1950).

74. See David Svaldi, *Sand Creek and the Rhetoric of Extermination: A Case Study in Indian-White Relations* (Lanham, MD: University Press of America, 1989). The comparisons to nazi rhetoric are obvious.

75. Richard Drinnon, *Facing West: The Metaphysics of Indian Hating and Empire Building* (Minneapolis: University of Minnesota Press, 1980); Reginald S. Horsman, *Race and Manifest Destiny: The Origins of Racial Anglo-Saxonism* (Cambridge, MA: Harvard University Press, 1981).

76. Stiffarm and Lane, "American Indian Demography," p. 34.

77. Roberto Mario Salmón, "The Disease Complaint at Bosque Redondo (1864–1868)," *Indian Historian*, No. 9, 1976.

78. W.W. Newcome, Jr., *The Indians of Texas* (Austin: University of Texas Press, 1961) p. 334.

79. James M. Mooney, "Population," in Frederick W. Dodge, ed., *Handbook of the Indians North of Mexico, Vol. 2* (Washington, D.C.: Smithsonian Institution, Bureau of American Ethnology Bulletin No. 30, 1910) pp. 286–87.

80. Thornton, *Holocaust and Survival*, p. 107. Also see Robert F. Heizer, ed., *The Destruction of the California Indians* (Salt Lake City/Santa Barbara: Peregrine Smith, 1974).

81. U.S. Department of Commerce, Bureau of the Census, Racial Statistics Branch, *Fifteenth Census of the United States, 1930: The Indian Population of the United States and Alaska* (Washington, D.C.: U.S. GPO, 1937) Table II: "Indian Population by Divisions and States, 1890–1930," p. 3.

82. The official record of the cumulative reductions in native landbase leading to this general result may be found in Charles C. Royce, *Indian Land Cessions in the United States: 18th Annual Report, 1896–1897* (Washington, D.C.: Smithsonian Institution, 1899). An additional 100 million acres were also being expropriated under provision of the General Allotment Act even as Royce completed his study; this left Indians with about fifty million acres total, or approximately 2.5 percent of their original land base; Janet A. McDonnell, *The Dispossession of the American Indian, 1887–1934* (Bloomington: Indiana University Press, 1991).

83. James M. Mooney, *The Aboriginal Population of America North of Mexico* (Washington, D.C.: Smithsonian Miscellaneous Collections, LXXX, No. 7, 1928) p. 33. For a more contemporary assessment of the situation in Canada, see Davis and Zannis, *Genocide Machine*.

84. On the boarding school system, see David Wallace Adams, *Education for Extinction: American Indians and the Boarding School Experience, 1875–1928* (Lawrence: University Press of Kansas, 1995).

85. On adoption policies, see Tillie Blackbear, "American Indian Children: Foster Care and Adoptions," in U.S. Department of Health, Education and Welfare, Office of Educational Research and Development, National Institute of Education, *Conference on Educational and Occupational Needs of American Indian Women, October 1986* (Washington, D.C.: DHEW, 1986) pp. 185–210. "Blind" adoptions are those in which the court orders adoption records permanently sealed in order that the person adopted can never know the identity of his/her parents or cultural heritage.

86. The goals of U.S. Assimilation Policy were summed up by Indian Commissioner Francis Leupp as "a mighty pulverizing engine for breaking up [the last vestiges of] the tribal mass"; see his *The Indian and His Problem* (New York: Scribner's, 1910) p. 93. Superintendent of Indian Education Daniel Dorcester described the objectives of his office as being to "develop the type of school that would destroy tribal ways"; quoted in Evelyn C. Adams, *American Indian Education: Government Schools and Economic Programs* (New York: King's Crown, 1946) p. 70. See more generally, Margaret Connell Szasz, *Education and the American Indian: The Road to Self-Determination Since 1928* (Albuquerque: University of New Mexico Press, [2nd ed.] 1999).

87. Brint Dillingham, "Indian Women and IHS Sterilization Practice," *American Indian Journal*, Vol. 3, No. 1, Jan. 1977, pp. 27–28. It should be noted that the government has conducted a comparable program against Puerto Rican and, to a somewhat lesser extent, African American women; *Women Under Attack: Abortion, Sterilization Abuse, and Reproductive Freedom* (New York: Committee for Abortion Rights and Against Sterilization Abuse, 1979).

88. U.S. Department of Commerce, Bureau of the Census, Racial Statistics Branch, *1980 Census*

of the Population, Supplementary Report: American Indian Areas and Alaska Native Villages (Washington, D.C.: U.S. GPO, 1984).

89. See Joseph G. Jorgenson, ed., *American Indians and Energy Development II* (Cambridge, MA: Anthropology Resource Center/Seventh Generation Fund, 1984).

90. These data derive from several sources, among them U.S. Senate, Committee on Labor and Human Resources, Subcommittee on Employment and Productivity, *Guaranteed Job Opportunity Act: Hearing on S.777* (Washington, D.C.: 100th Cong., 1st Sess., 1980); U.S. Congress, Office of Technology Assessment, *Indian Health Care* (Washington, D.C.: 103d Cong., 1st Sess., 1986); and Department of Health and Human Services, Public Health Service, *Chart Series Book* (Washington, D.C.: U.S. GPO, 1988). Also see *Conference on Educational and Occupational Needs of American Indian Women.*

91. See "A Breach of Trust," in this volume.

92. Jerry Kammer, *The Second Long Walk: The Navajo-Hopi Land Dispute* (Albuquerque: University of New Mexico Press,1980); Anita Parlow, *Cry, Sacred Ground: Big Mountain, USA* (Washington, D.C.: Christic Institute, 1988).

93. M.C. Barry, *The Alaska Pipeline: The Politics of Oil and Native Land Claims* (Bloomington: Indiana University Press, 1975).

94. Michael Garrity, "The U.S. Colonial Empire is as Near as the Nearest Reservation," in Holly Sklar, ed., *Trilateralism: The Trilateral Commission and Elite Planning for World Government* (Boston: South End Press, 1980) pp. 238–68.

95. As the Los Alamos Scientific Laboratory put it in its Feb. 1978 *Mini-Report*: "Perhaps the solution to the radon emission problem is to zone the land into uranium mining and milling districts so as to forbid human habitation."

96. Russell Means, "The Same Old Song," in my *Marxism and Native Americans* (Boston: South End Press, 1983) p. 25.

97. The 1887 "standard" was "one-half or more degree of Indian blood." This was subsequently lowered to one-quarter for "educational" purposes at the end of World War I (Act of May 25, 1918; 40 Stat. 564). On the origins of the Relocation Program and its effects of scattering Indians among the nonindian population, see Donald L. Fixico, *Termination and Relocation: Federal Indian Policy, 1945–1960* (Albuquerque: University of New Mexico Press, 1986).

98. Patricia Nelson Limerick, *The Legacy of Conquest: The Unbroken Past of the American West* (New York: W.W. Norton, 1987) p. 338.

99. See, as examples, Richard Arens, ed., *Genocide in Paraguay* (Philadelphia: Temple University Press, 1976); Robert M. Carmack, ed., *Harvest of Violence: The Maya Indians and the Guatemala Crisis* (Norman: University of Oklahoma Press, 1988).

100. Letter to the editor, *Rocky Mountain News,* Oct. 13, 1991.

101. This contention is readily borne out in a video tape prepared by University of Colorado media student Lori Windle, submitted as evidence in the case.

102. See, for example, Justice Jackson's remarks in the trial in Smith, *Reaching Judgement,* quoted throughout. Another U.S. prosecutor at Nuremberg, Telford Taylor, also takes up the issue in his book, *Nuremberg and Vietnam: An American Tragedy* (Chicago: Quadrangle, 1970).

103. Consider, for example, the instruction of Judge Paul F. Larrazolo to the jury at the end of the 1968 trial of participants in the celebrated 1968 Tierra Amarilla Courthouse Raid in New Mexico: "[A]nyone, including a state police officer, who intentionally interferes with a citizen's arrest does so at his own peril . . . since the arresting citizens are entitled under law to use whatever force is necessary to defend themselves in the process of making said citizen's arrest"; quoted in Peter Nabokov, *Tijerina and the Courthouse Raid* (Albuquerque: University of New Mexico Press, 1969) p. 264.

104. For instance, U.S. diplomat Ben Whitaker, Rapporteur of a 1985 U.N. study on implementation of the Genocide Convention, notes that this principle was "not new at [the Nuremberg] trial," and "was perfectly familiar in national legal systems [including that of the United States]." Consequently, "the doctrine was . . . not one invented *de novo* by the victors at Nuremberg," and there is

"little doubt that courts today would hold that the concept of individual responsibility will override any defense of superior orders"; U.N. Economic and Social Council, *Revised and Updated Report on the Question of the Prevention and Punishment of the Crime of Genocide Prepared by Mr. B. Whitaker* (25-26 U.N. Doc. E/CN.4/Sub.2/1985/6 (1985)) p. 24.

105. This position is articulated quite well in John Duffett, ed., *Against the Crime of Silence: Proceedings of the International War Crimes Tribunal* (New York: Clarion, 1970).

106. Whitaker, *Updated Report*, p. 26.

4. THE EARTH IS OUR MOTHER

1. On education, see David Wallace Adams, *Education for Extinction: American Indians and the Boarding School Experience, 1875–1928* (Lawrence: University Press of Kansas, 1995). On identification and recognition, see "Nullification of Native America?" herein.

2. See, e.g., Alan Van Gestel, "When Fictions Take Hostages," in James A. Clifton, ed., *The Invented Indian: Cultural Fictions and Government Policies* (New Brunswick, NJ: Transaction, 1990) pp. 291–312.

3. For a succinct and artfully constructed overview of this discourse, see Charles F. Wilkinson's *Indians, Time and Law: Native Societies in a Modern Constitutional Democracy* (New Haven, CT: Yale University Press, 1987). More comprehensively, see Rennard Strickland and Charles F. Wilkinson, eds., *Felix S. Cohen's Handbook on Federal Indian Law* (Charlottesville, VA: Michie, 1982).

4. I employ the term "hegemonic" in its specifically Gramscian sense; see Walter L. Adamson, *Hegemony and Revolution: A Study of Antonio Gramsci's Political and Cultural Theory* (Berkeley: University of California Press, 1980) pp. 170–79.

5. See my "Subterfuge and Self-Determination: Suppression of Indigenous Sovereignty in the 20th Century United States," *Z Magazine*, May 1997.

6. See generally, Paul A. Varg, *America: From Client State to World Power* (Norman: University of Oklahoma Press, 1990).

7. In the interim, the U.S. was by no means shy about picking up overseas colonies wherever it could, as is witnessed in its turn-of-the-century seizures of Hawai'i, the Philippines, Guam, "American" Samoa and Puerto Rico. The greater degree of sophistication generally manifested in its imperial ambitions can thus be attributed primarily to the fact that it had gotten into the game of overseas expansion rather belatedly, at a point when some 85 percent of the earth's surface had already been incorporated into the colonial dominions of one or another imperial power; see, e.g., Sidney Lens, *The Forging of the American Empire* (New York: Thomas Y. Crowell, 1971). On the juridical maneuvering occurring as a result, see Francis Anthony Boyle, *Foundations of World Order: The Legalist Approach to International Relations, 1898–1922* (Durham, NC: Duke University Press, 1999).

8. See Bernard Waites, *Europe and the Third World: From Colonisation to Decolonisation, c. 1500–1998* (New York: St. Martin's Press, 1999); David D. Newsome, *The Imperial Mantle: The United States, Decolonization, and the Third World* (Bloomington: Indiana University Press, 2001).

9. See Robert K. Thomas, "Colonialism: Classic and Internal," *New University Thought*, Vol. 4, No. 4, Winter 1966–67.

10. On America's formulation of Nuremberg Doctrine, and the resistance of its allies to the idea of a trial, see Bradley F. Smith, *The Road to Nuremberg* (New York: Basic Books, 1981).

11. Overall, see Eugene Davidson, *The Trial of the Germans: Nuremberg, 1945–1946* (New York: Macmillan, 1966); Bradley F. Smith, *Reaching Judgement at Nuremberg* (New York: Basic Books, 1977). On the correctness of the defendants' contention that they'd based their policies on the U.S. model, see Adolf Hitler, *Mein Kampf*, 2 vols. (New York: Reynal and Hitchcock, 1939) pp. 403, 591; *Hitler's Secret Book* (New York: Grove Press, 1961) pp. 106–8.

12. At the time the American submission was made at Nuremberg, there had been no less than 219 cases brought before the U.S. Court of Claims, none truly resolved and 86 of them still pending,

wherein one or more indigenous nations contended that its/their territory had been taken illegally— i.e., through fraud and/or armed force—by the United States; Walter Hart Blumenthal, *American Indian Dispossession: Fraud in Land Cessions Forced Upon the Tribes* (Philadelphia: G.S. McManus, 1955) p. 174; Harvey D. Rosenthal, *Their Day in Court: A History of the Indian Claims Commission* (New York: Garland, 1990) p. 24. It was also common knowledge that elsewhere—in the Philippines, for example—several hundred thousand people had been slaughtered in the process of U.S. takeovers only 40 years earlier; Stuart Creighton Miller, *"Benevolent Assimilation": The American Conquest of the Philippines, 1899–1903* (New Haven, CT: Yale University Press, 1983).

13. The relevance of Nuremberg to creation of the ICC is attested to by the fact that a virtually identical body had been proposed to the Congress on at least 20 occasions between 1910 and 1945, only to be shelved or voted down overwelmingly; Rosenthal, *Day in Court*, pp. 53–84.

14. This point is explored more thoroughly in my "Charades, Anyone? The Indian Claims Commission in Context," *American Indian Culture and Research Journal*, Vol. 24, No. 1, 2000.

15. *Public Papers of the Presidents of the United States: Harry S. Truman, 1946* (Washington, D.C.: U.S. GPO, 1962) p. 414.

16. Richard A. Nielson, "American Indian Land Claims: Land versus Money as a Remedy," *University of Florida Law Review*, Vol. 19, No. 3, 1973. Actually, there is one exception. In 1965, the ICC recommended (15 Ind. Cl. Comm. 666) restoration of 130,000 acres of the Blue Lake area to Taos Pueblo and, in 1970, Congress followed up by restoring a total of 48,000 acres (85 Stat. 1437); see R.C. Gordon-McCutchan, *The Taos Indians and the Battle for Blue Lake* (Santa Fe, NM: Red Crane Books, 1991).

17. An exception involved claims entered under provision of the Fifth Amendment, of which there were almost none. Interest was denied as a matter of course in other types of claim, based on the outcome of the *Loyal Creek Case* (1 Ind. Cl. Comm. 22 (1951)); Thomas LaDuc, "The Work of the Indian Claims Commission Under the Act of 1946," *Pacific Historical Review*, No. 26, 1957, pp. 1–16. A classic example of the more typical process is that in which the ICC purportedly established "quiet title" to virtually the entire state of California via an award of $29.1 million—about 47¢ per acre—in the 1964 "Pit River Land Claim Settlement"; *Thompson v. United States* (13 Ind. Cl. Comm. 369 (1964)). For further information, see M. Annette Jaimes, "The Pit River Indian Land Claim Dispute in Northern California," *Journal of Ethnic Studies*, Vol. 4, No. 4, Winter 1987; Howard Friedman, "Interest on Indian Land Claims: Judicial Protection of the Fisc," *Valparaiso University Law Review*, No. 5, Fall 1970.

18. John R. White, "Barmecide Revisited: The Gratuitous Offset in Indian Claims Cases," *Ethnohistory*, No. 25, Spring 1978.

19. *"Lone Wolf"* is covered in "The Tragedy and the Travesty," herein. Also see Ann Laquer Estin, *"Lone Wolf" v. Hitchcock*: The Long Shadow," in Sandra L. Cadwalader and Vine Deloria, Jr., eds., *The Aggressions of Civilization: Federal Indian Policy Since the 1880s* (Philadelphia: Temple University Press, 1984) pp. 214–45.

20. By the late 1990s, the amount "lost" in this fashion was estimated to have reached $40 billion; Peter Maas, "Broken Promise," *Parade Magazine*, Sept. 9, 2001, p. 6.

21. In the end, Indians were forced to expend some $100 million in legal fees—most of it mortgaged against our residual holdings—to obtain approximately $800 million in compensation for what the government would claim was clear title to about one-third of the continental U.S.; Rosenthal, *Day in Court*, p. 255.

22. John T. Vance, "The Congressional Mandate and the Indian Claims Commission," *North Dakota Law Review*, No. 45, 1969, p. 326.

23. *Congressional Record*, May 20, 1946, p. 5312.

24. See, e.g., the essays collected by Imre Sutton in his *Irredeemable America: The Indians' Estate and Land Claims* (Albuquerque: University of New Mexico Press, 1985).

25. In other words, "Congress cloak[ed] its own interests in a rhetoric of generosity to the Indian"; Wilcomb E. Washburn, *Red Man's Land, White Man's Law* (New York: Scribner's, 1971) pp. 103–4.

26. *Congressional Record*, May 20, 1946, p. 5319.

27. All told, 109 peoples, or portions of peoples, were terminated under a series of specific statutes accruing from House Concurrent Resolution 108 (1953), the great bulk of them by 1958 (one group, the Poncas of Oklahoma, was terminated in 1966); see generally, Donald L. Fixico, *Termination and Relocation: Federal Indian Policy, 1945–1960* (Albuquerque: University of New Mexico Press, 1986).

28. Statement of Utah Senator Arthur V. Watkins; quoted and discussed in Rosenthal, *Day in Court*, pp. 175–98.

29. U.S. House of Representatives, Committee on Indian Affairs, *Providing a One-Year Extension of the Five-Year Limitation on the Time for Presenting Indian Claims to the Indian Claims Commission* (Washington, D.C.: H. Rep. 692, 82d Cong., 1st Sess., 1951) pp. 593–601.

30. In 1956, the ICC was extended for a further five years. The process was repeated in 1961, 1967, 1972, and 1976; U.S. Congress, Joint Committee on Appropriations, *Hearings on Appropriations for the Department of Interior* (Washington, D.C.: 94th Cong., 1st Sess., 1976).

31. The original 852 claims had been consolidated into 615 dockets. Of these, the ICC had purportedly "disposed" of 547, 45 percent without awards (during the "Termination Era" proper, which lasted through the end of 1962, the tally was 105 dismissals versus 37 awards); see Indian Claims Commission, *Final Report* (Washington, D.C.: U.S. GPO, 1978). It should be noted that Indians began to appeal ICC dismissals towards the end of the 1960s. Of 206 such actions ruled upon by 1975, the Commission was affirmed in 96, partially affirmed in 31, and overruled in 79; U.S. Senate, Committee on Interior and Insular Affairs, Subcommmittee on Indian Affairs, *Hearings on S.876* (Washington, D.C.: 94th Cong., 1st Sess., 1975).

32. Rosenthal, *Day in Court*, p. 151.

33. U.S. Senate, Committee on Appropriations, *Hearings on H.R. 9390 for Appropriations for Interior and Related Agencies for 1957* (Washington, D.C.: 84th Cong., 2nd Sess., 1956) pp. 552–58.

34. U.S. Senate, Committee on Interior and Insular Affairs, Subcommittee on Indian Affairs, *Hearings on S.307, A Bill to Amend the Indian Claims Commission Act of 1946* (Washington, D.C.: 90th Cong., 1st Sess., 1967) p. 20.

35. U.S. Senate, Committee on Appropriations, *Hearings on H.R. 9417 for Appropriations for the Department of Interior and Related Agencies for 1972* (Washington, D.C.: 92d Cong., 1st Sess., 1971) pp. 1433–50; Committee on Interior and Insular Affairs, *Amending the Indian Claims Commission Act of 1946 as Amended* (Washington, D.C.: 92d Cong., 2d Sess., Rpt. 682., Mar. 2, 1972).

36. Attorney General Francis Biddle, who'd served as chief U.S. Justice at Nuremberg, had long since estimated that it would require billions of dollars to resolve even a very limited range of claims; U.S. Senate, *Terminating the Existence of the Indian Claims Commission* (Washington, D.C.: 84th Cong. 2d Sess., Rpt. 1727, Apr. 11, 1956).

37. Russel L. Barsh, "Indian Land Claims Policy in the United States," *North Dakota Law Review*, No. 58, 1982, pp. 1–82.

38. For the phrase used, see U.S. Department of Interior, Public Lands Law Review Commission, *One Third of the Nation's Land* (Washington, D.C.: U.S. GPO, 1970). On the size of the reservation landbase, see U.S. Department of Interior, Bureau of Indian Affairs, *Indian Lands Map: Oil, Gas and Minerals on Indian Reservations* (Washington, D.C.: U.S. GPO, 1978).

39. Several of these will be taken up in the section of the present essay devoted to Iroquois land claims. Another striking example is that of the 1861 Treaty of Fort Wise, in which the Cheyenne and Arapaho allegedly ceded the bulk of their territory in eastern Colorado. Among the problems with this arrangement are the facts that the majority of the native leaders supposedly signing the treaty were not even present—their signatures or "signs" were apparently forged—and that, in any event, the Senate subsequently and unilaterally rewrote the treaty text before ratifying and thereupon proclaiming it "binding" upon the Indians; Stan Hoig, *The Sand Creek Massacre* (Norman: University of Oklahoma Press, 1961) pp. 13–17.

40. Several of these will be discussed in the sections of the present essay devoted to the Iroquois and Black Hills land claims. Another pertains to the Cherokee, effectively dispossessed and interned at the

time they signed a treaty ostensibly ceding their homelands east of the Mississippi in exchange for territory in what is now the state of Oklahoma; see generally, Grant Foreman, *Indian Removal: The Immigration of the Five Civilized Tribes* (Norman: University of Oklahoma Press, 1953); Gloria Jahoda, *The Trail of Tears: The Story of the Indian Removals* (New York: Holt, Rinehart and Winston, 1975).

41. On the applicable customary law, see Sir Ian Sinclair, *The Vienna Convention on the Law of Treaties* (Manchester, U.K.: Manchester University Press, 1984).

42. Rodolfo Acuña, *Occupied America: The Chicano's Struggle Toward Liberation* (San Francisco: Canfield Press, 1972).

43. On the overall roles/performance of Jackson and Biddle, see Davidson, *Trial of the Germans*.

44. Robert H. Jackson, "Opening Statement for the United States Before the International Military Tribunal, November 21, 1945," quoted in Bertrand Russell, *War Crimes in Vietnam* (New York: Monthly Review Press, 1967) p. 125. More broadly, see Robert H. Jackson, *The Nürnberg Case* (New York: Alfred A. Knopf, 1947).

45. Truman, *Papers*, p. 414.

46. Vine Deloria, Jr., *Behind the Trail of Broken Treaties: An Indian Declaration of Independence* (Austin: University of Texas Press, [2nd ed.] 1984) p. 227.

47. See the 1967 statement of National Indian Youth Council representative Hank Adams included in *Hearings on S.307* at p. 91. Also see Robert T. Coulter and Steven M. Tullberg, "Indian Land Rights," in Cadwallader and Deloria, *Aggressions of Civilization*, p. 204.

48. Deloria, *Trail of Broken Treaties*; Paul Chaat Smith and Robert Allen Warrior, *Like a Hurricane: The American Indian Movement from Alcatraz to Wounded Knee* (New York: New Press, 1996).

49. See "The Law Stood Squarely on Its Head," herein. Also see Douglas Sanders, "The Re-Emergence of Indigenous Questions in International Law," *Canadian Human Rights Yearbook*, No. 3, 1983; Jimmie Durham, "An Open Letter on Recent Developments in the American Indian Movement/International Indian Treaty Council," in his *A Certain Lack of Coherence: Writings on Art and Cultural Politics* (London: Kala Press, 1993) pp. 46–56.

50. *Oneida Indian Nation v. County of Oneida* (414 U.S. 661 (1974)). For background on the strategy involved in such litigation, see Mark Kellogg, "Indian Rights: Fighting Back with White Man's Weapons," *Saturday Review*, Nov. 1978, pp. 24–30.

51. The letters were found in an old trunk by an elderly Passamaquoddy woman in 1957, and turned over to township governor John Stevens. It took the Indians fifteen years to bring the matter to court, largely because it was denied they had "legal standing" to do so; Paul Brodeur, *Restitution: The Land Claims of the Mashpee, Passamaquoddy, and Penobscot Indians of New England* (Boston: Northeastern University Press, 1985).

52. *Passamaquoddy Tribe v. Morton* (528 F.2d, 370 (1975)). For additional background, see Francis J. O'Toole and Thomas N. Tureen, "State Power and the Passamaquoddy Tribe: A Gross National Hypocrisy?" *Maine Law Review*, Vol. 23, No. 1, 1971.

53. Maine Indian Land Claims Settlement Act of 1980 (94 Stat. 1785).

54. *Narragansett Tribe of Indians v. S.R.I. Land Development Corporation* (418 F.Supp. 803 (1978)). The decision was followed by the Rhode Island Indian Claims Settlement Act of 1978 (94 Stat. 3498).

55. *Western Pequot Tribe of Indians v. Holdridge Enterprises, Inc.* (Civ. No. 76-193 (1976)).

56. The Mashantucket Pequot Indian Claims Settlement Act (S.366) was passed by Congress in Dec. 1982. For Reagan's veto, see *Congressional Quarterly*, Vol 41, No. 14, pp. 710–11.

57. The revised version of the Mashantucket Pequot Indian Claims Settlement Act (S.1499) was signed on Oct. 18, 1983.

58. *Mashpee Tribe v. Town of Mashpee* (447 F.Supp. 940 (1978)).

59. *Mashpee Tribe v. New Seabury Corporation* (592 F.2d (1st Cir.) 575 (1979), *cert. denied* (1980)). For further information, see Harry B. Wallace, "Indian Sovereignty and the Eastern Indian Land Claims," *New York University Law Review*, No. 27, 1982, pp. 921–50. Also see Brodeur, *Restitution*.

60. Douglas Sanders, "The U.N. Working Group on Indigenous Peoples," *Human Rights Quar-*

terly, No. 11, 1989. It should be noted that the U.S. has launched a veritable frontal assault in its effort to gut the proposed declaration; see Isabelle Schulte-Tenckhoff, "The Irresistible Ascension of the U.N. Declaration on the Rights of Indigenous Peoples: Stopped Dead in Its Tracks?" *European Review of Native American Studies*, Vol. 9, No. 2, 1995; Glenn T. Morris, "Further Motion by the State Department to Railroad Indigenous Rights," *Fourth World Bulletin*, No. 6, Summer 1998.

61. A problem here, of course, is the fact that the U.S., alone among U.N. member-states, has repudiated ICJ authority; "U.S. Terminates ICJ Compulsory Jurisdiction," *Department of State Bulletin*, No. 86, Jan. 1986.

62. For an assessment of the progress made in this arena, see S. James Anaya, *Indigenous Peoples in International Law* (New York: Oxford University Press, 1991). For the principles involved in resolving issues of this sort through such means, see Richard B. Lillich, *International Claims: Their Adjudication by National Commission* (Syracuse, NY: Syracuse University Press, 1962).

63. The general strategy described here is as applicable to Canada as to the U.S., a matter readily witnessed in the forms of struggle evident at Lubicon Lake, Oka, James Bay, and Gustafson Lake, to offer only the most prominent examples, over the past 30 years. See generally, John Goddard, *Last Stand of the Lubicon Cree* (Vancouver/Toronto: Douglas and McIntyre, 1991); Geoffrey York and Loreen Pindera, *People of the Pines: The Warriors and the Legacy of Oka* (Boston: Little, Brown, 1991); Grand Council of the Crees (Eeyou Astchee), *Never Without Consent: The James Bay Crees' Stand Against Forcible Inclusion Into an Independent Quebec* (Toronto: ECW Press, 1998); Janice G.A.E. Switlow, *Gustafson Lake: Under Siege* (Peachland, B.C.: TIAC Communications, 1997).

64. Florida Indian Land Claim Settlement Act (96 Stat. 2012 (1982)). For background, see Robert T. Coulter, "Seminole Land Rights in Florida and the Award of the Indian Claims Commission," *American Indian Journal*, Vol 4, No. 3, Aug. 1978.

65. See Winona LaDuke's "The White Earth Land Struggle," in my *Critical Issues in Native North America* (Copenhagen: IWGIA Doc. 63, 1989) pp. 55–71; and her "White Earth: The Struggle Continues," in my *Critical Issues in Native North America, Vol. 2* (Copenhagen: IWGIA Doc. 68, 1991) pp. 99–103.

66. Daniel McCool, "Federal Indian Policy and the Sacred Mountains of the Papago Indians," *Journal of Ethnic Studies*, Vol 9, No. 3, 1981.

67. Richard A. Lovett, "The Role of the Forest Service in Ski Resort Development: An Economic Approach to Public Lands Management," *Ecology Law Review*, No. 10, 1983. Also see George Lubick, "Sacred Mountains, Kachinas, and Skiers: The Controversy Over the San Francisco Peaks," in R. Lora, ed., *The American West: Essays in Honor of W. Eugene Hollan* (Toledo, OH: University of Toledo Press, 1980) pp. 133–53.

68. See the essay entitled "Genocide in Arizona? The 'Navajo-Hopi Land Dispute' in Perspective," in my *Struggle for the Land: Native North American Resistance to Genocide, Ecocide and Colonization* (Winnipeg: Arbeiter Ring, [2nd ed.] 1999) pp. 135–72.

69. Jack Campisi, "The Trade and Intercourse Acts: Indian Land Claims on the Eastern Seaboard," in Sutton, *Irredeemable America*, pp. 337–62.

70. For background, see M.C. Berry, *The Alaska Pipeline: The Politics of Oil and Native Land Claims* (Bloomington: Indiana University Press, 1975); John Berger, *Report from the Frontier: The State of the World's Indigenous Peoples* (London: Zed Books, 1987).

71. On the rejection, see U.S. House of Representatives, *House Report 15066* (Washington, D.C.: 94th Cong., 1st Sess., 1974). In 1980, the Congress passed an act (94 Stat. 3321) mandating formation of a Native Hawaiians Study Commission (six federal officials and three Hawaiians) to find out "what the natives really want." The answer, predictably, was *land.*

72. For the basis of the native argument here, see Haunani-Kay Trask, *From a Native Daughter: Colonialism and Sovereignty in Hawai'i* (Honolulu: University of Hawai'i Press, [2nd ed.] 1999). Also see Ward Churchill and Sharon H. Venne, eds., *Islands in Captivity: The Record of the International Tribunal on the Rights of Native Hawaiians*, 3 vols. (Cambridge, MA: South End Press, 2002).

73. Jefferson and other "radicals" held U.S. sovereignty accrued from the existence of the country

itself and did not "devolve" from the British Crown. Put another way, Jefferson—in contrast to John Marshall—held that Britain's asserted discovery rights in North America had *no* bearing on U.S. rights to occupancy of the continent; Gordon Wood, *The Creation of the American Republic, 1776–1787* (Chapel Hill: University of North Carolina Press, 1969) pp. 162–96; Merrill D. Peterson, *Thomas Jefferson and the New Nation* (New York: Oxford University Press, 1970) pp. 113–24.

74. This theme is explored by Vine Deloria, Jr., in an essay entitled "Self-Determination and the Concept of Sovereignty," in Roxanne Dunbar Ortiz and Larry Emerson, eds., *Economic Development in American Indian Reservations* (Albuqerque: University of New Mexico Native American Studies Center, 1979) pp. 22–28. Also see Walter Harrison Mohr, *Federal Indian Relations, 1774–1788* (Philadelphia: University of Pennsylvania Press, 1933).

75. Barbara Greymont, *The Iroquois in the American Revolution* (Syracuse, NY: Syracuse University Press, 1975). The concern felt by Congress with regard to the Iroquois as a military threat, and the consequent need to reach an accommodation with them, is expressed often in early official correspondence. See Washington C. Ford, et al., eds., *Journals of the Continental Congress, 1774–1789*, 34 vols. (Washington, D.C.: U.S. GPO, 1904–1937).

76. See Henry M. Manley, *The Treaty of Fort Stanwix, 1784* (Rome, NY: Rome Sentinel, 1932). The text of the Fort Stanwix Treaty (7 Stat. 15) as well as that of the Fort Harmar Treaty (7 Stat. 33) will be found in Charles J. Kappler, ed., *Indian Treaties, 1787–1883* (New York: Interland, 1973) pp. 5–6, 23–25.

77. Jack Campisi, "From Fort Stanwix to Canandaigua: National Policy, States' Rights and Indian Land," in Christopher Vescey and William A. Starna, eds., *Iroquois Land Claims* (Syracuse, NY: Syracuse University Press, 1988) pp. 49–65; quote from p. 55.

78. For an account of these meetings, conducted by New York's Governor Clinton during August and September 1784, see Franklin B. Hough, ed., *Proceedings of the Commissioners of Indian Affairs, Appointed by Law for Extinguishment of Indian Titles in the State of New York*, 2 vols. (Albany, NY: John Munsell, 1861) Vol. 1, pp. 41–63.

79. Clinton lied, bold-faced. New York's references to the Genesee Company concerned a bid by that group of land speculators to lease Oneida land which the Indians had not only rejected, but which the state legislature had refused to approve. In effect, the Oneidas had lost *no* land, were unlikely to, and the governor knew it; Campisi, "Fort Stanwix," p. 59.

80. The leases are covered at various points in *Public Papers of George Clinton: First Governor of New York*, Vol. 8 (Albany, NY: New York State Historical Society, 1904).

81. The price paid by New York for the Onondaga lease was "1,000 French Crowns, 200 pounds in clothing, plus a $500 annuity"; Helen M. Upton, *The Everett Report in Historical Perspective: The Indians of New York* (Albany: New York State Bicentennial Commission, 1980) p. 35.

82. Ibid., p. 38.

83. 1 Stat. 37, also called the "Nonintercourse Act." The relevant portion of the statute reads: "[N]o sale of lands made by any Indians, or any nation or tribe of Indians within the United States, shall be valid to any person or persons, or to any state, whether having the right of pre-emption to such lands or not, unless the same shall be made and duly executed at some public treaty, held under the authority of the United States." See generally, Francis Paul Prucha, *American Indian Policy in the Formative Years: The Trade and Intercourse Acts, 1790–1834* (Lincoln: University of Nebraska Press, 1970).

84. Upton, *Everett Report*, p. 40.

85. For ratification discussion on the meaning of the Treaty of Canandaigua, see *American State Papers: Documents, Legislative and Executive of the Congress of the United States, from the First Session to the Third Session of the Thirteenth Congress, Inclusive*, Vol. 4 (Washington, D.C.: Gales and Seaton, 1832) pp. 545–70. The text of the Canandaiga Treaty (7 Stat. 44) will be found in Kappler, *Indian Treaties*, pp. 34–37. On Tecumseh's alliance, see R. David Edmunds, *Tecumseh and the Quest for Indian Leadership* (Boston: Little, Brown and Company, 1984).

86. Paul D. Edwards, *The Holland Company* (Buffalo, NY: Buffalo Historical Society, 1924).

87. For background, see John Sugden, *Tecumseh's Last Stand* (Norman: University of Oklahoma Press, 1985); Allan W. Eckert, *A Sorrow in Our Heart: The Life of Tecumseh* (Boston: Little, Brown, 1992).

88. Henry S. Manley, "Buying Buffalo from the Indians," *New York History*, No. 28, July 1947.

89. For background, see Ronald Satz, *American Indian Policy in the Jacksonian Era* (Lincoln: University of Nebraska Press, 1975); Ernest Downs, "How the East Was Lost," *American Indian Journal*, Vol. 1, No. 2, 1975.

90. A good dose of the rhetoric attending passage of the Removal Act, and thus a glimpse of official sensibilities during the period, will be found in U.S. Congress, *Speeches on the Removal of the Indians, April-May, 1830* (New York: Jonathan Leavitt, 1830; New York: Kraus Reprints, 1973).

91. For text of the Treaty of Buffalo Creek (7 Stat. 550), see Kappler, *Indian Treaties*, pp. 502–16. An interesting contemporaneous analysis will be found in Society of Friends (Hicksite), *The Case of the Seneca Indians in the State of New York* (Stanfordville, NY: Earl E. Coleman, 1979 reprint of 1840 original).

92. Most principal leaders of the Six Nations never signed the Buffalo Creek Treaty. In the Senate, the treaty came up one vote short in successive polls of reaching the number necessary for ratification. On the third attempt, it was necessary for Vice President Richard Johnson to vote in order for the constitutional requirement of a two-thirds majority to be met. This in itself was illegal, since the vice president is empowered to cast a vote in the Senate only for purposes of breaking a tie; Manley, "Buying Buffalo from the Indians."

93. U.S. House of Representatives, H. Doc. 66 (Washington, D.C.: 26th Cong., 2d Sess., Jan. 6, 1841).

94. The text of the second Buffalo Creek Treaty (7 Stat. 586) will be found in Kappler, *Indian Treaties*, pp. 537–42.

95. The Tonawanda protest appears as U.S. Senate, S. Doc. 273 (Washington, D.C.: 29th Cong., 2d Sess., April 2, 1842). On the award, made on November 5, 1857, see *Documents of the Assembly of the State of New York* (Albany: 112th Sess., Doc. 51, 1889) pp. 167–70.

96. Upton, *Everett Report*, p. 53. The New York high court's invalidation of the leases is covered in *U.S. v. Forness* (125 F.2d 928 (1942)). On the court's deeming of the leases to be perpetual, see U.S. House of Representatives, Committee on Indian Affairs, *Hearings in Favor of House Bill No. 12270* (Washington, D.C.: 57th Cong., 2d Sess., 1902).

97 Assembly Doc. 51, pp. 43, 408.

98. 28 Stat. 887, Mar. 2, 1895. On the Ogden maneuver, see Upton, *Everett Report*, p. 161.

99. Allotment was a policy designed to supplant the traditional indigenous practice of collective landholding with the supposedly more "civilized" Euroamerican individuated property titles. For a survey of the impacts of the federal government's 1887 General Allotment Act (ch. 119, 24 Stat. 388) upon native peoples, mostly west of the Mississippi, see Janet A. McDonnell, *Dispossession of the American Indian, 1887–1934* (Bloomington: Indiana University Press, 1991).

100. *Hearings in Favor of House Bill No. 12270*, p. 23.

101. Ibid., p. 66.

102. The original case is *Seneca Nation v. Appleby* (127 AD 770 (1905)). It was appealed as *Seneca Nation v. Appleby* (196 NY 318 (1906)).

103. The case, *U.S. v. Boylan* (265 Fed. 165 (2d Cir. 1920)), is not important because of the negligible quantity of land restored but because it was the first time the federal judiciary formally acknowledged New York had never acquired legal title to Haudenosaunee land. It was also one of the very few times in American history when nonindians were actually evicted in order that Indians might recover illegally taken property.

104. New York State Indian Commission Act, Chapter 590, Laws of New York, May 12, 1919.

105. Upton, *Everett Report*, p. 99.

106. The final document is Edward A. Everett, *Report of the New York State Indian Commission*, Albany, NY, Mar. 17, 1922 (unpublished). The points mentioned are raised at pp. 308–9, 322–30.

107. Stenographic record of Aug. 21, 1922 meeting, Stillman files; New York State Historical Society, Albany.

108. Upton, *Everett Report*, pp. 124–29.

109. Ch. 576, 48 Stat. 948; now codified at 25 U.S.C. 461-279; also referred to as the "Wheeler-Howard Act," in recognition of its congressional sponsors. For a somewhat too sympathetic overview, see Vine Deloria, Jr., and Clifford M. Lytle, *The Nations Within: The Past and Future of American Indian Sovereignty* (New York: Pantheon, 1984).

110. The total amount to be paid the Senecas for rental of their Salamanca property was $6,000 per year, much of which had gone unpaid since the mid-30s. The judges found the federal government to have defaulted on its obligation to regulate state and private leases of Seneca land and instructed it to take an active role in the future; Laurence M. Hauptman, "The Historical Background to the Present-Day Seneca Nation-Salamanca Lease Controversy," in Vecsey and Starna, *Iroquois Land Claims*, pp. 101–22. Also see Arch Merrill, "The Salamanca Lease Settlement," *American Indian*, No. 1, 1944.

111. These laws, which were replicated in Kansas and Iowa during 1952, predate the more general application of state jurisdiction to Indians embodied in Public Law 280, passed in August 1953. U.S. Congress, Joint Legislative Committee, *Report: Leg. Doc. 74* (Washington, D.C.: 83rd Cong., 1st Sess., 1953).

112. This was based on a finding in *U.S. v. Minnesota* (270 U.S. 181 (1926)) that state statutes of limitations do not apply to federal action in Indian rights cases.

113. See Jack Campisi, "National Policy, States' Rights, and Indian Sovereignty: The Case of the New York Iroquois," in Michael K. Foster, Jack Campisi and Marianne Mithun, eds., *Extending the Rafters: Interdisciplinary Approaches to Iroquoian Studies* (Albany: State University of New York Press, 1984).

114. For the congressional position and commentary on the independent study of alternative sites undertaken by Dr. Arthur Morgan, see U.S. Senate, Committee on Interior and Insular Affairs, *Hearings Before the Committee on Interior and Insular Affairs: Kinzua Dam Project, Pennsylvania* (Washington, D.C.: 88th Cong., 1st Sess., May-Dec. 1963).

115. For further detail on the struggle around Kinzua Dam, see Laurence M. Hauptman, *The Iroquois Struggle for Survival: World War II to Red Power* (Syracuse, NY: Syracuse University Press, 1986).

116. *Tuscarora Indians v. New York State Power Authority* (257 F.2d 885 (1958)).

117. On the compromise acreage, see Laurence M. Hauptman, "Iroquois Land Claims Issues: At Odds with the 'Family of New York,'" in Vecsey and Starna, *Iroquois Land Claims*, pp. 67–86.

118. It took another ten years for this to be spelled out definitively; *Oneida Indian Nation v. United States* (37 Ind. Cl. Comm. 522 (1971)).

119. For a detailed account of the discussions, agreements and various factions within the process, see Upton, *Everett Report*, pp. 139–61.

120. Margaret Treur, "Ganiekeh: An Alternative to the Reservation System and Public Trust," *American Indian Journal*, Vol. 5, No. 5, 1979, pp. 22–26. On Wounded Knee, see, e.g., Robert Anderson, et al., *Voices from Wounded Knee, 1973* (Rooseveltown, NY: Akwesasne Notes, 1974).

121. *State of New York v. Danny White, et al.* (Civ. No. 74-CV-370 (N.D.N.Y.), Apr. 1976); *State of New York v. Danny White, et al.* (Civ. No. 74-CV-370, Memorandum Decision and Order, 23 Mar. 1977).

122. On the Moss Lake Agreement, see Richard Kwartler, "'This Is Our Land': Mohawk Indians v. The State of New York," in Robert B. Goldman, ed., *Roundtable Justice: Case Studies in Conflict Resolution* (Boulder, CO: Westview Press, 1980) pp. 7–20.

123. See Geoffrey York and Loreen Pindera, *People of the Pines: The Warriors and the Legacy of Oka* (Boston: Little, Brown, 1991).

124. *Oneida Indian Nation of New York v. County of Oneida* (14 U.S. 661 (1974)).

125. *Oneida Indian Nation of New York v. County of Oneida* (434 F.Supp. 527, 548 (N.D.N.Y. 1979)).

126. Allan Van Gestel, "New York Indian Land Claims: The Modern Landowner as Hostage," in Vecsey and Starna, *Iroquois Land Claims*, pp. 123–39. Also see the revisions published as "When Fictions Take Hostages," in James E. Clifton, ed., *The Invented Indian: Cultural Fictions and Government Policies* (New Brunswick, NJ: Transaction Books, 1990) pp. 291–312; and "The New York Indian Land Claims: An Overview and a Warning," *New York State Bar Journal*, Apr. 1981.

127. *County of Oneida v. Oneida Indian Nation of New York* (470 U.S. 226 (1985)).

128. Arlinda Locklear, "The Oneida Land Claims: A Legal Overview," in Vecsey and Starna, *Iroquois Land Claims*, pp. 141–53, quote at p. 153.

129. Ibid., p. 148.

130. This suit was later recast to name the state rather than the counties as primary defendant, and enlarged to encompass six million acres. It was challenged, but upheld on appeal; *Oneida Indian Nation of New York v. State of New York* (691 F.2d 1070 (1982)). Dismissed by a district judge four years later (Claire Brennan, "Oneida Claim to 6 Million Acres Voided," *Syracuse Post-Standard*, Nov. 22, 1986), it was reinstated by the Second Circuit Court in 1988; *Oneida Indian Nation of New York v. State of New York* (860 F.2d 1145).

131. *Oneida Nation of Indians of Wisconsin v. State of New York* (85 F.D.R. 701, 703 (N.Y.D.C. 1980)).

132. New York has attempted various arguments to obtain dismissal of the Cayuga suit. In 1990, the state's contention that it had obtained bona fide land title to the disputed area in leases obtained in 1795 and 1801 was overruled at the district court level; *Cayuga Indian Nation of New York v. Cuomo* (730 F.Supp. 485). In 1991, an "interpretation" by the state attorney general that reservation of land by the Six Nations in the Fort Stanwix Treaty "did not really" invest recognizable title in them was similarly overruled; *Cayuga Indian Nation of New York v. Cuomo* (758 F.Supp. 107). Finally, in 1991, a state contention that only a special railroad reorganization board should have jurisdiction to preside over claims involving areas leased to railroads was overruled; *Cayuga Indian Nation of New York v. Cuomo* (762 F.Supp. 30).

133. The terms of the agreement were published in *Finger Lakes Times*, Aug. 18, 1979.

134. Quoted in ibid.

135. Ibid.

136. For further details, see Chris Lavin, "The Cayuga Land Claims," in Vecsey and Starna, *Iroquois Land Claims*, pp. 87–100.

137. Ibid.

138. The one jurisdictional exception derives from a 1988 Second Circuit Court ruling that a federal statute passed in 1875 empowers the City of Salamanca, rather than the Senecas, to regulate zoning within the leased area so long as the leases exist; *John v. City of Salamanca* (845 F.2d 37).

139. The nonindian city government of Salamanca, a subpart of which is the Salamanca Lease Authority, filed suit in 1990 to block settlement of the Seneca claim as "unconstitutional," and to compel a new 99-year lease on its own terms (*Salamanca Indian Lease Authority v. Seneca Indian Nation*, Civ. No. 1300, Docket 91-7086). They lost and appealed. The lower court decision was affirmed by the Second Circuit Court on Mar 15, 1991, on the basis that the Senecas enjoy "sovereign immunity" from any further such suits.

140. P.L. 101-503 (104 Stat. 1179).

141. See, e.g., Frank Pommershine, "Tribal-State Relations: Hope for the Future?" *South Dakota Law Review*, No. 36, 1991; David E. Wilkins, "Reconsidering the Tribal-State Compact Process," *Policy Studies Journal*, No. 22, 1994.

142. This approach is entirely consistent with those advocated by several of the authors collected in Stephen Cornell's and Joseph P. Kalt's coedited volume, *What Can Tribes Do? Strategies and Institutions in American Indian Economic Development* (Los Angeles: UCLA American Indian Studies Program, 1992).

143. Glenn A. Phelps, "Representation Without Taxation: Citizenship and Suffrage in Indian Country," *American Indian Quarterly*, No. 9, 1985.

144. A useful survey of this and related situations will be found in K. Grover, et al., "Tribal-State Dispute Resolution: Recent Attempts," *South Dakota Law Review*, No. 36, 1991.

145. As the matter was framed by Dr. Martin Luther King, Jr., "those who make peaceful change impossible, make violent change inevitable"; quoted in a related context in my "Last Stand at Lubicon Lake: Genocide and Ecocide in the Canadian North," in *Struggle for the Land*, p. 228.

146. See, e.g., Felix S. Cohen's "Original Indian Title," in Lucy Kramer Cohen, ed., *The Legal Conscience: Selected Papers of Felix S. Cohen* (New Haven, CT: Yale University Press, 1960) pp. 273–304.

147. Everett Somerville Brown and Herbert E. Bolton, eds., *A Constitutional History of the Louisiana Purchase, 1803–1812* (New York: Beard Books, 2000).

148. The full text of the "Treaty of Fort Laramie with the Sioux, Etc., 1851" (11 Stat. 749), will be found in Kappler, *Indian Treaties*, pp. 594–96. For context, see Remi Nadeau, *Fort Laramie and the Sioux* (Lincoln: University of Nebraska Press, 1967).

149. Dee Brown, *Fort Phil Kearny: An American Saga* (Lincoln: University of Nebraska Press, 1971) pp. 184–90. For further background, see LeRoy R. Hafen and Francis Marion Young, *Fort Laramie and the Pageant of the West, 1834–1890* (Lincoln: University of Nebraska Press, 1938).

150. The full text of the 1868 Fort Laramie Treaty (15 Stat. 635) will be found in Kappler, *Indian Treaties*, pp. 998–1007. Lakota territoriality is spelled out under Articles 2 and 16.

151. 1868 Treaty, Article 17.

152. Ibid., Article 12.

153. William Ludlow, *Report of a Reconnaissance of the Black Hills of Dakota* (Washington, D.C.: U.S. Department of War, 1875). More accessibly, see Donald Jackson, *Custer's Gold: The United States Cavalry Expedition of 1874* (Lincoln: University of Nebraska Press, 1966) p. 8.

154. Ibid. Also see Walter P. Jenny's *Report on the Mineral Wealth, Climate and Rainfall and Natural Resources of the Black Hills of Dakota* (Washington, D.C.: 44th Cong., 1st Sess., Exec. Doc. No. 51, 1876).

155. This was the "Allison Commission" of 1875. For the most comprehensive account of the Commission's failed purchase attempt, see U.S. Department of Interior, Bureau of Indian Affairs, *Annual Report of the Commissioner of Indian Affairs*, 1875 (Washington, D.C.: U.S. GPO, 1875).

156. Frank Pommershein, "The Black Hills Case: On the Cusp of History," *Wicazo Sa Review*, Vol. IV, No. 1, Spring 1988, p. 19. The government's secret maneuvering is spelled out in a report prepared by E. T. Watkins published as *Executive Document 184* (Washington, D.C.: 44th Cong., 1st Sess., 1876) pp. 8–9.

157. Ralph Andrist, *The Long Death: The Last Days of the Plains Indians* (New York: Collier, 1964) pp. 276–292.

158. John Trebbel, *Compact History of the Indian Wars* (New York: Tower Books, 1966) p. 277. Also see J.W. Vaughn, *With Crook at the Rosebud* (Harrisburg, PA: Stackpole Books, 1956).

159. Dee Brown, *Bury My Heart At Wounded Knee: An Indian History of the American West* (New York: Holt, Rinehart and Winston, 1970) pp. 301–10.

160. For use of the term, see Jerome A. Greene, *Slim Buttes: An Episode of the Great Sioux War, 1876* (Norman: University of Oklahoma Press, 1982).

161. On the "total war" policy and its prosecution, see Andrist, *Long Death*, p. 297.

162. Brown, *Bury My Heart*, p. 312. Also see Mari Sandoz, *Crazy Horse: Strange Man of the Oglalas* (Lincoln: University of Nebraska Press, 1942); Robert A. Clark, ed., *The Killing of Chief Crazy Horse* (Lincoln: University of Nebraska Press, 1976).

163. 19 Stat. 254 (1877).

164. Act of August 15, 1876 (ch. 289, 19 Stat. 176, 192); the matter is well covered in "1986 Black Hills Hearings on S.1453, Introduction" (prepared by the office of Sen. Daniel Inouye); *Wicazo Sa Review*, Vol IV, No. 1, Spring 1988, p. 10.

165. Vine Deloria, Jr., "Reflections on the Black Hills Claim," *Wicazo Sa Review*, Vol. IV, No. 1, Spring 1988, pp. 33–38.

166. 18 U.S.C.A. § 1153 (1885) and 25 U.S.C.A. § 331 (1887), respectively.

167. Andrist, *Long Death*, pp. 351–52.

168. See the chapter entitled "The Politics of Repression" in Ronald Neizen, *Spirit Wars: Native North American Religions in the Age of Nation-Building* (Berkeley: University of California Press, 2000) pp. 128–60.

169. 8 U.S.C.A. § 140 (a) (2) (1924) and 25 U.S.C.A. 461 (1934), respectively.

170. See generally, Tom Holm, *Strong Hearts, Wounded Souls: Native American Veterans of the Vietnam War* (Austin: University of Texas Press, 1996).

171. A detailed examination of the IRA and its passage is to be found in Vine Deloria, Jr., and Clifford M. Lytle, *The Nations Within: The Past and Future of American Indian Sovereignty* (New York: Pantheon 1984). Also see Kenneth R. Philp, ed., *Indian Self-Rule: First-Hand Accounts of Indian-White Relations from Roosevelt to Reagan* (Salt Lake City: Howe Bros., 1986).

172. Thomas Biolosi, *Organizing the Lakota: The Political Economy of the New Deal on the Pine Ridge and Rosebud Reservations* (Tucson: University of Arizona Press, 1992).

173. Vine Deloria, Jr., and Clifford M. Lytle, *American Indians, American Justice* (Austin: University of Texas Press, 1983) pp. 17–18.

174. On the Menominees, see Nicholas C. Peroff, *Menominee DRUMS: Tribal Termination and Restoration, 1954–1974* (Norman: University of Oklahoma Press, 1982). On the Klamaths, see Theodore Stern, *The Klamath Tribe: The People and Their Reservation* (Seattle: University of Washington Press, 1965). For a more general view of U.S. termination/relocation policies and their place in the broader sweep of federal affairs, see Richard Drinnon, *Keeper of Concentration Camps: Dillon S. Myer and American Racism* (Berkeley: University of California Press, 1987). Also see "Like Sand in the Wind," herein.

175. This occurred as a result of an 1891 amendment (26 Stat. 794) to the General Allotment Act providing that the Secretary of the Interior ("or his delegate," meaning the BIA) might lease out the land of any Indian who, in his opinion, "by reason of age or other disability" could not "personally and with benefit to himself occupy or improve his allotment or any part thereof." As Deloria and Lytle observe (*American Indians, American Justice*, p. 10): "In effect this amendment gave the secretary of [the] interior almost dictatorial powers over the use of allotments since, if the local agent disagreed with the use to which [reservation] lands were being put, he could intervene and lease the lands to whomsoever he pleased." Thus, by the 1970s, the bulk of the useful land on many reservations in the U.S.—such as those of the Lakota—had been placed in the hands of nonindian individuals or business enterprises, and at *very* low rates.

176. R. Jones, *American Indian Policy: Selected Issues in the 98th Congress* (Washington, D.C.: Issue Brief No. 1B83083, Library of Congress, Governmental Division, [updated version] 2/6/84) pp. 3–4.

177. Department of Health and Human Services, Indian Health Service, *American Indians: A Statistical Profile* (Washington, D.C.: U.S. GPO, 1988).

178. The language accrues from one of President Woodrow Wilson's many speeches on the League of Nations in the immediate aftermath of World War I; Ray Stannard Baker and William E. Dodd, eds., *The Public Papers of Woodrow Wilson*, 2 vols. (New York: Harper, 1926) Vol. 2, p. 407.

179. 41 Stat. 738 (1920).

180. *Sioux Tribe v. U.S.* (97 Ct. Cl. 613 (1943)).

181. *Sioux Tribe v. U.S.* (318 U.S. 789 (1943)).

182. *Sioux Tribe v. U.S.* (2 Ind. Cl. Comm. (1956)).

183. *Sioux Tribe v. U.S.* (146 F.Supp. 229 (1946)).

184. Inouye, "Introduction," pp. 11–12.

185. *U.S. v. Sioux Nation* (448 U.S. 371, 385 (1968)).

186. *Sioux Nation v. U.S.* (33 Ind. Cl. Comm. 151 (1974)); the opinion was/is a legal absurdity insofar as Congress holds *no* such "power of eminent domain" over the territoriality of other nations.

187. *U.S. v. Sioux Nation* (207 Ct. Cl. 243, 518 F.2d. 1293 (1975)).

188. Inouye, "Introduction," p. 12.

189. *Sioux Nation v. U.S.* (423 U.S. 1016 (1975)).

190. Pommersheim, "Black Hills Case," pp. 18–25.

191. P.L. 95-243 (92 Stat. 153 (1978)).

192. *Sioux Nation v. U.S.* (220 Ct. Cl. 442, 601 F.2d. 1157 (1975)).

193. *Sioux Nation v. U.S.* (488 U.S. 371 (1980)).

194. Pommersheim, "Black Hills Case"; Deloria, "Reflections on the Black Hills Claim."

195. *Oglala Sioux v. U.S.* (650 F.2d 140 (1981), *cert.* denied).

196. *Oglala Sioux v. U.S.* (455 U.S. 907 (1982)).

197. *Sioux Tribe v. U.S.* (7 Cl. Ct. 80 (1985)).

198. An interesting study of this overall dynamic, in which the Black Hills cases figure prominently, will be found in David E. Wilkins' *American Indian Sovereignty and the Supreme Court*
(Austin: University of Texas Press, 1997) esp. pp. 217–34.

199. See note 192.

200. There are, of course, those like Chief Justice of the Supreme Court William Rehnquist who
consider anything other than a categorical refutation of any and all Indian contentions to be "one-
sided," "revisionist," and therefore "unfair." As was noted in the majority opinion written by Justice
Harry Blackmum in the Black Hills case, however, Rehnquist could cite *no* historians supporting his
"don't confuse me with the facts" version of history; analyzed in Wilkins, *Indian Sovereignty*,
pp. 225–31.

201. Peter Matthiessen, *In the Spirit of Crazy Horse* (New York: Viking, [2nd ed.] 1991) pp.
425–28.

202. Paul Chaat Smith and Robert Allen Warrior, *Like a Hurricane: The American Indian Movement from Alcatraz to Wounded Knee* (New York: New Press, 1996).

203. See "Bloody Wake of Alcatraz," herein.

204. This is well handled in Rex Weyler's *Blood of the Land: The Government and Corporate War
Against the American Indian Movement* (Philadelphia: New Society, [2nd ed.] 1992).

205. Durham's work is mentioned in Deloria, *Behind the Trail of Broken Treaties*, p. 267. Also see
the relevant material in Durham, *Lack of Coherence*, esp. the essays entitled "United Nations Conference on Indians" and "American Indians and Carter's Human Rights Sermons," pp. 27–29, 39–45.

206. United Nations Sub-Commission on Prevention of Discrimination and Protection of Minorities Resolution 2 (XXXIV) of 8 Sept. 1981; endorsed by the Commission on Human Rights by Resolution 1982/19 of 10 March 1982; authorized by ECOSOC Resolution 1983/34 on May 7, 1982.

207. See, e.g., Sadruddin Aga Khan and Hallin Bin Talal, *Indigenous Peoples: A Global Quest for
Justice* (London: Zed Books, 1987).

208. As concerns the study of conditions, this is the so-called "Cobo Report" (U.N. Doc.
E/CN.4/Sub.2/AC.4/1985/WP.5). Much of the content appears in Burger, *Report From the Frontier*.

209. For an overview of the drafting process, see my "Subterfuge and Self-Determination: Suppression of Indigenous Sovereignty in the 20th Century United States," *Z Magazine*, May 1997.

210. See Imre Sutton, "Configurations of Land Claims: Toward a Model," in Sutton, *Irredeemable
America*, pp. 121–26.

211. Perhaps the most comprehensive assessment of the meaning of the AIM action during this
period may be found in my "The Extralegal Implications of Yellow Thunder *Tiospaye*: Misadventure
or Watershed Action?" *Policy Perspectives*, Vol. 2, No. 2, 1982. Also see the chapter entitled "Yellow
Thunder" in Weyler's *Blood*.

212. *U.S. v. Means, et al.* (627 F.Supp. 247 (1985)).

213. P.L. 95-431 (92 Stat. 153 (1978)).

214. *Lyng v. Northwest Indian Cemetery Protective Association*, 56 *U.S. Law Week* 4292. For analysis, see Vine Deloria, Jr.'s "Trouble in High Places: Erosion of American Indian Religious Freedom in
the United States," in M. Annette Jaimes, ed., *The State of Native America: Genocide, Colonization
and Resistance* (Boston: South End Press, 1992) pp. 267–87. On the Circuit Court decision, see *U.S.
v. Means* (858 F.2d 404 (8th Cir., 1988)).

215. The bill was drafted by the Black Hills Sioux National Council, nominally headed by Gerald

Clifford and Charlotte Black Elk at Cheyenne River; for a reasonably thorough, if noticeably hostile, treatment of the Council, see Edward Lazarus, *Black Hills, White Justice: The Sioux Nation versus the United States, 1775 to the Present* (New York: HarperCollins, 1991) pp. 164, 186–87, 209, 226, 232–33.

216. Fergus M. Bordewich, *Killing the White Man's Indian: Reinventing Native Americans at the End of the Twentieth Century* (Garden City, NY: Doubleday, 1996) p. 230.

217. The full text of S.1453 may be found in *Wicazo Sa Review*, Vol IV, No. 1, Spring 1988, p. 3.

218. On Homestake, see Weyler, *Blood*, pp. 262–63. It should be noted that Homestake itself was briefly the defendant in a substantial damage suit; *Oglala Sioux Tribe v. Homestake Mining Co.* (722 F.2d 1407 (8th Cir. 1983)).

219. The figure was apparently arrived at by computing rent on the Black Hills claim area at a rate of eleven cents per acre for 100 years, interest compounded annually, plus $310 million in accrued mineral royalties. Much of the appeal of Stevens' pitch, of course, was that it came much closer to the actual amount owed the Lakota than that allowed in the Bradley Bill.

220. For instance, he made a cash donation of $34,000 to the Red Cloud School, on Pine Ridge, in 1987.

221. On Pine Ridge, for example, Stevens had attracted support from the influential elder Oliver Red Cloud and his Grey Eagle Society, as well as then-tribal attorney Mario Gonzales. His "plan" was therefore endorsed by votes of the tribal councils on Pine Ridge, Rosebud, and Cheyenne River; see generally Mario Gonzalez and Elizabeth Cook-Lynn, *The Politics of Hallowed Ground: Wounded Knee and the Struggle for Indian Sovereignty* (Urbana: University of Illinois Press, 1999).

222. Lazarus, *Black Hills, White Justice*, p. 423.

223. Ibid., p. 424.

224. Quoted in ibid., p. 425.

225. Ibid. Miller seems to have adopted his outlandish view of Black Hills regional history from Chief Justice Rehnquist (see note 200). In any event, it is included in *Wicazo Sa Review*, Vol. IV, No. 1, Spring 1988.

226. Lazarus, *Black Hills, White Justice*, p. 425.

227. Ibid. The resolution failed to pass the Senate by a narrow margin.

228. Ibid., p. 424.

229. Russell Means, conversation with the author, Apr. 1991.

230. Tim Giago, statement on National Public Radio, May 1988.

231. The text of the treaty (18 Stat. 689) will be found in Kappler, *Indian Treaties*, pp. 851–53.

232. Rudolph C. Ryser, *Newe Segobia and the United States of America* (Kenmore, WA: Center for World Indigenous Studies, 1985). Also see Peter Matthiessen, *Indian Country*, (New York: Viking, 1984), pp. 261–89.

233. Actually, under U.S. law, a specific Act of Congress is required to extinguish aboriginal title; *U.S. ex rel. Hualapi Indians v. Santa Fe Railroad* (314 U.S. 339, 354 (1941)). On Newe use of the land during this period, see Richard O. Clemmer, "Land Use Patterns and Aboriginal Rights: Northern and Eastern Nevada, 1858–1971," *Indian Historian*, Vol. 7, No. 1, 1974, pp. 24–41, 47–49.

234. Ryser, *Newe Segobia*, pp. 15–16.

235. Wilkinson had already entered into negotiations to represent the Temoak before the Claims Commission Act was passed; ibid., p. 13, n. 1.

236. The Temoaks have said consistently that Wilkinson always represented the claim to them as being for land rather than money. The firm is known to have run the same scam on other Indian clients; ibid., pp. 16–17.

237. Ibid., p. 16. Also see Robert T. Coulter, "The Denial of Legal Remedies to Indian Nations Under U.S. Law," *American Indian Law Journal*, Vol. 9, No. 3, 1977, pp. 5–9; Coulter and Tullberg, "Indian Land Rights," pp. 190–91.

238. Glenn T. Morris, "The Battle for Newe Segobia: The Western Shoshone Land Rights Struggle," in my *Critical Issues in Native North America, Vol. 2*, pp. 86–98.

239. Quoted in Jerry Mander, *In Absence of the Sacred: The Failure of Technology and the Survival of the Indian Nations* (San Francisco: Sierra Club Books, 1991), pp. 307–8.

240. Ibid., p. 309.

241. Quoted in ibid., p. 310.

242. Ibid., p. 308.

243. Quoted in ibid., p. 310.

244. Quoted in ibid., p. 309.

245. Ibid., p. 308.

246. Morris, "Battle for Newe Segobia," p. 90. The case is *Western Shoshone Identifiable Group v. United States* (11 Ind. Cl. Comm. 387, 416 (1962)). The whole issue is well covered in Jack D. Forbes, "The 'Public Domain' in Nevada and Its Relationship to Indian Property Rights," *Nevada State Bar Journal*, No. 30 (1965), pp. 16–47.

247. The first award amount appears in *Western Shoshone Identifiable Group v. United States* (29 Ind. Cl. Comm. 5 (1972)), p. 124. The second award appears in *Western Shoshone Identifiable Group v. United States* (40 Ind. Cl. Comm. 305 (1977)).

248. The final Court of Claims order for Wilkinson's retention is in *Western Shoshone Identifiable Group v. United States* (593 F.2d 994 (1979)). Also see "Excerpts from a Memorandum from the Duckwater Shoshone Tribe, Battle Mountain Indian Community, and the Western Shoshone Sacred Lands Association in Opposition to the Motion and Petition for Attorney Fees and Expenses, July 15, 1980," in *Rethinking Indian Law*, pp. 68–69.

249. *Western Shoshone Identifiable Group v. United States* (40 Ind. Cl. Comm. 311 (1977)). The final award valued the Shoshone land at $1.05 per acre. The land in question brings about $250 per acre on the open market at present.

250. Ryser, *Newe Segobia*, p. 8, n. 4.

251. Ibid, p. 20.

252. Quoted in Mander, *Absence of the Sacred*, p. 301.

253. Quoted in ibid., pp. 308–9.

254. Ibid., p. 311.

255. Quoted in ibid., p. 302.

256. *U.S. v. Dann* (572 F.2d 222 (1978)). For background, see Kristine L. Foot, "*United States v. Dann*: What It Portends for Ownership of Millions of Acres in the Western United States," *Public Land Law Review*, No. 5, 1984, pp. 183–91.

257. Quoted in Mander, *Absence of the Sacred*, p. 312.

258. Ibid.

259. *U.S. v. Dann* (Civ. No. R-74-60, Apr. 25, 1980).

260. *U.S. v. Dann* (706 F.2d 919, 926 (1983)).

261. Morris, "Battle for Newe Segobia," p. 94.

262. Quoted in Mander, *Absence of the Sacred*, p. 318.

263. Ibid., pp. 316–17.

264. Angela, Ursula and Alessandra, WSDP Activists, "U.S. Jails Clifford Dann," *Western Shoshone Defense Project Newsletter*, Vol. 1, No. 4, 1993. One of the problems experienced in this case was the intervention of Canadian attorney Bruce Clark, who counseled Clifford Dann to adopt a strict "sovereignty defense" in simply rejecting U.S. jurisidiction at trial. While Clark's position was techincally correct, it would have been pertinent—as Colorado AIM leader Glenn T. Morris, himself an attorney, pointed out at the time—to have *also* observed that Dann happened to be entirely innocent of the charges against him. For his part, presiding judge Bill McKibben imposed an especially harsh sentence because, he said, he wanted to "make an example that U.S. law cannot be ignored."

265. Mander, *Absence of the Sacred*, p. 317.

266. The Inter-American Commission is an organ mandated by the OAS Charter with the task of promoting observance of human rights among OAS member states, including the U.S. As a member of the OAS, the U.S. is legally bound to uphold the organization's human rights principles. The

Commission's action was taken in response to a petition filed by Mary and Carrie Dann on Feb. 19, 1998; "Inter-American Commission on Human Rights Requests United States to Stay Action Against Western Shoshone Sisters," Indian Law Resource Center Press Release, Apr. 7, 1988; "Inter-American Commission on Human Rights Considers the Danns' Case Against the United States," *Western Shoshone Defense Project Newsletter*, Vol. 5, No. 1, 1997.

267. Quoted in Mander, *Absence of the Sacred*, p. 313.

268. Ibid.

269. Quoted in ibid., p. 316.

270. Conversation with Raymond Yowell, Reno, Nevada, Apr. 1991.

271. Quoted in Mander, *Absence of the Sacred*, p. 314.

272. Ibid.

273. Quoted in ibid., p. 315.

274. Ibid.

275. Estimate provided by Raymond Yowell.

276. Anders Stephanson, *Manifest Destiny: American Expansion and the Empire of Right* (New York: Hill and Wang, 1995).

277. This, of course, was precisely the situation the entire Indian Claims Commission process of paying compensation rather than effecting land restorations was designed to avert; Leonard A. Carlson, "What Was It Worth? Economic and Historical Aspects of Determining Awards in Indian Land Claims Cases," in Sutton, *Irredeemable America*, pp. 87–110.

278. Christopher Sewall, "Oro Nevada Mining Company: The Trojan Horse," *Western Shoshone Defense Project Newsletter*, Vol. 5, No.1, 1997.

279. Ibid.

280. "In 1995, Canadian company Diamond Field Resources discovered the world's richest nickel deposit at Voisy Bay. Since then, over 300,000 mining claims have been filed by hundreds of companies and individuals on land that has never been ceded or sold by its original occupants. While currently pushing forward with their land claims, the Innu and Inuit were recently informed by the provincial government of Newfoundland that the land on which the mineral deposit is located will not be part of any land claims negotiations . . . On the southern portion of Innu territory (known as Nitassinan), along the north shore of the St. Lawrence River in Quebec, a similar mining rush has occurred"; ibid., p. 9. Also see Mick Lowe, *Premature Bonanza: Standoff at Voisey's Bay* (Toronto: Between the Lines, 1998).

281. Suharto, whose military until recently provided direct security for Bre-X's operations, has an especially bloody history. In 1965, he led the coup against Indonesian president Sukarno that left as many as a million people dead; Noam Chomsky and Edward S. Herman, *The Political Economy of Human Rights, Vol. 1: The Washington Connection and Third World Fascism* (Boston: South End Press, 1979) pp. 205–9. More recently, he oversaw the genocidal pacification of East Timor; John G. Taylor, *Indonesia's Forgotten War: The Hidden History of East Timor* (London: Pluto Press, 1991). The royalties paid by Bre-X, which claims to have discovered Indonesia's richest gold deposit, not only reinforced this ghastly régime, but augmented the personal fortune Suharto—estimated at $60 billion—siphoned from his generally impoverished people.

282. On Nov. 10, 1997, Oro-Nevada Resources Vice President for Government Affairs Tibeau Piquet announced the "Hand Me Down Project" to secure partners in opening mines in Crescent Valley. The Vancouver-based Placer Dome Corporation, a subsidiary of Kennecott, was most prominently spotlighted as a possibility, probably because of its existing mines in the area. Others mentioned were the Toronto-based Barrick Gold Corporation and Denver's Newmont Mining; "Oro Nevada Action Alert, Letters Needed!" *Western Shoshone Defense Project Newsletter*, Vol. 5, No. 2, 1997. On Cortez Gold, see Chris Sewall, "Cortez, The Conquest Continues," *Western Shoshone Defense Project Newsletter*, Vol. 3, No. 1, 1995. On the Pipeline Mine, see Christopher Sewall, "Pipeline's Dirty Little Secrets: Placer Dome's new mine in Crescent Valley experiencing problems," *Western Shoshone Defense Project Newsletter*, Vol. 5, No. 2, 1997. On South Pipeline, see Christopher Sewall, "South Pipeline: We Told

You So!," *Western Shoshone Defense Project Newsletter*, Vol. 5, No. 1, 1997. In addition to Pipeline and Pipeline South, another sixteen mines are operating in the area and a seventeenth, Echo Bay Mining's planned pit at Twin Creeks, has recently been approved; Tom Myers, "Twin Creeks Mine Approved by BLM," *Western Shoshone Defense Project Newsletter*, Vol. 5, No. 1, 1997.

283. Christopher Sewall, "Australian Mining Giant Has Eyes On Western Shoshone Land," *Western Shoshone Defense Project Newsletter*, Vol. 5, No. 1, 1997. Aside from WMC, other corporations with speculative interests in the area include Amax Gold, Independence Mining, Royal Gold, Battle Mountain Gold, Homestake Mining and Uranez; "Oro Action Alert."

284. On testing in Micronesia, see Jason Clay, "Militarization and Indigenous Peoples, Part I: The Americas and the Pacific," *Cultural Survival Quarterly*, No. 3, 1987. On testing in Nevada, see Dagmar Thorpe's *Newe Segobia: The Western Shoshone People and Land* (Lee, NV: Western Shoshone Sacred Lands Association, 1982) and "A Breach of Trust," herein.

285. Ian Zabarte, "Western Shoshone National Sovereignty Violated by Subcritical Nuclear Weapons Test," *Western Shoshone Defense Project Newsletter*, Vol. 5, No. 2, 1997.

286. Bernard Nietschmann and William Le Bon, "Nuclear States and Fourth World Nations," *Cultural Survival Quarterly*, Vol. 11, No. 4, 1988, pp. 4–7.

287. The Yucca Mountain plan is probably best handled in Gerald Jacob's *Site Unseen: The Politics of Siting a Nuclear Repository* (Pittsburgh: University of Pittsburgh Press, 1990) and Valerie L. Kuletz's *The Tainted Desert: Environmental and Social Ruin in the American West* (New York: Routledge, 1998).

288. Martha C. Knack, "MX Issues for Native American Communities," in Francis Hartigan, ed., *MX in Nevada: A Humanistic Perspective* (Reno: Nevada Humanities Press, 1980), pp. 59–66.

289. Quoted in Mander, *Absence of the Sacred*, p. 313.

290. Quoted in ibid., pp. 312–13.

291. Quoted in Nietschmann and Le Bon, "Nuclear States," p. 7.

292. Sanchez, an organizer with the Seventh Generation Fund, died of leukemia on June 30, 1993. He was 37 years old; Mary Lee Dazey and Dedee Sanchez, "Remembering Joe Sanchez," *Western Shoshone Defence Project Newsletter*, Vol. 1, No. 5, 1993.

293. Mander, *Absence of the Sacred*, p. 316.

294. Understandings on this score appear to be relatively well developed in some quarters of the nonindigenous opposition in Canada; see, e.g., discussion of the so-called Friends of the Lubicon in my "Last Stand at Lubicon Lake," in *Struggle for the Land*, esp. pp. 215–28.

295. There are those in the U.S. who seem to have taken, or are taking, the point to heart; see, e.g., Susan Zakin, *Coyotes and Town Dogs: Earth First! and the Environmental Movement* (New York: Viking, 1993) p. 246. Also see the chapter entitled "Black Hills Alliance," in Russell Means with Marvin J. Wolf, *Where White Men Fear to Tread* (New York: St. Martin's Press, 1996) pp. 397–402.

296. The sort of coalition at issue emerged with respect to opposing the Great Whale Project at James Bay; see, e.g., Grand Council of the Crees, *Never Without Consent*. Also see the section entitled "James Bay II" in "The Water Plot: Hydrological Rape in Northern Canada," in my *Struggle for the Land*, pp. 303–9.

297. This is exactly what I had in mind when I titled the introductory essay, "Journeying Toward a Debate," in my first edited volume, *Marxism and Native Americans* (Boston: South End Press, 1983) pp. 1–16.

298. Bernard Fall, *Hell in a Very Small Place: The Siege of Dien Bien Phu* (Santa Barbara: DeCapo Press, 1988 reprint of 1967 original).

299. Pierre Boudieu, *The Algerians* (Boston: Beacon Press, 1962).

300. Michael Perez-Stable, *The Cuban Revolution: Origins, Course and Legacy* (New York: Oxford University Press, 1998).

301. George Black, *Triumph of the People: The Sandinista Revolution in Nicaragua* (London: Zed Books, 1985); Editors, *The Sandinista Revolution* (New York: Monthly Review Press, 1986).

302. The actual quote was, "Be realistic, demand the impossible!"; Daniel Cohn-Bendit, *Obsolete Communism: The Left-Wing Alternative* (New York: McGraw-Hill, 1968) p. 131.

303. This point was long ago made from within the "Third World Revolution" itself; Régis Debray, *Revolution in the Revolution?* (New York: Monthly Review Press, 1968).

304. See, e.g., Thomas, "Colonialism." For theoretical underpinnings, see Antonio Gramsci's 1920 essay, "The Southern Question," included in his *The Modern Prince and Other Writings* (New York: International, 1957) pp. 28–51. For a classic study of the phenomenon, see Michael Hector's *Internal Colonialism: The Celtic Fringe in British National Development, 1536–1966* (Berkeley: University of California Press, 1975).

305. This is true, if for no other reason, because of the accuracy attending Sartre's equation of colonialism to genocide; Jean-Paul Sartre, "On Genocide," *Ramparts*, Feb. 1968 (included in Jean-Paul Sartre and Arlette El Kaim-Sartre, *On Genocide and a Summary of the Evidence and Judgements of the International War Crimes Tribunal* [Boston: Beacon Press, 1968]).

306. The point is made well, albeit in other connections, by Edward S. Herman and Noam Chomsky in their *Manufacturing Consent: The Political Economy of the Mass Media* (New York: Pantheon, 1988).

307. See, e.g., the various polemics analyzed in the essays "Assaults on Truth and Memory: Holocaust Denial in Context" and "Lie for Lie: Linkages Between Holocaust Deniers and Proponents of the 'Uniqueness of the Jewish Experience in World War II'," in my *A Little Matter of Genocide: Holocaust and Denial in the Americas, 1492 to the Present* (San Francisco: City Lights, 1997) pp. 19–62, 63–80.

308. Good illustrations of how this works will be found in the chapter entitled "Silencing the Voice of the People: How Mining Companies Subvert Local Opposition," in Al Gedicks' *Resource Rebels: Native Challenges to Mining and Oil Corporations* (Cambridge, MA: South End Press, 2001) pp. 159–80.

309. See, e.g., the exchange described by Jimmie Durham between himself and a member of the progressive Institute for Policy Studies on the issue of indigenous rights; Durham, *Lack of Coherence*, p. 174. Also see David Stock, "The Settler State and the U.S. Left," *Forward Motion*, Vol. 9, No. 4, Jan. 1991.

310. A devastating critique of this tendency will be found in J. Sakai, *Settlers: The Myth of the White Proletariat* (Chicago: Morningstar, 1983). Also see David Roediger, *The Wages of Whiteness: Race and the Making of the American Working Class* (London: Verso, 1991); George Lipsitz, *The Possessive Investment in Whiteness: How White People Profit from Identity Politics* (Philadelphia: Temple University Press, 1998).

311. A perfect illustration will be found in the "Indian Plank" of the *Program and Platform of the Revolutionary Communist Party, USA*, beginning with its 1980 iteration. For insight into the RCP's sentiments vis-à-vis native peoples, see its "Searching for the Second Harvest," included in my *Marxism and Native Americans*, pp. 35–58. For theoretical assessment, see "False Promises," herein.

312. See, as examples, Imre Sutton, "Indian Land Rights and the Sagebrush Rebellion," *Geographical Review*, No. 72, 1982, pp. 357–59; David Lyons, "The New Indian Claims and Original Rights to Land," *Social Theory and Practice*, No. 4, 1977; Richard D. Clayton, "The Sagebrush Rebellion: Who Would Control Public Lands?" *Utah Law Review*, No. 68, 1980.

313. For a sample of environmentalist arguments, see T.H. Watkins, "Ancient Wrongs and Public Rights," *Sierra Club Bulletin*, Vol. 59, No. 8, 1974; M.C. Blumm, "Fulfilling the Parity Promise: A Perspective on Scientific Proof, Economic Cost and Indian Treaty Rights in the Approval of the Columbia Fish and Wildlife Program," *Environmental Law*, Vol. 13, No. 1, 1982; and every issue of *Earth First!* from 1986–89. For another exemplary marxist articulation, see David Muga, "Native Americans and the Nationalities Question: Premises for a Marxist Approach to Ethnicity and Self-Determination," *Nature, Society, Thought*, Vol. 1, No. 1, 1987.

314. Russell Means, speech at the University of Colorado at Denver, Apr. 18, 1987 (tape on file).

315. Sakai, *Settlers*. Also see Patrick Wolfe, *Settler Colonialism and the Transformation of Anthropology: The Politics and Poetics of an Ethnographic Event* (New York: Cassell, 1999).

316. This should be contrasted to the standard government policy of evicting Indians whenever/wherever their property interests conflict with those of whites, corporate interests and, sometimes, even preferred indigenous groups; see, e.g., my earlier cited "Genocide in Arizona?" and Emily

Benedek, *The Wind Won't Know Me: A History of the Navajo-Hopi Land Dispute* (New York: Alfred A. Knopf, 1992). On comparable practices in Canada, see Geoffrey York, *The Dispossessed: Life and Death in Native Canada* (Boston: Little, Brown, 1992).

317. The quote can be attributed to Paleoconservative pundit Patrick J. Buchanan, delivered on the CNN talk show *Crossfire*, 1987.

318. This outcome would be quite in line with the requirements of international tort law; see, e.g., Istvan Vasarhelyi, *Restitution in International Law* (Budapest: Hungary Academy of Science, 1964). For application to the U.S. context, see the essay entitled "Reinscription: The Right of Hawai'i to be Restored to the United Nations List of Non-Self-Governing Territories," in my *Perversions of Justice: Indigenous Peoples and Angloamerican Law* (San Francisco: City Lights, 2002).

320. See my "The Crucible of American Indian Identity: Native Tradition versus Colonial Imposition in Postconquest North America," *American Indian Culture and Research Journal*, Vol. 23, No. 1, Spring 1999. Also see "Nullification," herein.

321. Ronald L. Trosper, "Appendix I: Indian Minerals," in American Indian Policy Review Commission, *Task Force 7 Final Report: Reservation and Resource Development and Protection* (Washington, D.C.: U.S. GPO, 1977); U.S. Department of Interior, Bureau of Indian Affairs, *Indian Lands Map: Oil, Gas and Minerals on Indian Reservations* (Washington, D.C.: U.S. GPO, 1978).

322. This theme is explored in greater depth in "I Am Indigenist," herein. Also see, *TREATY: The Platform of Russell Means' Campaign for President of the Oglala Lakota People, 1982*, appended to my *Struggle for the Land*, pp. 405–37.

5. A BREACH OF TRUST

1. *"Lone Wolf" v. Hitchcock* (187 U.S. 553, 557 (1903)). For context and analysis, see Blue Clark, "Lone Wolf" v. Hitchcock: *Treaty Rights and Indian Law at the End of the Nineteenth Century* (Lincoln: University of Nebraska Press, 1994).

2. See C. Harvey, "Congressional Plenary Power Over Indians: A Doctrine Rooted in Prejudice," *American Indian Law Review*, No. 10, 1982.

3. Ann Laquer Estin, *"Lone Wolf" v. Hitchcock*: The Long Shadow," in Sandra L. Cadwalader and Vine Deloria, Jr., eds., *The Aggressions of Civilization: Federal Indian Policy Since the 1880s* (Philadelphia: Temple University Press, 1984) pp. 214–45.

4. U.S. Department of Interior, Indian Claims Commission, *Final Report* (Washington, D.C.: U.S. GPO, 1979). For analysis, see Russel Barsh, "Indian Land Claims Policy in the United States," *North Dakota Law Review*, No. 58, 1982. On the notion of ownership reversion, see Felix S. Cohen, "Original Indian Title," *Minnesota Law Review*, No. 32, 1947.

5. The aggregate of reserved landholdings totals some fifty million acres (78,000 square miles), an area equivalent in size to the state of South Dakota. Of this, some 44 million acres are held in trust; Roxanne Dunbar Ortiz, "Sources of Underdevelopment," in Roxanne Dunbar Ortiz and Larry Emerson, eds., *Economic Development on American Indian Reservations* (Albuquerque: Institute for Native American Development, University of New Mexico, 1979) p. 61; "Native American Statistics—United States," in Susan Lobo and Steve Talbot, *Native American Voices: A Reader* (New York: Longman, 1998) p. 39.

6. See, e.g., Ronald L. Trosper, "Appendix I: Indian Minerals," in American Indian Policy Review Commission, Task Force 7, *Final Report: Reservation and Resource Development and Protection* (Washington, D.C.: U.S. GPO, 1977); U.S. Department of Interior, Bureau of Indian Affairs, *Indian Lands Map: Oil, Gas and Minerals on Indian Reservations* (Washington, D.C.: U.S. GPO, 1978).

7. The 1990 Census tallied 1.96 million American Indians. The count of indigenous peoples exceeds two million when Inuits, Aleuts, and Native Hawaiians are added in. This population is subdivided into some 500 federally recognized tribes and nations, including 200 native villages in Alaska; Lobo and Talbot, "Native American Statistics," p. 38. It should be noted that many analysts believe that the baseline indigenous population has been deliberately undercounted by approximately sixty

percent, and that serious estimates of the total number of native people in the U.S. run as high as fifteen million. See Jack D. Forbes, "Undercounting Native Americans: The 1980 Census and Manipulation of Racial Identity in the United States," *Wicazo Sa Review*, Vol. VI, No. 1, 1990; John Anner, "To the U.S. Census Bureau, Native Americans are Practically Invisible," *Minority Trendsetter*, Vol. 4, No. 1, Winter 1990–91.

8. U.S. Department of Commerce, Bureau of the Census, Racial Statistics Branch, *A Statistical Profile of the American Indian Population* (Washington, D.C.: U.S. GPO, 1988). These data may be usefully compared to those found in U.S. Department of Commerce, Bureau of the Census, *General Social and Economic Characteristics: United States Summary* (Washington, D.C.: U.S. GPO, 1983). For updated information, see *American Indian Digest: Contemporary Demographics of the American Indian* (Phoenix, AZ: Thunderbird Enterprises, 1995).

9. Rennard Strickland, *Tonto's Revenge: Reflections on American Indian Culture and Policy* (Albuquerque: University of New Mexico Press, 1997) p. 53.

10. See, e.g., U.S. Department of Health and Human Services, Public Health Service, *Chart Series Book* (Washington, D.C.: U.S. GPO, 1988); Karen D. Harvey and Lisa D. Harjo, *Indian Country: A History of Native People in America* (Golden, CO: North American Press, 1994) Appendix L.

11. Strickland, *Tonto's Revenge*, p. 53.

12. Lobo and Talbot, "Native American Statistics," p. 40.

13. Strickland, *Tonto's Revenge*, p. 53.

14. American Indian life expectancy on reservations during the 1990s is thus virtually identical to that of the U.S. general population a century earlier (46.3 years for men; 48.3 for women); Harold Evans, *The American Century* (New York: Alfred A. Knopf, 1998) p. xx.

15. Under Article II(b) of the United Nations Convention on the Prevention and Punishment of the Crime of Genocide (1948), any policy which intentionally causes "serious bodily or mental harm to members" of a targeted "national, ethnical, racial, or religious group, as such" is considered genocidal. Similarly, under Article II(c), acts or policies "deliberately inflicting on the group conditions of life calculated to bring about its physical destruction in whole or in part" constitute the crime of genocide; Ian Brownlie, *Basic Documents on Human Rights* (Oxford, U.K.: Clarendon Press, [3rd ed.] 1992) p. 31. Questions are habitually raised in some quarters as to whether the impacts of federal policy on American Indians are "really" intentional and deliberate. Let it be said in response that policies generating such catastrophic results over five successive generations cannot be reasonably understood in any other fashion.

16. Marjane Ambler, *Breaking the Iron Bonds: Indian Control of Energy Development* (Lawrence: University Press of Kansas, 1990) pp. 56, 66, 78, 140–41.

17. This is touched upon in connection with the so-called "heirship problem" by Wilcomb E. Washburn in his *Red Man's Land/White Man's Law: A Study of the Past and Present Status of the American Indian* (New York: Scribner's, 1971) pp. 150–51.

18. Lorraine Turner Ruffing, "The Role of Policy in American Indian Mineral Development," in Roxanne Dunbar Ortiz, ed., *American Indian Energy Resources and Development* (Albuquerque: Institute for Native American Development, University of New Mexico, 1980).

19. Michael Garrity, "The U.S. Colonial Empire is as Close as the Nearest Reservation," in Holly Sklar, ed., *Trilateralism: The Trilateral Commission and Elite Planning for Global Development* (Boston: South End Press, 1980) pp. 238–68.

20. It has been argued, persuasively, that without its domination of indigenous land and resources the U.S. military could never have achieved its present posture of global ascendancy; Valerie L. Kuletz, *The Tainted Desert: Environmental and Social Ruin in the American West* (New York: Routledge, 1998).

21. Eduardo Galeano, *The Open Veins of Latin America: Five Centuries of the Pillage of a Continent* (New York: Monthly Review Press, 1973) p. 12. Also see the essay entitled "The Open Veins of Native America: A Question of Internal Colonialism," in Leah Renae Kelly, *In My Own Voice: Essays in the Sociopolitical Context of Art and Cinema* (Winnipeg: Arbeiter Ring, 2001) pp. 112–15.

22. Anita Parlow, *Cry, Sacred Ground: Big Mountain, USA* (Washington, D.C.: Christic Institute, 1988).

23. Lobo and Talbot, "Native American Statistics," p. 40.

24. See generally, A. Rigo Sureda, *The Evolution of the Right to Self-Determination: A Study of United Nations Practice* (Leyden, Netherlands: A.W. Sijhoff, 1973).

25. Brownlie, *Basic Documents*, pp. 29–30.

26. Roxanne Dunbar Ortiz, "Protection of Indian Territories in the United States: Applicability of International Law," in Imre Sutton, ed., *Irredeemable America: The Indians' Estate and Land Claims* (Albuquerque: University of New Mexico Press, 1985) p. 260. More broadly, see Michla Pomerance, *Self-Determination in Law and Practice* (The Hague: Martinus Nijhoff, 1982).

27. Noteworthy examples are legion. Consider, as illustrations, the situations of the Scots and Welsh on the primary British isle, the Basques in Spain, and the Kurds in Turkey and northern Iraq; Peter Berresford Ellis, *The Celtic Revolution: A Study in Anti-Imperialism* (Talybont, Ceredigion: Y Lolfa, 1985); Cyrus Ernesto Zirakzadeh, *A Rebellious People: The Basques, Protests and Politics* (Reno: University of Nevada Press, 1991); Gerard Chaliand, ed., *People Without A Country: The Kurds and Kurdistan* (New York: Olive Branch Press, [2nd ed.] 1993). For a good overview of legal/political issues, see Gudmunder Alfredsson, "International Law, International Organizations, and Indigenous Peoples," *Journal of International Affairs*, Vol. 36, No. 1, 1982.

28. Dunbar Ortiz, "Protection," p. 261. Also see Ronald Fernandez, *Prisoners of Colonialism: The Struggle for Justice in Puerto Rico* (Monroe, ME: Common Courage Press, 1994); Edward Said, *The Question of Palestine* (New York: Vintage, [2nd ed.] 1992).

29. See generally, Haunani-Kay Trask, *From a Native Daughter: Colonialism and Sovereignty in Hawai'i* (Honolulu: University of Hawai'i Press, [2nd ed.] 1999).

30. A presumption underlying articulation of this principle in the Charter is, of course, that such territories have been legitimately acquired in the first place. With respect to the U.S., this is patently not the case. Leaving aside issues devolving upon coerced or fraudulent land cessions, the federal government's own Indian Claims Commission concluded in its 1978 final report that the U.S. possessed no basis at all for its assertion of title to/jurisdiction over approximately 35 percent of its claimed gross territoriality; Russel L. Barsh, "Indian Land Claims Policy in the United States," *North Dakota Law Review*, No. 58, 1982.

31. See especially the statement of U.S. State Department official Seth Waxman quoted in Glenn T. Morris, "Further Motion by State Department to Railroad Indigenous Rights," *Fourth World Bulletin*, No. 6, Summer 1998, p. 3.

32. Probably the best explication of the concept will be found in Michael Hector's *Internal Colonialism: The Celtic Fringe in British National Politics, 1536–1966* (Berkeley: University of California Press, 1975). For applications to the Native North American context, see, e.g., Robert K. Thomas, "Colonialism: Classic and Internal," *New University Thought*, Winter 1966–67; Menno Bolt, "Social Correlates of Nationalism: A Study of Native Indian Leaders in a Canadian Internal Colony," *Comparative Political Studies*, Vol. 14, No. 2, Summer 1981); my own "Indigenous Peoples of the U.S.: A Struggle Against Internal Colonialism," *Black Scholar*, Vol. 16, No. 1, Feb. 1985; and C. Matthew Snipp's "The Changing Political and Economic Status of American Indians: From Captive Nations to Internal Colonies," *American Journal of Economics and Sociology*, Vol. 45, No. 2, Apr. 1986.

33. Jean-Paul Sartre, "On Genocide," *Ramparts*, Feb. 1968.

34. It should be noted that this prognosis pertains as much to leftist states as it does to those oriented to the right; Walker Connor, *The National Question in Marxist-Leninist Theory and Strategy* (Princeton, NJ: Princeton University Press, 1984).

35. Kuletz, *Tainted Desert*, pp. 15–16.

36. A single defense contractor, the Vanadium Corporation of America, delivered all 11,000 tons of uranium consumed by the Manhattan Project; Hosteen Kinlicheel, "An Overview of Uranium and Nuclear Development on Indian Lands in the Southwest," *Southwest Indigenous Uranium Forum Newsletter*, Sept. 1993, p. 5.

37. Gerald D. Nash, *The American West Transformed: The Impact of the Second World War* (Bloomington: Indiana University Press, 1985) p. 177.

38. Richard Miller, *Under the Cloud: The Decades of Nuclear Testing* (New York: Free Press, 1986) p. 13.

39. Site selection procedures are reviewed in Richard Rhodes, *The Making of the Atomic Bomb* (New York: Simon and Schuster, 1986). Also see Henry DeWolf Smith, *Atomic Energy for Military Uses: The Official Report on the Development of the Atomic Bomb Under Auspices of the United States Government, 1940–1945* (Princeton, NJ: Princeton University Press, 1945).

40. As is now well known, there was even a fear among some participating scientists that the initial nuclear detonation might set off a chain reaction that would engulf the entire planet; Stephane Groueff, *The Manhattan Project* (Boston: Little, Brown, 1967) p. 19.

41. David Alan Rosenberg, "The U.S. Nuclear Stockpile, 1945–1950," *Bulletin of Atomic Scientists*, Mar. 1980.

42. The SBA risked little or nothing in funding these smallscale mining startups, since sale of all ore produced was guaranteed at a fixed rate by the AEC; Winona LaDuke, "The History of Uranium Mining: Who Are These Companies and Where Did They Come From?" *Black Hills/Paha Sapa Report*, Vol. 1, No. 1, 1979.

43. Robert N. Procter, "Censorship of American Uranium Mine Epidemiology in the 1950s," in Marjorie Garber and Rebecca L. Walkowitz, eds., *Secret Agents: The Rosenberg Case, McCarthyism and 1950s America* (New York: Routledge, 1995) p. 60. He is citing Robert J. Roscoe, et al., "Lung Cancer Mortality Among Nonsmoking Uranium Miners Exposed to Radon Daughters," *Journal of the American Medical Association*, No. 262, 1989.

44. On death rates among this almost entirely nonsmoking population, see Michael Garrity, "The Pending Energy Wars: America's Final Act of Genocide," *Akwesasne Notes*, Early Spring 1980. On attempts by Union Carbide representative Bob Beverly and others to nonetheless displace blame for the disaster onto cigarettes, see Jack Cox, "Studies Show Radon Guidelines May Be Weak," *Denver Post*, Sept. 4, 1979. Also see the quotations from Dr. Joseph Wagoner's unpublished paper, "Uranium Mining and Milling: The Human Costs," included in Leslie J. Freeman's *Nuclear Witnesses: Insiders Speak Out* (New York: W.W. Norton, 1982) p. 142.

45. In the Carpathians, "women are found who have married seven husbands, all of whom this terrible consumption has carried off to a premature death"; Georgius Agricola, *De Re Metallica* (London: Dover, 1912 translation of 1556 original) p. 214.

46. They also suggested that the death rate from lung cancer would have actually been far higher, were it not that numerous miners died from accidents—cave-ins and the like—before being diagnosed with the disease; F.H. Härting and W. Hesse, "Der Lungenkrebs, die Bergkrankheit in den Schneeberger Gruben," *Vierteljahrsschrift für gerichtliche Medizin*, No. 30, 1879.

47. P. Ludewig and S. Lorenser, "Untersuchung der Grubenluft in den Schneeberger Gruben auf den Gehalt an Radiumemanation," *Zeitschrift für Physik*, No. 22, 1924.

48. A shaft in Saxony with inordinately high radon levels was even known among miners as the *Todesschacht* (death mine); Wilhelm C. Hueper, *Occupational Tumors and Allied Diseases* (Springfield, IL: Charles C. Thomas, 1942) p. 441.

49. Egon Lorenz, "Radioactivity and Lung Cancer: A Critical Review of Lung Cancer in Miners of Schneeberg and Joachimsthal," *Journal of the National Cancer Institute*, No. 5, 1944.

50. Fred W. Stewart, "Occupational and Post-Traumatic Cancer," *Bulletin of the New York Academy of Medicine*, No. 23, 1947. Also see Angela Nugent, "The Power to Define a New Disease: Epidemiological Politics and Radium Poisoning," in Radid Rosner and Gerald Markowitz, eds., *Dying to Work* (Bloomington: Indiana University Press, 1986).

51. Proctor, "Censorship," p. 62.

52. Merril Eisenbud, *An Environmental Odyssey* (Seattle: University of Washington Press, 1990) p. 60.

53. Proctor, "Censorship," pp. 62–63.

54. Ibid., p. 64.

55. Ibid. Hueper was also branded a "security risk," accused alternately of being a "Nazi sympathizer" and a "communist," and prohibited for a time from traveling anywhere west of the Mississippi River.

56. Elof A. Carlson, *Genes, Radiation, and Society* (Ithaca, NY: Cornell University Press, 1981) pp. 356–67.

57. For an overview of Sternglass' findings and their suppression for over a decade, see his *Low Level Radiation* (New York: Ballantine, 1972). Also see Freeman, *Nuclear Witnesses*, pp. 50–77.

58. Gofman's AEC funding was revoked and the National Cancer Institute declined to replace it, effectively ending his research career; John W. Gofman and Arthur R. Tamplin, *Population Control Through Nuclear Pollution* (Chicago: Nelson-Hall, 1970); *Poisoned Power: The Case Against Nuclear Power Plants* (Emmaus, PA: Rodale Press, 1971; revised and rereleased in 1979 with a new subtitle, *The Case Before and After Three Mile Island*). Also see Freeman, *Nuclear Witnesses*, pp. 78–114.

59. Thomas F. Mancuso, et al., "Radiation Exposures of Hanford Workers Dying of Various Causes," *Health Physics*, No. 33, 1977. William Hines, "Cancer Risk at Nuclear Plant? Government Hushes Up Alarming Study," *Chicago Sun-Times*, Nov. 13, 1977.

60. Rosalie Bertell, *No Immediate Danger?* (London: Women's Press, 1985) pp. 83–88; Freeman, *Nuclear Witnesses*, pp. 22–49.

61. Duncan A. Holaday, et al., *Control of Radon and Daughters in Uranium Mines and Calculations of Biologic Effects* (Washington, D.C.: U.S. Public Health Service, 1957) p. 4; Howard Ball, *Cancer Factories: America's Tragic Quest for Uranium Self-Sufficiency* (Westport, CT: Greenwood, 1993) esp. pp. 49–51.

62. Proctor, "Censorship," p. 66. Archer is quoted in Ball, *Cancer Factories*, at pp. 46, 59–60; the judge is quoted at pp. 11–12, 49. Also see the legal analysis offered by George J. Annas in "The Nuremberg Code in U.S. Courts: Ethics vs. Expediency," in George J. Annas and Michael A. Grodin, eds., *The Nazi Doctors and the Nuremberg Code* (New York: Oxford University Press, 1992) pp. 209–10.

63. On weaponry, see Debra Rosenthal, *At the Heart of the Bomb: The Dangerous Allure of Weapons Work* (Menlo Park, CA: Addison-Wesley, 1990). With regard to reactors, of which there were only thirteen in 1952, all of them government owned and weapons production related, see David Dietz, *Atomic Science, Bombs and Power* (New York: Collier, 1962). In 1954, the 1946 Atomic Energy Act was revised to allow private ownership of reactors, all of which were publicly subsidized on a massive scale, an arrangement which brought corporate heavies into the game with a vengeance; Ralph Nader and John Abbott, *The Menace of Nuclear Power* (New York: W.W. Norton, 1977) pp. 275–76. Consequently more than a hundred additional facilities were built over the next thirty years; John L. Berger, *Nuclear Power: The Unviable Option* (Palo Alto, CA: Ramparts Press, 1976); Amory B. and L. Hunter Lovins, *Brittle Power: Energy Strategy for National Security* (Andover, MA: Brickhouse, 1982).

64. On profitability—35 corporations secured some $60 billion in federal contracts (over $200 billion in today's dollars) under the Eisenhower administration alone—see William F. Barber and C. Neale Ronning, *Internal Security and Military Power* (Columbus: Ohio State University Press, 1966) p. 13. More or less complete immunity from liability was provided under the 1957 Price-Anderson Indemnity Act; Jim Falk, *Global Fission: The Battle Over Nuclear Power* (New York: Oxford University Press, 1982) pp. 78–81.

65. Richard Hoppe, "A Stretch of Desert along Route 66—the Grants Belt—Is Chief Locale for U.S. Uranium," *Engineering and Mining Journal*, Vol. 79, No. 11, 1978; Sandra E. Bergman, "Uranium Mining on Indian Lands," *Environment*, Sept. 1982.

66. "In the Soviet Union and in other parts of Eastern Europe, prisoners were literally worked to death in mines, apparently as part of a deliberate plan to kill them. Outside North America, the largest single producer of uranium in the world was the German Democratic Republic, where, from 1945 to the end of the 1980s half a million workers produced some two hundred thousand tons of enriched uranium for Soviet bombs and reactors . . . A somewhat smaller program existed in

Czechoslovakia, on the southern slopes of the Erzgebirge. Tens of thousands of political prisoners were forced to work in seventeen uranium 'concentration camps' from the late 1940s through the early 1960s; epidemiological studies were conducted, but the State Security Police barred their publication"; Proctor, "Censorship," pp. 74–75. Also see Patricia Kahn, "A Grisly Archive of Key Cancer Data," *Science*, No. 259, 1993; Robert N. Proctor, "The Oberrothenbach Catastrophe," *Science*, No. 260, 1993.

67. J.B. Sorenson, *Radiation Issues: Government Decision Making and Uranium Expansion in Northern New Mexico* (Albuquerque: San Juan Regional Uranium Study Working Paper No. 14, 1978) p. 9.

68. Ibid. Also see Harold Tso and Lora Mangum Shields, "Navajo Mining Operations: Early Hazards and Recent Innovations," *New Mexico Journal of Science*, Vol. 12, No. 1, 1980.

69. Jessica S. Pearson, *A Sociological Analysis of the Reduction of Hazardous Radiation in Uranium Mines* (Washington, D.C.: National Institute for Occupational Safety and Health, 1975).

70. V. E. Archer, J.D. Gillan and J.K. Wagoner, "Respiratory Disease Mortality Among Uranium Miners," *Annals of the New York Academy of Sciences*, No. 271, 1976; M.J. Samet, et al., "Uranium Mining and Lung Cancer Among Navajo Men," *New England Journal of Medicine*, No. 310, 1984, pp. 1481–84.

71. Tom Barry, "Bury My Lungs at Red Rock: Uranium Mining Brings New Peril to the Reservation," *Progressive*, Oct. 1976; Chris Shuey, "The Widows of Red Rock," *Scottsdale Daily Progress Saturday Magazine*, June 2, 1979; Reed Madsden, "Cancer Deaths Linked to Uranium Mining," *Deseret News*, June 4, 1979; Susan Pearce and Karen Navarro, "The Legacy of Uranium Mining for Nuclear Weapons," *Earth Island Journal*, Summer 1993.

72. Garrity, "Energy Wars," p. 10.

73. Quoted in Shuey, "Widows," p. 4; Archer "conservatively" places the lung cancer rate among Navajo miners at 1,000 percent of the national average. Also see Robert O. Pohl, "Health Effects of Radon-222 from Uranium Mining," *Science*, Aug. 1979.

74. Norman Medvin, *The Energy Cartel* (New York: Vintage, 1974); Bruce E. Johansen, "The Great Uranium Rush," *Baltimore Sun*, May 13, 1979.

75. Kinlicheel, "Overview,"p. 6.

76. Kuletz, *Tainted Desert*, p. 31; Phil Reno, *Navajo Resources and Economic Development* (Albuquerque: University of New Mexico Press, 1981) p. 138.

77. Ambler, *Iron Bonds*, p. 152. For use of the term employed, see Raye C. Ringholz, *Uranium Frenzy: Boom and Bust on the Colorado Plateau* (Albuquerque: University of New Mexico Press, 1989).

78. The vents of one mine run by the Gulf Oil Company at San Mateo, New Mexico, for example, were located so close to the town's school that the State Department of Education ordered closure of the institution—but not the mine—because of the obvious health risk to the children attending it. Meanwhile, the local groundwater was found to have become so contaminated by the corporation's activities that the National Guard was forced to truck in drinking water (at taxpayer expense); Richard O. Clemmer, "The Energy Economy and Pueblo Peoples," in Joseph Jorgenson, ed., *Native Americans and Energy Development, II* (Cambridge, MA: Anthropological Resource Center/Seventh Generation Fund, 1984) p. 98.

79. Although the entire procedure of dewatering was/is in gross violation of both the Clean Water Act of 1972 (P.L. 92-500; 86 Stat. 816) and the Safe Drinking Water Act of 1974 (P.L. 93-523; 88 Stat. 1660), no criminal charges have ever been brought against Kerr-McGee or any other corporation involved in uranium mining; Ambler, *Iron Bonds*, p. 175; "Mine Dewatering Operation in New Mexico Seen Violating Arizona Water Standards," *Nuclear Fuel*, Mar. 1, 1982; Christopher McCleod, "Kerr-McGee's Last Stand," *Mother Jones*, Dec. 1980.

80. Clemmer, "Energy Economy," pp. 101–2.

81. Lora Mangum Shields and Alan B. Goodman, "Outcome of 13,300 Navajo Births from 1964–81 in the Shiprock Uranium Mining Area" (New York: unpublished paper presented at the

American Association of Atomic Scientists Symposium, May 25, 1984); Christopher McCleod, "Uranium Mines and Mills May Have Caused Birth Defects among Navajo Indians," *High Country News*, Feb. 4, 1985.

82. "Neoplasms Among Navajo Children" (Window Rock, AZ: Navajo Health Authority, Feb. 24, 1981).

83. Lora Mangum Shields, et al., "Navajo Birth Outcomes in the Shiprock Uranium Mining Area," *Health Physics*, Vol. 63, No. 5, 1992.

84. Kuletz, *Tainted Desert*, pp. 36, 40; quoting from U.S. Department of Health and Human Services, Indian Health Service, *Health Hazards Related to Nuclear Resources Development on Indian Land* (Washington, D.C.: U.S. GPO, 1983).

85. It has been estimated that it would require some 400 million tons of earth—enough to cover the entire District of Columbia 43 feet deep—to fill in the Jackpile-Paguate complex; Dan Jackson, "Mine Development on U.S. Indian Lands," *Engineering and Mining Journal*, Jan. 1980. Overall, see U.S. Department of Interior, Bureau of Land Management, *Final Environmental Impact Statement for the Jackpile-Paguate Uranium Mine Reclamation Project*, 2 vols. (Albuquerque: BLM New Mexico Area Office, 1986) Vol. 2, p. A–35.

86. Clemmer, "Energy Economy," p. 99.

87. Hope Aldrich, "The Politics of Uranium," *Santa Fe Reporter*, Dec. 7, 1978.

88. U.S. Comptroller General, "EPA Needs to Improve the Navajo Safe Drinking Water Program" (Washington, D.C.: U.S. GPO, Sept. 10, 1980) p. 5.

89. About 450 Lagunas, some three-quarters of the pueblo's labor force, as well as 160 Acomas worked for Anaconda at any given moment. Another fifteen to twenty percent of the Lagunas worked for the BIA or other federal agencies. Yet, even under such "full-employment" conditions, the median income on the reservation was only $2,661 per year (about $50 per week). This was less than half what a nonindian open pit miner was earning in an off-reservation locale during the same period; Clemmer, "Energy Economy," p. 99; Kuletz, *Tainted Desert*, p. 35.

90. R. Smith, "Radon Emissions: Open Pit Uranium Mines Said to be Big Contributor," *Nucleonics Week*, May 25, 1978; Linda Taylor, "Uranium Legacy," *The Workbook*, Vol. VIII, No. 6, Nov./Dec. 1983.

91. "Manpower Gap in the Uranium Mines," *Business Week*, Nov. 1, 1977. It should be noted that among other things the Labor Department was spending $2 million per year in tax monies to have Kerr-McGee train native workers to believe that "if they [did] not smoke, they [would] not develop lung cancer from exposure to radiation in the mines"; Dr. Joseph Wagoner, quoted in Denise Tessier, "Uranium Mine Gas Causes Lung Cancer, UNM Group Told," *Albuquerque Journal*, Mar. 11, 1980. There seem to have been no howls of protest from the surgeon general at the peddling of such quasi-official falsehoods. Instead, the country's "chief doctor" endorsed a battery of studies over the next several years, each of them reinforcing the credibility of such lies by purporting to prove that the "number one cause" of lung cancer among *non*smokers was the inhalation of "secondhand" cigarette smoke in even the most minute quantities rather than exposure to comparatively massive doses of military-industrial pollutants. There was not then—and is not now—the least evidence that tobacco smoke induces lung cancer in nonsmokers; see Peter N. Lee, "Difficulties in Determining Health Effects Related to Environmental Smoke," in Ronald R. Watson and Mark Witten, eds., *Environmental Tobacco Smoke* (Washington, D.C.: CRC Press, 2001) pp. 17, 18.

92. Ambler, *Iron Bonds*, p. 152.

93. The 1972 price of U.S.-produced uranium was $6 per pound. By 1979, the figure had risen to $42, a hugely illegal mark up which contributed greatly to the accrual of U.S. taxpayer-provided corporate superprofits during the final years of the AEC's ore-buying program (as well as the almost instantaneous bust of the domestic market when the program was phased out); David Burnham, "Gulf Aides Admit Cartel Increased Price of Uranium," *New York Times*, June 17, 1977. Shortly after its closure in 1982, Anaconda's Jackpile-Paguate complex was replaced as the world's largest open pit uranium mine by Rio Tinto Zinc's Rossing Mine, opened in 1976 in Namibia. Uranium from this de

facto South African colony, comprising about one-sixth of the "Free World" supply, was sold not only at a rate of less than $10 per pound to the U.S. and other NATO countries—a factor which drove the highly inflated price of U.S.-mined yellowcake back down to $15, thereby "busting" the profitability of production—but to Israel, making possible that country's illegal manufacture of nuclear weapons. It was also used to underpin South Africa's own illicit nuclear weapons development program; Richard Leonard, *South Africa at War: White Power and Crisis in Southern Africa* (Westport, CT; Lawrence Hill, 1983) pp. 60–69. On Australian uranium mining, and the resistance to it spearheaded by aboriginal peoples, see Falk, *Global Fission*, pp. 256–84. On northern Saskatchewan, see Miles Goldstick, *Wollaston: People Resisting Genocide* (Montréal: Black Rose Books, 1987). Overall, see A.D. Owen, "The World Uranium Industry," *Raw Materials Report*, Vol. 2, No. 1, Spring 1983.

94. W.D. Armstrong, *A Report on Mineral Revenues and the Tribal Economy* (Window Rock, AZ: Navajo Office of Mineral Development, June 1976); Joseph G. Jorgenson, "The Political Economy of the Native American Energy Business," in his *Energy Development, II*, pp. 9–20.

95. For a good summary of such practices, see Richard Nafziger, "Uranium Profits and Perils," in LaDonna Harris, ed., *Red Paper* (Albuquerque: Americans for Indian Opportunity, 1976). Also see Molly Ivins, "Uranium Mines in West Leave Deadly Legacy," *New York Times*, May 20, 1979; Bill Freudenberg, "Addictive Economies: Extractive Industries and Vulnerable Localities in a Changing World Economy," *Rural Sociology*, Vol. 57, No. 3, Fall 1992.

96. The federal program to undermine the Navajo self-sufficiency economy devolved upon wholesale impoundment of livestock during the 1930s and '40s; George A. Boyce, *"When the Navajos Had Too Many Sheep": The 1940s* (San Francisco: Indian Historian Press, 1974); Ruth Roessel, ed., *Navajo Livestock Reduction* (Chinle, AZ: Navajo Community College Press, 1975). At Laguna, which had enjoyed an agricultural economy since time immemorial, Anaconda's massive stripmining and related activities—which yielded an estimated $600 million in corporate revenues over thirty years—obliterated much of the arable landbase and irradiated most of the rest; Clemmer, "Energy Economy," pp. 97–98. More broadly, see Nancy J. Owens, "The Effects of Reservation Bordertowns and Energy Exploitation on American Indian Economic Development," *Research in Economic Anthropology*, No. 2, 1979.

97. Kinlicheel, "Overview," p. 6.

98. Laguna has been described as the "single most radioactively-contaminated area in North America outside of the military reservations in Nevada where nuclear bombs are tested"; Winona LaDuke, interview on radio station KGNU, Boulder, Colo., Apr. 15, 1986. Nevertheless, during 1986 "hearings for the environmental impact draft statement for the Jackpile-Paguate mine's reclamation project began with no less than ten Ph.D.'s and other 'technical' experts in a variety of scientific disciplines, including a mining engineer, a plant ecologist, a radiation ecologist, an expert in biomedicine, and others. All testified in obfuscating language that America's largest uranium mine could be safely unreclaimed. All were under contract to the Anaconda Corporation"; Marjane Ambler, "Lagunas Face Fifth Delay in Uranium Cleanup," *Navajo Times*, Feb. 5, 1986.

99. Quoted in Tom Barry, "The Deaths Still Go On: New Agencies Ignored Uranium Danger," *Navajo Times*, Aug. 31, 1978.

100. Freeman, *Nuclear Witnesses*, p. 140.

101. "Uranium-bearing tailings are constantly decaying into more stable elements and therefore emit radiation, as do particles of dust that blow in the wind and truck travel on dirt roads"; Clemmer, "Energy Economy," p. 102. Also see David Densmore Comey, "The Legacy of Uranium Tailings," *Bulletin of Atomic Scientists*, Sept. 1975.

102. Hoppe, "Grants Belt"; LaDuke, "History of Uranium Mining." In instances where milling was done in areas populated by "mainstream citizens," it was sometimes disguised as something else. For example, the AEC hid a milling operation, beginning in 1951, in Fernald, Ohio, near Cincinnati, behind the front that it was a "pet food factory." The ruse worked for 37 years; Helen Caldicott, *If You Love This Planet: A Plan to Heal the Earth* (New York: W.W. Norton, 1992) p. 90.

103. Lynn A. Robbins, "Energy Development and the Navajo Nation: An Update," in Jorgenson, *Energy Development, II*, p. 121.

104. Simon J. Ortiz, "Our Homeland: A National Sacrifice Area," in his *Woven Stone* (Tucson: University of Arizona Press, 1992) pp. 356–58.

105. Robbins, "Energy Development," p. 121. It should also be noted that the mill's tailings pile is located only about sixty feet from the San Juan River, Shiprock's only source of surface water, and less than a mile from a daycare center, the public schools, and the local business district. The closest residence is less than a hundred yards away; Tso and Shields, "Early Navajo Mining."

106. In 1979, several former mill workers with terminal lung cancer joined with eleven similarly afflicted Red Rock miners and the families of fifteen who'd already died in suing the AEC and Kerr-McGee for what had been done to them; "Claims Filed for Red Rock Miners," *Navajo Times*, July 26, 1979; Marjane Ambler, "Uranium Millworkers Seek Compensation," *APF Reporter*, Sept. 1980.

107. Luther J. Carter, "Uranium Mill Tailings: Congress Addresses a Long Neglected Problem," *Science*, Oct. 13, 1978.

108. See the map by Janet Steele entitled "Uranium Development in the San Juan Basin," in Freeman, *Nuclear Witnesses*, p. 139.

109. For example, the Sohio-Reserve mill at Cebolleta, a mile from the Laguna boundary, processed about 1,500 tons of ore per day during the late 1970s. Its tailings pond covers fifty acres, and the adjoining pile reached a record 350 feet; Clemmer, "Energy Economy," p. 98. Also see Hope Aldrich, "Problems Pile Up at the Uranium Mills," *Santa Fe Reporter*, Nov. 13, 1980.

110. Clemmer, "Energy Economy," pp. 97–98.

111. Report by Johnny Sanders (head of Environmental Health Services Branch of the Indian Health Service), T.J. Hardwood (IHS Albuquerque area director), and Mala L. Beard (the district sanitarian) to Laguna Pueblo Governor Floyd Corea, August 11, 1978; copy on file with the Southwest Research and Information Center, Albuquerque. To be "fair" about it, other corporations made similar use of tailings in several backwater nonindian communities on the Colorado Plateau during this period. These included Moab, Utah, and both Grand Junction and Durango, Colorado.

112. *Jackpile-Paguate Uranium Mine Reclamation Project*, pp. A-62–63.

113. The quantitative release of radioactive substances during the Church Rock spill was several times that of the much more publicized partial meltdown of a reactor at Three Mile Island, near Harrisburg, Pennsylvania, a few months earlier (March 28, 1979); Ambler, *Iron Bonds*, pp. 175–76; Mark Alan Pinsky, "New Mexico Spill Ruins a River: The Worst Radiation Accident in History Gets Little Attention," *Critical Mass*, Dec. 1979.

114. In the immediate aftermath, the Río Puerco was testing at over 100,000 picocuries of radioactivity per liter. The maximum "safe" limit is *fifteen* picocuries; Janet Siskind, "A Beautiful River That Turned Sour," *Mine Talk*, Summer/Fall 1982; Steve Hinschman, "Rebottling the Nuclear Genie," *High Country News*, Jan. 19, 1987. Although the July 16 "incident" was the seventh spill from this single dam in five years, United Nuclear had already applied for, and would receive, federal permission to resume use of its tailings pond within two months; Editors, "The Native American Connection," *Up Against the Wall Street Journal*, Oct. 29, 1979.

115. Report of the New Mexico Environmental Improvement Division (EID), dated Sept. 9, 1979, on file with the Southwest Research and Information Center, Albuquerque.

116. J.W. Schomish, "EID Lifts Ban on Eating Church Rock Cattle," *Gallup Independent*, May 22, 1980.

117. One company spokesperson reportedly informed community representatives that, "This is not a free lunch"; quoted in Dan Liefgree, "Church Rock Chapter Upset at UNC," *Navajo Times*, May 8, 1980. Such behavior is neither unique nor restricted to corporations. When, in 1979, it was discovered that well water in the Red Shirt Table area of the Pine Ridge Reservation in South Dakota was irradiated at a level fourteen times the EPA maximum—apparently as the result of the 3.5 million tons of tailings produced by an isolated AEC mining/milling operation begun in 1954 at Igloo, a nearby army ordnance depot—Tribal President Stanley Looking Elk requested $200,000 in BIA emergency funding to supply potable water to local Oglala Lakota residents. The Bureau approved Looking Elk's request in the amount of $175,000, but stipulated that the water be used *only for cattle*; Madonna

Gilbert, "Radioactive Water Contamination on the Redshirt Table, Pine Ridge Reservation, South Dakota" (Porcupine, SD: WARN Reports, Mar. 1980); Women of All Red Nations, "Radiation: Dangerous to Pine Ridge Women" *Akwesasne Notes*, Spring 1980; Patricia J. Winthrop and J. Rothblat, "Radiation Pollution in the Environment," *Bulletin of Atomic Scientists*, Sept. 1981, esp. p. 18.

118. On the cracks, see Chris Huey, "The Rio Puerco River: Where Did the Water Go?" *The Workbook*, No. 11, 1988. On the settlement, see Frank Pitman, "Navajos-UNC Settle Tailings Spill Lawsuits," *Navajo Times*, Apr. 22, 1985. On state facilitation, which took the form of discounting the extent and degree of damage done, see "EID Finds that Church Rock Dam Break had Little or No Effect on Residents," *Nuclear Fuel*, Mar. 14, 1983. The questions, of course, are why, if there was "no effect," at least one Navajo woman and an untold number of sheep sickened and died in 1979 after wading in the Río Puerco, why several other people died under similar circumstances over the next few years, and why the EID itself prohibited use of the river as a drinking water source until 1990, more than a decade after the spill; Loretta Schwarz, "Uranium Deaths at Crown Point," *Ms. Magazine*, Oct. 1979; Molly Ivins, "100 Navajo Families Sue on Radioactive Waste Spill," *New York Times*, Aug. 15, 1980.

119. D.R. Dreeson, "Uranium Mill Tailings: Environmental Implications," *Los Alamos Scientific Laboratory Mini-Report*, Feb. 1978.

120. Thadias Box, et al., *Rehabilitation Potential for Western Coal Lands* (Cambridge, MA: Ballinger, 1974).

121. On the extent of Peabody's coal stripping operations on Navajo at the time of the NAS study, see Alvin M. Josephy, Jr., "The Murder of the Southwest," *Audubon Magazine*, July 1971.

122. Although little uranium mining or milling had occurred in this region (with the exception of that at Igloo, which ended in 1972; see note 117 and accompanying text), it contains substantial deposits of uranium, low-sulfur coal and a wealth of other minerals. As was noted by one contemporaneous observer, overall, "the plans for the hills are staggering. They include a giant energy park featuring more than a score of 10,000 megawatt coal-fired plants, a dozen nuclear reactors, huge coal slurry pipelines designed to use millions of gallons of water to move crushed coal thousands of miles, and at least fourteen major uranium mines"; Harvey Wasserman, "The Sioux's Last Fight for the Black Hills," *Rocky Mountain News*, Aug. 24, 1980. Also see Amelia Irvin, "Energy Development and the Effects of Mining on the Lakota Nation," *Journal of Ethnic Studies*, Vol. 10, No. 2, Spring 1982.

123. The Nixon administration reputedly used this vernacular during discussions from 1972 onward. For the first known official articulation in print, see U.S. Department of Energy, Federal Energy Administration, Office of Strategic Analysis, *Project Independence: A Summary* (Washington, D.C.: U.S. GPO, 1974).

124. Nick Meinhart, "The Four Corners Today, the Black Hills Tomorrow?" *Black Hills/Paha Sapa Report*, Aug. 1979.

125. Means' statements were made during a speech delivered at the Black Hills International Survival Gathering, near Rapid City, South Dakota, June 12, 1980; included in my *Marxism and Native Americans* (Boston: South End Press, 1983); referenced material at p. 25.

126. All told, the official count is "approximately 1,000 significant nuclear waste sites" on Navajo alone; U.S. Department of Interior, Environmental Protection Agency, *Potential Health and Environmental Hazards of Nuclear Mine Wastes* (Washington, D.C.: U.S. GPO, 1983) pp. 1–23. During the National Citizens' Hearings on Radiation Victims in 1980, former uranium miner Kee Begay, dying of lung cancer, testified that he had "lost a son, in 1961. He was one of the many children that used to play in the uranium piles during those years. We had a lot of uranium piles near our homes—just about fifty or a hundred feet away or so—a lot of tailings. Can you imagine? Kids go out and play on those piles!"; Freeman, *Nuclear Witnesses*, pp. 143–44.

127. While Grants Belt mining and milling accounted for all but about ten percent of U.S. uranium production between 1941 and 1982, small amounts were done elsewhere in Indian Country. The AEC facility at Igloo has already been mentioned (see note 117 and accompanying text). Other examples include the Dawn Mining Company's mine and mill which operated at Blue Creek, on the

Spokane Reservation in Washington State, from 1964 to 1982, and Western Nuclear's Sherwood facility in the same locale, which operated briefly, from 1978 to 1982. The Blue Creek site in particular has generated contamination of local groundwater at levels forty times the EPA's maximum permissible limit for human consumption (4,000 times the area's natural level); Ambler, *Iron Bonds*, p. 176. Another illustration is the Susquehannah-Western Riverton mill site on the Wind River Reservation in Wyoming. Although it ceased operation in 1967, the corporations followed the usual practice of simply walking off and leaving the results for the local Indians, in this case Shoshones and Arapahos, to deal with; Marjane Ambler, "Wyoming to Study Tailings Issue," *Denver Post*, Feb. 5, 1984.

128. See generally, Anna Gyorgy, et al., *No Nukes: Everybody's Guide to Nuclear Power* (Boston: South End Press, 1979) p. 49.

129. Suzanne Ruta, "Fear and Silence at Los Alamos," *The Nation*, Jan. 11, 1993.

130. Concerned Citizens for Nuclear Safety, "LANL [Los Alamos National Laboratory] deliberately, secretly released radiation on at least three separate occasions in 1950," *The Nuclear Reactor*, Vol. 3, No. 1, Feb./Mar. 1994.

131. It appears that legal prohibitions against such "disposal" of nuclear wastes are being circumvented by shipping materials from other DoE facilities to Los Alamos, where they can be secretly burned in the lab's controlled air incinerator. It is estimated that 1,236 cubic feet of plutonium-contaminated substances are being dispersed in this way each year; Mary Risely, "LANCL Gropes to Find a New Way," *Enchanted Times*, Fall/Winter 1993, p. 6.

132. Ibid.

133. Since 1980, "physicians at the Santa Fe Indian Hospital have noticed an unusual number of thyroid cancer cases [associated with the atmospheric release of radioactive iodides] at the Santa Clara Pueblo, just north of Los Alamos"; Kuletz, *Tainted Desert*, p. 53. The rate of thyroid cancer at Santa Clara is triple the national average.

134. Ibid.

135. Risely, "New Way."

136. Kuletz, *Tainted Desert*, p. 53.

137. The Chernobyl explosion released, at a minimum, 185 million curies of atmospheric radiation during the first ten days. It has claimed 125,000 dead during the first decade, a rate which is not expected to peak for another ten years; Blanche Wiesen Cook, "Cold War Fallout," *The Nation*, Dec. 9, 1996, p. 32.

138. Elouise Schumacher, "440 Billion Gallons: Hanford wastes could fill 900 King Domes, *Seattle Times*, Apr. 13, 1991.

139. There were at least eleven tank failures at Hanford by 1970. Another, reputedly the worst, was discovered on June 8, 1973; Kenneth B. Noble, "The U.S. for Decades Let Uranium Leak at Weapons Plant," *New York Times*, Oct. 15, 1988.

140. Concerning shellfish as an indicator of the extent the Columbia River has been contaminated, it should be noted that a Hanford worker who dined on oysters harvested near the river's mouth in 1962 reportedly ingested sufficient radioactivity in the process that he triggered the plant's radiation alarm upon returning to work; Caldicott, *Planet*, p. 89.

141. Ibid. Also see Susan Wyndham, "Death in the Air," *Australian Magazine*, Sept. 29–30, 1990; Matthew L. Wald, "Wider Peril Seen in Nuclear Waste from Bomb Making," *New York Times*, Mar. 28, 1991.

142. Larry Lang, "Missing Hanford Documents Probed by Energy Department," *Seattle Post-Intelligencer*, Sept. 20, 1991.

143. Caldicott, *Planet*, p. 90.

144. The U.S. detonated a total of 106 nuclear devices in the Pacific between 1946 and 1958, 101 of them after 1950. Two atolls in the Marshall Islands, Bikini, and Enewetok—occupied by the U.S. in 1943—were subjected to 66 blasts of up to 15 megatons each. Among the tests conducted on Enewetok was that of the first hydrogen bomb in 1952. The local populations were forcibly relocated to Kili Island, where they were held against their will until 1968. The Bikinians were then told,

falsely, that it was safe to return to their homes, which were saturated with the radiation of 23 bombs. A decade later, the Enewetokans were also encouraged to return to their homes, despite the fact that a 1979 General Accounting Office study concluded they would be exposed to dangerously high radiation levels accruing from the 43 tests conducted there prior to 1958; Giff Johnson, "Nuclear Legacy: Islands Laid Waste," *Oceans*, Jan. 1980. The Bikinians were removed from their island again in 1978—at about the same time the people of Enewetok were going home—because cancers, birth defects, and other maladies had become endemic. It is likely that they'd been returned in the first place to serve as a test group upon which the effects of plutonium ingestion could be observed; Giff Johnson, "Bikinians Facing Radiation Horrors Once More," *Micronesia Support Committee Bulletin*, May/June 1978. Quite probably, the Enewetokans were slated to serve the same purpose.

145. David Loomis, *Combat Zoning: Military Land-Use Planning in Nevada* (Reno: University of Nevada Press, 1994) p. 10; citing Michael Skinner, *Red Flag* (Novato, CA: Presidio Press) p. 52.

146. The area was permanently reserved by the Shoshones in the 1863 Treaty of Ruby Valley; Dagmar Thorpe, *Newe Segobia: The Western Shoshone People* (Lee, NV: Western Shoshone Sacred Lands Association, 1982). Also see the map in Kuletz, *Tainted Desert*, p. 68.

147. On acreage, see Loomis, *Combat Zoning*, p. 31. With respect to the number of test detonations—five of which actually occurred north of the test site, on the Nellis bombing range—the official count was 702 U.S. and 23 British as of early 1992; U.S. Department of Energy, *Announced United States Nuclear Tests July 1945 through December 1991* (Washington, D.C.: U.S. GPO, 1992). On Dec. 8, 1992, however, the *New York Times* reported that there had been 204 *unannounced* U.S. tests conducted at the Nevada facility between 1952 and 1990; Anthony Robbins, Arjun Makhijani and Katherine Yih, *Radioactive Heaven and Earth: The Health and Environmental Effects of Nuclear Weapons Testing In, On, and Above the Earth* (New York/London: Apex Press/Zed Books, 1991) p. 91. Adding the six tests approved by the Clinton administration during 1992 yields a total of 953 nuclear bombings of Western Shoshone territory by that point.

148. See the subsection entitled "The Most Bombed Nation in the World," in Bernard Neitschmann and William Le Bon, "Nuclear Weapons States and Fourth World Nations," *Cultural Survival Quarterly*, Vol. 11, No. 4, 1987, pp. 5–7.

149. Howard Ball, *Justice Downwind: America's Atomic Testing Program in the 1950s* (New York: Oxford University Press, 1986) p. 85. Also see Miller, *Under the Cloud*.

150. For estimates of atmospheric releases, see Carole Gallegher, *America Ground Zero: The Secret Nuclear War* (New York: Random House, 1993).

151. Kuletz, *Tainted Desert*, p. 72.

152. U.S. Congress, Office of Technology Assessment, *Complex Cleanup: The Environmental Legacy of Nuclear Weapons Production* (Washington, D.C.: 105th Cong. 2d Sess., 1991) pp. 158–59. The half-life of several of these materials—e.g., the plutoniums—is estimated to be a quarter-million years.

153. "Report: Feds snub tribe's radiation exposure," *Reno Gazette-Journal*, June 7, 1994. On estimate of deaths, see James W. Hulse, *Forty Years in the Wilderness* (Reno: University of Nevada Press, 1986) p. 61.

154. During a 1956 effort by Nevada residents to enjoin further atmospheric detonations, a battery of the AEC's selected "scientific experts" perjured themselves by uniformly insisting, contrary to all logic and the results of their own classified studies, that nuclear weapons testing entailed "no public health hazard." Although the AEC later conceded that its witnesses had systematically lied under oath, no one was ever prosecuted in the matter; Kuletz, *Tainted Desert*, p. 73. Also see Bill Curry, "A-Test Officials Feared Outcry After Health Study," *Washington Post*, Apr. 14, 1979; Randall Smith, "Charge Ike Misled Public on N-Tests," *New York Daily News*, Apr. 20, 1979.

155. Kuletz, *Tainted Desert*, pp. 69–70.

156. China Lake, which encompasses 38 percent of the Navy's total landholdings, supports about 1,000 military personnel and over 5,000 civilian scientists, engineers, and technicians in more than 1,100 buildings on an annual budget of nearly $1 billion; ibid., pp. 62–63.

157. China Lake commands some 20,000 square miles of air space, as do each of the other three facilities. Quite literally, the sky over the entire Mojave has been appropriated by the military; Loomis, *Combat Zoning*, p. 70.

158. U.S. Navy, *Naval Weapons Center Silver Anniversary* (China Lake Naval Weapons Center: Technical Information Dept. Publishing Division, Oct. 1968).

159. One such group of Timbisha Shoshones have more or less established themselves as "squatters" in a Death Valley visitor's center. Others are clustered to the north and west, in the Owens Valley, the Tehachapi Mountains, and the Lake Isabella area. One of their areas of particularly sacred geography, the Coso Range, is now "officially called the Military Target Range, [and] constitutes some 70 square miles of mountainous area . . . with various targets—bridges, tunnels, vehicles, SAM sites—emplaced in a natural forested environment for tactics development and pilot training under realistic conditions"; R.E. Kistler and R.M. Glen, *Notable Achievements of the Naval Weapons Center* (China Lake Naval Weapons Center: Technical Information Dept. Publishing Division, 1990) p. 17. For further details, see William Thomas, *Scorched Earth: The Military Assault on the Environment* (Philadelphia: New Society, 1995).

160. Aside from the 1971 megablast—dubbed "Cannikan," it was about 350 times as powerful as the Hiroshima bomb, but carrying only one-third the force of the "Bravo" device exploded above ground on Bikini in 1954—the other two Amchitka detonations were "Long Shot" in 1965 (eighty kilotons) and "Milrow" in 1969 (one megaton); Robbins, Makhijani and Yih, *Radioactive Heaven and Earth*, p. 66.

161. David Hulen, "After the Bombs: Questions linger about Amchitka nuclear tests," *Anchorage Daily News*, Feb. 7, 1994.

162. Kristen Ostling and Joanna Miller, *Taking Stock: The Impact of Militarism on the Environment* (New York: Science for Peace, 1992).

163. Construction of the MX system—an entirely offensive weapon which was, of course, dubbed the "Peacekeeper"—promised to generate an estimated half-billion in profits for Weinberger's parent corporation; Tristan Coffin, "The MX: America's $100 Billion 'Edsel'," *Washington Spectator*, Oct. 15, 1980. It would also have eliminated the remaining habitable landbase of the Shoshones; Martha C. Knack, "MX Issues for Native American Communities," in Francis Hartigan, ed., *MX in Nevada: A Humanistic Perspective* (Reno: Nevada Humanities Press, 1980). Another fine study is Rececca Solnit's *Savage Dreams: A Journey Into the Hidden Wars of the American West* (San Francisco: Sierra Club Books, 1994).

164. Southwestern Arizona also includes another pair of huge military complexes, the half-million-acre Yuma Proving Grounds and adjoining million-acre Luke Air Force Base; see generally, Ostling and Miller, *Taking Stock*. The three native peoples in question are thus completely encircled by these facilities to their south, southern California's constellation of bases and test ranges to their west, the Nevada Test Site and related areas to their north, and the Navajo sacrifice zone to their east.

165. The latter include the 600,000-acre Hill Air Force Training Range, about thirty miles north of the somewhat larger Wendover Range. Adjoining Wendover to the south, is the equal-sized Deseret Test Center (containing the Tooele Arms Depot), below which is a much smaller parcel, the Fish Springs Nuclear Weapons Range. Abutting both Wendover and Deseret to the east is another equal-sized compound, the Dugway Proving Grounds. No public access is allowed on *any* of these approximately 2,750,000 acres, the combined controlled air space of which exceeds 20,000 square miles; see generally, Ostling and Miller, *Taking Stock*.

166. Karl Grossman, *Cover Up: What You Are Not Supposed to Know About Nuclear Power* (New York: Permanent Press, 1980) p. 13.

167. P.Z. Grossman and E.S. Cassedy," "Cost Benefit Analysis of Nuclear Waste Disposal," *Science, Technology and Human Values*, Vol. 10, No. 4, 1985.

168. As Dr. Helen Caldicott explains, "When exposed to air, plutonium ignites, forming very fine particles—like talcum powder—that are completely invisible. A single one of these particles could give you lung cancer. Hypothetically, if you could take one pound of plutonium and could put a

speck of it in the lungs of every human being [she estimates a single microgram is sufficient], you would kill every man, woman, and child on earth—not immediately, but later, from lung cancer"; Freeman, *Nuclear Witnesses*, p. 294. Also see David Burnham, "Rise in Cancer Death Rate Tied in Study to Plutonium ," *New York Times*, June 6, 1976.

169. Planning entails a "force reduction" in the number of such weapons to 3,500 by the year 2003; Charles Pope, "Nuclear Arms Cleanup Bill: A Tidy $230 Billion," *San Jose Mercury News*, Apr. 4, 1995.

170. Kuletz, *Tainted Desert*, p. 82; quoting William J. Broad, "The Plutonium Predicament," *New York Times*, May 2, 1995.

171. Pope, "Arms Cleanup."

172. U.S. Department of Energy, Office of Environmental Management, *Estimating the Cold War Mortgage: The 1995 Baseline Environmental Management Report* (Washington, D.C.: U.S. GPO, Mar. 1995); *Closing the Circle of the Closing of the Atom: The Environmental Legacy of Nuclear Weapons Production in the United States and What the Department of Energy is Doing About It* (Washington, D.C.: U.S. GPO, Jan. 1995).

173. U.S. Department of Energy, Office of Environmental Management, *Environmental Management 1995* (Washington, D.C.: U.S. GPO, Feb. 1995).

174. For analysis of the defects in this proposition, see Arjun Makhijana and Scott Saleska, *High-Level Dollars, Low-Level Sense: A Critique of Present Policy for the Management of Long-Lived Radioactive Wastes and Discussion of an Alternative Approach* (Takoma Park, MD: Institute for Energy and Environmental Research, 1992).

175. The Groundwork Collective, "The Illusion of Cleanup: A Case Study at Hanford," *Groundwork*, No. 4, Mar. 1994, p. 14. For the record, the classification scheme involved here, which is incorporated into the 1982 Nuclear Waste Policy Act (P.L. 97-425; 96 Stat. 2201), is problematic. The term "high-level wastes" pertains to spent fuel from nuclear power plants subject to reprocessing for extraction of plutonium and uranium-235. "Transuranic wastes" include substances like plutonium, neptunium and americium, "bred" from uranium-238. "Low-level wastes" include materials—e.g., worn out reactor parts—contaminated by exposure to high-level or transuranic substances. The classifications don't necessarily correspond to the degree of threat posed by a given material, only to the nature of the process by which it was produced; Concerned Citizens for Nuclear Safety, *The Nuclear Reactor*, early Spring, 1995.

176. Although tailings cleanup is mandated by the Uranium Mill Tailings Radiation Control Act of 1978, the program has been so chronically underfunded that it didn't really get started at all for eight years. When it did, its efforts consisted largely of moving tailings piles from particularly sensitive locations—such as downtown Edgemont, South Dakota, where the AEC had dumped about 3.5 million tons along the banks of the Cottonwood Creek, a quarter-mile upstream from the Cheyenne River—and relocating them to some "preferable" spot a few miles away, where they could be fenced off for "safety" reasons; Ambler, *Iron Bonds*, pp. 178–90. Arguably, the dispersal involved in such procedures worsens rather than alleviates the problem. The plain fact is that nobody has a clue what to do with this body of carcinogenic material which, by the mid-70s, was already large enough to "cover a four lane highway one foot deep from coast to coast"; Jeff Cox, "Nuclear Waste Recycling," *Environmental Action Bulletin*, No. 29, May 1976.

177. Nicholas Lenssen, *Nuclear Waste: The Problem that Won't Go Away* (Washington, D.C.: Worldwatch Institute, 1991) pp. 34–35.

178. Becky O'Guin, "DOE: Nation to burn and vitrify plutonium stores," *Colorado Daily*, Dec. 10, 1996.

179. The need for permanent repositories was formally enunciated for the first time in the Nuclear Waste Policy Act of 1982 (NWPA); the two-part scheme, authorizing establishment of MRS facilities as well as repositories, was included in the 1987 revision of NWPA; U.S. Department of Energy, Monitored Retrievable Storage Commission, "Nuclear Waste: Is There A Need For Federal Interim Storage?" in *Report of the Monitored Retrievable Storage Commission* (Washington, D.C.: U.S.

GPO, 1989); Gerald Jacob, *Site Unseen: The Politics of Siting a Nuclear Repository* (Pittsburgh: University of Pittsburgh Press, 1990).

180. Valerie Taliman, "Nine tribes look at storage: Signs point to nuclear dump on Native land," *Smoke Signals*, Aug. 1993.

181. "Plutonium is so hazardous that if you . . . manage to contain the [amounts projected to exist by the turn of the century] 99.99 percent perfectly, it would still cause somewhere between 140,000 and 500,000 extra lung-cancer fatalities each year . . . The point is, if you lose a little bit of it—a terribly little bit—you're going to contaminate the earth, and people are going to suffer for thousands of generations"; quoted in Freeman, *Nuclear Witnesses*, pp. 108, 111.

182. In 1995, the few residents of Lincoln County, Nevada, attempted to negotiate a hefty fee for themselves in exchange for accepting an MRS. The state government quickly quashed the initiative; Kuletz, *Tainted Desert*, p. 106.

183. Grace Thorpe, "Radioactive Racism? Native Americans and the Nuclear Waste Legacy," *The Circle*, Apr. 1995.

184. Taliman, "Nine tribes."

185. On the NCAI grant, see Randel D. Hansen, "Mescalero Apache: Nuclear Waste and the Privatization of Genocide," *The Circle*, Aug. 1994. On the CERT funding, see Winona LaDuke, "Native Environmentalism," *Earth Island Journal*, Summer 1993. CERT, created in the late 1970s by then Navajo Tribal Chairman Peter McDonald and federal lobbyist LaDonna Harris, has long been a major problem for those pursuing indigenous sovereignty; Philip S. Deloria, "CERT: It's Time for an Evaluation," *American Indian Law Newsletter*, Sept./Oct. 1982. Also see Geoffrey O'Gara, "Canny CERT Gets Money, Respect, Problems," *High Country News*, Dec. 14, 1979; Ken Peres and Fran Swan, "The New Indian Elite: Bureaucratic Entrepreneurs," *Akwesasne Notes*, Late Spring 1980; Winona LaDuke, "CERT: An Outsider's View In," *Akwesasne Notes*, Summer 1980.

186. Ambler, *Iron Bonds*, pp. 115, 234.

187. The lease, which will soon expire, generates about ninety percent of the reservation's revenues. Without the MRS facility, the Goshutes would not only continue to suffer a high degree of contamination, but be totally without income as well; Kuletz, *Tainted Desert*, p. 110.

188. Quoted in Randel D. Hanson, "Nuclear Agreement Continues U.S. Policy of Dumping on Goshutes," *The Circle*, Oct. 1995.

189. Unidentified Mescalero, quoted in Winifred E. Frick, "Native Americans Approve Nuclear Waste Dump on Tribal Lands," *Santa Cruz on a Hill Press*, Mar. 16, 1995.

190. Quoted in ibid.

191. Rufina Laws, cited in Kuletz, *Tainted Desert*, p. 108. Chino died in November 1998.

192. Such a sense of emotional/spiritual malaise is hardly unique to Indians, albeit it may manifest itself especially strongly among groups like the Mescaleros, who are placed in extremis; see Joanna Rogers Macy, *Despair and Personal Power in the Nuclear Age* (Philadelphia: New Society, 1983).

193. This, of course, leaves unaddressed the question of transuranic military waste—about 250,000 cubic meters of it—produced *before* 1970. Most of it is buried in shallow trenches at the Nevada Test Site and other locations, and is "difficult to retrieve" since the earth around it is now irradiated to an unknown depth. Present planning has gone no further than to leave it where it is, leaching into the environment at a steady rate; Rosenthal, *Heart of the Bomb*, p. 195.

194. Kuletz, *Tainted Desert*, p. 98; citing Concerned Citizens for Nuclear Safety, "What is WIPP?" *The Radioactive Rag*, Winter/Spring 1992.

195. National Academy of Sciences, Division of Earth Science, Committee on Waste Disposal, *The Disposal of Radioactive Waste on Land* (Washington, D.C.: NAS-NRC Pub. 519, 1957); Scientists' Review Panel on the WIPP, *Evaluation of the Waste Isolation Pilot Plant (WIPP) as a Water Saturated Nuclear Waste Repository* (Albuquerque, NM: Concerned Citizens for Nuclear Safety, Jan. 1988).

196. "Scientists Fear Atomic Explosion of Buried Waste," *New York Times*, Mar. 5, 1995.

197. About ten percent of Yucca Mountain's capacity is earmarked for military wastes. As to civil-

ian wastes, it will have been outstripped by the output of the country's 128 functioning commercial reactors before it is completed. Hence, a third repository is already necessary; Kuletz, *Tainted Desert*, p. 102.

198. Jacob, *Site Unseen*, p. 138.

199. The Low-Level Radioactive Waste Policy Act of 1980 makes the states responsible for the disposal of such materials, even if they've been federally/militarily produced (as they almost invariably are). California Governor Pete Wilson apparently opted to "assume the burden" of all 49 of his co-horts—on a fee-for-service basis—by dumping the aggregate contamination on a handful of Indians in a remote and unnoticed corner of his vast domain; Philip M. Klasky, "The Eagle's Eye View of Ward Valley: Environmentalists and Native American Tribes Fight Proposed Waste Dump in the Mojave Desert," *Wild Earth*, Spring 1994.

200. The plan is to "inter" the material—which contains plutonium, strontium, and cesium among a wide range of hyperactive and longlived substances—in five unlined trenches, each about the size of a football field. The facility is to be run by U.S. Ecology, formerly Nuclear Engineering, a corporation whose track record includes oversight of a similar—now closed and badly leaking—facility at Barnwell, Utah, as well as a disastrous West Valley enterprise in upstate New York; Kuletz, *Tainted Desert*, pp. 156–57; Berger, *Nuclear Power*, p. 104.

201. The phrase does not accrue from "radical" rhetoric. See the unabashed advocacy of the trend, both technically and politically, advanced in Charles C. Reith and Bruce M. Thompson, eds., *Deserts as Dumps? The Disposal of Hazardous Materials in Arid Ecosystems* (Albuquerque: University of New Mexico Press, 1992).

202. For a more panoramic view of the phenomenon in its various dimensions, see Donald A. Grinde, Jr., and Bruce E. Johansen, *Ecocide of Native America: Environmental Destruction of Indian Lands and Peoples* (Santa Fe, NM: Clear Light, 1995).

203. Felix S. Cohen, "The Erosion of Indian Rights, 1950–53: A Case-Study in Bureaucracy," *Yale Law Journal*, No. 62, 1953, p. 390.

204. Gyorgy, et al., *No Nukes*, p. 12.

205. There is simply no substitute for natural uranium. Neither enriched uranium nor plutonium can be produced without it, and the thorium-derived U-233 does not fulfill the same requirements; David R. Inglis, *Nuclear Energy: Its Physics and Social Challenge* (Reading, MA: Addison-Wesley, 1973).

206. David Burnham, "8,000 Pounds of Atom Materials Unaccounted for in U.S. Plants," *New York Times*, Aug. 5, 1977.

207. See, e.g., Gyorgy, et al., *No Nukes*; Falk, *Global Fission*.

208. Alex Haley, *The Autobiography of Malcolm X* (New York: Ballantine, 1965) p. 329.

209. For the most current overview, see Jay M. Gould, *The Enemy Within: The High Cost of Living with Nuclear Reactors* (New York: Four Walls Eight Windows, 1996). Also see Sternglass, *Low Level Radiation*; Gofman and Tamplin, *Poisoned Power*; Bertell, *No Immediate Danger?*

210. A solid case can be made that the whole antitobacco craze of the 1990s is more than anything a well-calibrated diversion intended to draw public attention away from the mounting health effects of radioactive contamination (tobacco, unlike plutonium, having no strategic value). For a classic illustration, see Stanton A. Glantz, et al., *The Cigarette Papers* (Berkeley: University of California Press, 1996), introduced by former U.S. Surgeon General C. Everett Koop. The entire 497-page text is devoted to explaining how tobacco smoke is responsible for virtually every disease known to man, and how the cigarette manufacturing industry knowingly suppressed such information for decades. Nuclear contamination is left altogether unmentioned—there are not even index references to substances like plutonium—as is the ongoing pattern of official suppression of relevant health data (overseen in part by Dr. Koop).

211. For elaboration, see Richard Leakey and Ronald Lewin, *The Sixth Extinction: Patterns of Life and the Future of Mankind* (Garden City, NY: Doubleday, 1995).

212. This is essentially the strategy advocated by Jay M. Gould in his "The Future of Nuclear

Power," *Monthly Review*, Vol. 35, No. 9, 1984. Also see the closing chapter of *Enemy Within*.

213. See, e.g., Richard Drinnon, *Facing West: The Metaphysics of Indian-Hating and Empire Building* (Minneapolis: University of Minnesota Press, 1980).

214. For articulation of the legal arguments, see Lee C. Buckheit, *Succession: The Legitimacy of Self-Determination* (New Haven, CT: Yale University Press, 1978); Catherine Iorns, "Indigenous Peoples and Self-Determination: Challenging State Sovereignty," *Case Western Journal of International Law*, No. 24, 1992.

215. Robert Jay Lifton and Eric Markusen, *The Genocidal Mentality: Nazi Holocaust and Nuclear Threat* (New York: Basic Books, 1988).

216. For a good treatment of an analogous phenomenon, see Deborah Lipstadt, *Denying the Holocaust: The Growing Assault on Truth and Memory* (New York: Free Press, 1993).

217. Analysis on each of these points will be found in my *A Little Matter of Genocide: Holocaust and Denial in the Americas, 1492 to the Present* (San Francisco: City Lights, 1997).

218. This goes to the notion of "enlightened self-interest" as explicated by Ernst Cassirer in his *The Philosophy of Enlightenment* (Princeton, NJ: Princeton University Press, 1951).

219. See, e.g., Cynthia Peters, ed., *Collateral Damage: The "New World Order" at Home and Abroad* (Boston: South End Press, 1992).

220. A snapshot of such possibilities is contained in Samir Amin's *Delinking: Towards a Polycentric World* (London: Zed Books, 1985).

221. On Manson, see Ed Sanders' *The Family* (New York: Signet, [rev. ed.] 1990).

6. LIKE SAND IN THE WIND

1. U.S. Department of Commerce, Bureau of the Census, *Report on Indians Taxed and Indians Not Taxed in the United States (except Alaska) at the Eleventh United States Census: 1890* (Washington, D.C.: U.S. GPO, 1894) pp. 637–38.

2. Overall, see Vine Deloria, Jr., and Raymond J. DeMallie, *Documents of American Indian Diplomacy: Treaties, Agreements, and Conventions, 1775–1979*, 2 vols. (Norman: University of Oklahoma Press, 1999).

3. U.S. Department of Commerce, Bureau of the Census, *1980 Census of the Population: Characteristics of the Population* (Washington, D.C.: U.S. GPO, 1983) Table 69, "Persons by Race and Sex for Areas and Places: 1980," pp. 201–12.

4. National Congress of the American Indian (NCAI), *Briefing Paper* (Washington, D.C.: NCAI, Apr. 1991).

5. See Jack D. Forbes, "Undercounting Native Americans: The 1980 Census and Manipulation of Racial Identity in the United States," *Wicazo Sa Review*, Vol. VI, No. 1, Spring 1990, pp. 2–26.

6. U.S. Department of Commerce, Bureau of the Census, *1980 Census of the Population, Supplementary Report: American Indian Areas and Alaska Native Villages* (Washington, D.C.: U.S. GPO, 1984) p. 24.

7. Ibid., Table I, p. 14.

8. Henry F. Dobyns, *Their Numbers Become Thinned: Native American Population Dynamics in Eastern North America* (Knoxville: University of Tennessee Press, 1983) p. 41.

9. Francis Paul Prucha, *Atlas of American Indian Affairs* (Lincoln: University of Nebraska Press, 1990) pp. 151–57.

10. *1980 Census, Supp. Rept.*, Table I. The American Indian population reported for Hawai'i in 1980 was 2,655. State by state break-outs are more readily accessible in Carl Waldman, *Atlas of the North American Indian* (New York: Facts on File, 1985) p. 201. Also see C. Matthew Snipp, *American Indians: First of This Land* (New York: Russell Sage Foundation, 1991) Appendix II: "Tribal Population Estimates by State," pp. 333–47.

11. Reginald Horsman, *Expansion and American Indian Policy, 1783–1812* (Ann Arbor: University of Michigan Press, 1967) pp. 6–7.

12. Thomas Perkins Abernathy, *Western Lands and the American Revolution* (Albuquerque: University of New Mexico Press, 1979).

13. The complete text of the 1783 Treaty of Paris may be found in Hunter Miller, ed., *Treaties and Other International Acts of the United States of America* (Washington, D.C.: University Publications of America, 1931) pp. 151–57.

14. This interpretation corresponds to conventional understandings of contemporaneous international law ("Discovery Doctrine"); see "The Law Stood Squarely on Its Head," herein.

15. Reflections on initial U.S. stature as a legal pariah are more fully developed in Vine Deloria, Jr., "Self-Determination and the Concept of Sovereignty," in Roxanne Dunbar Ortiz and Larry Emerson, eds., *Economic Development in American Indian Reservations* (Albuquerque: University of New Mexico Native American Studies Center, 1979) pp. 22–28.

16. On the Northwest Territory, see Randolph C. Downes, *Council Fires on the Upper Ohio: A Narrative of Indian Affairs on the Upper Ohio until 1795* (Pittsburgh: University of Pittsburgh Press, 1940). On the situation further south, see R.S. Cotterill, *The Southern Indians: The Story of the Five Civilized Tribes Before Removal* (Norman: University of Oklahoma Press, 1954).

17. A.L. Burt, *The United States, Great Britain, and British North America, from the Revolution to the Establishment of Peace after the War of 1812* (New Haven, CT: Yale University Press, 1940) pp. 82–105.

18. Arthur P. Whitaker, *The Spanish-American Frontier, 1783–1795* (Boston: Houghton-Mifflin, 1927); John W. Caughey, *McGillivray of the Creeks* (Norman: University of Oklahoma Press, 1938).

19. Allan W. Eckert, *A Sorrow in Our Heart: The Life of Tecumseh* (Boston: Little, Brown, 1992).

20. Horseman, *Expansion and American Indian Policy,* p. 7.

21. Letter from Schuyler to Congress, July 29, 1783, in *Papers of the Continental Congress, 1774–1789* (Washington, D.C.: National Archives, Item 153, III) pp. 601–7.

22. Letter from Washington to James Duane, Sept. 7, 1783, in John C. Fitzpatrick, ed., *The Writings of George Washington from Original Manuscript Sources, 1745–1799* (Washington, D.C.: U.S. GPO, 1931–1944) Vol. XXVII, pp. 133–40.

23. 1 Stat. 50 (1787). In actuality, conquest rights were never applicable anyway; see the section entitled "Rights of Conquest" in "The Law Stood Squarely on Its Head," herein.

24. For further analysis, see Horsman, *Expansion.*

25. Quoted from "Report and Resolutions of October 15, 1783," *Journals of the Continental Congress, Vol. XXV* (Washington, D.C.: U.S. GPO, no date) pp. 681–93.

26. The idea accords quite perfectly with George Washington's notion that all eastern Indians should be pushed into the "illimitable regions of the West," meaning what was then Spanish territory beyond the Mississippi (letter from Washington to Congress, June 17, 1783, in Fitzpatrick, *Writings of George Washington,* pp. 17–18). In reality, however, the U.S. understood that it possessed no lawful right to unilaterally dispose of the territory in question in this or any other fashion. In purchasing the rights of France (which had gained them from Spain in 1800) to "Louisiana" in 1803, the U.S. plainly acknowledged indigenous land title in its pledge to Napoleon Bonaparte that it would would respect native "enjoyment of their liberty, property and religion they profess." Hence, the U.S. admitted it was not purchasing land from France, but rather a monopolistic French right within the region to acquire title over specific areas through the negotiated consent of individual Indian nations. See generally, Alexander De Conde, *This Affair of Louisiana* (New York: Scribner's, 1973); Everett Somerville Brown and Herbert E. Bolton, eds., *A Constitutional History of the Louisiana Purchase, 1803–1812* (New York: Beard Books, 2000).

27. *Fletcher v. Peck* (10 U.S. 87 (1810)). Further elaboration on the implications of the cases mentioned herein may be found in my "Perversions of Justice: Examining the Doctrine of U.S. Rights to Occupancy in North America," in David S. Caudill and Steven Jay Gold, eds., *Radical Philosophy of Law: Contemporary Challenges to Mainstream Legal Theory and Practice* (Atlantic Highlands, NJ: Humanities Press, 1995) pp. 200–20. It should be noted here, however, that Marshall was hardly a disinterested party in the issue he addressed in *Peck.* Both the Chief Justice and his father were holders of the deeds to 10,000 acre parcels in present-day West Virginia, (then Kentucky), awarded for services

rendered during the revolution but falling within an area never ceded by its aboriginal owners; Leonard Baker, *John Marshall: A Life in Law* (New York: Macmillan, 1974) p. 80.

28. On the War of 1812, see Sidney Lens, *The Forging of the American Empire* (New York: Thomas Y. Crowel, 1971) pp. 40–61. On Tecumseh, see John Sugden, *Tecumseh's Last Stand* (Norman: University of Oklahoma Press, 1985). On the Red Sticks, see Joel W. Martin, *Sacred Revolt: The Muskogees' Struggle for a New World* (Boston: Beacon Press, 1991).

29. C.C. Griffin, *The United States and the Disruption of the Spanish Empire, 1810–1822* (New York: Columbia University Press, 1937).

30. Rembert W. Patrick, *Florida Fiasco: Rampant Rebels on the Georgia-Florida Border, 1810-1815* (Athens: University of Georgia Press, 1954); Henrietta Buckmaster, *The Seminole Wars* (New York: Crowell-Collier, 1966); J. Leitch Wright, Jr., "A Note on the First Seminole War as Seen by the Indians, Negroes and Their British Advisors," *Journal of Southern History*, No. 34, 1968.

31. *Johnson v. McIntosh* (21 U.S. (98 Wheat.) 543 (1823)).

32. Frederick Merk, *The Monroe Doctrine and American Expansionism* (New York: Alfred A. Knopf, 1967); Albert K. Weinberg, *Manifest Destiny: A Study of National Expansionism in American History* (Baltimore: Johns Hopkins University Press, 1935) pp. 73–89.

33. Indian Removal Act (ch. 148, 4 Stat. 411); *Cherokee v. Georgia* (30 U.S. (5 Pet.) 1 (1831)); *Worcester v. Georgia* (31 U.S. (6 Pet.) 551 (1832)). For further analysis, see Milner Ball, "Constitution, Court, Indian Tribes," *American Bar Foundation Research Journal*, No. 1, 1989, esp. pp. 23–9; Jill C. Norgren, *The Cherokee Cases: The Confrontation of Law and Politics* (New York: McGraw-Hill, 1996).

34. See generally, Grant Foreman, *Advancing the Frontier, 1830–1860* (Norman: University of Oklahoma Press, 1933); Frederick Merk, *Manifest Destiny and Mission in American History: A Reinterpretation* (New York: Alfred A. Knopf, 1963).

35. Grant Foreman, *Indian Removal: The Immigration of the Five Civilized Tribes* (Norman: University of Oklahoma Press, 1953); Gloria Jahoda, *The Trail of Tears: The Story of the American Indian Removals, 1813–1855* (New York: Holt, Rinehart and Winston, 1975).

36. Driven from Illinois, the main body of Sauks were trapped and massacred—men, women, and children alike—at the juncture of the Bad Axe and Mississippi Rivers in Wisconsin; Cecil Eby, *"That Disgraceful Affair": The Black Hawk War* (New York: W.W. Norton, 1973) pp. 243–61.

37. In many ways, the Seminole "hold outs" were the best guerrilla fighters the U.S. ever faced. The commitment of 30,000 troops for several years was insufficient to subdue them. Ultimately, the U.S. broke off the conflict, which was stalemated, and costing several thousand dollars for each Indian killed; John K. Mahon, *History of the Second Seminole War, 1835–1842* (Gainesville: University of Florida Press, 1967); Alan Axelrod, *Chronicle of the Indian Wars from Colonial Times to Wounded Knee* (New York: Prentice Hall, 1993) pp. 146–47; Buckmaster, *Seminole Wars*, pp. 71–109.

38. Wilcomb E. Washburn, *The Indian in America* (New York: Harper Torchbooks, 1975) p. 169.

39. Russell Thornton, "Cherokee Losses During the Trail of Tears: A New Perspective and a New Estimate," *Ethnohistory*, No. 31, 1984, pp. 289–300.

40. Ibid., p. 293.

41. *1980 Census, Supp. Rept.*; Prucha, *Atlas*, p. 157.

42. Duane H. King, *The Cherokee Nation: A Troubled History* (Knoxville: University of Tennessee Press, 1979) pp. 103–9.

43. Angie Debo, *A History of the Indians of the United States* (Norman: University of Oklahoma Press, 1977) p. 157.

43. Very little work has been done to document this proliferation of communities, although their existence has been increasingly admitted since the 1960s; see, e.g., the statement of Eastern Cherokee Principal Chief Jonathan Taylor quoted in "The Nullification of Native America?" herein.

44. Jackson's stated goal was not simply to defeat the Red Sticks, but to "exterminate" them. Some 800 Indians, many of them noncombatants, were killed and mutilated after being trapped within the Horseshoe Bend of the Tallapoosa River, in northern Alabama; David E. Stannard, *American Holocaust: The Conquest of the New World* (New York: Oxford University Press, 1992) pp. 121–23.

45. The text of Jackson's talk of Mar. 23, 1829, was originally published in *Documents and Proceedings relating to the Formation and Progress of a Board in the City of New York, for the Emigration, Preservation, and Improvement of the Aborigines of America* (New York: Indian Board for the Emigration, Preservation and Improvement of the Aborigines of America, 1829) p. 5.

47. The idea that America west of the Mississippi was ever seriously intended to be the exclusive domain of the continent's native peoples was belied even before removal was achieved by the creation of the territories of Missouri (1816), Arkansas (1819), and Iowa (1838). By 1821, Missouri had become a state; Malcolm J. Rohrbough, *The Trans-Appalachian Frontier: Peoples, Societies and Institutions, 1775–1850* (New York: Oxford University Press, 1978) pp. 159, 219, 321.

48. Quoted in Lens, *American Empire*, p. 100.

49. David M. Pelcher, *The Diplomacy of Annexation: Texas, Oregon and the Mexican War* (Columbia: University of Missouri Press, 1973). Actually, this transcontinental gallop represents a rather reserved script. As early as 1820, Luis de Onis, former Spanish governor of Florida, observed that, "The Americans . . . believe that their dominion is destined to extend, now to the Isthmus of Panama, and hereafter over all the regions of the New World . . . They consider themselves superior to the rest of mankind, and look upon their republic as the only establishment upon earth founded on a grand and solid basis, embellished by wisdom, and destined one day to become the sublime colossus of human power, and the wonder of the universe"; quoted in Lens, *American Empire*, pp. 94–95. It is also a matter of record that William Henry Seward, Secretary of State under Lincoln and Johnson in the 1860s, advanced a serious plan to annex all of Canada west of Ontario, but was ultimately forced to content himself with acquiring the Alaska Territory; see R.W. Van Alstyne, *The Rising American Empire* (New York: Oxford University Press, 1960) p. 141.

50. A map delineating the "permanent" territories assigned these peoples after removal is contained in Jack D. Forbes, *Atlas of Native History* (Davis, CA: D-Q University Press, n.d.).

51. The federal government recognizes less than half (32) of these nations as still existing; John W. Morris, Charles R. Goins, and Edward C. McReynolds, *Historical Atlas of Oklahoma* (Norman: University of Oklahoma Press, [3rd ed.] 1986) Map 76.

52. According to the *1980 Census, Supp. Rept.*, Table I, Oklahoma's Indian population of 169,292 is second only to California's 198,275. There were 4,749 people living on the reservation, or just 12.1 percent of the 39,327 members reflected on the Osage roll; ibid., p. 22.

53. On the War with Mexico, see George Pierce Garrison, *Westward Expansion, 1841–1850* (New York: Harper, 1937); Gene M. Brack, *Mexico Views Manifest Destiny, 1821–1846: An Essay on the Origins of the Mexican War* (Albuquerque: University of New Mexico Press, 1975).

54. David Svaldi, *Sand Creek and the Rhetoric of Extermination: A Case Study in Indian-White Relations,* (Washington, D.C.: University Press of America, 1989).

55. For a detailed overview, see my *A Little Matter of Genocide: Holocaust and Denial in the Americas, 1492 to the Present* (San Francisco: City Lights, 1997) pp. 222–45.

56. L.R. Bailey, *The Long Walk: A History of the Navajo Wars, 1846–68* (Pasadena, CA: Westernlore, 1978). More specifically, see Roberto Mario Salmón, "The Disease Complaint at Bosque Redondo (1864–1868)," *Indian Historian*, No. 9, 1976.

57. This episode is covered adequately in Edward Lazarus, *Black Hills, White Justice: The Sioux Nation versus the United States, 1775 to the Present* (New York: HarperCollins Publishers, 1991) pp. 71–95.

58. See Robert Clark, ed., *The Killing of Chief Crazy Horse* (Lincoln: University of Nebraska Press, 1976), and the concluding chapter of Stanley Vestal's *Sitting Bull: Champion of the Sioux* (Norman: University of Oklahoma Press, 1957).

59. The imprisonment program is described in some detail in the memoirs of the commandant of Marion Prison, later superintendent of the Carlisle Indian School; Richard Henry Pratt, *Battlefield and Classroom: Four Decades with the American Indian, 1867–1904* (New Haven, CT: Yale University Press, [reprint] 1964).

60. *Report on Indians Taxed and Indians Not Taxed,* pp. 637–38.

61. Lazarus, *White Justice*, p. 29. It should be noted that, contrary to myth, scalping was a practice introduced to the Americas by Europeans, not native people. It was imported by the British—who had previously used it against the Irish—during the seventeenth century; Nicholis P. Canny, "The Ideology of English Colonialism: From Ireland to America," *William and Mary Quarterly*, 3rd Series, XXX, 1973.

62. Lenore A. Stiffarm and Phil Lane, Jr., "The Demography of Native North America: A Question of American Indian Survival," in M. Annette Jaimes, ed., *The State of Native America: Genocide, Colonization and Resistance* (Boston: South End Press, 1992) p. 35. It is instructive that the Texas state legislature framed its Indian policy as follows: "We recognize no title in the Indian tribes resident within the limits of the state to any portion of the soil thereof; and . . . we recognize no right of the Government of the United States to make any treaty of limits with the said Indian tribes without the consent of the Government of this state"; quoted in Washburn, *Indian in America*, p. 174. In other words, extermination was intended to be total.

63. James M. Mooney, "Population," in Frederick W. Dodge, ed., *Handbook of the Indians North of Mexico, Vol. 2* (Washington, D.C.: Bureau of American Ethnology, Bulletin No. 30, Smithsonian Institution, 1910) pp. 286–87.

64. Sherburn F. Cook, *The Conflict Between the California Indian and White Civilization* (Berkeley: University of California Press, 1976) pp. 282–84.

65. Russell Thornton, *American Indian Holocaust and Survival: A Population History Since 1492* (Norman: University of Oklahoma Press, 1987) p. 49.

66. Thornton estimates the aboriginal North American population to have been about 12.5 million, most of it within what is now the continental U.S. In *Their Numbers Become Thinned*, Dobyns puts it as having been as high as 18.5 million. Kirkpatrick Sale, in *The Conquest of Paradise: Christopher Columbus and the Columbian Legacy* (New York: Alfred A. Knopf, 1990) splits the difference, placing the figure at 15 million. Extreme attrition due to disease and colonial warfare had already occurred prior to the American War of Independence. Something on the order of two million survivors in 1776 therefore seems a reasonable estimate. Whatever the exact number in that year, it had been reduced to 237,196 according to U.S. census data for 1900; U.S. Department of Commerce, Bureau of the Census, *Fifteenth Census of the United States, 1930: The Indian Population of the United States and Alaska*, (Washington, D.C.: U.S. GPO, 1937) Table 2, "Indian Population by State, 1890–1930," p. 3.

67. Cook, *Conflict*, p. 284.

68. Donald J. Berthrong, *The Cheyenne and Arapaho Ordeal: Reservation and Agency Life in the Indian Territory, 1875–1907* (Norman: University of Oklahoma Press, 1976).

69. Dan L. Thrapp, *The Conquest of Apacheria* (Norman: University of Oklahoma Press, 1967).

70. Merril Beal, *I Will Fight No More Forever: Chief Joseph and the Nez Percé War* (Seattle: University of Washington Press, 1963).

71. Kenneth Carley, *The Sioux Uprising of 1862* (St. Paul: Minnesota Historical Society, 1961).

72. See the section on "Iroquois Land Claims" in "The Earth Is Our Mother," pp. 73–84, herein. Also see Edmund Wilson, *Apology to the Iroquois* (New York: Farrar, Strauss, and Cudahy, 1960).

73. As of 1980, a grand total of 582 members of these amalgamated peoples were reported as living on the Stockbridge Reservation; *1980 Census of the Population, Supplementary Report*, Table I. Also see Patrick Frazier, *The Mohicans of Stockbridge* (Lincoln: University of Nebraska Press, 1992).

74. Appropriations Act of 1871 (ch. 120, 16 Stat. 544, 566), Major Crimes Act (ch. 341, 24 Stat. 362, 385 (1885)), *U.S. v. Kagama* (118 U.S. 375 (1886)). The next major leap in this direction was passage of the Assimilative Crimes Act (30 Stat. 717) in 1898, applying state, territorial, and district criminal codes to "federal enclaves" such as Indian reservations; Robert N. Clinton, "Development of Criminal Jurisdiction on Reservations: A Journey Through a Jurisdictional Maze," *Arizona Law Review*, Vol. 18, No. 3, 1976.

75. General Allotment Act (ch. 119, 24 Stat. 388 (1887)). Overall, see Janet A. McDonnell, *The Dispossession of the American Indian, 1887–1934* (Bloomington: Indiana University Press, 1991). On the blood quantum issue, see my "The Crucible of American Indian Identity: Native Tradition versus

Colonial Imposition in Postconquest North America," *American Indian Culture and Research Journal,* Vol. 23, No. 1, Spring 1999.

76. As is stated in the current procedures for enrollment provided by the Cherokee Nation of Oklahoma, "Many descendants of the Cherokee Indians can neither be certified nor qualify for tribal membership in the Cherokee Nation because their ancestors were not enrolled during the final enrollment [during allotment, 1899–1906]. Unfortunately, these ancestors did not meet the [federal] requirements for the final enrollment. The requirements at the time were . . . having a permanent residence within the Cherokee Nation (now the 14 northeastern counties of Oklahoma). If the ancestors had . . . settled in the states of Arkansas, Kansas, Missouri, or Texas, they lost their citizenship within the Cherokee Nation at that time."

77. McDonnell, *Dispossession;* D.S. Otis, *The Dawes Act and the Allotment of Indian Land* (Norman: University of Oklahoma Press, 1973).

78. James S. Olson and Raymond Wilson, *Native Americans in the Twentieth Century* (Urbana: University of Illinois Press, 1984) pp. 82–83.

79. Kirk Kicking Bird and Karen Ducheneaux, *One Hundred Million Acres* (New York: Macmillan, 1973).

80. The powers of individual agents in this regard accrued from an amendment (26 Stat. 794) made in 1891. The language describing these powers comes from Deloria and Lytle, *American Indians, American Justice,* p. 10.

81. This is known as the "Heirship Problem," meaning that if a family head with four children began with a 160-acre parcel of marginal land in 1900, his/her heirs would each inherit forty acres somewhere around 1920. If each of these heirs, in turn, had four children, then their heirs would inherit ten acres, circa 1940. Following the same formula, their heirs would have inherited 2.5 acres each in 1960, and their heirs would have received about one-half acre each in 1980. In actuality, many families have been much larger during the twentieth century—as is common among peoples recovering from genocide—and contemporary descendants of the original allottees often find themselves measuring their "holdings" in square inches. Wilcomb Washburn, *Red Man's Land, White Man's Law* (Norman: University of Oklahoma Press, [2nd ed.] 1994) pp. 150–51.

82. Henry E. Fritz, *The Movement for Indian Assimilation, 1860–1890* (Philadelphia: University of Pennsylvania Press, 1963); Frederick E. Hoxie, *A Final Promise: The Campaign to Assimilate the Indians, 1880–1920* (Lincoln: University of Nebraska Press, 1985).

83. Rebecca L. Robbins, "Self-Determination and Subordination: The Past, Present and Future of American Indian Governance," in Jaimes, *State of Native America,* p. 93. The quote from Leupp comes from his book, *The Indian and His Problem* (New York: Scribner, 1910) p. 93; that from Burke from a letter to William Williamson on Sept. 16, 1921 (William Williamson Papers, Box 2, File—Indian Matters, Misc., I.D. Weeks Library, University of South Dakota).

84. *Lone Wolf v. Hitchcock* (187 U.S. 553 (1903)). Among other things, the decision meant that the U.S. had decided it could unilaterally absolve itself of any obligation or responsibility it had incurred under provision of any treaty with any indigenous nation while simultaneously considering the Indians to still be bound by *their* treaty commitments. See Ann Laquer Estin, "*Lone Wolf v. Hitchcock*: The Long Shadow," in Sandra L. Cadwallader and Vine Deloria, Jr., eds., *The Aggressions of Civilization: Federal Indian Policy Since the 1880s* (Philadelphia: Temple University Press, 1984) pp. 215–45; Blue Clark, Lone Wolf v. Hitchcock: *Treaty Rights and Indian Law at the End of the Nineteenth Century* (Lincoln: University of Nebraska Press, 1994). This was an utterly illegitimate posture under international custom and convention at the time, a matter amply reflected in contemporary international black letter law; Sir Ian Sinclair, *The Vienna Convention on the Law of Treaties* (Manchester, U.K.: Manchester University Press, [2nd ed.] 1984).

85. Burke Act (34 Stat. 182 (1906)); Indian Citizenship Act (ch. 233, 43 Stat. 25 (1924)).

86. Much of this is covered—proudly—in Pratt, *Battlefield to Classroom.* Also see David Wallace Adams, *Education for Extinction: American Indians and the Boarding School Experience, 1875–1928* (Lawrence: University Press of Kansas, 1995).

87. Evelyn C. Adams, *American Indian Education: Government Schools and Economic Progress* (Morningside Heights, NY: King's Crown Press, 1946) pp. 55–56, 70.

88. The phrase used was picked up by the author in a 1979 conversation with Floyd Westerman, a Sisseton Dakota who was sent to a boarding school at age six. For a broader statement of the same theme, see Vine Deloria, Jr., "Education and Imperialism," *Integrateducation*, Vol. XIX, Nos. 1–2, Jan. 1982. For ample citation of the federal view, see J.U. Ogbu, "Cultural Discontinuities and Schooling," *Anthropology and Education Quarterly*, Vol. 12, No. 4, 1982.

89. On adoption policies, including those pertaining to so-called "blind" adoptions (where children are prevented by law from ever learning their parents' or tribe's identities), see Tillie Blackbear Walker, "American Indian Children: Foster Care and Adoptions," in U.S. Office of Education, Office of Educational Research and Development, National Institute of Education, *Conference on Educational and Occupational Needs of American Indian Women, October 1986* (Washington, D.C.: U.S. GPO, 1986) pp. 185–210.

90. The entire program involving forced transfer of Indian children is contrary to Article II(d) of the United Nations 1948 Convention on Prevention and Punishment of the Crime of Genocide; Ian Brownlie, *Basic Documents on Human Rights* (Oxford: Clarendon Press, [3rd ed.] 1992) p. 31.

91. Thornton, *Holocaust and Survival*, p. 227.

92. These estimates have been arrived at by deducting the reservation population totals from the overall census figures deployed in Prucha's *Atlas*, then subtracting the urban population totals deployed by Thornton (note 91).

93. The U.S., as is well known, undertook the Spanish-American War in 1898 primarily to acquire oversees colonies, notably the Philippines and Cuba (for which Puerto Rico was substituted at the last moment). It also took the opportunity to usurp the government of Hawai'i, about which it had been expressing ambitions since 1867, and to obtain a piece of Samoa in 1899. This opened the door to its assuming "protectorate" responsibility over Germany's Pacific colonies after World War I, and many of the Micronesian possessions of Japan after World War II; see Julius Pratt, *The Expansionists of 1898* (Baltimore: Johns Hopkins University Press, 1936); Richard O'Connor, *Pacific Destiny: An Informal History of the U.S. in the Far East, 1776–1968* (Boston: Little, Brown, 1969).

94. Emily Benedek, *The Wind Won't Know Me: A History of the Navajo-Hopi Land Dispute* (New York: Alfred A. Knopf, 1992) p. 142.

95. Olson and Wilson, *Native Americans*, p. 181.

96. For a good overview, see Craig H. Miner, *The Corporation and the Indian: Tribal Sovereignty and Industrial Civilization in Indian Territory, 1865–1907* (Columbia: University of Missouri Press, 1976).

97. This is brought out in thinly veiled fashion in official studies commissioned at the time. See, for example, U.S. House of Representatives, Committee of One Hundred, *The Indian Problem: Resolution of the Committee of One Hundred Appointed by the Secretary of Interior and Review of the Indian Problem* (Washington, D.C.: 68th Cong., 1st Sess., 1925). Also see Lewis Meriam, et al., *The Problem of Indian Administration* (Baltimore: Johns Hopkins University Press, 1928).

98. This was standard colonialist practice during the period; Mark Frank Lindsey, *The Acquisition and Government of Backward Territory in International Law*, (London: Longmans Green, 1926).

99. For what may be the first application of the term "internal colonies" to analysis of the situation of American Indians in the U.S., see Robert K. Thomas, "Colonialism: Classic and Internal," *New University Thought*, Vol. 4, No. 4, Winter 1966–67.

100. Indian Reorganization Act (ch. 576, 48 Stat. 948 (1934)). On assembly of the IRA "package," see Vine Deloria, Jr., and Clifford M. Lytle, *The Nations Within: The Past and Future of American Indian Sovereignty* (New York: Pantheon, 1984).

101. The classic example of this occurred at the Hopi Reservation, where some 85 percent of all eligible voters actively boycotted the IRA referendum in 1936. Indian Commissioner John Collier then counted these abstentions as "aye" votes, making it appear as if the Hopis had been nearly unanimous in affirming reorganization rather than overwhelmingly rejecting it. See Oliver LaFarge, *Running Narrative of the Organization of the Hopi Tribe of Indians* (unpublished manuscript in the LaFarge Collec-

tion, University of Texas at Austin). In general, the IRA referendum process was similar to—and served essentially the same purpose as—those more recently orchestrated abroad by the State Department and CIA; see Edward S. Herman and Frank Brodhead, *Demonstration Elections: U.S.-Staged Elections in the Dominican Republic, Vietnam, and El Salvador* (Boston: South End Press, 1984).

102. Robbins, "Self-Determination," p. 95.

103. See "Breach of Trust," herein.

104. Alvin Josephy, "Murder of the Southwest," *Audubon Magazine*, Sept. 1971, p. 42.

105. Bruce Johansen and Roberto Maestas, *Wasichu: The Continuing Indian Wars* (New York: Monthly Review Press, 1979) p. 162. The minimum rate was established by the Federal Coal Leasing Act of 1975, applicable everywhere in the U.S. except Indian reservations.

106. Olson and Wilson, *Native Americans*, p. 200.

107. The term "super-profits" is used in the manner defined by Richard J. Barnet and Ronald E. Müller in their *Global Reach: The Power of the Multinational Corporations* (New York: Touchstone, 1974).

108. U.S. Department of Interior, Bureau of Indian Affairs, *Indian Service Population and Labor Force Estimates* (Washington, D.C.: U.S. GPO, 1989). The study shows one-third of the 635,000 reservation-based Indians surveyed had annual incomes of less than $7,000. Also see the charts illuminating American Indian and Alaska native labor force participation as of 1980 deployed by Snipp, *American Indians*, pp. 214–40.

109. U.S. Senate, Committee on Labor and Human Resources, *Guaranteed Job Opportunity Act: Hearing on S.777* (Washington, D.C.: 100th Cong., 1st Sess., 23 Mar. 1987) Appendix A.

110. The classic image is that of Emma Yazzie, an elderly and very traditional Diné who subsists on her flock of sheep, standing forlornly before a gigantic Peabody coal shovel which is digging up her scrubby grazing land on Black Mesa. The coal is to produce electricity for Phoenix and Las Vegas, but Yazzie has never had electricity (or running water) in her home. She gains nothing from the enterprise. To the contrary, her very way of life is being destroyed before her eyes. See Johansen and Maestas, *Wasichu*, p. 141.

111. The term "underdevelopment" is used in the sense defined by Andre Gunder Frank in his *Capitalism and Underdevelopment in Latin America* (New York: Monthly Review Press, 1967).

112. U.S. Department of Commerce, Bureau of the Census, *A Statistical Profile of the American Indian Population* (Washington, D.C.: U.S. GPO, 1984); U.S. Department of Health and Human Services, Public Health Service, *Chart Series Book* (Washington, D.C.: U.S. GPO, 1988). An excellent summary is provided by Rennard Strickland in the essay "You Can't Rollerskate in a Buffalo Herd, Even if You Have all the Medicine: Indian Law and Politics," in his *Tonto's Revenge: Reflections on American Indian Culture and Policy* (Albuquerque: University of New Mexico Press, 1997) p. 53.

113. The terminology accrues from Eduardo Galeano, *The Open Veins of Latin America: Five Centuries of the Pillage of a Continent* (New York: Monthly Review Press, 1973).

114. Thus far, the only people able to turn this around have been the Northern Cheyennes, which won a 1976 lawsuit to have Class I environmental protection standards applied to their reservation, thereby halting construction of two coal-fired generating plants. For its part, the BIA had waived such protections in the Cheyennes' "behalf"; Johansen and Maestas, *Wasichu*, p. 174.

115. Rex Weyler, *Blood of the Land: The U.S. Government and Corporate War Against the American Indian Movement* (Philadelphia: New Society, [2nd ed.] 1992) pp. 154–55.

116. Tom Barry, "Bury My Lungs at Red Rock," *The Progressive*, Feb. 1979.

117. On tailings and associated problems such as radon gas emissions, see J.B. Sorenson, *Radiation Issues: Government Decision Making and Uranium Expansion in Northern New Mexico* (Albuquerque: San Juan Regional Study Group, Working Paper 14, 1978). On carcinogenic/mutogenic effects, see J.M. Samet, et al., "Uranium Mining and Lung Cancer in Navajo Men," *New England Journal of Medicine*, No. 310, 1984, pp. 1481–84. Also see Harold Tso and Laura Mangum Shields, "Navajo Mining Operations: Early Hazards and Recent Interventions," *New Mexico Journal of Science*, Vol. 20, No. 1, June 1980.

118. Richard Hoppe, "A stretch of desert along Route 66—the Grants Belt—is chief locale for U.S. uranium," *Engineering and Mining Journal,* Nov. 1978. Also see Nancy J. Owens, "Can Tribes Control Energy Development?" in Joseph Jorgenson, ed., *American Indians and Energy Development* (Cambridge, MA: Anthropology Resource Center, 1978). Also see "Breach of Trust," herein.

119. Amelia Irvin, "Energy Development and the Effects of Mining on the Lakota Nation," *Journal of Ethnic Studies,* Vol. 10, No. 2, Spring 1982.

120. Elouise Schumacher, "440 billion gallons: Hanford wastes would fill 900 King Domes," *Seattle Times,* Apr. 13, 1991.

121. Johansen and Maestas, *Wasíchu,* p. 154. They are referring to Thadis Box, et al., *Rehabilitation Potential for Western Coal Lands* (Cambridge, MA: Ballinger Publishing Co., 1974). The book is the published version of a study commissioned by the National Academy of Sciences and submitted to the Nixon administration in 1972.

122. Russell Means, "Fighting Words on the Future of Mother Earth," *Mother Jones,* Dec. 1980, p. 27.

123. See the section entitled "Genocide and the Genocide Convention," and accompanying citations, in "Confronting Columbus Day," pp. 44–46, herein.

124. Means, "Fighting Words," p. 27.

125. Robbins, "Self-Determination," p. 97.

126. The complete text of House Resolution 108 appears in Part II of Edward H. Spicer's *A Short History of the United States* (New York: Van Nostrum, 1968).

127. James E. Officer, "Termination as Federal Policy: An Overview," in Kenneth R. Philp, ed., *Indian Self-Rule: First-Hand Accounts of Indian-White Relations from Roosevelt to Reagan* (Salt Lake City: Howe Bros., 1986) p. 125.

128. Richard Drinnon, *Keeper of Concentration Camps: Dillon S. Myer and American Racism* (Berkeley: University of California Press, 1987).

129. Raymond V. Butler, "The Bureau of Indian Affairs Activities Since 1945," *Annals of the Academy of American Academy of Political and Social Science,* No. 436, 1978, pp. 50–60. The last dissolution, that of the Oklahoma Ponca, was delayed in committee and was not consummated until 1966.

130. See generally, Nicholas Peroff, *Menominee DRUMS: Tribal Termination and Restoration, 1954–1974* (Norman: University of Oklahoma Press, 1982).

131. Oliver LaFarge, "Termination of Federal Supervision: Disintegration and the American Indian," *Annals of the American Academy of Political and Social Science,* No. 311, May 1975, pp. 56–70.

132. See generally, Donald L. Fixico, *Termination and Relocation: Federal Indian Policy, 1945–1960* (Albuquerque: University of New Mexico Press, 1986); Alan L. Sokin, *The Urban American Indian* (Lexington, MA: Lexington Books, 1978).

133. Sharon O'Brien, *American Indian Tribal Governments* (Norman: University of Oklahoma Press, 1989) p. 86.

134. U.S. Department of Commerce, Bureau of the Census, *General Social and Economic Characteristics: United States Summary* (Washington, D.C.: U.S. GPO, 1983) p. 92; Thornton, *Holocaust and Survival,* p. 227.

135. NCAI *Briefing Paper.* In Susan Lobos and Kurt Peters, eds., *American Indians and the Urban Experience* (Walnut Creek, CA: AltaMira Press, 2001).

136. For use of the term "migration" to describe the effects of termination and relocation, see James H. Gundlach, Nelson P. Reid and Alden E. Roberts, "Native American Migration and Relocation," *Pacific Sociological Review,* No. 21, 1978. On the "discarded and forgotten," see American Indian Policy Review Commission, Task Force Ten, *Report on Terminated and Nonfederally Recognized Tribes* (Washington, D.C.: U.S. GPO, 1976).

137. See "The Nullification of Native America?" herein.

138. The term was coined in the mid-1970s to describe the self-destructive behavior exhibited by the Khmer Rouge régime in Kampuchea (Cambodia) in response to genocidal policies earlier ex-

tended against that country by the United States; Noam Chomsky, *Deterring Democracy* (New York: Hill and Wang, 1992) p. 380.

139. Alexis de Tocqueville, *Democracy in America* (New York: Harper & Row, 1966) p. 312.

140. "Hitler's concept of concentration camps as well as the practicality of genocide owed much, so he claimed, to his studies of British and United States history. He admired the camps for Boer prisoners in South Africa and for the Indians in the Wild West; and often praised to his inner circle the efficiency of America's extermination—by starvation and uneven combat—of the red savages who could not be tamed by captivity"; John Toland, *Adolf Hitler* (New York: Doubleday, 1976) p. 802. To have it in Hitler's own words, see his *Mein Kampf* (New York: Reynal and Hitchcock, 1939) pp. 403, 501; *Hitler's Secret Book* (New York: Grove Press, 1961) pp. 46–52.

141. Norman Rich, *Hitler's War Aims: Ideology, the Nazi State, and the Course of Expansion* (New York: W.W. Norton, 1973) p. 8.

142. John F.D. Smyth, *A Tour of the United States of America* (London: privately published, 1784) p. 346.

143. Quoted in Reginald Horsman, *Race and Manifest Destiny: The Origins of Racial Anglo-Saxonism* (Cambridge, MA: Harvard University Press, 1981) p. 198.

144. See the various quotes in Hutton, *Phil Sheridan*.

145. Fritz, *Assimilation*; Hoxie, *Final Promise*. Also see my *Little Matter of Genocide*, pp. 245–50.

146. The classic articulation, of course, is Joseph K. Dixon's 1913 *The Vanishing Race*, recently reprinted by Bonanza Books (New York). An excellent examination of the phenomenon may be found in Stan Steiner's *The Vanishing White Man* (Norman: University of Oklahoma Press, 1976).

147. Benedek, *Wind*. Also see Jerry Kammer, *The Second Long Walk: The Navajo-Hopi Land Dispute* (Albuquerque: University of New Mexico Press, 1980); Anita Parlow, *Cry, Sacred Ground: Big Mountain, USA* (Washington, D.C.: Christic Institute, 1988); the essay entitled "Genocide in Arizona: The 'Navajo-Hopi Land Dispute' in Perspective," in my *Struggle for the Land: Native North American Resistance to Genocide, Ecocide and Colonization* (Winnipeg: Arbeiter Ring, [2nd ed.] 1999) pp. 135–72.

148. Thayer Scudder, et al., *No Place to Go: Effects of Compulsory Relocation on Navajos* (Philadelphia: Institute for the Study of Human Issues, 1982).

149. See the section on the Western Shoshone Land Claim in "The Earth Is Our Mother," pp. 86–106, herein.

150. Alaska Native Claims Settlement Act (85 Stat. 688 (1971)). For details and analysis, see M.C. Barry, *The Alaska Pipeline: The Politics of Oil and Native Land Claims* (Bloomington: Indiana University Press, 1975); Thomas R. Berger, *Village Journey: The Report of the Alaska Native Review Commission* (New York: Hill and Wang, 1985).

151. The plan is known by the title of its sponsoring organization, the North American Water and Power Association (NAWAPA); see the essay entitled "The Water Plot: Hydrological Rape in the Canadian North," in my *Struggle for the Land*, esp. pp. 314–20.

152. The phrase is borrowed from Patricia Nelson Limerick's *The Legacy of Conquest: The Unbroken Past of the American West* (New York: W.W. Norton, 1987) p. 338.

153. See the essay entitled "Defining the Unthinkable: Towards a Viable Understanding of Genocide," in my *Little Matter of Genocide*, pp. 399–444.

154. For analysis, see Glenn T. Morris, "In Support of the Right to Self-Determination of Indigenous Peoples Under International Law," *German Yearbook of International Law*, No. 29, 1986; "International Law and Politics: Toward a Right to Self-Determination for Indigenous Peoples," in Jaimes, *State of Native America*, pp. 55–86.

155. This includes a rather large array of covenants and conventions pertaining to everything from the binding effect of treaties to the Laws of War. It also includes Ronald Reagan's postulation, advanced in October 1985, that the International Court of Justice holds no authority other than in matters of trade. A detailed examination of U.S. posturing in this regard will be found in Lawrence W. LeBlanc, *The United States and the Genocide Convention* (Durham, NC: Duke University Press, 1991).

7. THE BLOODY WAKE OF ALCATRAZ

1. On the fishing rights struggles, see American Friends Service Committee, *Uncommon Controversy: Fishing Rights of the Muckleshoot, Puyallup and Nisqually Indians* (Seattle: University of Washington Press, 1970). On the Alcatraz occupation, see Peter Blue Cloud, ed., *Alcatraz Is Not An Island* (Berkeley: Wingbow Press, 1972); Adam Fortunate Eagle (Nordwall), *Alcatraz! Alcatraz! The Indian Occupation of 1969–1971* (Berkeley: Heyday Books, 1992).

2. This is not to say that others—notably, members of the Black Panther Party—have not suffered severely and often fatally at the hands of official specialists in the techniques of domestic political repression in the United States. The distinction drawn with regard to American Indian activists in this respect is purely proportional. For comprehensive background on the experiences of nonindians, see Robert Justin Goldstein, *Political Repression in Modern America, 1870 to the Present* (Cambridge/New York: Schenkman /Two Continents, 1978). On the Black Panther Party in particular, see my "'To Disrupt, Discredit and Destroy': The FBI's Secret War against the Black Panther Party," in Kathleen Cleaver and George Katsiaficas, eds., *Liberation, Imagination and the Black Panther Party: A New Look at the Panthers and Their Legacy* (New York: Routledge, 2001) pp. 78–117.

3. Bruce Johansen and Roberto Maestas, *Wasíchu: The Continuing Indian Wars* (New York: Monthly Review Press, 1979).

4. Counterinsurgency is *not* a part of law enforcement or intelligence-gathering missions. Rather, it is an integral subpart of low intensity warfare doctrine and methodology, taught at the U.S. Army's Special Warfare School at Fort Bragg, North Carolina; see Maj. John S. Pustay, *Counterinsurgency Warfare* (New York: Free Press, 1965); Michael T. Klare and Peter Kornbluh, eds., *Low Intensity Warfare: Counterinsurgency, Proinsurgency, and Antiterrorism in the Eighties* (New York: Pantheon, 1988). For an illustration of the FBI's use of explicit counterinsurgency terminology to define its anti-Indian operations in 1976, see Ward Churchill and Jim Vander Wall, *The COINTELPRO Papers: Documents from the FBI's Secret Wars Against Dissent in the United States* (Boston: South End Press, 1990) p. 26.

5. U.S. Department of Justice, Commission on Civil Rights, *Events Surrounding Recent Murders on the Pine Ridge Reservation in South Dakota* (Denver: Rocky Mountain Regional Office, Mar. 31, 1976).

6. In his, at the time, definitive study of the Bureau, Sanford J. Ungar quotes a senior counterintelligence specialist to the effect that "success in this area is not measured in terms of arrests and prosecutions, but in our ability to neutralize our targets' ability to do what they're doing"; Sanford J. Ungar, *FBI: An Uncensored Look Behind the Walls* (Boston: Little, Brown, 1975) p. 311.

7. On the early days of the Black Panther Party, see Gene Marine, *The Black Panthers* (New York: New American Library, 1969). On the beginnings of AIM, and its obvious reliance on the Panther model, see Peter Matthiessen, *In the Spirit of Crazy Horse* (New York: Viking, [2nd. ed.] 1991) pp. 34–37.

8. On internal colonialism, see the section of that title in "Breach of Trust," pp. 114–16, herein.

9. On federal treaties with Indians and their implications, see "The Law Stood Squarely on Its Head," herein.

10. On native property rights within the U.S., see "The Earth Is Our Mother," herein.

11. U.S. Department of Labor, Bureau of the Census, *1970 Census of the Population, Subject Report: American Indians* (Washington, D.C.: U.S. GPO, 1972).

12. On plenary power doctrine, see "The Tragedy and the Travesty," herein.

13. On resource distribution, see generally Michael Garrity, "The U.S. Colonial Empire is as Close as the Nearest Indian Reservation," in Holly Sklar, ed., *Trilateralism: The Trilateral Commission and Elite Planning for World Government* (Boston: South End Press, 1980) pp. 238–68.

14. See generally, Joseph G. Jorgensen, ed., *Native Americans and Energy Development, II* (Cambridge, MA: Anthropology Resource Center/Seventh Generation Fund, 1984).

15. See generally, Roxanne Dunbar Ortiz, ed., *Economic Development in American Indian Reservations* (Albuquerque: University of New Mexico Native American Studies Center, 1980).

16. See "Breach of Trust," herein.

17. U.S. Department of Health, Education and Welfare (DHEW), *A Study of Selected Socio-Economic Characteristics of Ethnic Minorities Based on the 1970 Census, Vol. 3: American Indians* (Washington, D.C.: U.S. GPO, 1974). It should be noted that the economic and health data pertaining to certain sectors of other U.S. minority populations—inner city blacks, for example, or Latino migrant workers—are very similar to those bearing on American Indians. Unlike these other examples, however, the data on American Indians encompass the condition of the population as a whole.

18. U.S. Bureau of the Census, Population Division, Racial Statistics Branch, *A Statistical Profile of the American Indian Population* (Washington, D.C.: U.S. GPO, 1974).

19. Dennis J. Banks, speech before the United Lutheran Board, Minneapolis, Minnesota, March 1971.

20. Notable in this respect was resuscitation of the Lakota Sun Dance, forbidden by the BIA since 1881, when in August 1972 AIM members showed up en masse to participate in the ceremony at Crow Dog's Paradise, on the Rosebud Reservation. As the revered Oglala spiritual leader Frank Fools Crow put it in 1980, "Before that, there were only one, two Sun Dances each year. Just a few came, the real traditionals. And we had to hold 'em in secret. After the AIM boys showed up, now there are [Sun Dances] everywhere, right out in the open, too. Nobody hides anymore. Now, they're all proud to be Indian." The same principle pertains to the resurgence of numerous other ceremonies among a variety of peoples.

21. On the Indian Treaty Council (IITC), "AIM's international diplomatic arm," and establishment of the United Nations Working Group on Indigenous Populations, see Russell Means with Mavin J. Wolf, *Where White Men Fear to Tread: The Autobiography of Russell Means* (New York: St. Martin's Press, 1995) pp. 325–26, 356, 365.

22. The term "National Liberation Movement" is not rhetorical. Rather it bears a precise meaning under Article I, Paragraph 4 of Additional Protocol I of the 1949 Geneva Convention. Also see United Nations Resolution 3103 (XXVIII), 12 Dec. 1973.

23. Birgil Kills Straight, mimeographed statement circulated by the Oglala Sioux Civil Rights Organization (Manderson, S.D.) during the 1973 Siege of Wounded Knee.

24. By the mid-70s, even elements of the federal government had begun to adopt AIM's emphasis on colonialism to explain the relationship between the United States and American Indians. See, e.g., U.S. Commission on Civil Rights, *The Navajo Nation: An American Colony* (Washington, D.C.: U.S. GPO, Sept. 1975).

25. This remained true until the government's 1993 slaughter of 86 Branch Davidians in a single hour near Waco, Texas. The standard text on the 1890 massacre is, of course, Dee Brown's *Bury My Heart at Wounded Knee: An Indian History of the American West* (New York: Holt, Rinehart & Winston, 1970).

26. Robert Burnette with John Koster, *The Road to Wounded Knee* (New York: Bantam, 1974) p. 196.

27. Peter Matthiessen, *In the Spirit of Crazy Horse* (New York: Viking, [2nd. ed.] 1991) pp. 38, 110.

28. Yellow Thunder, burned with cigarettes, was forced to dance nude from the waist down for the entertainment of a crowd assembled in the Gordon American Legion Hall. He was then severely beaten and stuffed, unconscious, into the trunk of a car where he froze to death. See Rex Weyler, *Blood of the Land: The U.S. Government and Corporate War Against the American Indian Movement* (Philadelphia: New Society, [2nd ed.] 1992) p. 48. Also see Matthiessen, *Spirit*, pp. 59–60.

29. Quoted in Weyler, *Blood*, p. 49.

30. Alvin M. Josephy, Jr., *Now That the Buffalo's Gone: A Study of Today's American Indian* (New York: Alfred A. Knopf, 1982) p. 237.

31. The best overall handling of these events, including the complete text of the Twenty Point Program, is Vine Deloria, Jr.'s *Behind the Trail of Broken Treaties: An Indian Declaration of Independence* (Austin: University of Texas Press, [2nd ed.] 1984).

32. See Editors, *BIA, I'm Not Your Indian Anymore* (Rooseveltown, NY: Akwesasne Notes, 1973).

33. The money, comprised of unmarked twenty, fifty, and hundred dollar bills, came from a slush fund administered by Nixon's notorious Committee to Reelect the President (CREEP), and was delivered in brown paper bags. The bagmen were administration aides Leonard Garment and Frank Carlucci (later National Security Council chief and CIA Director under Ronald Reagan); Paul Chaat Smith and Robert Allen Warrior, *Like a Hurricane: The American Indian Movement from Alcatraz to Wounded Knee* (New York: New Press, 1996) pp. 163–65.

34. It was from these files that, among other things, the existence of a secret IHS program to perform involuntary sterilizations on American Indian women was first revealed; Brint Dillingham, "Indian Women and IHS Sterilization Practices," *American Indian Journal*, Vol. 3, No. 1, Jan. 1977.

35. The full text of administration response is included in *BIA, I'm Not Your Indian Anymore*.

36. The language is that of Webster Two Hawk, then President of the Rosebud Sioux Tribe and federally funded National Tribal Chairmen's Association. Two Hawk was shortly voted out of both positions by his constituents, replaced as Rosebud President by Robert Burnette, an organizer of the Trail of Broken Treaties. See my "Renegades, Terrorists and Revolutionaries: The Government's Propaganda War Against the American Indian Movement," *Propaganda Review*, No. 4, Apr. 1989.

37. One firm indication of this was the arrest by the FBI of Assiniboin/Lakota activist Hank Adams and Les Whitten, an associate of columnist Jack Anderson, shortly after the occupation. They were briefly charged with illegally possessing government property. The men, neither of whom was an AIM member, were merely acting as go-betweens in returning BIA documents to the federal authorities. The point seems to have been to isolate AIM from its more "moderate" associations; Deloria, *Behind the Trail of Broken Treaties*, p. 59.

38. Although he had stabbed Bad Heart Bull repeatedly in the chest with a hunting knife, Schmitz was charged only with second-degree manslaughter and released on a mere $5,000 bond; Weyler, *Blood*, p. 68.

39. Don and Jan Stevens, *South Dakota: The Mississippi of the North, or Stories Jack Anderson Never Told You* (Custer, SD: self-published pamphlet, 1977).

40. More broadly, AIM's posture was a response to what it perceived as a nationwide wave of murders of Indians by whites. These included not only those of Yellow Thunder and Bad Heart Bull, but of a 19-year-old Papago named Phillip Celay by a sheriff's deputy in Arizona, an Onondaga Special Forces veteran (and member of the honor guard during the funeral of John F. Kennedy) named Leroy Shenandoah in Philadelphia, and, on Sept. 20, 1972, of Alcatraz leader Richard Oaks near San Francisco; see my and Jim Vander Wall's *Agents of Repression: The FBI's Secret Wars Against the Black Panther Party and the American Indian Movement* (Boston: South End Press, 1988) p. 123.

41. The individual receiving the call was reporter Lynn Gladstone. Such calls are a standard FBI counterintelligence tactic used to disrupt the political organizing of targeted groups. See Brian Glick, *War at Home: Covert Action Against U.S. Activists and What We Can Do About It* (Boston: South End Press, 1989).

42. A Jan. 31, 1973, FBI teletype delineates the fact that the Bureau was already involved in planning the police response to the Custer demonstration. It is reproduced in my and Jim Vander Wall's *The COINTELPRO Papers: Documents from the FBI's Secret Wars Against Dissent in the United States* (Boston: South End Press, 1990) p. 241.

43. Weyler, *Blood*, pp. 68–69.

44. The average annual income on Pine Ridge at this time was about $1,000; Cheryl McCall, "Life on Pine Ridge Bleak," *Colorado Daily*, May 16, 1975. Wilson hired his brother, Jim, to head the tribal planning office at an annual salary of $25,000 plus $15,000 in "consulting fees"; *New York Times*, Apr. 22, 1975. Another brother, George, was hired at a salary of $20,000 to help the Oglalas "manage their affairs"; Wilson's wife was named director of the Reservation Head Start program at a salary of $18,000; his son, "Manny" (Richard, Jr.) was placed on the GOON payroll, along with several cousins and nephews; Wilson also upped his own salary from $5,500 per year to $15,500 per year, plus lucrative consulting fees, within his first six months in office; Matthiessen, *Spirit*, p. 62. When queried about the propriety of all this, Wilson replied, "There's no law against nepotism";

Robert Anderson, et al., eds., *Voices From Wounded Knee, 1973* (Rooseveltown, NY: Akwesasne Notes, 1974) p. 34.

45. In addition to this BIA "seed money," Wilson is suspected of having misappropriated some $347,000 in federal highway improvement funds to meet GOON payrolls between 1972 and 1975. A 1975 General Accounting Office report indicates that the funds had been expended without any appreciable road repair having been done, and that the Wilsonites had kept no books with which to account for this mysterious situation. Nonetheless, the FBI declined to undertake a further investigation of the matter.

46. The Gunnery Range, comprising the northwestern eighth of Pine Ridge, was an area "borrowed" from the Oglalas by the War Department in 1942 as a place to train aerial gunners. It was to be returned at the end of World War II, but never was. By the early '70s, the Oglala traditionals had begun to agitate heavily for its recovery. The deposits had been secretly discovered in 1971, however, through a technologically elaborate survey and mapping project undertaken jointly by the National Aeronautics and Space Administration (NASA) and a little known entity called the National Uranium Resource Evaluation Institute (NURE). At that point, the government set out to obtain permanent title to the property; its quid pro quo with Wilson seems to have been his willingness to provide it. See J.P. Gries, *Status of Mineral Resource Information on the Pine Ridge Indian Reservation, S.D.* (Washington, D.C.: BIA Bulletin No. 12, U.S. Department of Interior, 1976); Jacqueline Huber, et al., *The Gunnery Range Report* (Pine Ridge, SD: Office of the Oglala Sioux Tribal President, 1981).

47. Anderson, et al., *Voices*, pp. 17–26.

48. Quoted in Matthiessen, *Spirit*, p. 66.

49. Burnette and Koster, *Road*, p. 74.

50. The action was proposed by OSCRO leader Pedro Bissonette and endorsed by traditional Oglala chiefs Frank Fools Crow, Pete Catches, Ellis Chips, Edgar Red Cloud, Jake Kills Enemy, Morris Wounded, Severt Young Bear, and Everette Catches; Anderson, et al., *Voices*, p. 36.

51. Weyler, *Blood*, pp. 76–78.

52. On of their first actions was to meet with Colonel Vic Jackson, a subordinate of future FEMA head Louis Giuffrida, brought in from California to "consult." Through an entity called the California Civil Disorder Management School, Jackson and Giuffrida had devised a pair of "multi-agency domestic counterinsurgency scenarios" code named "Garden Plot" and "Cable Splicer" in which the government was interested. There is thus more than passing indication that what followed at Wounded Knee was, at least in part, a field test of these plans; Weyler, *Blood*, pp. 80–81. Also see Ken Lawrence, *The New State Repression* (Chicago: International Network Against the New State Repression, 1985).

53. Weyler, *Blood*, p. 83. The quantity of M-16 ammunition should actually read 1.3 million rounds. The military also provided state-of-the-art communications gear, M-14 sniper rifles and ammunition, "Starlight" night vision scopes and other optical technology, tear gas rounds and flares for M-79 grenade launchers, and field provisions to feed the assembled federal forces. All of this was in flat violation of the Posse Comitatus Act (18 USCS § 1385), which makes it illegal for the government to deploy the military in "civil disturbances." For this reason, Colonels Warner and Potter, and the other military personnel they brought in, wore civilian clothes at Wounded Knee in an effort to hide their involvement.

54. Bill Zimmerman, *Airlift to Wounded Knee* (Chicago: Swallow Press, 1976).

55. Clearwater was mortally wounded on April 17, 1973, and died on Apr. 25. Lamont was hit on April 27, after being driven from his bunker by tear gas. Federal gunfire then prevented anyone from reaching him until he died from loss of blood; Anderson, et al., *Voices*, pp. 179, 220.

56. Robert Burnette later recounted how, once the siege had ended, Justice Department Solicitor General Kent Frizzell asked his assistance in searching for such graves; Burnette and Koster, *Road to Wounded Knee*, p. 248. Also see Anderson, et al., *Voices*, p. 193.

57. The "hostages" were mostly elderly residents of Wounded Knee: Wilbert A. Reigert (aged 86), Girlie Clark (75), Clive Gildersleeve (73), Agnes Gildersleeve (68), Bill Cole (82), Mary Pike (72), and Annie Hunts Horse (78). Others included Guy Fritz (aged 49), Jeanne Fritz (47), Adrienne Fritz

(12), and Father Paul Manhart (46). When South Dakota Senators George McGovern and James Abourezk went to Wounded Knee on March 2 to "bring the hostages out," the supposed captives announced they had no intention of leaving. Instead they stated they wished to stay to "protect [their] property from federal forces" and that they considered the AIM people to be the "real hostages in this situation"; Burnette and Koster, *Road,* pp. 227–28.

58. The first federal casualty was an FBI agent named Curtis Fitzpatrick, hit in the wrist by a spent round on March 11, 1973. Interestingly, with his head swathed in bandages, he was evacuated by helicopter before a crowd of reporters assembled to witness the event; Burnette and Koster, *Road to Wounded Knee,* pp. 237–38. The second, U.S. Marshal Lloyd Grimm, was struck in the back and permanently paralyzed on March 23. Grimm was, however, facing the AIM perimeter when he was hit. The probability is therefore that he was shot—perhaps unintentionally—by one of Wilson's GOONs, who were at the time firing from positions behind those of the marshals; Anderson, et al., *Voices,* p. 128.

59. Quoted in ibid., p. 47.

60. Held was simultaneously serving as head of the FBI's Internal Security Section and as Special Agent in Charge (SAC) of the Bureau's Chicago Office. He had been assigned the latter position, in addition to his other duties, in order that he might orchestrate a cover-up of the FBI's involvement in the 1969 murders of Illinois Black Panther leaders Fred Hampton and Mark Clark. At the outset of the Wounded Knee Siege, he was detached from his SAC position—a very atypical circumstance—and sent to Pine Ridge in order to prepare a study of how the Bureau should deal with AIM "insurgents." The result, entitled "FBI Paramilitary Operations in Indian Country"—in which the author argued, among other things, that "shoot to kill" orders should be made standard—is extremely significant in light of subsequent Bureau activities on the reservation and Held's own role in them.

61. The terms of the stand down agreement are covered in Anderson, et al., *Voices,* p. 231. On the treaty, see "The Earth Is Our Mother" herein.

62. Federal representatives plainly prevaricated, arguing that they were precluded from responding to questions of treaty compliance because of Congress's 1871 suspension of treatymaking with Indians (Title 25 USC § 71). As Lakota elder Matthew King rejoined, however, the Indians were not asking that a new treaty be negotiated. Rather, they were demanding that U.S. commitments under an *existing* treaty be honored, a matter which was not only possible under the 1871 Act, but *required* by it; Anderson, et al., *Voices,* pp. 252–54.

63. Instead, a single marshal was dispatched to Fools Crow's home on the appointed date to deliver to those assembled there a note signed by White House Counsel Leonard Garment. The missive stated that "the days of treaty-making with Indians ended in 1871, 102 years ago"; quoted in ibid., pp. 257–58.

64. U.S. House of Representatives, Committee on the Judiciary, Subcommittee on Civil and Constitutional Rights, *1st Session on FBI Authorization, March 19, 24, 25; April 2 and 8, 1981* (Washington, D.C.: 97th Cong., 2nd Sess., 1981).

65. Weyler, *Blood,* p. 95; Burnette and Koster, *Road,* p. 253.

66. Subcommittee on Civil and Constitutional Rights, *FBI Authorization.*

67. Ibid. Means was convicted on *none* of the forty federal charges. Instead, he was finally found guilty in 1977 under a South Dakota law on "Criminal Syndicalism" and served a year in the maximum security prison at Sioux Falls. Means was, and will remain, the only individual ever convicted under this statute; the South Dakota legislature repealed the law while he was imprisoned. Amnesty International was preparing to adopt him as a Prisoner of Conscience when he was released in 1979; Amnesty International, *Proposal for a commission of inquiry into the effect of domestic intelligence activities on criminal trials in the United States of America* (New York: Amnesty International, 1980).

68. For excerpts from the transcripts of the "Sioux Sovereignty Hearing" conducted in Lincoln, Nebraska, during the fall of 1974, see Roxanne Dunbar Ortiz, ed., *The Great Sioux Nation: Sitting in Judgment on America* (New York/San Francisco: International Indian Treaty Council/Moon Books, 1977).

69. Tried together in a second "Leadership Trial," Crow Dog, Holder, and Camp were convicted of minor offenses during the spring of 1975. Holder and Camp went underground to avoid sentencing. Crow Dog was granted probation (as were his codefendants when they surfaced), and then confronted with charges unrelated to Wounded Knee the following November. Convicted, and sentenced to five years, he was imprisoned first in the federal maximum security facility at Lewisburg, Pennsylvania, then at Leavenworth, Kansas. The National Council of Churches and Amnesty International were preparing to adopt him as a Prisoner of Conscience when he was released on parole in 1977. See Amnesty International, *Proposal*, Weyler, *Blood*, p. 189.

70. As a congressional study concluded, this was "a very low rate considering the usual rate of conviction in Federal Courts and a great input of resources in these cases"; Subcommittee on Civil and Constitutional Rights, *FBI Authorization*.

71. This is a classic among the counterintelligence methods utilized by the FBI. For example, according to a Bureau report declassified by a Senate Select Committee in 1975, agents in Philadelphia offered as an "example of a successful counterintelligence technique" their use of "any excuse for arrest" as a means of "neutralizing" members of a targeted organization, the Revolutionary Action Movement (RAM) during the summer of 1967. "RAM people," the document went on, "were arrested and released on bail, but they were re-arrested several times until they could no longer make bail." The tactic was recommended for use by other FBI offices to "curtail the activities" of objectionable political groups in their areas. Complete text of this document will be found in *Agents*, pp. 45–47. More broadly, see U.S. Senate, Select Committee to Study Government Operations with Respect to Intelligence Activities, *Final Report: Supplementary Detailed Staff Reports on Intelligence Activities and the Rights of Americans, Book III* (Washington, D.C.: 94th Cong., 2d Sess., 1976).

72. This is the standard delineation of objectives attending the FBI's domestic counterintelligence programs (COINTELPROs); see the document reproduced in *COINTELPRO Papers*, pp. 92–93.

73. Quoted in Martin Garbus, "General Haig of Wounded Knee," *The Nation*, Nov. 9, 1974.

74. A complete list of those killed and dates of death is contained in *COINTELPRO Papers*, pp. 393–94.

75. Commission on Civil Rights, *Recent Murders*.

76. Johansen and Maestas, *Wasi'chu*, pp. 83–84.

77. FBI jurisdiction on reservations accrues under the 1885 Major Crimes Act (ch. 341, 24 Stat. 362, 385, now codified at 18 USC 1153).

78. As examples: Delphine Crow Dog, sister of AIM's spiritual leader, beaten unconscious and left to freeze to death in a field on Nov. 9, 1974; AIM member Joseph Stuntz Killsright, killed by a bullet to the head and apparently shot repeatedly in the torso after death on June 26, 1975.

79. Consider the case of the brothers Vernal and Clarence Cross, both AIM members, who were stopped along the road with car trouble outside Pine Ridge village on June 19, 1973. Individuals firing from a nearby field hit both men, killing Clarence and severely wounding Vernal. Another bullet struck nine-year-old Mary Ann Little Bear, who was riding in a car driven by her father and coming in the opposite direction, in the face, blinding her in one eye. Mr. Little Bear identified three individuals to police and FBI agents as being the shooters. None of the three were interrogated. Instead, authorities arrested Vernal Cross in the hospital, charging him with murdering Clarence (the charges were later dropped). No charges were ever filed in the shooting of Mary Ann Little Bear; Weyler, *Blood*, p. 106.

80. Quoted in Johansen and Maestas, *Wasi'chu*, p. 88. Actually, O'Clock's position fits into a broader Bureau policy. "When Indians complain about the lack of investigation and prosecution on reservation crime, they are usually told the Federal government does not have the resources to handle the work"; U.S. Department of Justice, *Report of the Task Force on Indian Matters* (Washington, D.C.: U.S. GPO, 1975) pp. 42–43.

81. In 1972, the Rapid City Resident Agency was staffed by three agents. This was expanded to eleven in March 1973, and augmented by a ten-member SWAT team shortly thereafter. By the spring of 1975, more than thirty agents were assigned to Rapid City on a long-term basis, and as many as

two dozen others were steadily coming and going while performing "special tasks; Johansen and Maestas, *Wasíchu*, p. 93; Department of Justice, *Indian Matters*, pp. 42–43.

82. In the Clarence Cross murder, for example, the killers were identified as John Hussman, Woody Richards, and Francis Randall, all prominent members of the GOONs. Or again, in the Jan. 30, 1976, murder of AIM supporter Byron DeSersa near the reservation hamlet of Wanblee, at least a dozen people identified GOONs Billy Wilson (Dickie Wilson's younger son), Charles David Winters, Dale Janis, and Chuck Richards as being among the killers. Indeed, the guilty parties were still on the scene when two FBI agents arrived. Yet the only person arrested was a witness, an elderly Cheyenne named Guy Dull Knife, because of the vociferousness with which he complained about the agents' inaction. The BIA police, for their part, simply ordered the GOONs to leave town; U.S. Commission on Civil Rights, *American Indian Issues in South Dakota: Hearing Held in Rapid City, South Dakota, July 27–28, 1978* (Washington, D.C.: U.S. GPO, 1978) p. 33.

83. On the CIA's relationship to Latin American death squads, see Penny Lernoux, *Cry of the People: United States Involvement in the Rise of Fascism, Torture, and Murder, and the Persecution of the Catholic Church in Latin America* (Garden City, NY: Doubleday, 1980).

84. Anderson, et al., *Voices*, p. 189. Frizzell himself has confirmed the account.

85. Ibid., p. 190.

86. The directive was issued on Apr. 24, 1973.

87. Anderson, et al., *Voices*, p. 213; Weyler, *Blood of the Land*, pp. 92–93.

88. See, e.g., Athan Theoharis, "Building a Case Against the FBI," *Washington Post*, Oct. 30, 1988.

89. See my "Death Squads in America: Confessions of a Government Terrorist," *Yale Journal of Law and Liberation*, No. 3, 1992. The interview was conducted by independent filmmakers Kevin Barry McKiernan and Michel DuBois several years earlier, but not released in transcript form until 1991.

90. "Det cord" is detonation cord, a rope-like explosive often used by the U.S. military to fashion booby traps. Brewer also makes mention of Bureau personnel introducing him and other GOONs to civilian right-wingers who provided additional ordnance.

91. Another example of this sort of thing came in the wake of the Feb. 27, 1975, beating and slashing of AIM defense attorney Roger Finzel, his client, Bernard Escamilla, and several associates at the Pine Ridge Airport by a group of GOONs headed by Duane Brewer and Dickie Wilson himself. The event being too visible to be simply ignored, Wilson was allowed to plead guilty to a petty offense carrying a $10 penalty in his own tribal court. Federal charges were then dropped on advice from the FBI—which had spent its investigative time polygraphing the victims rather than their assailants—because pressing them might constitute "double jeopardy"; Weyler, *Blood*, pp. 172–73; Matthiessen, *Spirit*, pp. 130–31.

92. At one point, the Bureau attempted to implicate Northwest AIM leader Leonard Peltier in the killing. This ploy was abandoned only when it was conclusively demonstrated that Peltier was in another state when the murder occurred; interview with Peltier defense attorney Bruce Ellison, Oct. 1987 (tape on file). Also see Matthiessen, *Spirit*, p. 133.

93. Both Moves Camp and Bissonette drove white over dark blue Chevrolet sedans. Goon leader Duane Brewer subsequently confirmed that his men had killed Bissonette by "mistake"; see "Death Squads." The victim, who was not herself active in supporting AIM, was the sister of OSCRO leader Pedro Bissonette, shot to death under highly suspicious circumstances by BIA police officer *cum* GOON Joe Clifford on the night of Oct. 17, 1973; *Agents*, pp. 200–3; Weyler, pp. 107–10.

94. Eastman, although a Crow, is directly related to the Dakota family of the same name, made famous by the writer Charles Eastman earlier in the century. Ironically, two of his relatives, the sisters Carole Standing Elk and Fern Matthias, claim to be AIM members in California.

95. "Death Squads," p. 96.

96. Structurally, the appropriation of the formal apparatus of deploying force possessed by client states for purposes of composing death squads, long a hallmark of CIA covert operations in the Third

World, corresponds quite well with the FBI's use of the BIA police on Pine Ridge. See A.J. Languuth, *Hidden Terrors: The Truth About U.S. Police Operations in Latin America* (New York: Pantheon, 1978); Edward S. Herman, *The Real Terror Network: Terrorism in Fact and Propaganda* (Boston: South End Press, 1982).

97. See, e.g., Commission on Civil Rights, *Recent Murders*.

98. In late 1973, Means took a majority of all votes cast in the tribal primaries. In the 1974 run off, however, Wilson retained his presidency by a 200-vote margin. A subsequent investigation by the U.S. Commission on Civil Rights revealed that 154 cases of voter fraud—non-Oglalas being allowed to vote—had occurred. A further undetermined number of invalid votes had been cast by Oglalas who did not meet tribal residency requirements. No record had been kept of the number of ballots printed or how and in what numbers they had been distributed. No poll watchers were present in many locations, and those who were present at the others had been appointed by Wilson rather than an impartial third party. There was also significant evidence that pro-Means voters had been systematically intimidated, and in some cases roughed up, by Wilsonites stationed at each polling place; U.S. Commission on Civil Rights, *Report of Investigation: Oglala Sioux Tribe, General Election, 1974* (Denver: Rocky Mountain Regional Office, Oct. 1974). Despite these official findings, the FBI performed no substantive investigation, and the BIA allowed the results of the election to stand.

99. As the Jumping Bulls' daughter, Roselyn, later put it, "We asked those AIM boys to come help us [defend ourselves against] Dickie Wilson and his goons"; quoted in an unpublished manuscript by researcher Candy Hamilton, p. 3 (copy on file).

100. See, e.g., a memorandum from SAC Minneapolis (Joseph Trimbach) to the FBI Director, dated June 3, 1975, and captioned "Law Enforcement on the Pine Ridge Indian Reservation," in which it is recommended that armored personnel carriers be used to assault AIM defensive positions.

101. No such warrant existed. When an arrest order was finally issued for Eagle on July 9, 1975, it was for the petty theft of a pair of used cowboy boots from a white ranch hand. Eagle was acquitted even of this when the case was taken to trial in 1976. Meanwhile, George O'Clock's assignment of two agents to pursue an Indian teenager over so trivial an offense at a time when he professed to be too shorthanded to investigate the murders of AIM members speaks for itself; Matthiessen, *Spirit*, p. 173.

102. Ibid., p. 156.

103. The agents followed a red pickup truck which, unbeknownst to them, was full of dynamite onto the property. In the valley, the truck stopped and its occupants got out. Williams and Coler also stopped and got out of their cars. They then began firing toward the pickup, a direction which carried their rounds into the AIM camp, where a number of noncombatant women and children were situated. AIM security then began to fire back. It is a certainty that AIM did not initiate the firefight because, as Bob Robideau later put it, "Nobody in their right mind would start a gunfight, using a truckload of dynamite for cover." Once the agents were preoccupied, the pickup made its escape. Northwest AIM was toying with the idea of using the explosives to remove George Washington's face from the nearby Mount Rushmore National Monument; interview with Bob Robideau, May 1990 (notes on file).

104. Matthiessen, *Spirit*, p. 158.

105. An additional indicator is that the inimitable William Janklow also seems to have been on alert, awaiting a call telling him things were underway. In any event, when called, Janklow was able to assemble a white vigilante force in Hot Springs, S.D., and drive about fifty miles to the Jumping Bull property, arriving there at about 1:30 p.m., an elapsed time of approximately two hours.

106. A further indication of preplanning by the Bureau is found in a June 27, 1975, memorandum from R.E. Gebhart to Mr. O'Donnell at FBIHQ. It states that Chicago SAC/Internal Security Chief Richard G. Held was contacted by headquarters about the firefight *at the Minneapolis field office* at 12:30 p.m. on June 26. It turns out that Held had already been detached from his position in Chicago and was in Minneapolis—under which authority the Rapid City resident agency, and hence Pine Ridge, falls—awaiting word to temporarily take over from Minneapolis SAC Joseph Trimbach. The only ready explanation for this highly unorthodox circumstance, unprecedented in Bureau his-

tory, is that it was expected that Held's peculiar expertise in political repression would be needed for a major operation on Pine Ridge in the immediate future; Johansen and Maestes, *Wasíchu*, p. 95.

107. Matthiessen, *Spirit*, pp. 483–85.

108. The FBI sought to "credit" BIA police officer Gerald Hill with the lethal long range shot to the head, fired at Killsright at about 3 p.m., despite the fact that he was plainly running away and therefore presented no threat to law enforcement personnel (it was also not yet known that Coler and Williams were dead). However, Waring, who was with Hill at the time, was the trained sniper of the pair, and equipped accordingly. In any event, several witnesses who viewed Killsright's corpse *in situ* —including Assistant South Dakota Attorney General William Delaney and reporter Kevin Barry McKiernan—subsequently stated that it appeared to them that someone had fired a burst from an automatic into the torso from close range and then tried to hide the fact by putting an FBI jacket over the postmortem wounds; Matthiessen, *Spirit*, p. 183.

109. The agents' standard attire was Vietnam-issue "boonie hats, jungle fatigues and boots." Their weapons were standard army M-16s. The whole affair was deliberately staged to resemble a military operation in Southeast Asia; see the selection of photographs in *Agents*.

110. Williams and Coler had each been shot three times. The FBI knew, from the sound of the rifles during the firefight if nothing else, that AIM had used no automatic weapons. Neither agent was stripped. There were no bunkers, but rather only a couple of old root cellars and tumbledown corrals, common enough in rural areas and not used as firing positions in any event (the Bureau would have known this because of the absence of spent cartridge casings in such locations). Far from being "lured" to the Jumping Bull property, they had returned after being expressly told to leave (and, in the event, they were supposed to be serving a warrant). Instructively, no one in the nation's press corps thought to ask how, exactly, Coll might happen to know either agent's last words, since nobody from the FBI was present when they were killed; Joel D. Weisman, "About that 'Ambush' at Wounded Knee," *Columbia Journalism Review*, Sept.-Oct. 1975. Also see my "Renegades, Terrorists and Revolutionaries."

111. The director's admission was made during a press conference conducted at the Century Plaza Hotel on July 1, 1975, in conjunction with Coler's and Williams' funerals. It was accorded inside coverage by the press, unlike the page-one treatment given Coll's original disinformation; Tom Bates, "The Government's Secret War on the Indian," *Oregon Times*, Feb./Mar. 1976.

112. Examples of the air assault technique include a 35-man raid on the property of AIM spiritual leader Selo Black Crow, near the village of Wanblee, on July 8, 1975. Crow Dog's Paradise, on the Rosebud Reservation, just across the line from Pine Ridge, was hit by a hundred heliborne agents on Sept. 5. Meanwhile, an elderly Oglala named James Brings Yellow had suffered a heart attack and died when agent J. Gary Adams suddenly kicked in his door during a no-knock search on July 12. By August, such abuse by the FBI was so pervasive that even some of Wilson's GOONs were demanding that the agents withdraw from the reservation; *COINTELPRO Papers*, pp. 268–70.

113. By September, it had become obvious to everyone that AIM lacked the military capacity to protect the traditionals from the level of violence being imposed by the FBI by that point. Hence, the organization began a pointed disengagement in order to alleviate pressure on the traditionals. On Oct. 16, 1975, Richard G. Held sent a memo to FBIHQ advising that his work in South Dakota was complete and that he anticipated returning to his position in Chicago by Oct. 18; a portion of this document is reproduced in *COINTELPRO Papers*, p. 273.

114. "Memorandum of Agreement Between the Oglala Sioux Tribe of South Dakota and the National Park Service of the Department of Interior to Facilitate Establishment, Development, Administration and Public Use of the Oglala Sioux Tribal Lands, Badlands National Monument" (Washington, D.C.: U.S. Department of Interior, Jan. 2, 1976). The Act assuming title is P.L. 90-468 (1976). If there is any doubt as to whether the transfer was about uranium, consider that the law was amended in 1978—in the face of considerable protest by the traditionals—to allow the Oglalas to recover *surface* use rights any time they decided by referendum to do so. Subsurface (mineral) rights, however, were permanently retained by the government. Actually, the whole charade was illegal inso-

far as the still-binding 1868 Fort Laramie Treaty requires three-fourths express consent of all adult male Lakotas to validate land transfers, *not* land recoveries. Such consent, obviously, was never obtained with respect to the Gunnery Range transfer; see Huber, et al., *Gunnery Range Report.*

115. The congressional missive read: "Attached is a letter from the Senate Select Committee (SSC), dated 6-23-75, addressed to [U.S. Attorney General] Edward S. Levi. This letter announces the SSC's intent to conduct interviews relating . . . to our investigation at 'Wounded Knee' and our investigation of the American Indian Movement . . . On 6-27-75, Patrick Shae, staff member of the SSC, requested we hold in abeyance any action . . . in view of the killing of the Agents at Pine Ridge, South Dakota."

116. The selection of those charged seems to have served a dual purpose: 1) to "decapitate" one of AIM's best and most cohesive security groups, and 2) in not charging participants from Pine Ridge, to divide the locals from their sources of outside support. The window dressing charges against Jimmy Eagle were explicitly dropped in order to "place the full prosecutorial weight of the government on Leonard Peltier"; quoted in Jim Messerschmidt, *The Trial of Leonard Peltier* (Boston: South End Press, 1984) p. 47.

117. Butler was apprehended at Crow Dog's Paradise during the FBI's massive air assault there on Sept. 5, 1975. Robideau was arrested in a hospital where he was being treated for injuries sustained when his car exploded on the Kansas Turnpike on Sept. 10; *Agents,* pp. 448–49.

118. Acting on an informant's tip, the Oregon State Police stopped a car and a motor home belonging to the actor Marlon Brando near the town of Ontario on the night of November 14, 1975. Arrested in the motor home were Kamook Banks and Anna Mae Pictou Aquash, a fugitive on minor charges in South Dakota; arrested in the automobile were AIM members Russell Redner and Kenneth Loudhawk. Two men—Dennis Banks, a fugitive from sentencing after being convicted of inciting the 1972 Custer Courthouse "riot" in South Dakota, and Leonard Peltier, a fugitive on several warrants, including one for murder in the deaths of Williams and Coler—escaped from the motor home. Peltier was wounded in the process. On Feb. 6, 1976, acting on another informant's tip, the Royal Canadian Mounted Police arrested Peltier, Frank Black Horse (a.k.a., Frank DeLuca) and Ronald Blackman (a.k.a., Ron Janvier) at Smallboy's Camp, about 160 miles east of Edmonton, Alberta; Matthiessen, *Spirit,* pp. 249–51, 272–78. On the outcome for Dennis Banks and the others, see my "Due Process Be Damned: The Case of the Portland Four," *Z Magazine,* Jan. 1988.

119. Poor Bear, a clinically unbalanced Oglala, was picked up for "routine questioning" by agents David Price and Ron Wood in February 1976 and then held incommunicado for nearly two months in the Hacienda Motel, in Gordon, Nebraska. During this time she was continuously threatened with dire consequences by the agents unless she "cooperated" with their "investigation" into the deaths of Coler and Williams. At some point, Price began to type up for her signature affidavits that incriminated Leonard Peltier. Ultimately, she signed three mutually exclusive "accounts"; one of them—in which Peltier is said to have been her boyfriend, and to have confessed to her one night in a Nebraska bar that he'd killed the agents—was submitted in Canadian court to obtain Peltier's extradition on June 18, 1976. Meanwhile, on March 29, Price caused Poor Bear take on the stand against Richard Marshall in Rapid City, during the OSCRO/AIM member's state trial for killing Martin Montileaux. She testified that she was Marshall's girl friend and that he had confessed the murder to her one night in a Nebraska bar. Marshall was then convicted. Federal prosecutors declined to introduce Poor Bear as a witness at either the Butler/Robideau or Peltier trials, observing that her testimony was "worthless" due to her mental condition. She has publicly and repeatedly recanted her testimony against both Peltier and Marshall, saying she never met either of them in her life. For years, members of the Canadian parliament have been demanding Peltier's return to their jurisdiction due to the deliberate perpetration of fraud by U.S. authorities in his extradition proceeding, and attempting to block renewal of the U.S.-Canadian Extradition Treaty because of the U.S. failure to comply. The Poor Bear affidavits are reproduced in *COINTELPRO Papers,* pp. 288–91. On her testimony against Marshall and recantations, see *Agents,* pp. 339–42. On the position of the Canadian Parliament, see, e.g., "External Affairs: Canada-U.S. Extradition Treaty—Case of Leonard Peltier, Statement of Mr. James Ful-

ton," in *House of Commons Debate, Canada* , Vol. 128, No. 129 (Ottawa: 1st Sess., 33rd Par., Off. Rept., Thurs., Apr. 17, 1986).

120. The disinformation campaign centered in the Bureau's "leaks" of the so-called "Dog Soldier Teletypes" on June 21 and 22, 1976—in the midst of the Butler/Robideau trial—to "friendly media representatives." The documents, which were never in any way substantiated but were nonetheless sensationally reported across the country, asserted that 2,000 AIM "Dog Soldiers," acting in concert with SDS (a long-defunct white radical group) and the Crusade for Justice (a militant Chicano organization), had equipped themselves with illegal weapons and explosives and were preparing to embark on a campaign of terrorism which included "killing a cop a day . . . sniping at tourists . . . burning out farmers . . . assassinating the Governor of South Dakota . . . blowing up the Fort Randall Dam" and breaking people out of the maximum security prison at Sioux Falls. The second teletype is reproduced in *COINTELPRO Papers*, pp. 277–82.

121. Defense attorney William Kunstler queried Kelley as to whether there was "one shred, one scintilla of evidence" to support the allegations made by the FBI in the Dog Soldier Teletypes. Kelley replied, "I know of none." Nonetheless the FBI continued to feature AIM prominently in its *Domestic Terrorist Digest*, distributed free of charge to state and local police departments across the country; *COINTELPRO Papers*, p. 276.

122. The initial round striking both Coler and Williams was a .44 magnum. Bob Robideau testified that he was the only AIM member using a .44 magnum during the firefight; Robideau interview, Nov. 1993 (tape on file).

123. Videotaped NBC interview with Robert Bolin, 1990 (raw tape on file).

124. FBI personnel in attendance at this confab were Director Kelley and Richard G. Held, by then promoted to the rank of Assistant Director, James B. Adams, Richard J. Gallagher, John C. Gordon, and Herbert H. Hawkins, Jr. Representing the Justice Department were prosecutor Evan Hultman and his boss, William B. Grey; memo from B.H. Cooke to Richard J. Gallagher, Aug. 10, 1976.

125. McManus professes to have been "astonished" when he was removed from the Peltier case; Matthiessen, *Spirit*, p. 566.

126. *U.S. v. Leonard Peltier*, (CR-75-5106-1, U.S. Dist. Ct., Dist. of North Dakota (1977)); hereinafter referred to as *Peltier Trial Transcript*.

127. Butler and Robideau were tried on the premise that they were part of conspiracy which led to a group slaying of Williams and Coler. Peltier was tried as the "lone gunman" who had caused their deaths. Similarly, at Cedar Rapids, agent J. Gary Adams had testified the dead agents followed a red pickup onto the Jumping Bull property; during the Fargo trial, he testified they'd followed a "red and white van" belonging to Peltier. The defense was prevented by the judge's evidentiary ruling at the outset from impeaching such testimony on the basis of its contradiction of sworn testimony already entered against Butler and Robideau; see *Peltier Trial Transcript* and *U.S. v. Darrelle E. Butler and Robert E. Robideau*, (CR76-11, U.S. Dist. Ct., Dist. of Iowa (1976)), for purposes of comparison; the matter is well analyzed in Messerschmidt, *Trial*.

128. No slugs were recovered from Williams' and Coler's bodies, and two separate autopsies were inconclusive in determining the exact type of weapon from which the fatal shots were fired. The key piece of evidence in this respect was a .223 caliber shell casing which the FBI said was ejected from the killer's AR-15 rifle into the open trunk of Coler's car at the moment he fired one of the lethal rounds. The Bureau also claimed its ballistics investigation proved only one such weapon was used by AIM during the firefight. *Ipso facto*, whichever AIM member could be shown to have used an AR-15 on June 26, 1975, would be the guilty party. The problem is that the cartridge casing was not found in Coler's trunk when agents initially went over the car with finetooth combs. Instead, it was supposedly found later, on one of two different days, by one of two different agents, and turned over to someone whose identity neither could quite recall, somewhere on the reservation. How the casing got from whoever and wherever to the FBI crime lab in Washington, D.C., is, of course, equally mysterious. This is what was used to establish the "murder weapon"; *Peltier Trial Transcript*, pp. 2114, 3012–13, 3137–38, 3235, 3342, 3388.

129. Agent Frank Coward, who did not testify to this effect against Butler and Robideau, claimed at the Fargo trial that shortly after the estimated time of Coler's and Williams' deaths, he observed Leonard Peltier, whom he conceded he'd never seen before, running away from their cars and carrying an AR-15 rifle. This sighting was supposedly made through a 7x rifle scope at a distance of 800 meters (a half mile) through severe atmospheric heat shimmers while Peltier was moving at an oblique angle to the observer. Defense tests demonstrated that any such identification was impossible, even among friends standing full-face and under perfect weather conditions. In any event, this is what was used to tie Peltier to the "murder weapon"; *Peltier Trial Transcript*, p. 1305.

130. Seventeen-year-old Wish Draper, for instance, was strapped to a chair at the police station at Window Rock, Arizona, while being "interrogated" by FBI agents Charles Stapleton and James Doyle; he thereupon agreed to "cooperate" by testifying against Peltier; *Peltier Trial Transcript*, pp. 1087–98. Seventeen-year-old Norman Brown was told by agents J. Gary Adams and O. Victor Harvey during their interrogation of him that he'd "never walk this earth again" unless he testified in the manner they desired; *Peltier Trial Transcript*, pp. 4799–4804, 4842–43. Fifteen-year-old Mike Anderson was also interrogated by Adams and Harvey. In this case, they offered both the carrot and the stick: to get pending charges dismissed against him if he testified as instructed, and to "beat the living shit" out of him if he didn't; *Peltier Trial Transcript*, pp. 840–42. All three young men acknowledged under defense cross examination that they'd lied under oath at the request of the FBI and federal prosecutors.

131. Crooks' speech is worth quoting in part: "Apparently Special Agent Williams was killed first. He was shot in the face and hand by a bullet . . . probably begging for his life, and he was shot. The back of his head was blown off by a high powered rifle . . . Leonard Peltier then turned, as the evidence indicates, to Jack Coler lying on the ground helpless. He shoots him in the top of the head. Apparently feeling he hadn't done a good enough job, he shoots him again through the jaw, and his face explodes. No shell comes out, just explodes. The whole bottom of his chin is blown out by the force of the concussion. Blood splattered against the side of the car"; *Peltier Trial Transcript*, p. 5011.

132. Peltier's being sent directly to Marion contravenes federal Bureau of Prisons regulations restricting placement in that facility to "incorrigibles" who have "a record of unmanageability in more normal penal settings." Leonard Peltier had no prior convictions and therefore no record, unmanageable or otherwise, of behavior in penal settings.

133. *U.S. v. Peltier*, 858 F.2d 314, 335 (8th Cir. 1978).

134. *U.S. v. Peltier*, 440 U.S. 945, *cert. denied* (1979).

135. Another 6,000-odd pages of FBI file material on Peltier are still being withheld on the basis of "National Security."

136. At trial FBI ballistics expert Evan Hodge testified that the actual AR-15 had been recovered from Bob Robideau's burned out car along the Wichita Turnpike in Sept. 1975. The weapon was so badly damaged by the fire, Hodge said, that it had been impossible to perform a match-comparison of firing pin tool marks by which to link it to the cartridge casing supposedly found in the trunk of Coler's car. However, by removing the bolt mechanism from the damaged weapon and putting it in an undamaged rifle, he claimed, it had been possible to perform a rather less conclusive match-comparison of extractor tool marks, with which to tie the Wichita AR-15 to the Coler Car Casing. Among the documents released under provision of the FOIA in 1981 was an Oct. 2, 1975, teletype written by Hodge stating that he had in fact performed a firing pin test using the Wichita AR-15, and that it failed to produce a match to the crucial casing; *United States v. Peltier*, Motion to Vacate Judgment and for a New Trial, (Crim. No. CR-3003, U.S. Dist. Ct., Dist. of North Dakota, (filed Dec. 15, 1982)). For the Eighth Circuit Court's decision to allow the appeal to proceed, despite Judge Benson's rejection of the preceding motion, see *U.S. v. Peltier*, (731 F.2d 550, 555 (8th Cir. 1984)).

137. During the evidentiary hearing on Peltier's second appeal, conducted in Bismarck, North Dakota, during late October 1984, it began to emerge that AIM members had used—and the FBI had *known* they had used—not one but several AR-15s during the Oglala Firefight. This stood to destroy the "single AR-15" theory used to convict Peltier at trial. Moreover, the evidentiary chain con-

cerning the Coler Car Casing was brought into question. In an effort to salvage the situation, Bureau ballistics chief Evan Hodge took the stand to testify that he, and he *alone*, had handled ballistics materials related to the Peltier case. Appeal attorney William Kunstler then queried him concerning margin notes on the ballistics reports which were not his own. At that point, he retracted, admitting that lab assistant Joseph Twardowski had also handled the evidence and worked on the reports. Kunstler asked whether Hodge was sure that only he and Twardowski had had access to the materials and conclusions adduced from them. Hodge responded emphatically in the affirmative. Kunstler then pointed to yet another handwriting in the report margins and demanded a formal inquiry by the court. Two hours later, a deflated Hodge was allowed by Judge Benson to return to the stand and admit he'd "mispoken" once again; he really had no idea who had handled the evidence, adding or subtracting pieces at will.

138. *U.S. v. Peltier*, CR-3003, "Transcript of Oral Arguments Before the U.S. Eighth Circuit Court of Appeals, St. Louis, Mo., Oct. 15, 1985," p. 19.

139. Ibid., p.18.

140. U.S. Eighth Circuit Court of Appeals, "Appeal from the United States District of North Dakota in the Matter of *United States v. Leonard Peltier*" (Crim. No. 85-5192, St. Louis, Mo., (Oct. 11, 1986)).

141. Ibid., p. 16.

142. The high court declined review despite the fact that the Eighth Circuit decision had created a question—deriving from a Supreme Court opinion rendered in *U.S. v. Bagley* (U.S. 105 S. Ct. 3375 (1985))—of what standard of doubt must be met before an appeals court is bound to remand a case to trial. The Eighth Circuit had formally concluded that while the Peltier jury might "possibly" have reached a different verdict had the appeals evidence been presented to it, it was necessary under *Bagley* guidelines that the jury would "probably" have rendered a different verdict before remand was appropriate. Even this ludicrously labored reasoning collapses upon itself when it is considered that, in a slightly earlier case, the Ninth Circuit had remanded on the basis that the verdict might *possibly* have been different. It is in large part to resolve just such questions of equal treatment before the law that the Supreme Court theoretically exists. Yet it flatly refused to do its job when it came to being involved in the Peltier case; see my "Leonard Peltier: The Ordeal Continues," *Z Magazine*, Mar. 1988.

143. Once again, the Supreme Court has declined to review the matter.

144. Jennifer Hoyt, "FBI agents protest clemency request: Clinton considers Peltier case," *Houston Chronicle*, Dec. 16, 2000; Chet Brokaw, "S.D. governor fought pardon for Peltier: Janklow takes credit for failure of clemency push," *Denver Post*, Feb. 3, 2001; Shannon Sorenson, "Clinton's Pardons Should Have Included Peltier," *South Florida Sun-Sentinel*, Mar. 17, 2001.

145. Holder moved into secondary education, and works for Indian control of their schools in Kansas and Oklahoma. Others, such as Wilma Mankiller, Ted Means, and Twila Martin, have moved into more mainstream venues of tribal politics. Still others, like Phyllis Young and Madonna (Gilbert) Thunderhawk have gone in the direction of environmentalism.

146. Examples include Jimmie Durham and John Arbuckle, both of whom now pursue—in dramatically different ways—careers in the arts.

147. Actually, this began very early on, as when AIM National President Carter Camp shot founder Clyde Bellecourt in the stomach in 1974 over a factional dispute instigated by Bellecourt's brother, Vernon. In the ensuing turmoil, Russell Means openly resigned from AIM, but was quickly reinstated; see Matthiessen, *Spirit*, pp. 85–86.

148. Banks was granted sanctuary by California Governor Jerry Brown in 1977, because of such campaign statements by South Dakota Attorney General William Janklow as "the way to deal with AIM leaders is a bullet in the head" and that, if elected, he would "put AIM leaders either in our jails or under them." An enraged Janklow responded by threatening to arrange early parole for a number of South Dakota's worst felons on condition they accept immediate deportation to California. During his time of "refugee status" Banks served as chancellor of the AIM-initiated D-Q University, near Sacramento; *Rapid City Journal*, Apr. 7, 1981.

149. Rebecca L. Robbins, "American Indian Self-Determination: Comparative Analysis and Rhetorical Criticism," *Issues in Radical Therapy/New Studies on the Left*, Vol. XIII, Nos. 3–4, Summer-Fall 1988.

150. An intended offshoot of the Peltier Defense Committee, designed to expose the identity of whoever had murdered AIM activist Anna Mae Pictou Aquash in execution style on Pine Ridge sometime in Feb. 1976 (at the onset, it was expected this would be members of Wilson's GOONs), quickly collapsed when it became apparent that AIM itself might be involved. It turned out that self-proclaimed AIM National Officer Vernon Bellecourt had directed security personnel during the 1975 AIM General Membership Meeting to interrogate Aquash as a possible FBI informant. They were, he said, to "bury her where she stands" if unsatisfied with her answers. The security team, composed of Northwest AIM members, did not act upon this instruction, instead incorporating Aquash into their own group. The Northwest AIM Group was rapidly decimated after the Oglala Firefight, however, and Aquash was left unprotected. It is instructive that, once her body turned up near Wanblee, Bellecourt was the prime mover in quashing an internal investigation of her death. For general background, see Johanna Brand, *The Life and Death of Anna Mae Aquash* (Toronto: James Lorimer, 1978).

151. Killed were Trudell's wife, Tina Manning, their three children—Ricarda Star (age five), Sunshine Karma (age three), and Eli Changing Sun (age one)—and Tina's mother, Leah Hicks Manning. They were burned to death as they slept in the Trudell's trailer home; the blaze occurred less than twelve hours after Trudell delivered a speech in front of FBI headquarters during which he burned an American flag; although there was ample reason to suspect arson, no police or FBI investigation ensued; *Agents*, pp. 361–64.

152. Personal conversation with the author, 1979.

153. None of this is to say that LPDC did not continue. It did, even while failing to fulfill many of the wider objectives set forth by its founders. In terms of service to Peltier himself, aside from maintaining an ongoing legal appeals effort, the LPDC is largely responsible for the generation of more than 14 million petition signatures worldwide, all of them calling for his retrial. It has also been instrumental in bringing about several television documentaries, official inquiries into his situation by several foreign governments, an investigation by Amnesty International, and Peltier's receipt of a 1986 human rights award from the government of Spain. Bill Clinton nonetheless failed to bestow clemency before leaving office.

154. *Keystone to Survival* (Rapid City, SD: Black Hills Alliance, 1981).

155. See "Breach of Trust," herein.

156. On the occupation, see my "Yellow Thunder *Tiospaye*: Misadventure or Watershed Action?" *Policy Perspectives*, Vol. 2, No. 2, Spring 1982.

157. See the section on the Black Hills Land Claim in "The Earth Is Our Mother," herein.

158. *Lyng v. Northwest Indian Cemetery Protection Association* (485 U.S. 439 (1988)).

159. See the essay entitled "Genocide in Arizona: The 'Navajo-Hopi Land Dispute' in Perspective," in my *Struggle for the Land: Native North American Resistance to Genocide, Ecocide and Colonization* (Winnipeg: Arbeiter Ring, [2nd ed.] 1999) pp. 135–72.

160. See the section on the Western Shoshone Land Claim in "The Earth Is Our Mother," pp. 96–106, herein.

161. On the early days of IITC, see the chapter entitled "The Fourth World," in Weyler, *Blood.*, pp. 212–50.

162. On Durham's recent activities, see his *A Certain Lack of Coherence: Writings on Art and Cultural Politics* (London: Kala Press, 1993).

163. See generally, my and Glenn T. Morris' "Between a Rock and a Hard Place: Left-Wing Revolution, Right-Wing Reaction, and the Destruction of Indigenous Peoples," *Cultural Survival Quarterly*, Vol. 11, No. 3, Fall 1988.

164. Colorado, Dakota, Eastern Oklahoma, Florida, Illinois, Maryland, Mid-Atlantic (LISN), Northern California, New Mexico (Albuquerque), Northwest, Ohio, Southeast (Atlanta), Southern California, Texas, Western Oklahoma, Wraps His Tail (Crow). These organized themselves as the

Confederation of Autonomous AIM Chapters at a national conference in Edgewood, New Mexico, on Dec. 17, 1993.

165. Means with Wolf, *White Men Fear*, p. 520. Also see "Confronting Columbus Day," herein.

166. Incorporation documents and attachments on file. The documents of incorporation are signed by Vernon Bellecourt, who is listed as a Central Committee member; the address listed for annual membership meetings is Bellecourt's residence. Other officers listed in the documents are Clyde Bellecourt, Dennis Banks, Herb Powless, John Trudell, Bill Means, Carole Standing Elk, and Sam Dry Water. Trudell, Banks, and Means maintain that they were neither informed of the incorporation nor agreed to be officers.

167. Expulsion letter and associated documents on file. Bill Means states that he was asked, but refused to sign the letter.

168. Statement during a talk at the annual Medicine Ways Conference, University of California at Riverside, May 1991.

169. Statement during a talk at the University of Colorado at Denver, Feb. 1988 (tape on file).

170. This assessment, of course, runs entirely counter to those of pro-Wilson publicists such as syndicated columnist Tim Giago—supported as he is by a variety of powerful nonindian interests—who has made it a mission in life to discredit and degrade the legacy of AIM through continuous doses of disinformation. Consider, as one example, his eulogy to Dickie Wilson—in which he denounced careful chroniclers of the Pine Ridge terror such as Onondaga faithkeeper Oren Lyons and Peter Matthiessen, described the victims of Wilson's GOONs as "violent" and "criminal," and embraced Wilson himself as a "friend"—in the Feb. 13, 1990, edition of *Lakota Times*. In a more recent editorial, Giago announced that his research indicates that "only 10" people were actually killed by Wilson's gun thugs on Pine Ridge during the mid-70s although the FBI itself concedes more than 40 such fatalities. Then, rather than professing horror that his "friend" might have been responsible for even his revised number of murders, Giago uses this faulty revelation to suggest that the Wilson régime really wasn't so bad after all, especially when compared to AIM's "violence" and irreverence for "law and order."

171. A good effort to render several of these lessons will be found in Glick, *War at Home*.

172. For superb analysis of this point, see Isaac Balbus, *The Dialectic of Legal Repression* (New York: Russell Sage Foundation, 1973).

173. A fine survey of the conditions prevailing in each of these sectors will be found in Teresa L. Amott and Julie A. Matthaei, *Race, Gender and Work: A Multicultural Economic History of the United States* (Boston: South End Press, 1991).

174. For details and analysis, see my and J.J. Vander Wall's edited volume, *Cages of Steel: The Politics of Imprisonment in the United States* (Washington, D.C.: Maisonneuve Press, 1992).

175. For a survey of the repression visited upon most of these groups, see *COINTELPRO Papers*.

176. For biographical information concerning those mentioned who are currently imprisoned by the United States, see *Can't Jail the Spirit: Political Prisoners in the United States* (Chicago: Committee to End the Marion Lockdown, [5th ed.] 2002).

8. FANTASIES OF THE MASTER RACE

1. Elizabeth Weatherford and Emelia Seubert, *Native Americans in Film and Video*, 2 vols. (New York: Museum of the American Indian, 1981, 1988). Also see the excellent 830-title filmography in Michael Hilger's *The American Indian in Film* (Metuchen, NJ: Scarecrow Press, 1986).

2. A number of works analyze this connection. Two of the better efforts are Hugh Honour's *The New Golden Land: European Images of America from the Discoveries to the Present Time* (New York: Pantheon, 1975) and Raymond F. Stedman's *Shadows of the Indian: Stereotypes in American Culture* (Norman: University of Oklahoma Press, 1982).

3. For exploration of this point in a number of facets, see Lester D. Freidman, ed., *Unspeakable Images: Ethnicity and the American Cinema* (Urbana: University of Illinois Press, 1991).

4. Most comprehensively, see Allen L. Wald and Randall H. Miller, *Ethics and Racial Images in*

American Film and Television: Historical Essays and Bibliography (New York: Garland, 1987). On African Americans in particular, see Donald Bogel's *Toms, Coons, Mulattoes, Mammies, and Bucks: An Interpretive History of Blacks in American Films* (New York: Viking, 1973) and Thomas Cripps' *Making Movies Black: The Hollywood Message Movie from World War II to the Civil Rights Era* (New York: Oxford University Press, 1993). On Latinos, see George Hadley-Garcia, *Hispanic Hollywood: The Latins in Motion Pictures* (New York: Carol Publishing-Citadel Books, 1993). On Asian Americans, see Jun Xing, *Asian America Through the Lens: History, Representations and Reality* (Walnut Creek, CA: AltaMira Press, 1998).

5. For a brilliant exposition on precisely this point, see Peter Biskind, *Seeing Is Believing: How Hollywood Taught Us to Stop Worrying and Love the Fifties* (New York: Pantheon, 1983).

6. Weatherford and Seubert, *Native Americans in Film and Video*, Vol. 2.

7. A poignant reflection on the ramifications of this situation will be found in Patricia Penn Hilden's *When Nickels Were Indians: An Urban Mixed-Blood Story* (Washington, D.C.: Smithsonian Institution Press, 1995).

8. Ralph Andrist, *The Long Death: The Last Days of the Plains Indian* (New York: Macmillan, 1964).

9. Such treatment is hardly reserved for Indians nor restricted to film. Rather, it is how the "West" has increasingly tended to treat all "Others" since medieval times. See Eric R. Wolf, *Europe and the People Without History* (Berkeley: University of California Press, 1982).

10. The case could of course be made that events transpiring 2–3,000 years ago in Egypt and the Near East have little or nothing to do with the heritage of Europe, which remained as yet uninvented. The point is, however, that in synthesizing itself Europe *claimed* these events as antecedents to its own tradition. Additionally, films such as *Cleopatra* do not devolve upon Egyptians so much as upon Roman interactions with Egyptians, and the Romans, to be sure, *were* antecedent Europeans. Thus, one might observe that Hollywood's handling of ancient Egypt is essentially the same as its handling of Indians: The people or culture involved has interest/meaning only insofar as Europeans are present to inject it. On the creation of what has become known as Europe, *circa* 800 C.E.; see Philippe Wolff, *The Awakening of Europe: The Growth of European Culture from the Ninth Century to the Twelfth* (New York: Penguin, 1968); Richard Hodges and David Whitehouse, *Mohammed, Charlemagne and the Origins of Europe* (Ithaca, NY: Cornell University Press, 1983).

11. Alan Axelrod, *Chronicles of the Indian Wars from Colonial Times to Wounded Knee* (New York: Prentice-Hall, 1993).

12. The Abbott and Costello flick was originally scheduled to be titled *No Indians Please*; Rennard Strickland, "Tonto's Revenge, or, Who Is That Seminole in the Sioux Warbonnet? The Cinematic Indian!" in his *Tonto's Revenge: Reflections on American Indian Culture and Policy* (Albuquerque: University of New Mexico Press, 1997) p. 29.

13. Ibid. The list presented here does not include several gambits by the Three Stooges. Also see Karen Wallace, "The Redskin and *The Paleface*: Comedy on the Frontier," in Daniel Bernardi, ed., *Classic Hollywood, Classic Whiteness* (Minneapolis: University of Minnesota Press, 2001) pp. 111–38.

14. Daniel Francis, *The Imaginary Indian: The Image of the Indian in Canadian Culture* (Vancouver, B.C.: Arsenal Pulp Press, 1992) p. 59.

15. Bill Holm and George Irving Quimby, *Edward S. Curtis in the Land of the War Canoes: A Pioneer Cinematographer in the Pacific Northwest* (Seattle: University of Washington Press, 1980); Ann Fienup-Riordan, *Freeze Frame: Alaskan Eskimos in the Movies* (Seattle: University of Washington Press, 1995). It should be noted that films such as *Nanook* and *Land of the Headhunters* dovetailed perfectly with the literary sensibility of the day. See, e.g., B.O. Flower, "An Interesting Representative of a Vanishing Race," *Arena*, July 1896; Simon Pokagon, "The Future of the Red Man," *Forum*, Aug. 1897; William R. Draper, "The Last of the Red Race," *Cosmopolitan*, Jan. 1902; Charles M. Harvey, "The Last Race Rally of Indians," *World's Work*, May 1904; E. S. Curtis, "Vanishing Indian Types: The Tribes of the Northwest Plains," *Scribner's*, June 1906; James Mooney, "The Passing of the Indian," *Proceedings of the Second Pan American Scientific Congress, Sec. 1: Anthropology* (Washington,

D.C.: Smithsonian Institution, 1909–1910); Joseph K. Dixon, *The Vanishing Race: The Last Great Indian Council* (Garden City, NY: Doubleday, 1913); Stanton Elliot, "The End of the Trail," *Overland Monthly*, July 1915; Ella Higginson, "The Vanishing Race," *Red Man*, Feb. 1916; Ales Hrdlicka, "The Vanishing Indian," *Science*, No. 46, 1917; J.L. Hill, *The Passing of the Indian and the Buffalo* (Long Beach, CA: n.p., 1917); John Collier, "The Vanishing American," *Nation*, Jan. 11, 1928. Overall, see Brian W. Dippie, *The Vanishing American: White Attitudes and U.S. Indian Policy* (Middletown, CT: Wesleyan University Press, 1982); Christopher M. Lyman, *The Vanishing Race and Other Illusions* (New York: Pantheon, 1982).

16. Jimmie Durham, "Cowboys and . . . " in his *A Certain Lack of Coherence: Writings on Art and Cultural Politics* (London: Kala Press, 1993) p. 176. The descriptive phrase used is taken from S.L.A. Marshall's *Crimsoned Prairie* (New York: Scribner's, 1972).

17. *Flap* is based on a novel by Claire Hussaker entitled *Nobody Loves a Drunken Indian* (1993 Buccaneer reprint of 1964 original). For its part, *Powwow Highway* is based upon a self-published novel of the same title written by an alleged Abenaki named David Seals and widely condemned by the native community as, at best, a travesty. While it does have the distinction of being one of the few movies that is far better than the book from which it originates—see, e.g., George Bluestone, *Novels Into Film: The Metamorphosis of Fiction Into Film* (Berkeley: University of California Press, [2nd ed.] 1973)—even a fine performance by Oneida actor Gary Farmer is insufficient to save it from being a waste of resources which might have been more usefully devoted to a worthy project.

18. It seems not to have occurred to Hollywood that the West also includes the Intermountain Desert of Utah/Nevada as well as the Great Basin of Idaho and eastern Washington/Oregon, and that peoples like the Utes, Paiutes, Shoshones, Bannocks, and others were always available for depiction, even within movieland's self-imposed spatial/temporal constraints. The explanation for this, of course, rests in the relative absence of Indian/white warfare in these areas. Indeed, the only significant exception to the subregional blackout comes with *I Will Fight No More Forever* (1979), a television tragedy focusing on the 1877 attempt by Idaho's Nez Percés to escape into Canada after fighting a brief defensive action against an overwhelming number of U.S. troops; Merril D. Beal, *"I Will Fight No More Forever": Chief Joseph and the Nez Percé War* (Seattle: University of Washington Press, 1963).

19. It is unclear exactly what geocultural disposition is supposed to be occupied by the Indians portrayed in "mountain man" films like *Yellowstone Kelly* (1959) and *Jeremiah Johnson* (1972). Apparently, they are consider to be of the "Plains type," or close enough to be treated as such.

20. In their thematic listing of major film releases through 1970, Ralph and Natasha Friar show a total of sixteen films focusing on Navajos, eight on Hopis, one on Zunis, eight on other Pueblos, one on the Yumas and none at all on Maricopas or Cocopahs. The Pimas are represented to some extent by a filmic biography of Marine war hero Ira Hayes; *The Only Good Indian . . . The Hollywood Gospel* (New York: Drama Books, 1972) pp. 317–19.

21. The Friars list 122 major films focusing specifically on Apaches, 100 on the Sioux; ibid., pp. 313–14. For more comprehensive listings reflecting more or less the same proportionality, see Weatherford and Seubert, *Native Americans*.

22. Wall and Miller, *Ethics and Racial Images*.

23. The first U.S. war against the Seminoles was waged in 1816–17 to "clear" Florida of its remaining native population. It was indecisive. A second was launched in 1835, but for "every two Seminoles who were sent West, one soldier died—1,500 in all. The war cost the federal government $20 million, and it ended in 1842 not through any victory on either side, but because the government simply stopped trying to flush out the remaining Seminoles who had hidden themselves deep in the Everglades." A third war was fought with these remnants from 1855 to 1858, with even less conclusive results; Axelrod, *Indian Wars*, pp. 146–47. On the protracted and almost equally costly nature of U.S. campaigns against the western Apaches, see E. Leslie Reedstrom, *The Apache Wars: An Illustrated Battle History* (New York: Sterling, 1990).

24. See generally, Ronald L. Davis, *John Ford: Hollywood's Old Master* (Norman: University of Oklahoma Press, 1995).

25. The nominations were for *Stagecoach* (1939) and *The Searchers* (1956). The other Monument Valley films were *My Darling Clementine* (1946), *Fort Apache* (1949), *She Wore a Yellow Ribbon* (1949), *Wagon Master* (1950), and *Cheyenne Autumn* (1964); J.A. Place, *The Western Films of John Ford* (Secaucus, NJ: Citadel Press, 1974). It should be noted that Ford actually won four Academy awards for best picture or best director. These were for *The Informer* (1935), *Grapes of Wrath* (1940), *How Green Was My Valley* (1940), and *The Quiet Man* (1952); Davis, *John Ford*.

26. Vine Deloria, Jr., talk at the University of Colorado/Boulder, June 1982 (tape on file). For more on the geocultural distortions involved in Hollywood westerns, see John Tuska, *The Filming of the West* (Garden City, NY: Doubleday, 1976).

27. Virtually all of the serial westerns coming out of the studios the 1930s and '40s were set in this fashion, among them the highly popular Gene Autry, Roy Rogers, Hopalong Cassidy, Lash Laroo, Sundown Carson, and Johnny Mac Brown movies. Among the top-rated weekly TV programs projecting the Plains to mass audiences in the same fashion during the 1950s and '60s were *Gunsmoke*, *Wagon Train*, *Wanted Dead or Alive*, *The Rebel*, *Cheyenne*, *Maverick*, *Rawhide*, and *Have Gun, Will Travel*. See C. L. Sonnischen, *From Hopalong to Hud: Thoughts on Western Fiction* (College Station: Texas A&M Press, 1978); Phil Hardy, *The Western: A Complete Film Sourcebook* (New York: William Morrow, 1986); Michael R. Pitts, *Western Movies: A TV and Video Guide to 4200 Genre Films* (Jefferson, NC: McFarland, 1986).

28. Strickland, "Tonto's Revenge," p. 20.

29. Ibid. In a weird kind of turnabout, albeit a very early one, the high plains-dwelling Lakotas are shown picking their way through a malaria-ridden subtropical swamp in *Ogallalah* (1912).

30. The Friars list another eight films on Seminoles as having been made between 1906 and 1911; one, *Ramshackle House*, in 1924; none in the thirties or forties; and one, *Johnny Tiger*, in 1966. None have been made since. The total number of films centering on Seminoles stands at fifteen; Friar and Friar, *Only Good Indian . . .* , p. 316. The count is not contradicted by information in either Weatherford's and Seubert's *Native Americans*, Wall and Miller's *Ethics and Racial Images*, or Hilger's *American Indian in Film*.

31. For more on Washburn, see my "Friends of the Indian? A Critical Assessment of Imre Sutton's *Irredeemable America: The Indians' Estate and Land Claims*," *New Studies on the Left*, Vol. XIII, Nos. 3–4, 1988.

32. George Catlin, *Letters and Notes on the Manners, Customs and Conditions of the North American Indians* (New York: Dover, 1973 reprint of 1844 original). In fairness, Curtis used exactly the same technique as Silverstein, carrying with him a trunk full of "typical Indian garb" in which to dress many of the subjects of his renowned turn-of-the-century photoportraiture; Holm and Quimby, *Edward S. Curtis*. For examples of the portraiture, see Edward S. Curtis, *Photos of North American Indian Life* (New York: Promontory Press, 1972).

33. See generally, Richard Erdoes, *The Sun Dance People: The Plains Indians, Their Past and Present* (New York: Vintage, 1962).

34. Catlin, *Letters and Notes*.

35. Skinner's query dates from 1914; quoted in Strickland, "Tonto's Revenge," p. 32.

36. Rogers, already having established himself as a popular syndicated columnist and radio commentator, was allowed to produce and star in three reasonably successful films directed by John Ford—*Doctor Bull* (1933), *Judge Priest* (1934), and *Steamboat Around the Bend* (1935)—before his untimely death in an airplane crash in the latter year; Davis, *John Ford*, p. 73.

37. Bunny McBride, *Molly Spotted Elk: A Penobscot in Paris* (Norman: University of Oklahoma Press, 1995) pp. 96–127.

38. It's not because none were available. James Young Deer, a Winnebago, directed several films. including the remarkable *Yacqui Girl* (1911), before setting out to make documentaries in France during World War I. Upon his return, he remained without assignment until the mid-30s when he was finally picked up as a second-unit director on "poverty row." Similarly, Edwin Carewe, a Chicka-

saw, directed several noteworthy films, including *The Trail of the Shadow* (1917) and *Ramona* (1928), before being abruptly "disemployed" by the major studios. At about the same time Carewe was being pushed out of the industry, Lynn Riggs, a Cherokee, wrote a play entitled *Green Grow the Lilacs*. It served as the basis for Rodgers and Hammerstein's *Oklahoma!*, although its author never received the praise, career boost, and financial rewards bestowed so lavishly on her Euroamerican counterparts; Strickland, "Tonto's Revenge," pp. 33–34. Also see Phyllis Cole Braunlick, *Haunted by Home: The Life and Letters of Lynn Riggs* (Norman: University of Oklahoma Press, 1988).

39. The comment was made by Oneida comic Charley Hill during a game of chess at my home in 1982.

40. In his memoirs, native actor Iron Eyes Cody recounts how an aging Thorpe actually broke down and wept after being denied a chance to play his father in the film based on his own life; *Iron Eyes: My Life as a Hollywood Indian* (New York: Everest House, 1982) p. 154.

41. At pages 281–83 of *Only Good Indian . . .* , the Friars provide a list of 350 white actors and actresses who've appeared in redface over the years. They do not, however, correlate the names to films or roles. An incomplete but nonetheless very useful resource in this connection is Roy Pickard's *Who Played Who on the Screen* (New York: Hipporene Books, 1988).

42. Ibid. For further analysis, see several of the essays included by Gretchen M. Bataille and Charles L.P. Silet in their coedited volume, *The Pretend Indians: Images of American Indians in the Movies* (Ames: Iowa State University Press, 1980), as well as Michael T. Marsden's and Jack Nachbar's "The Indian in the Movies," in Wilcomb E. Washburn, ed., *Handbook of the North American Indians, Vol. 4: History of Indian-White Relations* (Washington, D.C.: Smithsonian Institution Press, 1988) pp. 607–16.

43. Damien Bona, *Starring John Wayne as Genghis Khan: Hollywood's All-Time Worst Casting Blunders* (Secaucus, NJ: Citadel Press, 1996) pp. 30–31.

44. Hill conversation.

45. Davis, *John Ford*, pp. 184, 212, 224–25, 240.

46. Hill conversation. It should be noted that where Indians were featured more prominently, as when Cherokee actor Victor Daniels (Chief Thunder Cloud) was cast in the mostly nonspeaking role of *Geronimo* in 1939, he was required to don makeup so that he would resemble more closely the appearance of the white actors audiences were used to seeing portray Indians.

47. Strickland, "Tonto's Revenge," p. 28.

48. This articulation is often thought to derive from anthropology. Actually, it predates the "discipline" itself, comprising as it does the core rationalization for Europe's exercise of self-defined "conquest rights" elsewhere on the planet from about 1650 onward. Anthropology was subsequently invented for the explicit purpose of conjuring up pseudoscientific justifications for the whole enterprise. See generally, Sharon Korman, *The Right of Conquest: The Acquisition of Territory by Force in International Law and Practice* (Oxford: Clarendon Press, 1996) pp. 56–66.

49. The real nature of the white/Cherokee relationship in the Southeast, and the true measure of Euroamerican "benevolence," can be found in the fact that the Indians had been forcibly removed from their homeland during the 1830s and dumped on lands belonging to other native people west of the Mississippi. The whites of Georgia then took over the Cherokees' rich agricultural complex; Gloria Jahoda, *The Trail of Tears: The Story of the Indian Removals* (New York: Holt, Rinehart and Winston, 1975).

50. Most accessibly, see Jack Weatherford, *Indian Givers: How the Indians of the Americas Transformed the World* (New York: Crown, 1988).

51. On the destruction of Seneca croplands in particular, see Frederick Cook, *Journals of the Military Expedition of Major General John Sullivan against the Six Nations of Indians in 1779* (Auburn, NY: New York Historical Society, 1887). On "Mad Anthony" Wayne's destruction of Shawnee cornfields extending an estimated fifty miles along the Ohio River, see Richard Drinnon, *Keeper of Concentration Camps: Dillon S. Myer and American Racism* (Berkeley: University of California Press, 1987)

p. 23. On the destruction of the Navajos' extensive fields and orchards along the bottom of Cañon de Chelly, see Clifford E. Trafzer, *The Kit Carson Campaign: The Last Great Navajo War* (Norman: University of Oklahoma Press, 1982).

52. This polarity and its implications were well explored by Roy Harvey Pierce in his seminal *Savagism and Civilization: A Study of the American Indian in the American Mind* (Baltimore: Johns Hopkins University Press, 1953), and again in *The Savages of America: A Study of the Indian and the Idea of Civilization* (Baltimore: Johns Hopkins University Press, 1965).

53. See, e.g., Jay P. Kinney, *A Continent Lost—A Civilization Won: Indian Land Tenure in America* (Baltimore: John Hopkins University Press, 1937).

54. The "controversy" about the size of North America's precolumbian population, and the lengths to which "responsible scholars" have gone to falsify evidence to support superficially plausible underestimates is well handled in the chapter entitled "Widowed Land" in Francis Jennings' *The Invasion of America: Indians, Colonialism and the Cant of Conquest* (Chapel Hill: University of North Carolina Press, 1975). Suffice it here to say that twentieth century orthodoxy has decreed that the population of North America in 1492 numbered not more than a million, while the real figure was likely fifteen million or more.

55. Many of these are devoted to the reputedly "fierce" Mohawks and others of the Haudenosaunee, or Iroquois Six Nation Confederacy, as it is known. Examples include *Fighting the Iroquois* (1909), *A Mohawk's Way* (1910) and *In the Days of the Six Nations* (1911). A few later films—notably *Drums Along the Mohawk* (1939), *The Iroquois Trail* (1950), and *Mohawk* (1956)—were made following the same themes. Other significant exceptions to the rule include *Northwest Passage* (1940), *The Battles of Chief Pontiac* (1952), and *The Light in the Forest* (1958); Friar and Friar, *Only Good Indian . . .* , pp. 305–6.

56. *The Deerslayer*, for example, was first filmed in 1911, again in 1913, and then twice more, in 1943 and 1957. *The Pathfinder* was shot in 1911 and 1952. *Leather Stocking* appeared as a feature in 1909, before being serialized in 1924. *The Last of the Mohicans*, aside from its 1932 serialization, has appeared five times, in 1911, 1914, 1920, 1936, and 1992; ibid.

57. See the chapter entitled "'Nits Make Lice': The Extermination of North American Indians, 1607–1996," in my *A Little Matter of Genocide: Holocaust and Denial in the Americas, 1492 to the Present* (San Francisco: City Lights, 1997) esp. pp. 209–45.

58. One is never allowed to see the "Other" early in such films, but is kept continuously aware that "it" is out there somewhere, lurking, just waiting for a chance to commit the unspeakable. The imagination takes over, conjuring a fear and loathing among viewers that no literal imagery ever could. Usually, when the monster or space alien (or Indian) actually appears on screen, the audience experiences a sense of collective relief since whatever is shown is seldom as horrifying as what they've created in their own minds; Carlos Clarens, *An Illustrated History of Horror and Science Fiction Films: The Classic Era, 1895–1967* (New York: De Capo Press, 1997). One solution to the dilemma posed by such "emotional dissipation" was explored by director Sam Peckinpah in a 1961 episode of *The Alaskans* TV series (ABC; 1959–60), when he refused *ever* to reveal the beast which had terrified cast and viewers alike throughout the program; see generally, Paul Seydor, *Peckinpah: The Western Films* (Urbana: University of Illinois Press, 1980).

59. Friar and Friar, *Only Good Indian . . .* , p. 134.

60. Ibid.

61. Ibid., p. 215.

62. Stedman, *Shadows*, p. 116. The Indian as beast is a standard theme in American letters, analyzed very well by Richard Drinnon in his *Facing West: The Metaphysics of Indian-Hating and Empire Building* (Minneapolis: University of Minnesota Press, 1980). Mulligan's screenplay was based on Theodore V. Olson's *The Stalking Moon* (Garden City, NY: Doubleday, 1965).

63. Scalping and comparable forms of mutilation were actually primarily white practices, not Indian; see my "Nits Make Lice," pp. 178–88. As to Indians "slaughtering" large numbers of people, it was officially estimated in the 1890 U.S. Census that fewer than 5,000 whites had been killed in all

the Indian Wars combined. The rape of female captives is another case composed largely of transference; see my "The Crucible of American Indian Identity: Native Tradition versus Colonial Imposition in Postconquest North America," *American Indian Culture and Research Journal*, Vol. 23, No. 1, 1999.

64. There are only a handful of incidents on record in which Indians attacked a wagon train in anything resembling the manner commonly shown in the movies, and none in which we engaged in an outright assault on a fort anywhere west of the Mississippi. In reality, the cases where large numbers of Indians attacked *anything* are few (the Fetterman Fight, Wagon Box Fight, Beecher's Island, Adobe Walls, and the Little Big Horn are exceptional); see Andrist, *The Long Death*.

65. For more on this cinematic atrocity, see John Tuska, *The American West in Film: Critical Approaches to the Western* (Lincoln: University of Nebraska Press, 1988) p. 206. It should be noted that much the same device, that of having a white man excel Indians at their own skills, is hardly uncommon. Witness the Hawkeye/Natty Bumppo/Nathaniel character of *Last of the Mohicans* and other Fenimore Cooper sagas, or Fess Parker's title characterization *Davy Crockett: King of the Wild Frontier* (1955). Or, for that matter, consider the characters portrayed by John Wayne in *Hondo* (1953) and Rory Calhoun in *Apache Territory* five years later (both films based on Louis L'Amour novels, published in 1953 and 1957, respectively).

66. Rennard Strickland quotes his colleague, Oklahoma City University Professor Carter Blue Clark, as recalling such an experience during a Saturday matinee in the heart of Sioux country during the 1950s ("Tonto's Revenge," p. 18). I myself went through much the same thing at about the same time, albeit in a much more mixed-cultural setting, and have repeated the ordeal in several different localities since.

67. Quoted in Paul Andrew Hutton, *Phil Sheridan and His Army* (Lincoln: University of Nebraska Press, 1985) p. 180.

68. Scott Simmon, *The Films of D. W. Griffith* (Cambridge, U.K.: Cambridge University Press, 1993) p. 9.

69. Actually, six-shooters aren't needed. In *The Comancheros* (1961), a little boy armed with a blunderbuss manages to down three Indians with his one shot. For context, see John G. Cawelti, *The Six-Gun Mystique* (Bowling Green, OH: Bowling Green University Popular Press, 1975); Will Wright, *Sixguns and Society: A Structural Study of the Western* (Berkeley: University of California Press, 1975).

70. For analyses of this erosion in popularity, see George N. Fenin and William K. Everson, *The Western: From Silents to the Seventies* (New York: Grossman, 1973); William T. Pilkington and Don Graham, eds., *Western Movies* (Albuquerque: University of New Mexico Press, 1979).

71. See generally, Pierre Berton, *Hollywood's Canada* (Toronto: McClelland and Stewart, 1975); A.L. Haydon, *The Riders of the Plains: A Record of the Royal North-West Mounted Police of Canada, 1873–1910* (Toronto: Copp Clark, 1912); Gerald Friesen, *The Canadian Prairies: A History* (Toronto: University of Toronto Press, 1984).

72. On the Métis rebellions, and the NWMP's role—or, more appropriately, nonrole—in quelling them, see John Jennings, "The North West Mounted Police and Indian Policy after the 1885 Rebellion," in F. Laurie Barron and James B. Waldron, eds., *1885 and After* (Regina, Sask.: Canadian Plains Research Centre, 1986). On NWMP relations with the Lakota exiles, see Grant MacEwan, *Sitting Bull: The Years in Canada* (Edmonton, Alta.: Hurtig, 1973).

73. Francis, *The Imaginary Indian*, p. 80. Canadian filmmakers have done somewhat better with Mountie/Indian themes, as in the 1975 *Dan Candy's Law*.

74. Friar and Friar, *Only Good Indian . . .* , p. 188. On the Robinson Crusoe connection, see Stedman, *Shadows*, pp. 52–54, 179, 260. It should be noted that the Lone Ranger/Tonto duet appeared in a series of pulp novels beginning in 1936, and as a comic book series a year later. During the 1960s, they also formed the basis of a short-lived animated TV series.

75. Tonto was portrayed by two different Indians with virtually identical pseudonyms in the radio series and movie serials. Chief Thundercloud (Scott T. Williams) handled the airwave chores, while

Chief Thunder Cloud (Victor Daniels) appeared on the silver screen. Daniels' other credits include *Ramona*, the 1939 version of *Geronimo* and *I Killed Geronimo* (1950). The part in the TV series and 1950s films was handled by Mohawk actor Jay Silverheels, whose other credits include *Broken Arrow*, *The Battle at Apache Pass* and *Walk the Proud Land* (1956); Friar and Friar, *Only Good Indian . . .* , pp. 251–52.

76. Tonto was played in this instance by native actor Michael Horse, better known for his role in the 1980s David Lynch TV series *Twin Peaks*. Overall, see Lee J. Felbinger, *The Lone Ranger: A Pictorial Scrapbook* (Green Lane, PA: Countryside, 1988); James Van Hise, *Who Was That Masked Man? The Story of the Lone Ranger* (Las Vegas: Pioneer, 1990).

77. Rayna Green, *The Only Good Indian: Images of the Indian in American Vernacular Culture* (Bloomington: Ph.D. Dissertation, Indiana University, 1974) p. 382.

78. Francis, *The Imaginary Indian*, p. 167. If the formulation of Manifest Destiny sounds a bit Hitlerian, it should. The nazis modeled their *lebensraumpolitik* (politics of living space) directly on the example of the "Nordics of North America, who had ruthlessly pushed aside an inferior race to win for themselves soil and territory for the future"; Norman Rich, *Hitler's War Aims: Ideology, the Nazi State, and the Course of Expansion* (New York: W.W. Norton, 1973) p. 8. Also see Frank Parella, *Lebensraum and Manifest Destiny: A Comparative Study in the Justification of Expansionism* (Washington, D.C.: M.A. Thesis, Dept. of International Affairs, Georgetown University, 1950).

79. Robert S. Tilton, *Pocahontas: The Evolution of an American Narrative* (Cambridge, U.K.: Cambridge University Press, 1994) p. 56. On the notion of inherent racial inferiority bound up in the "Good Indian" stereotype, see Reginald Horsman, *Race and Manifest Destiny: The Origins of American Racial Anglo-Saxonism* (Cambridge, MA: Harvard University Press, 1981).

80. Fenin and Everson, for example, were still describing *Broken Arrow* as "a moving and sensitive film" a quarter-century later (*The Western*, p. 281). Analyst Robert Baird also continues to hold the movie in high regard, but then he is so knowledgeable on the subject that he continuously refers to the people depicted therein as "Cheyennes"; see his "Going Indian: Discovery, Adoption, and Renaming Toward a 'True American,'" from *Deerslayer* to *Dances with Wolves*," in S. Elizabeth Bird, ed., *Dressing in Feathers: The Construction of the Indian in American Popular Culture* (Boulder, CO: Westview Press, 1996) p. 201.

81. For comparison of Hollywood's stock treatments of American Indians with the handling of East Indians it borrowed from the Kipling tradition, see, as examples, *The Lost Patrol* (1934), *Lives of a Bengal Lancer* (1935), and *Gunga Din* (1939). For background, see, J. McClure, *Kipling and Conrad: The Colonial Fiction* (Cambridge, MA: Cambridge University Press, 1981).

82. Chandler had played Cochise twice more by 1954, as the Indian lead in *The Battle at Apache Pass*, and in a cameo at the beginning of *Taza, Son of Cochise*. Interestingly, the TV series cast Michael Ansara, an actor of actual native descent, in the same role; Friar and Friar, *Only Good Indian . . .* , p. 203; Stedman, *Shadows*, p. 218.

83. This is in the sense that virtually all westerns are at base simple moral plays; Wright, *Sixguns and Society*, p. 3.

84. Stedman, *Shadows*, p. 209.

85. S. Elizabeth Bird, "Not My Fantasy: The Persistence of Indian Imagery in *Dr. Quinn, Medicine Woman*," in her *Dressing in Feathers*, p. 249.

86. Stedman, *Shadows*, p. 211.

87. The main change-up in this drama was that Gable, as befitted his standing as a romantic lead, relied on a comely female played by Marie Elena Marques rather than a dignified male as his native counterpart; ibid., p. 29.

88. Friar and Friar, *Only Good Indian . . .* , pp. 303–4.

89. *The Outlaw Josey Wales*, it should be noted, was based on a book of the same title written by "Forrest Carter," a purported part-Cherokee who turned out instead to be Asa Earl "Ace" Carter, a "Ku Klux Klan thug and virulent racist, author not only of western novels but also of anti-semitic pamphlets and some of former Alabama governor George Wallace's strongest anti-Black speeches";

Francis, *Imaginary Indian*, p. 110. Small wonder that his depictions of Indians appeal to white sensibilities, so much so that, despite the truth of his background now being public information, another of his yarns, *The Education of Little Tree*, was made into a movie in 1997.

90. Annette M. Taylor, "Cultural Heritage in *Northern Exposure*," in Bird, *Dressing in Feathers*, p. 231.

91. The resemblance of the *Nakia* Indian character—it should actually be spelled *Nakai*—to that of Jim Chee in the novels of Tony Hillerman goes unremarked by Taylor; see the essay entitled "Hi-Ho Hillerman . . . (Away): The Role of Detective Fiction in Indian Country," in my *Fantasies of the Master Race: Literature, Cinema and the Colonization of American Indians* (San Francisco: City Lights, [2nd ed.] 1998) pp. 67–98.

92. Bird, "Not My Fantasy," p. 248. Also see John O'Connor, "It's Jane Seymour, M.D., in the Wild and Woolly West," *New York Times*, Feb. 4, 1993; Richard Zoglin, "Frontier Feminist," *Time*, Mar. 1, 1993.

93. For instance, during the program's opening credits, viewers are presented with a montage of close-ups portraiting Dr. Quinn and all other noteworthy characters. The Cheyennes, however, are depicted as a faceless group on horseback moving against the majestic panorama of Colorado's front range landscape; Bird, "Not My Fantasy," p. 248. On the extermination campaign, see Stan Hoig, *The Sand Creek Massacre* (Norman: University of Oklahoma Press, 1961).

94. Bird, "Not My Fantasy," p. 249.

95. Ibid., p. 251. The "Washita was the second two-hour special that focused on the Cheyenne—an episode from the previous season had followed the same pattern. Again, the suffering of the Cheyenne functions mainly to contrast [Dr. Quinn's] nobility with the brutality of the U.S. army and townspeople. In this show, Black Kettle [a real historical personality who stands in here as Cloud Dancing's "chief"] has been involved in peace talks with the army and is persuaded to accept to accept gifts of food and blankets as part of a settlement. Dr. Quinn helps persuade the Cheyenne to take the blankets, which turn out to be infested with typhus, and the Cheyenne begin to fall sick and die. This becomes a side issue, however, because Michaela's adopted son Matthew also has typhus. On learning this, she leaves the Indians and runs to Matthew, who of course survives . . . By the end of the episode, forty-five Cheyenne are dead, yet somehow the show presents a happy ending, as the townspeople perform a pageant for George Washington's birthday"; ibid., p. 252. The program leaves the impression that the whole thing was probably an "unfortunate accident." For a more accurate interpretation, see Stan Hoig, *The Battle of the Washita* (Garden City, NY: Doubleday, 1976). On the realities of U.S. bacteriological extermination of native peoples, see my "Nits Make Lice," pp. 151–56.

96. Quoted in Bird, "Not My Fantasy," p. 258.

97. Ibid., p. 251.

98. See, e.g., John Yewell, Chris Dodge and Jan DeSirey, eds., *Confronting Columbus: An Anthology* (Jefferson, NC: McFarland, 1992).

99. Bird, "Not My Fantasy," p. 246.

100. Quoted in Stedman, *Shadows*, p. 251. Sampson, a talented actor best known for his portrayal of Chief Broom in *One Flew Over the Cuckoo's Nest*, was habitually put in Tonto roles. Probably the worst example came in a 1976 potboiler, *The White Buffalo*, in which he was cast as Crazy Horse opposite Charles Bronson's Wild Bill Hickock. Together, the pair battle and destroy the most sacred animal of the Lakotas—which is depicted as a gigantic pillaging monster rather than as a normal buffalo with unique pigmentation—becoming "brothers" in the process.

101. Geoffrey York, *The Dispossessed: Life and Death in Native Canada* (Toronto: Little, Brown Canada, 1990) p. 55.

102. Stedman, *Shadows*, pp. 217–18; Tuska, *American West in Film*, p. 256. A clip of this scene is included in the excellent five-part PBS series, *Images of Indians*, produced by Phil Lucas and narrated by Will Sampson.

103. Quoted in Stedman, *Shadows*, p. 72.

104. Ibid., p. 62.

105. Quoted in ibid., p. 71.

106. Quoted in ibid., p. 62.

107. Like *Broken Arrow*'s Jeffords, both Clum and Davis are actual historical figures who wrote about their experiences during the "Apache Wars"; Britton Davis, *The Truth About Geronimo* (Chicago: Lakeside Press, 1951 reprint of 1929 original).

108. The sheer absurdity of placing a white woman on a buckboard amidst the desperately fleeing Cheyennes of the 1878 Breakout could not have been lost on Ford, since his script was ostensibly based on Mari Sandoz's superb *Cheyenne Autumn* (New York: Avon, 1954). Moreover, the author herself was available to serve as a consultant, had he desired. Inclusion of the teacher, however, allowed Ford to soften considerably the genocidal implications of what was actually done to the Cheyennes, and so he proceeded.

109. Little Big Man, be it known, is the name not of a white youngster adopted by the Cheyennes, but of the Oglala Lakota traitor who pinioned Crazy Horse's arms, allowing an army private named William Gentles to bayonet the great warrior through the kidneys in 1877; Robert A. Clark, ed., *The Killing of Chief Crazy Horse* (Lincoln: University of Nebraska Press, 1976). The name's (mis)usage in the Arthur Penn film stems from author Thomas Berger's having decided it was "catchy," and therefore entitling himself to reassign it to the main character of his 1964 novel. For analysis of the social function of the "protest flicks" themselves, see Stewart Brand, "Indians and the Counterculture, 1960s–1970s," in *Handbook of the North American Indian*, p. 570.

110. For "The Duke's" own views on the matter, see Randy Roberts and James S. Olson, *John Wayne: American* (Lincoln: University of Nebraska Press, 1995).

111. Bird, "Not My Fantasy," p. 251. Probably the most extreme example of a white character being scripted to stand in for Indians will be found in *Hombre* (1967), a film in which almost no native people appear at all (other than in a montage behind the opening credits). Instead, their culture is represented exclusively by a white man taken captive as a child and raised among them. At the end of the film, the character, played by Paul Newman, even fulfills the role of Hollywood's "Good Indians" by sacrificing himself to save a white woman in distress.

112. It's not just movies. "Progressive" academics like Werner Sollors and Sam Gill, not to mention the whole "New Age" movement, have been pushing exactly the same "inclusive" themes for nearly thirty years now. On Sollors, Gill, and their counterparts, see the relevant essays in this volume. On New Agers, see "Indians 'R' Us" herein.

113. On the realities of the Wounded Knee Massacre, see my "Nits Make Lice," pp. 244–45.

114. It should be noted that Wounded Knee was still officially designated as the site of a "battle" rather than a massacre until the mid-1970s. The myth of an Indian having fired the first shot still holds sway; Andrist, *The Long Death*, pp. 351–52.

115. Strickland, "Tonto's Revenge," p. 33. Worth noting is that early Lakota actor Chauncy Yellow Robe spent years trying to set the record straight with respect to the glaring inaccuracies so deliberately incorporated into *The Indian Wars Refought*.

116. As to the myth of Custer's being "massacred," it results in part from the unstinting efforts of his widow, Elisabeth Bacon Custer ("Libby"), to redeem his reputation during the remaining years of her long life. In this, she was joined by an army establishment deeply humiliated that one of its crack cavalry regiments had been obliterated by mere "savages." The upshot was/is an absurd contention— repeated some 250 times in books and articles; this relatively incidental battle is far and away the most written-about engagement in U.S. military history—that Custer and the 211 men under his immediate command had been unfairly pitted against about 5,000 Indians. In truth, there were likely fewer than 1,500 poorly armed native fighters in the Little Big Horn Valley on June 25, 1876, against which Custer had available roughly 750 well-equipped and -supplied troopers. See generally, W.A. Graham, *The Custer Myth: A Source Book of Custeriana* (Lincoln: University of Nebraska Press, 1986 reprint of 1953 original); Brian Dippie, *Custer's Last Stand: The Anatomy of an American Myth* (Missoula: University of Montana Press, 1976).

117. The semantics involved were of course not new, finding their origins in the earliest European

expositions on native people; see Honour, *The New Golden Land*; Berkhofer, *The White Man's Indian*. Their impact in cinematic format, however, *was* something new and far more totalizing than what had come before; Andrew Tudor, *Image and Influence: Studies in the Sociology of Film* (New York: St. Martin's, 1975). The insidious persistence of such term usage is perhaps best illustrated by the ubiquitousness with which it appears in serious histories such as Stan Hoig's otherwise excellent *The Sand Creek Massacre* (Norman: University of Oklahoma Press, 1961).

118. Custer—who had been appointed acting major general during the Civil War, but whose actual rank was lieutenant colonel—was court-martialed after deserting his troops in the field towards the end of his unsuccessful 1867 summer campaign against the Cheyenne. Relieved of his command, he was reinstated in time for the 1868 winter campaign—in which he scored his "great victory" at the Washita—only through the intervention of powerful friends like General Phil Sheridan. The triumph was marred, however, by Custer's military incompetence. Having failed to reconnoiter his target before attacking, he gleefully "pitched into" the noncombatant villagers of Black Kettle, thinking they were the only Indians at hand. The orgy of violence which followed—Custer ordered that even the Cheyennes' ponies be slaughtered—was interrupted by the appearance of large numbers of warriors who had been encamped, unnoticed, a bit further upriver. Realizing at that point that he might have an actual fight on his hands, Custer turned tail and ran so quickly that he abandoned a detachment of troops under Major Joel Elliott (a fact that led to the near complete disintegration of morale among the officers of his regiment). Embarrassed, Sheridan and others who had lobbied in his behalf covered up the sordid details. Walsh, for his part, leaves all of this unmentioned despite the fact that the information was readily available at the time he made his film. See generally, Frederick F. Van de Water, *Glory Hunter: A Life of General Custer* (New York: Bobbs-Merrill, 1934).

119. Donald Jackson, *Custer's Gold: The United States Cavalry Expedition of 1874* (Lincoln: University of Nebraska Press, 1966).

120. Although it is dubious that Custer's expedition actually discovered gold in the Black Hills, it is clear that the Custer himself, writing under a pseudonym, reported that it had in eastern newspapers. His purpose was to precipitate a gold rush into the sacred core of Lakota territory, a circumstance against which the Indians would have no alternative but to defend themselves. In the ensuing war, Custer reckoned to win another of his great victories, the glory of which he believed might prove sufficient to propel him into the White House. It was all working out splendidly until he repeated the blunder he'd committed at the Washita by charging into an unreconnoitered native encampment he apparently believed to be filled mostly with noncombatants. Having compounded his error by dividing his regiment into three parts—flanking elements were sent out in both directions so that the quarry would be unable to escape—Custer found himself overmatched when it turned out there were as many or more native fighters along the Little Big Horn as there were troopers in his 7th Cavalry. The chickens then came home to roost in a major way. Custer, far from being the gallant center of the "last stand" depicted in the famous Budweiser poster copied by Walsh and so many other filmmakers, was more likely the very first man hit during his assault. There is also prima facie evidence that he either committed suicide or was dispatched by one of his own men once it was clear that all was lost. One further reason it turned out this way is that Major Marcus Reno and Captain Frederick Benteen, commanders of the two flanking forces and embittered friends of Major Elliott, fatally abandoned by Custer at the Washita, appear to have returned the favor by refusing to come to his assistance once he came under heavy attack. See generally, Van de Water, *Glory Hunter*; Mari Sandoz, *The Battle of the Little Big Horn* (New York: Curtis Books, 1966).

121. Friar and Friar, *Only Good Indian . . .* , pp. 270–71; Tuska, *American West in Film*, pp. 204–9. Also see Rita Parks, *The Western Hero in Film and Television: Mass Media Mythology* (Ann Arbor, MI: UMI Research Press, 1982).

122. Robert M. Utley, *Cavalier in Buckskin: George Armstrong Custer and the Western Military Frontier* (Norman: University of Oklahoma Press, 1988).

123. Tom Hayden, for example, now an apologetic California legislator but then a very prominent antiwar radical, used a quote from Sitting Bull as the title of one of his books; *The Love of Posses-*

sions is a Disease With Them (New York: Holt, Rinehart and Winston, 1972). The sociocultural linkages between Vietnam and the Indian Wars were, however, brought out much better a bit later by Richard Drinnon in his *Facing West*. On the problems experienced by Hollywood in attempting to package the war in Southeast Asia in its customary triumphalist manner, see Gilbert Adair, *Vietnam on Film: From the Green Berets to Apocalypse Now* (New York: Porteus Books, 1981).

124. Tuska, *American West in Film*, p. 209.

125. Although he was never tried for it, three separate federal investigations concluded that Chivington had committed what would now be called crimes against humanity at Sand Creek; Hoig, *Sand Creek Massacre*, pp. 177–92. He is nonetheless treated quite sympathetically by Reginald S. Craig in his *The Fighting Parson: A Biography of Col. John M. Chivington* (Tucson: Western Lore, 1994 reprint of 1959 original). Nelson's screenplay for *Soldier Blue* was based on Theodore V. Olsen's *Arrow in the Sun* (Garden City, NY: Doubleday, 1969).

126. Friar and Friar, *Only Good Indian . . .* , p. 213.

127. Bird, "Not My Fantasy," p. 258.

128. This is hardly the only cinematic context in which such things hold true. For broader discussion, see John E. O'Connor and Martin A. Jackson, eds., *American History/American Film: Interpreting the Hollywood Image* (New York: Frederick Ungar, 1979); George McDonald Fraser, *The Hollywood History of the World* (London: Harvill Press, 1996); Peter C. Collins, ed., *Hollywood as Historian: American Film in a Cultural Context* (Knoxville: University Press of Kentucky, [rev. ed.] 1998).

129. On the pervasiveness and durability of scalp bounties, see my "Nits Make Lice," pp. 178–88. More generally, see Drinnon, *Facing West*; Svaldi, *Rhetoric of Extermination*.

130. Such "stabilizing" effects are examined in Tudor, *Image and Influence*.

131. This was the program dealing with typhus-infected blankets described in note 95. For explication of the phrases quoted, see Noam Chomsky and Edward S. Herman, *The Political Economy of Human Rights, Vol. 2: After the Cataclysm, Postwar Indochina and the Reconstruction of Imperial Ideology* (Boston: South End Press, 1979); Bertram Gross, *Friendly Fascism: The New Face of Power in America* (Boston: South End Press, 1982).

132. Quoted in Bird, "Not My Fantasy," p. 252. One question which is never posed is how a semiliterate frontiersman like Sully, who's plainly never been anywhere *but* the U.S., might be in a position to hold an informed judgment as to which country is best. Extrapolating, the same would hold true today for all the Pittsburgh hardhats and high school seniors who truly believe they are equipped to make that determination. Important glimpses of the answer will be found in books like Jacques Ellul's *Propaganda: The Formation of Men's Attitudes* (New York: Alfred A. Knopf, 1965).

133. Or, to paraphrase by way of borrowing from Noam Chomsky, "enjoy the new order, same as the old"; *World Orders, Old and New* (New York: Columbia University Press, 1996).

134. Eldridge Cleaver, "The Allegory of the Black Eunuchs," in his *Soul on Ice* (New York: Ramparts Books, 1968), pp. 155–75.

135. Ibid. Much has been made by white feminist analysts over the past thirty years of the idea that Cleaver's articulation of this male-centered schematic is evidence of his own virulent sexism; e.g., Robin Morgan, *The Demon Lover: On the Sexuality of Terrorism* (New York: W.W. Norton, 1989) pp. 167, 177. Without denying that he may have been—nay, undoubtedly *was*—a sexist of the first order, I would argue that making the charge on this basis is absurd. Cleaver, after all, was by no means advancing his own notion of how things should be. Rather, he was describing, and quite accurately, how white men saw it, and thus what had been imposed upon blacks and white women alike. Moreover, his conclusion, clearly drawn, is that the whole arrangement is sick, leading to pathological behaviors which he describes with a great deal of precision (but not endorsement). A much better job of treating what is actually objectionable in Cleaver's writing is provided by Michelle Wallace in her *Black Macho and the Myth of the Superwoman* (London: Verso, 1990).

136. Again, Cleaver is describing a white male projection, not endorsing it. White feminists like Susan Brownmiller have wrongly accused him of "justifying" or even "advocating" rape as a "liberatory strategy"; see Brownmiller's *Against Our Will: Men, Women and Rape* (New York: Simon and

Schuster, 1975) pp. 248–52. Rather, in describing his own resort to rape under the misimpression that it constituted a form of "insurrectionary activity," Cleaver was attempting to explain the kind of psychological *deformity* induced among black men by the structure of white male supremacy so that it might be understood and corrected through the formation of a genuinely viable liberatory praxis.

137. 3,724 lynchings were documented in the U.S. during this period; Arthur F. Raper, *The Tragedy of Lynching* (New York: Dover, 1970 reprint of 1933 original). To this tally must be added an unknown number, perhaps doubling the total, occurring between 1865 and 1889, undocumented lynchings occurring between 1889 and 1930, and a not insubstantial number occurring from 1931 onward. A reasonable estimate would thus be that roughly 8,000 black men have been murdered in an organized fashion by whites since the end of the Civil War, largely to deter their peers from even considering the "taking of liberties" with white women. And this does not speak to the thousands of others beaten, mutilated, and/or falsely imprisoned for the same purpose. It is important to bear in mind that much more than literal rape, real or invented, is at issue here. A classic example is that of 14-year-old Emmett Till, beaten to death in 1955 for having *whistled* at a Mississippi white woman. Brownmiller, who, against even this backdrop, is so prone to parsing Cleaver's impassioned prose, should be aware that her own hardly holds up to similar scrutiny. At one point she actually appears to "justify," "endorse," "advocate," or at least "apologize for" lynching and similar atrocities by explaining that she has come to "understand the insult implicit in Emmett Till's wolf whistle" and how such things now fill her with a "murderous rage"; Brownmiller, *Against Our Will*, p. 248. For analysis, see Angela Y. Davis' "Rape, Racism, and the Myth of the Black Rapist," in her *Women, Race, and Class* (New York: Random House, 1981) pp. 172–201.

138. Actually, one can trace the set of relations at issue all the way back to the Spanish system in mid-sixteenth-century Mexico; see, e.g., the section entitled "Notes on Genocide as Art and Recreation," in my *Little Matter of Genocide*, pp. 104–6. In North America, it first evidences itself in the more generalized régime of sexual repression imposed by John Endicott, periodic governor of the Plymouth Plantation, beginning in 1628; Frederick C. Crews, *Sins of the Fathers* (New York: Oxford University Press, 1966). Also see G.E. Thomas, "Puritans, Indians and the Concept of Race" (*New England Quarterly*, XLVIII, 1975) and Philip L. Berg, "Racism and the Puritan Mind" (*Phylon*, Vol. XXXVI, 1975).

139. The first dramatization which might be said to conform in some ways to Cleaver's schematic was James N. Barker's *The Indian Princess; or, La Belle Sauvage*, which opened in Philadelphia in 1808. This was followed by such notable productions as John Augustus Stone's *Metamora; or, the Last of the Wampanoags* (1829), George Washington Parke Custis's *Pocahontas; or, the Settlers of Virginia* (1830), Louisa H. Medina's stage adaptation of *Nick of the Woods* (1838), John Brougham's *Po-Ca-Hon-Tas; or, the Gentle Savage* (1855), David Belasco and Franklin Fyles' *The Girl I Left Behind Me* (1893), William C. De Mille's *Strongheart* (1905), and E.M. Royce's *The Squaw Man* (1905). On the literary front, there were Charles Brockden Brown's *Edgar Huntly; or, Memoirs of a Sleepwalker* (1799) and, of course, the Fenimore Cooper novels, beginning with *The Pioneers* (1823) and ending with *The Deerslayer* (1841). Meanwhile, Washington Irving had weighed in with *The Sketch Book* (1819) and his later trilogy of Indian-focused novels (1835–37), William Gilmore Simms published *The Yemasee* (1835), and Robert Montgomery Bird produced *Nick of the Woods* (1837). A few years later Henry Wadsworth Longfellow came forth with his epic *Song of Hiawatha* (1855). In 1860, the first of the Beadle dime novels (*Malaeska; the Indian Wife of the White Hunter*) was released. Following in the tradition of such early potboilers as *Frontier Maid; or, the Fall of Wyoming* (1819) and *Ontwa, Son of the Forest* (1822), the overwhelmingly positive reception of *Malaeska* laid the groundwork for *The Red Hand; or, Buffalo Bill's First Scalp for Custer*, the initial production of the Col. William F. Cody Theatrical Company in 1876. By 1882, there were a dozen such "Wild West Shows" touring the country. See generally, Albert Keiser, *The Indian in American Literature* (New York: Oxford University Press, 1933); Arthur Hobson Quinn, *Representative American Plays from 1767 to the Present Day* (New York: Appleton-Century-Crofts, 1953); Henry Blackman Sell and Victor Weybright, *Buffalo Bill and the Wild West* (New York: Oxford University Press, 1955) and "Legend Maker of the West—

Erastus Beadle," *Real West Annual*, 1970; Horace A. Melton, "King of the Dime Novels," *Western Frontier Annual*, No. 1, 1975.

140. Director D.W. Griffith appears to have lifted the scene whole from David Belasco's 1893 Broadway play, *The Girl I Left Behind Me*, Stedman, *Shadows*, p. 109.

141. Quoted in Tuska, *American West in Film*, p. 239.

142. Hill conversation.

143. In virtually all the early "captive narratives," such as that of Mary Rowlandson (1682), the women flatly denied that "threats to their chastity" had occurred. Some, like Isabella McCoy (1747), went so far as to assert that their own society's treatment of women was far worse than anything they'd experienced at the hands of Indians. Feminist analysts like Susan Brownmiller, in an effort to develop a transcultural "men = rape" paradigm, have sought to finesse this "problem" by claiming that each woman with firsthand experience was likely to have falsified the record in order to avoid stigma upon returning to white society. While the idea is superficially plausible, it is belied by Brownmiller's own citation of anonymous narratives where such potential consequences were not at issue, all of them saying essentially the same things as those to which names were affixed. Hence, to make their model seem to work, feminists subscribing to Brownmiller's outlook have not only discounted the accounts of female captives but accepted the secondhand libidinal interpretations of Cotton Mather and others among the women's white male counterparts, tracts which more careful researchers like Richard Drinnon have described as being little more than "violence pornography." Frederick Drimmer, compiler of one of the better collections of captive narratives, has concluded that, for a variety of reasons ranging from "medicine" to commerce, indigenous men east of the Mississippi almost never raped anyone, native *or* white, an assessment shared by such analysts as Richard Slotkin. Morris Edward Opler, one of the more knowledgeable students of Chiricahua Apache culture, concludes that these "most vicious of Indians" in the West "were traditionally reticent in sexual matters. The raping of women when on raids was looked upon by Chiricahua[s] with extreme disfavor and rarely took place." See *The Narrative of the Captivity and Restoration of Mrs. Mary Rolandson* (Boston: Houghton-Mifflin, 1930 reprint of 1682 original) p. 71; "Isabella McCoy," in Frederick Dimmler, ed., *Scalps and Tomahawks: Narratives of Indian Captivity* (New York: Howard-McCann, 1961) p. 13; Brownmiller, *Rape*, pp. 140–45; Drinnon, *Facing West*, p. 61; Richard Slotkin, *Regeneration Through Violence: The Mythology of the Western Frontier* (Middletown, CT: Wesleyan University Press, 1973) p. 357; Morris Edward Opler, *An Apache Life-Way: The Economic, Social, and Religious Institutions of the Chiricahua Indians* (Chicago: University of Chicago Press, 1941) p. 228.

144. Quoted in Stedman, *Shadows*, p. 105; Tuska, *American West in Film*, pp. 250, 246.

145. The Cheyennes do no such thing, but Arthur Penn has it that this is because the girl is too homely to arouse their desire rather than because they socially prohibit such conduct.

146. Bird, "Not My Fantasy," p. 249.

147. See Jack Nachbar, "*Ulzana's Raid*," in Pilkington and Graham, *Western Movies*.

148. Tuska, *American West in Film*, pp. 250, 256.

149. The Friars list another sixty such films prior to 1971 without even touching upon the Leatherstocking Tales, serial westerns and the like; Friar and Friar, *Only Good Indian . . .* , pp. 304–5.

150. The film is based on Will Cook's novel, *Comanche Captives* (New York: Bantam, 1960), which is in turn based on one of the more celebrated of the real-life captive stories, that of Cynthia Ann Parker. Taken as a nine-year-old during a Comanche raid along the Texas frontier in May 1836, she was raised as a Quahadi and was plainly viewed as such (not least, by herself). As an adult, she married Pina Nacona, a principal leader of the band, and had two sons and a daughter by him. After being forcibly "restored" to white society in 1860—her husband and several friends were killed in the process—she wasted steadily away and eventually died of what was described as a "broken heart"; Cynthia Schmidt Hacker, *Cynthia Ann Parker: The Life and the Legend* (El Paso: Texas Western Press, 1990). Tellingly, Susan Brownmiller neglects to mention this and a number of comparable examples when asserting that captive white women "had no say in the matter" of marrying Indians, thus conflating such marriages with rape. Worse, in the one case she *does* discuss, that of Mary Jemison,

Brownmiller misrepresents the woman's own account of her marriage by stating that the husband, Sheninjee, was "assigned." Moreover, Brownmiller fails to inform readers that, after her first husband died, Jemison personally selected a second husband, Hiakatoo; Brownmiller, *Rape*, p. 142. Also see James Seaver, *A Narrative of the Life of Mrs. Mary Jemison: Who Was Taken by the Indians When Only About Twelve Years of Age, and Has Continued to Reside Amongst Them to the Present Time* (Albany: n.p., 1824).

151. The film is based on Alan LeMay's novel of the same title, published by Harper & Row in 1954. The book is also based, loosely, on the story of Cynthia Ann Parker. Although Wayne's Ethan Edwards, who seems to be based on Robert Montgomery Bird's revenge-crazed Nathan Slaughter in *Nick of the Woods*, ultimately spares the girl, it is obviously a close call.

152. About the only time it is judged "okay" for celluloid Indians to abscond with Euroamerican females comes in Burt Lancaster's *The Scalphunters* (1968), a complicated and rather weird film, the screenplay for which was written by William Norton. Here, a group of Kiowas end up, with the hero's blessing, in possession of an entire wagonload of white prostitutes. This outcome is possible, presumably, because the women are to be assessed as having already forfeited whatever virtue they might once have possessed. Consignment to the savages is thus an appropriate moral penalty.

153. Tuska, *American West in Film*, p. 248.

154. Ibid.

155. This is another of those tidy inversions of reality at which Hollywood excels. As Leslie Fiedler notes in his *The Return of the Vanishing American* (New York: Stein and Day, 1968, pp. 45–46), to whatever extent native men may finally have come to practice rape, it was plainly in retaliation for the habitual and often systematic molestation of Indian women by white males. Nor can Euroamerican women be classified, or classify themselves, as mere "innocent bystanders and victims" in all this. White women no less than white men were and remain avid in their rationalization/celebration of the conquest/subjugation of native people, a process in which the rape of native women was integral. Often enough, such knowledge was/is explicit. The men of the 7th Cavalry, for example, including Custer himself, customarily raped their female prisoners. Indeed, it was common knowledge that Custer kept Monaseetah, the daughter of a slain Cheyenne leader, as his personal concubine for some months. Libby Custer not only knew it and turned a blind eye, but devoted her life to glorifying her husband's "accomplishments." While thus serving as the enabler in rape is not the same as being a rapist per se, it *is* to be complicit in the crime, and thus by no means "innocent" of it. Those who condone the abuse of others are in a poor position to register complaints when they themselves are subjected to its reciprocation. On Custer, Monaseetah, etc., see Van de Water, *Glory Hunter*.

156. Littlefeather (Marie Louise Cruz), is probably best known for having stood in for Marlon Brando at the Academy Awards ceremony in 1973, when he declined the Oscar for Best Actor as a protest of Hollywood's historical and ongoing misrepresentation of native people.

157. There were a total of six "American Indian-Speaking Females" listed by the Screen Actors Guild in 1971.

158. As is well known, love of the white man is supposed to have prompted Pocahontas to have thrown herself over the prostrate form of the English adventurer, John Smith, in order to prevent his being brained by her father's angry men after Smith had unprovokedly attacked them and gotten himself captured in the process. There is, however, no mention of this fabulous tale in Smith's original 1608 account of his exploits in the Virginia Colony. Rather, he appears to have fabricated it after the woman had already become a celebrity of sorts in England as the result of marrying another colonist, John Rolfe, then taking up residence in London. His motive seems to have been, purely and simply, to enhance the salability, hence profits, of his *General History of Virginia, New England, and the Summer Isles*, published in 1624. From there, the story became a mythic staple of Americana, anchored firmly in J.N. Barker's highly successful 1808 stageplay, *The Indian Princess; or La Belle Sauvage*, and Custis' *Pocahontas* 22 years later (note 139). See generally, Rayna Green, "The Pocahontas Perplex: The Image of Indian Women in American Culture," *Massachusetts Review*, Vol. 16, No. 4, 1975; Tilton, *Pocahontas*.

159. The Friars list nearly 200 such films under various headings; *Only Good Indian* . . . , pp. 309–11.

160. Tilton, *Pocahontas*, p. 3.

161. In the latest remake of *Last of the Mohicans*, director Michael Mann supposedly "solves" the problems of racism and sexism embedded in Fenimore Cooper's formulation by having *both* Uncas and the younger Munro daughter die, he while trying to save her from Magua, the film's "Bad Indian," she by resulting suicide. Hawkeye ("Nathaniel") and the elder daughter, Cora, are, however, allowed to live. Not coincidentally, both are white. The time-honored message thus remains exactly as it was described in other connections by John Tuska: "The ideology is simple: The races should not mix. When they do, the Indians are numerically the biggest losers, while an errant white may pay a penalty no less severe"; *American West in Film*, pp. 240–41.

162. Ibid., pp. 239–40. "The film was so popular that a sequel was made titled *The Squaw Man's Son* (Famous Players, 1917) . . . The next year DeMille directed a remake of the original. . . and he even made a subsequent talking version twice as long as the 1918 remake . . . An Indian actress named Redwing had played the Indian maiden in the original. Ann Little, who was not an Indian but who had played Sky Star in *The Invaders*, had the part in the remake and Lupe Valdez essayed the role in the talking version. In all three versions . . . the audience is reassured that Anglo-American culture is pre-eminent. Moreover, in vanishing, i.e., dying, the Indians give that culture their whole-hearted blessing and wish it well in a future which cannot include them"; ibid., p. 240.

163. Ibid., p. 244.

164. Probably the most duplicitous handling of the "issue" on record comes in *The Conquest of Cochise* (1953), when the Chiricahua leader, played by John Hodiak, is scripted to inform a young woman whom he desires that "Apache law" forbids her to marry a white army officer, Robert Stack, with whom she is in love. Thus is the white-imposed color line foisted off on the Apaches.

165. This is said despite Simone de Beauvoir's valiant effort to rehabilitate the Marquis in her "Must We Burn Sade?" *Les Temps Modernes*, Dec. 1951/Jan. 1952 (reprinted as an introduction to the 1966 Grove Press edition of Sade's *The 120 Days of Sodom and Other Writings*).

166. See Robert H. Rimmer, *The X-Rated Videotape Guide* (New York: Arlington House, 1984); *X-Rated Videotape Guide II: 1,200 New Reviews and Ratings* (Buffalo, NY: Prometheus Books, 1991).

167. It is credibly estimated that virtually all American blacks are to some extent genetically intermixed with whites at this point, and that more than a third are intermixed with Indians as well. By the same token, fewer than ten percent of those identified as American Indians can make any sort of legitimate claim to being free of Euroamerican and/or Afroamerican admixture. Less remarked upon is what this implies with respect to the "purity" of whites. Plainly, the nomenclature of "race" has no applicability in contemporary North America apart from its utility as a eurosupremacist ideological construction. See, e.g., Joel Williamson, *The New People: Miscegenation and Mulattoes in the United States* (New York: Free Press, 1980); Jack D. Forbes, *Black Africans and Native Americans: Race, Color and Caste in the Making of Red-Black Peoples* (London: Routledge, 1988); George M. Frederickson, *White Supremacy: A Comparative Study in American and South African History* (New York: Oxford University Press, 1981).

168. For a range of quotes by Jefferson to this effect, see Bernard W. Sheehan, *Seeds of Extinction: Jeffersonian Philanthropy and the American Indian* (Chapel Hill: University of North Carolina Press, 1973). Morgan's views are presented in Bernard J. Stern's *Lewis Henry Morgan: Social Evolutionist* (New York: Russell and Russell, 1931) and Carl Resek's *Lewis Henry Morgan: American Scholar* (Chicago: University of Chicago Press, 1960).

169. See, e.g., the quotes from phrenologist J.C. Nott and others in Berkhofer, *White Man's Indian*, pp. 58–59. More broadly, see William Stanton's *The Leopard's Spots: Scientific Attitudes Towards Race in America, 1815–1859* (Chicago: University of Chicago Press, 1960). For analysis of contemporary applications, see Troy Duster's *Backdoor to Eugenics* (New York: Routledge, 1990).

170. Wyn Craig Wade, *The Fiery Cross: The Ku Klux Klan in America* (New York: Simon and Schuster, 1987) pp. 119–39.

171. The Friars list 108 films pursuing this theme by 1970; *Only Good Indian . . .* , pp. 300–1.

172. Among the Cheyennes, there were the brothers George, Robert, and Charlie Bent, sons of William Bent, a noted white trader, and his native wife. While each struggled for their people's rights in his own way—George, for instance, fought briefly against the white invaders and testified on three separate occasions against perpetrators of the Colorado militia's infamous 1864 massacre of noncombatant Cheyennes and Arapahos at Sand Creek—Charlie is the better example (or at least the most reviled among mainstream commentators). Accepted into the Cheyennes' élite Crazy Dog Society ("Dog Soldiers"), he acquired an almost legendary status because of his courage in physically defending his homeland. Ultimately, Charlie Bent gave his all, dying an agonizingly lingering death in 1868 of wounds suffered during a skirmish with Pawnees fighting for the United States. It is instructive that while William Bent and his son George are frequently referenced in the literature, there is virtually no mention of Charlie. When his name comes up at all, it is almost invariably as a negative aside. Probably the best all-round study of the Bent family is David Lavender's *Bent's Fort* (Garden City, NY: Doubleday, 1954). On the Crazy Dogs, see, e.g., George Bird Grinnell, *The Fighting Cheyennes* (Norman: University of Oklahoma Press, 1956).

173. As Jerry Allen pointed out in his article "Tom Sawyer's Town" (*National Geographic*, July 1956), the real life personage upon whom Twain (Samuel Clemens) based the character was actually a man called "Indian Bill," a "kindly old rag-picker" in Hannibal, Missouri. There is of course no hint of this in such subsequent screen adaptations of Twain's novels as *The Adventures of Huckleberry Finn* (1960; 1985), *Tom Sawyer* (1973), *The Adventures of Mark Twain* (1985), *The Adventures of Huck Finn* (1993), and *Tom and Huck* (1995).

174. Alan LeMay, *The Unforgiven* (New York: Harper & Bros., 1957); quoted in Stedman, *Shadows*, pp. 124–25. Nomination of the film as "most racist" was made by Will Sampson in *Images of the Indian*. While I don't necessarily disagree with him, I feel the dubious distinction should be shared by *The Searchers*—also based on a LeMay novel—and perhaps *The Stalking Moon.*

175. Such lines were hardly a cinematic first. In *They Rode West* (1954), for instance, when the hero, an army captain, is told that there are "some people" moving around outside the fort, he responds: "*People?* You mean *Indians!*"

176. For an apt assessment of the schisms such racist value-loading has caused among Indians, see Hilden, *Nickels*. Perhaps the most crushing indictment of the entire conceptual structure will be found in Ashley Montague's *Man's Most Dangerous Myth: The Fallacy of Race* (Cleveland: World, [4th ed.] 1964). Also see Steven Jay Gould's *The Mismeasure of Man* (New York: W.W. Norton, 1981).

177. The *Ramona* films are based on Helen Hunt Jackson's factually based novel of the same title (Boston: Little, Brown, 1921 reprint of 1884 original), a classic of turn-of-the-century "reformist" literature. In it, a mixed-blood girl first "goes Indian" by way of marriage, then returns to the fold after her husband is murdered by a white man.

178. Strickland, "Tonto's Revenge," p. 21.

179. *Walker* premiered on Nov. 24, 1993. About the only thing observably "Indian" about the character is that he stops in, every episode, to visit with his "Uncle Ray," played by Floyd Westerman, an "actor" who can't for the life of him deliver a convincing line, but who apparently fulfills the show's requirements merely by looking like he just stepped off a nickel. Racism takes many forms, often subtle.

180. "Gregory Peck recalled that David O. Selznik delighted in the perversity of the casting. Jennifer Jones had recently won an Oscar as the saint in *Song of Bernadette* (1943) and Peck had just played a priest in *Keys to the Kingdom* (1944)"; Strickland, "Tonto's Revenge," p. 27.

181. Peter van Lent, "'Her Beautiful Savage': The Current Sexual Image of the Native American Male," in Bird, *Dressing in Feathers*, pp. 216–17.

182. Fabio, *Comanche* (New York: Avon, 1995). Van Lent himself notes the plot, but fails to draw the obvious conclusion.

183. See Peter G. Beidler, "The Contemporary Indian Romance: A Review Essay," *American Indian Culture and Research Journal*, Vol. 15, No. 4, 1991.

184. Phil Lucas, "Images of Indians," *Four Winds*, Autumn 1980.

185. Berkhofer, *White Man's Indian*.

186. Francis, *Imaginary Indian*, pp. 16–43. For background, see Robert J. Moore, Jr., *Native Americans, A Portrait: The Art and Travels of Charles Bird King, George Catlin, and Karl Bodmer* (New York: Stewart, Tabori & Chang, 1997); J. Russell Harper, ed., *Paul Kane's Frontier* (Toronto: University of Toronto Press, 1975). For specific applications, see Rennard Strickland, *Bodmer and Buffalo Bill at the Bijou: Hollywood Images and Indian Realities* (Dallas: DeGoyler Library, 1989).

187. Susan Sontag, *On Photography* (New York: Farrar, Straus & Giroux, 1977) p. 4; Francis, *Imaginary Indian*, p. 43.

188. Francis, *The Imaginary Indian*, p. 221.

189. Ibid., p. 194.

190. The poster, a major bit of Americana, derives from a painting entitled "Custer's Last Fight," done on a tent fly by Cassily Adams, purchased by St. Louis beer magnate Adolphus Busch and displayed in a saloon in that city while a somewhat altered copy was produced. The latter, retitled "Custer's Last Stand," was then cloned into a massively reproduced advertising poster by the Anheuser-Busch Corporation while the original was donated to the 7th Cavalry, who displayed it in their officer's club at Fort Bliss, Texas, until it was destroyed by a fire on June 13, 1946. Meanwhile, the poster was itself being imitated, most famously by Elk Eber, whose painting remains at present in the Karl May Museum in Dresden, Germany; Graham, *Custer Myth*, pp. 22, 348.

191. As Russell Means once put it, "[W]ho seems most expert at dehumanizing other people? And why? Soldiers who have seen a lot of combat learn to do this to the enemy before going back into combat. Murderers do it before they commit murder. SS guards did it to concentration camp inmates. Cops do it. Corporation leaders do it to workers they send into uranium mines and to work in steel mills. Politicians do it to everyone in sight. And what each process of dehumanization has in common for each group doing the dehumanizing is that it makes it alright to kill and otherwise destroy other people. One of the Christian commandments is 'thou shall not kill,' at least other humans, so the trick is to mentally convert the victims into non-humans. Then you can proclaim violation of your own commandment to be a virtue"; "The Same Old Song," in my *Marxism and Native Americans* (Boston: South End Press, 1983) p. 22. On material/physical conditions, see Rennard Strickland, "'You Can't Rollerskate in a Buffalo Herd Even If You Have All the Medicine': American Indian Law and Policy," in *Tonto's Revenge*, pp. 53–54.

192. Robin Wood, "Shall We Gather at the River? The Late Films of John Ford," *Film Comment*, Fall 1971.

193. Tuska, *American West in Film*, p. 237.

194. John H. Lenihan, *Showdown: Confronting Modern America in the Western Film* (Urbana: University of Illinois Press, 1980) p. 141. As Tuska observes in this connection, "A book such as Lenihan's, which was considered sufficiently well researched for him to earn a Ph.D. on the basis of it, actually does little more than extend the propaganda contained in the films themselves"; *American West in Film*, p. 251.

195. Nachbar, "*Ulzana's Raid*," p. 140. More extensively, see Jack Nachbar, *Focus on the Western* (New York: Prentice-Hall, 1974).

196. The phrase accrues from Thomas A. Harris's classic of "transactional analysis" (read: self-absorbed 1970s-style yuppism), *I'm OK—You're OK* (New York: Avon Books, 1973). It's a testament to how far affluent whites are from actually being "okay" that this volume still sells quite briskly.

197. This is really not that far off when one considers the implications of Ronald Reagan's 1986 state visit to the German military cemetery at Bitburg, during which he laid a wreath near the graves of SS men who, he said, "were victims, too." For various viewpoints on the meaning of Reagan's conduct, see Geoffrey Hartman, ed., *Bitburg in Moral and Political Perspective* (Bloomington: University Press of Indiana, 1986); also see Ilya Levkov, ed., *Bitburg and Beyond: Encounters in American, German, and Jewish History* (New York: Shapolsky, 1987).

198. No less than Steven Spielberg has already taken the first significant step in this direction with

his 1993 *Schindler's List*, a film explicitly devoted to a "good nazi." One still awaits an equally competent and compelling treatment of "bad nazis."

199. For examples of how this could work in practice, see David Stewart Hull, *Film in the Third Reich: A Study of German Cinema, 1933–1945* (Berkeley: University of California Press, 1969); Irwin Leiser, *Nazi Cinema* (New York: Macmillan, 1974); Eric Rentschler, *The Ministry of Illusion: Nazi Cinema and Its Afterlife* (Cambridge, MA: Harvard University Press, 1996).

200. Quoted in Friar and Friar, *Only Good Indian . . .* , p. 218.

201. See "Confronting Columbus Day" and "Let's Spread the Fun Around," herein. Also see the essay entitled "In the Matter of Julius Streicher: Applying Nuremberg Standards to the United States," in my *From A Native Son: Selected Essays in Indigenism, 1985–1995* (Boston: South End Press, 1996) pp. 445–54.

202. Tuska, *American West in Film*, p. 258.

203. Ibid.

204. Durham, "Cowboys and . . . ," pp. 18–19.

205. Jean-Paul Sartre, "On Genocide," *Ramparts*, Feb. 1968.

206. Anonymous respondant, quoted in Bird, "Not My Fantasy," p. 258.

207. On simulacra see Jean Baudrillard, *Simulations* (New York: Semiotext(e), 1983). More accessibly, see J.G. Merquoir, *The Veil and the Mask: Essays on Culture and Ideology* (London: Routledge & Kegan Paul, 1979); Noam Chomsky, *Necessary Illusions: Thought Control in Democratic Societies* (Boston: South End Press, 1989).

208. Strickland, "Tonto's Revenge," pp. 17–18.

209. For an excellent overview of the actual situations confronted by the men upon whom such characters are ostensibly based, see Tom Holm, *Strong Hearts, Wounded Souls: Native American Veterans of the Vietnam War* (Austin: University of Texas Press, 1996).

210. Laughlin (T.C. Frank) is a noted Jungian psychologist who seems in some ways to have approached his low-budget films as a kind of experiment in determining the extent to which certain "archetypes" might be substituted for quality—or even coherence—among movie audiences. He began with *The Born Losers* (1967), a self-produced travesty worthy of Turner Network Television's "Joe Bob Briggs Drive-In Theater." Although it suffered poor distribution, the film generated sufficient interest among younger viewers to warrant minor financial backing for a sequel. This turned out to be *Billy Jack*, a reworking and refinement of the original script which, despite an overload of wooden acting and a plot laced with absurdity, became a temporary sensation among the more self-consciously anti-establishmentarian of the country's young people. Apparently bemused by the magnitude of this success, Laughlin followed up with *The Trial of Billy Jack*, to all appearances a deliberately overlong (175 minutes) and nakedly implausible tale designed to test the outer limits of his *Billy Jack* formula. Convinced by the results that he'd seriously overreached, he tried again, seeking the middle ground with *Billy Jack Goes to Washington*, a marginally better picture—albeit an obviously contrived New Age remake of the classic *Mr. Smith Goes to Washington* (1939)—which flopped resoundingly, thus putting an end to Laughlin/Frank's research into American mass psychology; see generally, Brand, "Indians and the Counterculture."

211. Even so staid a reviewer as Leonard Maltin describes *War Party* as "an excuse for a cowboy and Indians movie" and "just another botched opportunity for Hollywood to shed light on the problems of the American Indian"; *Leonard Maltin's 1999 Movie & Video Guide* (New York: Signet Books, 1999) p. 1494.

212. *Son of the Morning Star* is based on Evan Connell's biography of Custer bearing the same title (San Francisco: North Point Press, 1984), but is too confused in its character development to classify. *The Broken Chain* is based on various biographies of the eighteenth-century Mohawk leader Joseph Brant as well as Francis Jennings' *The Ambiguous Iroquois Empire: The Covenant Chain Confederation of Indian Tribes with the New England Colonies* (New York: W.W. Norton, 1984), but is too thin to do its topic(s) justice. *Lakota Woman*, based very loosely on the already problematic autobiography of the same title authored by Richard Erdoes in behalf of Mary Crow Dog, may not even admit to being

marginally more accurate than the usual Hollywood fare. *Crazy Horse* seems based more than anything on Mari Sandoz's *Crazy Horse: Strange Man of the Oglalas* (Lincoln: University of Nebraska Press, 1942). It is the best of the lot, but by no means good cinema; "TNT Film Chronicles Sioux Legend from Crazy Horse's Point of View," *Sunday Oklahoman Television News Magazine*, July 7, 1996.

213. In an attempt to make it seem "progressive," the title of the last movie was consciously appropriated from Kirkpatrick Sale's benchmark study, *The Conquest of Paradise: Christopher Columbus and the Columbian Legacy* (New York: Alfred A. Knopf, 1990). Its content, however, was much closer to the stale mythology found in Samuel Eliot Morison's *Admiral of the Ocean Sea: A Life of Christopher Columbus* (Boston: Little, Brown, 1942).

214. Taylor, "*Northern Exposure*," p. 239.

215. On the series, see Kenneth C. Kaleta, *David Lynch* (New York: Twayne, 1993) pp. 133–55.

216. Unfortunately, most nonindian viewers seem to walk away with the misimpression that the vicious Indian character played by Graham Greene is intended to be real rather than a figment of the white lawyer's imagination. Actually, the attorney, played by Ron Lea, conjures the Greene character up in his own mind as a signification of how Indians seem to him entitled to respond to the kinds and severity of white transgression we suffer. Meanwhile, the lawyer is himself acting out the fantasy.

217. This is in some ways an extraordinarily complicated film; see, e.g., Gregg Rickman, "The Western Under Erasure: *Dead Man*," in Jim Kitses and Gregg Rickman, eds., *The Western Reader* (New York: Limelight, 1998) pp. 381–404.

218. Some years ago at a film festival in Toronto, Greene, who'd recently received an Academy Award nomination as Best Supporting Actor for his role in *Dances With Wolves*, explained that he wouldn't figure he'd really "made it" in his profession until, and not before, he could be cast in nonindian parts as readily as nonindians have been historically cast as Indians. By this definition, he "arrived" in the 1995 action flick, *Die Hard With a Vengeance*, when he was hired to play a New York City Police detective of no particular ethnicity. Farmer was also selected to play a nonethnic role in the 1996 Canadian release, *Moonshine Highway*. It should be noted that, despite the inclusion of numerous secondary white actors, there are entries for neither Greene nor Farmer—nor even Will Sampson—in such standard cinematic references as *Leonard Maltin's Movie Guide* and Ephraim Katz's *The Film Encyclopedia* (New York: HarperPerennial, [3rd ed.] 1998). See generally, Millie Knapp, "Graham Greene: Leading Man," *Aboriginal Voices*, Vol. 3, No. 2, 1996.

219. Strickland, "Tonto's Revenge," p. 32.

220. Ibid.

221. See note 102.

222. Strickland, "Tonto's Revenge," p. 35.

223. Ibid.

224. On Massayesva in particular, see the entry in Lori Zippay, ed., *Artists' Video: An International Guide* (New York: Electronic Arts Intermix and Abbeville Press, 1991) p. 139. More broadly, see Beverly R. Singer, *Wiping the Warpaint Off the Lens: Native American Film and Video* (Minneapolis: University of Minnesota Press, 2001).

225. Strickland, "Tonto's Revenge," p. 36.

226. Greg Sarris, *Grand Avenue: A Novel in Stories* (New York: Penguin, 1994). Also see Alison Schneider, "Words as Medicine: Professor Writes of Urban Indians from the Heart," *Chronicle of Higher Education*, July 19, 1996.

227. The *Times* comment was made by Modoc author Michael Dorris, quoted in Strickland, "Tonto's Revenge," p. 43. Also see Miles Morrisseau, "Irene Bedard: In a Place of Being," *Aboriginal Voices*, Vol. 4, No. 4, 1997.

228. See my and Leah Renae Kelly's "*Smoke Signals* in Context: An Historical Overview," in her *In My Own Voice: Explorations in the Sociopoloitical Context of Art and Cinema* (Winnipeg: Arbeiter Ring, 2001) pp. 123–31.

229. Sherman Alexie, *The Lone Ranger and Tonto Fistfight in Heaven* (New York: Atlantic Monthly Press, 1993); *Smoke Signals* (New York: Hyperion, 1998).

230. The first Pequot award, in the amount of $700,000, was made to Valerie Red-Horse/Red-Horse Productions in August 1997 to support a film entitled *Naturally Native*. Starring Irene Bedard and *Northern Exposure*'s Kimberly Norris Guerrero, the movie premiered at the 1998 Sundance festival and saw video release in early 1999; Millie Knapp, "A Fabulous First," *Aboriginal Voices*, Vol. 5, No. 3, 1998.

231. bell hooks, *Reel to Real: Race, Sex and Class at the Movies* (New York: Routledge, 1996).

10. INDIANS 'R' US

1. Bly's political dimension began to take form with publication of his interview "What Men Really Want" in *New Age*, May 1982. For an overview of his verse, see Robert Bly, *Selected Poems* (New York: Harper & Row, 1986). Earlier collections include *Silence in the Snowy Fields* (Middletown, CT: Wesleyan University Press, 1962), *This Body Is Made from Camphor and Gopherwood* (New York: Harper & Row, 1977), *This Tree Will Be Here for a Thousand Years* (New York: Harper & Row, 1979), *News of the Universe* (San Francisco: Sierra Club Books, 1981), *The Man in the Black Coat Turns* (Garden City, NY: Doubleday, 1981), and *Loving a Woman in Two Worlds* (Garden City, NY: Doubleday, 1985).

2. See Susieday, "Male Liberation," *Z Magazine*, June 1993, pp. 10–12. The author cites a *Newsweek* poll indicating that some 48 percent of Euroamerican males believe they are being "victimized" by a "loss of influence" in U.S. society. She points out that, by this, they appear to mean that they've been rendered marginally less empowered to dominate everyone else than they were three decades ago. Their response is increasingly to overcome this perceived victimization by finding ways and means, often through cooptation of the liberatory methods developed by those they're accustomed to dominating, of reestablishing their "proper authority."

3. Statements by Robert Bly during workshop session at the University of Colorado/Boulder, 1992.

4. Robert Bly, *Iron John: A Book About Men* (Reading, MA: Addison-Wesley, 1990). The title is taken from the fairy tale "The Story of Iron John" by Jacob and Wilhelm Grimm, of which Bly provides his own translation from the German.

5. As examples, see Patrick M. Arnold, *Wildmen, Warriors and Kings: Masculine Spirituality and the Bible* (New York: Crossroad, 1991); Robert Moore and Douglas Gillette, *King, Warrior, Magician, Lover: Rediscovering the Archetypes of Masculine Nature* (New York: Harper & Row, 1990); R.J. Stewart, *Celebrating the Male Mysteries* (Bath, U.K.: Arcania, 1991); and Kenneth Wetcher, Art Barker and F.W. McCaughtry, *Save the Males: Why Men Are Mistreated, Misdiagnosed, and Misunderstood* (Washington, D.C.: Pia Press, 1991). Anthologies include John Matthews' *Choirs of the God: Revisioning Masculinity* (London: HarperMandala, 1991); and Christopher Harding's *Wingspan: Inside the Men's Movement* (New York: St. Martin's Press, 1992). Or, in another medium, try Robert Moore, *Rediscovering Men's Potentials* (Wilmette, IL: Chiron, 1988; set of four cassette tapes).

6. Consider, for example, *Shaman's Drum* (produced in Willis, CA), described as a "glossy quarterly 'journal of experiential shamanism,' native medicineways, transpersonal healing, ecstatic spirituality, and caretaking the earth. Includes regional calendars, resource directory, information on drums."

7. Wallace Black Elk, an Oglala Lakota, is a former apprentice to Sicangu (Brûlé) Lakota spiritual leader Leonard Crow Dog and was a member of the American Indian Movement during the period of the Wounded Knee siege (*circa* 1972–76). Subsequently, he became associated with the late "Sun Bear" (Vincent LaDuke), a Chippewa who served as something of a prototype for plastic medicine men, and discovered the profit potential of peddling ersatz Indian spirituality to New Agers. Despite the fact that he is *not*, as he claims, the grand nephew of the Black Elk made famous by John Neihardt (*Black Elk Speaks* [Lincoln: University of Nebraska Press, 1963]) and Joseph Epes Brown (*The Sacred Pipe* [Norman: University of Oklahoma Press, 1953])—it's an entirely different family—"Grampa Wallace" has become a favorite icon of the Men's Movement. In fact, the movement has

made him something of a best-selling author; see Wallace Black Elk and William S. Lyon, *Black Elk: The Sacred Ways of the Lakota* (San Francisco: Harper, 1991).

8. The Sun Dance is the central ceremony of Lakota ritual life; the geographical reference is to "Crow Dog's Paradise," near Grass Mountain, on the Rosebud Reservation in South Dakota.

9. Another obvious alternative to "American Indianism" might be for the Men's Movement to turn toward certain warrior-oriented strains of Buddhism or even Shintoism. But then, Bly and the boys would be compelled to compete directly—both financially and theologically—with much more longstanding and refined institutions of spiritual appropriation like the Naropa Institute. Enterprises preoccupied with the various denominations of Islam are similarly well rooted in North America.

10. Statement made at the Socialist Scholars Conference, New York, 1988.

11. Letter to the author, Nov. 14, 1985.

12. The AIM resolution specifically identified several native people—Sun Bear, Wallace Black Elk, and the late Grace Spotted Eagle (Oglala Lakota) among them—as being primary offenders. Also named were nonindians, including Cyfus McDonald, "Osheana Fast Wolf," and "Brooke Medicine Eagle" (spelled "Medicine Ego" in the document), and one nonindian organization, Vision Quest, Inc. For the complete text, see my *Fantasies of the Master Race: Literature, Cinema and the Colonization of American Indians* (Monroe, ME: Common Courage Press, 1992) pp. 226–28.

13. The resolution was signed by Tom Yellowtail (Crow), Larry Anderson (Navajo), Izador Thom (Lummi), Thomas Banyacya (Hopi), Walter Denni (Chippewa-Cree), Austin Two Moons (Northern Cheyenne), Tadadaho (Haudenosaunee), Frank Fools Crow (Oglala Lakota), Frank Cardinal (Cree), and Peter O'Chiese (Anishinabe), all well-respected traditional spiritual leaders within their respective nations. For the complete text, see ibid., pp. 223–25.

14. For complete text, see *Oyate Wicaho*, Vol. 2, No. 3, Nov. 1982.

15. See "Declaration of War Against Exploiters of Lakota Spirituality," included as an attachment in my *Indians Are Us? Culture and Genocide in Native North America* (Monroe, ME: Common Courage Press, 1994) pp. 273–77.

16. See "Alert Concerning the Abuse and Exploitation of American Indian Sacred Traditions," included as an attachment in *Indians Are Us?*, pp. 279–81.

17. Sherman Alexie, "White Men Can't Drum: In Going Native for Its Totems, the Men's Movement Misses the Beat," *New York Times Magazine*, Oct. 4, 1992. For a Men's Movement perspective on the importance of drumming, and association (in their minds) with African and American Indian rituals, see George A. Parks, "The Voice of the Drum," in Harding, *Wingspan*, pp. 206–13.

18. Paul Reitman, "*Clearcut*: Ritual Gone Wrong," *Men's Council Journal*, No. 16, Feb. 1993, p. 17.

19. Paul Shippee, "Among the Dog Eaters," *Men's Council Journal*, No. 16, Feb. 1993, pp. 7–8.

20. Telephone conversation, June 7, 1993. Means' comparisons to Eichmann and the Aryan Nation are not merely hyperbolic. Adolf Eichmann, SS "Jewish liaison" and transportation coordinator for the Holocaust, actually asserted on numerous occasions that he felt himself to be a zionist; see Hannah Arendt, *Eichmann in Jerusalem: A Report on the Banality of Evil* (New York: Viking, 1963) p. 40. On the "True Jew" dogma of "Identity Christianity," religious creed of the rabidly antisemitic Idaho-based Aryan Nations, see Leonard Zeskind, *The Christian Identity Movement: A Theological Justification for Racist and Anti-Semitic Violence* (New York: Division of Church and Society of the National Council of Churches of Christ in the U.S.A., 1986).

21. Means' characterization of the process corresponds quite well with the observations of many experts on cultural genocide. Consider, for example, the statement made by Mark Davis and Robert Zannis in their book, *The Genocide Machine in Canada: The Pacification of the North* (Montréal: Black Rose Books, 1973, p. 137): "If people suddenly lose their 'prime symbol' [such as the sanctity of spiritual tradition], the basis of their culture, their lives lose meaning. They become disoriented, with no hope. A social disorganization often follows such a loss, they are often unable to ensure their own survival . . . The loss and human suffering of those whose culture has been healthy and is suddenly attacked and disintegrated is incalculable."

22. Statement made at the 1982 Western Social Science Association Annual Conference; quoted in *Fantasies*, p. 190.

23. Ibid., pp. 190–91.

24. Alexie, "White Men Can't Drum."

25. Ibid. The final example refers to an anecdote with which Alexie opens his article: "Last year on the local television news, I watched a short feature on a meeting of the Confused White Men chapter in Spokane, Wash. They were all wearing war bonnets and beating drums, more or less. A few of the drums looked as if they might have come from Kmart, and one or two of the men just beat their chests. 'It's not just the drum,' the leader of the group said, 'it's the idea of the drum.' I was amazed at the lack of rhythm and laughed, even though I knew I supported a stereotype. But it's true: White men can't drum. They fail to understand that a drum is more than a heartbeat. Sometimes it is the sound of thunder, and many times it just means some Indians want to dance."

26. Quoted in *Fantasies*, p. 194. It should be noted that Means' sentiments correspond perfectly with those expressed by Gerald Wilkinson, head of politically much more conservative National Indian Youth Council, in a letter endorsing an action planned by Colorado AIM to halt the sale of ceremonies to nonindians in that state by Sun Bear in 1983: "The National Indian Youth Council fully supports your efforts to denounce, embarrass, disrupt, or otherwise run out of Colorado, [Sun Bear's] Medicine Wheel Gathering . . . For too long the Bear Tribe Medicine Society has been considered repugnant but harmless to Indian people. We believe they not only line their pockets but do great damage to us all. Anything you can do to them will not be enough." Clearly, opposition to the misuse and appropriation of spiritual traditions is a transcendently unifying factor in Indian Country.

27. For an excellent overview of the German hobbyist tradition from its inception in the early twentieth century, see Hugh Honour, *The New Golden Land: European Images of the Indian from the Discovery to the Present Time* (New York: Pantheon, 1975).

28. Interestingly, at least some hobbyist replica objects—all of them produced by men who would otherwise view such things as "women's work"—are of such high quality that they have been exhibited in a number of ethnographic museums throughout Europe.

29. This seems to be something of a tradition on "The Continent." As examples, "William Augustus Bowles, an American Tory dressed up as an Indian, managed to pass in the upper crust of London's society in 1791 as 'commander-in-chief of the Creek and Cherokee' nations . . . A person calling himself Big Chief White Horse Eagle, whose somewhat fictional autobiography was written by a German admirer (Schmidt-Pauli 1931), found it profitable to travel Europe in the 1920s and 1930s, adopting unsuspecting museum directors and chairmen of anthropology departments into his tribe . . . None of them, however, could match the most flamboyant fake Indian to visit Europe . . . This party, named Capo Cervo Bianco (Chief White Elk), arrived in Italy during the 1920s, claiming to be on his way to the League of Nations to represent the Iroquois of upstate New York. He was received by Mussolini and for a time managed to live richly out of his believers' purses [until he was] exposed as an Italo-American by the name of Edgardo Laplant"; Christian F. Feest, "Europe's Indians," in James A. Clifton, ed., *The Invented Indian: Cultural Fictions & Government Policies* (New Brunswick, NJ: Transaction, 1990) pp. 322–23. The reference is to Edgar von Schmidt-Pauli, *We Indians: The Passion of a Great Race by Big Chief White Horse Eagle* (London: Macmillan, 1931).

30. Feest, "Europe's Indians," p. 323.

31. "Freesoul" claims to be the "sacred pipe carrier" of something called the "Redtail Hawk Medicine Society . . . established by Natan Lupan and James Blue Wolf . . . in 1974 . . . fulfill[ing a] Hopi prophecy that new clans and societies shall emerge as part of a larger revival and purification of the Red Road"; see John Redtail Freesoul, *Breath of the Invisible: The Way of the Pipe* (Wheaton, IL: Theosophical Publishing House, 1986) pp. 104–5. For a heavy dose of the sort of metaphysical gibberish passed off as "traditional Cherokee religion" by "Ywahoo" and her Sunray Meditation Foundation, see her *Voices of Our Ancestors* (Boston: Shambala Press, 1987).

32. Feest, "Europe's Indians," p. 323. For detailed exposure of Carlos Castaneda as a fraud, see

Richard De Mille, *Castaneda's Journey: The Power and the Allegory* (Santa Barbara, CA: Capra Press, 1976). In his recent essay "Of Wild Men and Warriors," moreover, Euroamerican Men's Movement practitioner Christopher X. Burant posits *Tales of Power* by "C.M. Castaneda" as one of his major sources; Harding, *Wingspan*, p. 176.

33. The Sun Dance is both culturally and geographically specific, and thus totally misplaced in the Black Forest among Germans. By extension, of course, this makes the series of Sun Dances conducted by Leonard Crow Dog in the Big Mountain area of the Navajo Nation, in Arizona, over the past twenty years equally misplaced and sacrilegious. A culturally specific ceremony is no more a "Pan-Indian" phenomenon than it is transcultural in any other sense.

34. Tipis were never designed to serve as mountain dwellings, which is why no American Indian people has ever used them for that purpose.

35. For a classic and somewhat earlier example of this sort of adoption of "Indian identity" by a German, see the book by Adolf Gutohrlein, who called himself "Adolf Hungry Wolf," *The Good Medicine* (New York: Warner, 1973). Also see the volume he coauthored with his Blackfeet wife, Beverly, *Shadows of the Buffalo* (New York: William Morrow, 1983).

36. Feest, "Europe's Indians," pp. 313–32. For a broader view on this and related matters, see the selections from several analysts assembled by Feest as *Indians and Europe: An Interdisciplinary Collection of Essays* (Aachen: Rader Verlag, 1987).

37. The roots of this perspective extend deep within the European consciousness, having been first articulated in clear form at least as early as the 1703 publication of a book by the Baron de Lahontan (Louis-Armand Lom d'Arce) entitled *New Voyages to North-America* (Chicago: A.C. McClurg & Co., 1905 reprint).

38. Feest, "Europe's Indians," p. 327.

39. Concerning the fantasy dimension of hobbyist projections about "Indianness," Dutch analyst Ton Lemaire probably put it best (in Feest's translation): "On closer look, these 'Indians' turn out to be a population inhabiting the European mind, not the American landscape, a fictional assemblage fabricated over the past five centuries to serve specific cultural and emotional needs of its inventors"; *De Indiaan In Ons Bewustzijn: De Ontmoeting van de Oude met de Nieuwe Wereld* (Baarn, Netherlands: Ambo S.V., 1986).

40. Implications attending use of the term "Wildman" in the European context, from which Robert Bly borrowed the concept, sheds a certain light on the U.S. Men's Movement's deployment of the term. From there, the real attitudes of both groups regarding American Indians stands partially revealed. See Susi Colin, "The Wild Man and the Indian in Early 16th Century Illustration," in Feest, *Indians and Europe*, pp. 5–36.

41. Absent the appropriative fetishism regarding American Indian spiritual life marking the Men's Movement, there is a remarkable similarity between its composition and sentiments and those of another group of "Indian lovers" whose activities spawned disastrous consequences for native people during the nineteenth century. See Francis Paul Prucha, *Americanizing the American Indian: Writings of the "Friends of the Indian," 1800–1900* (Lincoln: University of Nebraska Press, 1973).

42. There was some talk among German activists, while I was in Germany during May 1993, of disrupting Bly's planned tour in July.

43. For analysis of the extent and implications of such activities on U.S. and Canadian reservation lands, see my *Struggle for the Land: Native North American Resistance to Genocide, Ecocide and Colonization* (Winnipeg: Arbeiter Ring, [2nd ed.] 1999). Also see "A Breach of Trust," herein.

44. This represents an interesting inversion of the psychosis, in which the oppressed seeks to assume the identity of the oppressor, analyzed by Frantz Fanon in his *Black Skin, White Masks: The Experiences of a Black Man in a White World* (New York: Grove Press, 1967). Perhaps an in-depth study of the Men's Movement should be correspondingly entitled *White Skin, Red Masks*.

45. In terms of content, this comparison of nazi mysticism to that of the Men's Movement is not superficial. Aside from preoccupations with a fantastic vision of "Indianness"—Hitler's favorite author was Karl May, writer of a lengthy series of potboilers on the topic—nazi "spirituality" focused

upon the mythos of the Holy Grail; see Nicholas Goodrick-Clark, *The Occult Roots of Nazism: Secret Aryan Cults and Their Influence on Nazi Ideology* (New York: New York University Press, 1992). Bly and his bunch have mixed up very much the same stew; see Robert Cornett, "Still Questing for the Holy Grail," in Harding, *Wingspan*, pp. 137–42. Indeed, the movement pushes Emma Jung's and Marie-Louise von Franz's neonazi tract on the topic, *The Grail Legend* (London: Hodder and Stoughton, 1960), as "essential reading." Another movement mainstay is John Matthews' *The Grail Quest for the Eternal* (New York: Crossroads, 1981).

46. The Central Intelligence Agency, to name one governmental entity with an established track record of fabricating "social movements" which are anything but what they appear, has undertaken far more wacked out projects in the past; see John Marks, *The Search for the Manchurian Candidate: The CIA and Mind Control* (New York: W.W. Norton, 1979).

47. This is hardly a recent phenomenon, having been widely remarked in the literature by the mid-1960s. The semantic construction "dis-ease" accrues from British psychiatrist R.D. Laing's *The Politics of Experience* (New York: Ballantine, 1967).

48. Tapping into the malaise afflicting precisely this social stratum was the impetus behind the so-called "New Left" during the 1960s. For alternative approaches to organizing strategies in this sector, both of which failed, see Kirkpatrick Sale, *SDS* (New York: Random House, 1973), and Abbie Hoffman, *The Woodstock Nation* (New York: Vintage, 1969).

49. Occasionally, unsuccessful attempts are made to effect a synthesis addressing the whole. See, for example, Michael Albert, Leslie Cagan, Noam Chomsky, Robin Hahnel, Mel King, Lydia Sargent and Holly Sklar, *Liberating Theory* (Boston: South End Press, 1986).

50. For indigenous critique of marxism as being part and parcel of eurocentrism, see my edited volume, *Marxism and Native Americans* (Boston: South End Press, 1983). Also see "False Promises," herein.

51. Rudi Dutschke was a crucially important leader of the German SDS (*Socialistischer Deutscher Studentenbund*) during the first major wave of student confrontation with state authority during the late 1960s. On March 11, 1968, he was shot in the head at close range by a would-be neonazi assassin. The wounds severely and permanently impaired Dutschke's physical abilities and eventually, in 1980, resulted in his death. Since Deutschke was a seminal New left theorist on antiauthoritarianism, it is unfortunate that the great bulk of his writing has never been published in English translation. For the single exception I know of, see his essay "On Anti-Authoritarianism," in Carl Ogelsby, ed., *The New Left Reader* (New York: Grove Press, 1969) pp. 243–53.

52. As concerns American SDS (Students for a Democratic Society) founder Tom Hayden, he is now a very wealthy and increasingly liberal member of the California state legislature. Before his death, former SDS and YIPPIE! leader Jerry Rubin had become a stock consultant and operator of a singles club in Manhattan. Similarly, the late Eldridge Cleaver, one-time Minister of Information of the Black Panther Party and a founder of the Black Liberation Army, earned his living trumpeting right-wing propaganda. So does David Horowitz, once an editor of the radical *Ramparts* magazine. Rennie Davis, former SDS organizer and leader of the Student Mobilization to End the War in Vietnam, became an insurance hack and real estate speculator. Hayden, Rubin and Davis, defendants in the "Chicago 8" Conspiracy Trial, were considered at the time to be the "benchmark" Euroamerican radicals of their generation. The German SDS has surpassed all this: its first president, Helmut Schmidt, actually went on to become president of West Germany during the 1980s.

53. For a partial analysis of this phenomenon in the U.S., see Russell Jacoby, *The Last Intellectuals: American Culture in the Age of Academe* (New York: Basic Books, 1987).

54. Eldridge Cleaver, for instance, first became a "born again" Christian before converting to Mormonism. In 1971, Rennie Davis became a groupie of the then-adolescent guru, Maharaj Ji.

55. The trip was made with Bob Robideau, longtime AIM activist, codefendant of Leonard Peltier and former National Director of the Peltier Defense Committee, as well as M. Annette Jaimes and Paulette D'Auteuil.

56. The same recording is played in a seemingly endless loop in the United States. If I had a dollar

for every white student or activist who has approached me over the past decade bemoaning the fact that he or she has "no culture," I'd need no other income next year. If every American Indian received such payment, we could pool the proceeds, buy back North America and be done with it (just kidding, folks).

57. I personally date the advent of Europe from the coronation of Charlemagne as Roman Emperor in C.E. 800, and the subsequent systematic subordination of indigenous Teutonic peoples to central authority. In his book, *The Birth of Europe* (Philadelphia/New York: Evans-Lippencott, 1966), Robert Lopez treats this as a "prelude," and dates the advent about two centuries later. In some ways, an even better case can be made that "Europe" in any true sense did not emerge until the mid-to-late fifteenth century, with the final Ottoman conquest of Byzantium (Constantinople), the defeat of the Moors in Iberia, and the first Columbian voyage. In any event the conquest and colonization of the disparate populations of the subcontinent must be viewed as an integral and requisite dimension of Europe's coming into being.

58. For interesting insights on the 800-year—and counting—Irish national liberation struggle against English colonization, see Ciarán de Baróid, *Ballymurphy and the Irish War* (London: Pluto Press, 1990). On the Euskadi, see Cyrus Ernesto Zirakzadeh, *A Rebellious People: The Basques, Protests and Politics* (Reno: University of Nevada Press, 1991).

59. Although I doubt this is a "definitive" attribution, I first heard the matter put this way by the late Creek spiritual leader Philip Deer in 1982.

60. As Carolyn Merchant observes in her book, *The Death of Nature: Women, Ecology and the Scientific Revolution* (San Francisco: Harper, 1980, pp. 134, 140): "Based on a fully articulated doctrine emerging at the end of the fifteenth century in the antifeminist tract *Malleus Maleficarum* (1486), or Hammer of the Witches, by the German Dominicans Heinrich Institor and Jacob Sprenger, and in a series of art works by Hans Baldung Grien and Albert Dürer, witch trials for the next two hundred years threatened the lives of women all over Europe, especially in the lands of the Holy Roman Empire . . . The view of nature associated with witchcraft was personal animism. The world of the witches was antihierarchical and everywhere infused with spirits. Every natural object, every animal, every tree contained a spirit." Sound familiar? These women who were being burned alive, were thus murdered precisely because they served as primary repositories of the European subcontinent's indigenous codes of knowledge and corresponding "pagan" ritual.

61. The Cherokee artist Jimmie Durham tells a story of related interest. In 1986, after delivering an invited lecture at Oxford, he was asked whether he'd like to visit a group "who are actually indigenous to these islands." Somewhat skeptically, he accepted the invitation and was driven to a nearby village where the inhabitants continued to perform rites utilizing a variety of objects, including a pair of reindeer antlers of a species extinct since the last Ice Age (roughly 15,000 years ago). It turns out the people were of direct lineal Pictic descent and still practiced their traditional ceremonies, handed down their traditional stories, and so forth. The British government, getting wind of this, subsequently impounded the antlers as being "too important for purposes of science" to be left in possession of the owners. Those dispossessed were then provided a plastic replica of their sacred item, "so as not to disturb their religious life."

62. From Russell Means, "Fighting Words on the Future of Mother Earth," *Mother Jones*, Feb. 1981.

63. See Wilhelm Reich, *The Mass Psychology of Fascism* (New York: Farrar, Straus & Giroux, 1970). Also see George L. Mosse, *Nazi Culture: Intellectual, Cultural and Social Life in the Third Reich* (New York: Schocken, 1966).

64. An excellent early study of these dynamics may be found in Hermann Raushning, *The Revolution of Nihilism: A Warning to the West* (New York: Longmans, Green, 1939). More recently, see Fritz Stern, *The Politics of Cultural Despair: A Study in the Rise of Germanic Ideology* (Berkeley: University of California Press, 1961), and Robert A. Pois, *National Socialism and the Religion of Nature* (London/Sydney: Croom Helm, 1986).

65. During the two weeks I was in the newly reunified Germany, five refugees—all people of

color—were murdered by neonazi firebombings. Another forty were injured in the same manner. The German legislature repealed Article 16 of the Constitution, an important antinazi clause guaranteeing political asylum to all legitimate applicants, and opening the door to mass deportation of nonwhites. The legislature also severely restricted women's rights to abortions, while continuing its moves toward repeal of a constitutional prohibition against German troops operating anywhere beyond the national borders. Meanwhile, the government locked the Roma-Cinti Gypsies *out* of the former Neuengemme concentration camp where their ancestors had been locked *in*, en route to the extermination center at Auschwitz. This was/is part of an official effort to drive all Gypsies out of Germany (again); 120 million Deutschmarks were authorized for payment to Poland to convince it to accept an unlimited number of Roma deportees, while another 30 million each were earmarked as payments to Rumania and Macedonia for the same purpose (yet another such deal is being cut with Slovakia). Overtly nazi-oriented organizations are calling for the reacquisition of Silesia and parts of Prussia—eastern territories lost to Poland at the end of World War II—and are striking responsive chords in some quarters. See generally, Martin A. Lee, *The Beast Reawakens: Fascism's Resurgence from Hitler's Spymasters to Today's Neo-Nazis and Right-Wing Extremists* (New York: Routledge, 1999).

66. The *autonomen*, which may have been the defining characteristic of the German opposition movement during the 1990s, were quite proliferate and essentially anarchistic in their perspective; see generally, George Katsiaficas, *The Subversion of Politics: European Autonomous Social Movements and the Decolonization of Everyday Life* (New York: Humanities Press, 1997).

67. I was rather stunned by the sheer number of "squats"—usually abandoned commercial or apartment buildings in which a large number of people can live comfortably—in Germany. Some, like the Haffenstrasse in Hamburg and Keiffenstrasse in Dusseldorf—each comprising an entire block or more of buildings—have been occupied for more than a decade and serve not only as residences, but bases for political organizing and countercultural activities. For context, see Anders Corr, *No Trespassing: Squatting, Rent Strikes, and Land Struggles Worldwide* (Cambridge, MA: South End Press, 1999). On related phenomena in Holland, see Adilkno, *Cracking the Movement: Squatting Beyond the Movement* (Brookyn, NY: Autonomedia, 1990).

68. See Hamilton T. Burden, *The Nuremberg Party Rallies, 1923–39* (New York: Praeger, 1967).

69. On Wewelsburg castle, see Heinz Höhne, *The Order of the Death's Head: The Story of Hitler's SS* (New York: Coward-McCann, 1969) pp. 151–53. For photographs, see the section entitled "Dark Rites of the Mystic Order" in Editors, *The SS* (Alexandra, VA: Time-Life Books, 1988) pp. 38–49. The scenes of Wewelsburg should be compared to those described in Isabel Wyatt's *From Round Table to Grail Castle* (Sussex, U.K.: Lanthorn Press, 1979), a work highly recommended by leaders of the U.S. Men's Movement today.

70. For analysis of the settler state phenomenon, see J. Sakai, *Settlers: The Mythology of the White Proletariat* (Chicago: Morningstar Press, 1983).

71. This bizarre concept cuts across all political lines in settler state settings. In the U.S., to take what is probably the most pronounced example, reactionary ideologues have always advanced the thesis that American society comprises a racial/cultural "melting pot" which has produced a wholly new people, even while enforcing racial codes implying the exact opposite. Their opposition, on the other hand, has consistently offered much the same spurious argument. Radical Chicanos, for instance, habitually assert that they represent "la Raza," a culturally-mixed "new race" developed in Mexico and composed of "equal parts Spanish and Indio blood." Setting aside the question of what, exactly, a "Spaniard" might be in genetic terms—the contention is at best absurd. During the three centuries following the conquest of Mexico, approximately 200,000 immigrants arrived there from Iberia. Of these, about one-third were Moors, and another one-third were Jewish "conversos" (both groups were being systematically "exported" from Spain at the time, as an expedient to ridding Iberia of "racial contaminants"). This left fewer than 70,000 actual "Spaniards," by whatever biological definition, to be genetically balanced against nearly 140,000 "other" immigrants, and some thirty *million* Indians native to Mexico. Moreover, the settlers brought with them an estimated 250,000 black chattel slaves, virtually all of whom eventually intermarried. Now, how all this computes to leaving a "half-Spanish, half-

Indio" Chicano population as an aftermath is anybody's guess. Objectively, the genetic heritage of la Raza is far more African—black and Moorish—than European, and at least as much Jewish (Semitic) as Spanish. See Peter Boyd-Bowman, *Patterns of Spanish Immigration to the New World, 1493–1580* (Buffalo: State University of New York Council on the Humanities, 1973); Magnus Mörner, *Race Mixture in the History of Latin America* (Boston: Little, Brown, 1967) esp. p. 58.

72. The worst among them, of course, understands the nature of nazism and therefore embraces it; Howard Bushart, John P. Craig and Myra Barnes, *Soldiers of God: White Supremacists and Their Holy War for America* (New York: Pinnacle, 1999). The "mainstream," on the other hand—including the bulk of the state bureaucracy—simply accepts the privileges attending white supremacism as its collective "destiny"; George Lipsitz, *The Possessive Investment in Whiteness: How White People Profit from Identity Politics* (Philadelphia: Temple University Press, 1998).

73. For a classic articulation of this pervasive theme, see J.H. Elliott, "The Rediscovery of America," *New York Review of Books*, June 24, 1993: "Stannard takes the easy way out by turning his book into a high-pitched catalogue of European crimes, diminishing in the process the message he wants to convey. In particular, his emotive vocabulary seems self-defeating. 'Holocaust,' 'genocide,' even 'racism,' carry with them powerful contemporary freight . . . 'Genocide,' as used of the Nazi treatment of the Jews, implies not only mass extermination, but a clear intention on the part of a higher authority [and] it debases the word to write, as Stannard writes, of 'the genocidal encomienda system,' or to apply it to the extinction of a horrifyingly large proportion of the indigenous population through the spread of European diseases." Elliott is critiquing David E. Stannard's superb *American Holocaust: Conquest of the New World* (New York: Oxford University Press, 1992), in which official intentionality—including intentionality with regard to inculcation of disease as a means of extermination—is amply demonstrated.

74. Even Frank Parella, whose graduate thesis *Lebensraum and Manifest Destiny: A Comparative Study in the Justification of Expansion* (Washington, D.C.: Georgetown University, 1950) was seminal in opening up such comparisons, ultimately resorted to feeble "philosophical distinctions" in order to separate the two processes in his concluding section. For clarification of a sort unavailable to Parella, see Adolf Hitler, *Hitler's Secret Book* (New York: Grove Press, 1961) pp. 46–52.

75. James Axtell, presentation at the American Historical Association Annual Conference, Washington, D.C., Dec. 1992. For fuller elaborations of such inane apologia, see this "preeminent American historian's" *After Columbus: Essays in the Ethnohistory of Colonial North America* (New York: Oxford University Press, 1988) p. 44; *Beyond 1492: Encounters in Colonial North America* (New York: Oxford University Press, 1992) p. 261.

76. See, for example, Robert Roybal's observation in his *1492 and All That: Political Manipulations of History* (Washington, D.C.: Ethics and Public Policy Center, 1992): "Whatever evils the Spanish introduced [to the "New World" of the Aztecs]—and they were many and varied—they at least cracked the age-old shell of a culture admirable in many ways but pervaded by repugnant atrocities and petrification." Leaving aside the matter of Aztec "atrocities"—which mostly add up to time-honored but dubious Euroamerican mythology—the idea of applying terms like "age-old" or "petrified" to this culture, which existed for barely 500 years at the time of the Spanish conquest, speaks for itself. Roybal hadn't a clue what he was prattling on about.

77. For a good overview of traditional American Indian concepts and modes of warfare, see Tom Holm, "Patriots and Pawns: State Use of American Indians in the Military and the Process of Nativization in the United States," in Jaimes, *State of Native America*, pp. 345–70.

78. Revolutionary Communist Party USA, "Searching for the Second Harvest," in my *Marxism and Native Americans*, pp. 35–58. It is illuminating to note that the RCP, which professes to be totally at odds with the perspectives held by the Euroamerican status quo, lifted its assertion that ancient Indians consumed a "second harvest" of their own excrement verbatim from an hypothesis recently developed by a pair of the most "bourgeois" anthropologists imaginable, as summarized in that "cidatel of establishment propaganda," the *New York Times*, on Aug. 12, 1980. A better illustration of the

confluence of interest and outlook regarding native people in Euroamerica, between what the RCP habitually (and accurately) describes as "fascism," and the party itself, would be difficult to find.

79. In reality, about two-thirds of all vegetal foodstuffs commonly consumed by humanity today were under cultivation in the Americas—and nowhere else in the world—at the time the European invasion begin. Indians were thus the consummate farmers on the planet in 1492. Plainly, then, we taught Europe the arts of diversified agriculture, not the other way around (as eurocentric mythology insists). For further information, see Jack Weatherford, *Indian Givers: How the Indians of the Americas Transformed the World* (New York: Crown, 1988).

80. For example: George Wuerthner, "An Ecological View of the Indian," *Earth First!*, Vol. 7, No. 7, Aug. 1987. This rather idiotic argument is closely related to that of the quasiofficial Smithsonian Institution, adopted in toto by the RCP, that native people traditionally engaged in such environmentally devastating practices as "jumpkilling" masses of bison—that is to say, driving entire herds off cliffs—in order to make use of a single animal; RCP, "Searching for the Second Harvest, p. 45.

81. Consider, for instance, editor Jason Quinn's patronizing dismissal of the idea that, since nature itself functions in terms of multitudinous interactive hierachies, certain condemnations of social hierarchy might be "anti-natural." The very idea, he claims, is suitable only to an "authoritarian . . . not overly concerned with freedom"; *Anarchy*, No. 37, Summer 1993, p. 74. In the process, of course, he neatly (if unwittingly) replicates eurocentrism's fundamental arrogance, that of completely separating "social and institutional"—that is to say, *human*—undertakings from the rest of the natural world.

82. For solid rejoinders to such "worries" on the part of Euroamerican feminists, see Janet Stilman, ed., *Enough is Enough: Aboriginal Women Speak Out* (Toronto: Women's Press, 1987).

83. For a foremost articulation of the absurd notion that all or even most Indians were traditionally homosexual or at least bisexual—which has made its author a sudden celebrity among white radical feminists and recipient of the proceeds deriving from having a mini-bestseller on her hands as a result—see Paula Gunn Allen, *The Sacred Hoop: Recovering the Feminine in Native American Traditions* (Boston: Beacon Press, 1986, p. 256): "[L]esbianism and homosexuality were probably commonplace. Indeed, same-sex relationships may have been the norm for primary pair bonding . . . the primary personal unit tended to include members of one's own sex rather than members of the opposite sex." For a counterpart male proclamation, see Walter Williams, *The Spirit and the Flesh: Sexual Diversity in American Indian Culture* (Boston: Beacon Press, 1986). Both writers waltz right by the fact that if homosexuals were considered special, and therefore sacred, in traditional native societies—a matter upon which they each remark accurately and approvingly—then homosexuality could not by definition have been "commonplace" since that is a status diametrically opposed to that of being "special." Both Allen and Walters are simply playing to the fantasies of gay rights activists, using Indians as props in the customary manner of Euroamerica.

84. The language is taken from a note sent to me on June 7, 1993, by an airhead calling himself "Sky" Hiatt. It was enclosed along with a copy of Peter Singer's *Animal Liberation* (New York: New York Review of Books, 1975). Actually, the Euroamerican "animal liberation" movement is no joking matter to native people, as white activists—most of whom have never lifted a finger in defense of indigenous rights of any sort, and some of whom have openly opposed them—have come close to destroying what remains of traditional Inuit and Indian subsistence economies in Alaska and Canada; see Jerry Mander, *In the Absence of the Sacred: The Failure of Technology and the Survival of the Indian Nations* (San Francisco: Sierra Club Books, 1991) pp. 287, 296, 387.

85. This premise is simply a cultural paraphrase of the standard psychotherapeutic tenet that a pathology cannot begin to be cured until the person suffering from it first genuinely acknowledges that s/he is afflicted.

86. This is, of course, already happening. Witness, for example, the observation of Lance Morrow in the Aug. 19, 1991 issue of *Time*: "Bly may not be alive to certain absurdities in the men's movement . . . a silly, self-conscious attempt at manly authenticity, almost a satire of the hairy-chested . . . As a spiritual showman (shaman), Bly seeks to produce certain effects. He is good at

them. He [therefore] could not begin to see the men's movement, and his place within it, as a depthless happening in the goofy circus of America."

87. Quoted in Virginia Irving Armstrong, ed., *I Have Spoken: American History Through the Voices of the Indians* (Chicago: Swallow Press, 1971) p. 79.

11. FALSE PROMISES

1. James R. Walker, Raymond J. DeMallie and Elaine A. Jahner, *Lakota Belief and Ritual* (Lincoln: University of Nebraska Press, 1991).

2. See, e.g., Vine Deloria, Jr., "Native American Spirituality," in his *For This Land: Writings on Religion in America* (New York: Routledge, 1999) pp. 130–35.

3. Martin Bernal, *Black Athena: The Afroasiatic Roots of Classical Civilization, Vol. 1: The Fabrication of Ancient Greece, 1785–1985* (New Brunswick, NJ: Rutgers University Press, 1989); V.Y. Mudimbe, *The Idea of Africa* (Bloomington: Indiana University Press, 1994); Tsenay Serequeberhan, *Our Heritage* (Lanham, MD: Rowman and Littlefield, 2000).

4. Ermano Bencivenga, *Hegel's Dialectical Logic* (New York: Oxford University Press, 2000).

5. Marx would, no doubt, be supremely uncomfortable with this classification, if only because he subsequently defined his thought as having been antithetical to that of the Young Hegelians; Karl Marx, *The German Ideology* (New York: New World, 1963) pp. 5–7. The nature of the resulting synthesis is, however, explored rather thoroughly by Warren Breckman in his *Marx, the Young Hegelians, and the Origins of Radical Social Theory: Dethroning the Self* (Cambridge, U.K.: Cambridge University Press, 1999).

6. Karl Marx, *Economic and Philosophic Manuscripts of 1844* (New York: International, 1964).

7. As Marx put it, "My dialectic method is not only different from the Hegelian, but is its direct opposite. To Hegel, [mystical idealism] is the demiurgos of the real world . . . With me, on the contrary, the ideal is nothing else than the material world reflected by the human mind"; Karl Marx, *Capital, Vol. I* (London: Lawrence and Wishart, 1961) p. 19. Also see Karl Marx, *The Holy Family* (London: Lawrence and Wishart, 1956) pp. 115–16.

8. Marx, *Holy Family*, pp. 79–82.

9. See the essay entitled "White Studies: The Intellectual Imperialism of U.S. Higher Education," in my *From a Native Son: Selected Essays in Indigenism, 1985–1995* (Boston: South End Press, 1996) pp. 271–94.

10. Michael Albert, *Unorthodox Marxism: An Essay on Capitalism, Socialism and Revolution* (Boston: South End Press, 1978) pp. 52–53. Also see John Rosenthal, *The Myth of Dialectics: Reinterpreting the Marx-Hegel Relation* (New York: Palgrave, 1998).

11. Marx, *German Ideology*, p. 197.

12. Ibid., p. 7.

13. Genesis, 1:26.

14. See, as examples, "A Contribution to the Critique of Hegel's Philosophy of Right," in *Karl Marx: Early Writings* (London: C.A. Watts, 1963) pp. 43–44; Marx, *Holy Family*, p. 201.

15. Deloria, "Native Spirituality," pp. 131–32.

16. Genesis, 1:26–9.

17. Vine Deloria, Jr., "The Coming of the People," in his *For This Land*, pp. 235–42.

18. See generally, Robert Anchor, *The Enlightenment Tradition* (New York: Harper & Row, 1967); Terence M.S. Evens, *Two Kinds of Rationality* (Minneapolis: University of Minnesota Press, 1995). Concerning Marx specifically, see as examples, his *Economic and Philosophic Manuscripts*, pp. 105, 109, 111; *German Ideology*, pp. 13–4, 19–21; *Holy Family*, 79–82;

19. Russell Means, "The Same Old Song," in my *Marxism and Native Americans* (Boston: South End Press, 1983) pp. 28–29; Deloria, "Native Spirituality," pp. 131–32. For an interesting correlation to this view, coming from a completely different dirrection, see Bernard S. Silberman, *Cages of*

Reason: The Rise of the Rational State in France, Japan, the United States, and Great Britain (Chicago: University of Chicago Press, 1993).

20. For a very good, if unintended, survey of this theme, see Robyn M. Dawes, *Everyday Irrationality: How Pseudoscientists, Lunatics, and the Rest of Us Fail to Think Rationally* (Boulder, CO: Westview Press, 2001).

21. For what may be the best delineation of Marx's internal/external relations schema, see Bertell Ollman, *Alienation: Marx's Conception of Man in Capitalist Society* (Cambridge, U.K.: Cambridge University Press, 1976).

22. Gustav A. Wetter, *Dialectical Materialism* (London: Routledge, 1958).

23. See, as examples, Marx, *German Ideology*, p. 7; *The Poverty of Philosophy* (London: Lawrence and Wishart, n.d.) pp. 180–82; "Preface to *A Contribution to the Critique of Political Economy*," in *Karl Marx and Frederick Engels: Selected Works, Vol. 1* (London: Lawrence and Wishart, 1962) pp. 362–63.

24. Marx, *Economic and Philosophic Manuscripts*, pp. 72–73, 103. Also see Erich Fromm, *Marx's Concept of Man* (New York: Frederick Ungar, 1961).

25. As examples, Marx, "Wage Labour and Capital," *Selected Works, Vol. 1*, pp. 82–83; *German Ideology*, pp. 13–4, 19–21; *Capital, Vol. I*, p. 361; Marx and Frederick Engels, *Manifesto of the Communist Party* (Moscow: Progress, n.d.) pp. 80–81.

26. For one of the better overviews, see Stanley Aronowitz, *The Crisis in Historical Materialism: Class, Politics and Culture in Marxist Theory* (Minneapolis: University of Minnesota Press, 1990).

27. The classic in this connection is of course Mao Zedung's *On Contradiction*, included in *Selected Works of Mao Tse-Tung, Vol. I* (Peking: Foreign Languages Press, 1975) pp. 311–47.

28. As examples, Marx, *Economic and Philosophic Manuscripts*, pp. 113–14; *German Ideology*, pp. 9–13; *Poverty of Philosophy*, pp. 80–82; *Holy Family*, p. 125; Marx and Engels, *Communist Manifesto*, pp. 60–62. Overall, see Aronowitz, *Historical Materialism*.

29. Louis Althusser, *For Marx* (New York: Vintage, 1970).

30. Albert, *Unorthodox Marxism*, p. 58.

31. Jean Baudrillard, *The Mirror of Production* (St. Louis: Telos Press, 1975).

32. Means, "Same Old Song," p. 26.

33. As examples, Karl Karx, "Wages, Price and Profit," in *Selected Works, Vol. 1*, pp. 414–31; *Poverty of Philosophy*, pp. 40–42, 47–48, 53–54, 167; *Capital, Vol. I*, pp. 40, 395, 520, 522. Also see Samir Amin, *Law of Value and Historical Materialism* (New York: Monthly Review Press, 1979).

34. Means, "Same Old Song," p. 22.

35. Maurice Merleau-Ponty, *Adventures of the Dialectic* (Evanston, IL: Northwestern University Press, 1973).

36. Jean-Paul Sartre, *Critique of Dialectical Reason, Vol. 1: Theory of Practical Ensembles* (London: Verso, 2001); *Search for a Method* (New York: Alfred A. Knopf, 1963).

37. Theodor W. Adorno, *Negative Dialectics* (New York: Continuum, 1983); Herbert Marcuse, *Negations: Essays in Critical Theory* (Boston: Beacon Press, 1969). Overall, see Martin Jay, *The Dialectical Imagination: A History of the Frankfurt School and the Institute for Social Research, 1923–1950* (Berkeley: University of California Press, 1996).

38. David Ingram, *Habermas and the Dialectic of Reason* (New Haven: Yale University Press, 1989).

39. J.V. Stalin, *The Foundations of Leninism* (Peking: Foreign Languages Press, 1970); Neil Harding, *Leninism* (Durham, NC: Duke University Press, 1996).

40. For further amplification, see Ronald L. Meek, *Studies in the Labor Theory of Value* (New York: Monthly Review Press, 1956).

41. Aronowitz, *Historical Materialism*; Karl Bober, *Marx's Interpretation of History* (Cambridge, MA: Harvard University Press, 1950).

42. "Communism is the riddle of history solved, and it knows itself to be this solution"; Marx, *Economic and Philosophic Manuscripts*, p. 102.

43. Marx, "Preface," in *Selected Works, Vol. 1*, pp. 362–64.

44. See Elisabeth R. Lloyd, "Marx's General Cultural Theoretics," in my *Marxism*, esp. pp. 80–81.

45. As examples, see Marx, *Pre-Capitalist Economic Formations* (London: Lawrence and Wishart, 1964) pp. 68–83; *Capital, Vol. I*, pp. 356–58. For an illustration of where such conflation led, see the section entitled "The Old Feudal Society" in Mao Zedung's "The Chinese Revolution and the Chinese Communist Party," in *Selected Works of Mao Tse-Tung, Vol. II* (Peking: Foreign Languages Press, 1975) pp. 307–9.

46. For apparent confirmation of this suspicion, see Marx, *German Ideology*, pp. 9–13.

47. For discussion, see Judith Butler, Ernesto Laclau and Slavoj Zizek, *Contingency, Hegemony, Universality: Contemporary Dialogues on the Left* (London: Verso, 2000).

48. "In broad outlines, the Asiatic, ancient, feudal, and modern bourgeois modes of production can be designated as progressive epochs in the economic formation of society [and] the mode of production conditions the social, political, and intellectual life processes in general"; Marx, "Preface," pp. 363, 364.

49. It is worth noting that the cultural hierarchy thus elaborated is entirely consistent with the biological hierarchy preferred by contemporaneous scientific racists like Samuel George Morton and Josiah Clark Nott; William Stanton, *The Leopard's Spots: Scientific Attitudes Toward Race in America, 1815–59* (Chicago: University of Chicago Press, 1960). That Marx shared many of these ideas seems likely, given his favorable view of Charles Darwin's tendency to analogize evolutionary theory to social contexts; see, e.g., the letter written by Marx to Engels on June 18, 1862, included in *Marx and Engels: Selected Correspondence* (London: Lawrence and Wishart, 1956) pp. 156–57.

50. See generally, Shlomo Alvinari, *Karl Marx on Colonization and Modernization* (Garden City, NY: Doubleday, 1969).

51. This is brought out rather well by Vine Deloria, Jr., in his essay "Circling the Same Old Rock," in my *Marxism*, pp. 113–36.

52. Marx, *Pre-Capitalist Economic Formations*; Manuel Gottlieb, *Comparative Economic Systems: Preindustrial and Modern Case Studies* (Ames: Iowa State University Press, 1988).

53. For a good taste of this, see Samir Amin, *Un-Equal Development: An Essay on the Social Formations of Peripheral Capitalism* (New York: Monthly Review Press, 1976); *Maldevelopment: Anatomy of a Global Failure* (New York: Monthly Review Press, 1984).

54. "Our conception of history depends on our ability to expound the real process of production, starting out from the simple material production of life, and to comprehend the form of the intercourse connected with this and created by this." Hence, cultures which remain content with "the simple material production of life . . . have no history, no development, [unlike] men, developing their material production, and their material intercourse, [who] alter, along with their real existence, their thinking and the products of their thinking"; Marx, *German Ideology*, pp. 15, 28. For implications, see Eric Wolf, *Europe and the People Without History* (Berkeley: University of California Press, 1982).

55. Martin Jay, *Marxism and Totality: The Adventure of a Concept from Lukacs to Habermas* (Berkeley: University of California Press, 1984).

56. There is of course no other way the famous phrase in the *Communist Manifesto* concerning "workers of the world" *can* be understood. This is especially telling, given the book's opening sentence, which presents "a spectre haunting *Europe* (emphasis added)." In any event, to fill in the blanks, see C.L.R. James, *World Revolution, 1917–1936: The Rise and Fall of the Communist International* (New York: Hyperion, 1973); John Gerassi, ed., *The Coming of the New International* (New York: World, 1971).

57. Marx, *Early Writings*, pp. 27–31; *German Ideology*, pp. 67–69; *Capital, Vol. I*, pp. 762–64; *Capital, Vol. III* (London: Lawrence and Wishart, 1962) pp. 245, 252–53. Also see Marx and Engels, *Communist Manifesto*, pp. 55–57, 67–68.

58. Gavin Kitching, *Karl Marx and the Philosophy of Praxis* (New York: Routledge, 1988).

59. Mark Seldon, "Revolution and Third World Development: People's War and the Transformation of Peasant Societies," in Norman Miller and Robert Aya, eds., *National Liberation: Revolution in the Third World* (New York: Free Press, 1971) pp. 214–48; Gérard Chaliand, *Revolution in the Third Word: Myths and Prospects* (New York: Viking, 1977); Gordon White, "Revolutionary Socialist Devel-

opment in the Third World: An Overview," in Gordon White, Robbin Murray and Christine White, eds., *Revolutionary Socialist Development in the Third World* (Knoxville: University of Kentucky Press, 1983) pp. 1–34.

60. M. Tamarkin, *The Making of Zimbabwe: Decolonization in Regional and International Politics* (New York: Frank Cass, 1990).

61. For a broader view, see Alexander J. Motyl, *The Post-Soviet Nations: Perspectives on the Demise of the USSR* (Berkeley: University of California Press, 1992).

62. Ivo Banac, *The National Question in Yugoslavia: Origins, History, Politics* (Ithaca, NY: Cornell University Press, 1989); Aleksa Djilas, *The Contested Country: Yugoslav Unity and Communist Revolution, 1919–1953* (Cambridge, MA: Harvard University Press, 1996).

63. Jorge Palacios, *Chile: An Attempt at Historic Compromise During the Allende Years* (London: Banner Press, 1979).

64. Dennis Herbstein and John Evenson, *The Devils Among Us: The War for Namibia* (London: Zed Books, 1989).

65. See generally, Timothy P. Wickham-Crowley, *Guerrillas and Revolution in Latin America* (Princeton, NJ: Princeton University Press, 1993).

66. V.I. Lenin, *Questions of National Policy and Proletarian Internationalism* (Moscow: Progress, 1970).

67. For framing, see James Blaut, *The National Question: Decolonizing the Theory of Nationalism* (London: Zed Books, 1987); Nicole Arnaud and Jacques Dofny, *Nationalism and the National Question* (Montréal: Black Rose Books, 1996).

68. W. Ofuatey-Kodjoe, *The Principle of Self-Determination in International Law* (Hamdon, CT: Archon Books, 1972); A. Rigo-Sureta, *The Evolution of the Right to Self-Determination: A Study of United Nations Practice* (Leyden, Netherlands: A.W. Sijhoff, 1973).

69. See G. Stekloff, *History of the First International* (New York: Russell and Russell, 1968).

70. The formulation used here was advanced by Joseph V. Stalin, in a section entitled "The Nation" in his *Marxism and the National Question: Selected Writings and Speeches* (New York: International, 1942). Also see John Hall, "Nationalisms, Classified and Explained," S. Periwal, ed., *Notions of Nationalism* (Budapest: Central European University Press, 1995) pp. 8–33.

71. Ofuatey-Kodjoe, *Principle of Self-Determination*; Hannum Hurst, *Autonomy, Sovereignty, and Self-Determination* (Philadelphia: University of Pennsylvania Press, 1990).

72. Michla Pomerance, *Self-Determination in Law and Practice* (The Hague: Martinus Nijhoff, 1982).

73. Roxanne Dunbar Ortiz, *Indians of the Americas: Human Rights and Self-Determination* (London: Zed Books, 1984); Glenn T. Morris, "In Support of the Right to Self-Determination of Indigenous Peoples Under International Law," *German Yearbook of International Law*, No. 29, 1986; Catherine J. Jorns, "Indigenous Peoples and Self-Determination: Challenging State Sovereignty," *Case Western Reserve Journal of International Law*, No. 24, 1992.

74. Karl Marx and Frederick Engels, *Ireland and the Irish Question* (New York: International, 1972).

75. See, e.g., Karl Marx, "The Civil War in France," in *Selected Writings*, p. 527. Overall, see S. Shaheen, *The Communist Theory of Self-Determination* (The Hague: W. Van Hoeve, 1956).

76. Engels is quoted abundantly on the topic in Stekloff, *First International*.

77. Alvinari offers a truly remarkable selection of quotes in *Marx on Colonization and Modernization*.

78. Much of this is traced out by Renaldo Munck in his *The Difficult Dialogue: Marxism and the National Question* (London: Zed Books, 1986). Also see Blaut, *National Question*.

79. Again, ample quotation will be found in Alvinari, *Marx on Colonization and Modernization*. Also see Emmanuel Terray, *Marxism and "Primitive" Societies: Two Studies* (New York: Monthly Review Press, 1972).

80. A very good explication of the principles involved will be found in Alan Sica's *Weber, Irrationality and Social Order* (Berkeley: University of California Press, 1988). For a very solid rejoinder

to the Marx/Weber conception of rationality, see Leopold Kohr, *The Overdeveloped Nations: The Dis-economies of Scale* (New York: Schocken Books, 1978).

81. The implications of such thinking are traced rather well in Michael S. Teitelbaum's and J.M. Winter's *A Question of Numbers: High Migration, Low Fertility, and the Politics of National Identity* (New York: Hill and Wang, 1998).

82. Leon Trotsky, *History of the Russian Revolution* (New York: Pathfinder Press, 2001) p. 1157.

83. Roman Szporluk, *Communism and Nationalism: Karl Marx vs. Friedrich List* (New York: Oxford University Press, 1988). Also see John Schwartzmantel, *Socialism and the Idea of the Nation* (Hemel Hempstead, U.K.: Harvester Wheatsheaf, 1991).

84. The concept is set forth with reasonable clarity by V.I. Lenin in an essay entitled "The Principles of Socialism and the War of 1914–1918," in *Lenin on War and Peace* (Peking: Foreign Languages Press, 1970) esp. pp. 11–2, 26–27. Also see Ephraim Nimni, *Marxism and Nationalism: Theoretical Origins of a Political Crisis* (London: Pluto Press, 1991).

85. See, e.g., Mao Zedung's "The Chinese Communist Party and China's Revolutionary War," in *Selected Works of Mao Tse-Tung, Vol. I*, pp. 191–94.

86. For discussion, see Clifford Geertz, "The Integrative Revolution: Primordial Sentiments and Civil Politics in the New States," in his *Old Societies and New States: The Quest for Modernity in Asia and Africa* (New York: Free Press, 1963) pp. 107–13; Nicos Poulantzas, *State, Power and Socialism* (London: New Left Books, 1980); Erica Benner, *Really Existing Nationalisms: A Post-Communist View from Marx and Engels* (Oxford, U.K.: Clarendon Press, 1995); Berch Berberoglu, *The National Question: Nationalism, Ethnic Conflict, and Self-Determination in the 20th Century* (Philadelphia: Temple University Press, 1995).

87. Walker Connor, *The National Question in Marxist-Leninist Theory and Strategy* (Princeton: Princeton University Press, 1984) p. 14.

88. The thrust of Luxemburg's argument is set forth in *The National Question* (New York: International, 1976). Her ideas are carried forward to a considerable extent by Paul Brass, in his *Ethnicity and Nationalism: Theory and Comparison* (Beverly Hills, CA: Sage, 1991).

89. For an outline of Lenin's opposing position, see the sections entitled "Cultural-National Autonomy" and "The Utopian Karl Marx and the Practical Rosa Luxemburg" in his *Critical Remarks on the National Question, The Right of Nations to Self-Determination* (Moscow: Progress, 1971) pp. 14–20, 78–84.

90. Ibid., p. 26.

91. Stalin, *Marxism and the National Question*, p. 23.

92. Connor, *National Question*, p. 35.

93. Quoted in Jesse Clarkson, *A History of Russia* (New York: Random House, 1961) p. 636.

94. Jeremy Smith, *The Bolsheviks and the National Question, 1917–1923* (New York: Palgrave, 1999).

95. Connor, *National Question*, p. 77.

96. See Mark von Hagen, "The Russian Empire," and Victor Vaslavsky, "The Soviet Union," both in Karen Barkey and Mark von Hagen, eds., *After Empire: Multiethnic Societies and Nation-Building: The Soviet Union and the Russian, Ottoman, and Hapsburg Empires* (Boulder, CO: Westview Press, 1997).

97. Connor, *National Question*, p. 79. For detail, see Dick Wilson, *The Long March: The Epic of Chinese Communist Survival* (New York: Viking, 1971).

98. Connor, *National Question*, p. 87.

99. Ibid. For fuller background see the essays collected in Frank Dittmer and Samuel S. Kim, eds., *China's Quest for National Identity* (Ithaca, NY: Cornell University Press, 1993).

100. Robert L. Mole, *The Montagnards of Vietnam: A Study of Nine Tribes* (Rutland, VT: Charles E. Tuttle, 1970); Paul Seitz, *Men of Dignity: The Montagnards of South Vietnam* (Paris: Jacques Barthelemy, 1975).

101. See, e.g., Ho Chi Minh, *On Revolution: Selected Writings, 1920–1966* (New York: New American Library, 1967).

102. John Prados, *Presidents' Secret Wars: CIA and Pentagon Secret Operations since World War II* (New York: William Morrow, 1986) pp. 255–56.

103. Ibid., pp. 244–45, 251–55.

104. Ibid., p. 255–56.

105. In July 1985, while serving as a representative of the International Indian Treaty Council, I met with Vietnamese U.N. delegates in Geneva to discuss a possible trip to Vietnam. All went well until they realized that visits to the highlands provinces of Pleiku and Kontum were included in my proposed itinerary. These, I was informed, would be impossible insofar as the government could not guarantee my security therein. When I inquired whether this was because FULRO remained active in that area, my hosts appeared startled and abruptly terminated our meeting. To this day, reference to FULRO and/or the "Montagnard Question" remains absent from official Vietnamese statements.

106. See, e.g., Noam Chomsky, "The Wider War," in his *For Reasons of State* (New York: Vintage, 1973) pp. 172–211. Also see my and Glenn T. Morris'"Between a Rock and a Hard Place: Left-Wing Revolution, Right-Wing Reaction, and the Destruction of Indigenous Peoples," *Cultural Survival Quarterly*, Vol. 11, No. 3, Fall 1988.

107. For context, see George Black, *Triumph of the People: The Sandinista Revolution in Nicaragua* (London: Zed Books, 1981).

108. For a summary of the position(s) and agenda advanced by the representative Indian organization MISURASATA during the early 1980s, as well as maps delineating the territory involved, see the chapter entitled "Geopolitics and the Miskito Nation" in Bernard Neitschmann's *The Unknown War: The Miskito Nation, Nicaragua, and the United States* (Lanham, MD: Freedom House, 1989) pp. 1–57. Also see "MISURASATA Action Plan of 1981," in Klaudine Ohland and Robin Schneider, eds., *National Revolution and Indigenous Identity* (Copenhagen: IWGIA Doc. 47, 1983) pp. 89–94; "Proposal of MISURASATA for Autonomy and a Treaty of Peace Between the Republic of Nicaragua and the Indian Nations of Yapti Tasba," *Akwesasne Notes*, Vol. 19, No. 3, Late Fall, 1987.

109. Quoted in the *New York Times*, Apr. 26, 1985. It should be noted that Borgé had made almost identical statements to me during a brief meeting conducted in conjunction with a decolonization conference held in Havana during December of 1984.

110. Americas Watch, *The Miskitos in Nicaragua* (New York: Americas Watch, 1986); Amnesty International, *Nicaragua: The Human Rights Record* (London: Amnesty International, 1986).

111. Holly Sklar, *Washington's War on Nicaragua* (Boston: South End Press, 1988). For the record of negotiations between the Sandinistas and MISURASATA, see Neitschmann, *Unknown War*, pp. 67–89. On the Sandinista defeat, see Vanessa Castro and Gary Prevost, eds., *The 1990 Elections in Nicaragua and Their Aftermath* (Lanham, MD: Rowman and Littlefield, 1992).

112. Connor, *National Question*; Geertz, *Societies/States*; Ohland and Schneider, *Revolution/Identity*; Schmuel Eisenstadt, *Building States and Nations* (Beverly Hills, CA: Sage, 1973); P.N. Fedoseyev, *Leninism and the National Question* (Moscow: Progress, 1977); Leah Greenfeld, *Nationalism: Five Paths to Modernity* (Cambridge, MA: Harvard University Press, 1992).

113. For coinage, see Raphaël Lemkin, *Axis Rule in Occupied Europe* (Washington, D.C.: Carnegie Institution, 1944) p. 79. For legal codification, see Convention on Punishment and Prevention of the Crime of Genocide (U.N. GAOR Res. 260A (III) 9 Dec. 1948; effective 12 Jan. 1951), text included in Louis Henkin, Gerald L. Neuman, Diane F. Orentlicher and David L. Leebron, eds., *Human Rights: Documentary Supplement* (New York: Foundation Press, 2001) pp. 155–58.

114. Considerable amplification will be found in the essay entitled "Defining the Unthinkable: Towards a Viable Understanding of Genocide," in my *A Little Matter of Genocide: Holocaust and Denial in the Americas, 1492 to the Present* (San Francisco: City Lights, 1997) pp. 399–444.

115. On Avakian, see *Revolutionary Communist Party, USA: Program and Platform* (San Francisco: Revolution, n.d. [circa, 1980). Also see David A. Muga, "Native Americans and the Nationalities

Question: Premises for a Marxist Approach to Ethnicity and Self-Determination," *Nature, Society, Thought,* Vol. 1, No. 1, 1987.

116. Rudolf Bahro, *Red to Green: Interviews with New Left Review* (London: Verso, 1984); *Building the Green Movement* (Philadelphia: New Society, 1985).

117. We are confronted here with a phenomenon increasingly referred to as "post-marxism"; Stuart Kim, *Post-Marxism: An Intellectual History* (New York: Routledge, 2001).

118. The script conforms rather closely to that described by Walker Connor in his *Ethnonationalism* (Princeton, NJ: Princeton University Press, 1994). Also see Leopold Kohr, *The Breakdown of Nations* (New York: E.P. Dutton, 1975); Louis L. Snyder, *Global Mini-Nationalisms: Autonomy or Independence?* (Boulder, CO: Westview Press, 1982).

119. For an early articulation of this theme, see George Manuel and Michael Posluns, *The Fourth World: An Indian Reality* (New York: Macmillan, 1974). Also see Winona LaDuke, "Succeeding Into Native North America: A Secessionist View," the preface to my *Struggle for the Land: Native North American Resistance to Genocide, Ecocide and Colonization* (Winnipeg: Arbeiter Ring, [2nd ed] 1999) pp. 11–14.

120. Andrew McLaughlin, *Regarding Nature: Industrialism and Deep Ecology* (Albany: State University of New York Press, 1993); Phillip F. Cramer, *Deep Environmental Politics* (New York: Praeger, 1998).

121. Despite the book's many biases, a good enunciation is contained in Jerry Mander's *In the Absence of the Sacred: The Failure of Technology and the Survival of Indian Nations* (San Francisco: Sierra Club Books, 1991). Also see Chellis Glendenning, *My Name Is Chellis & I'm in Recovery from Western Civilization* (Boston: Shambala, 1994).

122. Several keystone texts in this connection will be found in John Zerzan's *Future Primitive and Other Essays* (New York: Autonomedia, 1994). More broadly, see Ulrike Heider, *Anarchism: Left, Right and Green* (San Francisco: City Lights, 1994).

123. Kohr, *Breakdown*; Snyder, *Mini-Nationalisms*; Chellis Glendenning, *Off the Map: An Exploration into Imperialism, the Global Economy, and Other Earthly Whereabouts* (Boston: Shambala, 1999).

12. THE NEW FACE OF LIBERATION

1. For background, see Peter Worsely, *The Third World* (London: Weidenfeld & Nicholson, [2nd. ed.] 1967), and the chapter entitled "The Making of a World" in Robert Malley's *The Call from Algeria: Third Worldism, Revolution and the Turn to Islam* (Berkeley: University of California Press, 1996) pp. 77–114.

2. See, e.g., Robert K. Thomas, "Colonialism: Classic and Internal," *New University Thought*, Vol. 4, No. 4, Winter 1966–67. With regard to Appalachian whites in particular, see Helen Matthews Lewis, Linda Johnson and Donald Askins, eds., *Colonialism in Modern America: The Appalachian Case* (Boone, NC: Appalachian Consortium Press, 1978).

3. George Manuel and Michael Posluns, *The Fourth World: An Indian Reality* (New York: Free Press, 1974).

4. The term "Host World" was coined by Winona LaDuke in her "Natural to Synthetic and Back Again," an essay written as the preface to my edited volume, *Marxism and Native Americans* (Boston: South End Press, 1983) p. vii.

5. Julian Burger, *Report from the Frontier: The State of the World's Indigenous Peoples* (London: Zed Books, 1987).

6. Noam Chomsky, *World Orders, Old and New* (New York: Columbia University Press, 1994).

7. The conceptual structure is basically Kantian, but has been shared in various ways by Western philosophers from Comte to Saint-Simon; Morris Ginsberg, "Progress in the Modern Era," in Philip P. Weiner, ed., *Dictionary of the History of Ideas: Studies of Selected Pivotal Ideas, Vol. III* (New York: Scribner's, 1973) pp. 633–50.

8. Paul Buhle, "Historical Materialism," in Mary Jo Buhle, Paul Buhle and Dan Georgakas, eds., *Dictionary of the American Left* (Urbana: University of Illinois Press, 1992) pp. 317–19.

9. According to the 1989 edition of *Webster's Ninth New Collegiate Dictionary*, which is what I happen to have closest at hand, the two primary meanings of "radical" are, "Of, relating to or proceeding from a root," and "Of or relating to an origin."

10. Russell Means, "The Same Old Song," in *Marxism and Native Americans*, pp. 19–33.

11. Vine Deloria, Jr., "Circling the Same Old Rock," in ibid., pp. 113–36.

12. A more detailed articulation will be found in "False Promises," herein.

13. This circumstance continues in "neocolonial" settings; Samir Amin, *Imperialism and Uneven Development* (New York: Monthly Review Press, 1977).

14. Lynn Dorland Trost, "Western Metaphysical Dualism as an Element in Racism," in John L. Hodge, Donald L. Struckmann and Lynn Dorland Trost, *Cultural Bases of Racism and Group Oppression: An Examination of Traditional "Western" Concepts, Values and Institutional Structures Which Support Racism, Sexism and Elitism* (Berkeley: Riders Press, 1975) pp. 50–89.

15. For perspectives on the racial/class tensions with which this circumstance has been imbued, see Napur Chaudhuri and Margaret Strobel, eds., *Western Women and Imperialism: Complicity and Resistance* (Bloomington: Indiana University Press, 1992).

16. Susan Brownmiller, *Against Our Will: Men, Women and Rape* (New York: Simon & Schuster, 1975).

17. Frantz Fanon, *The Wretched of the Earth* (New York: Grove Press, 1966); Albert Memmi, *The Colonizer and the Colonized* (Boston: Beacon Press, 1967).

18. Jean-Paul Sartre, "On Genocide," *Ramparts*, Feb. 1968.

19. Sadruddin Aga Khan and Hassan bin Talal, *Indigenous Peoples: A Global Quest for Justice* (London: Zed Books, 1987).

20. See the chapter entitled "Hegemony, Historical Bloc, and History," in Walter L. Adamson's *Hegemony and Revolution: A Study of Antonio Gramsci's Political and Cultural Theory* (Berkeley: University of California Press, 1980).

21. Jean-Paul Sartre, *Search for a Method* (New York: Alfred A. Knopf, 1963) p. 28.

22. Anyone doubting this should have a look at the "Resolution of the 5th Annual Meeting of the Traditional Elders Circle," published verbatim in my *Fantasies of the Master Race: Literature, Cinema and the Colonization of American Indians* (Monroe, ME: Common Courage Press, 1992) at pp. 223–25.

23. See, e,g., Martin Carnoy's *Education as Cultural Imperialism* (New York: David McKay, 1974).

24. Frantz Fanon, *Towards the African Revolution* (New York: Monthly Review Press, 1967); Amilcar Cabral, *Revolution in Guinea: Selected Texts* (New York: Monthly Review Press, 1969).

25. Virtually all of the internal convulsions wracking Africa since the wholesale post-World War II dissolution of European empires have devolved upon the efforts of indigenous nations to recover their own rights to self-determination vis-à-vis newly independent African states, each of which has set out to consolidate itself within one or another of the territorial "compartments" created for administrative purposes by European colonialism itself. See, overall, J.M. MacKenzie, *The Partition of Africa, 1880–1900* (London: Methuen, 1983); Stewart C. Easton, *The Rise and Fall of Western Colonialism* (New York: Praeger, 1964); John S. Saul, *The State and Revolution in East Africa* (New York: Monthly Review Press, 1974).

26. De Beauvoir's relationship to the Algerian liberation struggle is covered in the volume of her memoirs entitled *La Force des choses* (*The Force of Circumstances*). As for Sartre, he penned the preface to Fanon's *Wretched of the Earth* and an introduction to Memmi's *Colonizer and Colonized* while strongly and consistently endorsing the FLN's resort to armed struggle to free Algeria from French rule. The latter is covered well in B. Marie Perinbam's *Holy Violence: The Revolutionary Thought of Frantz Fanon* (Washington, D.C.: Three Continents Press, 1982). More broadly, see Lewis R. Gordon's *Fanon and the Crisis of European Man* (New York: Routledge, 1995).

27. Sartre, *Search for a Method*.

28. For the immediate context of Trotsky's famous remark, see Vladimir N. Brovkin, *The Menshe-*

viks After October: Socialist Opposition and the Rise of Bolshevik Dictatorship (Ithaca, NY: Cornell University Press, 1988).

29. Mark Poster, *Foucault, Marxism and History: Mode of Production versus Mode of Information* (Cambridge, U.K.: Polity Press, 1984).

30. Michel Foucault, *The Archaeology of Knowledge & The Discourse on Language* (New York: Pantheon, 1972).

31. V.I. Lenin, *What Is To Be Done? Burning Questions of Our Movement* (New York: New World, 1969). Attribution for the response goes to Michael Albert's *What Is To Be Undone? A Modern Revolutionary Discussion of Classical Left Ideologies* (Boston: Porter Sargent, 1974).

32. On the 1960s variants, see Mitchell Goodman's *The Movement Toward a New America: The Beginnings of a Long Revolution* (Philadelphia/New York: Pilgrim Press/Alfred A. Knopf, 1970). On those of the 1930s, see the chapter entitled "Self-Help in Hard Times" in Howard Zinn's *A People's History of the United States* (New York: HarperPerennial, 1980) pp. 368–97.

33. Herbert Marcuse, "Repressive Tolerance," in Robert Paul Wolff, Barrington Moore, Jr., and Herbert Marcuse, *A Critique of Pure Tolerance* (Boston: Beacon Press, 1965) p. 111.

34. See generally, Kenneth Alsop, *The Bootleggers and Their Era* (Garden City, NY: Doubleday, 1961).

35. Dan Baum, *Smoke and Mirrors: The War on Drugs and the Politics of Failure* (Boston: Little, Brown, 1996).

36. Probably the best enunciation of the thinking underlying this approach is contained in Lee Lockwood's *Conversation with Eldridge Cleaver: Algiers* (New York: Delta Books, 1970).

37. Bernstein was the first major marxian revisionist, arguing during the early 1900s that "objective conditions" had changed since Marx's day to the point that revolution was no longer necessary in industrial societies. He posed as an alternative the idea that socialism could be voted into being, thus forging the standard position of American progressivism; Eduard Bernstein, *Evolutionary Socialism* (New York: Schocken, 1961).

38. See "Spiritual Hucksterism: The Rise of the Plastic Medicine Men" in my *From a Native Son: Selected Essays in Indigenism, 1985–1995* (Boston: South End Press, 1996) pp. 355–66. On McGaa in particular, see "Do It Yourself 'Indianism,'" in my *Indians Are Us? Culture and Genocide in Native North America* (Monroe, ME: Common Courage Press, 1994) pp. 283–89. On Castaneda, see "Carlos Castaneda: The Greatest Hoax Since Piltdown Man," in my *Fantasies of the Master Race: Literature, Cinema and the Colonization of American Indians* (San Francisco: City Lights, [2nd. ed.] 1998) pp. 27–66.

39. See "Indians 'R' Us" herein.

40. A good selection will be found in Leonard I. Krimerman and Lewis Perry, eds., *Patterns of Anarchy* (New York: Anchor, 1966). Also see Peter Marshall, *Demanding the Impossible: A History of Anarchism* (London: Fontana Press, 1993).

41. Kirkpatrick Sale, *Dwellers in the Land: The Bioregional Vision* (Philadelphia: New Society, 1991); John Zerzan, *Future Primitive and Other Essays* (New York: Autonomedia, 1994); *Elements of Refusal* (Columbia, MO: Columbia Alternative Library, [2nd ed.] 1999). Another worthwhile read is Ulrike Heider's *Anarchism: Left, Right and Green* (San Francisco: City Lights, 1994).

42. See "I Am Indigenist," herein.

43. Manuel and Posluns, *Fourth World*.

44. Roxanne Dunbar Ortiz, *Indians of the Americas: Human Rights and Self-Determination* (London: Zed Press, 1984); John Mohawk, *A Basic Call to Consciousness* (Rooseveltown, NY: Akwesasne Notes, 1978).

45. Haunani-Kay Trask, *From a Native Daughter: Colonialism and Sovereignty in Hawai'i* (Honolulu: University of Hawai'i Press, [2nd ed.] 1999); Jimmie Durham, *A Certain Lack of Coherence: Writings on Art and Cultural Politics* (London: Kala Press, 1993).

46. See my *Struggle for the Land: Indigenous Resistance to Genocide, Ecocide and Expropriation in Contemporary North America* (Winnipeg: Arbeiter Ring, [2nd ed.] 1999).

47. For background, see Daniel Cohn-Bendit, *Obsolete Communism: The Left-Wing Alternative* (New York: McGraw-Hill, 1968).

48. Bernard Neitschmann, "The Third World War," *Cultural Survival Quarterly*, Vol. 11, No. 2, 1987; "The Fourth World: Nations versus States," in George J. Demko and William B. Wood, eds., *Reordering the World: Geopolitical Perspectives on the Twenty-First Century* (Boulder, CO: Westview Press, 1994) pp. 225–42.

49. Elaine Katzenberger, ed., *First World, Ha Ha Ha! The Zapatista Challenge* (San Francisco: City Lights, 1995).

50. See "The Bloody Wake of Alcatraz." herein.

51. Credit for crunching the numbers goes to Bruce Johansen and Roberto Maestas, who include this and an array of other comparative data in their *Wasíchu: The Continuing Indian Wars* (New York: Monthly Review Press, 1979).

52. Geoffrey York and Loreen Pindera, *People of the Pines: The Warriors and the Legacy of Oka* (Boston: Little, Brown, 1991); Linda Pertusati, *In Defense of Mohawk Land: Ethnopolitical Conflict in Native North America* (Albany: State University of New York Press, 1997).

53. Jancice G.A.E. Switlow, *Gustafson Lake: Under Siege* (Peachland, B.C.: TIAC Communications, 1997).

54. All of these are covered in my *Struggle for the Land.*

55. For background on some of the struggles mentioned, see Trask, *From a Native Daughter;* David Robie, *Blood on Their Banner: Nationalist Struggles in the South Pacific* (London/Leichhardt, N.S.W., Australia: Zed Books/Pluto Press, 1989); Gerard Chaliand, ed., *People Without a Country: The Kurds and Kurdistan* (New York: Olive Branch Press, [2nd ed.] 1993); Tony Hodges, *Western Sahara: Roots of a Desert War* (Westport, CT: Lawrence-Hill, 1983); Robert P. Clark, *Negotiating with ETA: Obstacles to Peace in the Basque Country, 1975–1988* (Reno: University of Nevada Press, 1990); J. Bowyer Bell, *The Irish Troubles: A Generation of Violence, 1967–1992* (New York: St. Martin's Press, 1993); Gwynfor Evans, *Fighting for Wales* (Talybont, Wales: Y Lolfa Cyf., 1991); Peter Beresford Ellis, *The Celtic Revolution: A Study in Anti-Imperialism* (Talybont, Wales: Y Lofla Cyf., 1985).

56. "A spectre is haunting Europe—the spectre of Communism"; Karl Marx and Frederick Engels, "Manifesto of the Communist Party," in *Karl Marx and Frederick Engels: Selected Works*, 3 vols. (Moscow: Progress Publishers, 1969) Vol. 1, p. 108.

57. Neitschmann, "Third World War."

58. Chomsky, *World Orders.*

13. I AM INDIGENIST

1. For what is probably the best available account of AIM, IAT, and WARN, see Paul Chaat Smith and Robert Allen Warrior, *Like a Hurricane: The American Indian Movement from Alcatraz to Wounded Knee* (New York: New Press, 1996).On Oka, see Gerald R. Alfred, *Heeding the Voices of Our Ancestors: Kahnewake Mohawk Politics and the Rise of Native Nationalism* (New York: Oxford University Press, 1995); Linda Pertusati, *In Defense of Mohawk Land: Ethnopolitical Conflict in Native North America* (Albany: State University of New York Press, 1997).

2. On James Bay, see Boyce Richardson's *Strangers Devour the Land* (Post Mills, VT: Chelsea Green, [2nd ed.] 1991). Also see the chapter entitled "Hydrological Rape in Northern Canada," in my *Struggle for the Land: Native North American Resistance to Genocide, Ecocide and Colonization* (Winnipeg: Arbeiter Ring, [2nd ed.] 1999) esp. pp. 298–309.

3. While it is hardly complete, a good point of departure for learning about many of the individuals named would be Alvin M. Josephy, Jr.'s *The Patriot Chiefs* (New York: Viking, 1961).

4. For implications, see Michel-Rolph Trouillot, *Silencing the Past: Power and the Production of History* (Boston: Beacon Press, 1995).

5. This problem is taken up in "Indians 'R' Us," herein.

6. From a movie, *The Outlaw Josie Wales* (1976).

7. George, Manuel and Michael Posluns, *The Fourth World: An Indian Reality* (New York: Free Press, 1974); Bernard Neitschmann, "The Fourth World: Nations versus States," in Geore J. Demko and William B. Wood, eds., *Reordering the World: Geopolitical Perspectives on the 21st Century* (Bounder, CO: Westview Press, 1994) pp. 225–42.

8. The bulk of those mentioned, and a number of others as well, appear in Roger Moody, ed., *The Indigenous Voice: Visions and Realities*, 2 vols. (London: Zed Books, 1988). Also see Alexander Ewen, ed., *Voice of Indigenous Peoples: Native People Address the United Nations* (Santa Fe, NM: Clear Light, 1994).

9. The term "Vichy Indians" comes from Russell Means, during a lecture at the University of Colorado/Denver in 1984.

10. For partial contextualization, see William E. Unrau, ed., *The White Man's Wicked Water: The Alcohol Trade and Prohibition in Indian Country, 1802–1892* (Lawrence: University Press of Kansas, 1996).

11. William Thomas Hagan, *Indian Police and Judges: Experiments in Acculturation and Control* (New Haven, CT: Yale University Press, 1966).

12. Kenneth R. Philp, ed., *Indian Self-Rule: First-Hand Accounts of Indian/White Relations from Roosevelt to Reagan* (Salt Lake City: Howe Bros., 1986).

13. Ross Swimmer is an alleged Cherokee and former Philips Petroleum executive who served as head of the U.S. Bureau of Indian Affairs under Ronald Reagan and argued for suspension of federal obligations to Indians as a means of teaching native people "self-reliance." Dickie Wilson was head of the federal puppet government on Pine Ridge Reservation during the early 1970s, and while in this position he formed an entity, called the GOONs, to physically assault and frequently kill members and supporters of AIM. Webster Two Hawk was head of the National Tribal Chairman's Association funded by the Nixon administration. He used his federally sponsored position to denounce Indian liberation struggles. Peter McDonald—often referred to as "McDollar" in Indian Country—utilized his position as head of the puppet government at Navajo to sell his people's interests to various mining corporations during the 1970s and '80s, greatly enriching himself in the process. Vernon Bellecourt is a former Denver wig stylist who moved to Minneapolis and became CEO of a state-chartered corporation funded by federal authorities to impersonate the American Indian Movement. David Bradley is a no-talent painter living in Santa Fe whose main claim to fame is in having made a successful bid to have the federal government enforce "identification standards" against other Indian artists; he has subsequently set himself up as a self-anointed "Identity Police," a matter which, thankfully, leaves him little time to produce his typical graphic shlock. To hear them tell it, of course, each of these individuals acted in the service of "Indian sovereignty." See generally, "Nullification of Native America?" and "Bloody Wake of Alcatraz," herein.

14. See Winona LaDuke's "Natural to Synthetic and Back Again," the preface to my *Marxism and Native Americans* (Boston: South End Press, 1983) pp. i–viii.

15. Guillermo Bonfil Batalla, *Utopía y Revolución: El Pensamiento Político Contemporáneo de los Indios en América Latina* (Mexico City: Editorial Nueva Imagen, 1981), p. 37; translation by Roxanne Dunbar Ortiz.

16. Ibid., pp. 37–38.

17. Ibid. p. 38.

18. Roxanne Dunbar Ortiz, *Indians of the Americas: Human Rights and Self-Determination* (London: Zed Books, 1984), p. 83.

19. Ibid. p. 84.

20. See Karl Marx, *Pre-Capitalist Economic Formations* (London: Lawrence and Wishart, 1964). Also see "False Promises," herein.

21. Dunbar Ortiz, *Indians of the Americas*, p. 85.

22. Manuel and Posluns, *Fourth World*, p. 1.

23. On the Irish and Welsh struggles, see Peter Berresford Ellis, *The Celtic Revolution: A Study in Anti-Imperialism* (Talybont, Wales: Y Lolfa, 1985). On the Basques, see Robert P. Clark, *Negotiating*

with ETA: Obstacles to Peace in the Basque Country, 1975–1988 (Reno: University of Nevada Press, 1990).

24. Dunbar Ortiz, *Indians of the Americas*, p. 89.

25. Bernard Neitschmann, "The Third World War: Militarism and Indigenous Peoples," *Cultural Survival Quarterly*, Vol. 11, No. 2, 1987. Also see his "Fourth World."

26. Geneva Offices of the United Nations, Press Release, Aug. 17, 1981 (Hr/1080).

27. See "The Law Stood Squarely on Its Head," herein.

28. On the Iberian legal tradition, see James Brown Scott, *The Spanish Origin of International Law* (Oxford, U.K.: Clarendon Press, 1934).

29. Hugo Blanco, *Land or Death: The Peasant Struggle in Peru* (New York: Pathfinder Press, 1972). Blanco was a marxist, and thus sought to pervert indigenous issues through rigid class analysis— defining Indians as "peasants" rather than by nationality—but his identification of land as the central issue was and is nonetheless valid.

30. The complete texts of 371 of these ratified treaties are compiled in Charles J. Kappler's *American Indian Treaties, 1778–1883* (New York: Interland, 1973). Additional treaty texts, plus a broad range of other relevant instruments, will be found in Vine Deloria, Jr., and Raymond J. DeMallie, *Documents of American Indian Diplomacy: Treaties, Agreements, and Conventions, 1775–1979*, 2 vols. (Norman: University of Oklahoma Press, 1999).

31. The constitutional provision comes at Article I, Section 10. Codification of customary international law in this connection is explained in Ian Sinclair's *The Vienna Convention on the Law of Treaties* (Manchester, U.K.: Manchester University Press, [2nd ed.] 1984).

32. See generally, Sidney L. Harring, *Crow Dog's Case: American Indian Sovereignty, Tribal Law, and United States Law in the Nineteenth Century* (Cambridge, U.K.: Cambridge University Press, 1994); David E. Wilkins, *American Indian Sovereignty and the U.S. Supreme Court* (Austin: University of Texas Press, 1997).

33. Anyone wishing to dig into this one is referred to Cornelius J. Moynihan's *Introduction to the Law of Real Property: An Historical Background of the Common Law of Real Property* (St. Paul, MN: West Legal Studies, 1987).

34. *"Lone Wolf" v. Hitchcock* (187 U.S. 553 (1903)). For analysis, see Blue Clark, *"Lone Wolf" v. Hitchcock: Treaty Rights and Indian Law at the End of the Nineteenth Century* (Lincoln: University of Nebraska Press,1999).

35. An even more straightforward enunciation of this fetid doctrine was made by the Supreme Court in its *Tee-Hit-Ton* opinion (348 U.S. 272 (1955)). For analysis, see Wilkins, *American Indian Sovereignty*, pp. 166–85.

36. See Quincy Wright, "The Law of the Nuremberg Trials," *American Journal of International Law*, No. 41, Jan. 1947. Also see "Bringing the Law Home," herein.

37. A fuller articulation of this thesis may be found in my "On Gaining 'Moral High Ground': An Ode to George Bush and the 'New World Order,'" in Cynthia Peters, ed., *Collateral Damage: The "New World Order" at Home and Abroad* (Boston: South End Press, 1992), pp. 359–72.

38. For the origins of such practices, see Dorothy V. Jones, *License for Empire: Colonialism by Treaty in Early America* (Chicago: University of Chicago Press, 1982). For a good survey of U.S. adaptations, see Donald Worcester, ed., *Forked Tongues and Broken Treaties* (Caldwell, ID: Caxton, 1975).

39. The travesty at Fort Wise is adequately covered in Stan Hoig's *The Sand Creek Massacre* (Norman: University of Oklahoma Press, 1961) pp. 13–17.

40. Deloria and DeMallie, *Indian Diplomacy, Vol. 2*, pp. 1237–1473.

41. See my "Charades, Anyone? The Indian Claims Commission in Context," *American Indian Culture and Research Journal*, Vol 24, No. 1, 2000.

42. See "The Earth Is Our Mother," herein.

43. The percentage is arrived at by juxtaposing the approximately fifty million acres within the current reservation landbase to the more than two *billion* acres of the lower 48 states. According to

the Indian Claims Commission findings, Indians actually retain unfettered legal title to about 750 million acres of the continental U.S.; see Russel L. Barsh, "Indian Land Claims Policy in the United States," *North Dakota Law Review*, No. 58, 1982.

44. Concerning Alaska, see M. C. Berry, *The Alaska Pipeline: The Politics of Oil and Native Land Claims* (Bloomington: Indiana University Press, 1975). On Hawai'i, see the Haunani-Kay Trask, *From a Native Daughter: Colonialism and Sovereignty in Hawai'i* (Honolulu: University of Hawai'i Press, [2nd ed.] 1999).

45. Those with questions should refer to Arnold Leibowitz, *Defining Status: A Comprehensive Analysis of U.S. Territorial Relations* (The Hague: Martinus Nijhoff, 1990).

46. The structure of oppression is delineated rather well in Pem Davidson Buck's *Worked to the Bone: Race, Class, Power and Privilege* (New York: Monthly Review, 2002).

47. An in-depth and very sharp articulation of this point will be found in J. Sakai, *Settlers: The Mythology of the White Proletariat* (Chicago: Morningstar Press, 1989). Also see George Lipsitz, *The Possessive Investment in Whiteness: How White People Profit from Identity Politics* (Philadelphia: Temple University Press, 1998).

48. The problem is partially but insightfully examined in Ronald Weitzer, *Transforming Settler States: Communal Conflict and Internal Security in Zimbabwe and Northern Ireland* (Berkeley: University of California Press, 1992). Also see Patrick Wolfe, *Settler State Colonialism and the Transformation of Anthropology: The Politics and Poetics of an Ethnographic Event* (New York: Cassell, 1999) pp. 1–8.

49. A good exposition of this phenomenon may be found in Paul Brodeur, *Restitution: The Land Claims of the Mashpee, Passamaquoddy, and Penobscot Indians of New England* (Boston: Northeastern University Press, 1985).

50. Several years ago, I illustrated this point by having a group of students do an examination of 100 randomly selected books, all of them purportedly offering progressive analyses of U.S. sociopolitical or economic relations, but not specifically devoted to the study of American Indian issues. More than two-thirds (64) of the books, including a dozen that professed to deal mainly with matters of race, ethnicity and class, failed to make any reference to Indians at all. Another 19 mentioned us only in passing, usually in a list of U.S. minorities. Only three contained anything resembling a substantive consideration of things Indian. The miniscule number of Indian-focused books published by left presses—Monthly Review and Verso, to offer primary examples—is another firm indication of what I'm talking about. It is worth noting that Native Hawaiians fare even worse, as do Samoans and the Chamaros of Guam.

51. See "False Promises," herein.

52. This, to be sure, militates against the recently fashionable postmodernist rejection of "hierarchy" in all forms, including the ordering of priorities; see Terry Eagleton, *The Illusions of Postmodernism* (Oxford, U.K.: Blackwell, 1996) 93–95, 113–14.

53. The form is in the first instance one of internal colonialism, the relations of which were first described by Antonio Gramsci in "The Southern Question," an essay included in his *The Modern Prince and Other Writings* (New York: International, 1957) pp. 28–51. For the most detailed case-study to date, see Michael Hector's, *Internal Colonialism: The Celtic Fringe in British National Development, 1536–1966* (Berkeley: University of California Press, 1975). For application to Native North America, see my "The Situation of Indigenous Populations in the United States: A Struggle Against Internal Colonialism," *Black Scholar*, Vol. 16, No. 1, Feb. 1985. It is worth noting that the Gramscian model has also been applied to Chicanos, blacks, and Appalachian whites: see, as examples, James Boggs, *Racism and Class Struggle: Further Pages from a Black Worker's Notebook* (New York: Monthly Review Press, 1971); Huey P. Newton, "Speech Delivered at Boston College, November 18, 1970," in his *To Die for the People: The Writings of Huey P. Newton* (New York: Random House, 1972) pp. 20–38; Mario Barrera, Carlos Muñoz and Charles Ornelas, "The Barrio as an Internal Colony," *Urban Affairs Annual Reviews*, Vol. 6, 1972; Rodolfo Acuña, *Occupied America: The Chicano's Struggle Toward Liberation* (San Francisco: Canfield Press, 1972); Helen M. Lewis, Linda Johnson and Donald Askins, eds., *Colonialism in Modern America: The Appalachian Case* (Boone, NC: Appalachian

Consortium Press, 1978); Ada F. Haynes, *Poverty in Appalachia: Underdevelopment and Exploitation* (New York: Garland, 1996).

54. Although, as was indicated in the preceeding note, several populations share the status of being internally colonized in the U.S., subjugation to colonialism in its "settler" form is a status unique to American Indians; see generally, Sakai, *Settlers*; Weitzer, *Settler States*; Wolfe, *Settler State Colonialism*.

55. The idea that the 13 American colonies' war for independence was somehow a "revolution" has always seemed curious to me. Insofar as the English monarchy was not overthrown—indeed, none of the "revolutionaries" involved sought such an outcome—it would be better understood as a decolonization or "national liberation" struggle. This and similar terminological/conceptual conflations greatly marred understandings of Third World liberation struggles in the twentieth century; see, e.g., Eric R. Wolf, "Peasant Rebellion and Revolution," in Norman Miller and Robert Aya, eds., *National Liberation: Revolution in the Third World* (New York: Free Press, 1971) pp. 48–67.

56. One of the slipperiest—and in some ways most self-serving—confusions can be found in the propensity of many recent theorists to simply declare colonialism to be over, irrespective of its ongoing forms of existence. That which no longer exists, of course, need be neither prioritized nor confronted. For critique, see Anne McClintock, "The Angel of Progress: Pitfalls of the Term 'Post-Colonialism',," in Patrick Williams and Laura Chrisman, eds., *Colonial Discourse/Post-Colonial Theory* (New York: Columbia University Press, 1994) pp. 291–304; Stuart Hall, "When was 'the Post-Colonial'? Thinking at the Limits," in Iain Chambers and Lidia Curti, eds., *The Post-Colonial Question: Common Skies/Divided Horizons* (London: Routledge, 1996) pp. 242–60; Arif Dirlik, *The Postcolonial Aura: Third World Criticism in the Era of Global Capitalism* (Boulder, CO: Westview Press, 1997).

57. This is entirely in line with the analogy of American Indians to a "miner's canary" affording early warning to other populations of what will surely befall them, should fundamental alterations in policy and attendant attitudes not be undertaken; Felix S. Cohen, "The Erosion of Indian Rights, 1950–53: A Case-Study in Bureaucracy," *Yale Law Journal*, No. 62, 1953, p. 390.

58. We were, to use Karl Marx's term, "primitive communists"; Marx, *Pre-Capitalist Economic Formations*, pp. 72–73. Also see Emmanuel Terray, *Marxism and "Primitive" Societies: Two Studies* (New York: Monthly Review Press, 1972).

59. Lewis Henry Morgan, *League of the Ho-de-no-sau-nee, Iroquois* (Rochester, NY: Sage & Bros., 1851). Morgan's work greatly influenced the thinking of Marx and Engels; see especially, Frederick Engels, *The Dialectics of Nature* (Moscow: Progress, 1954).

60. E. Morton Coulter, "Mary Musgrove, Queen of the Creeks: A Chapter in the Early Georgia Troubles," *Georgia Historical Quarterly*, Vol. 11, No. 1, 1927.

61. Evelyn Hu-DeHart, *Yaqui Resistance and Survival* (Madison: University of Wisconsin Press, 1984).

62. R. David Edmunds, *Tecumseh and the Quest for Indian Leadership* (Boston: Little, Brown, 1984).

63. See generally, Sharon O'Brien, *American Indian Tribal Governments* (Norman: University of Oklahoma Press, 1989).

64. Barbara Alice Mann, *Iroquoian Women: The Gantowisas* (New York: Peter Lang, 2000).

65. Norma Tucker, "Nancy Ward, Gighau of the Cherokees," *Georgia Historical Quarterly*, Vol.. 53, No. 2, 1969; Michael Wallis and Wilma Pearl Mankiller, *Mankiller: A Chief and Her People* (New York: St. Martin's, 1993); Melissa Schwartz, *Wilma Mankiller: Principal Chief of the Cherokees* (New York: Chelsea House, 1994).

66. Marla N. Powers, *Oglala Women: Myth, Ritual and Reality* (Chicago: University of Chicago Press, 1986).

67. Ruth Roessel, *Women in Navajo Society* (Rough Rock, AZ: Navajo Resource Center, 1981).

68. Valerie Shirer Mathes, "A New Look at the Role of Women in Indian Societies," *American Indian Quarterly*, Vol. 2, No. 2, 1975; Clara Sue Kidwell, "The Power of Women in Three American Indian Societies," (*Journal of Ethnic Studies*, Vol. 6, No. 3, 1979); Eleanor Burke Leacock, *Myths of Male Dominance: Collected Articles on Women Cross-Culturally* (New York: Monthly Review Press,

1981); Janet Silman, ed., *Enough Is Enough: Aboriginal Women Speak Out* (Toronto: Women's Press, 1987).

69. Although both books are deeply flawed, much good information on such matters can be obtained in Paula Gunn Allen's *The Sacred Hoop: Recovering the Feminine in American Indian Cultures* (Boston: Beacon Press, 1986) and Walter L. Williams' *The Spirit and the Flesh: Sexual Diversity Among Native Americans* (Boston: Beacon Press, 1986).

70. The Smithsonian view of Indians has been adopted even by some of the more self-consciously "revolutionary" organizations in the United States; see, e.g., Revolutionary Communist Party, USA, "Searching for the Second Harvest," in *Marxism and Native Americans*, pp. 35–58.

71. The thesis is, no kidding, that American Indians were the first "environmental pillagers," and it took the invasion of enlightened Europeans like the author of the piece to save the American ecosphere from total destruction by its indigenous inhabitants; see George Weurthner, "An Ecological View of the Indian," *Earth First!* Vol. 7, No. 7, Aug. 1987. For a fuller and more recent extrapolation, see Shepard Krech III, *The Ecological Indian: Myth and History* (New York: W.W. Norton, 1999).

72. Paul W. Valentine, "Dances with Myths," *Arizona Republic*, Apr. 7, 1991 (Valentine is syndicated, but is on staff at the *Washington Post*).

73. A fine selection of such early colonialist impressions can be found in the first few chapters of Richard Drinnon's *Facing West: The Metaphysics of Indian Hating and Empire Building* (Minneapolis: University of Minnesota Press, 1980). On the length of indigenous occupancy in the Americas, see George F. Carter, *Earlier Than You Think: A Personal View of Man in America* (College Station: Texas A&M University Press, 1980); Vine Deloria, Jr., *Red Earth, White Lies: Native Americans and the Myth of Scientific Fact* (New York: Scribner, 1995). On precontact population, see William Denevan, ed., *The Native Population of the Americas in 1492* (Madison: University of Wisconsin Press, 1976); Henry F. Dobyns, *Their Number Become Thinned: Native American Population Dynamics in Eastern North America* (Knoxville: University of Tennessee Press, 1983).

74. For a succinct but reasonably comprehensive survey of actual precontact indigenous material and intellectual realities, see Jack Weatherford, *Indian Givers: How the Indians of the Americas Transformed the World* (New York: Fawcett Columbine, 1988).

75. See Jack D. Forbes, *Black Africans and Native Americans: Race, Color and Caste in the Evolution of Red-Black Peoples* (New York: Oxford University Press, 1988). Also see my essay, "The Crucible of American Indian Identity: Native Tradition versus Colonial Imposition in Postconquest North America," *American Indian Culture and Research Journal*, Vol. 22, No. 2, 1998.

76. On federal quantum policy, see "Crucible"; also see "The Nullification of Native America?" herein.

77. This remains true even in such concerted recent efforts to prove otherwise as Steven A. Leblanc's *Prehistoric Warfare in the Southwest* (Salt Lake City: University of Utah Press, 1999).

78. Probably the best examination of Indian warfare and "militaristic" tradition is Tom Holm's "Patriots and Pawns: State Use of American Indians in the Military and the Process of Nativization in the United States," in M. Annette Jaimes, ed., *The State of Native America: Genocide, Colonization and Resistance* (Boston: South End Press, 1992) pp. 345–70.

79. See Gianfranco Poggi, *The Rise of the State* (Stanford, CA: Stanford University Press, 1974); Frank J. Harrison, *The Modern State: An Anarchist Analysis* (Montréal: Black Rose Books, 1996).

80. A brilliant articulation of this premise will be found in Otto Hintze's "Military Organization and the Organization of the State," in F. Gilbert, ed., *The Historical Essays of Otto Hintze* (Princeton, NJ: Princeton University Press, 1975). For a much fuller enunciation of the thesis, see Bruce D. Porter, *War and the Rise of the State: The Military Foundations of Modern Politics* (New York: Free Press, 1994).

81. One of the clearer historical examples of this concerns the creation of anarchist "autonomous zones" in Catalonia and elsewhere during the Spanish Civil War of the 1930s; see, eg., Sam Dolgoff, ed., *The Anarchist Collectives: Worker's Self-Management during the Spanish Revolution, 1936-1939*

(Montréal: Black Rose Books, 1974); Gaston Leval, *Collectives in the Spanish Revolution* (London: Freedom Press, 1975); Juan Gómez Casas, *Anarchist Organization: The History of the FAI* (Montréal: Black Rose Books, 1986).

82. Alexander J. Motyl, *The Post-Soviet Nations: Perspectives on the Demise of the USSR* (New York: Columbia University Press, 1992); Rogers Brubaker, *Nationalism Reframed: Nationhood and the National Question in the New Europe* (Cambridge, U.K.: Cambridge University Press, 1996).

83. Leon Trotsky, *History of the Russian Revolution* (New York: Pathfinder Press, 2001) p. 1157.

84. For articulation, and concurrence by nonindian radicals, see the videotape entitled *US Off the Planet: An Evening with Ward Churchill and Chellis Glendenning*, available from Pickaxe Productions (pickaxeprod@igc.org or www.cascadiamedia.org).

85. An excellent selection of very hardline nonindian statements to this effect will be found in Peter Stansill and David Zain Mairowitz, eds., *BAM [by any means necessary]: Outlaw Manifestos and Ephemera, 1965–1970* (Brooklyn, NY: Autonomedia, 1999).

86. A lot more could be said about it, but there is a certain sufficiency in the descriptor deployed by Robert Jay Lifton and Eric Markusen in their *Genocidal Mentality* (New York: Basic Books, 1990).

87. Brodeur, *Restitution*. Also see Alan Van Gestel, "The New York Indian Land Claims: An Overview and a Warning," *New York State Bar Journal*, Apr. 1981; "New York Indian Land Claims: The Modern Landowner as Hostage," in Christopher Vecsey and William A. Starna, eds., *Iroquois Land Claims* (Syracuse, NY: Syracuse University Press, 1988) pp. 123–39; "When Fictions Take Hostages," in James A. Clifton, ed., *The Invented Indian: Cultural Fictions and Government Policies* (New Brunswick, NJ: Transaction, 1990) pp. 291–312.

88. For a raft of comparable humor, see Deloria's *Custer Died for Your Sins: An Indian Manifesto* (New York: Macmillan, 1969).

89. Referred to here is the so-called "Bradley Bill" (S.1453); see the "Black Hills Land Claim" section of "The Earth Is Our Mother," herein, esp. pp. 93–5.

90. See "TREATY: The Platform of Russell Means' Candidacy for President of the Oglala Lakota People, 1982," in my *Struggle for the Land*, pp. 405–38.

91. Barsh, "Indian Land Claims." Also see Barbara Hooker, "Surplus Lands for Indians: One Road to Self-Determination," *Vital Issues*, Vol. 22, No. 1, 1972; R.A. Hodge, "Getting Back the Land: How Native Americans Can Acquire Excess and Surplus Federal Property," *North Dakota Law Review*, Vol. 49, No. 2, 1973; Laurie Ensworth, "Native American Free Exercise Rights to the Use of Public Lands," *Boston University Law Review*, No. 63, 1983.

92. See Bradford L. Thomas, "International Boundaries: Lines in the Sand (and Sea)," in George J. Demko and William B. Wood, eds., *Reordering the World: Geopolitical Perspectives on the 21st Century* (Boulder, CO: Westview Press, [2nd ed.] 1999) pp. 69–93.

93. For background, see Frank J. Popper, *The Politics of Land-Use Reform* (Madison: University of Wisconsin Press, 1981).

94. For contrast, see Kathleen Ann Pickering, *Lakota Culture, World Economy* (Lincoln: University of Nebraska Press, 2000).

95. Much of this is updated in the chapters entitled "Community and Economic Resources," "Great Plains Agriculture," and "Energy and Mineral Resources," in S.R. Johnson and Aziz Bouzaher, *Conservation of Great Plains Ecosystems: Current Science, Future Options* (New York: Kluwer Academics, 1995).

96. Paul Andrew Hutton, *Phil Sheridan and His Army* (Lincoln: University of Nebraska Press, 1985) p. 246. Also see William T. Hornaday, *Exterminating the American Bison* (Wasington, D.C.: Smithsonian Institution, 1899).

97. Unfortunately, the only reasonably accessible information on the Buffalo Commons proposal is contained in Anne Matthews' rather frothy *Where the Buffalo Roam: The Storm Over the Revolutionary Plan to Restore America's Great Plains* (New York: Grove Weidenfeld, 1992).

98. For detailed renderings, see Charles C. Royce, *Indian Land Cessions in the United States: 18th*

Annual Report, 1896–97, 2 vols. (Washington, D.C.: Bureau of American Ethnography, Smithsonian Institution, 1899). Also see the composite included in my *Struggle for the Land,* p. 10.

99. Pickering, *Lakota Culture, World Economy,* Also see John H. Moore, ed., *The Political Economy of North American Indians* (Norman: University of Oklahoma Press, 1993).

100. For data, see C. Matthew Snipp, *American Indians: First of This Land* (New York: Russell Sage Foundation, 1989).

101. Doing so, would of course necessitate some rather complex Indian/Indian negotiations as well. Fortunately, there is a very strong tradition in this regard; see Deloria and DeMallie, *Record of Diplomacy,* pp. 681–744.

102. See the maps deployed by Valerie L. Kuletz in her book, *The Tainted Desert: Environmental and Social Ruin in the American West* (New York: Routledge, 1998).

103. Royce, *Indian Land Cessions.*

104. David B. Knight, "People Together, Yet Apart: Rethinking Territory, Sovereignty and Identies," in Demko and Wood, *Reordering the World,* pp. 209–26. Also see the essays collected by Frederick Barth in his *Ethnic Boundaries* (Oslo: Norwegian University Press, 1969).

105. The Hawaiian sovereignty struggle is detailed in Trask, *Native Daughter.* Also see my and Sharon H. Venn's coedited *Islands in Captivity: The Record of the International Tribunal on the Rights of Indigenous Hawaiians,* 3 vols. (Boston: South End Press, 2002).

106. On the efforts of the Puerto Rican independence movement to obtain a plebiscite, etc., see Ronald Fernandez, *Prisoners of Colonialism: The Struggle for Justice in Puerto Rico* (Monroe, ME: Common Courage Press, 1994).

107. Along with Belorussia (now Belarus), the Ukraine held U.N. membership from the outset, but only as an extension of the Soviet vote included in a compromise arrangement designed to bring about participation of the USSR; Motyl, *Post-Soviet Nations,* p. 113. The independent functioning of both member states should be dated from 1991. Several other former Soviet "republics," none of which were previously U.N. member states, have also been recently accorded such standing in independent terms. These include Estonia, Latvia, and Lithuania (all on Sept. 17, 1991), Armenia, Azerbaijan, Kazahkstan, the Kyrgyz Republic, Moldova, Tajikistan, Turkmenistan, and Uzbekistan (all on Mar. 2, 1992), and Georgia (July 31, 1992). Although Serbia continues to refer to itself as Yugoslavia, and thus retains that country's U.N. member-state status, several of its former provinces have now gained equal standing. These include Croatia, Bosnia-Hervegovenia, and Slovenia (all on May 22, 1992), and Macedonia (Apr. 8, 1993). Additionally, while Czechoslavakia held member-state standing, its devolution into two countries—the Czech and Slovak republics—resulted in the admission of both to the U.N. on Jan. 19, 1993. Obviously, the principle of preserving the territorial integrity of existing member states against self-determining claims by peoples encapsulated within them is hardly set in stone; Knight, "Rethinking Territory," pp. 218–20.

108. The attainment of U.N. member-state status by the Federated States of Micronesia (Sept. 17, 1991) and Palau (Dec. 15, 1994) already points in this direction, as does the according of such standing to the tiny European protectorate of Monaco (May 28, 1993). On Palau, see Thomas, "International Boundaries," p. 90; on Monaco, see Saul B. Cohen, "Geopolitics in the New World Era: New Perspectives on an Old Discipline," in Demko and Wood, *Reordering the World* (2nd ed.), p. 60. Also see Walker Connor's *Ethnonationalism* (Princeton, NJ: Princeton University Press, 1994).

109. For indication of where this could lead, see Richard Falk, *The End of World Order: Essays in Normative International Relations* (New York: Holmes & Meier, 1983).

110. For one of the best elaborations of these principles, see Ved Nanda, "Self-Determination in International Law: Validity of Claims to Secede," *Case Western Reserve Journal of International Law,* No. 13 1981. Also see Lee C. Buchheit, *Secession: The Legitimacy of Self-Determination* (New Haven, CT: Yale University Press, 1978).

111. A very clear delineation of the available options will be found in Hannum Hurst's *Autonomy, Sovereignty, and Self-Determination* (Philadelphia: University of Pennsylvania Press, 1990).

112. A prototype for this sort of arrangement exists between Greenland (populated mainly by

Inuits) and Denmark. See Gudmundur Alfredsson, "Greenland and the Law of Political Decolonization," *German Yearbook on International Law*, No. 25, 1982.

113. This is essentially the idea advanced by Richard Falk in an essay entitled "Anarchism and World Order," in his *End of World Order*. Also see Harvey Starr, *Anarchy, Order and Integration: How to Manage Interdependence* (Ann Arbor: University of Michigan Press, 1999).

114. A good argument as to why megastates will "inevitably fall apart" is made by Martin Van Creveld in his *The Rise and Decline of the State* (Cambridge, U.K.: Cambridge University Press, 1999). Also see Leopold Kohr, *The Breakdown of Nations* (New York: E.P. Dutton, 1975).

115. Barth, *Ethnic Boundaries*; Connor, *Ethnonationalism*; John Hutcheson, *The Dynamics of Cultural Nationalism* (New York: HarperCollins, [2nd ed.] 1994); Kirkpatrick Sale, *Dwellers in the Land: The Bioregional Vision* (Philadelphia: New Society, 1991).

116. This is the basic idea set forth in "TREATY." Also see Reinhard Bendix, *Nation-Building and Citizenship* (Berkeley: University of California Press, 1964).

117. The concepts at issue here are brought out very well in William R. Catton, Jr., *Overshoot: The Ecological Basis of Revolutionary Change* (Urbana: University of Illinois Press, 1982).

118. Such ideas have even caught on, at least as questions, among some Euroamerican legal practitioners; see Christopher D. Stone, *Should Trees Have Standing? Towards Legal Rights for Natural Objects* (Los Altos, CA: William Kaufman, 1972).

119. For further elaboration, see Vine Deloria, Jr., *God Is Red* (New York: Delta, 1973); "Native American Spirituality" in his *For This Land: Writings on Religion in America* (New York: Routledge, 1999) pp. 130–34. Also see "False Promises," herein.

120. I base my estimate in large part upon the regional preinvasion demographic estimates extrapolated by Henry F. Dobyns towards the end of his *Their Number Become Thinned*.

121. CNN "Dollars and Cents" reportage, May 27, 1992. Interestingly, the same sort of thinking has marked the analyses of marxists with regard to the "developmental problems" confronting Africa; see, e.g., Gérard Chaliand, *Revolution in the Third World: Myths and Prospects* (New York: Viking, 1977) p. 114.

122. The idea is developed in detail in Jeremy Rifkin's *Entropy: A New World View* (New York: Viking, 1980). It should be noted, however, that the worldview in question is hardly "new," since indigenous peoples have held it all along; see, e.g., Russell Means, "The Same Old Song," in my *Marxism and Native Americans* (Boston: South End Press, 1983) p. 22.

123. I am, however, borrowing the "controversial" definition of insanity offered by R. D. Laing in his *The Politics of Experience* (New York: Ballantine, 1967).

124. One good summary of this, utilizing extensive native sources—albeit many of them go unattributed—is Jerry Mander's *In the Absence of the Sacred: The Failure of Technology and the Survival of Indian Nations* (San Francisco: Sierra Club Books, 1991).

125. If this sounds a bit scriptural, it is meant to. A number of us see a direct line of continuity from the core imperatives of Judeochristian theology, through the capitalist secularization of church doctrine and its alleged marxian antithesis, right on through to the burgeoning technotopianism of today. This is a major conceptual cornerstone of what indigenists view as eurocentrism (a virulently anthropocentric outlook in its essence); see Vine Deloria, Jr., "Secularism, Civil Religion, and the Religious Freedom of American Indians," in his *For This Land*, pp. 218–28. Also see "False Promises," herein.

126. The information is in André Gunder Frank's *Capitalism and Underdevelopment in Latin America: Historical Studies of Chile and Brazil* (New York: Monthly Review Press, 1967), but the conclusion is avoided.

127. See generally, Jerome Ch'en, *Mao and the Chinese Revolution* (New York: Oxford University Press, 1967); Alice Goldstein, ed., *China: The Many Facets of Demographic Change* (Boulder, CO: Westview Press, 1996); Kuttan Mahadevan, Chi-Hsien Tuan, Jing-Yuan Yu and P. Kishnan, *Differential Development and Demographic Dilemma: Perspectives from China and India* (New Delhi: South Asia, 1994).

128. Paul R. Ehrlich and Anne H. Ehrlich, *The Population Explosion* (New York: Simon and

Schuster, 1990); Michael Tobias, *World War III: Population and the Biosphere at the End of the Millennium* (New York: Continuum, 1998); United Nations, *World Population Prospects: A Report* (New York: United Nations, 2000).

129. I am extrapolating from the calculations of Catton in *Overshoot*.

130. This consideration, unfortunately, may have a certain bearing in China; see Song Jian, Chi-Hsien Tuan and Jing-Yuan Yu, *Population Control in China: Theory and Applications* (Westport, CT: Greenwood, 1985); H. Yuan Tien, *China's Strategic Demographic Initiative* (New York: Praeger, 1991); United Nations, *Case Studies in Population Policy: China* (New York: United Nations, 1991). It also has bearing in the U.S., however; see Brint Dillingham, "Indian Women and IHS Sterilization Practices, *American Indian Journal*, Vol. 3, No. 1, 1977; Committee for Abortion Rights and against Sterilization Abuse, *Women Under Attack: Abortion, Sterilization Abuse, and Reproductive Freedom* (New York: CARASA, 1979); Margarita Ostalaza, *Politica Sexual y Socialización Politica de la Mujer Puertorriqueña la Consolidación de Bloque Histórico Colonial de Puerto Rico* (Río Piedras, PR: Ediciones Huracán, 1989).

131. Sound arguments to this effect are advanced in Paul R. Ehrlich and Anne H. Ehrlich, *Population/Resources/Environment* (San Francisco: W. H. Freeman, 1970).

132. Paul R. Ehrlich and Anne H. Ehrlich, from their book *Healing the Earth*, quoted in CNN series *The Population Bomb*, May 1992.

133. This is yuppie self-indulgence disguised as a health issue. The fact is that, after decades of increasingly intensive and heavily-subsidized research, those who years ago proclaimed "environmental" tobacco smoke a "major public health hazard" are *still* unable to conclusively demonstrate that such "secondhand" or "passive" smoking produces any negative health effect whatever. To get the picture, one need only compare the chapter entitled "Smoke Exposure and Health" in Roy J. Shepard's seminal *The Risks of Passive Smoking* (New York: Oxford University Press, 1982) to Peter N. Lee's "Difficulties in Determining Health Effects Related to Environmental Tobacco Smoke," in Ronald A. Watson and Mark Seldon's coedited and currently definitive *Environmental Tobacco Smoke* (Washington, D.C.: CRS Press, 2001) pp. 1–24. Meanwhile, the official response to these nonfindings—that of banning smoking, which is primarily a poor people's behavior, from most public spaces—should be compared to the responses accorded the ongoing and massive environmental release of military/industrial contaminants, the negative health effects of which are exceedingly well documented; see, as examples, Lois Marie Gibbs, *Dying From Dioxin* (Boston: South End Press, 1995); Jay M. Gould, *The Enemy Within: The High Cost of Living with Nuclear Reactors* (New York: Four Walls Eight Windows, 1996). Also see "A Breach of Trust," herein.

134. This would be about fifty million, or about one-sixth of the present U.S. population; Catton, *Overshoot*, p. 53.

135. G. Wesley Johnson, Jr., ed. *Phoenix in the Twentieth Century: Essays in Community History* (Norman: University of Oklahoma Press, 1993).

136. Both the environmental and the social costs attending the L.A. catastrophe have been staggering. See Mike Davis, *City of Quartz: Excavating the Future in Los Angeles* (London: Verso, 1990); *Ecology of Fear: Los Angeles and the Imagination of Disaster* (New York: Henry Holt, 1998).

137. See, e.g., Mark Reisner, *Cadillac Desert: The American West and Its Disappearing Water* (New York: Viking, 1986).

138. See my "Water Plot," pp. 314–20.

139. Ronald L. Myers, ed., *Ecosystems of Florida* (Gainesville: University of Florida Press, 1990); John Ogden and Steve Davis, eds., *Everglades: The Ecosystem and Its Restoration* (Washington, D.C.: CRC Press, 1994).

140. See "A Breach of Trust," herein.

141. Although I take considerable exception to the blatant eurosupremacism lacing much of his work, some of the most powerful statements on why the dams must come down will be found in the work of the late Edward Abbey; see his *Down the River* (New York: E.P. Dutton, 1991).

142. On the human as well as environmental costs attending coal stripping in the Four Corners region, see the essay entitled "Genocide in Arizona: The 'Navajo-Hopi Land Dispute' in Perspective," in my *Struggle for the Land*, pp. 135–72.

143. See generally, U.S. Department of Commerce, Bureau of the Census, Economics and Statistics Division, *U.S. Census of Population: General Population Characteristics, United States* (Washington, D.C.: U.S. GPO, 1990). For background, see Kirkpatrick Sale, *Power Shift: The Rise of the Southern Rim and Its Challenge to the Eastern Establishment* (New York: Random House, 1975). For more recent contextualization, see Davis, *City of Quartz* and *Ecology of Fear*.

144. A good deal of the impact could also be offset by implementing the ideas contained in John Todd and George Tukel, *Reinhabiting Cities and Towns: Designing for Sustainability* (San Francisco: Planet Drum Foundation, 1981). Also see Sale, *Dwellers*.

145. For purposes of comparison, see *Funding Ecological and Social Destruction: The World Bank and International Monetary Fund* (Washington, D.C.: Bank Information Center, 1990). By contrast, the principle I advocate might be described as "Demanding Ecological and Social Preservation."

146. For the extent to which this is an issue, see Paul Harrison, *Inside the Third World: The Anatomy of Poverty* (New York: Penguin, [3rd ed.] 1993).

147. Many indigenous peoples take the position that all social policies should be entered into only after consideration of their likely implications, both environmentally and culturally, for our posterity seven generations in the future. Consequently, a number of seemingly good ideas for solving short-run problems are never entered into because no one can reasonably predict their longer-term effects; see Sylvester M. Morey, ed., *Can the Red Man Help the White Man? A Denver Conference with Indian Elders* (New York: Myrin Institute, 1970); also see the concluding chapter of Deloria, *God Is Red*.

148. For an analogous argument, see Thomas Kuhn's *The Structure of Scientific Revolutions* (Chicago: University of Chicago Press, [3rd ed.] 1996).

149. A contemporaneous description is offered by the man who in all probability coined the slogan; see Daniel Cohn-Bendit, *Obsolete Communism: The Left-Wing Alternative* (New York: McGraw-Hill, 1968). Ample contextualization will be found in George Katsiaficas' *The Imagination of the New Left: A Global Analysis of 1968* (Boston: South End Press, 1987).

·150. See, e.g., Virginia Irving Armstrong, ed., *I Have Spoken: American History Through the Voices of the Indians* (Chicago: Swallow Press, 1971).

151. Laing, *Politics of Experience*. Also see R.D. Laing, *The Divided Self: An Existential Study of Sanity and Madness* (New York: Routledge, 1999).

152. See generally, Daniel Burton-Rose, Dan Pens and Paul Wright, eds., *The Celling of America: An Inside Look at the U.S. Prison Industry* (Monroe, ME: Common Courage Press, 1998).

153. Armstrong, *I Have Spoken*, p. 79.

INDEX

ucation of Little Tree written by: 407n89; *The Outlaw Josey Wales* written by: 406n89

Carter, Pres. Jimmy: 179

Cassidy, Hopalong: 402n27

Castaneda, Carlos: 31, 231, 271

Castillo, Bobby: 276, 326n17

Castro, Fidel: 107

Catches, Chief Everett: 388n50

Catches, Chief Pete: 388n50

Catlin, George: 189, 190, 210

Cattaraugus Reservation: 76, 77, 78

Catton, William: 296

Caughnawaga Reserve (Canada): 79, 80

Ceausescu, Elena: genocide trial of: 305n29

Ceausescu, Nicolae: genocide trial of: 305n29

Celay, Philip: 387n40

Celts: 240; contemporary liberation movements among: 21; spiritual traditions of: 224, 227

Census Bureau, *see* U.S. Dept. of Commerce

Central Intelligence Agency (CIA): xi; and Latin American death squads: 172, 391–2n96; fabrication of "social movements" by: 423n46

Ceylon, *see* Sri Lanka

Chaco Declaration: 13

Chamberlain, Wilt: 191

Chanate, Rob: 276

Chaney, Lon: 193

Chandler, Jeff: 191, 195–6, 406n82

Chapman, Cathy: 326n17

Charlemagne: 237, 424n57

Charles, Norman: 174

Chechnya, revolts in: 21

Chernobyl, *see* Soviet Union

"Cherokee Cases": 1, 9–11; *also see Cherokee v. Georgia* opinion; John Marshall; *Worchester v. Georgia* opinion

Cherokees/Cherokee Nation: 10, 141, 143, 188, 189, 190, 192, 195, 326n10, 332n86; agriculture of: 403n49; Beloved Woman of: 285; coerced treaties and: 345n40; Cultural Heritage Center of: 25; Eastern Band of: 38, 231; enrollment criteria of: 380n76; "Etowah Band" of: 231; Great Seal of: 26; Keetoowah Band of: 28; of Oklahoma: 31–2, 40–1; Trail of Tears of: 56, 145–6; resistance to allotment of: 150; rolls of: 150, 326n10; *also see* Ward Churchill; Jimmie Durham; Wilma Mankiller; Rennard Strickland; Lynn Riggs; U.S. Indian Removal Policy; Will Rogers

Cheyennes: 16, 187, 189, 197–8, 200, 203,

290; Bent family and: 415n172; Camp Robinson massacre of (1878): 57, 84; decimation by disease of: 149; Crazy Dog ("Dog Soldier") Society of: 33, 205; environmental lawsuit of (1976): 382n114; Ft. Laramie treaties and: 170, 201; Ft. Wise Treaty and: 15–6, 170, 282, 344n39; ICC and: 15–6; mineral resources of: 153; Powder River territory of: 149; Sand Creek Massacre of (1864): 33, 56–7, 198, 202, 203, 415n172; 1868 Washita Massacre of: 57, 148, 198, 201, 407n95, 409n118, 409n120; 1875 Sappa Creek massacre of: 57; 1876–77 U.S. war against: 86; 1878 "breakout" of: 149; *also see* Arapahos

Chile: death squads in: 172; 1973–76 political murder rate in: 171, 272–3; "national question" in: 254

China/Chinese: 260; constitution of: 258; Han Empire of: 258; immigrants to U.S. of: xiv; immigrants to Vietnam ("Nungs") of: 258; internal colonization of indigenous peoples by: 20, 258, 266; "Long March" in: 258; Mongols and: 191, 258; the "national question" in: 254; population of: 295; 1949 maoist revolution in: 258

China Lake Naval Weapons Ctr. (Calif.): 131, 370n156

Chino, Wendell: 136

Chips, Chief Ellis: 388n50

Chivington, Col. John M.: 202, 203, 410n125

Chomsky, Noam: 273, 304n15

Christians/Christianity, value system of: 11

Chrystos: 276

Churchill, Ward: attacks upon: 28–9, 327n31, 328n37, 328n38; books published by: 29; Columbus Day protest trial of: 43; *From a Native Son* written by: 248; IITC work of: 433n105; Keetoowah Cherokee identity of: 28, 327n30; "North American Union of Indigenous Nations" proposal of: 290–1; *Struggle for the Land* written by: 272; teaching award bestowed upon: 29; 1984 German tour of: 235–40

citizen's arrest, right of: 341n103

City of Syracuse (New York), leases on: 83–4

Clark, Bruce: 355n264

Clark, Girlie: 388n57

Clark, Mark: 182, 389n60

Clark, William: 207

Clay, Sec. of State Henry: 160

1985 discussions with: 433n105; FULRO operations against: 258–9, 433n105; Hanoi government of: 259; internal colonization of Montagnards by: 20, 258–9; Kontum Province in: 433n105; National Liberation Front (NLF) of: 258 the "national question" in: 254; People's Army (PAVN; NVA) of: 258; Pleiku Province in: 433n105; Saigon government of: 258; U.S. Special Forces operations in: 258–9; U.S. war against: 88, 410n123

Vietnam War: xiv, 16

Vision Quest, Inc.: 420n12

Vitoria, Franciscus de: 5; Just War doctrine and: 12

Vizenor, Gerald: 215

Voisy Bay (Labrador): 104, 356n280

W

Wagoner, Joseph: 124

Wales/Welsh, secessionist movement among: 21, 273

Walker, Clint: 197

Walker-Rorex, Jeanne: 26, 30, 31, 37, 326n11

Walkingstick. Kay:332n86

Wallace, Gov. George: 406n89

Wallerstein, Immanuel: "World System" theory of: 19

Walsh, Raoul: 201, 202, 409n120

War of Independence (American): 7, 56, 71, 107, 143, 379n66; issuance of land scrip to troops during: 312n39; not a "revolution": 441n55

War of 1812: 145

"War on Drugs," the: 269

Ward, Nancy (Cherokee leader): 276

Waring, SA Gerard: 175, 393n108

Warner, Col. Volney: 169, 171, 388n53

Warren, Marquiz: 202

Warren, Shields: 118

Washburn, Wilcomb: 189, 201

Washinawatok, Ingrid: 276

Washington, Pres. George: 7, 70, 78, 107, 144, 277; desire to "remove" Indians of: 376n26; prefiguration of Hitlerian diplomacy by: 311–2n36

Washington Post: 285

Waterson, Sam: 214

Watkins, Arthur: 68

Waxman, Seth: 361n31

Wayne, Gen. Anthony: 192, 403n51

Wayne, John: 191, 199, 203, 206, 209, 405n65

weapons of mass destruction: xiv, 286; biochemical weapons (U.S.): 135; Soviet nuclear weapons testing and development: 116, , 363–4n66; U.S. nuclear weapons testing and development: 128–33; *also see* Atomic Energy Commission; Deseret Test Ctr.; Fish Springs Nuclear Weapons Range; Hanford nuclear weapons production facility; Marshall Islands; Nellis Gunnery Range; Pentagon

Webster, Judge William: 177; becomes FBI Director: 178

Weinberger, Sec. of Defense Casper: 133

Wendover Test Range (Utah): 371n165

West, Cornell: 328n33

West, Mae: 186

West Valley (NY) nuclear storage facility: 374n200; *also see* U.S. Ecology Corp.

West Virginia: absence of reservations in: 142; contemporary indigenous population of: 142

Westerman, Floyd: 381n88, 415n170

Western Nuclear Corp.: Sherwood facility of: 369n127

Western Sahara (Morocco): Polasario liberation movement in: 273

Western Shoshone Sacred Lands Assoc.: 100, alliances of: 105

Western Shoshones (Newes): AIM and: 273; compensatory awards to: 99, 101, 103, 136, 137; Court of Claims and: 99; Dann case and: 100–3; Duckwater community of: 103, 131; Ernest Wilkinson and: 97–8, 345n236; ICC and: 97–100; IRA and: 97; health conditions among: 131; land claims of: 72, 96–106; MX missile system and: 104–5, 131, 160; OAS request and: 102; Timbisha community of: 131; U.S. nuclear weapons testing and: 104, 130–3; 1863 Bear River massacre of: 57; Temoak Band of: 97, 98, 99; Timbisha Band of: 371n159; Yomba community of: 131; 1863 Treaty of Ruby Valley and: 96; treaty territory of: 96–7; *also see* Newe Segobia

Westlake, John: 12

Wetcher, Kenneth: 224

Weurthner, George: 285

Weyerhauser Corp.: 165

Whitaker, Ben: 61, 341n104

White Earth Chippewa Reservation: 71

White, Justice Edward D.: 313n69